CONVERSATIONS WITH
BARTH ON PREACHING

CONVERSATIONS
WITH
BARTH
ON PREACHING

William H.
Willimon

Abingdon Press

Nashville

CONVERSATIONS WITH BARTH ON PREACHING

This book is printed on acid-free paper.

Library of Congress Cataloging-in-Publication Data

Willimon, William H.
   Conversations with Barth on preaching / William H. Willimon.
    p. cm.
   Includes bibliographical references and index.
   ISBN 0-687-34161-2 (binding: pbk. : alk. paper)
   1. Preaching. 2. Barth, Karl, 1886–1968—Interviews. I. Title.

   BV4211.3.W52 2006
   251—dc22

                                              2006000564

06 07 08 09 10 11 12 13 14 15—10 9 8 7 6 5 4 3 2

MANUFACTURED IN THE UNITED STATES OF AMERICA

To Stanley, again, with gratitude

CONTENTS

Introduction 1

1. Barth the Preacher 9

2. Preaching the Bible with Barth 23

3. I Will Give You Words 47

4. How to Say What God Says? 83

5. Word Makes World 115

6. The Talkative God 143

7. Heralds of God 167

8. Troubled Preaching 197

9. Easter Speech 223

10. Called to Preach 239

Notes 267

Index of Scripture 317

Index of Names 319

Index of Subjects 323

"I like old Barth. He throws the furniture around."

Flannery O'Connor

INTRODUCTION

This book is the fruit of my four-decade engagement with the last century's greatest theologian. I encountered the work of Karl Barth shortly after his death while I was a student at Yale Divinity School in 1969. I had tried to meet him earlier but without success in an undergraduate reading of *Dogmatics in Outline*. But Barth met me just when I needed him—in the turbulent, invigorating, ultimately unproductive sixties wherein theology seemed so thoroughly to lose its nerve. I got interested in Barth because my best teachers—Childs, Holmer, Frei, and R. C. Johnson—reflected his great light in their own. Theologically, Barth restored my nerve in that distinctly unnerving period. When all seemed ready to jettison the Christian tradition in favor of "relevance," Barth's was a strong, assertive voice.[1] Barth saved me from the theological wasteland that decimated contemporary homiletics, gave me something to say as a preacher, and, later, gave me a way to say it.

Some time afterward I had the privilege of teaching homiletics in two universities where Barth made decisive turns in his theology—Bonn and Münster. My experiences there, attempting to teach German theological students, not only improved my German but also reawakened my interest in Barth. I had the almost mystical experience of speaking one afternoon in the very lecture hall where Barth had lectured in Bonn, and from whence the Nazis expelled him, and to which he returned after the war to lecture in the rubble that was left of the university. It occurred to me that afternoon that it had often been my fate to speak amid debris, whether in the ruins of the mainline Protestant church in North America or the rubble of all the theologies of this and that into which some of my own theological education had attempted to project me. In my first pitiful parish, in my frustrating attempts to preach, I discovered the inadequacy of much of my ministerial preparation. My discovery was not as dramatic as Barth's had been at his little church in Safenwil, but though both of us wandered from our parochial origins (Barth was pastor at Safenwil about as long as I served as a parish pastor), neither of us lost sight of what the parish taught us about the limits of our inherited theology and the difficulty of preaching the Word of God. Thank God.

Barth changed the title of his *Christian Dogmatics* to *Church Dogmatics* in service to the proclamation of the church (unlike too many contemporary theologians who write in servility to the academy). Yet few of us preachers profited from Barth's work. Although we have been through a rather remarkable resurgence of interest in the postmodern Barth—his thunderous voice continuing to roar whereas those of his contemporary opponents have become silent—little has been done on Barth as a preacher or Barth as a teacher of preachers.[2] I plan to put Barth in conversation with contemporary homiletics in a ministry of encouragement and empowerment for today's preachers. I want to tell you what Barth has taught me and why he points the way to a renewal of our preaching. After all these years and my many homiletical failures, Barth keeps me preaching.

Although James Barr charged that Barth "paid little attention to other people's opinions," the very worst of conversation partners, still Barth is, in my estimate, among the most "conversational" of theologians. His theology is constant listening and speaking, taking his primary conversation partner (the Trinity) with utmost seriousness, as well as his theological friends and foes seriously. As Barth said: "Conversation takes place when one party has something new and interesting to say to the other. Only then is conversation an event. One must say something engaging and original, something with an element of mystery. The Church must sound strange to the world if it is not to be dull. . . . As theologians we must be obedient to the Word."[3] We are able to converse because there are between us genuine differences. And we must be able to recognize genuine difference when we encounter it in a dialogue. And Barth managed always to be different and therefore rarely dull. The Christian difference means that Barth, as a conversationalist, (1) shows his dependence on those who have gone before him in the faith and (2) in his determination to construct an audience for the gospel. Barth also takes theological positions seriously enough to be fierce in his urgent opposition to those whom he believes to be wrong. The ferocity of his opposition shows the seriousness with which he takes them.

To prepare for this open conversation, I reread Barth. Rereading his early *Göttingen Dogmatics*, into which I had made an only halfhearted foray earlier, made a particularly powerful impression upon me. I can now say with some confidence that I have read everything that Barth published in English—a rather reckless claim—as well as having translated scores of Barth's sermons. While we have almost every sermon he ever preached, we have few of Barth's sermons in English. One reason Barth has not influenced us more is that he wrote so much—over 9,000 pages in the *Dogmatics* alone. What preacher has the time to read so massive a corpus?

Another reason Barth has exercised so little influence among preachers is that Barth is against almost everything that we have been taught.[4] We have been given inadequate theological preparation to read him. Often Barth sounds difficult when he is just being different. Most homiletics professors have never forgiven Barth for his assault upon them in his scathing *Homiletics*. Even if one wants willingly to follow Barth, he can be a demanding mentor. The sheer volume and obstinacy of Barth's work suggest to me that he fully intended for us not to be in communication with anyone else once we had taken up conversation with him.[5]

The huge volume, the very bulk of Barth's work, is a kind of rhetorical statement by Barth. Balzac said that he hoped to write so much fiction that the body of his stories would rival all the history and philosophy that was being written in his age. In other words, Balzac (one of Barth's most admired novelists) attempted to write so much that he would have the last narrative word on the story of his age. He would, in effect, write so much that his narrative would subsume every other narrative that attempted to name what was going on in the world of his day. Dickens comes to mind as another novelist whose output was so massive, so thoroughly done, that he commanded the attention, and the predominant descriptions, of his time.

I find Barth to be a similarly ambitious writer. When he writes, he shows that he has read everything that was written before, that he is in active and deep conversation with all that has preceded him, but that he is also clearly conversing with these earlier or contemporary interpreters in order to, in a sense, dispose of them, and move us to a renarration of the story of what God is doing with us in the world now. His little lectures on homiletics come to mind as an instance, not only of the way that Barth's mind works but also of the way that he rhetorically presents his material.[6] Before Barth can get to his own thoughts on homiletics, he must first dispose of Hollaz, Schleiermacher (of course), Vinet, Bauer, and any other continental homiletician of the present or previous century. When Barth tackles any subject, he must go back and laboriously demonstrate that he knows what has been said on the subject in order to demonstrate why what he says is different. And then, after writing so much, he has the gall to warn us that his theology is not for the facile "page turner" but for those who will plow through until the very end before making any judgments about his theology.[7] The sheer size of his work, its inertia, is in itself an argument.

I am not a "Barthian." For one thing, Barth was notoriously hard on his disciples (much like Jesus). For another, I'm too much the Wesleyan, sanctificationist, pietist (three things Barth despised) to follow him all the way to the end. And as a preacher, I care more for my listeners than Barth seemed to care. Yet because in so many ways I am so unlike Barth I have found him to be the most helpful of friends. His thought is a fascinating, architectonic, vast, and enthralling adventure as lively as the Trinity. I never cease to be surprised by his insights, nor do I doubt that he was the greatest theologian of our time and, perhaps, any time. Yet I hope that this book is more than simply an attempt to apply Barth's thought to homiletics. With Barth, there is no continuing what he began, but only beginning. He called his massive *Dogmatics*

> no more than the beginning of a new reflection on the Word of God. It is the beginning of a dialogue, necessary for the Church, with the doctrine of the last centuries but also with that of the Reformation and with the old and the new Catholicism. Every dialogue with the older and younger pioneers can be conducted more profoundly than has been done here, just as every problem can be thought over more profoundly and more extensively. . . . But especially every line of Holy Scripture can, on the basis of newer explorations, become better understood and formulated than in my work. I do not look upon my work as a new *Summa Theologica*, . . . on the contrary: many people will still be able to do very much and I would be glad to live to see the day when I would be thoroughly overtaken by someone or other.[8]

Thus, toward the end of his Gifford Lectures (that became *With the Grain of the Universe*), my friend Stanley Hauerwas says that, because Barth's *Church Dogmatics* was conceived as a mere beginning, as theological investigations along the way, the *Dogmatics* is too short rather than too long. Barth never completed his work, never finished his theology, as if to say that, with a living God, there is always something else left to be heard and left to be said. Thus we later preachers press on.

Those who are familiar with Barth's *Church Dogmatics* will recognize my attempt to mimic Barth's style with the periodic sections that are indented and in smaller type. Barth used these sections for various exegetical excurses as well as for more detailed arguments that gave additional support for his dogmatic sections. I use them for material that supports my main arguments. The reader can skip these excurses and stay with the main discussion or dip into them if time and interest allow. Some of Barth's best stuff is found in the small-print discourses; I hope that mine are half as interesting. I also include some of my recent sermons, just to demonstrate the homiletical effect of Barth upon a preacher like me. My thanks to Jacqueline Andrews, Wilson Nash, and Dan Rhodes for their help in this project, as well as to generous colleagues like Jason Byassee, Ralph Wood, Reinhardt Hütter, Gerhard Sauter, Richard Lischer, George Hunsinger, and Hinrich Stoevesandt, who looked over my work while in process and gave me their reactions. The resources of the Karl Barth Archive in Basel, and its generous director, Hans-Anton Drewes, proved to be indispensable. A generous grant from the Devonwood Foundation and Brenda and Keith Brodie enabled me to do the necessary research in Germany and Switzerland. As in any theological endeavor that I've attempted in the past twenty years, my debt to dear, difficult Stanley Hauerwas is huge.

Because of the massiveness and the difficulty of Barth's work, almost any generalization one makes about what Barth said or thought on a subject is open to contradiction and correction by Barth himself, not to mention his host of defenders and detractors. However, I forge ahead, not only because my subject is the proclamation of the church rather than Karl Barth (I'm sure that Barth would approve) but also because, as a preacher, I am in over my head on a weekly basis, saying far more than I know for certain, continuously bordering on blasphemy, overstating, risking, and fully exposed to contradiction and rejection. It's a tough way to make a living, but as Barth might add, it is the best living worth God's making.

In the beginning of his magisterial lectures that became *Protestant Theology in the Nineteenth Century*, Barth quotes Luther (the theologian whom Barth most resembles in his homiletic theology).[9] In a note written two days before his death, Luther wrote that no one can understand Virgil "unless he has been a shepherd or a farmer for fifty years," and no one can interpret Cicero unless "he has been involved for twenty years in the life of a powerful state," and "Let no one think that he has tasted Holy Scripture unless he has for a century . . . been responsible for the Church."[10] Barth goes on to comment that we know history only when it is something that has happened to us and sometimes happened against us, as we "participate in it." Perhaps this book is my confirmation of Luther's and Barth's observations. I have only been trying to preach, and teach others to preach, for thirty years, but I could only have understood Barth, to the degree that I have, by having Barth's thought be something that happened to me and sometimes against me. I could have only read Barth because, week-in and week-out having to come up with something to say to my congregation, I need Barth. In fact, considering the purposes of Barth's theology, and its peculiar challenges, I do not think that anyone should venture to interpret Barth who is not a preacher, that is, without being a participant in the Holy Spirit–dependent task that Barth assumes. However, for me to assume this intellectual challenge during the first years of my episcopacy, when I am responsible for the 650 pastors and well over 800 churches of my area of Alabama, when I am of necessity so consumed (as was Paul) by "the daily pressure upon me of my anxiety for all the churches" (2 Cor. 11:28 RSV), well, this is pushing Luther's demand for church experience to the extreme. While writing this book I preached an average of four sermons every week. Surely this risks overdoing the "practical" in practical theology! For some time now I've been knee-deep in the "preaching, baptizing, confirming, bell-ringing, and organ-playing, . . . religious moods and modes, . . . the community houses with or without motion-picture equipment, the efforts to enliven church singing, the unspeakably tame and stupid monthly church papers, and . . . the equipment of modern ecclesiasticism" that Barth despised.[11] Still, I forge ahead. The preachers of the North Alabama Conference say that they want more teaching from their anxiety-ridden, modernly ecclesiastical bishop, so here it is.

Two Portraits of a Preacher

At first glance, it is a crowd—simply a crowd. A throng of people, most of whom have their backs turned toward us, has gathered in a clearing in a wood. They are all dressed in sixteenth-century Flemish attire. Few are well dressed. Most of them appear to be poor, as most of the world's people always are. In the foreground, wrapped in a fine cloak, a man is having his fortune told. His palm is being read. An exotic figure, with a dog on his coat, is telling his fortune—a pastime specifically prohibited by the Reformed Church. They are by far the most prominent, most easily recognizable figures in the painting.

Why has this crowd gathered? All eyes, except for the gamblers, are turned inward toward the center of the painting. Three young peasants have clambered up trees to get a better view. Upon closer examination, we see that everyone, except for a gaping-mouthed sleeper toward the left of the picture, is listening to someone. The speaker is a man, dressed in brown peasant's clothing. He gestures with his left hand toward a man who stands at the crowd's perimeter, a stranger, his arms folded, listening, looking at the preacher, perhaps with a skeptical air.

This is Pieter Bruegel's *The Sermon of St. John the Baptist.*[12] One has to look, and look long and hard, to find the preacher, the Baptist, amid the crowd. He is lost amid his listeners. He has nothing that makes him stand out, no clerical dress, nothing that insists upon our attention. He is not in a church, but in a wilderness, far from a church. Many in the crowd ignore him, go on about their business or play their games. True, three of them have climbed a tree to get a better view, but some of the others are asleep. At whom is everyone looking? They appear to look toward an ordinary, none too special human being, gesturing toward another ordinary-appearing person.

Pieter Bruegel: *The Sermon of St. John the Baptist*

I take Bruegel's painting as a Barthian parable of preaching. On Sunday morning, we preachers stand up and speak of Jesus, pointing toward him with our words. Sometimes a crowd gathers. Sometimes a few go to some trouble to be there and get a look. There are distractions. But for the most part, the world goes on about its business. Games are played. People doze. One can hardly see Jesus for all that is going on around him. Still, this is the way that Jesus gets introduced to most people, through the gestures of our preaching.

Although he was averse to most artistic attempts to represent religious subjects, Karl Barth had a lifetime attraction for another painting of John the Baptist preaching.[13] It is by the German Expressionist painter Mathis Grünewald (his real name, it was discovered after three hundred years of misnomer, was Mathis Neithardt), a painter who preceded Bruegel by nearly a century. The preacher John the Baptist appears on the crucifixion panel of Grünewald's Isenheim Altar in the convent of the Antonites in Colmar. Barth appears to have discovered the painting the same summer that he finished the manuscript of his *Epistle to the Romans*, that fateful summer of 1918 as Europe began to disintegrate along with Barth's inherited theology. He kept a copy of this painting over his desk throughout his ministry, from his days as a young pastor until his death, referring to the painting fifty-one times in his writings—the only artist, other than his beloved Mozart, to be so honored.[14]

Barth commended Grünewald's John the Baptist as a worthy metaphor for Christian preaching. John holds an open Bible. He is preaching, pointing an incredibly long and bony finger toward the horribly crucified, dead Christ strung up before him on the cross. John is the "voice of one crying in the wilderness" (John 1:23, quoting Isa. 40:3). The Christian preacher merely points toward the Christ. The speaker ought to be transparent to the Light of whom John said, "he must increase but I must decrease" (John 3:30). The depiction of the Baptist on the Isenheim Altar was the perfect embodiment of two Barthian tests for faithful preaching: hint, pointing toward, indication (*Hinweis*), and distance, detachment (*Distanz*), themes first sounded by Barth in the first edition (1919) of his *Epistle to the Romans*. The preacher must point directly toward Christ, but the preacher must be reminded of the distance between the preacher and Christ. The Baptist's forefinger—exaggeratedly elongated—is pointing away from himself, drawing no attention to himself, gesturing imperatively toward Christ. In other words, Barth likes the painting because it commends Christ and does not draw attention to itself. Barth does not commend it for any of its intrinsic or artistic features but rather for its exclusively Christological focus.

Grünewald's *John the Baptist*

In the Isenheim Altar, John stands alone, pointing to the crucified Christ. There is no congregation to hear his sermon, except for the viewers of the painting. All is in darkness except for the central figures. Bruegel, in my viewing, puts a better point on the preacher's dilemma. The preacher is the one who stands up, amid a congregation of sometimes interested but more often than not disinterested listeners, and tries to say a word about One who stands quietly, arms folded, reflectively, on the edge of the crowd, a stranger whose name is God with Us. It is hard to get a hearing from the crowd; it is difficult to get them to pay attention, sometimes almost impossible to get them to see the Stranger as the Light of the World. Few listen, yet I can see from the painting that some are listening and, in listening, are beginning to see. Are they hearing? I know the rest of the story of this strange prophet and his baptismal candidate; despite everything against these two preachers, people did hear.

My favorite German artist is a contemporary, Anselm Kiefer, a man who is obsessed with narratives of life in the postwar, continually threatened modern world. I first met him in his massive, colorless, ashen, apocalyptic paintings. One day, while in the Modern Art Museum of Fort Worth, I saw a piece of sculpture that I could not get out of my head. It is a Kiefer sculpture on a theme that he has treated many times, *Book with Wings*.[15] The work is wonderfully displayed by itself in a circular, chapel-like setting at the museum in which the sun streams in from above, giving the area around a kind of mystical air. It is a large, ancient-looking gray book, fabricated from the beloved modern materials—steel, tin, and lead. The work is surely meant to be ironic—the book is ponderous, leaden, dead, and cold, yet the book has two large, graceful wings. Is the book—the word—attempting to ascend or descend? How can a thing like that get off the ground? Yet, despite itself, it does appear to float.

Anselm Kiefer sculpture on a theme that he has treated many times, *Book with Wings*.

The preacher in me has an immediate kinship with this sculpture. That's me on Sunday morning—ponderous big book in hand, attempting, with nothing more than leaden words, to take flight, to rise, to ascend. Preaching is impossible on most Sundays, an exercise in frustration, like attempting to take to the air in a lead-and-steel book.

Yet sometimes, by the grace of God, miracle of miracles, they hear. The Word rises, ascends; the Word condescends, descends. The old Bible takes wing, tabernacles among us, flutters, quivers, and, despite everything against it, hovers, and we miraculously hear. Every preacher knows the frustration of working with this ancient, weighty book that thuds like a lead brick when we try to talk about it. Every preacher knows the miracle when this old book takes wings and alights as a dove, speaks, and makes a way for itself despite us. It is a sight to behold. It is a triumph of God.

This book is about that triumphant miracle named preaching.

William H. Willimon
The Birmingham Area of The United Methodist Church
Pentecost
2006

CHAPTER ONE

BARTH THE PREACHER

Although Barth would be adamantly opposed to the current enthusiasm for theologizing from "experience," or theology that is "contextual," Barth's life, particularly his early years as preacher and pastor, illuminate his theology. His last assistant, Eberhard Busch, has given us our only Barth biography,[1] noted for its thorough but uncritical account of his life. Barth was born in Basel, Switzerland, in May of 1886. His father, Fritz, taught at the College of Preachers, but moved the family on to the University of Bern when Barth was very young. Later in life Barth noted what a strong example his father had given him of someone who took theology seriously. Barth's boyhood experience of Confirmation whetted his appetite for theology, so upon beginning his university studies in 1904, he focused on theology. There he was introduced to Kant's *Critique of Practical Reason,* calling it "the first book that really moved me as a student."[2] But Barth's encounters with the thought of Troeltsch and Herrmann at Marburg convinced him that he "must refuse to follow the dominant theology of the age,"[3] even though the exact form of that refusal was not yet clear in his mind.

The Young Pastor

Upon completion of his formal studies, he was called immediately as an assistant at Calvin's old pulpit in Geneva. Barth's initial attempt at preaching was unhappy. In Geneva, even when preaching from that historic pulpit, the people were unresponsive. Later, Barth excused his efforts by saying that he thought he did little real harm to people because he was heard by so few. Reflecting on his time in Geneva, he noted that though he attempted to lay his academic theological training on the congregation, foisting upon them "all that historicism and individualism," the people in Geneva "weren't having any."[4]

Though the nave was mostly empty, Barth continued to preach a mostly liberal gospel. The liberal "inner Jesus" of his teacher, *Wilhelm Herrmann* (1846–1922), seemed to Barth the most credible basis for the Christian faith to make contact with the modern world. While the search for a Jesus of history had ended in a dead end with the historical reconstruction of Jesus looking suspiciously like a mirror image of the historians themselves, Herrmann's answer had been to turn from a historical Jesus to a subjective, "inner Jesus." From Herrmann, Barth learned to be suspicious of historical Jesus reconstruction efforts as the attempt to step outside of faith into some objective security. Faith cannot be defended or justified by some means external to the faith itself. Historical research into scripture can therefore play an important but only secondary role. The important thing is a believer's individual experience with Christ, an experience which the liberal assumes is on a rather comfortable continuum between the believer and Christ.

By 1911, when Barth moved from Geneva to become pastor to a rather forlorn industrial village in Safenwil, canton of Aargau, he had the opportunity to focus more on his preaching, and when he did, he began to question some of his inherited theological assertions. Attendance in Safenwil was as poor as it had been in Geneva. However, now that Barth had

had the experience of preaching week-in and week-out to his own congregation, he was more consumed by the challenges of the preaching task and more starkly confronted by the weaknesses of the theology he received at the university. In Safenwil, Barth preached long, excruciatingly intellectual sermons that sailed over the heads of the simple folk in the pews. Though some said that his style was energetic and personal, Barth discovered that Herrmann's urbane liberalism was not at all helpful with a number of more challenging biblical texts. So Barth preached many topical sermons in these early years at Safenwil, preaching on such invigorating topics as "Mission" or "The Life of William Booth" and "The Heritage of the Reformation."

Gary Dorrien characterized Barth's early preaching in this way:

> He equated God with that which is "highest and best in our souls" and lauded Schleiermacher as "the brilliant leader of a new reformation." He taught that Christianity is rooted in the individual's experience of Christ and that Christ's victory over death lay in his calm acceptance of his impending crucifixion. Jesus was resurrected long before he died, Barth assured his congregation. . . . He later recalled that he and the people of Safenwil always seemed to be looking at each other through a pane of glass.[5]

The differences between his congregation and Harnack's or Herrmann's academic audience in Berlin and Marburg were sobering to Barth. He realized how much theology had tailored itself to fit the demands of the academy rather than the church. He also realized the limits of attempting to preach from an anthropological assessment of the "modern mind." When Barth attempted to share his own inner turmoil with his congregation in a sermon, that self-revelation only made them more suspicious of his preaching. Looking back on his first years as a young pastor, he said that he was sorry "for everything that my congregation had to put up with."

Later, when he visited his former congregation in 1935 as a renowned theologian, he apologized for not having preached the gospel more clearly when he was among them. "I have often thought with some trepidation of those who were perhaps led astray or scandalized by what I said at that time, or of the dead who have passed on and did not hear, at any rate from me, what by human reckoning they ought to have heard." Elsewhere he confessed that he was tormented "by the memory of how greatly, how yet *more* greatly, I failed as a pastor of Safenwil." Though they could not have known it at the time, the simple folk at Safenwil were witnessing the first stirrings of one of the century's remarkable theological transformations.

During this formative pastoral period an important influence came to Barth from a fellow pastor whose theology was very different from Barth's. *Christoph Blumhardt* (1858–1919) was a charismatic Christian socialist, son of a prominent Lutheran preacher and healer. The younger Blumhardt and Barth met for a series of conversations in 1915, just before Barth began his work on *Romans*. The thing that impressed Barth about Blumhardt, as he later explained, was that "Blumhardt always begins right away with God's presence, might, and purpose: he starts out from God; he does not begin by climbing upwards to Him by means of contemplation and deliberation."[6] From Blumhardt, Barth learned that theology commences with God, not with our pious yearnings or experience. The God of Blumhardt's theology was a strong, active, present God. What is God doing in the world? is a more important question than any of our questions about ourselves. Genuinely Christian thinking is oriented not to our supposed "religious experience"—the infatuation of nineteenth-century theology—but to God's actual work in the world. This realization, fostered in him through Blumhardt, had the effect of moving Barth away from some of his mild youthful socialism into an even more radical assessment of the relationship of Christianity in the world. The most radically political statement we can make is when we are able to say, in the face of the world's politics, "Thy kingdom come!" The world with its present political arrangements does not simply need improvement; it needs radical, sweeping, eschatological transformation that only God can give. That transformation cannot be fully characterized with the available language of socialist politics. Christianity demands its own distinctive speech to describe its distinctive vision. And from Blumhardt, Barth learned of the kingdom of God as a present reality that comes to us from beyond, a Kingdom that precedes and judges all of our concepts and experiences of the kingdoms of this world, particularly religiously derived concepts of the kingdom of God.[7]

Barth evidenced, from his earliest years, a distinctive characteristic of his thought—a wonderful naïveté about the personalities of history, entering into dialogue with them as if they were fully present contemporaries, testimony to his strong faith in the reality of the *communion sanctorum*. As Francis Watson said of Barth's commentary on the Epistle to the Philippians, "The disjunction between then and now has largely been abandoned."[8] To his great credit, Barth never lost this immediate, engaging naïveté that enabled him to converse with historical personalities and biblical texts with an open-eyed wonder that yielded stunning insights.

A peculiar influence upon the young Barth was *Franz Overbeck*, pariahic professor of New Testament in Basel and a friend of Nietzsche. Most theologians of the day regarded Overbeck as an erratic iconoclast, a crank. In 1920 Barth wrote "Unsettled Questions for Theology Today," a review of Overbeck's *Christentum und Kultur*, published posthumously. Barth took issue with those who thought that Overbeck was an atheist who was hostile to Christianity. If Overbeck was correct, said Barth, then "it is impossible for anyone really to be such a thing as a theologian." Overbeck said that contemporary theology had become a sham with its trumped-up historicism and intellectual pretense. Theology had reached a *cul de sac*. But Barth heard here a more positive message that he favorably (surprisingly) compared to the thought of the pious Blumhardt. Barth thought that both of these seemingly opposite thinkers said much the same thing: Christianity is essentially eschatological and demands an end to conventional modes of thinking. The peculiar subject matter of Christianity demands peculiar intellectual resources. Overbeck said that the option before us was either respectable history or outrageous Christianity. Christianity, he argued, was not something to be based upon historical events. Christianity claimed to be an end of history. It was not of this world, but rather a great contradiction to the world. Historical methods could not uncover or judge the claims of Christianity because those claims transcend history. Historians could never climb out of their own limited history in order to make judgments about history. Christianity was an in-breaking of the kingdom of God that obliterated all other kingdoms, including the "kingdom" that is served by historical study and its subservient historians.

Overbeck was not a Christian. He expected that Christianity would gradually fade away (as it indeed appears to have done in much of Switzerland). Yet Barth defends him, perhaps ironically, as a heroic thinker whose anti-theology suggests a return to the true purpose of theology. At least Overbeck was honest enough to know that there are few Christians left in the world and that Christianity cannot be supported or defended by the conventional intellectual means of making sense of the world—like history, a bogus application of Christianity that only reduces Christianity to another worldly philosophy and thereby erases Christianity's wild claims for itself.[9]

Barth loved Overbeck's eschatological emphasis (as much as he loved the eschatology of Blumhardt) and resonated with Overbeck's hyperbolic critique. From Overbeck he received a radically new awareness of the decisive difference between Christianity and our so-called history, curiously overlooking Overbeck's own loss of faith through his study of history. Christianity was a present eschatological experience, or it was not the Christianity of the Bible. History, said Overbeck, was an abyss "into which Christianity has been thrown wholly against its will."[10] Was Overbeck a theologian? Barth wrote (almost as if describing himself) that "a theologian who is determined not to be a theologian might perhaps—if the impossible is to become possible—be a very good theologian." Barthian irony is here apparent: one can only be a true theologian by denouncing and denigrating theology, constructing theology by dismantling theology, constantly turning theology against itself in order to adhere to its proper object—a God who is so distinctively different from us as to be a constant problem for theology.

We might also mention Barth's curious relationship to the thought of *Ludwig Feuerbach* (1829–1880). Like Overbeck, Feuerbach was a fierce critic of Christianity, yet his critique provided Barth with the insight he needed to assail the liberal theology of his student years. In an article he wrote in 1920, Barth praised Feuerbach for astutely unmasking the problem of theology. What Barth liked most in Feuerbach was not his notorious idea that Christianity was a mere projection of human religious yearnings, but rather Feuerbach's bald reduction of theology to nothing but anthropology, thus typifying the fate of most theology of the age. Theology had degenerated into anthropology, beginning with various assessments of the "human condition" rather than with, "And God said. . . ." Feuerbach furthered a process that began in Kant. Feuerbach merely exposed theology's nasty little secret: it had become more interested in humanity than God. From Feuerbach Barth learned his famous dictum that theology must be more than talking about humanity in a very loud voice. Otherwise, Feuerbach's charge against "theology" would simply be confirmed by our "theologians" themselves.

One of the few novelists who appealed to Barth was *Fyodor Dostoevsky*. Barth's good friend *Eduard Thurneysen* (1888–1978) introduced him to this wild Russian.[11] Barth was drawn to Dostoevsky's "Grand Inquisitor," a central chapter in his novel, *The Brothers Karamazov*. He found therein a sort of literary presentation of Overbeck's argument against church history. Dostoevsky's Inquisitor wants to improve the course of history, rather than to follow the narrow way of Christ. He offers people what they want: religion (namely miracle, mystery, and authority) in order to pacify them and keep them docile and happy. In fact, when Jesus appears to the Inquisitor, the church leader is repulsed by the sight of him. The Inquisitor accuses Jesus of caring nothing for the masses, those for whom the church must provide comfort and care, peace and security. Jesus only cared for the few heroic individuals who obeyed his revolutionary, "Follow me." In fact, the Inquisitor interpreted the three temptations Jesus overcame in Luke 4 as the three main tasks of the church: giving the people the means to believe, giving people bread before it gives them Spirit, and political order and security.

Barth read Dostoevsky's parable as a stark contrast between the way of Jesus and the conventional way of the church. The battle that raged was not the church against the world, but rather, Jesus against the institution that bears his name; not atheism against religion, but rather, Jesus against religion. The church attempted to save and preserve humanity, whereas it ought to point to Jesus as the only means of salvation. Jesus responds to the Inquisitor with a silent kiss, a reversal of Judas's betrayal of Jesus. This literary scene became a basis for Barth's sustained attack upon "religion," not only in *Romans*[12] but also throughout the *Dogmatics*.

One more influence upon the early Barth ought to be mentioned, the solitary Dane, *Søren Kierkegaard* (1813–1855). Barth was impressed by Kierkegaard's "infinite qualitative distinction" (stressed in the opening pages of *Romans*) between God and humanity, but he also subsumed Kierkegaardian irony into his style.[13] Barth seized upon Kierkegaard's metaphor of the "moment" to denote the time when God obliterates the slow progression of history and breaks into history as salvific event. But Kierkegaard was too depressed, sad, and anthropological for Barth's temperament. Kierkegaard seems to have influenced Barth's style more than his substance, making Barth's style richly metaphorical, ironic, and figurative, rather than abstract and systematic, demanding from us a decision and hoping to convert us in the process.[14] From Kierkegaard, Barth learned that Christianity is an invasion, an event whereby the eternal sweeps into time in this moment, demanding an either/or decision from us. Traveling in such disgruntled theological company, Barth could not help but radicalize and intensify his early dissatisfaction with the bland liberal theology that he had found to be so uninteresting in the pulpit.

Barth spent ten years as pastor in Safenwil, years he would look back upon as ten important years that led him, during this pastoral decade, to a complete abandonment of his youthful theological liberalism. As a pastor, he involved himself in local political arguments, arguments that led to considerable conflict not only with some of the economic and political leaders of the town, but with his congregation as well. His early socialist interest revealed to Barth the bourgeois confinement of his teachers and earned for him the title, among some in the village, of "the Red Pastor."

Barth did not spend all of his time criticizing Safenwil industrialists; in fact, most of his effort was spent on the Sunday sermon, sermon preparation being his most "political" activity. At Safenwil, Barth was a disruptive preacher: "My calling is to speak and to speak clearly. . . . If I wanted to be liked, I would keep quiet."[15] Barth set out boldly to let God speak in his sermons, without speaking for or about God. His sermons often seem to restate and repeat the biblical text because he was primarily concerned that the peculiar way of God's speech, as exemplified in scripture, be exemplified through repetition in his sermon.

Webb notes that Barth managed both to be assertive in his sermons, as early as Safenwil, and to qualify many of his boldest assertions. He spoke about God, and then he said that he was unable to speak about God; he said that we must work for the kingdom and then said that there is no work in the kingdom except God's work. In a 1916 sermon Barth said that the church was meant to be a place of crisis and disturbance, not refuge. Attending church, "you cannot go in and come out peacefully."[16] And it was the Bible, he thought, that was the ticking bomb that made the church so dangerous. He compared the Bible to a raging river that has swept over its banks, spreading destruction and yet also fertility in its flood. The message of the Bible is so great that it demands exaggeration. The message with which Barth threatened the congregation, also threatened the preacher who delivered it: "Everything in my position and words that you now think is directed against you was really directed against me and my own life long before."[17]

In Safenwil, Barth began to wonder why the spirited rhetoric of his pulpit work seemed to play no role in his theological reflection: "Why, I had to ask myself, did those question marks and the exclamation marks, which are the very existence of the pastor, play really no role at all in the theology I knew?"[18] He wondered if there was some way to transfer his pulpit penchant for irony and excitement from the sermon to his more academic discourse. The liberal theology that he inherited from seminary seemed limp and dated, "mere child's play." His Sunday sermonic socialism seemed no match for the great issues that were looming for the church. His was the preacher's dilemma of not only having something to say but also something pressing, interesting, and engaging to say. At one pastors' meeting, as the older pastors droned on, Barth said that he was filled "with the greatest unrest and anguish. . . . I wanted to shout out in the room, I have neither the voice nor the words, and I hang there wriggling like a roofer on his rope."[19] With his lifelong friend Eduard Thurneysen, then a young pastor in a nearby village, Barth began a fresh reading of the Bible.[20]

That some new beginning was stirring in him is evidenced in an address given in 1916, Barth's soon to become famous, "The Strange New World Within the Bible."[21] Here Barth not only announced his privileging of the Bible as a source for theology but also vividly described the shape of that source: the Bible is the rumbling of an earthquake, the thundering of ocean waves. People have asked too little of the Bible, yet the Bible has within itself a wonderful ability to break free of our meager questions and pose new, more sweeping questions to us, even as we thought we were questioning the Bible. The Bible has few answers to our questions, but rather negates our questions by raising before us the question that we have been avoiding: the question of God. This "strange, new world" did not simply want to speak to our world; it wanted to destroy and rebuild our world by the inbreaking of "the world of God." Barth, for instance, noted that the Bible was not all that helpful as a sourcebook for morality. It glorified war and had almost nothing to say about our bourgeoisie concerns in regard to business, marriage, and government. "It offer[ed] us not at all what we first seek in it," rather it offered an encounter with the "other" who resiliently stands against us and our questions, asserting only the tautology that devastates our theological probings: "God is God."

The Epistle to the Romans

When war broke out in 1914, Barth was horrified when he picked up the newspaper and saw that many of his once admired theological teachers had signed a Declaration of Support for the German government. His teachers' appeal to the German collective "religious war experience" distressed Barth because it seemed to him a sacralizing warrant for German militarism. To Barth this was the sad result of the theology of human experience, which he had learned from Schleiermacher and Herrmann. In September he told Eduard Thurneysen that the gospel was being "simply suspended for the time being and in the meantime a German war-theology is put to work, its Christian trimming consisting of a lot of talk about sacrifice and the like."[22] This spectacle made him doubt whether what had been preached as the gospel had ever been anything more than a "surface varnish" for nationalist ideology. "It is truly sad! Marburg and German civilization have lost something in my eyes by this breakdown, and indeed forever," he lamented.[23]

Barth said, in reading that Declaration of Support, "An entire world of theological exegesis, dogmatics, and preaching, which up to that point I had accepted as basically credible, was thereby shaken to the foundations, and with it everything that flowed at that time from the pens of the German theologians."[24] Yet it is wrong to describe Barth's distress, and the move it necessitated, as primarily related to current political events. As his friend Bonhoeffer said, "Barth's critical move in theology was not to be explained in terms of the collapse of the war . . . but in terms of a new reading of Scripture, of the Word which God has spoken in God's self-revelation. . . . This is not war-psychosis but listening to God's word. Barth does not come from the trenches but from a Swiss village pulpit."[25]

Barth began an intense period of intellectual searching centered upon scripture. During his search he rediscovered Paul. And consequently, he found in Paul a "real transcendence of the Bible," which became "the textual basis of my sermons." He engaged in an intensive study of the Epistle to the Romans. Seizing whatever time he could between his pastoral duties, Barth said, "I read and read and wrote and wrote." From this work, arising out of his parish and preaching experiences, emerged his *Commentary on Romans*, which he published in December 1918 and greatly revised in the more famous Second Edition of 1921. With *Romans*, twentieth-century theology began in a book by a village pastor that was said to fall like a bombshell on the playground of the theologians.

In his study of Paul, the Christian faith had become defamiliarized, something strange and alien to Barth, something far from the once comfortable fit with modern faith in human interiority and social progress. Barth stressed Christianity as something transcendent, eschatological, and thoroughly beyond the reach of our cognitive and communicative capacities.[26]

The kingdom of God is not a second world standing apart from the existing "real" world, he proclaimed. Rather, God's kingdom is this existing world made strange and new through the in-breaking power of the Spirit. The Kingdom is something that God does among us, rather than the outcome of our astute thought about God. In this strange new world, there are stark, either/or alternatives rather than easy alliances with the old world: "We are offered the magnificent, productive, hopeful life of a grain of a seed, a new beginning, out of which all things shall be made new," he declared. "One can only let it live, grow, and ripen within him. One can only believe—can only hold the ground whither he has been led. Or not believe. There is no third way." The Bible repeatedly made straight for the point at which one must decide whether to accept God's sovereignty or reject it. There was no third alternative. To accept it was to enter the new world of the Spirit of truth.

With the publication of *Romans* Barth found himself at the center of a theological movement known as "Dialectical Theology." In 1921 Barth was appointed as a professor of Reformed theology in Göttingen. As he left the parish ministry and headed for the university, he told Thurneysen in May 1921 that the muzzle of his gun was now trained upon Schleiermacher and that he was ready to declare war.[27] Later that year, his second edition of *Romans*, a more pointed and purer break with liberalism, blasted Schleiermacher for turning the world-shattering gospel into the tame provenance of "religion." Liberal theology attempted to make the gospel of Christ into one human possibility among many others, failing to see the gospel as the end of all human possibility. "Since Schleiermacher, this attempt has been undertaken more consciously than ever before in Protestant theology—and it is the betrayal of Christ."[28]

Barth cautioned that the Bible has little interest in most of the questions that people bring to their study of the Bible. People have been conditioned to think that it is their task to approach the Bible with the pressing questions of the day, there seeking moral guidance. Scripture, however, has the much greater calling of announcing the new world of God's reign. In various ways, and in many voices, scripture is about God's glory and sovereignty. The Bible is not about how we might climb up to God, Barth explained; scripture is always about how God has miraculously, triumphantly descended to us. When Schleiermacher based his "theology" upon anthropocentric claims and forsook any genuine appeal to revelation, Barth averred that Schleiermacher degraded the adventure of theology into a rehash of uninteresting, merely contemporary anthropological speculation. "And our fathers were right when they guarded warily against being drawn out upon the shaky scaffolding of religious self-expression."[29]

Though *Romans* was exciting biblical interpretation, the method of Barth's argument and much of its basis were still tainted with nineteenth-century liberalism. His concern with the problem of revelation, the problem of modernity, and the challenge of epistemology were thoroughly nineteenth-century preoccupations. However, Paul had Barth in his grip and was leading him toward a dramatic theological shift. Barth's newfound stress upon God's sovereignty and righteousness would soon have implications for his thought: "We have found in the Bible a new world, God, God's sovereignty, God's glory, God's incomprehensible love. Not the history of man but the history of God! Not the virtues of men but the virtues of him who hath called us out of darkness into his marvelous light! Not human standpoints but the standpoint of God!" Barth excitedly narrated Paul's word as a word addressed to our situation here and now, a word that had no need of the historical and psychological props that nineteenth-century hermeneutics had attempted to provide, because it has a living, speaking, revealing God to vouch for its claims. In the closing weeks of the war, after he had finished his commentary, Barth fretted that his conversion to a biblically oriented revelationism had come too late. "If only we had been converted to the Bible earlier so that we would now have solid ground under our feet!" he sighed to Thurneysen.[30]

Romans also showed evidence of Barth's new reading of Plato. For Paul, claimed Barth, salvation is the restoration of a broken existing ideal, the hunger for a new age beyond the transitory, faded quality of this age, an age that is "the truth of God written by the prophets of Israel, by Plato and their like." Like Plato and Kant, Barth surmised a "real reality" that lies beyond the world of mere appearances, a world that cannot be accessed through our normal, earthbound processes of thought, that is, God. And like Plato, Barth had no misgivings about daring to speak of that real, though invisible, world to a modern world that thought only the visible was real.

His theological insights demanded new ways of talking. Barth now worked in a style that many have regarded as "expressionistic," a style of theological writing with similarities to some of the expressionist novelists of the era who sought to break open the surface of language to reveal the real world underneath or beyond our usual modes of discourse. Though he mentions writers of fiction only rarely, Barth appears to have embraced expressionism's belief that true reality can be glimpsed only by disrupting or breaking open the world of superficial language. Historians tend to treat the world of appearances as the "real world," making of that world, which is readily available to our senses, an idol rather than inquiring into the infinitely more real world beyond our senses and historical retrievals. In Barth's hands, Paul's Letter to the Romans is a disruptive, uncontainable, idol-breaking critique of every merely human strategy for self-salvation.

Barth seemed, in *Romans*, shockingly indifferent to the methods of historical criticism of scripture, methods of "scientific exegesis" that had been developed in the previous century in the German university and which now had a hammer-hold on biblical interpretation. Methods of historical retrieval had little interest for Barth. Overbeck had soured Barth on that project. To Barth, "so-called history" was merely the empirically derived result of descriptions of the phenomenal world, history in which people find themselves and in which they experience past, present, and future. But Barth takes Paul's account of salvation in Christ and derives from it some interesting anti-historicist claims. "So-called history" is the history of the empirical world that lives under the judgment of sin and death, that is, under the God-imposed limits for human thought and cognition. Barth admitted that Paul perceived that ordinary history contained a hint of God's better world. This suggestion, this hint, Paul calls the Law. The Law can point us toward that new world, can show us the limits of our present world, but it cannot take us to the new world because the Law cannot generate the capacity within fallen human beings to fulfill its demands. Salvation is the new age that the Law promises but cannot deliver. Salvation is the pure gift that comes only from the Word of God through the "real history" of God's saving action.[31] The divinely given Word breaks into history not so much to transform the world as to shake it, to dismantle the world's reigning idols, and to throw the world into crisis.

When Barth revised *Romans*, his expressionistic rhetoric became even more vivid and provocative, filled with typically Barthian reiteration, repetition, exaggeration, and hyperbole. In the first edition, Barth was exuberant; now Barth seemed angry. The revised *Romans* reads like a sermon designed for provocation, full of overstatement and exaggeration in the intent to bring a crisis. In fact, this edition would give birth to a movement known as "Crisis Theology." Gary Dorrien notes of the second edition of *Romans*, "Nearly all of the book's academic reviewers made special note of its unusual rhetorical qualities. Philipp Bachmann remarked on Barth's 'burning zeal' and described his work as a type of 'pneumatic-prophetic exegesis redolent with an inexhaustible vividness.' In a generally enthusiastic review, young Emil Brunner noted that the book's apparent naïveté produced a first impression of astonishment and surprise. In a decidedly less favorable review, Adolf Julicher allowed that Barth 'knows how to speak penetratingly, at times charmingly, and always with colorful vividness.'" But then Julicher chided this young upstart for apparently turning his back on the lessons that had been learned and the articles of faith that had been affirmed in the university. Julicher found it galling that Barth, a graduate of prestigious, liberal Marburg, explicitly privileged the outmoded idea of supernaturalist biblical inspiration over the sober modern methods of historical criticism. With sadness, Julicher noted that for people like Barth and Friedrich Gogarten, nothing was more certain "than that there is no more progress in history, that development is forever at an end, and that no optimism in the interest of culture moves us anymore."[32] In other words, there is no more celebration among these young upstarts of the remarkable achievements of German Imperial high culture.

Even now, a preacher who reads the second edition of *Romans* will find, in Barth's strident cadences, the invigorating work of a fellow preacher who has been gripped by the gospel and thereby freed from the artificial restraints of culturally subservient theologies of this and that. Here is theology meant to be preached.[33]

By 1920 Barth's speeches and writings were inflaming the old liberal theological establishment, to Barth's apparent delight. At the Aarau Student Conference, Barth sharply dissociated himself from the historical-critical approach to religious studies, which falsely attempted to study, from the outside, the claims of faith that make sense only from the inside. Theology must speak from "inside and not outside . . . the knowledge of God and of the last things," said Barth. In his view, the key to biblical piety was precisely its antipathy to "religion" and the limp religious idea of "sacredness." Nothing in our experience is sacred; only God is sacred, and the Bible presents God as holy, incomparable, and unattainable. God cannot be grasped by even our highest concepts, nor put to use even in our most noble uses. God can only be served. "He is not a thing among other things, but the Wholly Other, the infinite aggregate of all merely relative others. He is not the form of religious history but is the Lord of our life, the eternal Lord of the world."[34]

In Kierkegaardian fashion, Barth saw Christ as "the paradox" and the great "divine incognito," describing faith as a "leap into the darkness of the unknown, a flight into empty air." Perhaps his disappointing experience with preaching in Basel and Safenwil prompted Barth to agree with Kierkegaard that faith cannot be communicated from one human being to another; it can only be revealed by God. There is no access from here to there except that which is divinely given. Paradoxically, the presence of Christ, standing before us, in history, is "the most complete veiling of His incomprehensibility." Through Christ, God is made known "as the Unknown, speaking in eternal silence." God, in Christ, was an embodied paradox for human perception and cognition. He came among us in a veiling/unveiling. Some of Barth's rhetoric can be explained by his embrace of the Kierkegaardian-like assertion that "the communication of God begins with a rebuff, with the exposure of a vast chasm, with the clear revelation of a great stumbling block." Faith is related to God in God's utter incomprehensibility and hiddenness, or it is false faith. Though in somewhat chastened tones, somewhat qualified cadences, these were the melodies that Barth sang for the rest of his life.

Luther had claimed that Romans 3:22-24 is the core of all scripture: "For there is no distinction, since all have sinned and fall short of the glory of God; they are now justified by his grace as a gift, through the redemption that is in Christ Jesus." With Luther and Kierkegaard, Barth proclaimed that the righteousness of God is displayed by the absolute separation between God and humanity, including especially those attempts by which humanity tries to attain God by evading him, namely, what Barth labels as "religion."[35] Dostoevsky strengthened Barth's contempt for "religion," seeing it as a false human attempt (represented by Dostoevsky's Grand Inquisitor) to set up some idol in the name of the living God, which gives people what they desire—mystery, authority, security, and miracle—rather than the world-shattering freedom that is theirs in Christ. Throughout his life, Barth was criticized for caring more about those who were outside the church than for those within. From his earliest days, Barth cultivated a thin differentiation between the "insiders" of the faith and the "outsiders." He really believed Paul when he said that "there is no distinction" except the distinction that the "religious" tend to delude themselves into thinking that their "religion" is actually a faith in the living God rather than a substitute for faith.

The Dogmatic Theologian

By 1925 Barth had been invited to teach at Münster. The move from the parish to the academy enabled Barth to further develop his theology, a theology that was born during his period as a pastor but which required a complete rethinking during his first years as a full-time academic. In the parish Barth had needed something to preach; now Barth needed to back up his assertions by reference to the theology that had gone before. He began an intense, systematic reading of classical dogmatic theology, especially the theology of the Reformation, which gave him a structure and a standpoint from which to rethink and to move out of the wreckage of theological liberalism.

Both his theology and his rhetoric became more chastened, more realistic as opposed to expressionistic, and more explicitly dogmatic as a result of his teaching duties in Münster. Although Barth resisted the label of "Reformed theologian" with good reason, he became not only a teacher of the Reformed tradition of Christian dogmatics but also a dogmatist within this tradition. The expressivist metaphors and word plays, which typified Crisis Theology and filled his early writings, gradually subsided from his work. He later recalled that in the mid-1920s he began to learn "along with a great centralization of what was material, to move and express myself again in simple thoughts and words." His language became more representational and mimetic as a function of his resolve now to serve the church as a dogmatic theologian whose thought was controlled by the cadences of scripture.[36]

Yet even when Barth launched his dogmatical work, he did so in service to preaching. He spoke of the sermon as "the starting point and the goal of dogmatics."[37] The basis of that dogmatic theology was Barth's conviction that "either God speaks, or he does not." During this period, Barth began his lifelong *opposition to apologetics*. There is no way to God but through God's self-revelation; our apologetic arguments only admit that God does not speak so we must. "When God speaks, God does not speak more or less, or partially, or in pieces, here a bit and there a bit. This is a contradiction in terms, an anthropomorphism, a basic naturalizing of revelation which fits Schleiermacher very well, but which ought not to have found any place among the older Reformed." The older Reformed dogmatists built a case for natural revelation from the confession that all truth is of God and, since Creation is from God, we can find revelation, in bits and pieces, within Creation. But Barth countered that the assumption of natural theology was less than the totality of truth that is God in Jesus Christ. "Truth that really goes back to God cannot be a particle of truth. It is either the whole truth or it does not go back to God and is not revelation at all." Barth was attracted to Zwingli's teaching that we can receive God's grace only through God's grace. Hence, Barth criticized the Reformed tradition for not sufficiently upholding Zwingli's insight about revelation as pure gift of God. He rather weakly attempted to invoke Calvin in support of his assertion of God's revelation as a pure gift of God, while at the same time criticizing Calvin's apologetic and natural theology arguments. Barth admitted that Calvin practiced apologetics as a means of asserting the glory of God but also noted that apologetic arguments play no real material importance in Calvin's theology. Unfortunately, said Barth, too many later Calvinists became mired in apologetics, thus undermining Calvin's earlier stress on the unapproachable glory of God. By the time of the Westminster Confession (1647), Barth noted, most of Reformed dogmatics was riddled with apologetic proofs based upon philosophical foundations other than the glorious self-revelation of God.[38]

Barth's study of Anselm in the early 1930s helped Barth *rid his thought of philosophical (that is, anthropological) foundations*. Anselm enabled him to begin the *Church Dogmatics* confessionally, writing and thinking without anxiety about finding some philosophical foundation from which to begin theology. All theology, Barth was now able to say with confidence, begins not with philosophical or anthropological assertions, but rather exclusively with the self-utterance of God in Jesus Christ. Anselm taught Barth that all theology is a practice of prayer. While Barth's theology became more rooted in the tradition, that is, more realistically and less expressionistically stated, Barth continued to speak of revelation as a miraculous, momentary gift of God, which occurs within the closed circle of Christian knowing. "For grace is the event in which God comes to us in his Word, an event over which God has sole control, and which is strictly momentary," said Barth. We have the possibility of knowing and experiencing the true God, not because we have alighted upon the right philosophical means to conceive of God, but rather because God graciously comes to us.[39] This Barthian "actualism" keeps his theology energetic, full of movement and excitement, and lively to the end.

Barth's theology also keeps its decidedly homiletical flavor, consistently pointing to speech and hearing as the basis for theological reflection. The Word of God will either speak for itself or not, Barth was declaring. The work of the theologian is to be open to the movement of the Word and to be tethered only to scripture for its substance. No human philosophical constructs can be allowed to obstruct the freedom of theology to listen to scripture and to testify to what is heard. His old colleague from Marburg, Rudolf Bultmann, complained that Barth thought he was emancipating himself from philosophy only to become the victim of an unstated, unacknowledged, outdated philosophy. Barth, however, remained undeterred in his determination to do theology without philosophical weapons to assist him. As Barth made a move to the University of Bonn, he was able to write and think with confidence that he could work within the "closed circle" of divine revelation, using the church's distinctive language, without having to borrow the speech of the world and without having to appeal to the world's reigning philosophies in order to justify his assertions.

From Herrmann Barth discovered that *revelation is self-authenticating*, a lesson he never forgot. While Barth appealed to scripture as the Word of God, he did so now, not on the basis of the liberal emphasis on reason and experience, but rather from the Herrmannian assertion that scripture creates a closed circle for itself through divine self-revelation. The gospel has no interpretive allies in the world. The words of the world, and the words evoked by the Word, are very differently derived words that evoke and point toward very different worlds.[40] Much later in his life Barth said, "I simply learned to speak the great word 'God' once again seriously, responsibly, and forcibly."[41]

Barth now strove to make his theology rigorously christological. Everything begins and ends with the Word made flesh. This circular, spiraling arrangement is the basic structure and the organizing metaphor for Christ is always the center, and our theological assertions surround this center, moving toward the center and out from the center. His *Church Dogmatics* is organized as a circle, the themes being like spokes of a wheel that move out from the center, Christ.

Hunsinger says:

> It is the metaphor of the circle comprising center and periphery—a metaphor which is constantly employed to bring out the centrality of Jesus Christ. The task of theology is to make clear at every point that Christ stands at the center of the gospel.
>
> To explain the Gospel is to expound, unfold and articulate its content, with no effacement of its unity and simplicity, but rather in enhancement of its unity and simplicity. It is to assert and honor it synoptically in all its richness, displaying the place and manner of each individual part. It is also to make known the periphery in each section as that of the true center, and the center as in every respect that of the distinctive periphery.[42]

Jesus Christ is understood as the central content of its witness, for Jesus Christ is the name of the God who deals graciously with sinful humanity. "To hear this is to hear the Bible—both as a whole and in each one of its separate parts. Not to hear this means *eo ipso* not to hear the Bible, neither as a whole, nor therefore in its parts." The one thing said in the midst of everything, the center which organizes the whole, is "just this: the name of Jesus Christ."[43] From beginning to end, Barth was grasped by the theological content, the christological substance of theology and preaching—Jesus Christ. He is therefore a wonderful corrective to contemporary theology and preaching, which has so often degenerated into various modes of self-presentation. Barth keeps asking us, in effect, "Do you really have anything to talk about other than yourself when you claim to be talking about God?"[44]

Yet in his first days at Bonn, Barth could not limit himself to purely theological concerns. The world now demanded Barth's attention, as the church faced a decision about what to do about Hitler. Barth's thinking about Hitler led to the *Barmen Theological Declaration* of 1934 and the formation of the Confessing Church. Against the pressures of national socialism upon the church, Barmen asserted that the church was to be defined, not by its alleged usefulness to the surrounding culture, but by listening only to its demanding Word and by confessing Jesus Christ "as the one Word of God which we have to hear and which we have to trust and obey in life and in death."[45] The Declaration employs a very Lutheran formulation, an embodiment of Luther's justification by faith alone in a theology of language. In Luther, the Word of God takes precedence over reason, experience, even over the church. "The church comes into being because God's word is spoken. The church does not constitute the Word but is constituted by the Word."[46] Hence, her subservience to the Word, and the Word alone, gives the church a marvelous freedom from all earthly sources of revelation, including Adolf Hitler. For our purposes let us note that Barth's chief opposition to Hitler, and Barth's main motivation in writing, was his insistence that the church must be free to preach what the church is told by God to preach. Barth's objections to the Nazis were first of all a matter of homiletics.

Barmen led to the surveillance of Barth by the Nazis, who stood at the back of his classroom as he lectured. He was quickly dismissed from his teaching position in Bonn and returned to Switzerland in 1935. Barth taught in Basel for the rest of his career. In Basel Barth produced his massive *Church Dogmatics*, first as lectures to students, and then volume upon volume, changing forever the landscape of theology and giving us preachers not only our most stirring rationale for proclamation but also the theological substance for some of our greatest sermons. There he frequently preached in the Basel prison, until just four years before his death, giving many of us American pastors our first and only sampling of Barth the preacher through a collection of his prison sermons, *Deliverance to the Captives*.[47]

And it all began in a forlorn little parish, in the every-Sunday challenge of speaking a word for God.

Or did it? Even after a survey of the life of Barth as a preacher and theologian, one is left with the nagging suspicion that one has not yet dug to the root or the origin of Barth's work. That his father was a pious preacher, that his professors so disappointed him by their support of the war, that his early homiletical efforts were a failure, that the rise of Hitler and the German Christians exposed the weaknesses of German liberal theology—none of this satisfyingly explicates the vast and unique counter-testimony that was the witness of Karl Barth. Later Barth would deny that *Romans* was in any way an attempt to base theological reflection on any kind of experience, including postwar death and despair. Revelation provides no adequate preparation for itself, said Barth. So Busch's biography is thorough but finally inadequate as far as explanation is concerned.

Perhaps Barth's biography is, in itself, a validation of his theology. This man, this preacher named Barth, is not to be explained by his life, but rather his life is to be explained as a miraculously divine construction. Barth preached what he preached, and thought what he thought, not merely because of prior intellectual and ecclesiastical influences, but because of what God gave Karl Barth. In preaching what he was told to preach, in telling what he heard, Barth brought down a theological world and offered another; and thus Barth's preaching, like our own at our best, was a credit, not to him, but to a God who speaks, who brings something out of nothing, who raises the dead, and who says to us that which we, and our intellectual and ecclesiastical influences, could never say. In short, Karl Barth is an instance of the triumph of the Word.

On the last afternoon of his life, Barth received a telephone call from his old pastoral friend Thurneysen. They talked about the troubling politics of the day with the Soviets about to put their foot on Hungary again. Barth ended what could have been a depressing conversation with a hearty, "He [Jesus] will reign!" Barth died in his sleep sometime during that night.

For Barth, preaching is one of the ways that Jesus reigns, and Barth's life and work is our hearty affirmation of the ultimate triumph of Christ's presently disputed but finally supreme sovereignty.

CHAPTER TWO

PREACHING THE BIBLE WITH BARTH

Preachers must not be boring. To a large extent the pastor and boredom are synonymous concepts. Listeners often think that they have heard already what is being said in the pulpit. They have long since known it themselves. The fault certainly does not lie with them alone. Against boredom the only defense is again being biblical. If a sermon is biblical, it will not be boring. Holy scripture is in fact so interesting and has so much that is new and exciting to tell us that listeners cannot even think about dropping off to sleep.[1]

One could read the *Church Dogmatics* as a vast, rollicking biblical commentary. Time and again Barth makes some theological assertion, then immediately turns to extended biblical exegesis and exposition, often treating surprising texts as sources for his theology. Over the years I have enjoyed studying some prescribed lectionary text by first studying the text in various contemporary commentaries and then, using a scriptural index, turning to Barth's exposition of that text in his *Dogmatics*.[2] For us preachers searching for something to say, Barth declares that "the message which Scripture has to give us, even in its apparently most debatable and least assimilatable parts, is in all circumstances truer and more important than the best and the most necessary things that we ourselves have said or can say." Biblical interpretation is where Barth's theology becomes actualized, embodied, and tested. Barth wants to be an exclusively biblical preacher. As one of the three forms of revelation, here scripture and preaching work together, complimenting and empowering one another. Therefore Barth's way with the Bible, and the way of the Bible with Barth, is crucial for understanding Barth and using his thought in our preaching.

Welcome to a World Made Strange

Barth's view of the Bible is best represented in his famous lecture of 1916, "The Strange New World within the Bible." There Barth describes scripture as primarily a work of God, the very voice of God, an invasion of our world through words:

> The Bible tells us not how we should talk with God but what he says to us; not how we find the way to him, but how he has sought and found the way to us; not the right relation in which we must place ourselves to him, but the covenant which he has made with all who are Abraham's spiritual children and which he has sealed once and for all in Jesus Christ. It is this which is within the Bible. The word of God is within the Bible.[3]

For Barth, the Bible is a witness to revelation, "an empty spot at the place to which the biblical writers point."[4] It is not in itself revelation. Nothing is, in itself, revelation. In *Romans* Barth spoke of revelation as being a circle (time) that is intersected by a tangent line (eternity), the two figures touching at a single point. The point is undeniably there, but those who dwell within the circle have no means of prolonging or utilizing the tangent line—it episodically intrudes into their world from another world, remaining alien, uncontrollable, mysterious.

The luminosity of the biblical text is not a matter of the reader's pious imagination, not a matter of the application of our interpretive skills—be they moral, historical, or exegetical—because "this revelation inspired by the Holy Spirit, can become luminous for us only through the same Spirit."[5] Here we see Barth's insistence on the reality of divine agency as a prerequisite for biblical interpretation. Our fertile imaginations are not the key to biblical interpretation but rather the work of the Holy Spirit. The source of any interesting interpretation is prayer.[6] When it comes to making sense of the biblical text, we are always quite beyond our own resources. At best, we can join in the Bible's effort to point to the reality of God that is found there. Reminded of Grünewald's crucifixion, where John stands to the right of Jesus and directs our gaze toward the crucified Christ, Barth says, "It is this hand which is in evidence in the Bible."[7]

I confess that as a preacher who is much energized through the work of literary criticism of scripture, and a lover of literature to boot, I sometimes have a tendency to get so caught up in and drawn toward the artistic devices of the biblical text that my preaching suffers. I become so enamored with the text and its multifaceted wonders that I give too little attention to the text as only a witness, even if sometimes an eloquent witness, to revelation. Of this, as a preacher, I am only a witness to the witness of God. Barth keeps our reading of the Bible relentlessly theological, not simply in its content but also in its agency. The text lives because of a living agent who graciously speaks through the text.

One of Barth's great gifts was his cultivation of naïveté. Whether he is being precritical or postcritical I cannot say for sure, but I love the way that Barth continues to be shocked, surprised, and filled with wonderment at biblical texts, all the way to the end of his life. In seminary courses in biblical interpretation we usually think of hermeneutics as a matter of acquiring increasing interpretive sophistication. However, Barth's childlike naïveté enables him to see and hear things that we more serious adults miss.

John Webster deems it significant that Barth said that his first theological instruction came through the children's songs of Burckhardt:

> As a child, he was taught Basel-German children's songs by his mother. These simple songs influenced Barth throughout his life. They were written by "'a theologian called Abel Burckhardt. He was not a great man, but I, at any rate, held him in high respect. He lived about a hundred years ago and was a contemporary of the more famous Jacob Burckhardt who was second pastor at the cathedral here in Basel."
>
> Barth said that these children's songs, "were the textbook from which I received my first theological instruction at the beginning of the last decade of the nineteenth century, in a form which was appropriate for my immature years. What made an indelible impression on me was the homely self-assurance with which these unpretentious verses spoke of the events of Christmas, Palm Sunday, Good Friday, Easter, Ascension, Pentecost, as though they could have taken place that very morning in Basle or nearby, like any other exciting event. You climbed the grim hill of Golgotha and walked in Joseph's garden at daybreak . . . Was it all rather naive . . . ? Indeed it was very naive, but perhaps the deepest wisdom, with its fullest force, lies in naiveté, and this kind of wisdom, once gained, can carry a man over whole oceans of historicism and anti-historicism, mysticism and rationalism, orthodoxy, liberalism and existentialism. He certainly will not be spared trial and temptation, but in the end he will be brought back relatively unscathed to firm ground."[8]

Barth maintained this childlike openness to scripture all his life. As a boy, he was so sure of the reality of Jesus that he spent Palm Sunday standing at his window, eagerly watching for the entry of Jesus into his Swiss town.[9]

Because of the centrality of scripture as source for theological reflection, when Barth was asked to say something specifically about preaching in his *Homiletics*, he mostly said something about the Bible:

> Preaching must be exposition of holy scripture. I have not to talk *about* scripture but *from* it. I have not to say something, but merely repeat something. . . . Our task is simply to follow the distinctive movement of thought in the text, to stay with this, and not with a plan that arises out of it.[10]

If you are looking for a Barthian homiletic of biblical preaching, there it is. Preaching arises from scripture, repeats scripture, and follows the "distinctive movement" of the text. For Barth, so many of the interpretive issues with scripture that have occupied us for more than a century are negated by the simple fact that "He speaks for Himself whenever He is spoken of and His story is told and heard"[11] (*CD*, IV, 1, pg. 227).

The text speaks: "The text as part of the Bible is thus primarily important to us as a document, a record. But let us add at once: Not just as a record or document that had authoritative significance for some group at a particular time, but one that very specially and exclusively speaks to none other than precisely us at this particular moment, and does so as the open and only witness to the revelation of God, a Word which God has spoken to this age."[12] Barth says that it is important always to consider every biblical text as a testifying "witness."[13]

Immersion in the Bible's nitty-gritty way of speaking disciplines the tongues of preachers. Elegance of speech and oratorical embellishment suggest that the import of the message is in the style used by the messenger. Barth taught that the Bible demands "honesty of speech" and simple, straightforward speaking that acknowledges the "poverty" and the utter dependence of the speaker upon a divine agent:

> Honesty of speech is demanded. Speak your own language! Do not put on the royal mantle of the language of Canaan or pass yourselves off as little Luthers. Precisely those who are committed to exegesis and the church cannot posture as apostles or reformers. Phrases from the Bible and the hymnal and sonorous perorations are not appropriate either. If quotations are introduced only to give momentum to what is said, there is every reason for mistrust. Stand behind your own poverty![14]

Barth thus counsels us against being too concerned with the "hermeneutical gap," the distance between our time and that of Christ's time on earth (*CD*, IV, 1, pp. 287ff.). He says that this gap is only a mere "methodological question" but not a "genuine theological problem" (pp. 288-89). Barth can say this because, for him, the main issue with scripture is the vociferous content, the speaking subject, the Word made flesh, and our prayerful willingness to hear God act and speak in our time. Barth's sermons are therefore characterized by an almost total lack of hermeneutical apparatus and a studied disregard for bridging alleged gaps of time or circumstances between the biblical text and us. Barth believed that most hermeneutical questions are an attempt to escape the truth of this revealing, lively content (pp. 289ff.). Jesus is the Truth, the Truth that does not stand mute before us but rather as a speaking subject. We have many resources for evasion of this communicative, personal truth. One of them is biblical interpretation!

So Barth said that the best service for Good Friday would be simple repetition of the Passion story, letting the Holy Spirit then do its work (*CD*, IV, 1, pg. 250). A sermon consists of the preacher's careful repetition of the biblical text in a homiletical restatement of what the Bible says:

> The proper way is to construct the corpus of the sermon in repetition of the text's own rhythm and with due regard to the proportions discerned by exegesis. In such repetition we need not deal with

the passage schematically verse by verse as in the work of preparation. That will sometimes be the appropriate way, but often the decisive point at which to begin will be the middle or the end of the verse or passage.[15]

Yet Barth says that "preaching is exposition, not exegesis. It follows the text but moves on from it to the preacher's own heart and to the congregation."[16] Preaching is biblical when it is a grateful, joyful, playful submission to and repetition of the biblical text that is a faithful exposition of what God says and is saying. "Christianity has always been and only been a living religion when it was not ashamed to be in all seriousness a book-based religion," said Barth.[17] When Barth was accused of being "biblicist," he replied:

> When I am named "Biblicist," all that can rightly be proved against me is that I am prejudiced in supposing the Bible to be a good book, and that I hold it to be profitable for men to take its conceptions at least as seriously as they take their own.[18]

Yet Barth counsels careful preparatory work for preaching from the scriptures. In fact, preparation for preaching is almost exclusively an exercise in the various arts of attentiveness to the specifics of the biblical text:

> Preachers must pay attention to the text, noting what is written in it. From first to last scripture says the same thing, but it constantly says the one thing in different ways. The Bible arose as a historical document speaking of a historical event in the midst of the flux of human life. Instead of attention one might say "diligence," i.e., concern for what is written in this text as in no other. This is why academic exegetical work is demanded, exact philological and historical study. The variety of scripture has another aspect, namely, that each time each passage will speak as needed to each person. For this reason more than philological attention is needed. Also needed is the attention which is an attempt to read the Word of God in the text and self and congregation. A sermon is not a good one if it is clear that the preacher lacks the attentiveness. For this reason ever new respect or *respicere* to this and that text is required. We must be on guard against the simple indolence that can be natural to even the industrious pastor who is always busy. On Sunday it will become apparent in the pulpit, for no industriousness or activity can compensate for indolence at the decisive point. Church boards should show flexibility in giving pastors more time for preaching, for sermon preparation is time-consuming labor. They should also see to it that only sermons that have been diligently prepared be presented from the pulpit.[19]

Barth also counsels us preachers to cultivate deferential modesty with the scriptures. The biblical preacher must practice a modest transparency, must be like John the Baptist in Grünewald's *Crucifixion*, standing at some respectful distance from the scriptures, pointing to them "in an almost impossible way,"[20] decreasing in importance as the scriptures take on more significance in the congregation:

> Preaching that is in conformity with scripture will be modest. Scripture itself enjoins us to be modest, and preachers ought to behave modestly and not to push themselves into the limelight with their more or less good qualities. If the attention to which we referred above is present, the preacher will be under the continuous instruction of scripture, will be contradicted by it, will be kept within bounds. An encounter will take place between the prophets and apostles on the one side and the pastor on the other. The latter must step back with any personal views or spirituality. No matter how vital we may be, we all tend to follow well-defined tracks. Even after the most arduous study, we still do not really know what to say.[21]

Biblical preachers must cultivate the art of relinquishment, letting go of our dearest insights in deference to the Bible's insights:

> The gospel is not in our thoughts or hearts; it is in scripture. The dearest habits and best insights that I have—I must give them all up before listening. I must not use them to protect myself against the breakthrough of a knowledge that derives from scripture. Again and again I must let myself be contradicted. I must let myself be loosened up. I must be able to surrender everything.[22]

At the same time that he speaks of preachers diligently disciplining themselves to the word of scripture, Barth stresses revelation as an event. We preachers must cultivate flexibility. The Bible becomes God's Word and, as the word of a living God, is in constant movement, alive and vital, demanding of its homiletical expositors energetic vitality too:

> Preachers must be flexible. The Bible is not God's Word in the sense of a state code that tells us precisely what the view of the state is. In reality we ought to say that the Bible *becomes* God's Word. Whenever it *becomes* God's Word, it is God's Word. What we have here is an event. Simply to have read somewhere that the Bible is God's Word is not the point. Preachers are summoned to a life history with the Bible in which something constantly takes place between them and God's Word. Flexibility means, then, that we have to plunge into this movement, submit to it, and let it lead us through the whole of scripture in all its statements and stages. The fact of the canon tells us simply that the church has regarded these scriptures as the place where we can expect to hear the voice of God. The proper attitude of preachers does not depend on whether or not they expect God to speak to them here.[23]

There is in each biblical text a "distinctive movement of thought in a text," great variation in the way biblical texts handle their witness.[24] Preachers must be willing to be flexible and supple enough, in our construction of sermons and in our choosing of appropriate forms of a sermon, to be faithful to the richness of the biblical text itself. We should "construct the corpus of the sermon in repetition of the text's own rhythm and with due regard for the proportions discerned by exegesis."[25] In other words, the form of the sermon ought to be cognizant of and faithful to the form of the biblical text. There is not some previous, predetermined rhetorical pattern or form that fits all biblical texts. The sermon must be made to fit the text, not the text to some preconceived notion of the form of the sermon. There is no prefabricated template for biblical preaching.

Barth gives lectionary-based preaching a qualified "yes." Lectionary preaching helpfully demonstrates to the congregation that we preach what we have been told to preach, that we do not select the text for our sermons on the basis of personal preference, but rather our text selects us. Although Barth has unspecified problems with the lectionary, he does seem to value it as a good discipline that keeps preachers "on the path suggested by the church":

> We may voluntarily follow the prescribed readings, even though much might be said against the ancient church lectionary. When following the readings we are at once compelled to say only what the prescribed text wants, and our own thoughts are held in check. Calvin calls the church the mother of believers, and a child lets its parents guide it, so a pastor may submit to what the church decides. It is not absolutely necessary, however, to stay on the path suggested by the church.[26]

Barth refuses to allow for "special occasions" when the text can be laid aside due to a "theme of the day":

On special occasions, e.g., the outbreak of war, the text must always stand above the theme of the day. Thoughts about the war must not be intruded into the text. More than ever in precisely these situations we must maintain obedience to the text. The church can execute its true task only if it is not caught up in the general excitement but tries to achieve mastery over it by proclaiming what is above all things human.[27]

Barth confesses that, during his misspent youth, he was a topical preacher:

In 1914, when the outbreak of war left the whole world breathless, I felt obliged to let this war rage on in all my sermons until finally a woman came up to me and begged me for once to talk about something else and not constantly about this terrible conflict. She was right! I had disgracefully forgotten the importance of submission to the text. It may come to the point that a member of the congregation has to call the pastor to order and counsel reconsideration. All honor to relevance, but pastors should be good marksmen who aim their guns beyond the hill of relevance.[28]

For Barth, prayer is not so much our speaking to God, but God's speaking to us. Evangelism is not a culmination of our search for God, but rather a by-product of God's search for us. Preaching is not so much what we say about God, but rather what God says about God's self. And scripture is not so much an account of our history of God, but God's history with us, not our experience of God, but *God's* experience of us! Barth really believes that biblical knowledge is knowledge of a person, a living, communicative person distinct from ourselves. That the Risen Christ addresses us is our great protection against mysticism, existentialism, Roman Catholic ecclesiology, Protestant biblical literalism, preoccupation with the great historical gap between us and the Bible, and all else of detriment to the continuing event of the Risen Christ among us. Any problems that we raise about hearing the Bible are met by Barth's grand assertions of the activity and freedom of the Holy Spirit. The distant possibility of miracles, of rising from the dead, and of understanding scripture is countered, not through argument, but by the fact of their actual occurrence in the real world that is rendered through scripture.

I must say that for a theologian who stresses the action and the restless movement of God's Word, Barth tends to speak with too much finality, asserting, pronouncing, and declaring. Some biblically induced hesitation on his part would be helpful. He ties too many things together, interlocks too many ideas too finally and too neatly, and talks too much. Too much of what he said is said with such conviction and confidence that it sounds conclusive and categorical. In other words, in some significant aspects, Barth's style of speaking and presentation does not match the actualism and vitality of his theology nor the peculiar way that scripture tends to present itself. Should not preaching that is faithful to the episodic, dialectic nature of thought in Christ be more open-ended?

Perhaps the open-ended quality of so many of Jesus' parables is not just an aspect of the parables that awaits a skillful preacher to bring the parables to conclusion, to explain them, and to fix them for the congregation, but the parabolic, open-ended form is itself a theological statement, a unique way of communicating the God who demands to be given room to work with us in God's own way rather than in our way. I wish that Barth had taken more seriously his own demand to be faithful to the biblical text both in substance and in form.

Still, Barth never wavers from his awe of scripture as a divine gift, a product not of human spiritual longing and striving but of God's speaking. Revelation, in any of its three forms, is neither initiated nor maintained by humanity, but is truly and completely the miraculous product of the Resurrection in the Holy Spirit. This is one of the reasons Barth keeps asserting the authority of the Bible as the best possible means of safeguarding God's freedom and sovereignty in God's self-revelation (*CD*, I, 2, pg. 534). In the Bible, God refuses to give himself over to human control. This refusal includes being boxed up in a collection of words and propositions. "As to when, where, and how the Bible establishes itself for us as the Word of God in such an event, we do not decide. Concerning that, the Word of God himself decides!" (*CD*, I, 2, pg. 530).[29]

In recent years there has been great stress upon the Bible as "the church's book," a product of the church and its struggle with revelation and its heritage, scripture, and tradition linked together in catholic fashion. While this stress is appropriate, I am sure that Barth would have none of this. Barth felt it absolutely essential to keep the Bible in a position above the church, against the church, the judge of the church rather than its product, in order that the church might be made faithful by some criterion and empowerment other than its own.[30]

"The Bible is the opportunity which the Revelation of God has created for itself by the appointment of human witnesses. It is offered to us as a possibility which waits to be realized by revelation because it offers itself to be found there. Thus Holy Scripture is *the* source of revelation."[31] Even though Barth characterized three forms of revelation, it is also clear that scripture holds a distinctively powerful place in Barth's scheme:

> The whole truth is that in spite of all appearances to the contrary, Holy Scripture has more power than all the rest of the world together. The whole truth is that all other world-principles are already unmasked and delimited in Holy Scripture, that they are already overcome for all their supposedly final and absolute validity, that their power is already surpassed and their triumph outstripped. The whole truth—hidden but complete—is that of the story of the young David (1 Sam. 17:23f.). It was not in the helmet and armour of Saul, but with his shepherd's sling, that he overcame Goliath. Very rashly, from a human point of view, he confronted Goliath in the name of Yahweh Sabaoth. (*CD*, I, 2, pg. 678. Cf. II, 1, pp. 435-39, 605-7; IV, 3, pp. 389ff.)

While he affirms that scripture is powerfully revealing and self-expressive—"God has spoken, speaks now and will again speak" (*CD*, I, 2, pg. 800)—Barth allows for some interpretation of scripture "in order to be proclaimed and heard again and again in the Church." But his robust sense of revelation will not allow Barth to do much more than "exegesis and application." Any interpretation of scripture ought to be a kind of restatement, a redescription rather than vigorous and imaginative interpretation:

> In order to be proclaimed and heard again and again in the Church and the world, Holy Scripture requires to be explained. . . . As the Word of God it needs no explanation, of course, since as such it is clear in itself. The Holy Ghost knows well enough what He has said to the prophets and apostles and what through them He wills also to say to us. . . . But this Word in Scripture assumes the form of a human word. Human words need interpretation because as such they are ambiguous, not usually, of course, in the intention of those who speak, but always for those who hear. Among the various possibilities, the sense intended by the speaker has to be conveyed, and as the sense which they have for the speaker, it has to be communicated to the thinking of the hearer, so that the words have now a meaning for him, and indeed the meaning intended by the speaker. Perhaps this twofold interpretation, which can be distinguished as exegesis and application, can be made at once by the hearer; perhaps the speaker himself is in a position to offer this twofold interpretation of his words, or, if not their application, at least their exegesis; perhaps a third party must intervene and perform this service of interpretation for speaker and hearer. All, human words without exception need one of these interpretations. Now, since God's Word in Scripture has taken the form of a human word, it has itself incurred the need of such interpretation. (*CD*, I, 2, pp. 712f.)

Because of our sin, our resilient disbelief, scripture needs prayerful, disciplined listening. But the good news is that ultimately none of our resources for evasion of the Word are equal to the self-revealing power of the Word. How do we make the Bible relevant to people in their various situations? Barth's simple answer is that we don't. It is the resurrected, speaking Christ who makes the story relevant to all people everywhere by fundamentally altering who they are and what their situation is.[32] Questions of interpretation are asked within a closed circle of the gospel narrative and the speaking, living presence of Christ. If we would hear the gospel, in order to have something to say about the gospel, it must be as an act of prayer. It must be prayer in Jesus' name, as he is portrayed in the gospel, an obedient submission to the command of God. There is thus in Barth not much interest in turning aside from this difficult endeavor to assess the historical reliability of these accounts. The story "works" because the resurrected Christ deems to make it work.

The biblical text "speaks" and "means," but only as a miracle. By "miracle" I do not mean miracle in the Enlightenment sense of some supernatural intrusion into the natural workings of the universe. That sense of miracle is an invention of the Enlightenment's attempt to push God out of God's world. For Christians there is no such thing as "natural" and therefore no such thing as intrusion by the "supernatural." What the world calls "natural" we call "Creation," the product of a creative God. In other words, it's all miraculous if by miraculous you mean a gracious work of God. With the fullness of the Christian tradition, I mean miracle in the sense of God's working among us in the world to accomplish God's purposes, not some strange, unnatural intrusion into the world. *Miracle* is a word that denotes God's work.[33]

Preaching must discipline itself to look away from the preacher and also not to be overly concerned about the listener. When Barth warns against "an arbitrary biblicism," because "preaching takes place in a very specific church at a very specific time," we think that he is going to say something positive about taking the congregational context into consideration in the preparation of sermons. But no, the "specific church at a very specific time" that Barth has in mind is "dogmatic history and dogmatics of the church" at our "particular location."

> In order to avoid the danger of an arbitrary biblicism, we must constantly remind ourselves that preaching takes place in a very specific church at a very specific time. Here then, we must seriously point out how important it is to work carefully on the dogmatic history and dogmatics of the church within which preachers must engage in proclamation at their own particular location. All preachers need a good dogmatics. In this regard attention should be drawn to the extraordinary importance of dogmatic studies at the university and later in the ministry. For an understanding of the bible we need particular guidelines which like buoys in the sea mark off the channel, and sometimes detours as well, but always serve to protect us against running aground through ignorance or negligence.[34]

The Defeat of History

A major problem for the biblical preacher is that, as modern people, we are the heirs of the historicist way of looking at things, a point of view that is a vast attempt to destroy the possibility of miracle. As modernists we do not believe in miracle; we believe in history. History is that objective, scientific-like methodology that enables us to get at what is real, to stabilize what "really happened." Historical events and forces explain the present so that we do not need to resort to miracle for explanations. All effects are due to exclusively human causes. We are all historicists now in that we tend to look at the present as the result of a series of orderly, explicable historical developments. We are where we are, not as the result of any suprahistorical intervention, but rather through a series of human developments. The way to explain something is to describe how it got to be that way through various prior causes and gradual historical unfolding. The past is determinative of the present. Faith comes through "faith development," a slow and orderly, even predictable process of gradual growth of an innate, generic human capacity called "faith." Faith is not something that comes to us but rather something within us awaiting development. The developmental view of the world, whether in its historical, psychological, or religious forms, is just one aspect of the modern world's attempt to rid itself of the miraculous and thereby render a silent cosmos safe from a God who speaks.

Bultmann was dismayed to find Barth's extended exposition on the exorcism that was performed by J. C. Blumhardt.[35] Bultmann apparently considered Barth's much-beloved Blumhardts, father and son, to be mentally unbalanced, sad throwbacks to a time that modernity had defeated. Barth saw the Blumhardts as radical critics of the closed-mindedness of modernity. When Barth considers how the exorcised evil spirit is reported to have shouted in Blumhardt's hearing, "Jesus is Victor!" Barth observes:

> Like similar events in the New Testament, the occurrence during which Blumhardt heard this cry: "Jesus is Victor," has three aspects. On the first, it is realistically explained in the sense of ancient and modern mythology. On the second, it is explained in terms of modern psychopathology, or depth psychology. On the third, it is not explained at all but can only be estimated spiritually on the assumption that the two former explanations are also possible and even justifiable in their own way.[36]

To me, the remarkable thing about Barth's exposition of this event is not only that he enjoys it as a sort of contemporary phenomenon that has obvious similarities to biblical events but also that he is quite willing to hear whatever "modern mythology" and "depth psychology" may have to say about these matters. Yet it is also clear that Barth privileges the explanation that is no explanation at all. Indeed, it could be said that one of Barth's major problems with historical-criticism and modernist explanations of biblical texts was that they attempt to be explanation rather than repetition and proclamation. Historical criticism of scripture, the insights from mythology, psychology, and so forth, may all be considered by the faithful preacher, but only if they are considered "in their own way."[37]

At first Barth seems to think (in *Romans*, for instance) that contemporary, skeptical biblical scholarship was an ally in the preacher's interpretive endeavor—searches for the "historical Jesus" had demonstrated that we can detect next to nothing about this historical Jesus! Barth says that this frees us to focus more intently (like John the Baptist would have us in Grünewald's painting) upon the cross. That is where the "real Jesus" is to be found, not in historical reconstruction. Later, in the *Dogmatics*, Barth seems to have become extremely suspicious of historical criticism, suspecting that it is an attempt at the false security of his much-hated "religion." More about that later.

Barth advised that when we preachers turn to historical criticism, we must do so "with tact." We must be tactful and respectful, not of the intellectual limits of our congregations, but out of respect for the intellectual limits of historical criticism. "Biblical criticism in the pulpit also falls under the need for tact. It should be introduced only in the context of ministry and done with respect, not under the pressure of a false ideal of truthfulness."[38] The vaunted "truthfulness" of historical criticism is a truthfulness that is honest about the limits of the biblical text but not about its own limits. It must therefore be used "with tact."

Barth had little interest in searching for and in defining what was "real," particularly through historical methodology and by attempting to uncover historical developments. "Realism" for Barth means an accurate description of what is. Barth does not begin on the basis of the modernist assumption that we and our actions are all that there is, but rather that we live in a created world, a world that is being continuously created by the Word. "And God said . . ." is the beginning of our world as it really is because God never retires as Creator. God continues to be significant in the creation of the real world every time there is, "And God said. . . ." Scripture is that great, imaginative, but truthful store of images, names, dates, ideas, and claims that constitute the "real world." The challenge of the preacher is to describe that world in such a way that people may recognize it as their home and are invited to take up residence in it as a trustworthy place.

In historical criticism, "realistic reading" meant attempts to reconstruct the event that lay behind the biblical, literary rendering. The historical was a better bearer of "truth" than the literal, which was an odd development, considering the history of how human beings have generally thought about themselves. Hans Frei, in *The Eclipse of Biblical Narrative*,[39] says that when we came to think of a biblical text's truth solely in terms of its historical "ostensive referent" behind the form of the text, rather than to see its literary form as conveying truth, then we acquiesced into the modern dichotomy between fact and value, history and fiction, reason and faith, and assumed that historical methodology was better suited to find the "facts" of the matter than various literary forms. This led to our present malaise with scripture. Modern people (and this applies both to those who think they are biblical "conservatives" as well as those who name themselves "liberals" or "progressives") believe that "scientific" methods yield more reasonable, unassailable truth than aesthetic methods.[40]

Barth, in neo-Kantian fashion, rejects history as a means of knowledge of the eternal. He has faith in literary forms as revealers of truth because of his theological commitments. Because Barth believes that Jesus is risen and alive, the "ostensive reference" in scripture is to a living, speaking person, who, through present actions, confirms scripture's message. Everywhere in the text, when the text speaks of "God," Barth refers to the living Christ. When the Bible attempts to communicate, it does so through a wide range of sophisticated literary devices rather than through a primitive attempt at historiography. Perhaps this is because a living God, a God of the Resurrection, refuses to be constrained by the limits of history. Therefore Barth does not think of scripture as stories about the historical Jesus in the past, but has confidence that, in these narratives, the Risen Christ is present and speaking as the agent who makes scripture work.[41] These stories render an active author, a subject, a speaker, an agent who is Christ. To attempt to disrupt these stories in order to get to the history behind them, to somehow peer through them to some idea that is beyond or beneath them, is to do violence to the referent of the stories. This is why Barth utterly rejects any attempt, be it Marxism or existentialism, Protestant orthodoxy or the Roman Catholic magisterium, to try to find some interpretive standpoint outside or above the text that will help us hear the text. The only way to understand the text is a willingness to stand within the all-embracing interpretive world of the texts and the Lord of the texts.

Hans Frei noted that Barth believes that Jesus Christ in his life becomes that chain of events to which all of human life is figurally related. That is, the reader or hearer must realize that this story is a real description of the real world, and the central character of this story is busy helping one to discover one's place within this real world. Proust speaks of reading a text and, as one is reading, having a hand reach out from the text and take your hand. This is something akin to Barth's view of reading scripture.

I required my freshman seminar to read Augustine's *Confessions*. We had been reading various novels in a course in "The Modern Self in Literature." I gave the students Augustine without giving them more information than "this is the story of a person's life." They dutifully took up the *Confessions* and read it. Some of them thought that they were reading fiction, others thought it a sort of primitive autobiography. The thing that amazed me was how much they heard in the book, how many things they saw, as first-time readers, that I had never seen, despite my repeated readings of *Confessions*. This ancient book spoke to them as vividly as Cicero's *Hortensus* spoke to Augustine when he was about their age. (Augustine said of that work, "This book inflamed me.") It is remarkable how these ancient texts, as classics, as fine literature, speak to us across all of our barriers.

Yet even this is not what Barth has in mind. His hermeneutics is based on theology, not on aesthetics. Christology, the living Christ who really speaks in the text, not just the illuminating possibilities within the text, is what enables the Bible to speak to us so that we might speak of and from the Bible in our sermons.

God's Story

For Barth, the most dangerous stand that we may attempt to take outside this world of the text is not in some philosophical point of view but rather in that last pitiful asylum of the modern person: our own subjectivity. Because the Holy Spirit is busy penetrating and informing our subjectivity, even subjectivity is no real refuge from the Holy Spirit. Still, subjectivity is the attempted last refuge of the modern scoundrel attempting to evade the voice that addresses us through the text. A deep concern about our flight to subjectivity, a deep longing to return to the "object,"[42] was at the heart of Barth's criticism of Schleiermacher and Bultmann. Barth thought it dangerous to refocus our attention from the person of Jesus to ourselves, or even upon our church—thus his fierce polemic against Roman Catholicism. Barth's reading of scripture is "realistic" in that it stays focused on the Other. It attempts to be controlled by the object of its reading, not by reader intention. Barth keeps claiming a true *extra nos* objectivity of the Christ that speaks through the *verbum externum* of scripture.

Edward Farley has an extended meditation upon preaching, which he calls "the impossible task." Preaching is "biblical," but that is just the problem: How to get from the Bible to us? Farley says that, while there are some variations in the process, most preachers attempt to "build a bridge." This, the average preacher does through taking bits and pieces of scripture, "texts," and thereby reducing preaching to a "message," "that-which-is-preached." Then the preacher connects "that-which-is-preached" to "the situation of the congregation" by the construction of a "rhetorical vehicle."

Farley calls this "a failed paradigm," because we preachers have switched from "preaching the gospel," to preaching various passages as the contents of scripture. We are called, says Farley, "to proclaim the good news," not a series of ideas extracted from scripture. He is mainly critical of the way such an approach fragments scripture into various atomistic texts that do injustice to the literary shape and movement of scripture. Farley's criticisms seem to me a fair critique of much of contemporary preaching's use of scripture.

Against this preaching of various biblical passages, Farley proposes "a counter view." That view is based upon his definition of the gospel as "not a thing to be defined." "It is not a doctrine, a delimited objective content," a view with which we Barthians might agree. But then he says that the content of this gospel proclamation "means to bring to bear a certain past event on the present in such a way as to open the future." This is "ever the content and source of the proclamation of the Christian church: the bringing to bear of the event of Jesus onto the present in such a way that the present is both judged and drawn in hope and redemption."

At this point we struggle to find much substance within Farley's definition of preaching's gospel content. He says that preaching vaguely proclaims "the mystery of God's salvific action and how that transforms the world. To proclaim the Gospel then is to enter the world of Gospel, struggling with questions of suffering, evil, idolatry, hope, and freedom." About the best that Farley has to offer in terms of specifics is that the gospel always has a "prophetic element—disruption, an exposure of corporate oppression and individual collusion, and, at the same time, an uncovering of redemptive possibilities." Paul Tillich could not have been more evasive.

Farley's main target is what he calls "biblicist preaching," that preaching that turns the Bible into an idol. "For those who need certainty, utter clarity, or simplicity, this new paradigm will be insufficient." He sees himself as a "prophetic" critic of "popular piety," but I fear that Farley doesn't appreciate how his presentation, his "new paradigm" is itself an expression of the old "popular piety" of the academy—keep preaching a matter of "mystery" and "metaphor" and call this vague abstraction "prophetic." But "prophetic" on what basis?

Farley does say that gospel preaching renders, not an idea or a principle, but rather a "presence." The trouble is, Farley's "presence" never seems actually to speak, or at least to speak in any way that challenges the hearers' situation as they themselves define it. "Prophetic," in a biblical sense, means more than simple expressionistic "disruption" of the present order. It means disruption of the present order by the invasion of a specific presence, a God who has an identity and specific demands, a God whom we cannot make into anything we please, a God with a name and a face, Jesus. The remedy against our tendency toward idolatry is not the vague and mysterious, generic "God" who is no God but rather a vision of and a receptivity to the true and real God who comes to us in complex but specific triunity.

Yet mostly Farley unintentionally reminds us that, without God as an active agent in preaching, biblical preaching really is impossible.[43]

David Kelsey says that, for Barth, the Bible is "one vast loosely-structured non-fictional novel."[44] Kelsey's is an important insight for a preacher who attempts to be in conversation with Barth. In order to read the Bible as a "vast loosely-structured non-fictional novel," most of us must get over the methods of scripture reading that we were taught in seminary, taught to us by historians. We must get beyond modern prejudice that fiction is inferior to history and that novels are less important for revelation of what is real than biographies. And we must get over our subjectivist prejudice that encourages us to read and to value a fictional text mainly as a projection of our interiority rather than a challenge to our subjectivity through confrontation with a distinct literary artifact.

Our consciousness is not a sufficient bridge toward the Bible. We learn from Stephen Crites that consciousness is story-created, rather than story being consciousness-created.[45] It is not that we make up stories out of our subjectivity but rather that stories make up us. It occurred to me, in my freshman seminar, that the novel has become so important in the modern world because we are desperate for some means of order and experience, now that we no longer believe in an Orderer of experience. The novel becomes our means of attempting to make up a story in order to make up a life. Self-construction of the world, and ourselves, is a modern North American imperative, though a deluded one. Frank Kermode noted that the novel has become our epic, our *Odyssey* in a world that has been abandoned by God, our great substitute for biblical narrative, our encouragement to create a world through our subjective experience.[46]

The notion of art as constructive projection rather than realistic description is the sort of thing that worried Plato about art. Plato dismissed art as nothing more than "imitation" and at times dangerous imitation, inferior to life, and sometimes terribly misleading to those who ought to be dedicated to reality. Art therefore is a lower sort of "reality" at best, a delusion at worst. Because I live in a world where most "art" tends to be cinematic, I can see Plato's point about the delusional qualities of art. Hollywood gives empty lives an alternative, though fake, world.

But Plato did not sufficiently appreciate the ability of art to point toward reality, to be more real than much that passes for "reality." Art, when it attempts to portray the truth, is a way of thinking, an encounter with a world outside our subjectivity, a means of apprehending the truth about ourselves. There is a sense in which we know more about what "really happened" by reading a novel about a particular historical character than we know about that character by reading a biography or history. Much that passes for historical biography— the facts, just the facts—is more novelistic than it is willing to admit (if it is interesting biography), and the truth that is given us in a novel is more "factual" than the forced, unimaginative arrangement and presentation in most biography. Has the novel given us something that is less real or more real? As has been noted, Barth reads the Bible like a loosely structured historical novel, with the singular additional insight that the object of this loosely structured historical novel is none other than Christ himself. Just because scripture consists of artfully constructed narratives, Barth will not allow us to dismiss scripture as merely fiction. And just because the reconstructions of historical criticism presume to use scientific methodology, Barth will not allow us to embrace them as more real than the narrative, history-like texts of scripture themselves.

Hunsinger says that Barth understood the narrative quality of scripture in a way that differentiates him from both the scriptural literalists and the scriptural expressivists. The literalists tend to view biblical narratives as "factual reports." The expressivists tend to see them as "mythological pictures." Barth speaks of biblical narratives as "legendary witnesses." Though the literalists tried to avoid using critical-historical-exegetical methods of interpretation, attempting to continue to read scripture in essentially "precritical" terms, they eventually succumbed to historical-critical methods, believing that by uncovering the "real" history of the text, it would serve their literalist intentions. (As I noted earlier, in my experience, about the only ardent, uncritical defenders of the methods of historical criticism tend to be conservative Evangelicals who believe that history gives them their best defense that the biblical narrative "report" can be secured, stabilized, and made certain through the unassailable historical "fact" recovered by the historian.) To these literalists I would say that if historical methodology has enabled you to secure a text that is truly "inerrant" and "infallible," then you certainly do not need the Holy Spirit to help you read and interpret scripture. Nor should you bother with the living, speaking, resurrected Christ. Go worship your unassailable, inerrant, infallible fact and life will be easier for you than attempting to worship the living Christ.

This, by the way, is why Barth not only rejects topical preaching, be it catechetical, ethical, or occasional, but also rejects expository preaching—if what is meant is extraction of some idea from the biblical text. In expository preaching this extracted idea is then expounded and applied, turning biblical narrative into abstract, general concepts and allegedly "biblical principles." Barth criticized expository preaching for representing a "bondage to the letter" and an abuse of the Bible, making it into a source rather than a witness. It privileges the text over its context (who is Jesus Christ) and fixed principles of living agency.[47] The only proclamation worthy of the name is the self-proclamation of the Word of God.

As for the expressivists, their view of scripture as a more or less evocative series of mythological pictures led them to expand historical-critical methods to include also literary criticism of scripture. Historical criticism enabled them to point to the gaps and discrepancies between the narratives and the results of historical research; literary criticism enabled them to approach the texts as poetic metaphors, figures of speech that were aesthetic artifacts to be examined and interpreted as symbols that evoke a variety of reactions in a variety of readers, not really "true" in any strict sense of truthful to what really is.

In reaction to all this, in calling the biblical narratives "legendary witnesses," Barth attempted to read scripture in essentially "postcritical" terms. He neither simply accepted nor simply rejected the fruits of historical criticism of scripture. He rather subordinated such insights to the primary task of the theological (that is, christological) reading of scripture.[48] The assertions of the Bible are confessional in character and therefore tend to be categorically beyond the reach of historical criticism, said Barth. Scripture's most interesting assertions—like the creation of the world, the incarnation of the eternal Word, the resurrection of Jesus—are all presented in unmistakably imaginative and legendary depictions. They were neither "actual reports," nor "mythological pictures." They are not past history nor are they expressions of our subjectivity. They are unique and unrepeatable events that demand a particular sort of attention and a particular sort of narration. Barth prefers to call them "Legends," or even the more obscure, "Sagas." Hunsinger says that, by taking this approach to biblical narrative, Barth is able to hold together the imaginative and the eventful quality of these biblical accounts. (See *CD*, I, 1, pp. 326-29; III, 1, pp. 80-94; IV, 2, pp. 478-79 for Barth's discussions of these "Legends.")

Through his approach to scripture as a history-like narrative, Barth stimulates an imaginative reading of scripture. He throws himself into his interpretations, identifies with the characters, treats biblical personalities as contemporaries, delights in discovering some detail of the text that has eluded others, focuses on one word of a text as potentially pregnant with meaning, and, in general, brings a wonderfully naive, childlike approach to his reading.[49] Barth's vivid imagination is formed through the reading of scripture. It is not an unconstrained imagination (I suppose that no imagination is completely unconstrained). He really attempts to discipline himself to the specifics of the text, to allow the text to grasp his full attention. Nevertheless his is a freely utilized imagination. Barth protests against "a ridiculous and middle-class habit of the modern Western mind which is supremely phantastic in its chronic lack of imaginative phantasy" (*CD*, III, 1, pg. 81). Imagination, too, belongs no less legitimately than analysis, to the human possibility of knowing. He once said that a person without imagination is more of an invalid than one who lacks a leg.[50]

These imaginative invalids (historians and biblical literalists?) should not be allowed to dictate how the Bible may express its truth. Imagination is used by the Holy Spirit to awaken us to our place in the middle of God's struggle to regain the world. Preachers work the biblically inspired imagination, helping our people retell their lives in the light of the story of Christ. Through an inspired (literally infused with Spirit) imagination, we come to see our little lives lifted up, incorporated into, His Life. Our lives thereby become a figuration of the story of Jesus.

> I simply do not understand how the current search for the "historical Jesus," at least as it is represented by the Jesus Seminar and its aftermath, is much of an advance over the work of D. F. Strauss and his 1864 *Life of Jesus*. All attempts to reconstruct a "life of Jesus," or "the essential Jesus," or the "real Jesus" tend to begin with an assumption, even if that assumption is unstated, that Jesus is dead. Once they finish rummaging around in the pitifully small historical leftovers from "the historical Jesus," about the only theological claims they can make for Jesus tend to be sentimental assertions about some vaguely sacred aura that appears to have surrounded him and appears to have attracted many to him. What's dead stays that way.

> Barth charged that the goal of Strauss's project, even if Strauss did not know it, was to render a sentimental, bourgeois Jesus, a Jesus that could be useful to the aspirations of the rising nineteenth-century European middle class, without hindering their upward movement. Far from being a revolutionary, Barth said, Strauss was an accommodationist. The results of this work in Strauss (or in the contemporary Jesus Seminar) give us (to quote Barth on Strauss), "a Jesus reduced in stature and hammered into shape, perhaps, a Jesus who is perhaps a trifle groomed, domesticated, and made practicable when compared with all the strange things which are said of him in the texts."[51] Barth said that just about no one in his day has been able to improve on the rigorously a-theological work of Strauss, work which every real theologian must understand and then laugh at its bourgeois enslavement, moving on to a more rigorously theological and revolutionary reading of the biblical texts. I agree.

> Though some of the Jesus Seminar think of themselves as "progressive Christians," they are really reactionary in their rendition of the new California, upper-middle-class accommodationist Jesus.

David Ford characterized Barth's position on revelation in scripture in this way, "Because of the presence of the living Jesus Christ witnessing to himself through the text of the Bible, that text despite its imperfections and errors, can convey all the truth that we need for faith. . . . This particular story is unique in demanding a decision about whether Jesus is alive today, a decision which can only be taken in faith which is the result of Jesus' initiative."[52] In reading scripture, one is forced, at nearly every turn in text, to believe in and witness to the Resurrection. Christ is present in scripture, not only to unveil but also to demand, to call and to summon, to unveil and, in calling, to enable us to hear and to respond in faith. Preaching, as one of the three forms of revelation, participates in this lively, demanding ability of the living Christ to reveal in scripture and in preaching.

> James F. Kay has a wonderful study of what the older dogmatics called the problem of *Christus praesens*, that is, how Christ is present in preaching.[53] Kay is specifically concerned with the vivid and powerful way in which Christ is present in preaching as asserted in the theology and biblical interpretation of Rudolf Bultmann. Kay says that it is clear that in the primitive church of the New Testament, Jesus Christ is the agent who renders revelation, not simply the object who is rendered by revelation. Jesus communicates the kerygma,

rather than just being communicated by the kerygma. Kay shows decisively that Rudolf Bultmann has a robust sense of the presence of Christ in preaching. He quotes Bultmann: "Christ is the eschatological event not as a figure of the past . . . but as the *Christus praesens*. And indeed he becomes present in the Word proclaiming Him and in the sacraments, . . . insofar as by them the death and resurrection of Christ becomes present events for the recipient, i.e., as *verbum visible*."[54] In Bultmann the *parousia* of Christ occurs in preaching, only in preaching.[55] (Barth criticized Bultmann for depersonalizing the presence of Christ in preaching, saying that Bultmann made the Risen Christ a sort of ideal possibility rather than a concrete and specific personality, a real actuality.)[56]

Like Barth, Bultmann stressed the great gap, the great distance between us and God. Bultmann criticized pietism for overlooking the Johannine departure of Jesus, a departure that means "a vast *distance* persists . . . which precludes all familiarity, all mysticism."[57] Neither in his coming nor in his going does Jesus "yield himself up to man's tender emotions: for he is none other than the Revealer, in whom God addresses man."[58] Bultmann says that preaching must always retain this eschatological quality of being here and not here, now and not yet.

Like Barth, Bultmann stresses that God is to be known only through the work, the presently revealing work, of the Risen Christ. God is to be known in Christ and nowhere else. Yet Kay believes that Bultmann overstepped Barth in claiming that the kerygma, the preached message, is the exclusive locus of the presence of Christ. "Christ, the Crucified and Risen One, encounters us in the Word of Proclamation—nowhere else."[59] Bultmann has no threefold manner of revelation, like Barth. In fact, when Bultmann says "Incarnation," he is not referring to the historical Jesus, but to the phenomenon of the Word who is continually enfleshed as "an ever new event in the event of Proclamation" (Bultmann, *Theology of the New Testament*, pg. 130). In 1948, he said, "I am turning my back on all historical encounters and toward the unique encounter with the proclaimed Christ, who encounters me in the kerygma which concerns me in my historical situation . . . I still deny that the historical search can encounter traces of epiphany of God in Christ. . . . It can only bring us to a historical encounter with the historical Jesus; but the *kyrios christos* encounters us only in the kerygma of the church."[60] (Barth, it seems to me, even with his doubts about the revelatory capacity of history, strikes a way between modernist radical historicism and the rather radical anti-historicism of Bultmann.)

Kay addresses us preachers in saying that "what gives Bultmann's work such perennial prospects is that no other theology in this century provides such a majesty of understanding of preaching as the primary *locus* of Christ's presence in the world. Christ is our contemporary, investing us with a demand and promise and grace. Christ presides over our time, and every time, from his place in the pulpit."[61] Although Bultmann powerfully invests preaching with revelatory potentiality, I think it unfortunate that he exclusively invests preaching with such power. Fortunately, Barth is not as reductionistic. Barth stresses revelation as a threefold, Trinitarian affair. Furthermore, I see little indication that Bultmann's theology has "perennial prospects." There is no postmodern renewal of interest in Bultmann, unlike Barth. I also, on the basis of my investigations, challenge Kay's contention that "no other theology in this century provides such a majesty of understanding of preaching" as Bultmann's. Barth is better.

I think it important to note that when Barth uses the language of "event" or actualization, he does not mean "event" in a merely episodic and occasional way, but rather "event" in the sense of an occurrence that is unintelligible if it is not from God. When Barth says "event" he means "miracle." In Barth, Christ is theologically, miraculously present in preaching in a way that Bultmann does not indicate.

In his famous exchange of letters with Bultmann about demythologization, when they are locked in a discussion of Romans 5:21, Barth finally says that when he gets to heaven, he will inquire of Paul just what he means by what he says in Romans 5:21. However, he will not do so before he has first sought out W. A. Mozart. This indicates to me that Barth may have believed that Bultmann was sadly too pedestrian, too prosaic, and lacked a sufficient aesthetic imagination for the peculiar demands of biblical literature.

Yet Kay is absolutely right that contemporary preaching suffers, to a great degree, because it lacks a theological spokesperson like Barth or Bultmann to assert that preaching is important because of the radical possibility and undeniable reality of Christ present in preaching.

Being encountered by the living Christ in scripture, we are in a similar position to the first disciples in John 20–21. In fact, take John 20–21 as a parable for our encounter with scripture. In these stories we, like them, are encountered by the Risen Christ, something considerably more real and obstinate than a figment of our imagination. As John says, all that Jesus did and said could fill a hundred books, but "these things are written that you may believe." We are hunkered down behind the locked doors of all our modern epistemologies and means of analysis. Then the Risen Christ comes to us, and lets us touch him, feed upon him, and he speaks to us, and thereby he becomes the proof we need in order to believe.

Untimely Word[62]

Acts 2:12-18

> "*These are not drunk, . . . for it is only nine o'clock in the morning. No, this is what was spoken through the prophet Joel: . . . upon my slaves, both men and women, in those days I will pour out my Spirit; and they shall prophesy.*"

Let me just say, in beginning: this is no way to preach. For one thing, this is no place to preach. Sorry setting. When I preach I prefer to preach with a soaring neogothic erection to back me up. Duke Chapel. Not in a poorly furnished campus theater. For another, sermons are not meant to be preached before an evaluation panel of gimlet-eyed professors, stripped of the church and its liturgy. This is no model for preaching. It's the wrong time, wrong place, wrong purpose. It's the wrong congregation! A panel sitting there just waiting to pounce on my heartfelt homiletical efforts! Look at them!

There's a time and place for preaching, and this ain't it.

I did a wedding years ago (when I was a promiscuous young pastor without standards) at a yacht club, on a Saturday night. Hardly knew the people, but they were cousins of somebody in my congregation and as a favor, well, there I was. Yacht club. By the time I got there they had already been boozing for an hour. Champagne corks flying. The bride's father finally staggers over and says, "Okay, preacher, you're on. Everybody shut up and come over here! The service is starting. Bride? Groom? Get over here!"

The bride and the groom had asked for a "little sermon."

"Not on your life," I replied, in love. I sailed through the wedding liturgy like Columbo reading a crook his rights and got out of there, resolved never to get caught again in such impropriety. Wrong time, wrong place, wrong people.

Not more than a month later, a grandmother in our congregation was keeping her little grandchild while the mother was at work. In an instant, the child dashed out into the street and his little body was thrown thirty feet into the air. The child lived a few more hours and we stood by the bed and watched him die. Such grief! Such guilt!

We gathered at a cheap funeral parlor because I couldn't talk them into having the funeral at the church. I sat there, surrounded by sprays of plastic flowers and a family so mad at God they couldn't look at me. And at some point, somebody came up to me and said, "Reverend. It's time. Would you say just a word?"

Wrong way, wrong time, wrong place for preaching.

September 16, 2001. I stood on the steps of Duke Chapel and watched people running—that's what they were doing, running into church. I could read the desperation on their faces, the hunger for some word more eloquent and comforting than those of the president. I called Hauerwas the evening before, seeking theological guidance. Help me! I said. What should I say? Hauerwas replied, "I thank God I'm not a preacher tomorrow!"

What good are words in the face of the horror, the evil, the falling towers, and death? Wrong time, wrong place for preaching.

Aristotle said that it's easy to tell somebody the truth but difficult to tell them the truth at the right time. With truth-telling, says Aristotle, there's a question of timing. That's why friends are best to tell us the truth. Friends know us well enough to know when to speak the truth to us.

As a teacher, the way I figure it, about 90 percent of what I teach is the right material—taught at the wrong time. I can tell by looking into their zombie-like eyes. It's the wrong time. They're not yet ready to be taught.

I teach for the sacred privilege of being there for the right time when the eyes light up, and the face startles, and I know that I have been there with the right word at the right time. There's no time better for a teacher than that.

Thus the book of Ecclesiastes says that for everything there is a time, for everything there is a season (3:1). There's a time to speak and a time to keep silent (3:7). God "made everything suited for its time," says Ecclesiastes (3:11). God has built into creation a sense of timing. There is the right time, the due season.

But then in the next verse Ecclesiastes says: and you can never know the right time. There is a time for everything and only God knows what that time is! There's a time to speak and a time to keep silent, but you'll never know when that time is!

I despise Ecclesiastes.

Well, we had a wonderful service on Pentecost. Quite a crowd that Sunday—Parthians, Medes, Elamites, Iraqis, and other Mesopotamians—simultaneous translation, descent of the Holy Spirit, fire. No sermon because the church was so new and so full of the Holy Spirit it didn't yet need professional preachers. Words were everywhere. When the service ended and the commotion settled, we opened the doors of the church and looked out into the street and there gathered a mob of scoffing rabble.

"Look, them Christians is doing the same thing they did when Jesus was with 'em. They're drunk!"

And Peter—who could think of nothing to say just a few weeks earlier when confronted by that maid at midnight in the courtyard—Peter said, "Well, er, it's only ten in the morning. We're not drunk. Yet."

Not the most promising beginning for a sermon.

It was the wrong time (Peter hadn't been an apostle but for a few weeks). No time for homiletical training. It was the wrong place (in the middle of Times Square and a mob?). And Peter preached, preached a short, four-minute homily (strange that we later preachers learn nothing from that!), and even though Peter used no sappy illustrations from daily life, had no snappy opening lines, made absolutely no reference to their felt needs, or purpose-driven lives, and had a lousy conclusion—three thousand people heard, were cut to the heart, asking, "What do we have to do to be saved?"

The first Christian homily in history was delivered in the wrong place, at the wrong time, in the wrong way, except that God spoke and began to transform the world through preaching.

It was as if God said, "I'm going to take back what belongs to me! The Revolution begins now! I'm going head-to-head with Satan."

How? "With preaching."

And we asked, "Here? Now?"

Some people think that John Wesley was converted when he had his "heartwarming experience" at Aldersgate. Others think that Wesley's real conversion came when he wrote in his diary, "This afternoon I submitted to be even more vile and descended to the level of field preaching." See this proper little Oxford Don descend at the wrong time, at the wrong place, and preach?

Second Timothy 4:2 says, "Preach the word, . . . in season and out of season." Yet, really now, is God's word ever in season, in sync, in step, in place—except that there, then, God speaks?

Acts 17. Paul is wandering around the Agora in Athens (Greece, not Georgia), marveling at how many gods these pagans worship, doing a very Jewish thing—arguing with anybody who will talk to him. A mocking crowd again gathers—a mocking, academic, pagan crowd (which I can tell you from twenty years of personal experience is one of the worst kinds of crowds!). And though nearly everybody is there for the wrong reasons, and though it is the wrong time, and nobody is there to have church or to hear about Jesus, Paul preaches, preaches one of the most succinct and perfectly formed classical orations in all of scripture. And three people come forward to follow Jesus.

(You say, "Only three?" Hey, it's a college town, three isn't bad, considering the location!)

This dear, devout, dumb Divinity School student said to me, "Must be quite a challenge preaching at Duke Chapel, where most of the people aren't there out of real commitment to the practices of discipleship but rather for the music, or the beautiful building. Must be hard to preach to them."

"Not at all," I replied. "The way I figure it, in any church, on any Sunday, most of the people are gathered for all the wrong reasons. They think they've come to be made a little less miserable, or to find a little more meaning, or because they are going to get help with their problems, there to be unexpectedly jumped by Jesus, who wants to make them even more miserable than when they got there."

Hey, if we're going to wait for the right time, the right place, the right people with the right reasons before we preach, I guess we'll never get to preach!

It's God's business to make time for the Word. It's up to us only to preach. Only Word made flesh can make my words the Word made flesh.

Jonah said to God, "I'm not going to preach to those Iraqis. We've tried negotiation, the UN, they won't listen! It's not the right sort of setting for preaching." Jonah takes a swift boat to Tarshish. But after being vomited up on the beach, he reluctantly goes to Baghdad and there—*without illustration, modulation, or gesticulation*—preaches the shortest, lousiest sermon on record: "Forty days, Nineveh will be overthrown."

"There, I've preached it, now can I go back to Durham?"

And just out of meanness the LORD caused everyone in that great city to repent. The people repented, the king repented, even the cows repented. Not much of a sermon, except . . .

Why did I preach thirty-two sermons in this past year at Duke Chapel, in the heart of a modern, secular, scoffing university campus? Because somebody told me the story of Jonah, the world's worst preacher, whom God made to preach the world's most effective sermon.

Philip is told to go to the middle of the desert. And at noon! There, in the worst heat of the day, he encounters, of all people, an Ethiopian, an Ethiopian eunuch, who's somehow got an Isaiah scroll on him. "'Like a lamb he was led to the slaughter.' Who's the writer talking about," the Ethiopian asks, "himself, or somebody else?"

Philip says, "He's talking about Jesus, of course. To use an impenetrable metaphor for an Ethiopian eunuch, Jesus is that Lamb led to the slaughter."

The Ethiopian asks, "What do I have to do to be among the Lamb's people?"

"Well," says Philip, "we have this ritual called baptism. And nothing would make me happier than to get all the saints in Jerusalem riled up by baptizing a eunuch, but unfortunately, we must have water in order to baptize, and we're out here in the desert so a rule's a rule and, sorry, wrong place."

"Look, here's water, what's to hinder me?" asks the eunuch.

Wrong time, wrong person. Except God took time.

I taught this sheep-dip of a course when I was here, "Introduction to Christian Ministry." I always began the course by having each student tell about his or her call to the ministry. How did you get here? I would ask.

One by one they told their stories. Many of them seemed to feature light on a patio in the afternoon, and Jesus. We finally got to Carol and I was excited. Carol had told me, in an advising session, that she owned a multimillion-dollar medical lab business. She had walked off that business, disposed of everything, and had come to seminary. My, Carol must have a story to tell of blinding light and thunderous voice that would make Paul's conversion be as nothing.

Carol said, "Well, our pastor had asked me to be the lector for a Sunday service. I read the Epistle and the Gospel. At the end of the service, as we were leaving church, this older woman came up to me and said, 'Dear, you read so well, you probably ought to be a pastor.'"

And I said, "That's it? Nothing more? You have walked off a good-paying job and come to Durham on the basis of some old lady's telling you that you can really read?"

"You would have to have been there to get it."

We can't know the right time. I can't always figure out when a sermon is in season. Only God knows. Thus Bullinger says, "The preached word is God's word." And Karl Barth says, "Only Christ can preach."

I'm not the right preacher and you're not the right listener, and this is neither the right time nor the right place, unless God makes it so.

Thus Peter comes out, faces the scoffing mob, and bumbles through a sermon. Although it was neither the right time, nor the right place, three thousand people heard and were saved. Peter didn't do that.

Barth's Limitations as a Biblical Interpreter

Generally, Barth is held in low regard by most biblical scholars.[63] Considering what Barth said about many of them and their work, and considering Barth's own intentions in biblical interpretation, the critics' low regard for Barth is no surprise. However, even for those of us who love Barth's interpretation, we must admit that Barth may not be as "biblical" as he claims.

Although Barth says that he is listening carefully to scripture, Barth listens to a limited range of scripture. He has, in the words of Graham White, "a very narrow range of stories at his disposal."[64] It is interesting to note which scripture Barth virtually omits from his "canon": wisdom literature, the Sermon on the Mount, and apocalyptic literature, to mention a few.

Furthermore, his rigorously christological reading of all texts leads to some curious interpretations, and not only of the Old Testament texts that Barth submits to christological interpretation.[65] To read all texts on the basis of the second person of the Trinity is a defensible hermeneutical practice. But to read all texts to the virtual exclusion of the other two persons of the Trinity seems not only limited but also not true to Barth's intentions to be rigorously Trinitarian in his theology. Barth gives the Holy Spirit the central role in the miracle of hearing. The Bible becomes the Word of God through the actions of the Holy Spirit. But the Holy Spirit is not some sort of "magical, mystical, indefinable whispering and compelling" source of inspiration "from the human soul" (*CD*, IV, 2, pg. 360). The Holy Spirit is Trinitarian, not a third separate "person" who works in some obscure, mystical, independent way of the Father and the Son. Rather, the Holy Spirit is precisely the same God who was incarnate as the man Jesus now effectively uniting himself with us in mutual self-disclosure (*CD*, IV, 2, pg. 331). The "miracle" of hearing is always a thoroughly Trinitarian one that is made possible by the work of the Holy Spirit. Barth surely has the essential work of the Holy Spirit in mind when he says that prayer is a requisite for biblical interpretation: "Because it is the decisive activity, prayer must take precedence even of exegesis" (*CD*, I, 2, pg. 695).

But the Holy Spirit is not only the means whereby revelation occurs, as Barth repeatedly stresses, but also the substance of revelation. The Holy Spirit is not only a means and mode of God's being present to us, but is also God's being. It is the nature of the Trinitarian God, as experienced in the third person of the Trinity, to be alive, energetic, moving, vital, and uncontainable. Pentecostalism, while it may do an injustice to the first or second person of the Trinity, is a great reminder and corrective to my church that the church lives in the power of the Spirit, that the church is a gift of the Holy Spirit or the church degenerates into being an antiquarian society or a merely humanly contrived organization. One might say much the same about the creative, fecund work of the Father. When we are gripped by some insight into scripture, it's Genesis 1 all over again, the work of a God who loves to create something out of nothing, bringing into being that which was not. I am sure that Barth would want to affirm this, but his biblical interpretation does not show an actual dependence upon the full Trinity.

One of the reasons for some of Barth's more bizarre interpretations is that Barth makes such a strong Christocentric interpretation that Christ completely takes over the story in a way that the stories themselves do not bear.[66] It is typical of biblical narrative, for instance, to portray Christ as a sort of reflection on the faces, questions, and actions of those around him. But Barth simply subsumes all of these characters as icons of Christ in a way that I do not find in the story itself. Because Barth claims to be working exclusively and strictly from the story itself, this is a problem. Brent Strawn has also criticized Barth's interpretation of the Old Testament on the basis that Barth's rigorously christological readings of scripture are not sufficiently Trinitarian, a charge that I am sure would cut Barth to the quick.[67]

In Barth, Christ becomes the interpretive key to nearly every passage everywhere. When, in his vivid interpretation of the prodigal son, Barth portrays Christ as the son who went into the far country, Barth over-interprets a parable, albeit beautifully.

For Barth to claim that his dogmatics is based directly on scripture is a claim that boggles the minds of many who plow through the *Dogmatics*.[68] Barth expends so much time on matters like the Trinity, the origin and reality of the demonic, angels, the realm of nature, subjects on which the Bible tends to be terse. He makes his statements on all of these subjects with such seeming finality, with such earnestness and in such seriousness and detail, saying so much more on these issues than the Bible says, taking them so much more seriously than the Bible takes them, that he appears to be in danger of making his dogmatics a kind of revelation in itself.

I think David Ford amply demonstrates that Barth's claim to be working exclusively from scripture to scripture, exclusively within the scriptural world, in order to write a theology that is exclusively tied to scripture, is not always supported by Barth's use of scripture. For instance, Barth's Doctrine of Election, which von Balthasar rightly calls "the heartbeat of Barth's theology," including its forty-eight-page treatment of Judas Iscariot, while wonderfully creative and marvelously challenging to traditional theological treatments of election, nevertheless claims to hear far too much from the text than the text itself will allow.[69] Barth gives Judas a prominence, pushes Judas into the story of salvation, despite Judas's own actions, and makes Judas one of the most interesting and prominent of the disciples. Little of this is supported by the biblical texts themselves.[70]

Paul McGlasson has said that when Barth reads the Bible for Christology, Barth uses two differing reading approaches that result in two different sorts of readings.[71] When Barth is primarily working for concepts of Christ, the identity of Christ is described in rather abstract and impersonal terms. Jesus becomes more logical than personal.[72] When Barth is working from narratives, like the narrative of the prodigal son in "The Royal Man" (*CD*, IV, 2, pp. 154-264), Jesus' identity is more concrete and personal. In his article on Barth's ecclesiology, Nicholas M. Healy complains that, in writing about the church, "Barth uses Scripture primarily as a source of doctrinal concepts rather than narratives. He applies these concepts directly to the church, which he describes in an abstract rather than a concrete way."[73] In other words, when Barth is a truly narrative reader, he has more interesting and ultimately coherent things to say than when he begins with certain concepts for which scripture becomes a mere illustration of the concepts.

Yet as a preacher I cannot help but enjoy the imaginative range of Barth's engagement with scripture, and all my criticisms pale before Barth's great exposition. Barth's exegetical passages, and his metaphors and images, may be the strongest and most imaginative and invigorating aspects of his theology.[74] I dearly love his portrayal of Christ as the prodigal son. I also find wonderfully suggestive his discussion on Judas and election. Barth's exegesis shows the fruitfulness of reading scripture from a strictly theological point of view and, by comparison with much contemporary academic exposition, the fruitlessness of reading scripture without any acknowledged theological commitments.

This is not to claim that Barth is a model reader of scripture. I wish Barth had used more analogical language in his discussions, and less propositional speech. I wish he had been more the poet and less the propositionalist. In other words, I wish that he had more closely followed his own homiletical advice to follow the "distinctive movement of the text." I think this is due to more than the preacher in me. It is a pleading with Barth to be more true to his own claims for the peculiarity of Christian thinking and the peculiar shape of that thinking in scripture. Barth did say that, when it comes to scripture, "the writing is obviously not primary but secondary. It is the deposit of what was once proclamation by human lips" (*CD*, I, 1, pg. 102). It is the homiletical, oral-aural quality of scripture that puts us close to the very voice of God.

Barth's Bible is an animated, speaking presence, not an inanimate object. Thus Barth has unbridled faith that there is nothing wrong with the church that cannot be cured through a homiletical rediscovery of the Bible. The church is that community that has no other support than that offered through the upholding by the scripture:

> Right up to our own days the Old and New Testament Scriptures have never been reduced to a mere letter in Christian circles, but have continually become a living voice and word, and have had and exercised power as such. To be sure, they have sometimes been almost completely silenced in a thicket of added traditions, or proclaimed only in liturgical sing-song, or overlaid by bold speculation . . . or torn asunder into a thousand shreds (each more unimportant than the other) by unimaginative historico-critical omniscience. But they have always been the same Scripture . . . which can speak and make itself heard. . . . But at some point, as a fellowship of those who hear Scripture's voice, the threatened community begins to group and consolidate and constitute itself afresh around the Bible, and in so doing it again finds itself on solid ground when everything seems to totter.[75]

Toward the end of his *Homiletics*, after having given his rules for reading scripture, Barth confesses the need humbly to keep biblical mystery as mystery, to remain as an "astonished child":

> We should not try to master the text. The Bible will become more and more mysterious to real exegetes. They will see all the depths and distances. They will constantly run up against the mystery before which *theology* is like trying to drain the ocean with a spoon. The true exegete will face the text like an astonished child in a wonderful garden, not like an advocate of God who has seen all his files.[76]

As he boarded the train to return to Switzerland, victim of the Nazis' purge of the German universities, Barth's parting exhortation to the students and pastors whom he left behind, his last gift to them for the fight ahead, was to urge them toward "exegesis, exegesis and yet more exegesis! Keep to the Word, to the scripture that has been given to us."[77]

CHAPTER THREE

I WILL GIVE YOU WORDS

It is difficult to conceive God, but to define him in words is an impossibility. . . . But in my opinion it is impossible to express God, and yet more impossible to conceive God. For that which may be conceived may perhaps be made clear by language. . . . But to comprehend the whole of so great a subject as this is quite impossible and impracticable, not merely to the utterly careless and ignorant, but even to those who are highly exalted, and who love God. (Gregory of Nazianzus, "Second Theological Oration")

What to preach? The Saturday evening dilemma of the hapless modern preacher— what shall I say in a sermon?—may be a uniquely contemporary situation. Preachers, by the nature of their vocation, are those who speak because they have been told something to say. Can you imagine Paul pacing about his prison cell, agonizing because "I have nothing to say to First Church Corinth"?

Jesus warned his disciples that "they will arrest you and persecute you; they will hand you over to synagogues and prisons, and you will be brought before kings and governors because of my name." But then in the same breath he calls these persecutions "opportunity to testify" (Luke 21:13). Even the worst things that happen to a Christian are to be seen as opportunities to witness, a golden opportunity to preach. To prepare for such crucial speaking, Jesus commands avoidance of preparation. "So make up your minds not to prepare your defense in advance; for I will give you words and a wisdom that none of your opponents will be able to withstand or contradict" (Luke 21:14-15). I will give you words (literally in the Greek, "I will give you a mouth"). We have something to say because God speaks. "I believed, and so I spoke," says Paul (2 Cor. 4:13). Or as Barth puts it, "Cognizance becomes knowledge when man becomes a responsible witness."[1] That is, we Christians think with our mouths open. We know, really know, that which we are able to speak, and we are able to speak only because God speaks.

In a quick survey of homiletics, Thomas G. Long notes how, at least since Augustine, Christian preaching was happily married to the art of rhetoric. Christian preachers saw the Bible as a source of preaching's *content*, then used the insights and procedures of classical rhetoric for the *form* and *style* of sermons. It was, says Long, a reasonably happy and productive "mixed marriage" lasting for many centuries. But then, says Long, the marriage between rhetoric and homiletics suffered a "Barth attack."[2]

Barth thundered forth that preaching is interesting, as a form of communication, for primarily theological rather than rhetorical reasons. Preaching is the Word of God. As preachers, we must speak God's word. That is a frightening task, particularly on a weekly basis. Yet we must not begin with the preacher, with the preacher's words, or with our fears. We must begin in faith, specifically, faith in a God who speaks.

Trevor Hart says, "Karl Barth's entire theological project might legitimately be described as a 'theology of proclamation.' The assumption upon which it is predicated and with which Barth concerns himself as (he insists) the only legitimate starting point for truly theological activity, is the claim made by faith that God has spoken, that he has proclaimed his Word to humankind, that he has revealed himself."[3] Theology for Barth is the church's reflection upon God's speech and our speech about God. Theology is that secondary enterprise that comes along after the church's conversation (*CD*, II, 1, pg. 49). Barth said, "As the theological discipline, Dogmatics is a scientific self-examination of the Christian Church with respect to the content of its distinctive talk about God" (*CD*, I, 1, pg. 3). Eugene Peterson asserts that the Christian life in general, and the preaching ministry in particular, is renewed only when we begin at "square one" for all Christian thought and action. "Square one," says Peterson, is the simple, astounding, always surprising event, "And God said. . . ."[4]

Barth discusses the miracle of revelation in *CD* I, before he discusses anything else, and no matter what he discusses, throughout the rest of the *Dogmatics*, he never gets beyond his primal wonder that "God speaks." This is theology's only warrant, proclamation's only reason.

We have within us no inherent capacity to know what to say about God. Yet, curiously, Barth's theology gives scant attention to the Reformation problem of human sin. For Luther and Calvin, sin kept us from hearing God's plainly spoken Word. For Barth, the problem is human ignorance, unknowing, which is a symptom of our sin. Whereas the Reformers, when they talk about preaching, must talk about human sin in our attempts to communicate the gospel, for Barth the problem is epistemological, how to speak of God to those who have little conceptual apparatus for hearing what God has already done about sin. Any alleged feeling of absolute dependence (Schleiermacher), yearning for some ground of being (Tillich), or desire for a more fulfilling life (contemporary advocates too numerous to mention) will not provide access to God. As Barth famously said, God talk is not talk about humanity in a loud voice. There is no anthropological starting point for theology (theology = God talk). There is not within the hearer some divine spark, point of contact, or inchoate inclination that only awaits a skillful preacher's development to make it a bridge to God. A sermon is not our attempt to construct Jacob's ladder. Acts of human imagination are only creaturely constructions that never adequately image the Creator. Feuerbach perceptively saw that all such talk is mere projection, talk by inflated selves without any real reference to anything outside ourselves. Barth thunders against such tame communication that cuts God down to ourselves:

> We suppose that we know what we are saying when we say "God." We assign to Him the highest place in our world: and in so doing we place Him on fundamentally one line with ourselves and with things. We assume that He needs something: and so we assume that we are able to arrange our relation to Him as we arrange our other relationships. We press ourselves into proximity with Him . . . We make Him nigh unto ourselves. We allow ourselves an ordinary communication with Him, we permit ourselves to reckon with Him. . . . We serve the No-God.[5]

A few years ago, teaching a course on "The Rhetoric of Preaching," I found myself in the embarrassing position of admitting to the students (at the last class session!) that the class, despite my good intentions, had been a mistake. I had begun, as the study of rhetoric tends always to do, by having them read Aristotle's *On Rhetoric*. (Almost all of the best of Western rhetoric is a series of footnotes on Aristotle.) We had marveled at Aristotle's taxonomy of a speech, his insightful psychological analyses of various sorts of audiences, his stress upon the importance of the character of the speaker and other aspects of the art of public speaking. Yet at the end I was forced to confess that the course was a failure.

"Aristotle was a brilliant, skillful philosopher of public speaking. When it comes to analysis of the challenges of rhetoric, no one is better," I admitted. "His one limitation is that he was not a Christian. That means that Aristotle did not believe in the Holy Spirit, did not know a God who speaks, who discloses, reveals. He marveled at human beings' ability to speak but did not know a God who speaks.

"Unfortunately, I have conducted this course as if that made no difference to the task of preaching. I would say this. If there is not a talking God who loves to raise the dead, then go with Aristotle. There is no one more helpful for the task of speaking without God. But if this course has been extended training in how to preach as if God were dead and therefore silent, then it has been a sad atheistic mistake."

Barth is determined to eschew rhetorical concerns in order to leave our proclamation in a highly vulnerable position—that is, speech that appeals to revelation alone as the basis for its assertions. As preachers, we are called upon not to try to speak of God without God, for that would be merely a compromise with atheism; we are to bear witness to the Word we have received.

We know, we speak, only because of the biblical assertion, "And God said. . . ."[6]

How Do We Know What We Know?

Christians must learn and relearn how odd it is to have a God who speaks, who discloses and reveals. Otherwise we know nothing about God and therefore have nothing to say. *How do we know what we know?* Epistemology has been a major concern for modern philosophy. For Christians the great challenge is to respond to the epistemological question—how do we know what we know—through revelation. We know what we know only as it has been given, revealed by a God who shows us that which we could never, on our own, uncover.

Philosophy is love of, and hot pursuit of, wisdom (*philo* + *Sophia*). Barth was notoriously suspicious of "philosophy." Though he had a deep, wide-ranging knowledge of philosophy from Plato through the then-contemporary Existentialists, Barth repeatedly warned of the dangers of Christian thought attempting to make too easy an alliance with philosophy. Philosophy must never set theology's agenda, although it can be used by an eclectic theologian. Because philosophy tends toward systemization and generalization, it tends to distort Christian theology's attentiveness to its peculiar subject, making that subject (God) seem more orderly and humanly conceivable than the subject really is.

A major reason for his misgiving about philosophy was Barth's conviction that Truth is the Way, the Truth, and the Life, that is, Jesus Christ. That embodied Truth is not to be apprehended by the way that philosophy normally goes after the truth. Truth is a Way, a movement, a journey; Truth is a person, personal, Jesus of Nazareth.[7] Because of the peculiar nature and personality of Christian Truth, philosophy has difficulty with this sort of Truth. Philosophy begins in questions, but invariably the wrong questions, questions like, "How can we know God?" whereas Barth was more impressed with the amazing, philosophically inexplicable questions like, "How does God so well know us?"

What is there and how do we know it is there? This is the sort of epistemological question on which philosophy feeds. There is a parable in the Hindu Vedas in which a person, entering a darkened room, sees a snake coiled in a corner. Though filled with terror at the thought of a venomous snake ready to strike, the person examines the snake more closely. Is it a snake or only a harmless coil of rope? It is only a piece of rope. What once was thought to be a threat, perceived in the right way, is no longer a threat. This, implies the Vedas, is a purpose of philosophy; to disarm the world by removing the threat of the unknown. Telling the truth about the world is what ultimately makes the world bearable.

Plato (427?–347? BCE) said that human beings seem born to ask *why*?[8] We naturally want to know the truth. If we know the truth, we will do it, thought Plato; therefore knowledge is the engine that drives Plato's ethics. But getting knowledge is no easy task. Paul says of humanity, "For what can be known about God is plain to them, because God has shown it to them. Ever since the creation of the world his eternal power and divine nature, invisible though they are, have been understood and seen through the things he has made" (Rom. 1:19-20). But in this rare Pauline outburst of incipient natural theology, Paul is not fully acknowledging how strange the world is to us.

The world is not presented to us in a simple, fixed, self-evident way. Plato was deeply suspicious that the world we have before our eyes is not the world that is actually there (e.g., Plato's "Allegory of the Cave"). Our perceptions of and experience of the world are notoriously flawed. The truth about things is not apparent. Philosophy is that hard, hazardous human struggle to get right about what is real, to perceive what is really there, and to discover, through reason, the ideals. When Plato spoke of philosophy beginning in wonder, he also meant wonderment that our perception of the world is so terribly flawed. Philosophy can therefore be described as criticism of our ways of conceiving of our world, a critique of our means of knowledge. How do we know what we know? And how do we know what we know is true?

Though Plato had his doubts about our perception of the world, he rejected the radically skeptical view that we can never reliably know. Radical doubt about our knowledge was fostered by the Sophists like *Gorgias* (fifth century BCE). The Sophists said that it is doubtful that anything exists and, if it does, any true knowledge of it would be difficult to communicate. Plato, following his teacher, Socrates, believed that there existed a world behind, beyond the visible world. That world beneath the apparent world is the world of unchanging, stable ideas, a world that can be known and described, but only with the greatest of difficulty. Plato condemned the Sophists for being cynical, intellectually lazy, and doubting too much the validity of human perception. It is possible, through reason, to have reliable and even certain knowledge of this ideal world, the world as it is in perfection. Philosophy is a search that moves beyond tangible things to contemplation of the pure, ideal form whereby there is certitude.

As a young pastor Barth was influenced by his close rereading of Plato. Against a radically skeptical, sophistic view of knowledge, Plato convinced Barth that it is possible to gain reliable knowledge of reality. Yet any true knowledge of the world must be transcendent from the world, must be more certain than the changing, deceptive appearance of things in this world in order to be real knowledge. In other words, to know this world accurately we must have some nonworldly referent, particularly when the knowledge being sought is knowledge of that which transcends our normal means of knowledge.

Aristotle (384–322 BCE) begins his monumental *Metaphysics* (*meta+physics*, literally, that which comes after physics, that thought that comes after thinking about the physical, tangible world) with the assertion, "All men by nature desire to know." For evidence, Aristotle points to our senses. Consider the delight we take in our senses such as smell or hearing, totally apart from any usefulness that we may obtain through such sensation. All creatures must seek knowledge of the world, if they are to survive, but the incessant pleasure that human beings take in our acquisition of knowledge of the world is beyond even our need for brute survival. Through our experience of probing and testing the world, we gain knowledge of the world. Our reason enables us to make sense of our experience, to arrange the vast array of perceptions into configurations that make sense, and thereby we are enabled to move in the world with confidence.

Aristotle was unimpressed with Plato's appeal to some transcendent, beyond-this-world source of knowledge. We know through experience of the world, this world, not through high-flown thought about some invisible, ideal forms that lie behind the world. The way to know is to keep close to the stuff of this world through careful observation of the way the world works.

Aristotelian linkage of knowledge with the actual experience of the world was to be broken by Descartes. *René Descartes* (1596–1650) ran away from his French Jesuit school of La Fleche at sixteen and joined the French army operating against the German states. In a way, Descartes enabled the modern world to run away from the church, at least in its thought. His 1637 *Discourse on Method* was a declaration of independence from scholastic and medieval modes of authority in thought. This is what Jeffrey Stout has called the "flight from authority."[9] And yet at the same time Descartes's was a touchingly naive confession of faith in the possibilities for mathematical analysis. Above all, Descartes desired *certitude* by means of deductions from self-evident propositions, a mode of thought that not only showed great faith (and I use the word *faith* intentionally) in mathematics and mechanistic philosophies but also a way of thought that goes back, in some of its aspects, at least to Socrates. Descartes substituted faith in the authority of an infallible method for faith in an infallible ecclesiastical or social authority. This method was the way toward systematic, self-evidently demonstrative knowledge. Trustworthy knowledge must be based upon experience, and there can be a universally agreed-upon way to get to that knowledge.

Descartes's Socratic starting point is *methodological skepticism,* doubting everything that can be doubted in order eventually to arrive at certitude. Once one has reached the indubitable, then it is possible for one rationally to build a system of necessary consequences that will constitute certain, irrefutable truth. Thus, Descartes gave birth to modern ways of thinking and their consequences.

Descartes also achieved a "flight to objectivity."[10] From Descartes, the modern world received an "objectivist" view of knowledge. Knowledge consists of neutral "facts" that have been separated out from unverifiable "values." The mastery of these facts, their transfer to the mind, constitutes thought. Descartes split the person into a mind-body dichotomy, with the mind being the true essence of a human being. Said Descartes:

> I concluded that I was a substance whose whole essence nature consists only in thinking, and which, that it may exist, has need of no place, nor is dependent on any material thing; so that "I," that is to say, the mind by which I am what I am, is wholly distinct from the body and is even more easily known than the latter, and is such, that altogether the latter were not, it would still continue to be all that it is.[11]

Whereas Aristotle urged us to look carefully at the world that we have before us, note in Descartes's statement the Cartesian devaluing of the material world, as well as social and bodily existence, in favor of the sovereign, detached, thinking self. Here is the disconnected self, neutrally receiving the "facts" of the world as they come, unfettered by any historical or social contingencies—other than attachment to the newly conceived Cartesian sovereign self.

Descartes claimed that his principles were derived from "clear and distinct ideas." Attempting to extend simple mathematical formulae to all things, he conceived of a mechanical universe. As it turned out, Descartes simply provided new proofs for old convictions. In his unqualified self-confidence in human reason, in his self-assurance that he was objectively observing the "Book of the World," rather than merely building upon mere prejudiced feeling or faith, Descartes demonstrated a new kind of "faith."

Descartes began his *Discourse on Method* by praising "Good sense," which he claimed to be "most equally distributed" throughout humanity. By "Good sense" he means detached, allegedly innate "reason." The great challenge, according to Descartes, is not simply to have a vigorous mind—because he believes that all people have such a mind—but the "prime requisite is rightly to apply it." He announced to the world that he had "formed a Method that gives me the means, as I think, of gradually augmenting my knowledge, and of raising it by little and little to the highest point."

Descartes had found a way to get to sure knowledge, a methodical way to truth, without recourse to external authority or revelation, other than the authority of his Method. Truth is to be gotten, not from the church and its teachings, but rather from the thinking, detached self. His 1637 *Discourse on Method* dominated modern philosophic method until Hume and Kant demonstrated its limits.

Here is how Descartes described his project in his *Meditations:*

> It is sometime ago now since I perceived that, from my earliest years, I had accepted many false opinions as being true, and that what I had since based on such insecure principles could only be most doubtful and uncertain; so that I had to undertake seriously once in my life to rid myself of all the opinions I had adopted up to then, and to begin afresh from the foundation, if I wish to establish something firm and constant in the sciences.[12]

Systematic doubt, arising from the detached, sovereign self, is the way to absolute certitude.

Barth said that once Descartes had so severely limited his method of thought to those ideas that were exclusively derived from himself,

> it is quite impossible to reach out either to the transcendence of a God who confronts man in sovereign omnipotence, existing for Himself and therefore existing for man, to the transcendence of a subject of human thought which is not exhausted in the act of thinking, or to the transcendence of a real external world attained by our thought but not included within it. The God of Descartes is hopelessly enchained within the mind of man. Neither in the description given of Him nor in the role ascribed to Him does He bear the divine character which would distinguish Him as the being to whom objective existence beyond all human imagining must be ascribed, for the simple

reason that it is He Himself who has inexorably and inescapably prescribed these thoughts for man.[13]

Barth ridiculed the Cartesian notion of objectivity in modernity. He says of modern observers,

> They sit at their telescope . . . observing and reflecting upon what they have seen. They do not allow themselves to be personally affected, for all their interest in these things. It is they who decide and regulate the distances in relations between themselves and things. It is they who observe and experiment and note the inner connection of things and their detailed and general harmony and usefulness. They are the masters who are able to put everything to rights . . . things do not really touch them, either for evil or for good.[14]

Barth charged that Descartes's method produced not an extension of human consciousness into knowledge about the world but rather only a "confrontation" with itself.[15] Barth asserted that revelation was knowing of a quite different order than the knowing of Descartes. Revelation is knowledge that confronts "a givenness which is wholly grounded in itself. All theological thought must start with that which is given and return to it."[16]

Descartes invented the denuded knower. The way to sure and certain knowledge is for the knowing subject intentionally to strip itself of all preconceptions, prejudices, and prior convictions and attempt a kind of intentional innocence. Apprehend the objects of the world as they are, without reading upon those objects any prior convictions. The way to knowledge is through objectivity and detached observation.

Descartes turned to the subject. His claim of neutral observation was eventually uncovered as a different sort of subjectivism now disguised as detached objectivity. Charles Taylor shows that Descartes's *Cogito, ergo sum* gave birth to the subjective, autonomous self of the Enlightenment.[17] Barth called this the invention of the "Absolute Man":

> [Enlightenment] man knows that he is linked with, and ultimately of the same substance as, the God significant for him in this double function. God is spirit, man is spirit too. God is mighty and so is man. God is wise and benevolent, and so is man. But he is all these things, of course, infinitely less perfect than God. Man's way of being these things is confused and fragmentary, but it is the same way. . . . Has not [this Enlightenment] man in fact asked himself and himself given the answer he apparently wished to hear from some other source? This is the question of which, thus expressed, man in the eighteenth century was not aware. This was the absolutism also inherent in his inner attitude to life; he assumed it to be self-evident that in taking himself into account, and himself answering the account, and then acting in obedience to it he was also showing the existence of God. . . . believed—even in this inmost place we find him prey to a strange vicious circle—that by virtue of the reality of his own existence he could vouch for God.[18]

In Descartes's account of knowledge, knowledge consists of insights, detached ideas that come to the knower without corruption or external coercion. *John Locke* (1632–1704) took this a step further. Locke gave this example: Take a prince and a peasant. While each of them sleeps, their brains are exchanged. When they awake, there will be a peasant with the brain of a prince and a prince with the brain of a peasant. Will they be the same people? Locke said that he would not deny that each would appear to be the same man as before, but each is now *a totally different person*. We are who we are, said Locke, because of the way our minds have been stocked.

In his *Essay Concerning Human Understanding* Locke asked, "How is the mind furnished?" Answer: Through human experience and perception. Obviously, this conception of knowledge led to our modern overweening faith in education, to developmental theories of the self, and to the notion of human beings as determined by their environment. I know what I know because of the way my environment has stocked and furnished my brain.

Locke's famous *tabula rasa* depicts the human intellect as an essentially innocent, disinterested blank slate upon which experiences are written, lives are formed, and humans are made to think what we think. Locke taught that we have certain sensory experiences that we pull together and, on the basis of experience, form certain ideas. Our thoughts are a sort of consortium of our experiences of the world. Experience precedes and enables thought. What we call "thought" is our collection of, inference from, and arrangement of our experiences. In this sort of thinking, thinking moves forward by analogy, by arranging our thought on the basis of experience.

Gottfried Leibniz (1646–1716) accused Locke of reviving the old medieval scholastic assertion that there is nothing in the mind that has not been put there by the senses. If our mind is able to receive and to arrange experience, then something must precede experience in the mind. Leibniz thus made the ironic observation that there is nothing in the mind that has not been put there by the senses *except the mind itself*. Leibniz began what was to be a thoroughgoing critique of the Lockean assertion of human experience as the royal road to sure knowledge. Despite Locke and his modern progeny, experience may not be all that it is made out to be. Experience would count as nothing but a barrage of incessant stimulation without the selectivity and integration that come into play through our mental processes of conceptualization and arrangement. As a professor of mine was fond of saying, "You haven't had an experience just because it happened to you." Our experiences provide the crude data—very crude—that the mind must make into something worth knowing.

No mind is ever a *tabula rasa*, innocent, free from some prior conceptual framework. The whole notion of "experience" arises from our having something that we are able to recognize and to name as "experience." Perception is grounded in apperception. We not only have sensory stimulation, but we know that we are having such stimulation, and we are busy making something of it that is considerably more than sensory stimulation. Our experience cannot be the result of only experience. Perception is inexplicable on purely material, mechanical grounds. Something precedes the mechanism. If you enter our brains, you can see various cells and mechanisms, but you will never see "ideas," or colors, notions, or principles, and yet they are "there." The mind is active. Perception is dependent upon apperception. A materialist, reductionist idea of the mind doesn't work. There is a sense in which theory precedes experience. That is why "theologizing from experience" is an inadequate source for theology. No person has had the "white male experience" until that person has inculcated the theory that there is such a thing as that experience and that there are certain aspects of that experience that ought to be noted. That also means that my "white male experience" will be so different from another white male's experience because of all the things that I bring to interpretation of that experience. To think on the basis of some allegedly universal experience is not to think at all.

Bishop George Berkeley (1685–1753) (the "If a tree falls in the forest, and no one is there to hear it, does it make a sound?" Bishop Berkeley) therefore sought to show that a Lockean purely materialistic notion of knowing can't be defended. Berkeley attacked

Locke's theories of human knowing as being too empiricist. There is no *Tabula nuda*, and if there were, it would be a jumble of meaningless information. Berkeley rejected the notion that matter is the source of our mind, seeing therein a sort of materialism that terribly reduced human mental life.

For one thing, said Berkeley, the material world does not have independent existence. There is, in a deep sense, no "there, there" without certain processes that are nonmaterial. We not only "make sense" of the material world but we also "make" that world through our perceptions of the world. Berkeley did not say, in the fashion of some radical skeptics, that there is no material world. Rather, he said that there is no independently existing material world, independent of all perception, all ideation, all conceptualization, without imposed thought, wisdom, and understanding. There remains brute, empty, thoughtless matter going its way, not depending on our recognition of it to exist. Yet for it to exist *pro nobis* it must be formed by our perception, it must be recognized, it must be describable.

What do we say, when we say, "That is a tree"? Anything we say is a means of according attributes to it—green, large, spreading, beautiful—that enable us to know "tree." What do you have left when all the attributes are removed, when there is nothing that is describable?

Nothing. What we call "the material world," that good, solid stuff of "facts," is a complex of attributes that have been ascribed from our mental world. What are these attributes? Perceptions. Absent these perceptions, we have little in the world to notice. For a thing to be, said Berkeley, it must be the result of a perception, a result of a complex organizational operation of the mind that makes analogies, connections, and categories. To be is to be perceived. If we say, "There she is," we are making a report of our perception, our mental arrangement of attributes that makes *her*, and makes her *there*. For there to be attributes, these attributes must reside in some percipient. For a property to be, it must be perceived. (Barth, by the way, was unimpressed that we seem to have a strong urge to know and to be with and to speak of God. Barth thought it more amazing that God had noticed and had spoken to us. For Barth the big question can never be the conventionally modern, "Does God exist?" but rather, "Do we exist?" We have no existence, as human beings, apart from those who have been perceived and addressed by God.)

The good bishop thus said, "An idea cannot be anything other than another idea." When we say, "That is a tree," that is an idea. If you see a tree, and know it, you are really drawing upon an idea, not upon the object itself. You can have no knowledge of a thing that is not first an idea of a thing. Theory precedes experience. Words make the world. All knowledge is ideational knowledge. Everything that you say about the physical world derives from an ideational world.

Perhaps this sounds radically skeptical of our ability to know anything real about the world. But this is not to say that there is no material world. This is rather to say that all the external entities in our world must first subsist in the perceptions and minds of those who know them in order to know them as entities.

One sees where Berkeley is going with this. If there were no realm of mind and spirit, no transcendent realm, there could "be" nothing else, because for there to be anything else there must be attributes and percipients. All attributes are ideas, the result of some consciousness. The material universe subsists in the mind of the One who made it and in the minds of those who experience the world. Thus Bishop Berkeley attempted to refute the skepticism, materialism, and incipient atheism in the empirical view of knowledge that was expounded by Descartes and given great support by the successes of Newtonian physics, as well as the thought of John Locke. Though Locke, the great empiricist, never thought of himself as a skeptic or an atheist, Bishop Berkeley saw that Locke's *Essay Concerning Human Understanding* had removed God as an agent of human knowledge by stressing that all knowledge is the result of human experience. The Lockean mind knows nothing except that which is attained by the mind through experience, through sense perception. Lockean knowledge is basically the result of physics, that is, the impact of various bodies within the world upon the human consciousness.

Berkeley accepted Locke's contention that the test of all knowledge is in experience, but he stressed that any such knowledge is still *knowledge of ideas*. There is no objective world of matter "out there" that intrudes on the senses "in here." Even "matter" is a notion, an abstraction derived by progressively stripping the perceived world of its perceived qualities, leaving only an idea of matter as the substance of the world, a substance that is not perceived or perceivable, but is rather an idea. Science consists of generalized descriptions of a course of observed events, sequences, and conjoined perceptions.

Berkeley warned that our ideas not only help us perceive the world but also limit our perceptions of the world. "For we are apt to lay too great a stress on analogies, and, to the prejudice of truth, humour that eagerness of the mind, whereby it is carried to extend its knowledge into general theorems" (Paragraph 106, Berkeley, *Of the Principles of Human Knowledge*). The mind is busy working upon the world. The perceiver intrudes powerfully into what is perceived. We are always attempting to universalize and to generalize our observations, to inflate them to apply to all situations, and thus what we call "the world" may not be as factual, as stable and reliable as we think, because the world is also a product of what we think.

Augustine had earlier made a distinction between perception and understanding, a distinction that also appears later in Descartes. I can perceive a square when I see one. I can look at a shape and immediately know that I am looking at a square. Furthermore, I can conceive of a square. That is, even though I am not actually looking at a square, I can sit here and, just through thought, picture in my mind a square. In my experience, perception has preceded conception. That is, I have seen enough squares to be able to conceive of a square in my mind when I want to.

But it is also possible, noted Augustine, to conceive of something that cannot be viewed. That is, I can perceive a square when I see it, but I am not able to perceive a chiliagon. A chiliagon, a thousand-sided shape, has so many sides that when I look at it, it will look like an ordinary circle to me. However, in my mind, I can easily conceive of a chiliagon, a thousand-sided shape. Scientists conceived of the atomic structure long before they had any means of perceiving the structure of the atom.

Though I may be limited in my ability to perceive of God, I can conceive of God. This human ability to conceive is otherwise known in scripture as "idolatry."

David Hume (1711–1776) continued this critique of experience and sensation as sources of knowledge by forcing us to reexamine the fundamental assumptions upon which our convictions rest. Hume unveiled the precarious character of most of our fundamental assumptions and allegedly self-evident convictions. He showed that the Enlightenment picture of the world as an essentially uniform, unified, and orderly realm that is available to us through the senses, said more about the percipient than it did about the world.[19]

Hume showed that there is little purely rational justification for our beliefs, much less adequate empirical evidence. Whereas religion, for Hume, has its origin in fear, science has its origin in action, but even science gives us little more than probable knowledge. Mathematics, while appearing to be wonderfully certain, is mostly built upon agreed-upon definitions. Most of our beliefs have their origin in experience, but these beliefs have only practical validity. Our thought is more constrained than we like to admit: "Nothing, at first view, may seem more unbounded than the thought of a free thinking human being who can not only rebel against all human authority but is not even restrained within the limits of nature and reality." Said Hume, "To form monsters, and join in congress shapes and appearances, cost the imagination no more trouble than to conceive the most natural and familiar objects. And while the body is confined to one planet, along which it creeps with pain and difficulty, the thought can in an instant transport us into the most distant regions of the universe. . . . But though our thoughts seem to possess this unbounded liberty, we shall find, upon a nearer examination, that it is really confined within very narrow limits, and that this created power of the mind amounts to no more than the faculty of compounding, transposing, augmenting, or diminishing the materials supported us by the senses and experience" (13, *An Enquiry Concerning Human Understanding*).

Hume notes that Adam, though he may have had all of his rational faculties about him, could never conceive, just by looking at water, that water would suffocate him. Adam could discover nothing by simply observing the qualities of an object, the causes which produced it, or the effects that will arise from it. Hume said that reason, "unassisted by experience, [cannot] draw any inference concerning real existence and matter of fact" (Paragraph 23, Section IV, Part 1, *Skeptical Doubts Concerning the Operation of the Understanding*). Reason is not some detached, innate quality of the mind. Reason requires an interplay with experience to do its work.

On this basis Hume was dismissive of theological reasoning as a peculiar kind of thinking that utilizes a mode of thought not found in other types of thinking, namely, faith, faith that devalues both reason and experience. "Divinity or Theology, as it proves existence of a Deity, and the immortality of souls, is composed partly of reasonings concerning particulars, partly concerning general facts. It has a foundation in *reason*, so far as it is supported by experience. But its best and most solid foundation is *faith*, and divine revelation." (Paragraph 132, Part III, Section 12, of the *Academical or Skeptical Philosophy*)

This "faith," Hume found to be a cheap evasion of the necessity to let reason and experience do their work in showing us the world as it truly is. "If we take in our hand any volume; of divinity or school metaphysics, for instance; let us ask, *Does it contain any abstract reasoning concerning quantity or number?* No. *Does it contain any experimental reasoning concerning matter of fact existence?* No. Commit it then to the flames: for it can contain nothing but sophistry and illusion."

Empiricist Hume struck another even more decisive blow against the received tradition in casting doubt on the *notion of causation*. For Hume, human thought is a distinctly *human* enterprise. We think what we think because what we think is shaped by human nature as well as our prior habits of thought and expression.

Following Locke, Hume believed that the contents of the mind come through experience, through our perception. Unlike Locke, Hume taught that perception consists of both impressions and ideas. Impressions are sensations, emotions, and our record of external stimulation. In our reflections, the mind examines its received impressions. Ideas are simply weaker forms derived from our impressions.

Hume thought it important to note that all of our knowledge is mediated. Nothing comes at us directly. The mind filters through, arranges, notices, and ignores experience. We have no direct knowledge of the external world. What we call our "mind" or our "self" is the bundle of our received perceptions that have been organized in the mind in certain ways. Hume conceived of the self as analogous to a military parade. All of the soldiers are marching in formation. Occasionally, one soldier drops out and another soldier will take his place in the parade, but essentially this is how thoughts come to us and stay with us, as an ordered procession of thoughts that have been arranged to make the world come to us in a reasonably orderly way.

Real knowledge of the world begins in perception, says Hume. We have no direct knowledge of the world, but only knowledge that is mediated by the sense organs. We can never know the "real world" except by way of these representations. What we call "knowledge" is a name for a set of "ideas" about what is going on in the world, but we really do not have any means of validating these ideas by direct, unmediated cognition of the world.

To demonstrate his idea of mediated knowledge, Hume attacked the received philosophical tradition of causation. Hume wrote during the nascent age of science, and science was then essentially a search for causes. He says that our notion of causation arises out of our experience of association. As human beings we note repetition, similarity, and contiguity, and we develop these into theories of cause and effect. When two or more experiences are together, in the same sequence, we see a pattern. Having observed repetition, we assume that something that happened earlier caused the latter in causal sequence. This we call "causation." But Hume said that this concept of causation is simply the result of our experience. When A and B are associated together, and in our observation A always precedes B, we feel that we are correct in saying that A "caused" B. But Hume challenges this notion, saying that we really have no basis for conceiving A to be the cause of B except that these two phenomena have been "constantly conjoined" in our experience, and that one seems to precede the other.

Hume says that the concept of causation cannot be established by purely detached, rational analysis. Rather, the concept of causation is testimony to the way we human beings like to think of things, to the habitual manner in which the mind treats phenomena that are constantly conjoined. If I see one billiard ball move and strike another, I have not seen the "cause." I may assume that some force made the first ball strike the second ball, but as Hume notes, a goose looking at the same phenomenon would not see this "cause."

In one of his famous assertions, Hume says, "The future is under no logical obligation to mimic the past." That we assume that what has happened in the past is determinant of what will happen in the future, says more about the yearnings, aspirations, even fantasies of human beings than it says about the facts of natural events. We may have subjective grounds for assuming that the future is determined by the past, but we have little rational justification for this assumption.

Human beings, alone in the world, desperately need to believe that the world is an orderly place. The mind can take only so much disorder. Therefore we observe various repetitions in nature and we come up with certain natural "laws." A major role of science is moving from observed probability to predictability, dependability. When phenomena occur that do not seem to fit into our pattern, we experience cognitive dissonance. For instance, as I write this, we have experienced a number of shark attacks on the East Coast. The reporters reiterate that shark attacks of humans are a relatively rare phenomenon. But this summer alone, three people have already been killed in the waters of the eastern coast by sharks. The reporter has just told me that autopsies will be performed on the bodies of the victims. They hope to identify the sharks that perpetrated this act.

"If we can understand more about what caused these attacks and why, we will be able to prevent these attacks in the future," the reporter assures us. Really? What faith we modern people have in our ability to know in order to control!

Hume lived in a world where God was being removed from the picture as a First Cause. When the root cause of the world is no longer perceived as a benevolent—if often incomprehensible—figure, the world becomes frightful. Hume thus attacks our historical and later scientific determinism. Such notions of predictable, dependable cause and effect say more about the world we wish we had, says Hume, than the world we have got. The world is much more surprising, confusing, and new than we like to imagine. Or, to put it less positively than Hume, the world is emptier, more terrifyingly devoid of direction than we dare to think.

Epistemologically, *the modern world was an attempt to create a closed system, where there were no intrusions from the outside.* Everything could be explained by reference to processes within the system. While Hume indicated the limits of this sort of knowing, he also asserted that as far as epistemology goes, this is the only game in town. The world may be eventually fully knowable because everything we need to make sense of the world is before us if we can just get the configurations right in our minds. And yet, we are constantly reminded that the world doesn't really work like that. There are constant, inexplicable phenomena that are beyond the reach of our perceptive abilities and that evade our attempts to categorize and systematize. As Hume noted, despite our efforts to keep the system predictable, in lock-step cause and effect predictability, the world keeps eluding our grasp and reality is more confusing, more anxiety provoking than we would like. (David Hume, "An Inquiry Concerning Human Understanding," in *Essential Works of David Hume*, R. Cohen, ed., NY, 1965)

Immanuel Kant (1724–1804) said that Hume's skepticism shook him out of his "dogmatic slumber" and made him question the extent, validity, and limits of human knowledge. Kant learned that knowledge is determined not merely by our empirical investigations into the nature of the object that we wish to know, but is determined also by the nature of the knower, the knowing subject, and by the nature of knowledge itself. Knowledge, and the means of arriving at that knowledge, is peculiar to the object of that knowledge.

Kant was a sort of defender of the faith, or more properly faith in the validity of science against skepticism, and faith in religion and morals against the doubts engendered by critical inquiry. He divided the known world into two realms—one of "pure reason," that domain of time and space where reason could stand alone, the world that is perceptible through objective, rational inquiry. The other realm was that of "practical reason" or faith, that realm that cannot be touched by the inquiry or criticism of empirical science, the realm of God. Kant thereby saved science from Hume's skepticism. And yet he also saved religion and the realm of faith from the withering gaze of scientific skepticism. True, religion can find no ground in "pure reason," whose range is that of our sense experience. It must seek its grounding elsewhere. God's essential quality, said Kant, was immortality, and immortality cannot be found in the realm of time and space, and therefore cannot be apprehended by reason and experience. Our attempts to know must respect that object of our knowing. If we would know God, then, that way is not through rational inquiry, but through conscience, through faith.

Kant made a great impression on Barth in his early years. He convinced Barth that thinking about God required a very different sort of thought, though Barth eventually disagreed with Kant's removal of God from the area of the rational and Kant's implied reduction of thought about God to the thinking subject.

Hume helped to free Kant from the confines of the objective, Newtonian, mechanistic world. Hume enabled Kant to see that our assumptions form our thought about anything beyond the immediate sensations given in the here and now. We have these momentary impressions of the world, but the moment we try to go beyond these momentary impressions, into claims of cause and effect, purpose and meaning, we are in the realm of assumption engendered by habit. Hume felt that about the best we could claim for our knowledge of the world was probability. We can trust the habitual and the plausibly predictable conjunction of events, but not much more.

To Kant, the mathematician, probability was not enough. He wanted divine necessity, but knew that human experience alone could not provide it. Kant found hope by reconceiving of the nature of knowledge, by thinking about knowing itself, epistemology. In order to defend faith, Kant divided the world into the *phenomenal* and the *noumenal*. Though noumenal realities are not known the same way that we know phenomenal realities, they are still known as realities. Though we cannot know noumenal truth the same way that we know phenomenal truth, noumenal truth is just as truthful, though in a very different way, as phenomenal truth. Said Kant, we all have a sense of moral obligation that is distinct from any experience we might have had. This is the sort of reality that is revealed in the "inner voice of duty" within the conscience. Kant's *categorical imperative*, the moral law within us that is universalized throughout humanity, testifies to a moral order that is beyond the vicissitudes of our experience and perception. That innate sense of duty points to a world of freedom where duty is not hindered by empirical necessity. Kant went further to assert that the existence of the categorical imperative implies a God, a source of immitigable demand. Conscience points to a realm in which duty may be fulfilled, exempt from limitations of time and space, free of contingent considerations.

Kant's solution was influential on theologians, but it had two deleterious consequences: it made religion subservient to ethics, and it tended to seal religious thought within the subjectivity of the individual, thus negating comparison of religious thought with any other kinds of thought. (This is what John Milbank, on the first page of his magisterial *Theology and Social Theory*, called the "false humility" of the Enlightenment: Christianity must think by translating its thoughts and assertions into more rational, more intellectually acceptable ways of thinking.[20] Barth's work fairly well ended this aspect of the Enlightenment project.)

Georg Hegel (1770–1831) thought that the Kantian denial of rational knowledge of God was a tragic dead end for philosophy, and said so in his *Lectures on the Philosophy of Religion* given in 1821. Kant had preserved God from the attacks of the empiricists, but had now removed God out of the reach of sense experience and into a realm where nothing could be rationally said or debated about God. Hegel attacked the Kantian notion that we can know nothing of God, an insight that had become an intellectual dogma after Kant. Without knowledge of God, Hegel could not see how there could be any great human knowledge worth having. Hegel hoped, through these lectures, to restore to religion "the courage of cognition."[21]

Hegel noted that there is no feeling we have that is not at the same time an act of representation. Animals may appear to express sadness or joy, but when these emotions go beyond mere mechanical response, as they do in human beings, they are in the realm of ideas, of words and pictures. When he lectured on religion again in 1824, Hegel openly stated his opposition to the Kantian relegation of reason exclusively to areas where we have sense experience, and the correlative relegation of religion to the realm of feeling. Hegel said that it was odd to think of God as that one idea that exists only as vague idea, without substance, as some ethereal "Supreme Being." For Hegel, God is Trinity.[22] Any attempt to think of "God" without this substantial determination leaves us with a meaningless and vague "hollow abstraction." True, we are not permitted, by the nature of God, to inspect God as we might inspect any other "thing" within our world. "God does not offer himself for observation," said Hegel. Observation is too detached and abstract a way to think about thinking about God.

The only way to think about God, said Hegel, was in relationship with God, and the only way to be in relationship with God is for God to offer himself to us. God can only be known as God is, as a movement of speaking, as loving relationship. We cannot know that subject by gazing at some theoretical representation of it, by making God into a hypothetical possibility, but only by participating in God. "Religion is our relation to God," says Hegel. It is not that we are unable to know God but rather that knowledge of God requires a different sort of knowing. These thoughts of Hegel were quite influential upon the young Barth, as was the form of Hegel's dialectical philosophy.

While he was at it, Hegel criticized the theologian *Friedrich Schleiermacher* (1768–1836) for relegating religion to the "realm of contingent subjectivity; that is the realm of feeling." Schleiermacher, following Kant, sought to protect religion by fencing it off where the rationalists and empiricists could not get to it. In his famous, *On Religion: Speeches to the Cultured Among Its Despisers*, he argued that religion is prior to theology. The test of the validity of a religion is the experience of the divine in a person's life. Thus he would be able to make an appeal to Christianity's "cultured despisers." But by relegating religion to the vague world of "feeling" (that which Schleiermacher called "the innermost sanctuary of life"[23]), Hegel said that Schleiermacher was in danger of "atheism." God has become a mere product of my joy, or my pain, or whatever feeling happens to be working on me at the moment.

Against Schleiermacher's romantic subjectivity, Hegel countered that it is the essence of knowing to know something that is, something that has some independent existence beyond the figments of my imagination. In any rationality, we must show that what we are talking about has a reality beyond my own subjectivity. Rationality also has a communal, social dimension. At some point I must demonstrate that what I think and feel makes contact with what someone else is thinking and feeling. This is a major purpose for conversation. So Hegel says that by making God a product of feeling, Schleiermacher has no way of demonstrating that his "God" is any more than "a God for me." Hegel thus notes the relational, communal nature of our knowledge about God. To know a thing is in some manner to be in conversation with, in relationship with, that which we want to know.

Thus *Nicholas Lash* observes that Hegel's critique of atheism raises the bar on what we mean when we say that "we know":

> Atheism, for Hegel, cuts far deeper than any mere matter of disbelief in a supreme being. It is the condition of those who . . . are so locked into narcissistic self-absorption as to be cut off from relationship with God, deprived of that redemptive knowledge of God which is our human participation in the reality of God's self-movement. Atheism, then, is the result of those who get *stuck* in their finitude, where "finitude" means, not contingency, but egotism.[24]

When Schleiermacher speaks of religion as that "feeling of absolute dependency," that "feeling" must be derived from somewhere other than in the feeling subject. The feeling itself is not, by itself, capable of generating "absolute dependency." Thus, in saying that we have a feeling of absolute dependency, we are saying that we have an idea of God that is derived from God.

So Barth later noted that *Schleiermacher renders revelation into a "general capacity of humanity" rather than a gift of God.* This also led Barth to accuse Schleiermacher of a "strict nominalistic" view of language whereby statements regarding God are "purely subjective ideas and descriptions that do not correspond to anything in [God's] nature."[25] Against this Barth argued not only for the "objectivity" of God but, more important perhaps, for God's personality. There can be encounter only between persons—identifiable, real personalities that are more than feelings.

Lash says that when later generations conflated "feeling" and "experience," even though Schleiermacher certainly intended to be talking about God, it is all too easy to get the impression that "all he was *really* talking about were 'subjective,' psychic phenomena."[26]

Considerations of this sort led to Barth's continuous and withering attack on Schleiermacher throughout the *Church Dogmatics.* "One can not speak of God simply by speaking of man in a loud voice," Barth famously countered.[27] Barth managed both greatly to admire Schleiermacher and to assert continuously that he was dead wrong on the issue of knowledge of and talk about God.[28] The trouble is, thought Barth, Schleiermacher's subjectivity leads to Feuerbach's projection; theology that presumes to work from the inside out too easily leads to a theology trapped on the inside.

Before we leave this survey of the epistemologies that Barth resisted, mention should be made of *William James* (1842–1910), our homegrown American philosopher whom Barth appears never to have read, but who deeply influenced how many of us think about "the varieties of religious experience."[29] James sought to rescue religious faith from the devastation of empirical psychology and mechanistic views of the world, an attempt that earned James, at least here in North America, the affection and devotion of intellectually nervous Christians ever since. To effect this rescue, James established a pragmatic, functional view of the religious faith. James claimed that our religious faith, while having shaky justification in any external, absolute sense, was biologically functional. He criticized what he called both "gnosticism" and "agnosticism," criticizing both the notion that abstract truth is the ultimate end of thought and the notion that faith is a handicap to knowledge.

The mind is a servant of our biological will, in the sense of the mind being an instrument for gaining us intellectual "satisfaction." James said that what we call "truth" is a servant to human needs, particularly the human need to make satisfying sense of the "big, blooming, buzzing confusion" of immediate human experience. When we say something is "true" we mean that it satisfies our need for explanations. We believe in certain things, James reasoned, for "moral reasons." That is, when we say that we know something to be "true," we mean that we know it to be reliable, workable, and helpful in negotiating our way through the world. Ideas must have "cash value."

William James taught that we each have a right, no, a solemn duty, to take our experience with utmost seriousness.

Josiah Royce (1855–1916) immediately charged that *James had reduced religion to purely subjective motives.* James had come close to suggesting that religion was of merely functional significance: religion is good for us because it works in satisfying human need to believe in something that explains the mystery of the world. When Royce criticized James, James replied by saying that "if his absolutist critics" refused to accept his pragmatic, utilitarian, and functional view of the absolute, then "the absolute is true in *no* way then, and least of all, by the verdict of the critics, in the way which I assign!" In other words, if our faith in God cannot be believed to be at least useful, then there is not much to believe about God.

In his essay "Reflex Action and Theism," James attempted to take a biological view of human thinking. "The acts we perform are always the result of outward discharges from the nervous centres, and that these outward discharges are themselves the result of oppression from the external world, carried in or along one or another of our sensory nerves." But then James predicted that theism would not be destroyed by such biological, rather mechanical modern explanations because theism, "by reason of its practical rationality, is certain to survive all lower creeds." The main justification for theism's survival was "practical rationality." To conceive of a mind as a Lockean blank slate, passively awaiting experience to write upon it, was "immoral." We have a moral duty to think, to sculpt and to craft the world, and "theism" has been one of the most creative and eloquent means of that moral action of humanity in the world.

Said James,

> Man's chief difference from the brutes lies in the exuberant success of his subjective propensities—his pre-eminence over them simply and solely in the number and in the fantastic and unnecessary character of his wants, physical, moral, esthetic, and intellectual. Had his whole life not been a quest for the superfluous, he would never have established himself as inexpugnable as he has done in the necessary. And from the consciousness of this he should draw the lesson that his wants are to be trusted; but even when their gratification seem farthest off, the uneasiness they occasioned is still the best guide of his life, and lead him to issues entirely beyond his present powers of reckoning. Prune down his extravagance, sober him, and you undo him. The appetite for immediate consistency at any cost, or what the logicians call the "law of parsimony"—which is nothing but the passion for conceiving the universe in the most labor-saving way—will, if made the exclusive law of the mind, end by blighting the development of the intellective self quite as much as that of the feelings for the will. The scientific con-

ception of the world as an army of molecules gratifies this appetite after its fashion most exquisitely. But if the religion of exclusive scientism should ever succeed in suffocating all other appetites out a nation's mind, and imbuing a whole race with the persuasion that simplicity and consistency demand a *tabula rasa* to be made of every notion.

One reason James had such a powerful influence on us was the power of his prose.

But in the end, James's "theism" does not have much of a God to offer other than the God who is useful to some specified human need. As Nicholas Lash says, "Anyone interested in finding out why Karl Barth was so hostile to what he called 'religion,' has only to read William James!"[30] When Hauerwas prepared his Gifford Lectures in 1999, he wisely credited William James with being the father of American "theologians" like Reinhold Niebuhr, and also wisely made Barth the very antithesis of the thought of William James. If anyone wants to know how theology in North America degenerated into anthropology, one has only to read Hauerwas's Barthian critique of William James.

Surely it was *Feuerbach* who gave birth to James's functional idea of religion. For Feuerbach, a functional view of religion was a way of dismissing religion, or reducing it to a purely subjective phenomenon. For James, establishing the function of religion was a means of rescuing religion from the ravages of modern skepticism—just as for Marx, noting the function of religion as "opium of the people" was meant to wake people from the chief tranquilizer offered by the state. Barth wanted to wake people up from their dogmatic slumber induced by life in a world where, thanks to the work of modern, skeptical, instrumentalist epistemologies, we thought we were at last safe from any information that was not self-constructed, self-derived, secure from being disturbed by any other voices than our own.

The *modern occurred when the world decided to get along without Christianity, and though the world surely did not fully appreciate this at the time, it was also a decision to get along without God, to think without (in Voltaire's words) "the God hypothesis."* This long excursus is, in part, an attempt to understand how philosophy helped produce modernity and helped produce the thought that it is possible to think without our thoughts being gifts of God.

Though modernity has been a huge challenge for the preaching of the gospel, all times between the times are always bad. Modernity is no worse than another time, except that modernity enjoys thinking of itself as the way things are, not a moment in history or an intellectual construct, but rather a "fact," the very consummation of history to which proclamation of the gospel must adopt itself or else sound silly. It has always been a challenge to bring the gospel to speech, because the gods do not give up their ground easily. And one of modernity's peculiar challenges is its cunning refusal to acknowledge its gods.

Preachers think in order to have something to say. We also speak in order to think. We think with our mouths open in a complex interplay of hearing, speech, and thought. The major task in our present situation is to rescue our epistemologies from the limits of the subjective, to free ourselves from the modern enslavement (begun in Descartes, further developed by Kant) to the detached modern self. We are due for a recovery of the objectivity in our thought and a renewed sense of thought as encounter with something other than ourselves.

Our thinking and knowing are analogous to the work of the artist. The artist is never merely about self-expression. (Auden is reported once to have said, "If art is only self-expression, keep it to yourself.") To make a work of art is never to begin *ex nihilo*, not only in the sense that the artist brings to the task all of the insights, ideas, and inclinations of the person of the artist but also in that the artist must confront the stuff of his or her art—a piece of stone, a canvas and some paint, or the limitations and potential of a musical instrument. The violinist speaks of wrestling with the violin. The writer tells of the terror of staring at the blank page. Art requires respect for the medium, constant practice with the limitations and possibilities that are inherent in the medium. The artist must be willing to risk his or her subjectivity in the task of creation, must be willing to be challenged, confronted, and limited by the otherness and the malleable objectivity of the medium. Some of the artist will need to be sacrificed in the task of bringing the medium to visible or audible expression. The artist must be willing to be surprised by what can and cannot be done with the given medium. Art is never the unconstrained exercise of the artist's will upon the medium. Most artists I know have a great respect for, sometimes a great fear of, often a deep love and infatuation for the medium of their art. They speak of the clay telling them what sort of pot ought to be made, they complain of the stone that demands to be cut in a certain way, of the characters in a novel taking on a life of their own and leading the artist in ways that the artist never intended to go, indeed would not have gone without the encounter with and submission to the stuff of the work.

It is precisely in relationship to the specific stuff of the world that the sheer "otherness" of the world becomes most clear to the artist. The world is not a mere projection of my feelings and thoughts. The world stands there in defiant, sometimes loving, otherness. It is not infinitely pliable to my will. It has secrets that it may or may not tell me. At least this is what I, as a biblical preacher, have found to be true of the world that is a biblical text. Sunday upon Sunday, it is the sheer otherness of the text that overwhelms me, challenges me, demands to be spoken in a voice not exclusively my own.

The Defeat of Subjectivity

Artistic-like respect for the objectivity, the otherness of the biblical text and for the otherness of a loquacious God is a virtue to be cultivated for Christian knowing and speaking. There is, to be sure, a great distance between us and God, huge problems with any claim of knowledge about God, yet the Creed reminds us that, in the words of Nicholas Lash,

> It is only because the absolute difference between the world and God has been bridged by *God*, in his address and presence, that we are able to live in his presence and respond to his address. But we are able to do so in the measure that we do not, in our insecurity and nervous Gnosticism, attempt to *overcome* that absolute difference by seeking to substitute *possession* of his word and spirit for that relationship to him which always remains relationship to holy mystery.[31]

The way Barth put this was that, in revelation, there is no having and holding, only receiving, continually dependent receiving. In saying this, Barth does not mean that what God reveals to us is insubstantial and ethereal, but rather that it is always an event, a gift not of our own devising. We have no epistemological means for moving from here to there. With God, knowledge comes only by God's miraculous move from there to here.[32]

Barth liked to use the image of "awakening" to describe what God works in us when we are awakened by the revelatory Word of God:

We should set alongside the concept of illumination that of awakening, not putting it either above or below the other but side by side with it in order to gain a deeper view. Under the influence of Pietism and Methodism this has become an important word in the Christian vocabulary. Yet it is not so compelling a New Testament word as illumination. To be precise there are only two passages which are expressly dominated by it (Rom. 13:11 and Eph. 5:14), and even in these it appears only in the closest connection with illumination, from which we cannot separate it materially if we are really to describe the vocation of man. . . . Awakening is instructive, thirdly, because the reference in both the New Testament passages which mention it is not to Jews or Gentiles or children of the world but quite unmistakably to Christians and therefore to those who are already called but who obviously . . . both need and are granted a new and further calling; just as elsewhere in the New Testament Christians are continually addressed as people who are indeed awakened, roused and awake, but in such a way that they, too, are not prevented from falling asleep again, like even the wise as well as the foolish virgins who slept according to Mt. 25 and thus stand in constant need of, and are constantly granted, a new call to awaken. This is the extent to which the vocation of man is concerned with the establishment of the totality and not merely of a part or beginning of Christian existence. What makes a man a Christian is that the One who has wakened him once is not content with this, but as the faithful One He is (I Thess. 5:24) wakens him again and again, and always with the same power and severity and goodness as the first time. What makes him a Christian is that he has a Lord who to his salvation will not leave him in peace but constantly summons him to wake up again.[33]

And again:

According to the speech and thought-forms of the Bible, concepts such as light, illumination, revelation and knowledge do not have . . . a more narrowly intellectual or noetic significance. . . . The light or revelation of God is not just a declaration and interpretation of His being and action. . . . In making Himself known, God acts on the whole man. Hence the knowledge of God given to man through his illumination is no mere apprehension and understanding of God's being and action, nor as such a kind of intuitive contemplation. It is the claiming not only of his thinking but also of his willing and work, of the whole man, for God. It is his refashioning to be a theatre, witness and instrument of His acts. Its subject and content, which is also its origin, makes it an active knowledge, in which there are affirmation and negation, volition and decision, action and inaction, and in which man leaves certain old courses and pursues new ones. As the work of God becomes clear to him, its reflection lights up his own heart and self and whole existence through the One whom he may know on the basis of His own self-declaration. Illumination and therefore vocation is the total alteration of the one whom it befalls. The light seen by seeing eyes becomes the light of the body, of the person of a man, in the shining of which it becomes wholly clear (Lk. 11:34f.) and is set wholly under the judgment and grace, the promise and command, of the One who calls him. The light thus bears "fruit" (v. 9). There is an "armour" of light which those whom it lightens must immediately put on (Rom. 13:12). Far from being a mere spectator of the light, man becomes and the Christian is a "child of light" (Jn. 12:36; I Thess. 5:5; Lk. 16:8), or "light in the Lord" (v. 8). (*CD*, IV, 3, pg. 510)

Barth claimed that the problems in our knowing God—and they are real problems, problems so real as to be insurmountable by any human contrivance—are surmounted by the revealing God. It was Barth's contribution to epistemology to assert that God initiates and brings to completion the act of knowing by, on the one hand, enabling himself objectively to be known, and on the other, entering into us, creating the faith that enables us to respond appropriately to God's self-objectification. This is the objective and subjective dynamic of revelation, and it is an act of God rather than a human work.[34] That this happens, that God's Word is heard and known, is not a matter of human capability or responsibility, but utterly by God's sovereign freedom. But happen is precisely what it does. Revelation, the Word of God, is an event in which actual humans find themselves miraculously drawn into a circle of knowing in which they are enabled to share God's own knowledge of himself.[35] Trevor Hart says that this knowledge

> can in no way be abstracted from this happening and frozen or codified, any more than it can be provoked or coerced by human effort. . . . We can no more hold on to it or recreate it than we can cause it. We can only live in faith recollecting that it has happened in the past, and trusting God's promise that it will happen in the future. We can even identify the places where it has happened and where we trust it will happen again. But we can not confuse those places with the event itself than we would confuse an empty concert hall with the rapturous symphony which we heard performed there or the site of some long distant romantic encounter with the love which once infused it. To employ the word revelation to refer to any reality other than the dynamic happening itself is, for Barth, to confuse the issue, and to mistake purely human realities for that which is for God alone.[36]

Socrates birthed philosophy as a dialectical endeavor, a give-and-take conversation in which subjects are considered, reconsidered, stated, restated, so that there is growth in understanding in the process, far more growth than would be possible if philosophers went about merely monologically stating unassailable, incorrigible propositions. Barth wrote theology dialectically (*dia*, two + *lectos* speaker) because the dynamic subject matter (the Trinity and its perichorietic movement) demanded a means of engagement that was dynamic and energetic. Theology must find a language that describes the Truth in a way that is complex enough to be truthful to the subject under consideration. When the subject is very God, and very Human, the Word made flesh, then dialectic (God is, God is not) is demanded.[37] When the subject is the triune God in which these three distinct modes of God's being are one—in which the Father speaks to the Son and the Son speaks to the Father and the Son speaks to and is constantly addressed by the Holy Spirit and all three are constantly speaking to humanity—only dialectic catches some of the richness and energy of Trinitarian discourse. Subject speaks to object, object addresses subject, and object changes the subject in the act of dialogue. "For now we see in a mirror, dimly, but then we will see face to face. Now I know only in part; then I will know fully, even as I have been fully known" (1 Cor. 13:12).

I have characterized this book as a conversation with Barth. Barth believed that the entire Christian life was a conversation that is begun at Christmas:

> It is in His birth from above, the mystery and miracle of Christmas, that we are born again. It is in His baptism in the Jordan that we are baptized with the Holy Spirit in the fire. It is in His death on the cross that we are dead as old men, and His resurrection in the Garden of Joseph of Arimathaea that we are risen as new men. Who of us then, in relations to our own conversion or that of others, can seriously know any other terminus for this event in the day of Golgotha, in which He accomplished in our place and for us all the turning and transforming of the human situation, and as He did so, was crowned as the royal man He was our Lord? (CD, IV, 2, pg. 583)

The Trinity is inherently conversational, constantly drawing us up into a conversation in which we participate in the story of God and in which we are changed in the process. Barth is a Trinitarian because he is Christocentric. After meeting Jesus as the Word, we now know that it is of the nature of this God to be a lively, revealing, demanding presence to us. It is not only true that God speaks but that *this* God who, being Trinity, is a speaking Subject, a revealing Subject, and an engaging Subject speaks.

Modernist attempts to ground theological speech in human subjectivity have been put in peril by the increasing tentativeness of the subject in our age. The great question for us, stated so well by Nietzsche, is not so much whether the world, or God, or anything outside of us exists, but whether we exist. This is what Martin Buber called "the questionableness of man."[38] By the twentieth century, Descartes's subjective "I think, therefore I am" was asserted with less confidence. An atheistic world called upon our subjectivity to do far too much work in constructing the consciousness and in naming the world. In the process, the self has become thin and insubstantial, an unworthy source for meaning and knowledge of the world. Detached from the world, withdrawn into the sovereign self, modern thinking did not grow; it shrank.[39] Kant's grand faith in the "solitary individual," standing alone, thinking alone, gazing up into the starry heavens, increasingly came to be seen as a tragedy rather than as an inspiring image of humanity come of age.

Nicholas Lash calls attention to the way that Martin Buber spoke of the "eclipse of God," rather than Nietzsche's "death of God" metaphor as an attempt to describe what had happened to us in the unbridled subjectivity of modernity. "An eclipse of the sun is something that occurs between the sun and our eyes, not in the sun itself," said Buber.[40] The failure to perceive is not in the disappearance of the sun but in the limits of our own perception in modernity. Buber also called this a problem of "the silence of God," but, he said, "since I cannot conceive of any interruption of the divine revelation, a condition that works on us as a silence of God."[41] The miraculous nature of divine communication helps explain the complex interplay between resurrection and preaching in Romans 15:16-19. As Paul says, if there is no resurrection, then preaching is impossible and all is "in vain." On the other hand, the fact that preaching is possible is, for Paul, a kind of validation of the reality of the Resurrection.

Seeing Is Believing[42]

John 20:1-18

> *I recently heard a distinguished historian declare, "Once the modern world convinced itself that nothing is real except what we can see and touch, it's been downhill ever since."*
>
> *Thumbing through the cantaloupes in the vegetable department, I couldn't find any that looked appealing, so I asked, "Do you have any more cantaloupes?" The reply: "Well, what you see is all there is; you can either takes 'em or leaves 'em."*
>
> *I found this a grand summary of modern higher education. You look at the world, some things don't seem quite right, things don't quite fit. But growing up means to be the sort of person who quits whining and says, "Well, this is all there is. What you see is what you get."*
>
> *Most of us learn to take it rather than leave it, asking only for the guts to live with the world that we see, not as we would wish it to be. What we see is what we get. And there is a certain dignity in not consoling ourselves with fairy tales, to soberly aspire to be that well-adjusted person who lives by the facts. What is real is only what you can see.*
>
> *Sometimes some student—being young and still maladjusted—whines about present arrangements, or gets depressed, or seeks some chemical relief from reality. I say, "Kid, live with it. You will love the rest of your life in a minivan with inflatable passenger restraints and adjustable rate mortgage. What you see is what you get."*

And yet this doesn't do justice to the mystery of vision. You don't have to live long before you realize what you see might not necessarily be what there is. The brain filters out most of the visual impressions that stimulate the optic nerve. What we see is a product of a sort of template in the brain. When sensory stimuli are fed through the optic nerve, the brain sorts through its collection of previously experienced images, makes matches, fits what we see into a pattern, and we say, "There it is! That's a tree." And when you've seen one tree, you've seen 'em all; you stop seeing the trees for the tree. Or as Jesus put it: "Seeing, they do not see."

And yet what does the brain do with things that don't fit into previously experienced patterns? What if something truly new, not easily categorized and pigeonholed, comes along?

What if seeing is limited by what we expect to see? What if it is not so much a matter of "you get what you see," but also a matter of "you see what you have already gotten"?

You've seen that optical illusion that, when you first look at it, seems to have scrambled black and white letters on it. You look and it is hard to recognize anything. But focus on it again, you see the word "JESUS."

Plato said that most philosophy was based on the discovery that you can't trust what you see. Perception is conditioned, warped, constricted, and unreliable. And now I'm trying to move you from an Aristotelian notion of knowledge to a Platonic one.

Thus, Mary Magdalene appeared at the tomb of Jesus early Easter. When Mary saw that the huge stone at the door of the tomb had been rolled away, and that the tomb was empty, she immediately "saw" what had happened—someone had stolen the body of Jesus. Was it not enough that they horribly tortured him to death on the cross? Now they've desecrated the body. Even when an angel appears and asks her why she is weeping, Mary still says, "Someone has stolen Jesus' body."

It is not until Jesus appears to Mary and calls her by name that she begins to see. Even then, she at first thinks that the Risen Christ is a gardener. Mary just can't get out of her mind that she is at a cemetery, place of death and loss. She can't refocus her gaze, even when an angel tells her, even when the Risen Christ stands right in front of her.

And Thomas. When Thomas hears that Jesus' body is missing and that Jesus has appeared before other disciples, Thomas says that unless he sees the wounds in the side of Jesus, he won't believe. After all, the one believable thing about Jesus is that he is dead, crucified and buried, with large holes in his hands and a gaping wound in his side. That's reality. That's one reason we flocked to Mel Gibson's The Passion of the Christ. We may not believe that "Jesus Christ is Lord," but everybody believes that death is dominant and is the end of Jesus, as it will be the end of everyone here. You can see death. What you see of death is what you get.

A study done years ago on the grieving process said that one of the most significant moments in grief is when the living view the body of the deceased, something my family never did. Why is it important for grieving people to view the embalmed body of the deceased? Thereby death becomes real. Death is not real as an abstraction, an idea. Seeing is believing, touch is real.

And thus John says that the Risen Christ appears, tells Thomas to touch his wounds, and Thomas sees and exclaims, "My Lord and My God."

It's not fair to call him "Doubting Thomas." It wasn't that Thomas refused to believe. He believed. But like us, he believed in what he could see. And what he could see was death, failure, annihilation, wound, and defeat. Mary saw the same. Until Jesus called her by name, her vision was out of focus. Until the Risen Christ asked Thomas to touch his wounds, Thomas was blinded by the visible facts.

What does it take to see? It is not enough to say, "Well, what you see is what you get." There is this matter of failed vision, inadequate perception. We've all had that frustrating experience of seeing something at some distant point across the landscape. And then we say to the friend beside us, gesturing, "Look, over there!"

What enables us to see? What grabs our gaze, turns our eyes in the right direction, and brings all into focus?

For Mary and for Thomas, it was the Risen Christ. Jesus not only rose from the dead, but appeared to the very ones who had forsaken him. He did not leave them to their own devices or their misperceptions. He came to them. He spoke to one, calling her by name; he encouraged the other to touch his very body. He turned their gaze away from that which was expected and accustomed toward that which was revealed.

Maybe that is why we call Christianity a "revealed religion." You can't "see it" until it is shown you. You are given the gift of the presence of the Risen Christ, and then you see and then you believe.

I have now endured three successive versions of The Matrix. Phenomenally successful film. Many of the students just love it and eagerly await the next Matrix sequel. Most of the film I couldn't figure out. Wrong generation. But I did carry away one insight. I think a lot of you in the student generation have a hunch that the so-called real world is a sham, a facade, a front. What we call real may be real in the sense that Disney World is real. On top, what we can clearly see, is this wonderful, clean, colorful, and bright world, but underneath is the dark, clanking machinery, levers being pulled by Michael Isner, and Kmart that make the fantasy look real, when it is only a capitalist contrivance designed to bamboozle you.

What if seeing, real seeing, is not an intellectual achievement of hard work and a good epistemological method, but a gift? You see, I think the story of Mary at the tomb, and Thomas in doubt, is a story about you. You got Easter the same way they got Easter. You are here, not because you did an analysis of various Near Eastern immortality myths and concluded that the resurrection of Jesus made sense. You are here because the Risen Christ, in some way or another, called your name. "Mary." "George." "Courtney." And hearing your life addressed, you saw.

Others of you are the Thomas type. You are not good with abstractions. You need visible, tangible proof. One of you told me that you drove three hours this morning, arising at daybreak to be here for the service in Duke Chapel. When I said that I—having seen a preview of the sermon—thought it not worth such a drive, you said, "I'm not coming for the sermon. I'm coming for the building, the music, the bells." You explained, "I'm not that great a believer. Never have been. Can't get all those fancy theological ideas. I need something large and tangible if I'm to believe."

I think you had been reading the twentieth chapter of John's Gospel. Seeing really is believing. Most of the time we "see through a mirror dimly," as Paul put it. We're in the dark. Occasionally, by the grace of God, things come into focus and we see. We see, not as an intellectual achievement on our part, but as a gift on God's part. The Risen Christ loves us enough to give us what we need to see and to believe—our name called in the darkness, his body and blood given into our probing fingers. John's Gospel ends with John say-

ing, "I wrote this gospel down in order that you might believe." The Risen Christ gives us what we need.

A few years ago a young man came to me complaining that he was "losing my faith." He had real problems with the virginal conception of Jesus, with the miracles, with resurrection. I talked with him, reasoned with him, argued with him. I suggested a book he might read. I remember it as a frustrating conversation. I hadn't seen him since his graduation from Duke until, this past January, preaching up at Harvard, he greeted me at the door of Memorial Church, just as bursting with belief as he could be. What happened? I told him I recalled that afternoon we discussed his faith.
He had no recollection of ever having had a conversation with me.

I won't bore you with the details, but he said there had been a series of interesting events, a voice in the night, coincidences. In short, he had been addressed, encountered. Now, he was home. He believed on the basis of having his name called.
I think that you are here this morning for exactly the same reason. In one way or another, your name has been called by the Risen Christ. You have heard, you have seen, you have believed.
Everybody says Mel Gibson did a great job of realistically portraying the death of Jesus. Big deal. Even the Durham Morning Herald can do a good job on death. But to see life, to believe life wrenched from death, risen, triumphant—that takes more than a good movie. It takes a blindness-to-light miracle. Fortunately, we've got a God who loves to do that.[43]

We can speak about God because God has broken the silence between us and turned to us. God has become objective to us and thereby rescued us from our subjectivity. Furthermore, because of the nature of God, and the way God has turned to us, quite beyond the reach of our epistemological capacities, *we respond in faith.* Barth says, "God has turned to us in such a way that we can answer only with faith. . . . We may not give this answer, but when we do it is an answer to God, an answer to this confidential turning and address of his. The address is not an expression of faith. Faith, if it is faith, finds its generative basis in it."[44]

Barth said that God is the object that stimulates our thought and talk about God, not anything subjectively arising from within us. He criticized that sort of modern theology "which starts with pious experience or faith," and then proceeds on the belief that "grasping God as truth is possible only on the condition of the presence of certain presuppositions in those who grasp it."[45] Barth says that subjective appeals all rest on Descartes's proof of God, which Barth dismisses as simply the subjectively based syllogism that, "because the idea of God exists in us, therefore God exists in himself."[46] This insight of Barth negates preaching as I most often hear it within my own ecclesiastical family. Much of the preaching that I hear is mainly in the evocative mood, attempting to tap into what is assumed to be the innate religious experience of humanity.

Barth, of course, would have no patience with attempts to "do theology from experience." James H. Cone wrote: "To put it simply, Black Theology knows no authority more binding than the experience of oppression itself. . . . Concretely, this means that Black Theology is not prepared to accept any doctrine of God, Christ, or Scripture which contradicts the black demand for freedom now."[47] Cone's statement raises all sorts of questions, from a

Barthian point of view. Who defines "black experience"? How is the demand for the abstract ideal of "freedom" a specifically Christian, or even a generally theological demand?

Experience, even the experience of oppression, is not much of a point of departure for theology. For one thing, there is no raw "experience" that comes to us without interpretation. Nicholas Lash notes that when we speak of "religious experience," we often do so as if that experience were from out of nowhere, a strange, momentary intrusion without any precedent.[48] Nietzsche showed that, in a deep sense, interpretation precedes experience. When we say that we have experienced something, we are also saying that we have learned something, that something has happened to us that we are trying to understand.

To quote my professor again: "You haven't had an experience just because it happened to you." What happens to us requires interpretation, is interpretation. Why else would the same thing happening to different people result in differing experiences? Most people who met Jesus did not experience him as the Son of God. Those who did must have had a quite different experience of Jesus that arose from somewhere other than their raw, untutored experience. We are learning that what we call "experience" is amazingly "external," shaped, determined, linked to social configurations that are far from being purely subjective.

Christians are those who believe that any account of "human experience" must take account of the possibility of God's graciousness, of God's continuing creation of the world, of God's direction and shaping of discourse through the Word, through relationship, and through the gift of institutions (i.e., church). For all these reasons, Barth was dismissive of any theology that begins in experience, having had such bad experiences with that theology that attempted to think from the experience of nineteenth-century German theological liberalism.

Thus Barth advocated that theology must work "as though nothing had happened."[49] And the "nothing" that happened was Hitler. It took a great deal of theological reflection on Barth's part to know that Hitler was, after all, a "nothing." When one can dismiss so significant a subject as Hitler as a stimulus for theology, one really is opposed to theologizing from experience! Reading through Barth's wartime and immediately postwar sermons, I found no more than a dozen passing, cryptic references to the wartime experience. As a preacher, Barth disciplined himself not to allow himself to be jerked about by "experience," even so significant an experience as the Second World War.

Shortly after the events of September 11, 2001, I edited a collection of sermons by campus ministers that were preached the day after that tragedy.[50] Most of those sermons, including my own, were reflections on that event; most were therapeutic attempts to console people who were in grief. Notable exceptions were the sermons by the Roman Catholic campus ministers at Notre Dame University. Two of their sermons simply announced the prescribed lectionary text for the day and proceeded to explicate the text, "as if nothing happened." I found their freedom exhilarating. The lectionary had enabled them to refuse giving the perpetrators of the 9/11 tragedy yet another tragedy: the forsaking of the church's important biblical business.

George Hunsinger explains that

> the hiddenness of our being in Christ, its imperceptibility and its incomprehensibility, means, when taken together with the truth and actuality of this being, that any attempt

72

to understand our salvation by looking directly to ourselves can only bring results that are frustrating. Considered in itself, our experience of salvation will always be abstract, ambiguous, and unreliable. Experience is therefore a category which Barth typically treated with suspicion, especially since it had been made into the object and source of theological reflection ever since the days of Schleiermacher. Experience, Barth acknowledged, can scarcely be presented as absent from the life of faith, but neither can it be regarded as central to the life of faith. We believe in Christ, he insisted, not in our experience of Christ; we attempt to listen to the gospel, not to our experience of the gospel; we believe in salvation, not in our experience of salvation. Jesus Christ is not an experience but an event, the gospel is not an experience but the news of an event, and the presence of salvation is "not an experience, precisely because and as it is the divine decision 'concerning us'" (*CD*, I, 2, pg. 532). That is to say, none of these realities is to be perceived, postulated, conceived, or defined directly on the basis of whatever may happen to be its subjective or experiential content in the life of faith. Jesus Christ, the gospel, and the presence of salvation are rather to be perceived and defined as events that transcend (while including) our experiences, precisely because their apprehension is gracious and miraculous (actualism), their content is hidden, self-grounded, unique, and mysterious (particularism), and (as has yet to be developed) their experiential accompaniments are, at best, provisional and filled with promise (objectivism).[51]

Barth has so little to say about our experience because it has so little bearing on salvation and on the Christian life. Experience, being relative and ambiguous, "cannot be the object of our faith and witness" (*CD*, I, 2, pg. 209). "Thus, while I can and must say that I know from my own experience the help which I have to attest, this experience of mine must not be put in the center, it must not be the autonomous theme of what I say, if my word is not to lose the character of true witness" (*CD*, I, 2, pg. 442). That center lies elsewhere, in the work of Jesus Christ. "I am not really concerned to speak at all about myself and my sin and my experiences as an independent theme, but only about . . . the name of Jesus Christ as the essence and existence of the loving kindness in which God has taken to himself sinful humanity, in order that we should not be lost but saved by him" (*CD*, I, 2, pg. 443).[52]

Barth conceived of preaching as always in the vocative mood, a form of address, something that was said to us rather than something arising out of us.[53] Barth would have us preachers reclaim the formative quality of our preaching. He would tell us to preach in such a way that we do not attempt to evoke or to elicit some variety of human religious experience, but rather to discipline our talk to talk about that objective reality (God) who is beyond our experience, the One who is the source of what we call our "experience of God," who is the provocation of that experience rather than the experience itself.

Sitting in prison, awaiting his certain execution, punishment for a crime he never mentions, Boethius (executed in 524 CE) writes *The Consolation of Philosophy*, a book dearly beloved by the first Christian philosophers. Though he was a noble, well-educated Roman, Boethius spent most of his time in Greece, and it was there, no doubt, that he met Dame Philosophy.

How to handle misfortune in life? When bad things happen, how do you cope? For the early Greeks, for instance the Thebian tragedies of Sophicles, the best thing to do with tragedy is nobly to accept tragedy as your lot in life. Fate. There is nothing to be done. We are, said Homer, only playthings of the gods. Mere mortals cannot control events. Humanity is at its best, in Greek drama, through honest artistic depiction of its tragic destiny.

In jail, awaiting death, Boethius looks at what has happened to him and is determined not to be defeated by it. As he sits in his prison cell, lamenting his fate, the artistic muses one by one appear and attempt to entertain him, attempt to distract him from his sad situation. This is often the function of art—entertainment, distraction. Then noble Dame Philosophy enters, and she tells all the muses to be gone. Then philosophy engages Boethius in dialogue. *The Consolation of Philosophy* consists of a dialogue between Boethius and Dame Philosophy about the nature of God, providence, fate, and grace. In turning his fate into philosophy, rather than art, Boethius sets a pattern for much of Western thought. Greek philosophy told Boethius that any circumstance can be turned to good advantage. Even sad, terribly tragic events can be transformed through a better attitude that is engendered by clear thinking. Though we do not know whether or not Boethius was Christian or pagan, eventually, the church declared him to be a saint, so impressed was the church with his heroic philosophizing.

Boethius suggests that what the world calls "reality" ought to be critically examined. We ought not to take things as they are presented to us. Critical interpretation is required to know where we are. Are we in prison, or are we free? It is possible, through thought, to change our position relative to the world. The world does not present itself to us as self-evident. The stuff of life demands our active creation and fabrication. We are created, it appears, to ask, why?

In turning his prison cell into a philosopher's study, Boethius comes to the conclusion, through this dialogue, that there really is no such thing as bad luck. It all depends upon how you look at it. What the world calls imprisonment may be transformed into the habitat of a free man. What the world regards as free may be involuntary servitude. The wise person is able to see the grace of God, even within the sad events of life.

At one point Dame Philosophy says to Boethius, "There are lots of people who would be delighted to trade places with you. In turning away from your fate, you are turning away from God."

Dame Philosophy convinces Boethius that happiness is the true end of humanity. We are made to find *eudaemonia*. We are meant, despite life's setbacks, for happiness, but not happiness based on material things. Rather, we are made for philosophical happiness—detached, serene contentment, that consolation that the world's wrong cannot thwart, that home to which one can return during times of tragedy. This is the goal of philosophy.

Although the *Consolation* is an appeal to earnest philosophizing, it is significant that Boethius personifies Philosophy, as if Philosophy is something external to him, Truth that comes to him rather than his coming to Truth. There can be no real help to us, in this prison cell called life in this world, that is not external to us. Furthermore Boethius portrays Philosophy as a person, not a set of abstract ideas, but a person who encounters him in his misery, cajoles and challenges him, argues with and seduces him. That Truth that dares to speak to us, that reaches to us, is that Truth worth knowing. Thus read from another angle, the Consolation presages the death of all earnest, heroic, subjective philosophizing, namely, the advent of Jesus Christ.

God speaks to us as address, summons, and vocation. All our talk about and to God is the response of those who have been addressed. Thus Barth would care little for my excursus into epistemology because Barth does not stress (at least after *Romans*) the epistemic incapacity of humanity but rather the gracious, effusive, generative initiative of God, who generously bridges the gap through constant self-giving.[54]

Barth does not, like the fideists, reject natural knowledge of God on the basis of radical skepticism of reason, nor on the basis of a Bultmannian Gnostic theology of negation—we can only say for sure what God is not, not what God is. Barth rejects all *via negationis*. We do know God because God does speak. Our God is named Jesus. The Incarnation is the rebuke to all docetic heresies. The Word really did become flesh and continues, when scripture is faithfully read, to do so again and again in our midst through revelation.

Although what God graciously revealed to us is so much greater than our possibilities of conception, God does reveal, giving not only the substance but the means for revelation. We know Christ, not by some independent human means, but rather by divine gift. Thus when Paul says in 1 Corinthians 12:3 that "no one can say 'Jesus is Lord' except by the Holy Spirit," he took the first step in the direction of the dogmatic statement that Christian knowing, and Christian speaking, is dependent upon divine revealing. Ephesians 3:18-19 prays "that you may have the power to comprehend, with all the saints, what is the breadth and length and height and depth, and to know the love of Christ that surpasses knowledge, so that you may be filled with all the fullness of God."

Therefore Barth will not submit to some naturalistic worldview that believes that, if Christianity is to be comprehensible, it must be framed within a worldview that is within the range of modern imagination. His epistemology is developed on the basis of the nature of things, on the basis of that object that we are attempting to know, without *a priori* assumptions about what we are going to know. In this sense, Barth could claim to be "scientific" in his theology, "scientific" in the sense of that mode of thought that is radically determined by the object of its inquiry.

Theologically, Barth's stress upon revelation was an attempt to devise an epistemology on the basis of the Lutheran assertion of the priority of grace alone. If we know anything of God, our knowledge has come exclusively by an undeserved, unmerited, unearned gift of God.

Barth quotes Calvin's words, uttered near the beginning of his *Institutes of the Christian Religion*: "There is within the human mind, and indeed by natural instinct, an awareness of divinity. . . . To prevent anyone from taking refuge in the pretense of ignorance, God has implanted in all men a certain understanding of his divine majesty. . . . Since, therefore, men one and all perceive that there is a God and that he is their Maker, they are condemned by their own testimony because they have failed to honor him and to consecrate their lives to his will" (*CD*, I, 3, pg. 1). Barth then challenges Calvin's "conviction . . . that there is some God, is naturally inborn in all, and is fixed deep within, as it were in the very marrow. . . . It is not a doctrine that must be first leaned in school, but one of which each of us is master from his mother's womb and which nature itself permits no one to forget, although many strive with every nerve to this end" (*CD*, I, 3, pg. 3). Begin with the world and the human mind as creations of God, and work toward God from there; such is the basis for all attempts at "natural theology."

Schleiermacher showed his indebtedness to Calvin's line of reasoning when he began his theology with epistemology, assuming that if we can just understand human experience, then it is possible to explain and defend Christianity to non-Christians, for they also have the same experience. We can find some neutral terms, derived from our allegedly common human experience—such as a feeling of "absolute dependence"—and work from there.

Luther would have demurred from such attempts, insisting that any real knowledge of God is an experience of God's grace:

> The Gospel commands us to look, not on our own good deeds or perfection but at God Himself as He promises, and at Christ Himself, the Mediator. And this is the reason why our theology is certain: it snatches us away from ourselves and places us outside ourselves, so that we not depend on our own strength, conscience, experience, person, or works but depend on which outside ourselves [*extra nos*], that is, on the promise and truth of God who cannot deceive.[55]

The predella of the altar of the city church of Wittenberg, where Luther preached, depicts the Reformer in the pulpit. Luther is not facing the congregation, but rather pointing to the crucified Christ, who is exalted between the congregation and the preacher, so that the eyes of all, both the eyes of the preacher and the congregation, will fall on Christ alone and not on the eloquent preacher. This is a wonderful image of the externality of the Word in the best of Protestant preaching. Preaching is pointing toward what God has done outside us, for us. The preacher is not the mediator between Christ and his people, for there is no mediation to be had except that of the grace of Christ. Both preacher and congregation always stand in need of that grace that comes only as a gift from Christ and not from our techniques for thinking about Christ.

Barth can be called a "realist" in that he assumes an objective reality to which our thought must conform if we are to know, a reality whose validity is independent of our ability to recognize that objective reality as true. (This was one of Barth's debts to his early reading of Plato.) Theology starts and remains within the sphere of religious language. It does not begin with our theories of knowledge but rather it builds upon the facts as received in revelation and works from there. Theological assertions therefore cannot be easily translated into nonreligious language. Barth is trying to establish a rigorously realistic conception of religious language. This flies in the face of the empiricism and the skepticism of much modern epistemology.[56]

Barth said that theology simply begins with the assumption that knowledge of God is given in revelation. It cannot question this assumption on the basis of some position outside itself, some epistemology that is more suited for the understanding of other phenomena and objects, but moves strictly within this logical circle (CD, II, 1, pp. 4, 250; I, 2, pg. 535). "The veracity of the revelation of God verifies itself by verily laying claim to the thinking and speaking of man" (CD, II, 1, pg. 211). In regard to the authenticity of scripture, for example, there is no way to justify scriptural authenticity on the basis of some other criterion such as historical verifiability. It is the authoritative canon "just because it is so" and for no other reason that could be given from humanity's side of the epistemological divide (CD, I, 1, pg. 120).[57]

By recognizing theology as a closed linguistic system, Barth accentuates a quality that is found in many other closed linguistic systems that describe entities other than divine. We are learning, in philosophy after Wittgenstein, to respect the integrity of different linguistic systems. Just as one cannot easily move from the language employed by physics to that employed by chemistry, because each of these scientific languages is attempting to be true to its object, so we cannot easily slide from the language of theology to that of anthropology. As Graham White notes, "There are many statements that refer to rationally inaccessible entities, but which are true and meaningful (if indeed, they are true or meaningful) solely by virtue of that reference, independently of any experiences that we might have or means of verification that we might employ."[58] The path is not from any alleged common human experience of God to thoughts about God but rather the path is from statements about revelation to an account of who God has been revealed to be.[59]

Barth mocked the "temptation of all theology" that asks first what God is free to do, and then proceeds to investigate God's freedom.[60] First we define what it is possible for God to be—omnipotent, omniscient, and various other (nonbiblical!) alleged divine attributes—and then we busily construct a God who can meet our qualifications.[61] Yet Barth claims God is always free to surprise and to reveal in ways that do not conform to our criteria. God is not limited by what we are able to think. Knowledge of God is in God's hands, not ours, and God's hands are open to us through God's Word.

> In *Romans*, Barth stressed the sheer otherness, the distance of God, the human inconceivability of God. If he had stopped there, with his thought in 1922, then Barth could well have been criticized for undercutting any possibility of divine-human conversation. (This is what von Hugel criticized in Kierkegaard's "infinite qualitative distinction" between God and humanity. He said that Kierkegaard so "exalted" the "difference of nature between man and himself and God . . . as to cut away all ground for any experience or knowledge sufficient to justify him in even a query as to what God is like or not like."[62])

> There are those who believe that Barth has nothing but an anti-epistemology. In 1922, in *Romans*, Barth gave an exclusively dialectic answer to the question "What can we know of the true God?" hovering somewhere between Yes and No, impressed by the great gap between the Word of God and the words of humanity. But by 1927, when Barth said that he was ready to become a "regular theologian," he was ready to affirm the Word of God as the definitive mediation between God and humanity. As Torrance notes, Barth had an epistemology, but it was not that of the philosophers:

>> It is sometimes argued that Barth excludes natural theology only in the name of Biblical revelation and faith in Christ and not on epistemological grounds. But this is hardly true, for Barth does develop a very powerful epistemological structure in the heart of his theology which through its intrinsic integration with the material content of our knowledge of God in Christ can allow no place for an *independent* natural theology in the body of theology proper or even as a preamble to the faith.[63]

> As Barth says, God can be known through God's works, for God's works are God's.[64] However, it is important to remember that "they are bound to Him, but He is not bound to them." God miraculously gives himself to be known by us. That is the only Barthian epistemology there is. All knowledge of God is gracious, miraculous. So Barth is against apologetics, not only because, in apologetics, believers concede too much in advance, but also because he must defeat our ingrained modern tendency always to begin with ourselves. When it comes to knowing about God, Jesus Christ has graciously made us insiders. We are able actually to hear the words of God and to know God because, as the scriptures teach us, God is love.

> Barth saw no reason to begin theology with a theory of knowledge. Knowing begins, not with theories of knowledge, but with scripture's actual account of a God who speaks, who is revealed to be the preacher, Jesus the Christ.

To all my preacherly frustration about the limits of language and the inability of knowledge, Barth replies that "only revelation in the strict sense overcomes the dilemma which haunts all religious philosophy, namely, that the object escapes or transcends the subject. Revelation means the knowledge of God through God and from God. It means that the object becomes the subject. It is not our own work if we receive God's address, if we know God in faith. It is God's work in us."[65] That work in us is called the Word, the subjective and objective revelatory miracle.[66] When God reveals God's self to us, it is as Word, not as some vague, foggy spiritual experience. God graciously comes to us in a form and with discernible content, as both objective content and as speaking subject. God graciously self-objectifies himself for us by becoming the speaking subject who initiates the conversation and, by the Holy Spirit, enables us to engage in the dialogue. The Holy Spirit miraculously gives us words.[67]

Therefore we do well to be suspicious of any "spirituality" that attempts to have intercourse with God by means other than the Word, the Word made flesh. The Book of Job is filled with long speeches—speeches to, about, and from God. One of the strangest is the first speech by one of Job's friends, Eliphaz. Eliphaz has little sympathy with Job's plight. He tells Job that he must deserve his suffering because of his sin. Eliphaz's authority is based upon his claim to have received special, nonverbal revelation:

> Now a word came stealing to me,
>   my ear received the whisper of it.
> Amid thoughts from visions of the night,
>   when deep sleep falls on mortals,
> dread came upon me, and trembling,
>   which made all my bones shake.
> A spirit glided across my face;
>   the hair of my flesh bristled.
> It stood still,
>   but I could not discern its appearance.
> A form was before my eyes;
>   there was silence.
>   (Job 4:12-16)

Despite the strange reverie, Eliphaz launches into a conventional—and what will become by the end of his preaching boring and redundant—reiteration of commonplace wisdom about suffering:

> Can mortals be righteous before God?
> Can human beings be pure before their Maker? (Job 4:17)

Job rejects such visionary banalities. He wants the Word. He wants conversation, dialogue with God that has more form and substance than Eliphaz's vision.

In an age of insubstantial, often nonverbal "spirituality"—of labyrinths and candles, of meditation gardens and silent, Zen-like contemplation of the void—Barth reminds us preachers that the practice of the Christian faith is verbal rather than spiritual, continuing conversation with the Word made flesh, and therefore a word that cannot be made to mean anything we want. The Christian faith is quite "spiritual," but mostly in the sense that Spirit is Word, Word is flesh.

As divinely initiated and sustained conversation, "Revelation" for Barth is not some datum that is deposited before us for our consideration, examination, and affirmation.

Rather, "Revelation" refers to God's self-disclosure *and* to God's enablement of our hearing and active response.

Thus Barth *overcomes the modern subject-object split by stressing the continuing, dialogical, dynamic nature of knowledge of God* as that which comes in relationship, in conversation with God. There is no receiving and holding this knowledge, rather there is only constant, moment-by-moment, day-by-day response, fresh every morning. This is knowledge that demands not simply assent but rather continuing, self-forgetful obedience. Again, "Only revelation in the strict sense overcomes the dilemma which haunts all religious philosophy, namely, that the object escapes or transcends the subject. Revelation means the knowledge of God through God and from God. It means that the object becomes the subject. It is not our own work if we receive God's address, if we know God in faith. It is God's work in us."[68]

So we are not to labor to construct a Christian theory of knowing in order to have something to say about God. Rather, we are to acknowledge a God who has something to say, whose very being is Word, self-disclosure, and whose exercise of divine freedom is to reveal. That divine self-disclosure is gift, grace. As an event of divine initiative and freedom, it cannot be systematized, categorized, fixed, and codified. It can only be witnessed. This knowledge is not readily available to us on our terms but is an event that happens on God's terms.

This is a threatening word to those who must come up with something to say on a weekly basis. It is a frightening thing to come before the people of God each week—blank sheet of paper before us, blank-faced congregation before us—knowing that we can speak only on the basis of faith in a God who speaks. Yet that threat is balanced by the weekly experience of a loquacious, resourceful, revealing God.

Amid all these thoughts on the possibility and impossibility of knowledge, we preachers may be tempted to despair. It is so difficult to know anything about God; it is equally difficult to say what we know. The thing that Barth honors in preachers is that "preachers dare."[69] He says that they dare "as though the history of philosophy had ended with the most satisfying or at least the most definite result." All of the significant epistemological problems that have been uncovered in the history of philosophy, including the ones that we have so laboriously discussed toward the beginning of this chapter, are the problems that arise when daring preachers "dare to bracket all these things and deal with them from outside by tossing out such words as eternity, assurance, victory, forgiveness, righteousness, Lord, and life, as though they could and should do so."[70] Barth calls the preaching task the supreme "venture," "the beginning of dogmatic wisdom," "an enterprise in which we realize that there are many things against the possibility of their success." Preachers dare.

> "How lonely are those who dare to speak about God, how far removed from the broad way of the many or even the quiet paths of the finest and noblest among us."[71] Barth admits not everybody is born to be a "knight of faith" like Kierkegaard.[72] "And unfortunately the stroke by which one becomes such can be given neither at university nor at ordination."[73]

Barth says that those who attempt to preach from an "exposed position," without prior philosophical foundations, without adequate philosophical justification, props, and without being able to build upon innate human capacity are those whom the church should honor for their daring.[74] There is no certain knowledge of God, all is gift, and that is where preachers have the guts to work. Preaching is "an unheard-of, an absolute venture." Preachers are thus those who know firsthand 2 Corinthians 6:9, "As dying, and see—we are alive." On a weekly basis we must die to ourselves and to all philosophical underpinnings in order to be resurrected by a living God. We are those who are left "up in the air," without foundations, all our efforts must be "lit up by a word which in the first instance cannot really be on our own lips. It *is* possible to speak about God, but the basis of this possibility does not cancel out in the least what has been said about the impossibility of finding any other basis for this venture."[75]

A favorite word of Aristotle's was *logos*, meaning "word," from whence we get our word "logic." *Logos* can mean "reason." When the word appears in the Gospel of John, chapter 1, "In the beginning was the *logos* . . ." it is normally translated as "Word," and Barth loves to stress Christ as a "word," the Word, thus depicting the Christ as pure communicative event. But logos could also mean the reason for a thing, the *telos*, the purpose, the rationale that drives a being toward fulfillment. Aristotle certainly concerned himself with the reasonableness of things, by which he meant the purpose of things. In the beginning was the reason.

We Christians have yet to appreciate the oddness that the *logos*, the reason, the purpose for which we are here, the rational beginning of our thought, is the *Logos*, Jesus, the Christ. He is the reason for, the prior condition of our knowledge and thinking. In the beginning was, not our search for reasons, but rather the *Logos*, the personification of God's search for us, the preexistent source of who we are and what we are to be about. We can think about God joyfully, exuberantly, because God in Jesus Christ has first thought of us.[76] When we Christians say that we want to know, we mean that we passionately desire this distinctive, impersonated, incarnated knowledge.

So significant is this matter of knowledge for Barth that Gustaf Wingren accused Barth of substituting "revelation" for the place of "justification" and "forgiveness of sins" in classical Protestant theology.[77] Wingren astutely noted that Barth's theology had a curious nineteenth-century quality—with its lack of emphasis upon sin, its stress upon human knowing as the problem rather than human redemption. Despite all of Barth's desire to write theology rather than anthropology, Wingren found Barth's obsession with the dynamics of human knowledge about God to be a disturbing, nineteenth-century, Schleiermachian twist to Barth: "It is strange that we must make this statement, but it is necessary: In Barth's theology man is the obvious center. The question about man's knowledge is the axis around which the whole subject matter moves."[78]

True, for Barth, sin is mostly a form of unknowing. In *CD*, III, 3, Barth develops in great detail his thoughts about evil as non-being, what he calls *das Nichtige*. This "nothingness" lacks objective existence and only exists "in our blind eyes," because we erroneously regard it as something when it is really nothing. What we regard is "something" to our veiled eyesight that tends to confuse nothing as something. Barth says this evil, this "nothingness," is what God "despised and passed by" in God's sovereign act of Creation, turning to create something, rather than concerning himself with Nothing. In *CD*, III, 3, in the section "God and Nothingness," Barth discusses evil as, "Under the control of God. . . . God has judged nothingness by His mercy as revealed and effective in Jesus Christ. Then in the final revelation that it is already refuted and abolished, God determines the sphere, the manner, the measure and the subordinate relationship to His Word and work in which it may still operate" (*CD*, III, 3, pg. 289). "Nothingness is that which brought Jesus Christ to the cross, and that which he defeated there. Only from the standpoint of Jesus Christ, his birth, death and resurrection, do we see it in reality and truth, without the temptation to treat it as something inclusive or relative, or to conceive of it dialectally and thus render it innocuous. From this standpoint we see it with fear and trembling as the adversary with whom God and God alone can cope" (*CD*, III, 3, pg. 305). Nothingness must not be taken too seriously because it is defeated. "Nothingness is the past . . . and consigned to the past in Jesus Christ, in which death it has received its desserts, being destroyed with consummation of the positive will of God which is as such the end of his non-willing" (*CD*, III, 3, pg. 363).

Evil is primarily a noetical phenomenon, rather than an ontological phenomenon. There is justification for Wingren's comment that, in Barth's view of sin, "the fundamental sin is false thinking and that on the contrary, faith becomes correct thinking. The verb *denken*, prevails in the description [of sin]."[79]

> Barth's refusal to regard sin and evil with greater seriousness than they deserve is a function of his great confidence in the victory of Christ on the cross and in the Resurrection. God's work has taken place in Christ. There is no evil power in controversy with God, except in our blinded eyes. We feel pessimism, defeat, and hopelessness as signs of our lack of knowledge. In other words, one of the things that revelation does for us is to show evil to be an illusion. "That man lacks knowledge of God . . . is Barth's fundamental, anthropological presupposition," says Wingren.[80] Our greatest challenge is not to overcome our sin; only God can do that, and God has done that in the death and resurrection of Jesus. Nor are we even challenged to appropriate the saving benefits of that victory in our lives; we have no work to do that has not already been done in our behalf by God in Christ, reconciling the world to himself. We are simply to let our eyes be opened to a completed, accomplished reality. We have no greater work than simple acknowledgment of what is. For Barth, salvation is therefore a noetic phenomenon, the grateful acknowledgment of the work that has been done for us by God in Christ rather than any work of our own.

>> We cannot impress upon ourselves too strongly that in the language of the Bible knowledge . . . does not mean the acquisition of neutral information, which can be expressed in statements, principles, and systems. . . . What it really means is the process or history in which man, certainly observing in hearing, using his senses intelligence, intelligence and information, but also his will, action and "heart," and therefore is a whole man, becomes aware of another history in which in the first instance encounters him as an alien history from without . . . and such a compelling way that he cannot be neutral towards it, but finds himself summoned to disclose and give himself to it in return.[81]

> Wingren criticizes Barth for saying so little about the seriousness of sin but then also criticizes Barth for so severely stressing that "God and man are set in opposition to one another" that nothing can be said to humanity about God. This is a rather strange observation, considering that it was Wingren who fulminated against Barth's making the Incarnation more important than reconciliation or redemption. Wingren says that Barth's "intention is to make God holier and more divine by setting him in opposition to man, but, in reality, in this way God becomes very like us in his basic attitude and in his reactions. The Incarnation cannot work a miracle—that of grace and love—in God's being and heart: even in Christ the divine and the human natures stand opposed to each other. . . . For Luther, it is just *majesty* that is humble. *Majesty* lies in the manger and hangs on the cross."[82] It seems to me that Barth, in his stress upon the divine condescension in the Incarnation, is very Lutheran. I think that if Wingren could have been more attentive to volume 4 of *Church Dogmatics*, he would have found a more satisfying Barthian treatment of reconciliation.

There are those who say that, for Barth, salvation is "a merely noetic matter." We can see the problem of the word *merely*.

In a section titled "The Awakening to Conversion," Barth vividly describes this noetic moment of awakening that is his idea of conversion:

> Christians . . . are those who waken up. This . . . biblical picture (v. ii) tells us more clearly than any abstract term that we might substitute what is really at issue. As they awake they look up, and rise, thus making the counter-movement to the downward drag of their sinfully slothful being. They are those who waken up, however, because they are awakened. They do not waken of themselves and get up. They are roused, and they are thus caused to get up and set in this counter-movement. Thus strictly and finally this awakening as such is in every sense the source in whose irresistible flow they are set in the obedience of discipleship. . . . Where someone is awakened and therefore wakes and rises, he has previously been asleep, and has been lying asleep. Christians have indeed been lying asleep like others. What distinguishes them from others is that this is now past; that they have been awakened and are awake. Or is it not the case that they are still asleep, or fall asleep again? Is there not still a Christianity which sleeps with the world and like it? (*CD*, IV, 2, pg. 554)

The difference between a Christian and a non-Christian is a noetic difference, a matter of waking up to the facts of what is going on in the world now that God has reconciled the world to himself. Both the Christian and the non-Christian are saved, reconciled, forgiven in Jesus Christ. Christian preachers have, as our vocation, like John the Baptist, to point to that fact. The difference between the Christian and non-Christian is one of belief: the Christian knows the fact of redemption and therefore lives in accordance with that knowledge, whereas the non-Christian does not yet know this.

Barth quotes Luther, who taught that even old Adam was a Christian, justified by faith, as are all Adam's progeny. All are justified, though not all know of their justification:

> Therefore behold how boldly the Old Testament speaketh of matters. There it standeth that Adam was already a Christian so long before Christ was born, for he had precisely the faith in Christ which we have, for time maketh none difference to faith. Faith is the same from the beginning of the world to the end. Therefore he did receive by his faith that which I have received, Christ he saw not with his eyes any more than we did, but he had Him in the Word, so we also have Him in the Word. The sole difference is that then it should happen, now it has happened. The faith is all the same, so all the fathers just like ourselves were justified by the Word and faith and also died therein." (Luther, *Sermons on Genesis*, 1527, and quoted in *CD*, I, 2, pg. 77)

It is not the Christian's knowledge that redeems, but rather redemption is the fact and the means of the Christian's acknowledgment.[83] While this sounds like a rather modest account of salvation—and is intended by Barth to be modest, giving God the glory—it is also an account of the Christian faith that puts preaching at the center. As those who traffic in the knowledge of God in Christ—as those who keep pondering why it is so difficult for us to know the Truth that makes us free, so hard to get us to open our eyes to what is what, so difficult to hear what is plainly, effusively being said to us in Christ—we preachers have an essential part to play in God's salvation of the world. It is our vocation to dare to tell the truth, to announce the victory, merely to point to the facts.

Did I say "merely"?

CHAPTER FOUR

HOW TO SAY WHAT GOD SAYS?

Rhetoric, Style, and Barth

The tongue is a small member, yet it boasts of great exploits. How great a forest is set ablaze by a small fire! And the tongue is a fire. The tongue is placed among our members as a world of iniquity; it stains the whole body, sets on fire the cycle of nature, and is itself set on fire by hell. For every species of beast and bird, of reptile and sea creature, can be tamed and has been tamed by the human species, but no one can tame the tongue—a restless evil, full of deadly poison. With it we bless the Lord and Father, and with it we curse those who are made in the likeness of God. From the same mouth come blessing and cursing. (James 3:5-10a)

In John Updike's novel *Roger's Version*, the main character, a divinity school professor, explains why he prefers Barth to Tillich. It is a matter of style. It is not simply that Tillich's thought is turgid and tepid, but rather it is "the superb iron of Barth's paragraphs, his magnificent seamless integrity and energy in this realm of prose—the specifically Christian—usually conspicuous for intellectual limpness and dishonesty . . . it caresses and probes every crevice of the unknowable."[1]

Barth's style is notoriously resistant to paraphrase and classification, despite my efforts to do so. What Barth wanted to do was so revolutionary that he was forced, in the words of Stephen Webb, "to write against theology, against, in fact, himself, in order to make evident what was hidden."[2] What Barth felt compelled to say required a distinctive way of speaking. Furthermore, the subject of Barth's discourse—the God who is named Trinity—required a distinctive rhetoric. Just as Mark had to invent a new literary device, a form called gospel, in order to bear the weight of the story that was Jesus the Christ, so Barth had to devise a way of speaking that enabled him to more adequately point to what he had discovered about the event of revelation. Thus Maurice Wiles has called Barth a kind of "theological poet."[3]

Stephen Webb characterizes Barth's style in this way:

Barth's metaphors proliferate his sense of an eternally impending crisis, and yet that crisis is such that he can never fully comprehend it. Instead, he hyperbolically distances humanity from its perception of God and denounces all religious and cultural attempts to bridge the gap from here to there. This prophetic approach claims to know too much, however, and so it too is subject to the crisis. In the end, his own attempt to make sense of the crisis is rendered incoherent; ironically, he cannot mean what he has set out to say. Throughout each phase of this tropical journey, then, from metaphor through hyperbole to irony, Barth's work is nearly unreadable. Barth does not write about God but reenacts the religious situation by displaying a theology under an impossible pressure, a discourse deprived of its subject matter. There is, thus, an unavoidable connection between his style and the content of his theology; one cannot be understood without the other.[4]

Barth developed an explosive, expressionistic style of theological discourse, not out of concern for the reader, but rather out of concern with the subject matter of theology—the God who is before us and among us, the Word made flesh. That move is counter to the way most of us contemporary preachers have been conditioned to think about stylistic matters. We tend to think of style as a matter that is dictated by the desired effect upon the audience. Style is determined by the listener's limits. A major difference between Barth and us is his almost cavalier disregard for the reader of his theology or the listener of his sermons.[5] "Preaching must conform to revelation,"[6] says Barth, not to our judgments about the listeners, which puts Barth at odds with most of present-day homiletics.[7]

Thomas G. Long has said that preaching's "turn to the listener" is the most significant homiletical trend of the twentieth century, and I believe him to be right.[8] Contemporary homiletical thought has been consumed with rhetorical, rather than theological, concerns, which accounts in great part for the impoverishment of contemporary preaching. Rhetoric might be defined as the art of listening to the listeners in order that the speech may be better adapted to the audience. Certainly the audience and its varied ways of hearing were of great concern to Aristotle. It is this preoccupation with the listener and with the listening abilities of the audience that contemporary homiletics has most concerned itself with when it concerned itself with rhetoric. Barth has taught me that listening to God is so much more interesting than listening to the listeners and that Christian preaching rests upon certain theological assumptions and works through certain theological mechanisms, having goals that are strictly theological, or it is a trivial endeavor hardly worth the effort.

Permit me a few examples of Barth's theologically generated, vivid, and energetic rhetoric:

The Christian's love for God, which is identical with his love for Jesus, consists in the fact (if we may be permitted an expression which sounds banal but in the strict sense is full of content) that he is a man who is *interested* in God, i.e., in "God in Christ." God has him, and therefore for good or evil he must have God. God is for him, and so he has no option but to be for God. He is this not merely peripherally but centrally; not merely momentarily but—no matter how often he may, like Peter, forget or deny it, in the continuity of his existence, his life-act. He does not cease to confess that he is a great sinner. But like Jeremiah (1:5) and Paul (Gal. 1:15) he will think of himself as predestinated to love, and therefore, although his love may and will grow cold, there can be no question of its complete extinction. . . . He is God's prisoner, and therefore stands strongly on this rock and is solidly at home in this fortress.[9]

There have to be in the world (according to God's will) men who even in the night, perhaps only at midnight or before, look forward to the morning, to the rising sooner or later of the Sun of righteousness, to the end and goal of all things and therefore to their new beginning in light, which no further end can follow. There have to be men by whose irrepressible and constant unrest at least a few and even perhaps quite a number of their fellows are prevented from falling asleep as though nothing had happened and nothing out of the ordinary could happen in the future. In so doing, they do provisionally, and in great weakness and frailty, as God's representatives, that which He Himself will finally do with unequivocal and irresistible power when His day comes.[10]

Preaching is preaching, not because it adopts a particular way of talking, but rather because it is God talk—talk about God and talk by God. Preaching is preaching because of exclusively theological, rather than rhetorical, concerns. Although Barth said that he wrote theology in service of preaching, nowhere does Barth show any interest in the rhetorical interests that consume so much of contemporary homiletics. While I consider Barth to be a master rhetorician, I doubt that he would take that as a compliment. Usually the best rhetoricians are those who are sly in their use of rhetoric. Yet all of his rhetoric arises, not from any concern for the audience, but rather under pressure from the subject.

What makes preaching different from other public speaking? Augustine, in his discussion of different sorts of rhetorical styles that ought to be matched to different purposes of persuasion (in *De Doctrina Christina*[11]), seems to struggle with the issue of just what sort of style befits the peculiar quality of the gospel. Augustine notes that a rational, careful, and precise presentation of ideas works for much of public speaking. Yet, "if listeners have to be moved rather than instructed, in order to make them act decisively on the knowledge that they have . . . then greater powers of oratory are required. In such cases what one needs is entreaties, rebukes, rousing speeches, solemn admonitions, and all the other things which have the power to excite human emotions."[12]

Shortly thereafter he asserts, as if to qualify himself, "Eloquent speakers give pleasure, wise ones salvation,"[13] though he admits that the medicine is more effective if it can be delivered with sweetness. Yet later Augustine admits that sometimes listeners demand the grand style and eloquent words as just another means of evasion of the gospel's demands, simply for the "sake of delight."[14] (Barth might have said that the thing that makes our speaking specifically Christian preaching is the subject of our speaking—the Trinity—who determines the purposes of our speaking and the means of our speaking.) I think that Augustine betrays a Platonic rather than a Hebraic conception of the use of words. He privileges reading over speaking, believing that in reading it is easier for memory to fix the truth in our minds forever (in my experience it is easier for me to remember a word that is spoken aloud than a word that is silently read).[15] Ambrose had taught Augustine to read silently (many believe that Augustine then became among the first people in the West to foster the art of silent reading, a new thing in this history of our use of words). Augustine's ambivalence toward rhetorical and stylistic issues in preaching typifies much of the history of Christian homiletics. It is an ambivalence that may be seen in my own discussion of rhetoric and in my criticisms of contemporary homiletics' rhetorical infatuations.

Rhetoric has been defined as the art of using the available means of persuasion, or, how messages influence people. Aristotle defined rhetoric as "the faculty of observing, in any given case, the available means of persuasion."[16] Rhetoric is the study of how speakers and listeners develop and communicate knowledge. Aristotle portrayed rhetoric as an analytical art or skill of attempting to discern the resources upon which we can draw to make claims that will influence other people through reason. In calling rhetoric the art of persuasion, Aristotle frankly admits that rhetoric has to do with an exercise of power. Rhetoric is the study of the ways in which speakers attempt, through the power of words, to mold an audience's opinion. Like any exercise of power, rhetoric can be abused in order to manipulate, oppress, and seduce people, or it can heal, empower, and move people. Thus, Aristotle's thought on rhetoric tended to be linked to his *Politics* rather than to his *Poetics*, as an astute admission by the philosopher that speaking is a politically significant power play that ought to be used with care. Most preachers I know do not think of themselves as powerful people.

Yet anyone who has the gift of words has the potential to alter the world, to kill and make alive. Power is most dangerous when it is unacknowledged, undisciplined, and denied. Anyone who stands up and utters, "Thus saith the Lord . . . ," is thrust into a situation where issues of power and language become primary.

Rhetoric began as a formal field of study in fifth-century BCE Greece. During the chaotic, despotic reign of the tyrant from Syracuse, property had been seized and great injustices done. After his overthrow, when democracy was reestablished, people needed a means for arguing their cases before the court in order to retrieve their property. They had to justify their claims through argument. A class of itinerate teachers developed who went from place to place teaching skills of effective argumentation. (It is interesting that the study of rhetoric appears to have been born in an argument about property and who owns what. Perhaps that is the perennial basis for most important arguments, particularly theological ones—Who owns what?) These teachers of talk were called "Sophists." One of the earliest Sophists was *Protagoras* (481 BCE), the father of debate. Protagoras taught that there were always two sides to every argument. The outcome of the question was not self-evident or given, but was relative to the arguments and claims that could justifiably be made. The Sophist *Gorgias* (483–375 BCE) focused on the different styles of language to be used in different kinds of argument. Isocrates (436–338 BCE), however, accused the Sophists of trickery. He taught that the orator must be trained in philosophy and must be a person of good character who will not use words to deceive and to persuade at all costs. Isocrates focused on the different probabilities at work within an argument. He was one of the leading opponents of Plato. Plato and Isocrates came to represent the two differing attitudes toward rhetoric in antiquity. Plato emphasized philosophical truth and certainty over verbal ornamentation; Isocrates emphasized the importance of style and probability as a justification for our beliefs. Plato was a man of contemplation and reflection; Isocrates a man of decision and action.

The *Sophists* believed that there were certain storehouses of the mind, common places where one could go to find the available appeals that could be used. If one could learn these common places, these *topoi*, then one would have the arguments needed to make one's case in a moving speech.

Most famously, Plato criticized the Sophists because they regarded winning as an end in itself, regardless of one's purpose, regardless of the soundness of the argument. They would "make the weaker appear the stronger case, the worse, the stronger case," complained Plato. They were accused of making technique an end in itself, regardless of the substance or the ethics of the matter.

In making this charge, Plato assumed that there is *a priori*, a fixed notion about what is right and what is wrong. He thought that these notions could be known and applied. Plato said that the Sophist infatuation with technique was inherent in the practice of rhetoric itself—style was more important for the Sophists than substance. One of Plato's most famous dialogues, *Phadrus*, seems to establish the requirements for good rhetoric in such a way that they cannot possibly be met. In order to practice good rhetoric, one must be fully aware of the complex nature of the soul. Plato analyzes all of the different kinds of souls in such a way that the speaker is overwhelmed at the diversity of audiences and the impossibility of speaking to the audience in the proper way. The subtext behind *Phadrus* is that, if you employ rhetoric, by its very nature you are going to do so in an unethical, nonphilosophically justified way. Rhetoric tends to be focused on mere appearances, rather than reality, what is fleeting rather than what is eternal, and, as we all know, Plato was concerned with the timeless and the eternal. Plato argued with Isocrates, saying that all rhetoric tends to rely on mere opinion, on the conflicted, particular, fragile nature of truth rather than upon the trustworthy, stable nature of truth. Plato sought to base utterance on true knowledge—philosophy. In his *Gorgias* he accuses rhetoric of being merely shrewdness, cleverness, "flattery," akin more to "cookery" than to true art. (It is odd that Plato would have excluded poets from his Republic, since Plato was a master of parable and metaphor and a great rhetor himself.) Only through dialectic, through philosophy, are we led to secure truth, taught Plato, though the successful rhetoric of his own work gives us reason to be suspicious of Plato's critique of rhetoric.

Plato's famous student *Aristotle* defined a human being as that animal who uses words. Other animals are better fitted for survival; any number of beasts are more fleet of foot. Only women and men defend themselves with words, hurt with words, think with words, build a whole world with nothing but words. Aristotle (ca. 384–322 BCE) attempted to develop a synthesis of the conflicted positions of Plato and the Sophists by observing the way words actually work on us and on the world. He argued that rhetoric was neither moral nor immoral; it was a tool, a technique that could be used for good or evil. Rhetoric was that skill for discovering the available means of persuasion in a given case. This led Aristotle to complex audience analysis, to a consideration of various appeals and their appropriateness or inappropriateness. He classically defined rhetoric as "the faculty of observing in any given case the available means of persuasion."[17] After dividing the means of rhetoric into three parts: pathos, ethos, and logos, Aristotle stressed that the astute speaker tailored the mode of the address to suit the nature of the audience. Thus, Aristotle gives us our first "psychology" in his attempt to analyze and categorize the various sorts of audiences, noting what sort of rhetorical approach would be best for each audience. In contrast, Barth shows no interest in his audience and expends little energy in analysis of the limitations, desires, or condition of the audience. His is rhetoric quite different from that of Aristotle, more like Plato, in that the subject matter determines the shape and form of the message, rather than the audience.

The *Romans* took the theories of rhetoric developed by Aristotle and adapted them to teaching, using them as a means of instruction. The questions that interested the Romans most, in regard to rhetoric, were How do we teach? and How do we learn? How does the mind operate in sorting out various claims? How are people moved to action through words? Romans like *Cicero* (ca. 106–43 BCE) were particularly fond of the systemization of rhetoric. Building upon Aristotle's distinctions, they divided the study of rhetoric into five parts, five "canons": invention, arrangement, style, memory, and delivery. *Invention* went through the storehouses of the mind, identified the available resources for persuasion, and then selected them. *Arrangement* was the organization and pattern of a speech. *Style* focused on the use of language, the selection of particular words and phrases and how they suggest tone and appeal. *Memory* referred to the process of keeping in mind what one was about to say. *Delivery* involved an appropriate way of actually speaking the speech, elocution. There was eventually a study of all sorts of devices to aid in the memory, observing the way that the mind keeps certain ideas and disposes of others. Note the Roman stress on technique, the outward presentation of the speech rather than the philosophical substance of the speech. A good speech consists of an important idea, to be sure, but it must be an idea that is presented, through wise structure and the ornamentation of speech, so that the speech does what it is intended to do.

The Romans saw rhetoric as the goal of education, the development of the citizen orator, the one whose speech was characterized, by *Quintilian* (ca. 40–95 CE), as "the good person speaking well." Aristotle, in listing the various appeals that operate within a speech, considered ethos, the character of the speaker, to be the most important. Thus rhetoric was linked to ethics.

> For the Sophists, rhetoric was an art; for Plato, it was a knack; for Cicero, it was a name for the speech itself; for Quintilian, it was a pedagogical system. For Aristotle, rhetoric was, instead, a "faculty" . . . a capacity, an ability, a way of organizing and making sense of the practical exigencies of the world.[18]

Augustine (354–430), trained in Classical rhetoric, advocated the careful use of rhetoric to advance the Christian message:

> While the proponents of error know the art of winning an audience to good will, attention, and open mind, shall the proponents of truth remain ignorant? While the [Sophist] states facts concisely, clearly, plausibly, shall the preacher state them so that they are tedious to hear, hard to understand, hard to believe? While the one attacks truth and insinuates falsehood by fallacious argument, shall the other have too little skill either to defend the true or refute the false?[19]

In the early Renaissance, an obscure theologian-philosopher named *Peter Ramus* (1515–1572), in attempting to adapt classical rhetoric for a theory of preaching, took the five canons of the Romans and split them into two groups: invention and arrangement on the one hand; style, memory, and delivery on the other. Invention and arrangement were lifted from rhetoric and given over to philosophy, since these related to the process of discovery of what was true. Style, memory, and delivery were relegated to rhetoric. Ramus's division implied that the process of discovery of what was true was different from the process of presenting what was true, though Aristotle had astutely held these two together. In separating the truth of a speech from its presentation, Ramus gave Christian rhetoric a perennial problem: How can rhetoric mean more than mechanics, delivery, gesture, and other factors related to elocution? Theology was given the issue of truth.

Under the influence of *René Descartes* (1596–1650) and his search for certitude, invention and arrangement withered away as rhetorical concerns. The branch of philosophy called logic was linked to rhetoric as the best means toward certitude. Descartes saw invention and arrangement as outmoded methods of achieving knowledge. All ideas must at least aspire to the standards of formal logic, for logic was the most compelling force of the mind, reasoned Descartes. He developed methods of reasoning that claimed to be purely deductive. Philosophy was about the demonstration of self-evident truths, almost a form of mathematics. Once Descartes separated "facts" from "values," there was no need for the ornamentation of rhetorical persuasion, because the facts themselves speak for themselves. Thus did rhetoric, as a legitimate means of intellectual investigation, die during the Enlightenment, when knowledge tended to be dominated by rationalism and empiricism. *John Locke* (1632–1704) called rhetoric "an art of deceit and errour" and wanted to banish figures of speech from serious discourse. And *Immanuel Kant* (1724–1804) rejected rhetoric because it made persuasion a merely subjective, emotional matter.

Philosophers of language in the late twentieth century, however, rejected this logically positivistic approach because it did not give significant consideration to many important intellectual processes, clearly denying the way speech works upon us. The positivistic view regarded all statements of value, good, and beauty as simply a report of our personal preference. Statements that led to certitude were valued over statements that were inherently conflicted and ambiguous. This is all part of the conventional fact-value dichotomy of modernity. Furthermore, *Ludwig Wittgenstein* showed that words not only express or represent but also construct, create, and constitute a "world."[20] Hence, there was, by the second half of the twentieth century, a great revival of interest in rhetoric and a reclaiming of the power of language, not only in speech but also for action.

The literary critic and theorist *Wayne Booth* said that the modern, positivistic approach led to "two modern dogmas" (Booth uses the word *dogma* with intention), which we accept "on faith":

(1) "Scientism." Nonscientific claims are all of equal value, for there is no way to verify or deduce them with certainty. One is as good as another. Only science leads us to true knowledge.

(2) "Irrationalism." Things that cannot be decided with scientific certainty can only be decided with force; the strong will prevail. Therefore discussions that are about value rather than fact (such as all discussions related to art, religion, and philosophy) are inherently conflicted and deadly.[21]

But we must ask if these are the only two choices in persuasive speech. Booth argues for a more nuanced, complex view of the rhetorical process, one that goes beyond the false dogmas of modernity. Booth believes that all authors are rhetorical, even if they write without consciousness of their rhetoric, because all authors try to persuade readers of their point of view about the world: "The author cannot choose whether to use rhetorical heightening. His only choice is the kind of rhetoric he will use."[22] Barth, however, would probably contest Booth's claim of the pervasiveness and unavoidability of rhetoric. In contrast to Booth's model, Barth spoke of the language of the sermon being like a pane of polished glass through which we see through the words to the object at hand, thus advocating the sermon as a sort of anti-rhetorical event. For Barth, the only rhetoric worth practicing is that employed by scripture itself. Also, Jesus, the Word made flesh, is the rhetoric of the Trinity.

Contemporary rhetoric moved from debates about the character and attributes of the speaker, the form and arrangement of the speech, and the logic of the argument toward a rediscovery of the listener. Drawing upon psychological and sociological studies of how listeners process and construct information, of the ways in which listeners intrude powerfully into the making of a speech, rhetoric turned energetically toward the listener and the reader.

Kenneth Burke stressed the constitutive power of speech by which, through words, we attempt to make and remake the world through language. Meaning-making through words is a joint project of both the speaker and the listener. Hence, there has been much talk in contemporary rhetoric about the linguistic construction of all reality. *Feminist interpreters* have spoken about the importance of the political, social locations of the speaker and the listener and the way that meaning is a function of the configurations of power. *Elisabeth Schüssler Fiorenza* was among the growing number of biblical interpreters who applied rhetorical insights to the study of scripture. She writes that

> a rhetorical hermeneutic does not assume that the text is a window to historical reality, nor does it operate with a correspondence theory of truth. It does not understand historical sources as data and evidence but sees them as perspectival discourse constructing their worlds and symbolic universes. . . . Not detached value-neutrality but an

explicit articulation of one's rhetorical strategies, interested perspectives, ethical criteria, theoretical frameworks, religious presuppositions, and sociopolitical locations for critical public discussion are appropriate in such a rhetorical paradigm of biblical scholarship.[23]

Sallie McFague pioneered a "rhetorical theology," arguing that it is of the nature of "religious reality" to be apprehended only figuratively, never abstractly: "The point is that difficult, strange, unfamiliar matters must be approached with the utmost cunning, imagination, and indirection in order to them to be seen at all."[24] McFague says that we must do more than simply admit to the rich poetic and literary basis of first-order religious language—scripture, hymns, confessions, prayers—but that second-order theological reflection must also admit its essentially rhetorical character.

The rhetorical "turn to the listener" has a long history, particularly in North American preaching. *Harry Emerson Fosdick,* the father of liberal preaching in North America, described the preacher's task as an aggressively persuasive, rhetorical task:

> The preacher's business is not merely to discuss repentance, but to persuade people to repent: not merely to debate the meaning and possibility of Christian faith, but to produce Christian faith in the lives of his listeners; not merely to talk about the available power of God to bring victory over trouble and temptation, but to send people out from their worship on Sunday with victory in their possession. A preacher's task is to create in his congregation the thing he is talking about.[25]

Fosdick's admission of his own rhetorical concerns may explain why we preachers are the inheritors of a long history of theological prejudice against rhetoric. Preachers who stressed rhetoric were those who forsook the theological rationale for preaching. Rhetoric was often regarded as ornamentation, style, subservient to dialectical and philosophical modes of thinking, merely on the margin of serious thought. Perhaps there was, among many theologians, the fear that, if rhetorical claims were true, if factors other than logic and reason contributed to our theology, then these other factors were thereby contributing to the destruction of the science of theology. If language did no more than merely point to and represent more stable and substantial ideas, then, in fact, we find that we have undercut our theological search for stable and substantial ideas.

Rhetoric has been usually relegated by theologians to the intellectually suspect field of "practical theology" in general and homiletics in particular. Today rhetoric has emerged as the major concern of homiletics, suggesting that those critics who suspect that practical theology lacks a significant theological base are right.[26]

Barth's Expressionism

Barth wrote theology with style. His style of theological exposition was one of the most distinctive aspects of his theology, and, consequently, changes in his style were indicative of changing emphases in his thought. Barth's theology seems at times more self-consciously "rhetorical" than his preaching. His theology shows that Barth was a master of style, an astute rhetorician (though perhaps unconsciously), and a Christian communicator who exemplifies how the subject matter of our speaking ought to determine the style of our speech.

Hans Urs von Balthasar was among the first to call Barth's early style, the style of *Romans* (and to some degree *The Göttingen Dogmatics*), "theological expressionism."[27] His interpretation of Barth, however, is rather wooden, part of the tireless (and at times tiresome) search for Barth's theological, rather than his stylistic, antecedents. Wilhelm Pauck also used the expressionist analogy to describe *Romans*.[28] Von Balthasar makes the seminal observation that Barth "did not write well because he had a gift for style. He wrote well because he bore witness to a reality that epitomizes style, since it comes from the hand of God."[29] However, he does not develop that insight to any great degree. Stephen Webb takes von Balthasar's comment as a starting point for his own extensive examination of the theological significance of Barth's expressive style.[30]

Webb notes that *Romans* is

> a very figurative work, a vast and feverish swamp across which one can easily lose all sense of direction. In fact, Barth recognizes, even in *Romans*, that rhetorical language is essential to what he has to say. Due to the otherness of God and the sinfulness of humanity, Barth does not think that theologians or preachers can use direct language about God any more. "We think we know what we are about when we dare to use this direct language. . . . Broken men, we dare to use unbroken language. We must not forget that we are speaking in parables and after the manner of men."

In other words, because we are fallen, sinful creatures who use language in sinful, fallen ways, our language must be figurative, metaphorical, standing at some poetic distance from the subject we are attempting to talk about through our broken images. As the poet T. S. Eliot said, poetry is a "raid on the inarticulate." When it comes to theology, this is even more the case. The great gap between our human linguistic abilities and the divine objects of our verbal rendering is a recurring theme in Barth.[31]

> *Nietzsche* rediscovered the essentially metaphorical quality of most of our language, even language that claims to be nonmetaphorical and reasonable. "What is truth? A noble army of metaphors, metonyms, anthropomorphisms—in short, a sum of human relations that were poetically and rhetorically heightened, transferred, and adorned, and after long use seem solid, canonical, and binding to a nation. Truths are illusions about which it has been forgotten that they *are* illusions."[32] It was Nietzsche's frank acknowledgment of language as metaphorical that undermined the Enlightenment's confidence in its transparent, rational speech and helped give birth to a postmodern evaluation of language as figurative act, a way of thinking that is not less than the rational but considerably more. In this way language is always both an excess and an absence.

> A contemporary theoretician of rhetoric, *Paul de Man*, defines rhetoric, not simply as a matter of speech for persuasion but as an inherent figurative capacity within language. "Rhetorical," according to de Man, is any language that does not mean what it seems to say. Rhetoric is thus synonymous with the language of literature.[33] Rhetoric refers to the suppleness of language, that linguistic means of disrupting a one-to-one relationship between words and things in order to make room for imagination and possibility. Rhetoric mines the disruptive, explosive, and contentious nature of language, encouraging a plurality of interpretation. Thus, in rhetoric, language is recognized as disruptive, making reading a more difficult activity than it is sometimes thought to be. Poetry is violence rendered to prose, all in the interest of a more full and truthful apprehension of reality.

Barth, while acknowledging the inability of our speech and thought as a result of the Fall, refuses to despair of our ability to talk about God. Barth sees our ability to talk about God, despite our inability to talk about God, as evidence of God's redemptive condescension to sinful humanity in the Christ. As we speak about God, we must always cultivate honesty about our basic sin-conditioned inability to speak about God. Our broken, metaphorical language about God has the virtue of not pretending to know or to say more about God than God says. Metaphorical speech keeps pointing to the eschatological gap between our time-bound, limited assertions about God and the God who is. As Barth said in *Romans*, "If Christianity be not altogether thoroughgoing eschatology, there remains in it no relationship whatever in Christ."[34] Precisely at those honest moments when we acknowledge our inability to speak about God, God speaks to us, and we hear and thus are enabled to speak about God. The Christian life is always an eschatological interplay between speech and silence, having and not having.

Barth taught that the church never gets beyond its *eschatological expectation*. There must always be, within the church and its ministrations, a sense of now-and-not-yet, a sense of having-and-not-having, of the end of language. There must be, in the church, gratitude for what it has been and is being given in its preaching and ministrations, yet also a sense that nothing we say or do in the church is fixed, final, fully consummated, all that it ought to be and one day will be. Here is the way Barth states, in his later writing, the eschatological quality of the Christian faith:

> Can the Christianity and the Church which really derive from and are grounded in the resurrection of Jesus Christ ever be anything better than the place where, from out of and beyond all the required representations of Jesus Christ, the kingdom, the covenant, reconciliation and its fruit, men can only cry and call out: "Lord, have mercy upon us! Even so, come, Lord Jesus"? Is not perhaps the surest test of genuine Christianity and Church life whether the men united in it exist wholly in this expectation and therefore not at all in a supposed present possession of the glorious presence of their Lord? Will not His truly promised and therefore undeniable presence among them necessarily show itself in the fact that they exist as those who know an honest and basic lack, and thus hope for His conclusive appearing and revelation and their own and the whole world's redemption and consummation, looking and marching towards it in Advent in a movement from Christmas, Good Friday and especially Easter? What other time or season can or will the Church ever have but that of Advent?[35]

Of the many instances of the figures that Barth uses to communicate indirectly about God, one of the most famous is the geometrical image of the tangent and the circle: "In the Resurrection the new world of the Holy Spirit touches the old world of the flesh, but touches it as a tangent touches a circle, that is, without touching it. And, precisely because it does not touch it, it touches it as its frontier—as the new world."[36] No sooner does Barth give us this image, than he takes it away, saying that the divine never actually touches the world, for the divine is qualitatively different from the world.

Elsewhere in *Romans* Barth says that grace is "the effulgence, or, rather, the crater made at the percussion point of an exploding shell, the void by which the point on the line of intersection makes itself known."[37] Barth uses wartime images—the explosion of a shell. He thus notes not only how dramatic is God's grace but also how difficult it is to describe the workings of grace in words. After the assault of grace, there is nothing left to point to but its results. Webb says that the best metaphor for the divine is a metaphor that does not make any "as if" identification at all, but dissolves itself or points to absolutely nothing.[38] So Barth describes the intersection of planes in geometry, the algebra of a minus sign before brackets, a signpost, tangents, frontiers, prison bars, and others. Grace intrudes upon the world but is in no way tied to the world. It cannot be grasped or contained but only pointed toward, indicated, not analyzed.[39]

The heightened language of crisis and conflict permeates *Romans:* "The man under grace is engaged unconditionally in a conflict. This conflict is a war of life and death, a war in which there can be no armistice, no agreement—and no peace."[40] Real religion "spells disruption, discord, and the absence of peace";[41] it is a terrorist's bomb that somebody has had the nerve to deck out with pretty flowers, but it "will sooner or later explode. Religion breaks men into two halves."[42] To read Barth is to be lured into a new world where grace threatens at every turn in the road.

Barth beckoned his readers into the "strange new world of the Bible." Though he said that he wanted to effect a mere replication of biblical speech in his language, Barth was constructing that "strange new world" through his flood of expressionist rhetoric. Postmodernists have noted the *constitutive, creative, world-forming quality of language.*

Augustine's description of himself at the beginning of his *Confessions* is a paradigmatic account of the way *we mold the world, and the world molds us, with nothing but words.*[43] Augustine begins an account of his life, not with birth, but rather with speech. The First Book of the *Confessions*[44] begins with Augustine's early childhood fascination with and frustration over words. "Little by little, I began to be aware where I was and wanted to manifest my wishes to those who could fulfill them as I could not. For my desires were internal; adults were external to me [could be translated: my wishes were inside me, while other people were outside, *intus eras et ego foris*] . . . so I threw my limbs about and uttered sounds, signs resembling my wishes."[45] Without the means of communication, the infant Augustine is totally isolated from the human community.

Reaching into his infantile past, Augustine discovers that words were the mechanism whereby he was enabled to make connections. Words enabled his interior to be made exterior as he gradually learned that by making certain sounds, he was able to reveal his wants and needs to adults around him. Words also enabled the infant Augustine to order the world and make it more bearable, to make it his world. Through words he moved out into the world. He celebrates that he is "now a boy with the power of speech. I made my wants known to my family and they made theirs known to me, and I took a further step into the stormy life of human society." Language is the means to community; it is the mediator of communion.

By the end of his story, furthermore, we learn that these words were also the tether by which Augustine was drawn by the Word. He is converted upon hearing a child sing, "Take up and read," and by turning to scripture.[46] I believe this to be a major purpose of the *Confessions,* that is, to chronicle Augustine's movement from words to the Word. As he matures, we see a man gradually accumulate enough words so that eventually he is able to hear the Word. He moves in his conversation from monologue to dialogue. The *Confessions* begins with "I," "I," and ends with "You," "You." All of our little words gesture toward the Word. "What has anyone achieved in words when he speaks about you? Yet woe to those who are silent about you because, though loquacious with verbosity, they have nothing to say."[47]

Augustine's book is about this movement through words to the Word, a movement Augustine teaches us to name as salvation. Augustine lures the reader in with the expectation that we are going to read an autobiography. But we have not read long before we realize that we are not merely reading an autobiography, an account of events in a person's life. We are witnessing a healing. From the first frustration of the infant who is in the world, knowing not the world and neither being known by the world, from the frustration that accompanies the pain of not possessing the words to fit in the world, to that rest in God that is the culmination of Sabbath rest in the Word, this is the story of a catharsis. We are also witnessing the creation of the Christian sense of the self, a self that does not exist except as one who is addressed. Until words come to us, it is as if we do not exist at all.

Augustine's love of words makes his deep suspicion of, indeed, his baleful hostility to, the art of rhetoric in which he was trained seem rather remarkable. He remarks that he was educated to be a "peddler of words." As we noted, he condemns those whose classical education gave them a string of flowery words that enabled them to say nothing but to say it well. Though a masterful rhetorician, Augustine sets the tone for an historic Christian suspicion of the art of rhetoric. Throughout the Christian tradition, rhetoric has almost exclusively negative connotations—flowery, excessive, deceitful speech, appearance rather than reality in sermons.

Recognition of the constitutive quality of language for human beings, which we see demonstrated in Augustine's account of his childhood, has figured prominently in the "*linguistic turn*" in late twentieth-century philosophy.[48] In fact, the general claim could be made that there has been growing consensus in the fields of philosophy of language, linguistics, and literary theory that language is not only or perhaps not at all reflective of reality but instead constitutes what it sets out purportedly to describe and to imitate. That is, language is not the servant of an already existing "something out there," but rather, as a mediator, it shapes and even creates what loosely can be called knowledge: our intuitions, perceptions, and conceptions of what really is.

Words come before world. Theory plays upon experience just as much as experience constitutes theory. We have beliefs about the world before we can make sense of the world. Belief gives us a perspective, somewhere to stand, a way to move out into the world. Without these prior convictions, we would never have the courage to move out and thus would never have a world.

William James, in an almost "postmodern" turn, asserted that every time that we say, "I know," that claim to knowledge is based on the prior affirmation that "I believe."[49] In a series of lectures published in 1908, James challenges the Kantian notion that somehow we can escape to a world of rock-solid "facts," untainted by belief. As James said, "Our faith is faith in someone else's faith, and in the greatest matters this is mostly the case."[50] James said that life always exceeds logic: "It is the practical reason for which the theoretic reason finds arguments after the conclusion is once there." The universe is never complete, but is always becoming, or coming into existence.

Richard Rorty, working in the Jamesean American pragmatic tradition, argues that philosophy has been captured by visual and, in particular, mirroring metaphors that mislead it to seek a stable and certain—the term he uses is "Cartesian"—foundation for all of knowledge.[51] Against this view, Rorty argues that the mind is not a mirror of nature that needs to be continuously polished and repaired by philosophy. That which we privilege with the name "Truth" is not so much an increasingly accurate representation of reality (a matter of "seeing") as the present results of an endless conversation (a matter of "doing") that seeks to edify and enhance our lives rather than to control and explain nature. Words make the "world." That which we call "reality" is not something standing below, beneath, or beyond the words, but rather it is language all the way down. Rorty's concern is that we understand our language because language is how we understand and constitute ourselves: language is not a mere dressing or cover that can be stripped away to show the naked essence of reality; language is the material with which we construct what we call "reality."

Heidegger called language the "house of being." We can only live in the world that we are able to talk about. Finding words for the world makes the world.[52] The nature of those words, for Heidegger, tends to be poetic, metaphorical, and evocative, for only poetic language is capable of dealing with the complexities of our lives in the world. This is different from philosophy's general practice of using abstract concepts and general principles to probe reality.

As Nicholas Lash puts it, theologians work with other people's conversations, attending to our words about God.[53] When the talk is with the God of Israel and the church, the conversation is infinitely interesting. Barth is among the most fascinating of conversationalists, a theologian who manages both to attack and assault the rhetorical enterprise, while at the same time to be the most skilled of rhetoricians. Perhaps the most skilled of rhetoricians are always those speakers and writers whose rhetorical stratagems are so adept as to not appear to be stratagems at all.

Barth knows that our words are much more than mere windows through which to peer into reality or tools that we use to get at the world. Words are the way that reality looks at us. Words form us; words are the tools whereby God both creatively forms us and vocationally uses us. The transformative, formative, constitutive power of language has been somewhat of an obsession for me, but then, I am a preacher who enjoys thinking that my words, by God's grace, make a difference.

It does not take long, wandering through the *Dogmatics*, to realize that Barth is about the creation of a world through his words. He never speaks as a detached, dispassionate academic, but rather as a preacher seeking to persuade. Barth constitutes a distinctive linguistic world by constant reference to the biblical text, privileging that text over other vocabularies, metaphors, and descriptions; by employing his own sometimes maddening repetitive quality, continually circling a theological construct, then returning again, moving forward, coming back, gradually expanding our understanding of the given concept by viewing it from a number of perspectives, gradually moving forward through repetition; by the sheer volume of his work, insisting that we read all of him before we make a judgment upon him, thereby forcing us to read so much of him that we hardly have time to read anyone else; and by his vigorous declarative, assertive style, which impressed Bonhoeffer as a "take-it-or-leave-it" attitude.

We have been conditioned to think of preaching as an activity that makes contact between speaker and audience. The audience is external to the speaker, and preaching negotiates the great gap between speaker and listener. This way of conceiving of public speaking makes speaking and hearing analogous to the technological process of transmission and reception. David Cunningham criticizes this conception of preaching because in it "both audience and speaker are reified, and the argument itself becomes no more specifiable than a radio wave."[54] Aristotle clearly knew that the audience is active in the shaping and the receiving of a message (what Derrida would refer to as the countersignature). Speaking is also a matter of audience and speaker in dynamic dialogue that defies the reduction of speaking to the mere sending and receiving of information. Speaking is also a matter of formation.

Speakers construct audiences. Aristotle expends much effort in analyzing and categorizing his various audiences. But Aristotle is also, in ways he never acknowledges, constructing an audience, attempting to produce hearers who are worthy of his arguments.[55] When Lincoln delivered his Gettysburg Address, he was not simply offering them information, but he was also reconstructing their rationale for the Civil War, reconceiving the war and changing his hearers in the process.[56]

As we have said, Barth expresses little interest in his audience, little concern to tailor what he has to say to their expectations and interests. Yet early in his *Dogmatics* Barth specifies an audience, namely, the Protestant Church—that group whose language he uses, sometimes using that language against them in his dogmatic appeal:

> We must be consistent here and confess that it is not possible for us suddenly to speak undogmatically about the confessional attitude of dogmatics, instead of standing ourselves within the confessional attitude. Negatively, the confessional point of view undeniably means this at least, that other confessional positions are excluded with a final seriousness, i.e., as heretical.[57]

Barth not only wants to speak to this audience through his words, but he also wants to change them, as this statement implies.

A few pages later, Barth claims that his seemingly "intolerant" and "confessional" specification of an audience need not exclude those who do not share his presuppositions (i.e., Catholics) if they are willing to encounter the true differences that exist between the speaker and the listener, and if they are willing to listen to a speaker who is open and honest about his presuppositions (and presumably, if they are willing to risk the possibility that they just might be changed in the listening).

Speakers ought to acknowledge, at least to themselves, the constitutive, audience-forming qualities of their speaking, ought to have some self-definition of whom their speech is intended to serve. I say this under the assumption that *all speech is connected to some power configuration,* that it serves some social order. Christian speakers who are not clear, at least to themselves, about their "politics"—that is, about who is in charge, where this world is heading, and who sits on the throne—are most likely to serve the dominant social order of the epoch. They engage in an only soft construction of their audience, speaking in ways that do little to challenge the audience's previous external formations. They tend to speak in ways that merely express or underscore the received world of the listeners rather than to speak in ways that potentially transform, reform, and deconstruct that world.

I admit that many of my rhetorical observations relate little to Barth's own interests. Barth had no desire, so far as I can tell, to develop an abstract theory of language and its use, and he never turns from his theological exposition to admit his own rhetorical commitments. He was too sly a communicator for that. His interests were disciplined to the exclusively theological. I surmise that Barth, if asked about language, would assert that all language begins with God, including human language. God's speaking is prior to our speaking. Not all human language is helpful in talking about God; in fact, much human language is evasion of God. As in the story of the tower at Babel, we use language to get ourselves organized against God as part of our idolatrous attempt to make ourselves a stairway to heaven through our speech. Yet Barth also constantly reiterated his conviction that God graciously, generously uses language to self-reveal.[58] That is the main reason we care, according to Barth, for language at all—this is the Trinity's self-appointed, most extensively used means of self-revelation.

Stephen Webb points to the energetic, explosive quality of Barth's style, particularly during his "Expressionist" period of *Romans* as a rhetorical result of his theological assertions. It was Barth's style, as much as his substance, if I may use that questionable modernist dichotomy, that led people to characterize Barth's work as a bomb thrown into the playground of the theologians.[59] Many of Barth's metaphors and analogies from this period are military ones of invasion, explosion, frontal assault, and enemy resistance. He describes true Christians as those who are the victims of a successful surprise attack by God.[60]

Barth describes revelation in much this way: On the field in battle, a fierce enemy with superior forces has roused itself and has taken the initiative, going on the attack; troops in the front line send a courier to warn of the beginning of the attack to the reserves in the rear. The troops on the front line are like prophets, apostles who warn the second line of defense, the church, of the impending attack. The report of the attack, this call to arms, to those in the rear who are awaiting the attack, is called scripture. Even before this report (scripture) is produced, the enemy has begun to attack those on the front line. This initial action, this opening assault, is revelation. *And the enemy is God.* Barth says that anyone who does not understand revelation in this way "does not know what he says when he uses the word revelation."[61] This is a rather amazing metaphor and shows Barth's belief that even as revelation discloses God's will to be with humanity, revelation also indicates the great threat and difference that God is to humanity.

Though in the same article Barth apologizes for using "such a military point of view," he says that this metaphor indicates the crises, struggle, and eventual victory that are inherent in the nature of revelation. God has made war on humanity. God intends to overthrow us. And that warfare is called God's revelation.

Barth scorns, insults, and derides his opponents. Langdon Gilkey complained that, with Barth, "there is no arguing with this man while you are reading him—his thought has entirely too much dominating or overwhelming power. If you wish to dispute with him, close the book, lock it in a closet and move away—preferably quite out of the house. Then and only then can you succeed in constructing a critique."[62]

I vividly recall how I, as a seminarian, deep in a semester-long reading of Tillich with David Kelsey at Yale, read Barth's long discussion of Tillich in *Church Dogmatics* I. After Barth considers Tillich from a number of points of view, poses a number of questions to his contemporary, Barth had the nerve to end his discussion of Tillich by saying, "Finally, he is just not interesting."[63] In a self-deprecating moment Barth said that he was guilty of resembling that wandering gypsy who, having only a few leaky kettles of his own, for compensation occasionally sets someone else's house on fire. The inflammatory quality of his rhetoric was, as we have noted, that which attracted the novelist John Updike's interest in Barth's work, recognizing in him a fellow rhetorician.[64] The great Southern gothic Christian novelist Flannery O'Connor confided to a friend, "I like old Barth. He throws the furniture around."[65]

These observations may help answer the question: Why is Barth so perennially fascinating, particularly in this postmodern age, even to those who vehemently disagree with him and wish to disregard him? Webb contends that Barth's great respect for the lively, sovereign quality of God's speech made Barth search for new speech and made Barth continually suspicious of all human descriptions of God, including his own descriptions. This led him to speech that is strong and assertive, but supple and full of movement and energy. When this God graciously speaks, it is as a "shattering disturbance, an assault which brings everything into question."[66] Grace is not a warm embrace but "a lightning bolt" that both enlightens us about our existence and destroys our present existence at the same time. Webb says that Barth, "faced with the blank page of theology . . . tries to erase his marks just as he is making them." Webb points to Barth's often exasperating "bombastic exclamations" followed by equally exasperating "cunning retractions" that keep the reader off balance, expecting more, having no place finally to settle in and take root. Webb recalls that Hans Frei called Barth a "thinker of extremes," whose extreme position can be not only strong but also mutually contradictory.

Barth's rhetoric, and not just in the early *Romans* but all the way through to the end of the *Church Dogmatics*, reminds me of the overheated rhetoric of the Gospel of Mark in which Jesus is presented as one who always goes "ahead of them" on a relentless journey, making cryptic assertions along the way, and then "immediately" (one of Mark's favorite words) moving on elsewhere to a new place that we would not have gone had we not been following him. Through his distinctive gospel rhetoric, Mark is rendering a crucified God as well as forming a church that is able to walk behind a crucified God.

Steven Webb complains that John Bowden is typical of the many scholars who note Barth's rhetorical power without seeing the theological implications of his rhetoric. Yet Bowden observes: "Several analogies have been used to sum up Barth's style. He has been seen as an architect, building on mediaeval scale and with a mediaeval freedom that is not afraid of inconsistency. He has been seen as a poet or painter, setting down what has escaped less penetrating eyes. And probably most appropriately of all, he has been compared with the great musicians. . . . 'Symphonic' is a good adjective for Barth."[67] But then Bowden denies that Barth's style is integral to his arguments. Bowden says that Barth's "long hours in the study were not spent polishing style."[68] Barth was more concerned with being right than being eloquent, says Bowden. Webb, however, counters that Bowden "is an example of the tendency of writers to praise Barth's style but also to draw back from the use of rhetoric as an explanatory tool in theology."[69]

Sophistry taught that figures of speech are decorative and expendable parts of language that can be replaced by more literal statements when maximum clarity and precision are needed more than emotional appeal, such as when one is speaking philosophy or science. The Sophists thus reduced rhetoric to dispensable, interchangeable ornamentation, mere foliage. *Descartes*, as we have noted, subscribed to this Sophistic view. Descartes made epistemology the main concern of philosophy, privileging the question: how do we attain sure and certain knowledge? Skepticism was philosophy's great challenge, Hume having not yet attempted to develop the notion of probability as a way of mediating between the empirical demonstration and authority.[70] Descartes sought an almost mathematical basis for knowledge by simplifying arguments and making them as clear and distinct as possible. Through systematic doubt, Descartes sought to clear away all derivative and inconsequential "opinions" in order to discover those truths that would commend themselves directly and immediately to the natural light of "reason." From these truths, then, a system of reliable, virtually irrefutable propositions could be ascertained.

The rhetorical implications of the Cartesian project were significant: language became a tool of reason by which we seek accuracy, clarity, transparency, and precision. Descartes saw language as either a tool of our prejudices and unfounded opinions; a poetic, relativistic misrepresentation of reality; or a means of discovering the sure and certain foundation of rational thought. The British empiricist *John Locke* (1632–1704), by separating emotion from the realm of reliable thought and reason, reduced figures of speech to mere poetic exaggeration. For Locke, language was at best a sort of window, sometimes fully transparent, sometimes opaque, through which we are able to see through words to reality, the "thing itself." In his *Essay Concerning Human Understanding*, Locke, the defender of reason against emotion, emotionally condemns rhetoric's figurative speech as the provenance of "the fair sex," saying,

> If we would speak of things as they are, we must allow that all the art of rhetoric, besides order and clearness; all the artificial and figurative application of words eloquent hath invented, are for nothing else but to insinuate wrong ideas, move the passions, and thereby mislead the judgment; and so indeed are perfect heats; and therefore, however laudable or allowable oratory may render them in harangues and popular addresses, they are certainly in all discourses that pretend to inform or instruct, wholly to be avoided; and where truth and knowledge are concerned, cannot but be thought a great fault, either of the language or person that makes use of them. . . . It is evident how much men love to deceive and be deceived, since rhetoric, that powerful instrument of error and deceit, has its established professors, is publicly taught, and has always been had in great reputation: and I doubt not but it will be thought great boldness, if not brutality, in me to have said thus much against it. Eloquence, like the fair sex, has too prevailing beauties in it to suffer itself ever to be spoken against. And it is in vain to find fault with those arts of deceiving, wherein men find pleasure to be deceived.[71]

Locke's strong, sexist dismissal of rhetoric, which reduces discourse to that which only pretends to instruct, vainly calling attention to itself with its superficial artistry, is an interesting piece of rhetoric in itself. More important, Locke shows the modernist tendency to separate the aesthetic from the cognitive, the pleasurable from the reasonable, the artistic from the real, writing the sort of dualism and reductionism for which modern thought is noted. Metaphorical speech is the sort of speech that modernity overcame. Metaphors are expendable, and substitutable for more explicit and direct speech.

Which is to say that Barth, in using metaphoric, figurative speech, used that speech that is despised by modernity.

In his explosive, expressionistic speech in Romans, Barth is the preacher whose limited language will not allow him to do justice to the subject under discussion, yet he must speak. Exaggeration, hyperbole, and metaphor enable Barth to keep up the tension between what he wants to say and his human inability to say it. Here Barth is the preacher, stretched between the necessity of speaking of God and knowing full well that almost anything said about God is a misrepresentation of God. Figurative speech enables Barth to keep up the tension in our talk about God while not retreating into silent, apophatic mysticism about God-talk. "So long as we endeavor to speak about grace," Barth explains, "our speech must labor under a necessary obscurity."[72] To those who complained that Barth's rhetoric in *Romans* was unintelligible and unduly complicated, Barth retorted, "Those who claim to speak simply seem to me to be—simply speaking about something else."[73]

Barthian Irony

Webb gives us a grand exploration of the ironic aspects of Barth's theology. It is ironic that, in speaking about God, we preachers speak for God. Webb finds this homiletical dilemma to be a major concern of Barth's 1922 speech, during the time that he was revising *Romans*, "The Word of God and the Task of the Ministry." In his speech, delivered before a group of clergy, Barth underscores the ironic tension within preaching. Preachers are caught in the ironic, impossible situation of having to speak a word that cannot be spoken. Barth dismisses current academic theology as "the turning over of a sick man in his bed for the sake of change."[74] Because it attempts to speak from the sad emptiness of human life, rather than exclusively from God's revelation, contemporary theology is always lusting after some new way to say what it says, flitting from this to that source for its "revelation." What one generation finds interesting the next will reject as boring. Where can preaching turn for its strong word of proclamation?

Forget attempting to address people and their problems. Barth rejects any notion of preaching being helpful to people and their daily dilemmas. "The people do not need us to help them with the appurtenances of their daily life."[75] The people lust after some affirmation of their value and significance, but what they really need is knowledge of God. Yet this is the sort of knowledge that is incommunicable, even for a preacher. "We cannot speak of God. For to speak of God seriously would mean to speak in the realm of revelation. To speak of God would be to speak God's word, the word which can come only from Him, the word that God becomes man."[76] To simply speak "God" directly to someone is not to speak of God. Echoing Kierkegaard, Barth insists that God cannot be communicated as information that people lack. We can speak mostly in negatives, saying what God is not: God is not our "religion," not our highest human aspirations, not our needs or their fulfillment. But even our negations are not saying enough. We must speak. "We hear the imperative even from history: we ought to speak of God! It is an imperative which would give us perplexity enough even if we were in a position to obey it."[77] How dare preachers to speak of the unspeakable?

This brings Barth to one of his most famous paradoxical statements, and one of his most important assertions about preaching: "As ministers we ought to speak of God. We are human, however, and so we cannot speak of God. We ought therefore to recognize both our obligation and our inability and by that very recognition give God the glory."[78] Preachers are those who recognize the paradox of Christian speaking, who live every Sunday morning with the paradox, and yet go ahead and speak despite the paradox, and "give God the glory."

Barth does not say much more to explicate this aporia because he wants to let it stand and not prematurely deliver the preacher from the tension within the preaching task, the absurdity and the bold foolishness of the gospel of a crucified savior.

Paul notes the peculiar "Word of the cross" in 1 Corinthians 1:18-25. Preaching about the cross, says Paul, sounds weak to the world, but it is the power of God. He contrasts "wisdom"—that special knowledge of the world and the ability to express that knowledge in a powerful, polished way—with words "about the cross." The peculiar subject matter of Christian proclamation—a crucified savior—is *moria* ("foolishness") to the world. But such "foolishness" in preaching will *apolo* ("destroy") the *sophia* ("wisdom") of the world. The cross is the destruction of worldly rhetoric. "Where is the one who is wise?" "Where is the debater of this age?" The *moria* of our *kerygma* is an overturning of the human standards of what is wise and what is foolish. The cross is the world's *skandalon*. The "wisdom of God" is a crucified savior. The "power of God" is a cross. This passage from 1 Corinthians seems to me to be the *locus classicus* of a peculiarly Christian account of rhetoric and a good example of how the peculiar subject matter of preaching demands a peculiar approach to rhetoric.

Preaching must be redeemed by God's grace if it is to be Christian preaching. Preaching must be an act of God or it is not Christian. Only God can speak the Word made flesh that we so desperately need to hear. Later, Barth will say that we can speak of God because God has spoken and God will speak again; therefore our preaching is bound to have a repetitive quality about it. Preaching is always a reenactment of the primal miracle, "And God said . . ." (Gen. 1).[79]

Barth slashes away at orthodox theology's dogmatism, which treats God as a silent object, an inert system that can be adequately described in human language. He also attacks the way that mysticism treats God as pure, unmediated being who can be known only through negation and refusal to know and to speak. Mysticism may attempt to cloak its own dogmatism under the guise of epistemological humility, but it is still another arrogant human technique to get God to stay quiet and still through human means. Barth commends his dialectical theology as the best way to maintain the tensions that are unavoidable and even essential to faithful talk about God. Only dialectic keeps theology as lively as its subject:

> On this narrow ridge of rock one can only walk: if he attempts to stand still, he will fall either on the right or left, but fall he must. There remains only to keep walking—an appalling performance for those who are not free from dizziness—looking from one side to the other, from positive to negative and from negative to positive.[80]

Dialectics is the only means of keeping one's balance as one attempts to walk that tensive way that is the knowledge of God.

Of course, in commending dialectics as the best way to speak of God, Barth runs the risk of inventing just another fatal human attempt to get up to God through our methods and philosophies. Why not simply confess to our sinful human inadequacy and fall silent? But silence is no real option. Silence, Barth says, could be a commendable discipline for some theologians, but it hardly befits the vocation of a preacher! The preacher must embrace the paradox and speak with irony, speaking of God and acknowledging that one does not speak about God. Dialectic, Barth says, is the most true form of theological discourse but also full of failure. In its tensive, inconclusive, broken, and ragged way of speaking, dialectics keeps pointing toward the necessity of God to make our words mean what we believe them to mean. Theologically speaking, theology is impossible. Thus Barth's theology is an attack upon theology. It is notable as an attack upon theology from the inside, keeping close to the assigned task of theology, criticizing theology on its own terms rather than on some external, worldly criterion of judgment. This is the only way for theology to find its voice. Otherwise, there is nothing but silence. Only from within theology can the statement of theology's impossibility be made, and in fact that is the only statement that theology can make.[81] Though he renounced the classification of himself as a "dialectical theologian" by the early 1930s, Barth continued to practice dialectical rhetorical form. He never tired of pointing to the dialectic of God's veiling and God's unveiling, God's silence and God's revelation, God's distance and God's nearness, preaching's impossibility and preaching's necessity. God is, is not, God is wholly other and God is fully present in human form as the Word made flesh. God both is, is not, present and is, is not, absent.

The impossible possibility of theological discourse is behind one of Barth's renowned metaphors: "The religion which we are about to detect in ourselves and in others is that of human possibility, and, as such, it is a most precarious attempt to imitate the flight of a bird."[82] Most theology is static in its use of language, as if it were talking about some inert object, a lifeless portrait that points to where God once was but now is not. Barth wants a theology that is as dynamic and uncontainable as God, like a bird in flight. This is a major reason why my attempts to describe Barth's prose, and to exemplify it through a few excerpts, cannot do justice to Barth's symphony. My book about Barth thus tends to be more readable than Barth, for Barth writes in a way that is frustrating, elusive, and defeating of the reader's attempt to grasp him and understand him, to fix and define him. Hence, his theology beautifully embodies his theological claim about the fragile, tensive, dependent quality of our existence before God. As Webb puts it, in a disturbingly ironic phrase, "Reading Barth parallels the experience of trying to know God. . . . Barth's rhetoric is his theology—to the extent that he has one."[83]

Barth's Realism

Steven Webb sees in Barth's thought a move from his 1920s style of "Expressionism" in *Romans* toward the "Realism" that characterizes the later *Church Dogmatics*.[84] Webb attributes this move in great part to Barth's move from the pulpit to the Göttingen classroom in 1921, in which Barth was no longer "the outsider, a radical pastor in a small village," but had to "assume the responsibilities of carrying on and communicating the tradition of academic theology." In other words, the move from pulpit to lectern necessitated a move in Barth's rhetoric as well. Webb says that in so doing, Barth no longer focused upon "the particular problem of preaching, now he sought the necessary foundation for teaching."

True, nearly all of the sections of the *Church Dogmatics* began as lectures, a format in which Webb says that Barth "had to build a consensus and give a convincing account of his views by developing the proper credentials."[85] In 1927, now at Münster, Barth decided that dogmatics should not focus on preaching but on the more general proclamation of the Word of God in the church. Barth did not even mention preaching when he published his *Die Christliche Dogmatik im Entwurf (Christian Dogmatics in Outline)*.[86]

Later, in Bonn, Barth continued to purge his thought of his earlier existentialism by beginning his final great work, the *Church Dogmatics*, a rigorously christological attempt to rethink the faith, as the title implies, as church dogma. He was now, says Webb, writing as a "realist" in protest against the Romantic tradition, observing with clear-eyed realism the objects at hand and not so concerned to persuade and influence the reader through strong, dazzling rhetoric to explicate the center of Christian thought—Jesus the Christ. Realistic language differs from expressivistic language in that realism sees language as representational and analogous, allowing itself to be determined by the reality under scrutiny.

Von Balthasar was among the first to note a shift in Barth's thought from the early, volcanic expressionism of *Romans* to the more staid realism of the *Dogmatics*. Other commentators have noted that Barth retained expressionistic stylistic tendencies all the way to the end. However, there is no denying that Barth now gave much more stress to the objective, realistic aspects of revelation. Rebelling against the romantic subjectivism that characterized so much of the thought of the age, Barth stressed that theological language really does point to a reality, God, who gives our language meaning it could never have on its own.[87] Our theological statements are much more than subjective projections (Feuerbach, Freud), but are real descriptions given to us, projected upon us, as it were, by the reality we are attempting to communicate—God. We can communicate because God first communicates with us.

Busch tells us that in 1931 Barth's favorite author at that time was Balzac,[88] master of the realistic genre. In 1944, in a rare comment on literature, Barth defends realism in literature as the sole purpose of the literature:

> I expect him [the modern novelist] to show me man as he always is in the man of today, my contemporary—and vice versa, to show me my contemporary in man as he always is. I expect the novel to give evidence on every page that its author not only knows this man properly and sees right through him, from the depths of his heart to his outward manners and mode of speaking, but also treats him honestly, i.e. loves him as he is and as he is not, without regret or contempt. . . . It should tell me what its author finds special in this man—that and no more. In other words, it should have no plans for educating me, but should leave me to reflect (or not) on the basis of the portrait with which I am presented. . . . Its form should correspond to the portrait of the man whom it presents; its form should be necessary, strict and impressive to the extent that I do not forget the man I have been shown in his temporal and timeless aspects. I should be able to live with him, and indeed perhaps have to live with him again and again.[89]

Barth expects realism from the novelist, in which the style is subordinated to the subject, simply, directly describing the subject and then allowing the reader to see the reality of the matter under consideration.

Donald Phillips describes Barth's style as one of "complete fidelity to the object of inquiry as determining the nature of scientific activity, rationality and discourse."[90] Thomas Torrance also stresses the scientific and objective nature of Barth's dogmatics.[91] Barth says, "The goal of language must be determined by the unique object in question."[92]

Barth regards theology as a "science." By this Barth means that branch of inquiry that is characterized by strict fidelity to the object of inquiry.[93] At the beginning of *Evangelical Theology* he says:

> Theology is one among those human undertakings traditionally described as "sciences." Not only the natural sciences are "sciences." Humanistic sciences also seek to apprehend a specific object and its environment in the manner directed by the phenomenon itself; they seek to understand it on its own terms and to speak of it along with all the implications of its existence.[94]

The special object of theology determines the methodology of its investigation.

He rejects an "arbitrarily chosen basic view" for theology. While it is impossible to think about anything without presuppositions, Barth insists that such conceptions "must not usurp the position of the object." Instead, "the choice of dogmatic method can be made only with the intention of placing human thinking and speaking on the path of total surrender to the controlling power of its object."[95] Barth thus constructs his theology as if Christ were the center of a wheel, with the spokes of the wheel radiating from this "object" of investigation. Theology keeps attempting to discipline itself to allow its object to speak for himself.[96] Barth says that "the goal of thought and language must be determined entirely by the unique object in question."[97]

Gary Dorrien says that Barth's theological rhetoric was powerful and conflicted "because of his uncompromising insistence on doing theology as exegesis of the Spirit-illuminated Word without any resort to philosophical preunderstandings or apologetic stopgaps or demythologized worldviews." Barth "demonstrated the possibility of doing theology as a Word-following dialectic of divine hiddenness and presence that trusted in the sufficiency of the revealed object of faith."[98] The nature of the external reality with which theology works (God) dictates the sort of language used. And our language in no way fixes that reality into one sovereign form because God is completely free to reveal in freedom. Our use of language must be supple and adaptive, willing to change as the subject changes.

George Hunsinger warns those of us who would label Barth as an expressionist that Barth's "expressionism" was of a peculiar kind. It was an expressionism that was guided by his theological commitments. Unlike many so-called expressivists, Barth always kept his language tied to a particular external referent (God as rendered in scripture). German artistic expressionism sought to disrupt, to break free of the cultural restraints of German bourgeois society of the post–World War I years. Much of the fictional and dramatic expressivism of the era saw language as symbolic, as representing some relatively inaccessible emotive or noncognitive experience. Theological expressivism, such as that articulated by Tillich, stressed that symbols are not to be taken literally, for in themselves they are essentially incapable of conveying any cognitive information about God or of supplying any definite predicates of God. They are far more symbolic of human emotive experience than of some divine source. Hunsinger says that, while this sort of expressivism has a better appreciation of God's linguistic transcendence than does literalism, literalism has a better appreciation of God's readiness to be known. On the other hand, literalism underestimates the miraculous, dynamic, and gifted quality of God's self-revelation.

Barth says that we can actually speak in a reliable way about God but only because of the miracle of God's self-revelation. Nothing, not even expressivistic language, overcomes our linguistic incapacity to speak about God. Only God can do that. Whereas literalism tends to be equivocal, Hunsinger reminds us that the Barth of the *Dogmatics* stressed that our language about God can be analogical. What we say about God may be more or less true or untrue, but what makes it reliable is its dependency upon the miracle of grace, upon the resourcefulness of that which we are attempting to analogue.[99]

Augustine stressed that preachers must, through prayer, be told something from God before we can speak:

> The aim of our orator, then, when speaking things that are just and holy and good . . . [is to pursue them] to the best of his understanding, with pleasure, and with obedience. He should be in no doubt that any ability he has and however much he has oratory; and so, by praying for himself and for those he is about to address, he must become a man of prayer before becoming a man of words. . . . Before he opens his thrusting lips he should lift his thirsting soul to God so that he may utter what he has drunk in and pour out what has filled him.[100]

Hunsinger says that "Barth's realism differed from literalism and expressivism with respect not only to the 'mode of reference,' but also to the 'mode of address.' Theological language, as Barth understood it, addressed its subject matter to the whole person. By contrast, literalism and expressivism each tended, whether implicitly or explicitly, to single out some special aspect of human nature as having privileged access to divine revelation (as variously conceived). Literalism, for which the linguistic form of revelation was essentially propositional, tended to grant privileged status to modes of apprehension and address that were cognitive. Expressivism, on the other hand, for which the linguistic form was essentially symbolic, tended to grant privileged status to modes of apprehension and address that were emotive. Perhaps without great exaggeration it may be said that literalism saw revelation as addressed to the head without the heart, whereas expressivism saw it addressed to the heart without the head. From a Barthian standpoint, both failed to see that revelation was primarily a form of personal address from God to the whole person as meditated through the witness (in word and deed) of the church. Both underestimated the primacy of God as the acting and addressing subject. For both literalism and expressivism, revelation was overlooked as an essentially 'kerygmatic' event . . . an event of personal encounter that was as wholly self-involving for the initiator (God) as for the recipient (the human being)."[101]

The Hard Part About Prayer[102]

Luke 11:1-13

That you have come to be with God this day—mid-summer, mid-vacation—even when many are cutting church, suggests to me that you want to be here, says to me that you are expecting a pleasant experience here with God this day.

Lord, come to us. God, speak to us. Jesus, show us thy glory. Thus we pray, and thus we are here to be with God.

"Lord, teach us to pray, teach us to be with God, just like John taught his disciples."

This is about the only request for teaching that the disciples made to Jesus. They did not say, "Lord, teach us to interpret scripture correctly," or "Lord, teach us to be peacemakers," they said, "Lord, teach us to pray, like John taught his disciples."

And in response Jesus taught them a word-for-word, concise, precise prayer. He did not say to them, "First get alone with your thoughts and dredge up some spiritual feeling within yourself." He said, "When you pray, pray just like this." Prayer in the manner of Jesus does not come naturally, is not something that suits our inclinations. This sort of prayer has to be taught to you, word for word.

He loved them enough to teach them a prayer so that they might, in Spirit and in truth, pray in Jesus' name. "Write this down, commit this to memory, learn it by heart.

"When you come before God, say, 'Our Father, thy name be hallowed, thy kingdom come, thy will be done on earth just like it is in heaven.'" Jesus then goes on and tells some parables about prayer. But to my mind, this summer Sunday, nothing that Jesus later says about prayer is as challenging, as tough, as these six opening words of prayer. Thy name, thy kingdom, thy will. There's the rub with prayer. If prayer were in our name, about our kingdoms, and in the interest of our will, prayer would be easy. But prayer in his name, in the service of his kingdom and his will—that's hard.

Perhaps that is why Jesus had them commit this prayer to memory, why we say it through rote memorization every Sunday. I was at an Episcopal church in Texas. The group was talking about what they loved about their church. One person said, "I've only been an Episcopalian for a few years. I grew up a Methodist."

I said, in love, "Lady, don't brag about leaving the Methodist church. You're nobody special! Millions have left it before you."

She continued, "But the one thing I have difficulty with in the Episcopal Church is that we pray these fixed, printed prayers out of the Book of Common Prayer. I think prayer ought to be more spontaneous, more from the heart."

And I replied, in love, "Really now, do you think that you would pray for your enemies, for rain, or even for George W. Bush if we left you to your own devices? No, you have to read it out of the book in order to pray this boldly."

Pat Henry gave me a great business book. I don't read business books, save the ones Pat makes me read. Fierce Conversations is the name of the book. It's a book on how to have a significant, substantive conversation with other human beings, because most of business, and just about all of leadership, is a matter of conversation. Here are lessons on how to have active, engaging, fierce conversation.

The first request for a "fierce conversation"? Courage. Guts. The courageous willingness to let the other speak, the openness to enter the deep, unfathomable mystery of another, the risk of having another make a claim on your life.

People have criticized me: You don't make eye contact, you talk too much and listen too little, you fail to focus on what I'm saying.

And I think, "Well, hello? I've had conversations with people before—just talking, just exchanging information, just hanging out—and I came away different, changed." We don't risk true conversation, real engagement, because we fear that we might be changed in the interaction.

Years ago, like you seated in the pew, fellow church member at the end of the pew smiles. "How are you?" I ask. It's a little ritual, a habit: "How are you?" It's what we say when we see somebody, a social convention. And she says, "Not good, actually. Tom left us last week, and I don't know what the girls and I are going to do."

And I said, "Look, it's just a little social convention. When I asked, 'How are you?' I didn't actually expect you to take me that seriously and get that intimate with me in church! I hardly know you, and though Jesus commands me to call you 'sister,' I'm frightened by the responsibilities that might entail."

Alas, most of my conversations are facile rather than fierce. I say, "I didn't say anything to him because I didn't know what to say." To tell the truth, "I didn't risk the conversation because I didn't know what I might hear."

Mother Teresa was asked by Dan Rather, "Mother Teresa, what do you say when you pray?" She responded, "I don't say anything. I listen."

Jesus said, "When you pray, when you go head-to-head with God, let the very first thing you say be, 'Thy name is holy, thy kingdom come, thy will be done.'" In other words, prayer is the gutsy willingness to let God be God in your life.

Some misconceptions: Prayer is not so much what we say but a determined willingness to let God have God's say. Prayer is not so much an articulation of what I want but rather a risk of being exposed to what God wants. Prayer is the possibility that I might be changed in the conversation. Note that in the Lord's Prayer, Jesus does not begin with us and our need but rather with God and God's nature, with exposure to the demands of a living God—thy name be hallowed, thy will be done, thy kingdom come, on earth as in heaven.

I remember the advertising slogan from years ago, "Prayer changes things," followed by the slogan, "And sometimes what prayer changes is us."

One of the last conversations that Jesus had was in the Garden of Gethsemane—a no-holds-barred, white-knuckled, blood-sweat-and-tears argument—a conversation that ended with Jesus', "Nevertheless, not my will but thine be done."

What faith, what courage to say that, to pray that and to mean it!

I pray, "Lord, take away this cup from me. Deliver me from this distress. Save me from this dilemma. Solve this problem. Salve this pain. Er, (long pause) amen."

I want God to know my will, my will be done on earth and right now. But that's not prayer like Jesus taught us.

I told my Freshman Seminar, "We're almost mid-semester. I think it would be good to *get some feedback on this course. Don't be bashful, speak up, give me some mid-course evaluation. How is the course going? How am I doing as your teacher?"*

Immediately one said, "Sometimes you seem kinda disorganized." Another, "You let the discussion go on too long." Yet another, "Have you ever taught this course before?"

And I said, "You're just freshmen! What do you know?"

A few weeks ago I had lunch with a man who has suffered terribly from a painful back problem for as long as I have known him. At lunch, he looked different. I commented on how he looked: "Joe, have you finally gotten the medical treatment you needed to take away some of your back pain? You look like you feel better."

He replied, "No, I have not gotten the medical treatment I needed. I'm still in pain, but a few weeks ago, while in prayer, I prayed to God the prayer that I always have prayed, 'Lord, I beg you, take away some of my pain so that I may live without the suffering I've endured.' And you know what God said to me? 'Now what gave you the notion that I was against your being in some pain? Read the New Testament! I put people in pain! Live with it and show people through your life that the life I gave you is good.'"

There was someone who had been taught to pray by Jesus.

The day that we began our invasion of Iraq, with "shock and awe" from the air, a group of us showed our concern by gathering in front of the chapel for prayer at eight in the morning. We stood in a circle in front of the chapel and prayed anguished, sometimes angry, prayers of lament and protest. "Lord, rebuke our national leaders for their violent and hostile actions," prayed one. "Lord, in your mighty power restrain the murderous intent of those who would lead this peaceful nation into an unprovoked war." On and on went the anguished prayers.

Finally, as we had decided, Professor Stanley Hauerwas, a professional Christian pacifist, ended our time of prayer with, "Lord, please be with George Bush. He is probably a well-intentioned man who is trying, through this war, to protect us and give us the security that we demand. Forgive us, Lord, for being the sort of fearful, faithless people who have deluded George Bush into thinking that his job is to protect us, to make us secure and safe on our own. Forgive us for our part in this war through our own fantasies and presumption and for relying on anyone, even our President, other than you to protect us. Amen."

Prayer that begins as a projection of my yearnings, desires, and needs upon God ends in encounter with the living God. This is prayer as Jesus taught us.

In speaking about God, we cannot get there by any human faculty—cognitive or emotive, practical or theoretical. Speech about God is always miraculous in origin and characterized by humble gratitude that, despite our incapacity, we do hear and thus we do speak. Hunsinger also notes that literalism's rather modernist desire for certitude in religious discourse distinguishes it from Barth's realism. Literalist realism—with its preference for univocal reference, propositions, and cognitive forms of address—violates the peculiar nature of biblical speech (which tends to be metaphorical, evocative, and multivalent) and, perhaps unintentionally, attempts to circumvent the necessity for inspiration by the Holy Spirit through its presumed adequacy of its theological assertions. Expressivism, on the other hand—with its equivocation, and its preference for noncognitive address—tended to reduce theological truth to merely metaphorical, poetic truth. Theological words, among expressivists like Tillich or Bultmann, were not so much true or false as functional or dysfunctional in their ability to express or to evoke human experience of the divine.

By keeping his language eschatological, analogical, provisional, and essentially keryg-matic, Barth is able to use theological terms without claiming certitude. He claims congru-ence and sufficiency. Thus he is able to say that his language, despite its deficiencies, is a true enough rendition of God. None of this is the final word about God, all that can be said or must be said, but it is what can be legitimately said. It is "realistic" in that it really does refer to some reality outside itself, and it is "objective" because its validity does not depend upon merely human experience to confirm its truth. Biblically derived theological language was so dependable, so confident of God's miraculous work in and through it, that Barth could advise us preachers that all we must do is hear, then repeat, without ornament or anx-iety, the Word of God, and thereby others will be given the grace to trust this word in life and in death.[103]

We see Barth struggling to keep his language sufficiently tied to its peculiar subject mat-ter when Barth describes scripture. Barth calls biblical narratives "legendary witnesses." Biblical narratives are not merely historical reports, nor are they fictional, imaginative fab-rications, they are "witnesses." Their imaginative, legendary quality was intrinsic to their theological content, the communicative form that was demanded by their very real, but very unusual subject matter. A witness is not to create the event that the witness reports, but rather is truthfully to report on the event, to witness to its eventuality.[104] The witness ensures the objectivity, the reality that the testimony under consideration is faithful and true.

Thomas G. Long draws out the implications of the Barthian scripture as witness, and preacher-as-witness image:

> Consider what happens in a court trial. The trial is conducted in a public place because what happens is a public matter. A trial is designed to get at the truth, and the people have a vested interest in the truth. In order to get at the truth, a witness is brought to the stand to testify. Now this witness is in every way one of the people, but he or she is placed on the stand because of two credentials: The witness has seen some-thing, and the witness is willing to tell the truth about it—the whole truth and nothing but the truth. In one sense, the personal characteristics of the witness do not matter. The court is interested in the truth and in justice, not in the witness per se. In another sense, however, the character of the witness is crucial. If the witness lies—bears false wit-ness—the ability of the people to discover the truth will receive a grievous blow. "False testimony," writes Ricoeur, "is a lie in the heart of the witness. This perverse intention is so fatal to the exercise of justice and to the entire order of discourse that all codes of morality place it very high in the scale of vices."
>
> The court has access to the truth only through the witness. It seeks the truth, but it must look for it in the testimony of the witness. The very life of the witness, then, is bound up into the testimony. The witness cannot claim to be removed, objectively pointing to the evidence. What the witness believes to be true is a part of the evidence, and when the truth told by the witness is despised by the people, the witness may suffer, or even be killed, as a result of the testimony. It is no coincidence that the New Testament word for "witness" is *martyr*.[105]

In Luke 24:45-49, Jesus becomes the preacher, interpreting the scriptures to his disciples. As he interprets for them, he calls them his "witnesses," telling them that they are sent out but that they must wait "until you have been clothed with power from on high." David Bartlett gives what could be a good summary of the Barthian view of the source of preaching.

It is not as though when the church comes together to hear the Word proclaimed and share the meal we become second-hand interpreters of the story that rightly belongs to generations long gone. It is rather that we become witnesses to that reality to which we bear witness. The life of the preacher, like the life of every Christian, is nurtured in word and sacrament. We receive in order that we may share.[106]

Long put this well when he wrote,

The preacher as witness is not authoritative because of rank or power, but rather because of what the preacher has seen and heard. When the preacher prepares his sermon by wrestling with the biblical text, the preacher is not merely gathering information about the text. The preacher is listening for a voice, looking for a presence, hoping for the claim of God to be encountered through the text.[107]

But how does a witness to the Resurrection bring that sort of event to speech? The events were real but inconceivable and therefore nearly indescribable. The biblical stories were acts of inspired human imagination, told by witnesses, but they were not merely the product of human inventiveness. Human imagination, disciplined by the mystery of the events themselves, gave us these biblical stories. Stories like the empty tomb narratives of the Gospels do not refer to historically discrete, locatable, and datable historical "facts" as conceived by modernity. Yet neither do they merely express subjective human "experiences." They bear adequate witness to a living, active, surprising subject who acts in the world, yet often in ways that are difficult to bring to speech. To my mind, some of the evidence for the validity of the empty tomb accounts in the Gospels is their conflicted diversity. That the Gospel writers had such differing testimony to the aftermath of Resurrection is assurance that something happened, something undeniable in its reality but also almost indescribable in its occurrence.

Thus Barth thinks of scripture as, from the beginning, of mainly kerygmatic significance. Biblical witnesses speak of the divine self-proclamation to those who were not present at the event in such a way that the story becomes eventful in the lives of those who hear. These stories are acts of analogical imagination that show the difficulty as well as the success of the first narrators of these events.[108] When we attempt to convince through speaking, we draw upon structures of reasoning that are available to us, building upon the presumed world, making connections with previous experiences. And yet this is just the problem when we are attempting to convince people of divine events, because, by their nature, such events are not part of our received modes of thinking, not part of our presumed world, with little connection to previous experience. The presumed structure of the world, into which we have all been inculcated—that is, the modern world—is too limited and confining in its structures of meaning. Thus, Barth speaks of the impossibility of preaching.

Whether Barth impresses one as an expressivist or a realist in style, he provides for us preachers a wonderful example of a kerygmatic theologian who works in service to the proclamation of the church. He demonstrates the rhetorical implications of a theology that keeps strictly tied to its subject. One of the important insights of contemporary homiletics is the idea that the form of a sermon ought to be shaped by the formative demands of the biblical text. Scripture uses a wide array of literary forms to convey the richness and complexity of the Trinitarian God. There is something about this God, and the communication of this God, that demands poetry, saga, history, invective, blessing, genealogy, polemic, forensic argument, and virtually all the rich rhetorical possibilities available in the gift of human speech.[109]

Barth at his best mirrors some of this richness in his own resourceful stock of theological rhetoric. One of the things that baffles me about Barth is the way in which his theology at times seems more "homiletical" than his sermons. His sermons have a rather predictable form of straightforward pronouncement on the basis of a biblical text, the development of some insight from the text, attention to some detail of the text, with a simple and reiterated declaration of faith at the end of the sermon. Aside from those sermons that embody a single word of announcement from the biblical text like, "Nevertheless!" or "All!" Barth generally seems to be oblivious to the rhetorical shape or the stylistic intent of the biblical texts. I find this troubling in one who was so gifted a rhetor himself and who claims to be adhering so strictly to the text. Barth seems still to be in the grip of the rather Platonic notion that a biblical text is mainly important for the idea that it contains or communicates. In such a view, the shape of the biblical text is likely to be regarded as a merely disposable, arbitrary container for the kernel of truth inside. While Barth clearly marvels at some of the particularities and peculiarities, the surprising movements within a given biblical text, those insights seem to have little effect upon the shape of his sermon from that text.

George Hunsinger denies that it is possible to take the richness that is Barth and reduce that richness to some single motif in Barth. Still, Hunsinger helpfully identifies five key themes in Barth.[110] Webb asks whether "multiplying motifs is really the best way to resolve the problems inherent in the thematic approach." I expect that any stylistic analysis of Barth that tries to label him as either an expressivist or a realist, or even a bit of both, does injustice to the rhetorical richness that is found throughout the Barthian corpus. I think the best stylistic characterization of Barth's writing, particularly the *Dogmatics*, is that of a symphony. Hunsinger himself notes the symphonic qualities, the repetitions and negations, the expansions and the retractions found in the *Dogmatics* that resist attempts to categorize and thematize Barth. Others have compared the form of the *Dogmatics* to a vast, sprawling, constantly upwardly soaring Gothic cathedral.[111] Barth requested that readers approach his work not with the intention of finding in it some school or theme but rather to read all of it. Rather than analyze Barth by discovering a theme, or a variety of themes, a style or mix of styles, perhaps we would do better to approach Barth in a more aesthetic manner, reading him as a symphony rather than as a dissertation. This became apparent to me when, at the same time I was engaged in a close reading of *Church Dogmatics* III, I attended a performance by my choir of Bach's *St. Matthew Passion*. Somehow, sitting there with Bach for such an extended period of time, as those waves of music swept over me, hearing so many repetitions, repetitions that became expansions of an earlier theme, a subtle further development of the theme that at first seemed only a repetition, the fatigue and the sense of being taken by the music to some other world, it all seemed very much like the experience of reading Barth. His work really does need to be taken as a whole, not taken apart and mined for certain abstract themes, but experienced, encountered, changing us in the process.[112]

Like the Mozart whom he loved, Barth crafted his thoughts like a symphony, with sharply contrasting themes resolved into higher unities and marked by frequent recapitulations. Themes or fragments of themes, once dominant, are constantly carried forward into a new setting where other themes become ascendant.[113] Part of what Barth seems to share with Mozart, in other words, is a taste for thematic interplay, a taste that includes the custom of complex recapitulation, modification, and allusion. The more deeply one reads Barth, the more one senses that his use of repetition is never pointless. Rather, it serves as a principle of organization and development within an ever-forward elliptical theological whole.[114]

In these similarities with Mozart, Barth once again shows a connection between the form of his theology and his subject matter. For Barth, theology is a vast, interconnected, complex symphony in which every theme is connected to every other theme. David Ford says that it is as if Barth saw the Christian faith as a multifaceted crystal, taking that crystal in hand and saying, "Now we are going to look at the basic structure of the crystal through this facet, this particular doctrine, of the Christian faith. Notice how it connects not only with those facets that adjoin it but also with those more remote and those on the opposite side. Above all, notice that the light which infuses the whole is the very light which refracts through this facet as well."[115] Having conducted this examination, Barth then turns the great crystal in his hands and directs our attention in a similar way to yet another facet of the whole. Theology attempts to look at God from all sorts of different angles, and then celebrates how all the aspects are interconnected in the whole. It is a grand performance of theology.

Thus a president of a major protestant seminary, when I mentioned Barth to him, said of his own continuing encounters with the *Dogmatics*, "Barth feeds my soul. He moves me beyond my issues of agreement and disagreement with him to the rejuvenating joy of simply being with him as he sings an anthem to the triumph of God."

Among the implications of Barth's theological style for us preachers are these:

1. *Preaching is the proclamation of the Word of God.* It is neither moral exhortation (the gospel is demeaned and our human situation is denied by reducing preaching to moral exhortation), nor a heartfelt expression of the preacher's personal piety (who cares?). Preaching is not a skillful representation of God's word (the task of theology). Preaching is not, despite the history of rhetoric, primarily a matter of persuasive speaking. Persuasive speaking is God's problem, not ours. A sower goes out to sow and, without careful preparation or planning, just begins slinging seed. Of course, in such effusive sowing, there is much waste, for this sower seems determined to overwhelm the world with words. In fact, most of the seed falls on infertile ground. It is up to God to give the growth, not us preachers. The hearing of God's word is not an example of democracy in action, with the hearers making savvy choices in what they will accept or reject. Preaching is dramatic, effusive presentation of God's word, so that God's word is heard through it, if God wills. "Proclamation is human speech in and by which God Himself speaks like a king through the mouth of his herald."[116] Whether God speaks through preaching is God's free choice: "When and where it pleases God, it is God's own Word,"[117] but preaching is nevertheless that dangerous, confident adventure of letting God be God in the church.

Throughout the history of the church's preaching, one senses a certain nervousness within the church, a recurring lament about the current state of the church's preaching. The church is right to worry about its preaching because every Sunday sermon is a sort of experiment, a test, a public demonstration of the church's claim that Jesus Christ was indeed raised from the dead and continues to speak to the very ones who betrayed him. As Word of God, something that God says before we say anything, preaching is one of the three forms of God's revelation (preaching, scripture, and Christ—the Eternal Word) and a unique way that the Trinity communicates with us.

Yet, the freedom of God's voice also implies that God's speaking is not limited to the proclamation of the church. "God may speak to us through Russian Communism, a flute concerto, a blossoming shrub, or a dead dog."[118] However, Barth suggests that, unless we are prophets, preachers are not free to rummage around in other competing texts until we have presented the biblical text, for there is no independent proclamation, only the proclamation of the church, Jesus Christ.[119] Preaching is always more critical of the church than the world, more abusive of those who listen on the inside than those who may hear on the outside. Judgment always begins with God's own house, including the judgment that is the frustration at our inability to listen to God's word.

2. *The great gift that encounters with Barth may have for many of us contemporary preachers is a recovery of nerve, of gospel-induced boldness.*[120] In an age in which preaching seems to have lost its voice, in which Christian convictions seem so in need of a thousand qualifications, and we preachers continue to grope for some socially acceptable means of speaking of the Word made flesh, Barth offers an invitation to join him, as well as our weaker voices can, in a great anthem. Later in his career, long after he had written *Romans*, Barth reread his work. And even after his many misgivings about his theological method used there, Barth said to himself, "Well roared, lion!"[121]

What does it mean if preaching is God's Word? It obviously does not mean that pastors in the pulpit cease to be pastors and become instead the

> flutes of the Holy Spirit. They are just this as little as Isaiah or Paul. . . . What they say does not suddenly cease to be human talk about God and therefore to be in itself talk about something else and not God. No, they are now really aware what it means to stand within that bracket with the last and highest that they can bring by way of authority or freedom. . . . Yet it is nonetheless a miracle, a reality of the Spirit, of God, no less incomprehensible, unfathomable, and nonderivable than revelation itself or its communication through the prophetic and apostolic Word. . . . We can never be too bashful or restrained or modest in thinking and speaking about this third presupposition. . . . It is a great thing to presuppose that Jesus Christ is the Logos. It is an even greater and more daring thing to presuppose that the same Logos still speaks today through the Word of these witnesses. But from our standpoint it is indubitably the most dangerous and ambivalent and burdensome thing to presuppose that the same Logos speaks again and will constantly speak as Christian preaching, especially when we are not just as spectators of the process but participants in it.[122]

Theology, language, and communication are inseparably related. By nature and etymology, "theology, is a *logia*, logic, or language bound to the *theos*, which both makes it possible and also determines it."[123] Israel and the early church were great talkers about God because of their conviction that they had really heard something of God that no one else had heard.

3. *Barth demonstrates to us that to be a Christian communicator is to be engaged in a struggle, a conflict, a kind of war.* As Christians, we ought never to forget that we speak from a minority viewpoint—and always have. We are, in our speech, speaking against the presumed world of the majority. Therefore, in our assertions, we will not find many interpretive allies in the weapons of the world. The world is accustomed to getting its messages from psychology, the vaunted ego, or clear-eyed reason. Our message requires a miracle to make it comprehensible.[124] Conflict and disruption are inherent in Christian discourse because the claimed stability of the world, the presumption by which the world carries on its business, is being challenged.[125] We North American preachers today may be among the first generations in our context to realize that the political ground has shifted under our feet. We are no longer deferentially addressing a culture that can claim, even in its unguarded moments, to be "Christian." Every Sunday we are issuing a declaration of war against some of the most cherished idols of our culture. The world in which we live is adamantly set against the gospel— and always has been. This culture in which we work is arranged, in all sorts of subtle but powerful ways, against the claims that Jesus Christ is Lord—and always has been. The world is a world at war—and always has been. Sovereignty is under dispute—and always has been. Thus the Bible is full of violence and war, for there was something about Jesus that brought out the worst in the world. Christians are contentious. It is not because we want to be critical and contentious, but rather it is because of the inability of the presumptive world to relinquish its tight, imperialistic grip upon the imagination, that there is conflict. "Common

sense," always a great foe of gospel foolishness, is really social consensus. Thus Barth's sustained rhetorical belligerence—his biting sarcasm,[126] his contempt for the glittering images of much that passes for "theology," his refusal to use the approved intellectual weapons that were offered to him by the academy, his denial of a natural point of contact between our self-constructed world and the world of the gospel—make him an inspiring example for the contemporary tongue-tied preacher.

The voice of the L ORD *is over the waters;*
  the God of glory thunders,
  the L ORD*, over mighty waters.*
The voice of the L ORD *is powerful;*
  the voice of the L ORD *is full of Majesty. . . .*
The voice of the L ORD *causes the oaks to whirl,*
  and strips the forest bare;
  and in his temple all say, "Glory!"
      (Psalm 29:3-4, 9)

CHAPTER FIVE

WORD MAKES WORLD

In two large rooms in the Pompidou Center, the Museum of Modern Art in Paris, there is an installation by the artist *Joseph Beuys* (1921–1986). A large, black grand piano occupies the center of one of the rooms. The top of the piano is nailed shut. The two rooms are covered, walls and ceiling, with about a foot of thick, sound-absorbent padding. The piece is entitled *Plight* (1958/1985). Here is our plight as communicators, as workers in words and sound. There is an instrument for making music, but contextual factors within modern life smother and suppress the sound. Thus the plight of the contemporary preacher.

When I was in seminary, learning to preach, I got the impression that my greatest challenge as a communicator of the gospel was the skeptical, critical, analytical "modern world." My plight, as a preacher, was to stand in the premodern, prescientific world of the Bible and yet speak to the modern world. The preacher, so I assumed, artfully bridges the two-thousand-year gap between the Bible and the modern world.

Concern over this historical gap was the great preoccupation of most of the theology, homiletics, and biblical interpretation that I learned in seminary: how to generate communication, how to speak to the modern world.

Barth displays a studied disregard (if not contempt) for the modern world. In an almost postmodern fashion, Barth realized that the modern world was an intellectual construction dating back not much further than Descartes, a way of viewing reality but a view that need not necessarily be honored as the last word on "reality." He refused to accommodate his theology to the philosophical limitations of modernity. Rather, he thought that modernity ought to be unmasked as a limited way of looking at the world and then dethroned in our consciousness as we dared to be lured into the "strange new world" of the Bible.

In preaching, we are moving people, little by little, Sunday by Sunday, toward new and otherwise unavailable descriptions of reality. We are on our way, in the sermon, toward a new heaven and a new earth, a new world. The pragmatic, typically American charge against Christian preaching is that Christians fail to "practice what you preach." To charge preaching with being hypocritical is not to understand the pushy, imperialistic quality of Christian preaching. Christian preaching is not merely the skillful description of the world as it is but a bold, visionary, and demanding call to be part of a world that is to be. The result of proclamation is performance and we are not, in most of our performances, there yet. Christian preachers are heralds who proclaim the true sovereignty of God in territory whose ownership is still under dispute. We are not there yet. Jesus Christ is Lord but not in fullness and completion. Therefore the easiest thing in the world is to point to the gap between what Christians profess ("Jesus Christ is Lord") and how we presently live ("George W. Bush is Lord"). We are thus accused of hypocrisy in saying so much more than we are able to live. Of course we say more than we yet have.

Christians must not allow the charge of hypocrisy to bowdlerize our speech. We must not trim our proclamation to our meager abilities to embody it. In preaching, it's the listening, rather than the speaking, that can be the greatest risk. (Barth even defines preaching as "speech which obediently listens" and describes the best of all churches as "the listening church."[1]) It is the risk of having our little lives judged by bold, visionary, eschatological speech, the pain of having our world rocked by another world that comes sweeping in upon us in the sermon. To take up residence in a new world, to become a citizen of a new order, I must first hear about it. It's speaking that constructs a world, and it's hearing that changes the world. To charge us with the hypocrisy of not yet living what we profess is to demand that preaching be merely descriptive or interpretative rather than announcement.

With Barth I came to see that my challenge, as a preacher, was not to speak in terms that could be readily accessible to the modern world as it is, but rather to speak in a way that made sense in the light of the Word made flesh. My task was not to find the words that fit the modern world but rather to find a world of words that fit a God who is Trinitarian in being and operation and therefore constantly creating the world. The modern world began as a search for sure knowledge but ended in the construction of the world where severe limits were put on knowledge, limiting knowledge to that knowledge that was most conducive to the modern world's methods of thought. Thus the modern world was an attempt to have a world that successfully excluded a living, revealing God. It is no coincidence that the world thereby constructed may have been history's most inhuman age, an age that is known, not for its creative arts, but rather for the production of the biggest bomb and the bloodiest wars. Without God, anything that humanity can dream is possible—genocide, environmental degradation, the extermination of species, and other nightmares of human ingenuity.

The modern world was born in the great confidence that we humans had the power to know without restraint. The postmodern world began with the acknowledgment that, in modernity, our knowledge did not grow but shrank. Postmodernism knows that it is difficult for us to know something like the Trinity when we live in twenty-first-century North America and are therefore extremely circumscribed in our ability to know.

We have noted Barth's preoccupation with noetics. Barth is more concerned with revelation than with redemption. Our redemption is done, accomplished in Jesus Christ; therefore, that fact is uncontested, except among those who do not know.[2] What remains conflicted, contested, and awaiting realization is our knowledge of that fact. Barth is amazed both that we do not know this world-changing fact and also that, despite our distance from God, we do occasionally know the fact. Barth rhapsodically sings to revelation as the only ground upon which we stand, the only basis for our life in God:

> It is the ground on which we stand, the horizon by which we are bounded, the atmosphere in which we breathe. It is the life of our life. It is inaccessible and concealed just because it is so real—with a divine reality over which we have no control, but which controls us with a force with which none of the known and accessible elements of our life can even remotely compete. It is not in the sphere of our knowledge because it is wisdom itself, without whose light our knowledge would not be possible even in its limitation. We have no power over it because it is omnipotence, by which all our power is created, and without which it would be impotence. It does not exist as one of the facts which we seek and can discover because it is we who are searched and discovered in our existence by it. (*CD*, II, 2, pg. 777)

God's gracious revelation of the "fact" of our redemption in Christ does not mean that it is no longer a mystery, and that it is a mystery does not mean that God is unable to reveal it to us. Through the mysterious grace of God, God's knowledge of us "becomes the object of our knowledge; it thus finds a way of becoming the object of our experience and our thought; it gives itself to be apprehended by our contemplation and our categories" (*CD*, I, 2, pg. 172).

However, as a given "object," revelation remains a great mystery, "beyond the range of what we regard as possible for our contemplation and perception, beyond the confines of our experience and our thought," something new and fresh, challenging and unexpected, uncontainable and unmanageable. "It comes to us as a Novum which, when it becomes object for us, we cannot incorporate in the series of our other objects, cannot compare with them, cannot deduce from their context, cannot regard as analogous to them. It comes to us as a datum with no point of connection with any other previous datum." Faith is a mode of apprehension as unique and mysterious as the object of its apprehension: "The act of knowing it is distinctive as one which we actually can achieve, but which we cannot understand, in the sense that we simply do not understand how we can achieve it." Our ability to know God and to assent to what we know is not ours but rather a gracious gift of God: "We can understand the possibility of it solely from the side of the object, i.e., we can regard it not as ours, but as one coming to us, imparted to us, gifted to us. In this bit of knowing we are not the masters but the mastered."[3]

George Hunsinger says that our knowledge of God is the gift of revelation: "Mystery precludes mastery, just because it confronts the human mind with something it can never control—an event inconceivable though real and real though inconceivable. Its inconceivability does not detract from its reality, and its reality does not detract from its inconceivability. It can therefore only be acknowledged, confessed, described, and received as the utterly unique and mysterious act of God."[4] Or, as Barth puts it (in a way that has implications for preachers who often use analogies, proofs, and illustrations), "Those who want to talk about revelation, those who want to explain what it means . . . must not try to strengthen their work with analogies, proofs, and references of some other provenance. They should perhaps let themselves be strengthened as Elijah was on the way to Horeb, the Mt. of God, that is, by an angel."[5]

Barth said that the one thing that he hoped, throughout all of the twists and the turns in the *Dogmatics*, would remain "inexorably unchanged" to his life's end was "the mystery of God in his relationship to man and not . . . the mystery of man in his relationship to God."[6] He said this in 1939, just after completing volume 1 of the *Dogmatics*. He sought throughout the *Dogmatics* to proclaim, to explore, and yet to preserve the mystery of God's work in Jesus Christ. And the main miracle and mystery is God's being present to humanity in the Trinity. The Trinity for Barth is God's being both transcendent and immanent at the same time in Jesus Christ. And the Incarnation is the great mystery of God's being veiled and unveiled, tenting among us, as the Word.

Incarnational Knowledge

Barth regarded revelation as an utterly miraculous incarnational event. Our preaching is a demonstration of, and is dependent upon, the relentless, continuing determination of this God to be incarnate:

> Thou dost beset me behind and before,
> and layest thy hand upon me.
> Such knowledge is too wonderful for me;
> it is high, I cannot attain it.
> Where shall I go from thy Spirit?
> Or wither shall I flee from thy presence? (Psalm 139:5-7 RSV)

In recent years, there as been considerable interest shown in the "person of the preacher," in the strengths and weaknesses of the humanity of the preacher.[7] Thus "incarnate" preaching primarily focuses on the Word dwelling in the humanity of the preacher. Barth has no concern, so far as I can tell, in such speculation. It is not the humanity of the preacher that makes preaching interesting but rather the humanity of God that makes preaching work. In this chapter we shall explore some of the homiletical implications for Barth's stress upon the revelatory quality of the Incarnation.

Eberhard Jüngel opens his wonderful, difficult book on the Trinitarian significance of Barth's thought with a deceptively simple sentence, "Barth thinks as a theologian."[8] He goes on to say that this means, in Barthian thought, that God is not the result of our theological assertions but prior to them. God's being goes before anything we know or say about God. We raise no question about God before God has put a question to us. God has already proceeded and preceded us. Thus our knowledge of God is linked to our worship of the true God. All attempts to know God without the grace of God in revelation are idolatrous. Barth says that so many of our attempts to gain knowledge of God are based upon the idolatrous lust to "be like God" (Gen. 3:5). "We shall never be as God is. We can never put ourselves in God's place. It is to our shame that we continually want and try to do so."[9] Only God can reveal God.[10] And God has revealed God in the Word made flesh. All knowledge begins there, including knowledge of ourselves: "At no level or time can we have to do with God without having also to do with this man. We cannot conceive ourselves and the world without first conceiving this man with God as the witness of the gracious purpose with which God willed and created ourselves and the world and in which we may exist in it and with it."[11]

Against the Catholics, with increasing emphasis as the *Church Dogmatics* moves along, Barth reiterates his conviction that the Incarnation is "the one and only sacrament" (*CD*, IV, 2, pg. 55).[12] Whereas the Medieval Catholic Church focused on "transubstantiation" of the elements in the Eucharist, Barth focuses on how Jesus Christ transforms us, makes us present in this history, not how participation in the Eucharist makes us participants in Christ's history.

To say that God is incarnate, appearing in the flesh, is to say that God's revelation is always both unveiled and veiled, both revealed and concealed. Jesus was never self-evidently the Messiah. He was "veiled," and preaching ought never to attempt to tear away that veil. He was something to be seen only by those who were given "eyes to see." All of our possible knowing about God "rests with God."[13] That we do indeed, despite all the epistemological problems, see and know God is a miracle, a miracle that is as amazing as the Nativity or the Resurrection. Our words become an event of God's word because again and again God graciously wills it to be so.[14] Just as we describe the Incarnation in the Creed, so we can say that preaching can be the Word of God, says Barth, when it is "conceived by the Holy Ghost."[15]

Barth has a scathing denunciation of the Mariology in the Catholic Church, saying that the important thing about Mary is that she is someone to whom "the miracle of revelation" happens:

> Mariology is an excrescence, i.e., a diseased construct of theological thought. Excrescences must be excised. . . . The greatness of the New Testament figure of Mary consists in the fact that all the interest is directed away from herself to the Lord. It is her "low estate" (v. 48), and the glory of God which encounters her, not her own person, which can properly be made the object of a special consideration, doctrine and veneration. Along with John the Baptist Mary is at once the personal climax of the Old Testament penetrating to the New Testament, and the first man of the New

Testament (v. 38). She is simply man to whom the miracle of revelation happens. (*CD*, I, 2, pp. 138-40)

George Hunsinger says, "In Barth's theology, the saving work of the Spirit is Trinitarian in ground, Christocentric in focus, miraculous in operation, communal in content, eschatological in form, diversified in application, and universal in scope."[16] The work of the Holy Spirit is always miraculous. It is the sole effective agent by which communication with God is made humanly possible. In our present state, we human beings cannot on our own recover communication with God. Sin obfuscates and enslaves us and debases our desires. Yet through the proclamation of the gospel, what is impossible is made possible, the miracle of revelation happens. The only condition necessary is the Spirit's incarnational operation in the human heart. Our communication with God, says Hunsinger, never depends on regenerated capacities (Wesley), infused virtues (Aquinas), acquired habits (Aristotle), or strengthened dispositions in the soul (contemporary humanists too numerous to mention). Those who are once awakened to lifelong conversion by the Spirit never cease to be sinners, yet the Spirit never ceases to reach out to sinners. This seems utterly opposed to Wesley and to the current emphasis on spiritual "practices" whereby we can improve our situation before God. There is in Barth no "synergism" or "cooperation" with divine grace, no "point of contact" between us and God. It is all miracle, a miracle on the level of the virginal conception of Jesus. In preaching, we see a "miracle of God" in which just as "he does not regard the lowliness of his handmaiden . . . or view the unclean lips of Isaiah as an obstacle . . . does not think it impossible to pitch his tent in what is at best our poor and insignificant and stammering talk about God."[17]

One more aspect of Barth's incarnational treatment of preaching was his insight that revelation is both the unveiling and the veiling of God, both the revelation and the concealment of God.

In *Romans* (1933 ed., pg. 39) Barth, building on Luther and Kierkegaard, said that "the Gospel requires faith. . . . It can therefore be neither directly communicated nor directly apprehended . . . it can appear among us . . . only as contradiction. . . . It withdraws itself when it is not listened to for its own sake." Kierkegaard has said, "Truth is not nimble on its feet." It is of the nature of the gospel not to be self-evident. Barth fulminates against taking the gospel, which ought to be "truth that is new every morning," and attempting to ossify it "into a sacred reality." Preaching is meant to be "a marvel to which one may quietly point" (*GD*, I, pg. 59). Barth's epistemology is based upon the assumption that "God does not belong to the world. Therefore he does not belong to the series of objects for which we have categories or words by means of which we draw the attention of others to them, and bring them into relation with Him. Of God it is impossible to speak, because He is neither a natural nor a spiritual object" (*CD*, I, 2, pg. 750). As Trevor Hart explains, Barth was reacting against "the somewhat optimistic and imperialistic epistemology of the Neo-Kantian philosophy in which something is known as it is 'objectified' or 'made into an object,' that is to say classified and labeled by the mind in accordance with universally given sets of categories" (Hart, "The Word and the Words and the Witness," p. 96). On the other hand, Barth rejects an epistemology based upon subjectivity (as in Schleiermacher, then Bultmann) that makes God into an existentially encountered nonobjective entity.

"If God's concealment is really to be his revelation, if the barrier before which we stand is also to be a door that opens, if God is to make himself known, then this must take place by

God's concealing his pure deity, by his emptying himself" (see Phil. 2:6). Barth distinctly believes that it is precisely in God's revealing that we most dramatically experience God's concealing because what is revealed is so far afield from our expectations and conceptions of God. Barth says that God's unveiled "yes" to us in the Christ is also God's veiled "no." "The Yes itself means a No, that in the very closeness of God our distance from him is disclosed."[18]

Barth says that in church history, the fathers of the church labored so hard, at Chalcedon and elsewhere, to define the nature of the Trinity and Incarnation, not because they "mischievously wanted to pierce a secret. It was rather that they thought they stood before a secret, before the basis of the church and Christian preaching." "They thought it essential that this secret should be recognized and perpetually acknowledged as such, and that they should thus establish it fundamentally against all caprice or pressure. Thus they fix for all time the notion of fully human and fully divine."[19]

Christians claim that, in Jesus Christ, we have seen—that is, we know—as much of God as we ever hope to see or to know. This is the great scandal of Christianity, expressed in the Incarnation and in the Atonement. Thus Nicholas Lash quotes Pamela Vermes saying, "Israel in terms of religious history means direct relation between man and a Being who allows himself to be seen in events and natural phenomena yet remains invisible. To this form of God, Christianity *opposed* one with a particular human face."[20] Christianity is born in an assertion that it is virtually impossible not to see God. Whereas Israel's story is a long record of an attempt to be faithful to the first commandment, the church's story is a long story of attempting to be faithful to the first commandment (the prohibition against images) by saying that we are not to make an image for God because we already have the supreme image for God—Jesus Christ.

Yet Lash also notes that such statements do not do justice to the nuances of our claim of God in Christ. There is, amid Christian claims of unveiling, a strong claim of veiling that is tied, not to God's inherent obscurity, but rather to the identity of the God revealed in it—the crucified, suffering servant, the weak and poor one from Galilee. In both the person and the work of Christ, we are struck by our unknowing. God came to us, in the flesh, and the way God came to us led us to say, in the words of the Spiritual, "We didn't know who you was."

The Jewish challenge to Christian claims of knowledge rests not only in the unique and surprising person of Christ but also in his work. To put it bluntly, if Jesus is the Redeemer, the faithful Jew wants to know, then why does the world not look more redeemed? Why don't we as Jesus' followers look more redeemed? This is a serious question for the Christian. Undoubtedly, to persecuted Israel, our claims of the "now and not yet" quality of the kingdom of God seem a bit limp, and our pointing to the church as the foretaste of Jesus' complete redemption seems, at best, comical.

Yet, while Christian theology must confess its uncertainty, the constant contestableness of its most cherished concepts, its inherently unstable affirmations, it would do better to admit to its dependency, to receive with thanksgiving the revelation it has, to dare, despite all we do not know, to testify to what we know. It is the nature of the Crucified Messiah to be veiled and unveiled at the same time.[21]

Flannery O'Connor once said that the good realist writer must learn to be "humble in the face of what is."[22] Through his dialectical thought, Barth both stresses all that we cannot know of God—the elusive, ungraspable, apophatic quality of God's being—and at the same time affirms with critical "realism" the objectiveness of God, the sheer "thatness" of the

Word made flesh.[23] This Barth does by reflections about the communicative quality of the Trinity and by God's self-revelation in the incarnation of Christ. Both the Trinity and the Incarnation assure us that God has intruded into human understanding in a way that graciously gives us confident knowledge of God.[24] And yet, that God has intruded in the Trinity and Incarnation is that which keeps shattering and frustrating our knowledge.

From his earliest writings until his latest, Barth maintains that there is an implicit paradox in the very nature of revelation. God reveals himself, yet God does so in such a way and in such a format that even in the midst of God's revealedness God remains hidden. Thus in Romans, citing Kierkegaard and Luther for moral support, Barth writes:

> The Gospel requires—faith. . . . It can therefore be neither directly communicated nor directly apprehended . . . it can appear among us, be received and understood by us, only as contradiction. The Gospel does not expound or recommend itself. It does not negotiate or plead, threaten or make promises. It withdraws itself always when it is not listened to for its own sake. . . . "Indeed only when that which is believed on is hidden, can it provide an opportunity for faith. And moreover, those things are most deeply hidden which most clearly contradict the obvious experience of the sense" (Luther).[25]

Trevor Hart says of this passage from Barth that

> the same precise point undergirds Barth's view of Scripture and preaching as developed in GD and CD. Thus, "To deny the hiddenness of revelation even in Scripture is to deny revelation itself, and with it the Word of God. For God's Word is no longer God's Word when the truth that is new every morning . . . is made into sacred reality, when the miracle of God that is encircled with the possibility of offense is made into a marvel to which one may quietly point."[26]

In Jesus, in our encounters with scripture, in our preaching, there is therefore always a veiling/unveiling. These three forms of revelation both reveal and conceal. In those moments when any of these forms of divine self-communication become revelation, God has miraculously torn the veil away, making comprehensible the incomprehensible. The veil remains in place, but for those with "eyes to see" it becomes transparent, while for others it is and remains utterly opaque.[27]

Trevor Hart says Barth's paradoxical, now and not yet, revealed and not revealed quality of revelation is a reflection of his belief in the paradoxical quality of the Incarnation itself: "For Barth, the *scandalon* must be allowed to stand. . . . God's Word comes to us in fully human form. It is veiled from us by this very creatureliness, and becomes 'visible,' as it were, only in the event of revelation. The real presence of the word in human words cannot be guaranteed, coerced, pinned down or held on to. As in the sacrament, it can only be prayed for and received by faith in, with and under the creaturely elements. There is no magical transubstantiation."[28]

Real proclamation, therefore, is defined by Barth as "human talk about God on the basis of the self-objectification of God which is not just there, which cannot be predicted, which does not fit into any plan, which is really only in the freedom of His grace, and in virtue of which He wills at specific times to be the object of this talk, and is so according to His own good pleasure."[29] Furthermore, "It must be so solely the truth and miracle of God if his Logos, as he does not regard the lowliness of his handmaiden . . . or view the unclean lips of Isaiah as an obstacle . . . does not think it impossible to pitch his tent in what is at best our poor and insignificant and stammering talk about God."[30]

There have been those who have charged Barth with an inadequate or one-sided theology of Incarnation. Trevor Hart recalls how, in 1948, John Baillie charged Barth with a practical (if not a theoretical) Nestorianism,[31] that is, a separation of Jesus (the man from Nazareth whom the searchers for the historical Jesus had futilely tried to exhume), from the divine Word that is the focus of faith. Baillie acknowledges that Barth was probably reacting against the failure of the nineteenth-century quest for the Jesus of history in insisting that faith could not then, in the New Testament, nor now in our age, be based upon the results of historical research.

In Baillie's judgment, Barth showed a shocking disregard for the "actual concrete manifestation" of Jesus, and no interest in any assessment by historians and textual critics about what Jesus was "really like."[32] To show such disregard for the historical presentation of Jesus in the Gospels, said Baillie, is to risk an uncarnate Word, a Word that does not really become flesh. This damages the logic of incarnation.[33]

What Baillie missed was not only Barth's real concern with history but also Paul's influence upon Barth. If Barth is nonchalant about the movements of the "historical Jesus," he is disinterested in much the same way that Paul was unconcerned about the "historical Jesus." For Paul and for Barth, the cross and resurrection of the historical Jesus so thoroughly shattered the presumed world, that too much interest in that shattered world's history and to Jesus' movements in it seemed inappropriate, a failure to appropriate the radical effects of the Cross and Resurrection upon history.

As a teacher of theology, Barth always had his students begin by reading Feuerbach. Barth thought that Feuerbach's accusation—talk about God is, in the end, only talk about humanity—was an accurate judgment upon the theology of the nineteenth century. Any theology that attempted to begin with history stayed fixed in history, thus capitulating to Feuerbach's charge. Theological statements ought to be about God, not some aspect of human experience and consciousness about God. Christian theology is always a response to the revelation of God, not a source for our thoughts about God.

In saying this, as Trevor Hart carefully notes, Barth is not saying that God is not present with us in creation but rather saying something about the peculiar way that God is present. Barth believes that God is effusively, luxuriantly present to us, through the work of the Holy Spirit, as a gift of God's grace. But God is present as the God-Man Jesus, so much so that we are not free to point to anything else in all creation as if that were revelation (pantheism). Hart quotes Barth:

> Revelation and it alone really and finally separated God and man by bringing them together. For by bringing them together it informs man about God and about himself, . . . it tells him that this God (no other) is free for this man (no other). . . . The man who listens here, sees himself standing at the boundary where all is at an end. . . . The revelation that crosses this boundary, and the togetherness of God and man which takes place in revelation in spite of this boundary, make the boundary visible to him in an unprecedented way.[34]

God is really present with us in history, but God is present distinctively as the Christ. God elects to be among us as fully human and fully divine.[35] Revelation is revelation because God elects it to be so. If God is present to us in revelation, it is "not a condition (*ein Zustand*), not an opening through which any Tom, Dick or Harry may look into heaven, but a happening (*ein Geschehen*)."[36] God is not available to us through some general human ability to comprehend, but remains both the free subject and the free object of our knowing. We know, Barth asserts, only indirectly, incarnationally, as an event that is both veiled and unveiled.[37]

Gustaf Wingren complained that "Barth has a tendency to shift the emphasis in the Gospel of Christ from the death and resurrection to the Incarnation, the birth, the miracle of Christmas. When the death and resurrection stand in the center—as they do in all four Gospels and in the rest of the New Testament—the Gospel has the character of struggle. There is a kingdom of evil, which must be destroyed, and Christ came in order to destroy it. . . . Barth's propensity for concentrating attention on the miracle of Christmas depends on the central position given to the unqualified concept of 'revelation.'"[38] When Barth does this, Wingren says, "God's appearance in human form becomes the center of the Gospel, and the primary function of faith is to apprehend this appearance of God in human form. Faith apprehends God and requires knowledge of him—a knowledge which man does not previously possess. This dominant position of the problem of knowledge and Barth's theology here is in his emphasis on the Incarnation as such over the death and resurrection."[39] In a stinging critique of Barth's stress upon the problem of the lack of a point of contact between humanity and God, Wingren says, "Man without means of contact with God is not the kind of man described in the biblical writings. This man without means of contact with God is the modern, atheist man for whom the question of knowledge is the one essential question whenever the conception of God is discussed."[40]

I can see the force of Wingren's criticism of Barth because I know the theological danger of making Christmas more important than Good Friday and Easter, of making Incarnation more important than cross and resurrection. In short, I know the theological dangers of life in the contemporary mainline Protestant Church. Yet I would defend Barth to Wingren by noting that Barth is so focused on the problem of knowledge of God and how that knowledge is given in the eternal Word made flesh, that he quite naturally tends to stress (overstress?) Incarnation. This stress seems rather "homiletical" of Barth, a theologian for whom issues of knowledge, communication, and proclamation tend to be central, whereas problems of redemption, atonement, and reconciliation are considered accomplished, finished, and completed in the work of cross and resurrection.

Barth's stress on knowledge rather than sin is a curious counter-tendency to much of the theology of the twentieth century, so concerned have we been with evil. It must also be admitted that Barth's is a counter-tendency to the New Testament itself. Wingren points to the "struggle" that characterizes the Gospel accounts of Jesus' work, the struggle that characterizes the story of cross and resurrection, and the absence of this struggle in Barth. Barth's theology does have about it a sort of serenity based upon Barth's supreme confidence that the struggle is over due to the work of God in the cross and resurrection of Christ. It seems to me that Barth is being heavily influenced by the Gospel of John, and its stress on belief, on seeing and understanding (though, of course, John has no "Virgin Birth" of Jesus). The Gospel of John is fascinated by the incomprehension of nearly everyone around the Christ and also by the radical nearness of the One who attended wedding parties, funerals, and so patiently, and rather redundantly, talked to his disciples. Barth is simply overwhelmed with the fact of revelation, that this God has made himself known in Incarnation, that the Word has dwelt among us, full of grace and truth, and that we have beheld the glory of the Word as the only begotten of the Father.

Barth's theology makes the Incarnation, *die Fleischwerdung des Wortes*, one of its most persistent themes. It is especially the element of human passivity in this event that is important to Barth's theology. The birth in Bethlehem implies that God "makes room for himself among us." God enters in among us without our work. The Incarnation is a miracle that signifies God's determination to be with us (*CD*, I, 2, pg. 209).

Furthermore, this incarnational "knowledge," as Barth speaks of knowledge, is an active, engaging event that embraces both personal and cognitive, subjective and objective elements. The modern world tended to have a fixed, inert view of knowledge. Knowledge is what we get when we do empirical research on the fixed stuff of the world and thereby uncover the irrefutable "facts." Barth comes to a much more lively view of knowledge by basing his view of knowledge upon scripture's use of the term (which he explicates in *CD*, IV, 3, pp. 183-85). Barth points out that the Bible has a considerably involved notion of what it means "to know" God. Theology must work, not from any cool, dispassionate standpoint but rather from intense self-involvement. In his Trinitarian thought, Barth always links knowledge of God and love of God, similar to the way they are linked in Calvin (*CD*, I, 1, pg. 480). (Plato had taught that there is a kind of erotic quality to true knowledge; we can know something well only when we are willing to fall in love with the object of our knowledge. Barth speaks of knowledge as if it were a kind of coitus.) Barth's dynamic, gifted view of knowledge is behind his statements that link theology to prayer: "Theological work is surely inconceivable and impossible at any time without prayer" (*CD*, IV, 3, pg. 882).[41] Prayer, as conversation with God, a matter of God's speaking and our listening, is the primary mechanism of revelation; therefore, it is the primary method of knowing. Prayer is the peculiar way that Christians think.

> In the act of the knowledge of God, as in any other cognitive act, we are definitely active as the receivers of images and creators of counter-images. Yet while this is true, it must definitely be contested that our receiving and creating owes its truth to any capacity of our own to be truly recipients and creators in relation to God. It is indeed our own viewing and conceiving. But we ourselves have no capacity for fellowship with God. . . . He is far from us and foreign to us except as he has of himself ordained and created fellowship between himself and us—and this does not happen in the actualizing of our capacity, but in the miracle of his good-pleasure.[42]

"In many and various ways God spoke of old to our fathers by the prophets; but in these last days he has spoken to us by a Son" (Heb. 1:1-2 RSV).

Knowledge and Obedience

Barth teaches that knowledge of God requires not just assent, acknowledgment from the recipient, but also obedience. ("Disobedience" means literally, failure to listen, *obedire*, Latin, "to listen.") It is homiletically significant that Barth teaches that all theological understanding is a form of vocation, a summons, not simply to assent but also to obedience. "Knowledge of God is obedience to God. Observe that we do not say that knowledge of God may also be obedience, or that of necessity it has obedience attached to it, or that it is followed by obedience. No, knowledge of God as knowledge of faith is in itself and of essential necessity obedience. It is an act of human decision corresponding to the act of divine decision; corresponding to the act of grace, in which faith is grounded and continually grounded again in God."[43]

Barth has been often accused of so stressing the miraculous divine giftedness of revelation that he leaves no room for human response to that gift. But Hart reminds us that the self-objectification of God for our sakes in the Incarnation "is not the terminus but only the start-ing point and the vital means for God's self-disclosure to his creatures. In order for this same human form to become transparent with respect to God's own being there must be a corre-sponding reception, hearing and response within the human sphere."[44] Faith and obedience are linked, and both are gifts bestowed by God in the event of revelation itself. Here too, though, in dealing with both faith and responsive obedience we are dealing not with a per-manently bestowed condition of receptivity and response, but with a capacity created fresh and new in the happening of divine self-giving. God, through the creative agency of the Spirit, draws us into communion, and in doing so lifts us up beyond the limits of our own natural capacity into the self-transcending circle of the knowledge of God. Faith is therefore not some capacity that we bring to the divine-human conversation, through which we meet and respond to God's revelation; faith is itself a gift that enables us to hear what is being said by God in Christ and to see what is being shown.[45]

"God has turned to us," Barth writes, "in such a way that we can answer only with faith. We may not give this answer, but when we do it is an answer to God, an answer to this con-fidential turning and address of his. The address is not an expression of faith. Faith, if it is faith, finds its generative basis in it."[46] Thus the proper basis of Christian talk about God, of knowledge of God, is precisely this unexpected and undeserved incarnational address of God: God's own proclamation to humanity, God's speaking of the divine Word. And the proper form of all theological endeavor is response. Christian preachers, says Barth, dare to speak about God. But they can do so only on the presupposition that God has spoken first, that God has addressed human beings, has addressed them as human subjects, and that God's address compels them also to speak. Otherwise their speech would be the ultimate presumption.

What power Barth ascribes to the Word:

> Gospel and Law as the concrete content of God's Word imply always a seizure of man. No matter what God's Word says to man *in concretissimo*, it always tells him that he is not his own but God's. If in the light of its origin in revelation, in Jesus Christ, we understand the Word of God as the epitome of God's grace, grace means simply that man is no longer left to himself but is given into the hand of God. . . . If a man knew nothing of this power that both sustains and stimulates, both protects and punishes, both pacifies and disturbs, if he merely heard about it without knowing it as a power, he would only give evidence that he knew nothing of the Word of God. We are acquainted with the Word of God to the degree that we are acquainted with this power. We speak of God's Word when we speak in recollection and expectation of this power, and when we do so in such a way that we realize that this power of the Word of God is not one power among others, not even among other divine powers, but the one unique divine power which comes home to us, to which we are referred, in face of which we stand in decision between the obedience we owe it and the unfath-omable inconceivability of disobedience, and consequently in the decision between bliss and perdition. . . . Where God has once spoken and is heard, i.e., in the Church, there is no escaping this power, no getting past it, no acknowledgment of divine pow-ers that are not summed up in this power, that are not related to the manner of this power and active in its mode.[47]

And the promise is that when we preachers simply stand up and obey, dare to speak what we have been given, then God makes our words God's own. Barth says, "When we are obedient . . . we have the promise that God Himself will acknowledge our obedience

. . . and this means that He will confer upon our viewing, conceiving and speaking His veracity."[48]

As George Hunsinger has demonstrated, Barth's theology is thoroughly Chalcedonian, a constant demonstration of the theological significance of the hypostatic union of human and divine natures in the Incarnate Word. Within the fully human act of preaching lies a text of scripture, but even the text is not the ultimate referent for our sermons. These words of preaching or scripture point to the Word, that event and person who is Jesus Christ. In preaching we reverse the order in which the Word came to us. Whereas the Incarnate Christ gave rise to the word of scripture, which in turn fuels and substantiates the preaching of the church, in preaching we move in a closed circle from our words in the sermon to their words in scripture, to God's Word in Christ.

Hart says that each of the three forms of divine communication has a human counterpart: the humanly told story of Jesus, the texts of scripture, and the human words of the preacher. Yet even as these acts of communication reveal, each also conceals. Nothing within any of these human forms themselves compels our faith or makes God obvious to our perception. As every preacher knows, it is quite possible to hear the words of a sermon and to hear nothing of God, just as it was possible for many to encounter Jesus and not to confess, "You are the Messiah, the Son of God." In order for the words of scripture, the words of a sermon, or even the Incarnate Word to speak, there must be some activity of God that enables them to be instruments, agents of God's self-revelation. Nothing else but miraculous divine intervention can give us the ears to hear and the eyes to see. No human capacity can make this occur. Just as in the Incarnation, Jesus is fully human and fully divine, so the words of the preacher, while never ceasing to be fully human, are used by God, commandeered for God's speaking.

Barth's three forms of revelation and proclamation are distinctive. Each has its own essential function. True, in the Incarnate Word, God speaks distinctively and directly as the reality of God himself in a way that neither scripture nor preaching speaks. The words of preaching and scripture bear witness to that reality of the Word, but they are, in themselves, not the Word. Trevor Hart notes that the Fathers spoke of Jesus' humanity as "anhypostatic," having had no prior existence apart from the Incarnation as Son of God.[49] Jesus is, and always has been, and always is again, the Word, fully human and fully divine.

Yet when it comes to scripture and preaching, as one of the three forms of divine self-disclosure, we have human phenomena that have independent existence prior to the Word. The Word graciously intrudes into, commandeers these realities in the event of revelation. Their identities, as distinctive realities, do not change, but the Word has moved in among them (John 1) not permanently, but temporarily, making these communicative phenomena—scripture and preaching—mean more than they could mean without the incarnating Word.[50] On those gracious, surprisingly frequent moments when this union occurs, scripture and preaching resemble John the Baptist, who points away from himself toward the Incarnate, crucified Word, witness to a reality that would otherwise be hidden without this divine infusion, this inspiration of our human forms. Preaching and scripture function as revelation, but they are not, in themselves, revelation. Jesus Christ, the Word, as fully human and fully divine, is revelation that enables our human means to be revealers.

Yet when we focus not so much on their human aspects but their divine activity, all three forms of Barthian revelation really do function as God's own self-disclosure to humanity. Whether it happens through encounter with the body and blood of the Incarnate Word, through the Bible, or through preaching, this is truly, engagingly the real revelation of God. True, scripture and preaching become the Word of God through the use by them of the Incarnate Word; still, all three are aspects of God's gracious, miraculous willingness to come to us through these three.

The church has a constant struggle to be true to the Chalcedonian character of God in Christ—fully human, fully divine. The inadequacies and frailties of the preacher seem greater than the disorder and fallibilities of the biblical text with which the preacher works. Docetism (from the Greek "to appear," "to seem") can be a temptation in regard to our dealings with the second form of revelation—scripture—as it seems somehow more eternal, fixed, authoritative, and sacred than any words we preachers can say. Who can watch the average preacher at work and think that in this preacher's words we have an exclusively divine phenomenon that only appears to be through a human agent? All talk of our preaching being God's appointed means of self-disclosure seems rather silly when one considers the average Sunday sermon. But no, Barth's Chalcedonian theology of the Incarnation affirms that scripture is not only divine but also human and that our preaching is not only human but also divine.

On the other hand, there may be the fear that, if we acknowledge the humanity of preaching—its fumbling, mundane quality—we will reduce preaching to "nothing but" human words that are too low ever to reach the Word. This tempts us toward a docetic view of preaching, tempted to make exaggerated claims for preaching to match some of biblical literalism's exaggerated claims for scripture, elevating preaching as an exclusively divine work untouched by human judgments, human errors, and human hearing. But no, as Barth says, "Fallible men speak the Word of God in fallible human words."[51]

In my experience, this tendency to neglect the human, fallible side of preaching is less pronounced in the mainline Protestant Church than the tendency to undervalue preaching as less than revealing and less divinely empowered in comparison with scripture. Barth makes the unashamed claim (with Bullinger in the Second Helvetic Confession) that the preaching of the Word of God is nothing less than the Word of God. We preachers have good reason both to tremble and to take heart from the use of that little word *is*. In preaching we have nothing less than "God's own proclamation."[52]

Barth not only asserts that God has elected to use the words of scripture as God's Word but also in a similar way elects the words of preaching. Both preaching and scripture, by the grace of God, really do witness to that revelatory reality who is Jesus the Christ, the Word. Thus preaching is a demonstration of the Incarnation, of the Chalcedonian affirmation that Christ comes to us as fully human and fully divine. There is no mystical fusion in which preaching is supernaturally lifted out of the realm of the human, nor is there a radical dissociation of preaching from the actual voice of God.[53]

Miraculous Trinitarian Preaching

In a pointed statement in *Romans*, Barth writes, "He who says 'God' says 'Miracle.' "[54] This is the best summary both of Barth's understanding of God and of Barth's epistemology. God can only be spoken of, really, by God. In fact, this is the miracle of the Incarnation to which Christianity witnesses: through Jesus Christ, God speaks about Godself. Otherwise, God is the Wholly Other, the eternal one who is in complete contradiction to all things in time, including our time-bound attempts to know and to speak of God.

Though Barth's stress upon the miraculous, gifted quality of Christian communication may seem to some preachers a shaky foundation upon which to build a sermon, it takes off the preacher's shoulders the burden of finding the right words, the right technique, and the right form in order that a sermon "works." It also suggests that some of our sermonic "failures" are due to God and not to us! Preaching is, for Barth, something that God does, a gift. A gift that cannot be withheld is not a gift. It is not our job to make preaching "effective" or "relevant." That task belongs to the Holy Spirit. Jesus Christ is not only the proclaimed but also the Proclaimer, not only the object of revelation but also the Revealer.

While theology must retain its dialectical character, it is able to proceed with confidence toward speech about God because God has, through the three forms of revelation, proceeded toward humanity. While revelation is always uncontainable, uncontrollable "event," a "miracle of God," something "hidden" and "veiled," it is nevertheless given, disclosed, and unveiled in objectivity and specificity.

Barth is utterly consistent in his insistence that, in this matter of communication between us and God, the movement is always from God and not from us. We do not initiate or continue the divine-human conversation. God's freedom and mystery are set over against human language. This was Barth's bombshell in *Romans,* but is a recurring theme that is accentuated in the last volumes of the *Church Dogmatics* in various ways. Our knowledge of God is nothing short of miraculous:

> Nothing could be further from our minds than to attribute to the human creature as such a capacity to know God and the one Word of God, or to produce true words corresponding to this knowledge. Even in the sphere of the Bible and the Church there can be no question of any such capacity. If there are true words of God, it is all miraculous.[55]

One of the ways in which Barth's thought was not Orthodoxy *redivivus* was in his placement of his discussion of the Trinity, placing it at the beginning of his theology, giving us the most developed treatise on the Trinity since the Reformation, making the Trinity and its work the essential source for all theological discourse:

> Treatment of the doctrine of the Trinity belongs to dogmatic prolegomena. Its significance, as a presupposition of the basic principles that must be set forth in dogmatics proper. . . . [The Trinity] does not come out well in the traditional position assigned to it. (Usually at the end of the specific doctrine of God.) Again, it does not have any natural force, or at most only decorative force, after the manner of Schleiermacher it is put right at the end of dogmatics.[56]

Note how Barth bases everything he says about God first upon the Trinity, which is not only the content of God but also the means by which we know God.

It was Barth's rediscovery of the Trinity that enabled him both to affirm the transcendence and the immanence of God. God, in the Trinity, is both indissoluble subject and object of revelation. When Christians say, "Word," they mean Jesus Christ, the unique self-revelation of God. He is the living Word, the particular, concrete revelation of a triune God. This insight, said Barth, caused him to "take all that had been said before and to think it through once more and freshly and to articulate it anew as a theology of the grace of God in Jesus Christ."[57]

Revelation is revelation of the very nature of God as (1) a God who speaks, (2) a historical reality of Jesus Christ, and (3) One who is actually heard by humanity. God has come to us as Father, Son, and Holy Spirit. These three are one. As early as his *Göttingen Dogmatics* (1924), Barth spoke of the threefold form of God's self-proclamation. The biblical witness is a testimony to God as Revealer, Revelation, and Revealedness. These are the three modes of being of God. The Doctrine of the Trinity rightly stands at the beginning of anything that we are able to say about God and is God's self-giving of the mysterious inner nature of God.

Against Schleiermacher's attempt to make human subjectivity into humanity's way up to God, Barth countered that there is simply no way from human, subjective, autonomous knowledge to God. "The closed circle of man's self-understanding must be broken from without and made accessible to something outside itself." Indeed, Barth holds that the criterion of objectivity is most important for a proper theology (*CD*, I, 2, pg. 7). It is on the basis of this strong emphasis on the objectivity of revelation over against humanity's subjective notions about God that Barth is often interpreted as having a "realistic epistemology."[58] While that assessment is too simple for the dynamic, subject-object interaction that characterizes Barth's idealistic epistemology, Barth is a "realist" in his stress that revelation is something outside us, something against our subjectivity rather than an extension of our subjectivity. Theology is that sort of thinking in which the knower is decisively changed by the object of knowing, in which the object of our knowing (the God named Trinity) speaks to us, reaches out to us, becomes objective to us because of love.[59]

So when Barth discusses Creation, he does so as to make clear that the creature is created to be in conversation with the Trinity. "As God in Himself is neither deaf nor dumb but speaks and hears His Word from all eternity, so outside His eternity He does not will to be without hearing or echo, that is, without the ears and voices of the creature."[60] This is all speculation, for who knows what took place at the creation of the world? Yet we do know what takes place in Jesus Christ and, out of that speaking and hearing, we have a clue to what God was like from the beginning of the world—a creative, communicative, resourceful Trinity. At Creation, in what Barth calls a "divine soliloquy,"[61] we find that God is sound before God is light, speech before sight. Did not God say, "Let us . . . ," even before there was light?[62]

Having stressed that God is so close to us as Trinity, Barth immediately asserts that when we say that God is "transcendent," we ought not to mean that in the sense of being an abstraction who is at a distance from our powers of conception. On the contrary, when God has come near to us in Jesus Christ, we discover that it is the majestic freedom of this God to "condescend" to the creature, to show unfathomable grace to the creature. And in this peculiar nearness, this condescension is the chief proof of God's distance and sovereign transcendence. Barth said that God's "transcendence stands out as the presupposition of His condescension fulfilled in the saving turning . . . to that which is not an equality with Himself."[63]

Barth talks about these three modes of revelation in ways that are at times maddeningly dialectical, but always dynamic, eventful, and unified. They are distinct realities; we preachers must not confuse our words with the words of the prophets and apostles whose words are the source for our preaching. Just as we are not free, in Trinitarian faith, to detach, prioritize, or elevate one person of the Trinity from the others, so we are not free to detach or to elevate one mode of God's proclamation over another.[64] A sermon cannot be a simple recitation of the words of scripture; the sermon is the scriptural word made manifest, contemporary, and present. Scripture is not to be equated with the incarnate manifestation of God who is Jesus the Christ. Nor can preaching be demeaned as less trustworthy or significant than scripture simply because people like us, in a time like ours—rather than the apostles in their time and place—are doing the preaching.

The Extravagance of Trinitarian Faith[65]

Matthew 28:16-20

"*Good teachers are big talkers,*" *he said to me. I found this an interesting observation coming from a man who had spent his entire life preparing teachers to teach in elementary schools.*

"*I haven't worked this out in any exact way, but from my observations, good teachers are big talkers. They are people who are effusive, ubiquitous in their interaction with people. They are everywhere, all the time, talking, interacting with the children.*"

And I thought about some of the great teachers I have known, particularly teachers of young children. It seemed to me that he was right. Good teachers are good talkers. I am thinking now of a woman who taught one of my children. When you visited her classroom, you saw a person who somehow managed to be everywhere, all the time, moving, interacting with the children, talking to them, full of opinions about their work, full of encouraging words and constant conversation. Good teachers' constant reaching toward their students evokes the best from their students. There does seem to be a sort of effusiveness and loquaciousness about good teachers.

Scripture says that our God is a big talker—effusive, loquacious. Think of the Bible as a long story of God's attempted conversation with humanity. We keep rejecting the words of God, turning in another direction, worshiping false Gods, and attempting to hide, evade, or end the conversation. But God keeps coming back to us. God comes to us in the lives of the patriarchs, in the words of the prophets, in the gift of God's law. Then, stopping at nothing, God comes to us as the Son, comes to us as Jesus. Then—even when we killed his only Son, hung him on a cruel cross, thinking that that had probably ended relations between us and God—in three days, God came back to us as the Risen Christ, came back and resumed the conversation with the same disciples who had forsaken him. God keeps coming back, again, and even again.

We are now, on this Sunday, ending the church's celebration of the Great Fifty Days of Easter—God's supreme coming back to talk to us as the resurrected Christ. But we end Easter in the confidence that we do not thereby end God's continuing conversation with us. What we thought, with the Cross, was the end was, with the Resurrection, the beginning because it is of the nature of this God to be loquacious, effusive.

Our appointed scripture comes from the very end of Matthew's Gospel, when the Risen Christ tells his followers to "bed down here, get some real estate, build a church for me with accessible parking, and hold on tight to the experience that we have shared together." No! Christ resurrected and victorious tells his people to "Go!" "Get out of here and go into the whole world and make disciples. Tell them, baptize them, teach them in the name of the Father, the Son, and the Holy Spirit."

The same God who had come to them now tells them to go to others. The same resourceful, creative, talkative God who had spoken to them, in life and in death, now commands them to speak to others about him. To say that they are to do this in the name of the "Father, Son, and Holy Spirit" is not just a pious tag added on to Christ's mission mandate. It is the source of that mandate. It is the nature of this God whom we call Father, Son, and Holy Spirit—the Trinity—always to reach, always to go, to address, to summon, and to speak; and those who would be in the world (us) in his name must also be on the go, always talking as we go. Wasn't that what we heard the angel say to the women at the tomb, "Go! Tell!"? Act toward the world the same way that God as Father, Son, and Holy Spirit has acted toward you!

Martin Luther, in speaking of the real presence of Christ in the Lord's Supper, spoke of God's "ubiquity." Our God is ubiquitous, everywhere, and at all times present, though peculiarly, particularly, and especially present in the Eucharist, the Lord's Supper. Our God is not only loving, caring, and acting, our God is ubiquitous.

There is a kind of effusiveness about God, an effervescent, overflowing quality.

Augustine spoke of this in a passage in his great book The City of God. Augustine spoke of the "plentitude" of God. As evidence of this, Augustine mentioned the effusiveness whereby God created all of the flowers in the world. We might have stopped creating flowers after one or two beautiful specimens. But God didn't stop. God kept creating multitudes of flowers, all in different shapes and colors and kinds. Not only are they beautiful, Augustine notes, but see the glory in how they will turn their heads toward the sun, bending toward the light. We might have been content, as humans, with just a few flowers and their splendor. God didn't stop with a few, because God is effusive, overflowing with love and creativity. God is ubiquitous, plenitudinous.

I feel sorry for Fundamentalist Christians, who earnestly attempt to reduce this effusive, overflowing God to five or six "fundamentals." It is tough to get this God down to a list of five or six of anything, because our God is effusive.

I sorrow for the self-described "Progressive Christian" scholar who recently dumbed things down to "the essence of Christianity"—five or six vague platitudes that allegedly sum up Jesus. This isn't progress but regress to a "god" who is considerably more flat and dull than the Trinity.

So, as Christians, we don't have one Gospel, we have four. Four Gospels! One might have thought that we could have stopped with one, saying to ourselves, "Matthew fairly well got it right, let's all go with Matthew. Why confuse the children with all these Gospels? Let's go just with Matthew." But no, an effusive, ubiquitous, plenitudinous, and overflowing God requires at least four Gospels to talk about God and Christ.

And one way the church has historically attempted to talk about God's plenitudinousness and effusiveness, God's ubiquitousness and loquaciousness, is through the Trinity. Don't think of the Trinity as some incomprehensible doctrine of the church, though God's plenitudinousness is beyond our comprehension. Think of the Trinity as our earnest, though groping attempt, somehow to put into words what has been revealed to us of the overflowing love of God.

Sometimes you hear people say, "Well, you are a Christian, and I am not, but the important thing is that we all try to believe and serve God. Right?"

Wrong.

Christians are not those who believe in some amorphous, vague concept of "god."

Christians are those who believe that God is best addressed as Trinity. God is not simply a monad, "God." God is the Father, God is the Son, and God is the Holy Spirit. And these three are One.

We might have been able to say, at some early point, "Well, we all believe in the same God." However, we believe that God came to us as Jesus. We believe that Jesus is God in the flesh, the fullness of God. The one from Nazareth was as much of God as we ever hope to see. This crucified Jew was raised from the dead, which was God's way of saying, "You wonder what I'm like? Here's what I'm like—crucified, suffering, forgiving love."

And after experiencing that, all of our notions of God had to go back to the drawing table. If Jesus Christ is God, then we have a challenge in talking about God. After Easter, it just wouldn't do to talk about God as anything less than Trinity. In the Trinity Christians attempt to account for the complex biblical testimony that (1) God is always completely transcendent and omnipotent; and yet (2) Jesus, who died horribly and was raised miraculously by God, was somehow fully God; and that (3) the Spirit, poured out on the church, is also God; and yet (4) there is only one God.

When God came to us as the Son, Incarnate in Jesus, God did not say, "Call me by my proper name, Trinity." God didn't have to. We did. That is, on the basis of our experience of God as complex, ubiquitous, and overflowing with love as the Father, the Son, and the Holy Spirit, we just naturally started speaking of God as Trinity. We experienced one God in these three ways. Though it was the same God whom we had experienced as the great Creator of the world, the Father of Israel, now we also experienced that God in the flesh as the Son, as well as the power flowing from God, the Holy Spirit.

Augustine, one of the greatest minds of the Western World, put his head to thinking about the Trinity. Augustine, a master of words, took fifteen books to talk about the Trinity, fifteen books that took him over a decade to write. Augustine's On the Trinity continues to be helpful in thinking through that which is difficult to think about, namely the nature of God, who comes to us as Father, Son, and Holy Spirit.

Early on in his massive treatise, Augustine had seven statements about God: The Father is God. The Son is God. The Holy Spirit is God. The Son is not the Father. The Father is not the Holy Spirit. The Holy Spirit is not the Son. And then, after these six statements, Augustine adds one more. There is only one God.

This is the thinking that is tough to get into our brains. We have experienced three rather distinctive modes of the one God's presence. God is the Father, the Creator of us and the world. God is the Son, the One who comes to us as Jesus, living, suffering, dying, and rising among us. We experience God as Holy Spirit, that power that has intruded into our world as the near presence and power of God.

And yet, we are not tritheists, we don't believe in three gods. We know, with Israel, that there is only one God. These names—Father, Son, and Holy Spirit—are not three names for the same thing. They are the three names that describe the nature of one God.

In Book 7 of On the Trinity, Augustine tried to think of an analogy of God and he looked within himself. In looking within himself, Augustine noted how the human soul itself is Triadic, Trinitarian. There is a kind of triune way in which we experience ourselves, as if the Trinity is built right into the structure of our reality.

We say, for instance, "I love myself." According to Jesus, it is all right to love ourselves, for we are to love our neighbors as we love ourselves. So we can say, "I love myself." When we do so, we are speaking in a triune way. When I say, "I love myself," there is a lover that is doing the loving, namely me loving myself. There is also the beloved, the object of my love, which is also me; then, there is the loving, the act and energy of the lover upon the beloved. So even with the one there is the lover, the beloved, and the loving.

Thus, within our own hearts, in our own experience, Augustine said that there is the *vestigia trinitatis*, vestiges of the Trinity. Reality is Trinitarian—complex, revealing, and communicative.

One of the church fathers said, "When we talk about the Trinity, we must forget how *to count." He was simply recognizing that, at first glance, the Trinity is a mathematical impossibility. After all, how can one equal three?*

We must throw away our math, not because the Trinity is a logical muddle, but because we need a different kind of logic. It took Augustine fifteen books to try to think about it, because God is God and we are not. Because God comes to us with a complexity and effusiveness, a ubiquity and a plenitude that boggle our modest minds; no wonder we have trouble thinking about God. No wonder the Trinity boggles our imaginations. And that is probably the right way to put it. The problem with the Trinity is not that this is a bunch of nonsense, but that God is God, in God's particularly glorious, effusive way, and we are creatures, the recipients of a love so deep we cannot find words to describe it. When we think about the Trinity, we must forget how to count.

Watch a newborn infant coo and smile, and reach toward you and interact with you, and you may rightly conclude that we ourselves are Trinitarian in being—we have been created to reach out, to speak, to be in relationship, and we are restless until we make contact.

There is a modern word for talking about this dynamic structure—synergy. Within the Trinity, there is constant movement, interaction, as the Father gives to the Son, the Son is constantly returning praise and glory to the Father, the Father and the Son give to the Holy Spirit, and the Holy Spirit constantly draws everything back to the Father and the Son. There is the Beloved, the Lover, and the Love.

So in today's scripture the last thing that the Risen Christ commands us to do is to go out of here and live in the world as he—Father, Son, and Holy Spirit—is in the world. A church that doesn't reach out, that is not going and telling, is not the church formed by the effusive Trinity. A Christian who doesn't want, in love, to go out and tell somebody is not one who is formed by the relentlessly reaching out and drawing in that is the Trinity.

Thank God that our relationship with God is not dependent upon our talking to, listening to, reaching toward, and loving God. The Trinity refuses to leave it all up to us. In Jesus Christ, through the promptings of the Holy Spirit, in the wonder of a good Creation, the Trinity keeps reaching toward us, keeps leaving hints for us, indications that we live every moment of our lives upheld by a living, resourceful, loquacious God.

As one of you put it to me, when you were in the midst of a terrible, life-threatening illness and I asked you if you were afraid of death, you said to me, "Not really. When I think of all the trouble that God has gone to for me, all the tricks that God has used to grab me, all the traps that God has lain to catch me, I can't believe God will let a little thing like death stump him."

That struck me as a very Trinitarian sort of observation, the fruit of a life lived in the light of the God who is the talkative Father, Son, and Holy Spirit.

Preaching, scripture, and the Incarnate Christ work together in Barth as a perichoretic event. (He discusses perichoresis in *CD*, I, 1, pp. 45f.) Father, Son, and Holy Spirit interpenetrate one another in and with their hypostatic distinctions. "The Holy Spirit is the Spirit of Jesus Himself" (*CD*, IV, 2, pg. 325). Just as Barth refuses to ascribe any greater or lesser importance to any of the three manifestations of God in the Trinity, so Barth refuses to ascribe any greater or lesser value to any one mode of the three modes of proclamation. Can we live with such an exalted vision of preaching? We are more accustomed to thinking of preaching as subservient to the words of scripture, and scripture as subservient to the person of Christ. But Barth dares to claim that the proclamation of the church is a tri-unity (he prefers to speak of the Trinity as "triunity") in which the Word of God is present in each of three forms.

Can Barth really mean this?[66] Is my faltering preaching of the same order and on the same revelatory level as the writings of Paul? Are the words of Paul in scripture of equal significance to the presence of Christ in the church? Just as in the Trinity there is unity but also distinction, Trevor Hart says that we "need to draw a careful distinction between the humanity of the three forms and what we might legitimately term their divinity."[67] Hart would have us turn toward the Incarnation as a way of understanding proclamation as human and divine.

> The Doctrine of the Trinity is what basically distinguishes the Christian doctrine of God as Christian, and therefore what . . . distinguishes the Christian concept of revelation as Christian, in contrast to all the possible doctrines of God are concepts of Revelation. (*CD*, I, 1, pg. 301)

The Trinity is our concept of where and how God gives God's self to be known, experienced, recognized, acknowledged, and obeyed as God. What impresses me about the New Testament's rare, explicit reference to the Trinity in Matthew 28 is the Risen Christ's statement: "I am with you always." Is this to be taken as a promise or a threat? This is said to the disciples, those who best knew Jesus, who had been with him throughout his ministry and therefore knew firsthand what a threat a fully present Jesus was to their existence. Therefore, is it good news or bad to be told, by the Christ, in effect, "I only had a few years to harass you before I was killed, but now that I am raised I am with you always"?

David Ford and Rowan Williams both emphasize that for Barth, theology is a form of *nachdenken*, "reflection," about God in the light of the triune God's actual and quite successful self-giving to be thought and to be understood. Our lives in Christ are our reflections of his revealed glory, our response to God's self-presentation and address.[68]

In hearing, Barth says we have an inconceivable miracle of grace, in which, in hearing, the human being is reconciled, and reconstituted, by participation in the Word of God. God is knowable in and through the Trinity.

Through the Trinity, we break that old rhetorical dichotomy between the hearer and the speaker. We do not begin with the speaker—with the speaker's gifts or limitations. Nor do we begin, as so much of contemporary homiletics, with considerations of the hearer's gifts and limitations. In conceiving of communication in Trinitarian form, speaker and hearer are inseparably bound. This God not only speaks but listens. Barth stressed that the Trinity is not only God's being, that aspect of the Trinity that so interested the classical theologians, but the Trinity is also God's knowing. "He has seen to it that He is to be found by those who seek Him where He Himself has given Himself to be found" (*CD*, II, 1, pg. 197).[69]

The Word, the eternal Word, Jesus the Christ, is the foundation for any of our words, in scripture or in preaching, for speaking of either scripture or preaching as forms of the "Word of God." Nicholas Wolsterstorff says emphatically: "The speech of the preacher remains purely human speech. Barth makes the point emphatically, over and over: Scripture and contemporary proclamation as such are not the Word of God. . . . God speaks by way of a human being only if God is that human being—Jesus Christ. This is fundamental in Barth!"[70]

Nevertheless, to specific persons and on specific occasions, both scripture and preaching do actually become the instruments of God's speaking. The structure of the *Church*

Dogmatics shows that Barth views the Word as primary. (He begins with "Word of God," vol. 1, before moving to "Doctrine of God," vol. 2.) The Trinity is first known to us as a God who speaks. Torrence says that "central to the Doctrine of the Trinity, therefore, is the doctrine of the knowledge of God—not *our* knowledge of God, but rather that knowledge of God internal to the mutual indwelling of the Godhead. Thus our articulation of the Trinity stems from the church's acknowledgment of the self-articulation which derives from the divine self-knowledge—a divine self-disclosure which constitutes its life, its ethics and, indeed, its having any warrant whatsoever for the dubious and dangerous activity of theological discourse."[71] The Trinity is the content and the means, not only for what we know about God but also God's knowledge of Godself, since the Trinity represents that constant conversation that goes on in the heart of God.

Jesus told a parable about an unproductive fig tree (Luke 13:6-8). The servant asked, "Master, do you want me to cut down this fruitless fig tree? It has had long enough to bear fruit." But the master somewhat surprisingly replies, "No, let it alone *(aphetes)*. Dig around it and put some manure *(koprion)* on it and we'll see." This parable strikes me as a vivid overhearing of a conversation that occurs in the heart of the Trinity. On the one hand is the righteousness of the Father communicated to the Son ("cut it down"); on the other hand we have the intercession of the Son to the Father ("leave it alone," literally *aphetes*, "forgive it"). Theology might be defined by Barth as overhearing a conversation that occurs in the heart of the triune God.

Barth's long reflections on the Trinity seemed to some of his pastor readers to be far removed from the actual demands of preaching the gospel. One of Barth's students in Bonn in the 1930s, the great preacher Helmut Thielicke, complained of Barth's "otherworldliness." Though Thielicke later recalled that Barth was an engaging professor whose polemics "darted like tongues of fire from the precipitous towers of his theological system," the preacher in Thielicke refused to accept Barth's claim that the Word possesses a power of its own to create its own audience. From Thielicke's neo-orthodox Lutheran standpoint, Barth replaced the dialectic of law and gospel with a nearly magical concept of the Word that "robbed the Gospel of its concreteness and brought back the old heresy of docetism in a new and extreme form." Thielicke's charge of docetism reminds us, if we need reminding, that Barth has a most robust sense of the power of God to make our preaching God's Word. Pastor Thielicke also complained that Barth's almost exclusive focus on the theological, rather than the ethical aspects of the Christian faith, "left the human being with no theological guidance in life." Instead of developing the practical implications of his theological assertions, said Thielicke, Barth kept floating off into ever more "remote metaphysical spheres, expending his intellectual energy in speculation on the Holy Trinity and other 'heavenly' themes."[72]

But Barth's reflection on the Trinity is one of his means of accounting for God's constant and concrete communication with us, a means of resisting the tendency of theology to drift off into "heavenly themes." The Trinity will not allow us to think of God in terms of some supreme essence, some absolute. The Trinity is a phenomenon of communication and intimate relationship. Perichoresis stresses the fellowship within God's self—as Father, Son, and Holy Spirit and claims that such fellowship is built right into the grain of the universe.[73] This God is therefore the free Subject rather than a graspable object of our knowledge.[74] The amazing thing is that, though God is the self-sufficient One in the Trinity, free to live "from and by Himself,"[75] this God graciously reaches out to us:

This God has no need of us. This God is self-sufficient. This God knows perfect beatitude in Himself. He is not under any need or constraint. It takes place in an inconceivably free overflowing of His goodness if He determines to co-exist with a reality distinct from Himself. . . .[76]

Unlike the poor creature who does not have being within itself, for whom self-giving may be a threat to the integrity of the self, God is free to be for and with another. The complete self-giving of God is a kind of validation that God can be closer to creatures than we creatures can be with ourselves, or with one another.[77]

Luther and Calvin taught that subject and object are identical in faith. The later Barth demonstrated an unwillingness to grant much significance to our demonstrations and professions of faith. Barth is so impressed by the objective, given act of God in faith that he was unimpressed by our rather modest, subjective "yes" that characterizes what we call our "faith."[78] Barth taught that faith is merely "the subjective realization of an objective res." Faith "only finds what is already there both for the believing and the unbelieving man." Emil Brunner found Barth's objectification of faith to be counter to the concept of faith in the Reformers. Brunner noted that the Reformers stressed the place of faith in the triune formulation of 1 Corinthians 13, where hope and love are bound together in a unity with faith, all three having equal importance. Brunner charged that Barth had an intellectualized preoccupation with the object of faith that overwhelmed any other concern, particularly any concern for human response in faith. In Barth's hundreds of pages on the Trinity as the supreme *objectum fidei*, he seems unperturbed that neither Luther nor Calvin shared his subordinated view of human responsiveness to the work of the Trinity. He doesn't even discuss "faith" as having any special significance of its own until a rather brief discussion of faith toward the very end of the *Church Dogmatics*. Brunner charged that Barth had departed from the biblical testimony, and from Reformed dogmatic concerns as much as Schleiermacher (only in a different way), with all of Barth's Trinitarian speculation on God's inner being.[79]

Trinitarian epistemology has implications for our talk about God. When Christians talk about God, we are the inheritors of a tension between two tendencies within the history of Christian theology. There is frequent testimonial of encounters with God as being numinous in quality, quite mystical. God is ineffable, beyond our ways of knowing and understanding. Thus, there is within the faith a sense that God is beyond human understanding and therefore human description. We have difficulty applying our meager store of words to God, unless we have a great change of meaning in the words.

Gregory Nazianzus complained of the difficulty one has of conceiving of and thinking about the Trinity:

No sooner do I conceive of the One than I am illuminated by the splendour to the Three; no sooner do I distinguish them than I am carried back to the One. When I think of any One of the Three, I think of him as the whole. . . . I cannot grasp the greatness of that One so as to attribute a greater greatness to the rest. When I contemplate the Three together, I see but one torch, and cannot divide or measure out the undivided light.[80]

Again, Barth adores God as Revealer. Scripture is full of words about God; therefore, through the gift of these words we can meaningfully talk about God. This was the answer given by Neo-Thomism with its doctrine of the analogy of being. That is, words applied to God shift their meaning in accordance with intelligible analogies that human beings use for the being of God. Karl Barth was a great critic of the Thomistic analogy of being. (Many critics have found Barth himself to be incomprehensible and incoherent on this matter of the analogous use of language.[81])

We preachers need to note some of the debate about the proper use of and source for our analogies because preaching works so often through analogy. Barth stresses that our analogies are dangerous, since we are apt to move from conceptual analogies, from human experience, to God, whereas God would have us move the other way around, moving from the analogies that God gives us through faith to formation of and understanding of human experience (*CD*, I, 1, pg. 336). Barth is critical of the way Augustine used analogies from human experience (Trinity as memory, reason, and will, etc.) to talk about the Trinity, believing that Augustine utilized the wrong order of knowing.[82] Barth talks about the role of analogy in Christian epistemology under the general heading of "The Limits of the Knowledge of God," and under the more specific topic of "The Veracity of Man's Knowledge of God." He asserts a genuine possibility: "We cannot open our mouths, to speak about God without recourse to the promise that we shall seek the truth in the analogy of his truth itself" (*CD*, II, 1, pg. 231). We speak about God under the divine promise that God will give us truthful analogies that will enable us faithfully to speak of God the unspeakable.

Barth maintained that the correspondence between God and our language is established only by the grace of God, through faith, not by our natural reasoning ability. In speaking of God, we never can contain the truth of God, cannot capture or control the Creator. Yet our language does reflect the truth of God's true being, if we speak of God in what we genuinely know through faith in Jesus Christ, if we use that language that God has sanctified and chosen in becoming one with us in Jesus Christ. We don't have to make analogies out of our own experience and being because God is an analogy-making, analogy-giving Creator.

Among the fruitful places to look for Barth's thoughts on God talk is the *Church Dogmatics*, volume II, part 1, section 27, as well as Barth's *Humanity of God*.[83] Barth is really not interested in "religious language," indeed he is completely negative about the whole idea of "religion."[84] He asks the question in this way: "Where do we find the veracity in which we apply to God words which are inadequate to describe Him, as we all do in every point when we speak directly or indirectly about God? Does there exist a simple parity of content and meaning when we apply the same word to the creature on the one hand and to God's revelation and God on the other?"[85] There cannot be, as some of the Neo-Thomists call it, "Equivocity" because, when speaking about God says Barth, "There remains only what is generally meant by analogy, similarity, partial correspondence and agreement."[86]

Barth denies that we have the ability to speak of God positively—applying attributes such as "good," or "loving"—or even negatively—such as "incomprehensible," or "infinite." Human descriptions, be they positive or negative, cannot be applied to God unless God "bestows" or "gives" truth to them. Negative expressions for God are no closer to the truth about God than positive ones. In fact, Barth says that some of our crude anthropomorphisms may be more adequate than some of our negations (incomprehensible, inaccessible, unapproachable, etc.), which are abstract and vague. All human words are unreliable apart from God's grace in giving them truthfulness. Even our negative notions about God are still human notions and therefore woefully inadequate and misleading when applied to God unless God elects to give them adequacy.

And yet Barth firmly rejects agnosticism in our talk about God. He bases his thoughts on the limits of human knowledge, not on Kantian or Empiricist philosophical reflection concerning the limits of human thought, but rather on the peculiar nature of God's revelation to humanity. God reveals God's self as distant from humanity. And yet God permits our words to serve as designations for God. Human words apply to God simply by the grace of God, who gives our words their truthfulness when applied to God.

For Aquinas, human knowing proceeds from the creature to the Creator through the order of being as the Creator reaches to the creature. Barth, however, true to his interest in epistemology more than ontology, insists that the order of being must correspond to the order of knowing and signifying. We must attend to the peculiarity of the reality that is signified.[87]

All knowledge of God is derived from words applied to God by God. It is of the nature of the Trinity to be alive with conversation, overflowing, effusive conversation. Otherwise, we know not God, but some God-substitute, a mere idol, some inadequate human projection—from the paucity of our human experience—that we call "God." It is futile to keep trying to find a source for thought about God, not from God, but from ourselves. Barth can say this because Barth believes that our language originates with God. Language is God's invention, a phenomenon that exists at God's initiation, God's peculiar means of generativity and creativity. "And God said. . . ." God, by the unique nature of God's being, "owns" words about God. All our language is God's idea, the unique way in which this God has chosen to relate to the world. Genesis 1, followed by John 1, is Barth's biblical justification for these sorts of claims.[88]

Language and Election

Revelation for Barth is not only a function of his doctrine of the Incarnation, and not only related to his thought on the Trinity, but is also an exemplification of Barth's Doctrine of Election. Barth claims that God selects particular words and lays aside other words when God reveals to humanity the ways in which we must think about God.[89] Here Barth has a view of language that is quite similar to his view of the importance of God's Election. God's sovereign and gracious choice of Israel is paralleled with God's sovereign and gracious choice of such words as "Father," or "Lord," words that graciously, truthfully signify that reality who is "God."

According to Barth's Doctrine of Election, scripture teaches that when God chooses Jane Jones for some task, God's choice has nothing to do with the alleged virtues or appropriateness of Jane. Jane is a sinner and cannot be a vehicle for divine work on the basis of who she is or might aspire to be. However, God justifies Jane, sanctifies her, and grants her great power through Christ's resurrection. Jane is a witness to God, despite her human limitations, of the power of God to summon and to empower those whom God has summoned. In a similar way, God elects some of our human words to do the work of communication, which links epistemology to the Doctrine of Election.[90]

Revelation is always a dialectic of the unveiling of our incapacity to know God and at the same time the gift of the capacity to know God. The hiddenness of God denotes our distance from God, and yet, God's revelation enables us to know God, which means that revelation enables us, in seeing God, to see more clearly the distance of God. Just as God "adopts" women and men as witnesses, so God "adopts" words.[91]

Barth describes the election of words by God to be God's word as a form of divine vocation:

God's real revelation simply cannot be chosen by us and, as our own possibility, put beside another, and integrated with it into a system. God's real revelation is the possibility which we do not have to choose, but by which we must regard ourselves as chosen without having space or time to come to an arrangement with it within the sphere and according to the method of other possibilities. By treating it as if it does not do the choosing but is something to be chosen, not the unique but just one possibility, Christian natural theology very respectfully and in all humility recasts revelation into a new form of its own devising . . . making revelation into non-revelation. (CD, II, 1, pp. 139-40)

Election of language is not an utterly miraculous matter. In making a word like "father" communicate to us of the "Father," or a word from the law courts like "redemption" to communicate God's work on the cross of Jesus, God makes our words do what they cannot do by making them genuinely correspond to the divine being, but God "does not perform a violent miracle" (CD, II, 1, pg. 229). Nor does God "alienate" our words from their proper and original sense or usage. Nor does God endow them with "a purely fictional capacity," as if they did not enter into genuine correspondence but were surrounded by a haze of equivocation. On the contrary, when God gives our words this correspondence in the act of self-revelation, God does no more than give us words. The German word that Barth sometimes uses for this is *Aufhebung*, literally lifting our words up to make them mean what God means them to mean.

Barth discusses the word "father" as an analogy:

By the name "father" we do, of course, denote the natural human author of our existence. But our natural human father is not our Creator. He is not the lord of our existence, not even the lord of our life, let alone our death. When Scripture calls God our Father it adopts an analogy only to transcend it at once.

Hence we must not measure by natural human fatherhood what it means that God is our Father (v. 16). It is from God's fatherhood that our natural human fatherhood acquires any meaning and dignity it has (Eph. 3:15).

God our Father means God our Creator (cf. for this Deut. 32:6 and Is. 64:7). And it should be clear by now that it is specifically in Christ, as the Father of Jesus Christ, that God is called our Creator. That God is our Creator is not a general truth that we can know in advance or acquire on our own; it is the truth of revelation. Only as that which we know elsewhere as father-son relation is transcended by the Word of Christ, the Crucified and Risen, only as it is interpreted by this Word, which means, in this case, only as it acquires from this Word a meaning which it cannot have of itself, only in this way may we see what creation means. But in this way we can see. The Father of Jesus Christ who according to the witness of Scripture is revealed in Jesus His Servant has the qualities of a Lord of our existence. The witness to Him leads us to the place where the miracle of creation can be seen. It bears witness to the holy God who alone is God, the free God. (CD, I, 1, pg. 398)

God comes to us and takes our words like "father" and makes them mean something, gives them a truthfulness that they cannot have on their own, lifts up our language to make it God's language. Barth says, "When we are obedient . . . we have the promise that God Himself will acknowledge our obedience . . . and this means that He will confer upon our viewing, conceiving and speaking His veracity."[92] It can never be that our word for "father," can be analogously applied to God, as if we could thereby define God on the basis of our experiences of human fatherhood. There are too many problems with our conceptions of, and practice of, the word "father" to enable us to move from here to there with such a word. Rather, God's revelation of Godself as "Father" enlightens and defines all human notions of fatherhood. God restores our words to their proper and original sense and usage, and freely endows them with true and genuine reference.

> Concepts and words have no claim on him, that he shouldbe their object. He himself, however, has every—the best founded and most valid—claim on us and on all our views, concepts and words, that he should be their first and last and proper subject. Therefore, he does not annul his truth or deny it, nor does he establish a double truth, nor does he place us in the doubtful position of an "as if" cognition, when he allows and commands us in his revelation to make use of our views, concepts and thoughts to describe himself, his Word and his deeds. On the contrary, he establishes the one truth, his own, as the truth of our views, concepts and words. (CD, II, 1, pg. 229)

In our preaching, through the miracle of a divine *Aufhebung*, our views, concepts, and words point toward a genuine conformity with their original and proper object, the unique particularity and particular uniqueness of God.

The same event may also be described from the human side or "from below," for just as God does not act inappropriately in giving our words this determination, so we do not act inappropriately in receiving it. Everything depends, Barth argued, on seeing that God's act of revelation is performed with pure grace. "That is, in a bestowal which utterly transcends all our capacity, being and existence as such, but does not destroy us, does not consume and break our being and existence" (CD, II, 1, pp. 197-98). Or perhaps it might be said more dialectically that the bestowal of grace in the knowledge of God utterly annuls our capacity, being, and existence by utterly transforming them, destroys us by renewing us, consumes and breaks our being and existence only to reestablish them at a higher level of wholeness. In any case, "from our point of view this is a miracle, an inexhaustible reality that cannot be established, deduced or explained—it is present to us, to our salvation, and it can be affirmed and grasped by us in faith, to become a determination of our being and existence" (CD, II, 1, pg. 198). The grace of this miracle and the miracle of this grace are therefore to be met with gratitude. "It . . . lies in the nature of this revelation that we can meet it only with the praise of thanksgiving" (CD, II, 1, pg. 198).[93]

Is there a problem here in making language a matter of exclusively divine creativity? Barth (following Hegel?) certainly wants all of our talk about God to be self-involving, a matter of relationship, not merely abstract definitions. And yet for Barth, human self-involvement, even very deep and earnest human involvement with God, cannot provide even a provisional basis for our understanding of God. Knowledge of God comes always as a gift, as unmerited grace, and a gift given can also be a gift withheld. As we speak of God, we have not within our power to control or to rest assured that our speech about God truthfully describes God. All is God's gift rather than human possession or achievement.

Must grace, as revelation, be so occasional? Donald Evans says, "It seems to me that what is at the root of Barth's difficulty concerning language is a defective concept of Divine grace. Barth makes grace, like creation, a work *ex nihilo*. He does not allow any initial basis or provisional contribution or pre-existing capacity in human beings as such."[94] Evans objects to the way in which Barth has applied Reformation (specifically Lutheran) soteriology of salvation by grace alone to Christian Epistemology. It appears that, in his thought on words, Barth has allowed a stress upon the instantaneous event of divinely conferred meaning to overshadow a fair consideration of meaning as an ongoing, cumulative, dependable experience of language. In other words, has not Barth rendered our words about God into highly unstable, unmanageable events?

Most of us preachers know, from firsthand experience, that our speech about God is highly unstable, unmanageable, and a constant pain. Our words about God grow limp from overuse, mean one thing to one set of hearers and quite another thing to others, are culturally contingent, tradition dependent, and notoriously insubstantial. Sometimes we say "God" and really do appear to be faithfully representing a reality and at other times our speech falls on deaf ears. We repeat the same word, or the same set of words, words which have previously worked quite well, but now they clearly do not do the work for which they are intended.

Yet sometimes they do. By the grace of God we preachers also experience our words miraculously being raised from the dead, enlisted, elected to mean more than they could, by our efforts, mean. Barth can make such sweeping claims for the utter meaninglessness and ineffectiveness of our speech about God, without the electing grace of God, because Barth is so utterly convinced of the effusive, irresistible triumph of the grace of God. By the grace of God, we *do* speak about God, and our speech about God graciously, rather effusively, effects that which it indicates. Our words about God have about them a disarmingly performative "meaning."

"My word shall not return to me in vain. . . ." (Isa. 55:11). In my experience, preachers, particularly mainline Protestant preachers, tend to have too little faith in preaching rather than too much. And I use the word "faith" here with intention. How curious, among those who make their living talking about God in sermons, to find so little confidence in the ability of our sermons to render God. Too many preachers can tell you all the factors responsible for people's inability to encounter the Word of God in a sermon—laziness, sin, ignorance, distraction, and so forth, but have no means of accounting for why, despite all of these conventional reasons for not hearing, sometimes people do hear. Some pastoral psychologists have suggested that this curious sort of pastoral lack of confidence in the efficacy may have something to do with the preacher's unconscious fear that if preaching really is effective, if preaching is truly God's appointed means for intruding upon the world, then that means that preachers must be considerably more invested in the preaching.[95] If preaching is potentially powerful, for good or ill, then preachers must be willing to exercise more care and responsibility in their preaching. Better to whine about the pointlessness of preaching and its ineffectiveness than to admit to its possible power.

I expect that the reasons for this pastoral devaluation of preaching may be more due to theological problems in pastors. Too many of us have opted for a Deistic deity who is mostly silent and ineffective. Lacking a robust theology of Election, or more specifically, a resourceful God who wills to elect both us and our words, then there is no way for preaching ever to be effective. With the great effort that has been expended, in recent decades, to make preaching more rhetorically effective, much of the preoccupation with narrative in preaching and matters of sermonic form and style may stem from a kind of a-theism.

And lest we speak of this world-rendering-word as an episodic, actualistic, occasional affair, we need to be reminded that the Christian now lives, by the power of the Word, in a new world. The Word of God creates, for the one who is summoned by this Word, a great security. Our faith rests, not on our ability, through our good works or our good concepts, to climb up to God. Rather, our situation with God always originates with the Word climbing down toward us. This Word gives the Christian confidence and hope. Our faith is not a fragile, come-and-go sort of thing because it rests upon the continuous, effervescent self-communication of God in Christ. As he approached the end of his life, Barth said,

> The Christian can never in any circumstances . . . think and speak and act as though God were unknown to him. . . . He cannot reverse his election and calling, which are not his own work but God's. He cannot make himself again a man to whom God's Word has not been spoken. . . . He cannot alter the fact that the precedence of the Word over all the other factors in his life pertains to him and that he knows very well that it does. . . . A Christian is a person who is grasped and held by God and cannot escape his claim. He can undertake and do many things against God but not against the fact that God knows him and is also and always well known to him.[96]

When contemporary homiletics puts too much stress upon the listener, rather than upon the Speaker (God's eternal word), it undercuts the security that is to be had from a strong, resourceful, faithful, electing God. The Christian is the one who has been addressed and thereby awakened to the fact of a whole new world and cannot go back no matter how hard you try. Jesus Christ is more than personal. He is the full "alteration of the whole world situation" (*CD*, IV, 3, pg. 191).

The words of Scripture tend toward announcement, promise, address, and command. Therefore, these words demand, like any gift, trust, gratitude, and obedience. Jesus Christ is the Paradigm for Christian epistemology. Jesus Christ is the decisive clue for how it is possible for us to know God on the basis of words at all. He is the decisive analogy of being and the analogy of faith, the basis for any meaningful speech about God. Thus, Barth's epistemology, like his theology in general, is rigorously christological. Barth asks, "Can the principle of theology be sought anywhere but in God himself and known in any way but from God himself, that is from revelation? Can man know himself except as he is primarily known by God himself?"[97]

In one of his aphorisms, Nietzsche asks, "What if truth were a woman?" At first the statement sounds sexist, and may be, but I sense an irony. Then I remembered John 14:16 where Jesus says clearly, "I am the way, the truth, and the life." He did not say I have come to tell you the truth, or to share some truths with you. He says directly, "I am the truth." What if truth were not as we usually think of it—an abstraction, a principle, an idea? What if truth were a person, personal? What if truth has a name and a face, a personality, an ability to reach out and embrace us? What if truth does not await our discovery of it, does not inertly sit there awaiting our affirmation but initiates an encounter, reaches out to us, and enables us to respond in kind?[98] What if truth were a resurrected Jew from Nazareth?

CHAPTER SIX

THE TALKATIVE GOD

Christian preachers dare to talk about God. Even on the presupposition of the mediation of revelation by holy scripture this venture would always be impossible without the third presupposition that God acknowledges it and will himself speak as we speak, just as he spoke to the prophets and apostles and still speaks through them. . . . It is pure doctrine if the word of the preacher gives free play to God's own Word.[1]

We come up here against the painful and tragic riddle of Christian preaching. In a thousand tongues it speaks about God, and truly without quoting a last and supreme authority and claiming last and supreme freedoms. Why, then do people not hear that we are talking about God? Why does everything remain so dumb, gray, dull, and dead around us as though we were talking about something else? . . . "The preaching of the Word of God is the Word of God?" One has to make a choice here. Either this is an arrogant exaggeration, postulate or hyperbole, one of the piously shameless acts that religion is always perpetuating . . . or else it is reality, the wholly new reality of the Spirit, of God, which we can only await afresh, understand afresh, and need to seek and find and thankfully receive afresh. There is no other option.[2]

Shortly before his death, Barth said in a radio broadcast: "My whole theology, you see, is fundamentally a theology for parsons. It grew out of my own situation when I had to teach and preach and counsel a little."[3] Barth never acquired the German equivalent of the Ph.D. and did not think it his choice that he was led to deviate from his plan to spend his life as a pastor in the Swiss Reformed Church. He never got beyond his pastoral origins. His ministry began as a preacher, as a pastor at Safenwil, where he labored for ten rather frustrating years. His work was born out of the homiletical question: How is preaching possible?[4] I wonder if his early preaching experience convinced him of the impossibility of speaking up for God in a sermon or anywhere else. Our words simply cannot do justice to the Word. The failure of our speech in the pulpit is similar to our failure to speak and to listen to one another: "Most of our words, spoken or heard, are an inhuman and barbaric affair because we will not speak or listen to one another. We speak them without letting ourselves be found or helped."[5]

"It is not the words that are really empty. It is men themselves when they speak and hear empty words," says Barth.[6] Empty words produce empty people. We would be thoroughly justified in cynicism, disillusionment, and suspicion about our words; and most good preachers are often victims to these three maladies on more Sundays than not. Yet Barth says that we preachers must never allow cynicism, disillusionment, and suspicion to make a home among us.[7] We are Trinitarians who believe in a restless, relentlessly communicative God. Particularly in Romans, but elsewhere throughout his writing, Barth shows a disbelief that our speaking can be God's speaking—*except that it is, by the grace of God, God's speaking.* Barth's theology demonstrated the preacher's dilemma: he was compelled to preach the Word of God, but he was uncertain that his words could carry the Word, but he was also convinced that God graciously speaks and that we, by the grace of God, hear. This is Barth's own formulation of this problem:

> Is one single word of mine even the word that I am seeking, a word which I out of my great need and hope want to say? Can I speak in such a manner that one word does not negate another?[8]

And yet his monumental theological writings, as well as his own preaching, demonstrated Barth's extravagant faith that God has, in Jesus Christ, overcome the problem of preaching.

The Word of the Lord Came to Me, Saying

At this particular junction in the history of Christian preaching, I believe that the first gift that Barth has to give us preachers is his contagious optimism about the gratuitous extravagance of the Trinity. This God is nothing if not capacious. We have had quite enough skepticism about the possibility of communication. In the present moment we must again affirm that we can preach because God wills to be known. Barth writes a great deal because God speaks a great deal. In fact, when one objectively considers all of the evidence in scripture and elsewhere for the loquaciousness, the tirelessly revelatory work of a self-revealing God, one is hard-pressed to figure out why contemporary thinkers have thought so much on the alleged silence, absence, and elusiveness of God. The Trinity refuses to be a *Deus Absconditus:*

> Creation begins as an aspect of the speech of God. Creation is the result of a series of divine proclamations, "Let there be light . . ." (Gen. 1:3). Who was God addressing? As we have said, the Trinity seems to be internally conversational, "Let us . . ." (Gen. 1:26), and that conversation seems to have the quality, from the first, of being public, of being able to be overheard. God comes to Adam, addressing the earthling, initiating a conversation before one is sought. All hope of Christian proclamation rests upon this persistently communicative God. The world in all its formlessness has been addressed.

> In the Old Testament, prophets are those who have been addressed, who are given something to say. For instance, the book of Jeremiah begins, "The words of Jeremiah son of Hilkiah . . ." (Jer. 1:1), but the story gets going, just four verses later, with, "Now the word of the LORD came to me saying . . ." (Jer. 1:4). There is no Jeremiah, no words of the prophet Jeremiah, no story until there is the "word of the LORD." "Now I have put my words in your mouth . . ." (1:9). Dozens of times, throughout the prophecies of Jeremiah, at every turn in the story of the prophet's life, the story resumes with, "The word of the LORD came to me, saying . . ." (2:1; see also 2:5; 3:6; 7:1; 10:1; 11:1, etc.). At certain wonderful moments Jeremiah despairs, is angry with God, turns away, and says that he will now be silent, but then, "the word of the LORD came to me, saying. . . ."

> A prophet speaks because a prophet has been spoken to. The prophetic task is to bring God's being to speech: "Now the word of the LORD came to me saying, 'Before I formed you in the womb I knew you. . . . See, today I appoint you over nations and over kingdoms, / to pluck up and to pull down, / to destroy and to overthrow, to build and to plant'" (Jer. 1:4, 10). How absurd that this youth, who has no credentials, training, or

status, is appointed by God "over nations," to destroy and to build up. All of this is given to the one who is given the words of God. Preachers are powerful people.

The story of Easter is thus a prophetic story, a story of the way in which this God will not keep silent (Luke 24; John 20), will not let the conversation (the argument?) between God and humanity be ended simply because of the sin of humanity, will not be defeated by human intransigence. The Risen Christ comes back to the very ones who betrayed the Crucified Jesus, came back to them and resumed the conversation.

This is the hope upon which every church is built, the hope upon which every sermon is preached: Christ comes back to his betrayers and talks to them.

In the *Göttingen Dogmatics*, Barth says that despite all of the potential obstacles to communication and all of our sinful evasion of the divine communication, we

> must start with the presupposition that man knows, understands, and accepts God's Word. We must not start, then, with his ungodliness or his ignorance or incomprehension or contradiction. These things are certainly present, but they are a presupposition which falls away the moment I proclaim God's Word to him. . . . I must count him to be God's with the same axiomatic certainty with which I place myself under the *Deus Dixit*. I must stop all contrasting of myself with him, all complaining and judging, all trying to win him or persuade him or bring him over as if he were not already along beside me. This could rest only on the secret denial of revelation.[9]

Thus Barth shows a huge confidence in the power of the gospel to communicate itself. Any of Barth's doubts about epistemology or revelation about human capacity for comprehension, are bracketed out by his dominant, irrepressible epistemological optimism. He can be so honestly pessimistic about the possibilities of human speaking about God because he is so optimistic about the possibilities for God's speaking to humanity. Again, when Barth speaks of God's self-revelation as "event" he is speaking positively, not negatively, about revelation. Our God talks, and talks a great deal. It is of the inner nature of the Trinity to be outwardly reaching, seeking, and communicating. The believer is not some lonely hero but rather the one who is constantly, even if episodically, grateful for the faithfulness of a God who refuses to leave us to our own devices.

Why should we preachers venture into the intimidating theology of Karl Barth? Barth's lively lectures in Göttingen in 1924 demonstrate the primacy of his homiletical concerns. My own rereading of those lectures helped rekindle my interest in Barth and preaching. Barth begins his *Göttingen Dogmatics* by saying that dogmatic theology has always been "mortally dangerous"[10] but that it is "bitterly necessary."[11] Dogmatics is necessary because it is essential service to the homiletical question, "*What* will you say? And what will *you* say of God?"[12] Dogmatics exists to serve the ministry of the Word of God. What we will say begins, not with scholarly rumination on abstractions, but with "the concrete situation of preachers mounting the pulpit steps."[13]

Barth said that his break with liberalism around 1915 occurred "simply out of what we felt to be the 'need and promise of Christian preaching.'"[14] In the first few weeks of his lectures at Göttingen Barth wrote to his friend Thurneysen that the purpose of his teaching was to address "the situation of the preacher in the pulpit."[15] Homiletics was defined by Barth as the science of the practice of preaching. Dogmatics is the science, the principles, and the norms for Christian proclamation.

After reading some of Barth's early theology in the first two editions of *Romans*, Harnack accused Barth of being at heart "a despiser of academic theology" and someone who wanted to turn his lecture hall into a preaching hall, his professor's chair into a pulpit.[16] Barth replied that the purpose of dogmatics is not to preach, but to test preaching. Dogmatics is needed because "in every age the church's preaching has been sick."

Barth says that dogmatic theology is like Socrates standing before the Sophist rhetorician Gorgias and asking the speaker questions about the presupposition for the proclamation. This questioning by the theologian is needed to ensure that preaching keeps its "own proper point" (*GD*, pg. 27).

Another of the gifts of dogmatics to preaching is the corrective of the whole, the lifting up of the "big picture," a constant prodding to do justice to the full sweep of the gospel. Dogmatic theology cannot be the source of preaching, nor can it be the final judge of preaching, but it can be preaching's conversation partner who keeps reminding preaching of the whole. Preaching, by its very nature, tends toward focus upon part of the gospel, dangerously neglecting the full sweep of the gospel. A preacher usually begins with a pericope, with a piece of a book of the Bible, which is itself a piece of the Bible. In the time allowed, the preacher cannot say all that could be said about even that portion of scripture. To be fair to us preachers, sermons that are too carefully qualified, too cognizant of all the larger issues surrounding that particular passage, overly concerned to do justice to all truths that are counter to this truth are dull sermons. This is one of the reasons few academic theologians are noted preachers.

Dogmatics, which rarely worries about being dull, comes along after the sermon to remind the preacher and congregation (who almost never, ever read dogmatics) of what else could be said, of what needs to be said next Sunday if we are to be true to the grand sweep of the gospel.

In a letter to Professor Norman Porteus in St. Andrews,[17] Barth tells the professor that preaching follows the Bible in a way that systematic theology does not, because preaching, unlike systematic dogmatics, is attempting to hear the voice of the Trinitarian God. Therefore preaching has a directness about it. It works between the acts and speech of a creative, redeeming, atoning God and must be an attempt to "describe the way between these three points." (Note that these triune "points" are a description of Barth's own theological organization.) Theology can be for preaching "only a corrective," a "reminder of the totality and fullness of the Word of God," and a "warning against heretical overstress on other points." At the same time, dogmatics can never become an "absolute critic" of preaching. Dogmatics can only place questions to the preacher from the "wholeness of the Word of God which preaching is not permitted to lose sight of."

Preaching can be allowed to stress a single point of view, only as it keeps at least in view the other points. Dogmatics is there to remind the preacher and congregation that every sermon ends in mid sentence, that sermons cannot stand alone, that every sermon ends with a plea for everyone to return next Sunday and resume the conversation. Every sermon begins, from the point of view of the "whole counsel of God," with the preacher saying, in effect, "As I said last Sunday, let me amplify and correct by saying this Sunday. . . ."

We preachers can be glad that Barth said that dogmatic theology is never the stuff of preaching, but rather the "academic exercises that we must have done before we can preach and teach."[18] Theology is the preparatory calisthenics and the stretching exercises that reflect upon the words of the Christian faith and help the preacher know what these words mean in their Christian specificity. Dogmatics is the essential homework that preachers must have behind them when they preach, but need not be explicitly present with the preacher in the sermon. Our dogmatics that we learn in seminary "have no place in the pulpit, but pastors in the pulpit should give evidence that they know them by their silent adherence to them. They should preach non-dogmatically but with a solid dogmatic behind them."[19] For instance, Barth says that the Doctrine of Predestination is the great defense against all Pelagianism, but he advises preachers to avoid preaching on the doctrine "too often or expressly."[20]

While dogmatics and homiletics are closely related, they are distinct activities and must be respected as such. Christian preaching is speech that builds up the church; dogmatics draws upon and scientifically examines this speech. There is this intimate bond between dogmatics and preaching throughout the *Göttingen Dogmatics*. Barth orders his material as "the logical content of Christian preaching."[21] He would later speak of "the unavoidable affinity between knowledge and preaching."[22]

Barth says that dogmatics summons preaching to reflection "by reminding it of its origin and purpose. It does this by literally taking it at its word, by understanding it better than the pastors who engage in it do. By uncovering its relations to the past, by bringing out plainly as possible its links to its origins, by underlying, completing, and clarifying the reference preaching itself makes either well or badly . . . this is a modest ministry which is not even to be compared with the glory of the ministry of the Word itself. It is also a dangerous ministry. . . ."[23]

Gerhard Sauter puts the relationship between the glorious ministry of preaching and the more modest ministry of dogmatics in a very Barthian way:

> Dogmatics inquires into the foundations of the proclamation that is entrusted to the church. These foundations do not consist of a distant goal or a norm or ideal. Rather, they can be heard in proclamation as God's speech. To this extent, preaching is a form of the Word of God—not even mere revelation!—and for this reason dogmatics is rooted in preaching as a phenomenon, even though this phenomenon is the word of humans. But dogmatics has to deal with the possibility that God's speech can be heard through preaching; that this actually happens is due to God alone. For the sake of such hope, the talk of the church about God is the theme of dogmatics. The theme is not God himself in a direct form. God has willed to express himself in preaching. Faith, too, is not the theme. Faith arises only through preaching, and preaching constantly confirms it. Only God himself can verify what is said with reference to him.[24]

The Bible is unconcerned with our modern infatuation, the existence of God, "Is there a God?" Rather, the Bible is obsessed with the extravagant self-communication of God. In so many ways, scripture marvels at the range of God's interests and modes of self-revelation. The skeptical "Did God say . . . ?" is not a typical biblical question. Satan is the first theologian when he asks, "Did God say . . . ?" (Gen. 3:1). We preachers are much more optimistic about revelation. We preachers ask, "Congregation, can you believe what God has the nerve to say to us today?" Barth says that preachers assemble people not by the statement "God is" but rather by the announcement, "God spoke." "For even the statement 'God is' is obviously a reference back to God's self-knowledge in his Word. God's action in relation to the world and us, what does it consist of but simply his making Himself known in this relation as the one who Himself and alone acts?" Thus, "the Content of revelation is God alone, Holy God, God Himself. Christian preaching must be aware of this."[25]

> Word of God preached means human talk about God which by God's own judgment . . . is for us not just human willing and doing characterized in some way but also and primarily and decisively . . . God's own speech. . . . The Word of God preached means . . . man's talk about God in which and through which God himself speaks about Himself.[26]

The Impossibility of Atheism

Barth's studied disregard for even the possibility of atheism is an outgrowth of his optimistic confidence in the extravagant self-revelation of God in Jesus Christ. For Barth, what we might call "atheism" is not just the passive failure to believe in God, but the active refusal to believe in the God who is so well revealed to us in Jesus Christ. Atheism is just another form of insidious "religion." Atheism arrogantly attempts to say something about God—that God does not exist, or that God is unjust or cruel, unapproachable, or a figment of our imagination—that is purely self-derived. Atheism is not humble intellectual inability to believe in God but the arrogant refusal to believe in God as a Jew from Nazareth, the God who is made manifest to us in the three forms of revelation. Unwilling to believe that God could come to us in this particular form, we adopt a more generalized, generic form of "god" and either believe or disbelieve in this self-constructed idol.[27] Upon hearing Jesus refer to his own disciples as an "unbelieving generation" in Luke 10, Barth says that "what we are dealing with here . . . is the extremely fundamental fact that the disciples, while Jesus has called them, and they are His followers, belong to an 'unbelieving generation' (v. 19). They are wholly and utterly outside even while they are wholly and utterly inside. So far as they stand on their own feet . . . they are wholly and utterly outside. It is clear that they have their religion, but it is equally clear that their religion is unbelief."[28] All that we call "religion," Barth calls "unbelief."[29] In my experience, most collegiate "Departments of Religion" are thus, from a Barthian perspective, aptly named. Their main work is defense against a living, speaking God. Most churches too.

> Barth has not been served well by the translation of the original German, *Unglaube* by "unbelief" in his *Church Dogmatics*. It is better rendered into English as "faithlessness," or even better, "unfaith." Thus our problem is not an unwillingness to entertain certain beliefs, but rather an unwillingness to yield to divine, disruptive grace, to surrender all purely human attempts to know and to speak of God's work. We are always sinful, self-justifying creatures. Our anxiety over *how to preach*, as if God has not spoken and is not speaking, is an exercise of this faithlessness.

> I wonder if Barth could even understand what we call "atheism" because he was so convinced that the Trinity is so utterly self-revealing. "Atheism" is another "religious" attempt to contain the living God, to define God, to have God at our disposal, to silence God.[30] One of Barth's great contributions was to say that "religion" equals "atheism" and "atheism" is a variety of "religion." "Religion is unbelief. It is a concern, indeed, we must say it is the one great concern, of godless man."[31]

> Garrett Green says that the great challenge for Barth is to affirm "the priority of revelation over religion without denying the religious nature of revelation." Religion is an

unavoidable human phenomenon. Religious rites, rituals, practices, and disciplines may be helpful in placing us in those situations where revelation may reach us. (I doubt that Barth would allow me to put the matter in this way, but as a practitioner of religion, I believe it.) However religion can degenerate, and usually does in one way or another, into an evasion of revelation, a last-ditch effort on our part to protect ourselves against the demanding, commanding event of revelation; therefore, Barth teaches us to be especially careful when we are in the sphere of religion.[32] If one is looking for the betrayers of Christ, one ought to look first among those who are gathered regularly at the table of Christ.

At the same time Barth, the indomitable optimist about revelation, stresses that no human being can ever become "ontologically godless."[33] Thus, real atheism, a life without God, is for Barth an impossibility. Barth taught that the human being "cannot really escape God. His godlessness . . . can make God a 'manless' God . . . [but the good news is that] man has not fallen lower than the depth to which God humbled himself for Him in Jesus Christ." We may be able to construct an inhuman "god," but we cannot be truly godless humans, says Barth. The Christ reveals the truth about God, namely that this God is, from eternity, our God. This God is utterly *pro nobis*, one with humanity. Even when humanity lowers itself to the foolishness of saying, "There is no God" (Ps. 14:1), God is there, condescending, stooping—in Jesus Christ—to our level. So God's act in the Incarnation has made "atheism" an ontological (and I would add, epistemological) impossibility.[34] Thus Barth cannot conceive of the human being outside of relationship with God. "This commandment . . . is not too hard for you, nor is it too far away. It is not in heaven. . . . Neither is it beyond the sea. . . . No, the word is very near to you; it is in your mouth and in your heart for you to observe" (Deut. 30:11-14).

Barth's low estimate of "religion" and his refusal to give disbelief any ontological status account for why the church's preaching can never be a strictly "in house" activity because, although there may be those who are outside the church, they can never—because of the nature of this incarnational, Trinitarian, relentlessly reaching God—be completely outside the reach of God's grasp and therefore beyond the bounds of Christian communication. Thus Barth would have us preachers not take "atheism" too seriously, or at least to take it seriously in the wrong way. Also, Barth would have us not be too troubled about speaking to folk who self-designate themselves as "religious" or "irreligious." In the eyes of God, we're all "religious," and that's our problem.

In Marilynne Robinson's second novel, *Gilead*,[35] the protagonist, a pastor, says of a little Baptist church that was destroyed by a lightning strike, "That was always a major part of my idea of a church. When I was a child I actually believed that the purpose of steeples was to attract lightning. I thought that they must be meant to protect all the other houses and buildings, and that seemed very gallant to me."[36] The church is here to protect people from God. On the page after this statement, the narrator says that his two favorite theology books are Barth's *Epistle to the Romans* and Calvin's *Institutes*.

Stanley Hauerwas gave me *Gilead*, telling me, "This is the first truly Barthian novel ever written."

The old preacher says toward the end of his life, "I have found Barth's work to be full of comfort. . . . But in fact, I don't recall ever recommending him to any tormented soul except my own."[37]

Barth's writing, and not just his early writing, sounds homiletical. He writes with urgency, stridency, dogmatic assertion, and vivid imagery. His theology at times sounds more homiletical than his sermons. The *Church Dogmatics* in places reads as if it were dictated, which much of it was, in a breathless tempo,[38] to faithful Charlotte von Kirschbaum, with Barth pacing back and forth across his study. One can hear the human voice behind Barth's written word, an echo of the voice of the Other.

Rhetoric Against Itself: Turning Away from the Listener

The great misunderstanding, especially in modern times, Barth believed, was to suppose that a personal encounter with God was somehow given in the structure of human nature itself. The preacher need only uncover that point of contact within the listener's self and build a bridge to that innate point of contact.[39] Barth's denial of that point of contact was due, not only to his great pessimism about human nature but also due to his great optimism about the self-revelatory capacity of the Trinity. Barth thought that preaching that thinks it has uncovered some human yearning for the Word was only deceiving itself, offering the world nothing more than a false god. As for the true God, the Word made flesh, the Word "completes its work in the world in spite of the world."[40]

The great nineteenth-century theological error was to suppose that divine revelation is problematic, not sufficiently given in Christ; and therefore revelation must be derived from the depths of human self-consciousness or human moral experience. There, said theology of the nineteenth century, God was somehow waiting to be discovered and encountered. The condition for the possibility of encountering God was thus found in the interior depths of the self. Yet when our personal encounter with God was understood in these terms—the terms set by human nature—it was inevitable, Barth argued, that two things would and did eventually happen. First, Jesus Christ would cease to be understood unequivocally as the Lord; and second, we ourselves would consequently come to usurp the center, which rightfully belongs to him. (Here, I am virtually paraphrasing the first thesis of the Barmen Declaration.)[41] Rather than understanding ourselves from him, we would come to understand him from ourselves. Rather than take him on his own terms as the Lord—that is, as God's unique, final, and binding revelation—we would take him on our own terms as a postulate of our experience, "as an ideal case or an idea of our possibility and our reality."[42] In other words, we would refuse to give God glory (Rom. 1:21), devising some means of getting to God through our own glorious selves.

Most of the preaching I hear in my church family is in the evocative mode. Preaching makes contact with something within the human consciousness, awakens or evokes that something, often using the biblical witness but more often using the subjective experience of the preacher, and calls that product of evocation "faith." This project has as its progenitor (who else?) Schleiermacher. Redemption, said Schleiermacher, is an evocation of God-consciousness, arising from out of the depths of the human soul where God has been only partially forgotten but of which, through skillful preaching, people can be reminded.[43] Preaching makes contact with some inner, spiritual essence that is primarily a matter of "feeling."[44]

Barth is so dismissive of any "point of contact" through human faculties because he is so confident that the point of contact is provided by revelation itself.[45] Humanity can only speak to humanity. Humanity is the basis for any "point of contact," but it is not our humanity; it is the humanity of Christ. "Everyone as such is a fellow of Jesus."[46]

Baptism Miracle[47]

When Jesus also had been baptized . . . the heaven was opened, and the Holy Spirit descended. . . . And a voice came from heaven, "You are my Son." Luke 3:21-22

I am learning how to preach. I've only been trying to preach for the last thirty years and, after thirty years, I know less about how to preach a sermon than when I began.

I've learned: When it comes to sermons, people don't listen; more accurately, people don't hear—too many obstacles to successful communication. Skeptical modern world, science, attention deficit disorder, sophomore hormones, sin.

I work on a sermon, do my homework. Then I stand up here and thrash about for twenty minutes. Tell some sappy stories. Gesture from the torso. But you don't hear! Even though the lights are in my eyes up here, I can see that you don't hear!

I don't know how to preach. Tried every technique, different forms and arrangements. It's hard to hear the things of God, particularly things of God. How can you talk to someone about God? How do you speak in such a way that people don't just hear about God but are brought to God? I have learned that it is just about impossible to get people to get a sermon.

But sometimes, they do. People undeniably hear. Most of you keep coming back because, having had the lightning strike once, it could well strike again, and you want to be here for it. Having once shuffled in here—distracted, unfocused, unsure—you have, despite all, irrefutably heard.

You know what annoys me about all of you? It's when I preach a sermon, that I meant to be good, but it isn't, say a sermon that could have been a good sermon if I had only had a month more to work on it, a sermon like that—poorly illustrated, badly supported, turgid, and opaque—that sort of sermon, and here you come out, tears in your eyes, grip my hand, and say, "Thank you. That was wonderful. That was life-changing! Got it!"

Got what? I have the manuscript for that sermon. I'm an expert on preaching, and I know a bad sermon when I hear one. Nothing there!

Now why, despite my worst efforts, why did you hear? Who pulled back the veil between us and God? Not me.

Clergy friend of mine, for his sabbatical, didn't read books and write thoughts. He chose to travel about the country, visiting churches, listening to sermons. I asked him what he learned in his thirty-sermon tour, and he said, "I think it's a miracle that anybody ever hears anything."

And yet, you do. Why? I think it's a miracle.

Pascal's Pensées. One of the greatest minds ever, incisive, probing, struggling with the big questions, looking for answers, frustrated. Then in the middle of the night, Pascal writes, "Not the God of the philosophers, but the God of Abraham, Isaac, and Jacob. Fire! Fire! Fire!"

Even so great a mind as Pascal couldn't climb his way up to God, so the living God inflamed him.

Today's gospel: It was another day at the river. John was baptizing, washing people up, getting ready for the Messiah. It was a ritual that Jews sometimes went through, a kind of purification rite, sometimes associated with preparation for the coming of the Messiah.

"Messiah's coming," John preached. "Someday, sometime, someplace, Messiah's coming." People were filled with expectation. John didn't say, "Messiah's here!" No, John preached, "Messiah's coming."

Just going through the motions, expecting the Messiah. People interrupted his sermon with, "Are you the Messiah?"

"No," John answered them. "I couldn't tie the shoelaces of the one who is coming after me, the one you are expecting. I baptize with water; the one who is coming after me, more powerful than I, he will baptize with wind and fire!"

John said, "I just wash you up; he will burn you up! Purify you!"

Heap of difference between expecting the Word of God and hearing it. A great distance between anticipating the possibility of the Presence of God and getting God.

Well, John is baptizing. "Next." Wade in the water, stoop to the water, up out of the water. "Next." Wade, stoop, up. "Next."

And then, with this one from Nazareth—Dove, Spirit, Voice, the heaven ripped open, the veil torn asunder, fire.

This dove, spirit, voice is a "Bible" way of saying that God was present.

That great dove, Spirit hovering over the muddy Jordan waters, reminds of that primal Spirit that hovered over the waters at Creation, bringing life, light.

We have begun Year C in the Lectionary; that's the year of Luke. All year, just about every Sunday, the Gospel is Luke. Jesus in Luke can be so enigmatic—tells these cryptic, incomprehensible, often pointless parables. Who can understand him? But here, in this moment, at the first of the year, the veil is pulled back, there is a voice all the way from heaven, and we see, hear, "You are my Son, you're Beloved." A voice, directed not at us, but at Jesus, a conversation within the heart of the Trinity, but we get a miraculous overhearing. And it is enough.

The voice is "from heaven." It is not of the earth. It is not a voice, like most of what you hear, that arises out of your infantile background, the damage that your mother inflicted upon you during your latent stage, something you are dealing with from adolescence, an upsurge of the human spirit. It is a word not psychologically, sociologically, anthropologically derived. It is "from heaven," that is, from God. It's a miracle.

I don't know how many heard the voice that day. I'm glad that somebody heard it, saw the dove, felt the fire, and had the guts to tell us. Because maybe then we, though sorely limited by our modern epistemological restraints, might be open to such a voice, and such a vision.

We baptize babies. Why? A baby can't believe the Apostles' Creed, can't think theology, can't obey the Ten Commandments—which makes a baby totally, utterly dependent upon the grace of God to do for the baby what the baby can't do for herself.

If this baby is going to get back to God, it will take a miracle.

Get my drift. We baptize in promise, expectation. God will work in this child's life. We baptize anybody, any age, into the same promise. Everybody here requires a voice, a dove, a heavenly aperture, not of our own devising or you won't get home.

One of you has been attending Duke Chapel for years. And yet you told somebody that you haven't understood but one sermon in a hundred in all those months of Sundays! Man keeps coming to Duke Chapel. Doesn't understand one sermon in a hundred! Why? I don't mean, "Why don't you understand," because, as we have noted, there are dozens of reasons why people don't hear God's Word. I mean, "Why do you keep coming?"

> *Because four years ago, in a sermon, by a guest preacher, Fire! The heavens opened, a dove descended, and down to the tips of your toes, you heard: God, so close you could feel the breath.*
>
> *I can't preach God's Word to you. Forgive me when I try to explain Jesus, attempt to talk you into the faith. I can't. And it's not because I'm not so hot as a preacher; it's because revelation, recognition—when it's about God—is always a gift. A miracle. It's got to come "from heaven."*
>
> *I can't preach, you can't hear, except as miracle.*
>
> *I'm not saying that the baptism of Jesus happened just that way, with a literal dove, descending upon an unembellished baptism, with an actual, audible voice. I'm not saying that this "fire" was not somewhat figurative. I'm not saying that visions like this happen every day.*
>
> *I am saying that it will happen to you!*
>
> *You're being baptized, or you're taking a bath, or you're taking a break, you're listening to a sermon, you're staring off into space doing nothing, and then, just when you think you've got your world all safe and silent, the once hushed heavens open, a voice, inexplicable but undeniable, some big bird swoops, wind. And you, despite reservations, dare wade into the water. You draw near the fire. You ignite.*
>
> *It's Epiphany. The Word has been made flesh and moved in with us. Watch your back. Be careful.*

Barth's great confidence in the self-revelation of God, his decision to begin all theological discourse with the faith that "and God said . . . ," tends to put Barth at odds with the rhetorical turn of contemporary homiletics.[48] One of Barth's most notable differences when compared with contemporary homiletics is his anti-rhetorical attitude. I hope it is clear by now that my long discourse on the history of rhetoric in the early part of this book was a Barthian attempt to examine rhetoric in order to defeat it. God's strategies for speaking (that is, the three forms of divine self-communication: the eternal Word, Jesus Christ; the inspired word of scripture; and preaching) are the basis of our preaching. Our rhetorical stratagems are not. Therefore, we preachers need not overly trouble ourselves with methods and means of proclamation, with a turn toward the listener, because the triune God already has turned toward us in cross and resurrection.

Beverly Zink-Sawyer demonstrates that the contemporary "turn to the listener" is a tendency that can be seen throughout the history of preaching.[49] She chastises Calvin's famous definition of the church as that place where "the word is purely preached and the sacraments rightly administered"[50] as "ignoring those who hear the preached word. The results are a conception of homiletics as one-way communication and a dangerous neglect of a crucial component of the homiletical task." Zink-Sawyer shows how attentive Augustine was to the need "to teach, to delight, and to persuade" the listener, how wonderfully aware Augustine was of the need to select various styles of homiletical discourse.[51] She says that Augustine "advocated a delicate balance between rhetorical preparation and trust in divine intervention in order to produce effective preaching."

But then came Alan of Lille's twelfth-century *Art of Preaching*, where the attentiveness to the biblical text subsumed concern for the listener and, according to Zink-Sawyer, the listener got lost. She praises Calvin for defining the marks of the church as that place where "the Word of God is purely preached *and heard*" (emphasis Zink-Sawyer's). She then praises American Puritan preachers like Jonathan Edwards for their concern with the impact of preaching upon the hearts and minds of their listeners (which I believe to be a strange reading of Edwards's preaching), as well as the preachers of the Great Awakenings. She also has surprising praise for the "New Measures" of Charles G. Finney, as well as Horace Bushnell who, according to one commentator, "opened the floodgates of human experience for preachers of the religious mainstream."[52]

The floodgates swept in preachers of experience like Henry Ward Beecher who, in his Yale Lectures on Preaching said, "There is a force—call it magnetism or electricity or what you will—in a man, which is a personal element, and which flows from a speaker who is *en rapport* with his audience." Beecher even had his church building designed as an "auditorium" in order to produce the maximum impact on his hearers. "No speech is successful that does not do something to an audience," said Beecher.

Zink-Sawyer then praises early women preachers and African-American preachers for peppering their sermons with homely anecdotes and illustrations that made contact with the everyday struggles of their hearers, though she does not demonstrate that these preachers were any more attuned to the listeners than other preachers of their day.

Of course, Zink-Sawyer attributes Harry Emerson Fosdick's "What Is the Matter with Preaching?" as the precursor to contemporary concern with the listener. The trouble is, said Fosdick, that preachers have lost their nerve in the face of modern discoveries and knowledge. A mediocre sermon is one that "establishes no connection with the real interests of the congregation."[53] A good sermon specializes, said Fosdick, in "problem solving" and the "felt needs" of the people in the pews.[54] Fosdick confidently places a great burden upon the back of the preacher: "The preacher's business is not merely to discuss repentance but to persuade people to repent. . . . A preacher's task is to create in his congregation the thing he is talking about. . . . A good sermon is an engineering operation by which a chasm is bridged so that spiritual goods on one side . . . are actually transported into personal lives upon the other. . . . It need never fail to make a transforming difference in some lives."[55]

Zink-Sawyer says that the one deviation in this nearly thousand-year concern for the listener was Karl Barth who, though he did show some concern for the state of his congregations, led a "biblical theology movement" that was the precursor of "neo-orthodoxy" and "the entrenchment of fundamentalism" in mid-century North America.[56] Fortunately, American homiletics has gotten over this temporary setback with Barth and "we have witnessed another major turn toward the listeners in preaching theory," says Zink-Sawyer.[57] She praises, or at least notes, those churches that have "abandoned traditional homiletical and liturgical models" for "more familiar styles of communication," those preachers who have found the Myers-Briggs Type Indicator a helpful wedge into the consciousness of the hearers, the women preachers, African-American preachers, Liberationist preachers who place their listeners' real-life context at the center of their concern, and especially Fred Craddock, who noted the fundamental weakness of contemporary preaching in its "monological character."[58] She also cites David Buttrick, who she says has turned us once again to worry about the "how" of preaching. She says that, thanks to Buttrick, "preachers are called to name God, the God we come to know through the Christian story, in the world of lived experience: a world reconstructed within shared consciousness through the careful appropriation of hermeneutical insights, linguistic strategies, and meaningful imagery. Through words deliberately chosen and organized."[59]

Before she is finished with her survey of the "turn to the listener," Zink-Sawyer admits that the trend that she has been praising has some dangers: the possible loss of "theological integrity," in which preachers are too eager to embrace contemporary forms and content in their preaching without considering the theological implications; the loss of authority, which, she says, can be addressed by "more attentiveness to the text, more awareness of the listeners, and more dependence on the grace of God."[60] This last section of her article is revealingly titled, "Mediating the Sacred Space Between Pulpit and Pew," a testimony to the impossible assignment that Zink-Sawyer has assigned to preaching.

If she were writing her article today, I wonder if Zink-Sawyer would be more critical of this "turn to the listener," if she would be more concerned about the theological substance and purpose of preaching, if she might be more willing to specify some of the content of the sermon, the "what" or "who" of the sermon rather than the "how" of the sermon. Probably not, since her article is a testimony to the pervasive, traditional homiletic concern with effects. Yet she does show how out of step Karl Barth is with conventional homiletics.

Richard Lischer,[61] in answer to Lucy Hogan's championing of the turn-to-the-listener rhetorical strategies in preaching, wrote, "Why I Am Not Persuasive." Lischer noted how rhetoric, from the beginning, was a matter of persuasion. He says that it is not enough to say, "Well, in one way or another, all speaking wants to persuade." Nor is it enough to rework "persuasion" in postmodern fashion so that it is made to mean something less persuasive. Any rhetorical attempt to be persuasive rests upon the essentially a-theistic assumption (this is my way of putting Lischer's argument, not his) that it is up to the preacher to persuade, move, argue, demonstrate, and convince. Hogan says that Lischer has such a low estimation of the sinfulness of humanity (because Lischer is a Lutheran?) that he cannot believe that rhetoric will work on sinful listeners. Lischer counters that his objections to rhetorical strategies of persuasion are based upon theological rather than merely anthropological considerations—"Christology, soteriology, ecclesiology, and pneumatology." He believes that the rhetoric that is attempted by us preachers usually arises from a failure to understand that we really do have a God who redeems our speech, who breathes, discloses, and declares in a way that is beyond all of our rhetoric.

Lischer also notes that he has never seen a preacher improve by becoming more concerned about rhetoric. Rather, preachers get better at preaching when they catch fire by "surrendering themselves to the Holy Spirit, or renewed their devotion to Christ, or gave themselves to some practice of ministry only to be surprised by renewal."

Lischer (who wrote the definitive book on the preaching of Martin Luther King) says, "Martin Luther King, Jr. was a B+ preacher until he got caught up in something larger than himself." It is fine to study rhetoric, to admit to it, to attempt to use it and not abuse the congregation with it, but Lischer says that preaching will work only by theological means, only when it is "grounded in the church's mission and not a rhetorical theory. . . . Real transformations will occur but, disturbingly, at some remove from our most cherished homiletical rules. Homiletics must sustain its age-old dialogue with rhetoric but on a new footing. It must challenge conventional categories such as persuasion with the strength of its own message, the New Utterance of the gospel."

Barth could not have said it better.

James F. Kay, Engle Professor of Homiletics and Liturgics at Princeton, delivered an influential address at Princeton on November 6, 2002, in which he attacked the tendency of homiletics in America to concern itself with rhetorical matters.[62] After reviewing the history of attempts to Christianize classical (i.e., pagan) rhetoric, Kay notes the curious way in which rhetoric has once again captured the field of homiletics, citing the book on rhetoric by Hogan and Reid as a prime example.[63]

Kay says that the great contribution of Karl Barth to rhetoric, as seen in his lectures in *The Word of God and the Word of Man*,[64] was the depiction of the subject of a sermon as being God. Furthermore, God was not merely the subject matter of the sermon but its Agent. Only when God speaks in preaching as Agent is preaching truly the Word of God. Here Kay cites Barth's speech "The Need and Promise of Christian Preaching,"[65] first delivered in 1922. Kay says, "Within this new theological framework [of Barth] . . . rhetoric cannot package or deliver the living God. Simply put, if the human words of the sermon are to become God's Word, then God must make them so . . . for the power of rhetoric is not the power of the gospel."

Kay says that Barth discovered in the world crisis of 1914–1918 that everything human, including the art of rhetoric, belongs to the dominion of death. Barth's friend Eduard Thurneysen declared that "the pulpit must be the grave of all human words." This was followed by his slogan "No eloquence!" Clearly Barth's project was, at least in part, an attack on any simple linkage of preaching to the arts of rhetoric

Kay notes that Barth did not so much want to dispose of rhetoric but rather Barth wanted to move homiletics from being a peculiar kind of rhetoric, to making it a subfield of dogmatics. He quotes Long's vivid statement, "Barth gladly drove a stake into the heart of rhetoric and called upon the newly widowed homiletics not to mourn but to dance on the grave."[66] Kay says that what Barth rejected was "not rhetoric, as such, but an autonomous rhetoric, theologically ungoverned, that claims for its eloquence the power to make God real for people."[67] In short, Barth would have rejected just about every contemporary homiletical appeal to rhetoric.

Hogan and Reid attempt to construct an updated rhetoric of preaching. While Hogan and Reid say that preaching is definitely "more" than rhetoric, as James Kay points out in some detail, Hogan and Reid never specify what that "more" is.[68] Hogan and Reid say that rhetoric is "the study of what is persuasive in human communication, whether intentional, or simply consequence of the human condition."[69] This anthropological, nontheological approach characterizes their book. Again they define *rhetoric* as an "intentional, created, polished attempt to overcome the obstacles in a given situation with a specific audience on a given issue to achieve no particular end."[70] In other words, we are thoroughly back in the tradition of rhetoric being mostly "eloquence," even what was at one time dismissed as "ornamentation."

Interestingly, Hogan and Reid put great stress on the ethos of the speaker. This of course follows Aristotle and Quintilian. They say that all Christian speakers must "strive for personal virtue because virtue matters in the proclamation of the gospel."[71] Kay says that comments like this are attempts to "baptize Aristotle" (Kay, pg. 28).

Hogan and Reid use a number of theological terms like "gospel," "grace," and "good news," and refer to theological subject matter, but nowhere do they suggest that the subject matter of theology demands a specific sort of sermonic rhetoric, or that the "sermonic subject matter exercises agency."[72] For them, "rhetoric is the constant; theology is the variable."[73] Hogan and Reid say that preaching is "a good person offering good reasons to good people."[74]

Kay's response to this rhetorical turn sounds almost Barthian (though in Kay's case it is probably Bultmannian): "The God of Christian preaching is the speaking God of the scriptures. We cannot preach as if this subject matter of our preaching were at our disposal or under our control. We do not create the Creator of the Gospel, and the Word of God is not a commodity we pedal (cf. II Corin. 2:71). Rather, as Paul reminds the Corinthians, 'We are ambassadors *for* Christ, *God making this appeal, through us* . . . ' (2 Cor. 5:20 RSV)." Kay says that rhetoric is absolutely right, that who preaches the gospel is the most important thing. For Christians the who who preaches is Christ![75] As Kay says, about the matter of form, that we cannot preach "as if the subject matter were indifferent to our words of witness."[76]

I expect Hogan and Reid would counter that effective preaching is effective rhetoric, "and we cannot begin a theory of preaching pietistically devoid of an understanding of the art of rhetoric."[77] Hogan and Reid would probably accuse Barth of beginning "pietistically," but they would be, again, wrong.

In the opening volume of the Church Dogmatics[78] Barth charged that the yearnings of "religion" had been exchanged for reflection upon revelation and thereby "theology lost its object." Yet true knowledge of God comes only through the grace of divine revelation. In other words, theology has lost something to preach. Preaching is not a human endeavor: *It is a miracle*. Preaching is in trouble today, not because it has difficulty finding the proper form or style, but because it has lost its subject matter. Grace *negates* preaching. When grace is given to hear, we preachers realize that God has taken over our sermon, that our sermon is now part of an event of proclamation that is out of our hands. The sermon has become God's word and has, in a sense, died in the process.

On the other hand, when grace is not given (because grace is a gift and a gift can be withheld or it is not a gift), then no matter how skillful our sermon, we usually do not have to be told that it did not become true proclamation. Many of our homiletic failures are due to God. Preaching is always dependent upon grace to elevate it (*Aufhebung*) to the Word of God. Our preaching is negated and exalted, devastated and birthed, judged and justified by the grace of God in revelation. The last words of Luther, "We are all beggars, this is true," were surely the last words of a preacher.

Barth's Homiletical Implications

Which brings us at long last to Barth's homiletics. It is high time for me to share some of my discoveries that have become my presuppositions in this conversation with Barth on preaching:

First, *Barth's helpfulness to preachers will be found more in his theological works than in his brief homiletical writings. Second, although some of Barth's basic convictions about proclamation remain throughout his life, Barth's actual practice of preaching shows development and change throughout his life. Third, we therefore do Barth a disservice to take his Bonn lectures on homiletics (that were much later published as* Homiletics) *as fully representative of Barth's homiletic. Fourth, Barth may not be as helpful to us preachers as a homiletical role model than as an engaging and encouraging critic of our preaching.*

In 1995 Hartmut Genest published a fine survey of Barth's preaching that stressed the changes in Barth's sermons and his thought about preaching.[79] He shows, through numerous examples from Barth's sermons, how Barth developed as a preacher. Recall that Barth was against abstract principles, foundational concepts, and eternal truths in theology. Genest cites three epochs of Barth's own preaching. *First* there is the young pastor, fresh out of theological studies, who shows the influence of his teachers Herrmann and Von Harnack with their stress, respectively, upon religious subjectivity and individualism, and historical relativity. Barth's Safenwil sermons of 1913–1914 present numerous examples of these liberal tendencies. A 1914 sermon clearly shows Barth's concern to link his new Kingdom of God interests with religious socialism. Many of the sermons from this period are long dissertations on various theological concepts and experiences, or biographical sermons like "The Life of William Booth." Yet the young Barth is a lively, engaging preacher who, according to Genest, works within the hermeneutical concept that his role as a preacher is to "look behind the historical through to the spirit of the Bible." The preacher is to point to and to elucidate the "spirit of the Bible" within the lives of the congregation.[80] These early sermons are quite different from Barth's almost exclusively christological sermons that were published in the 1960s.

Genest sees the early collection, "Come Creative Spirit," closely connected to *Romans*,[81] as representative of Barth's *second* homiletic phase. He also demonstrates that, although Barth clearly broke with Schleiermachian theology by the time *Romans* appeared, Barth continued to show a multidimensional connection with Schleiermacher's preaching for years to come. The feelings that Barth sought to make contact with were more akin to the feelings that concerned "dialectical theology," but it was still a homiletic of feeling.

The *third* phase of Barth's preaching is characterized by his prison sermons. In these sermons, regardless of the biblical text, Barth always points his hearers toward the living Christ, the work of Christ in their behalf, and the theological significance of their daily struggles, in those rare moments when their struggles are mentioned.

Genest then does a nice study of the question, "Just how wide was the influence of Barth upon homiletics from 1930 until 1970 in the German speaking area of Europe," particularly Barth's demand that preaching limit itself to pure biblical exposition. Genest finds only limited influence. German-speaking preachers, in the whole, tended to be much too abstract, conceptual, and (somewhat significantly) too "dogmatic" to suit Barth's ideas and practices of preaching.

Genest also shows how Barth's prison sermons (*Deliverance to the Captives*) show great interest in and sensitivity toward the hearer. He thus pleads with homileticians (such as Rudolph Boren) for an "end to the conversation blockade" between them and Barth over the tension between "theology and empirical insights."[82]

My own examination of the sermons of Barth confirms these three major periods of Barth's preaching. There is the early Safenwil period in which Barth preaches unashamedly topical sermons, rather long, on some theme of current or historical interest. Around 1920, after the publication of *Romans*, I sense that Barth is searching for a new approach to preaching. At about the same time that he attempts to write a commentary on Ephesians, his sermons seem much more biblical, yet very long and complicated. He still begins with some social problem and, only toward the end, will say something like, "Which brings us to St. Paul's insights on this subject. . . ."

During this period he writes to his friend Thurneysen, admitting that he preached to as few as eighteen or twenty people on a Sunday. His sermons are still what one might call "thematic," or "topical," which is remarkable considering his ideas in Romans. In other words, his homiletic does not seem to keep pace with his theological discoveries. For instance, in August 1919, he preached a sermon on parents and children, and as his major illustration of this theme, Barth has an extended reflection upon the relationship of the elder and younger Blumhardt (this was soon after the elder Blumhardt's death).

Barth preached only occasionally during his years as a professor from the 1920s to the 1940s. In a 1948 letter to Emil Brunner, he says that he wants to be open to change and development in his preaching but at the same time acknowledges a sense of failure when it comes to preaching. Many of Barth's sermons during this period begin to show that tendency that characterized his preaching for the rest of his life, that is, the Barthian inclination to seize upon one word in the biblical text like "All," or "Nevertheless," and preach an entire sermon on that word. He seems so convinced of the effusive power of the Word of God, that just one word is enough for a sermon. His sermons are also strictly, limitedly biblical, sounding much like his exegetical excurses in the *Dogmatics*.

After 1957 Barth began preaching at the Basel prison. Most English readers know Barth's preaching, if they know it at all, through these sermons, which show a much less complicated, direct, simple, and self-confident style, with almost no illustration, few allusions to contemporary situations, and an almost exclusive focus upon the biblical text, often one word in the text.

My analysis of an audio recording of two of these prison sermons was an ear-opening experience.[83] How much more lively, pastoral, and energetic was Barth as an actual preacher than were Barth's printed sermons! The actual oral presentation is more passionate and vivid than the German text, vastly more so than the English translation. These later sermons embody a more fully realized Barthian homiletic that exemplifies the strong principles that were enunciated in the homiletical lectures of 1933, yet with a vivid christological center.

I believe it is a mistake to regard Barth's 1933 *Homiletics* as either a fair representation of Barth's homiletic or as Barth's most significant word on homiletics. For Barth there is no final word on anything, no guiding principles for anything—including homiletics. Everything is in motion, in reformation—that is, everything that he says or writes attempts to honor a living, moving, active God. With Barth we begin all theological reflection "in the middle," in the middle of our time with God, in the middle of a conversation. There is no final word on anything, particularly no final word on preaching.

In reading his *Homiletics* we must remember that these are the notes taken by an admiring student, that were presented to Barth nearly thirty years after Barth delivered the lectures. Though some of his friends urged Barth not to allow them to be published, an aging Barth agreed, so Barth must have considered them to be a fair representation of his thought about preaching at a specific time in his life. Barth's *Homiletics* did not intend to lay down principles for preaching in all times and places. To do so would be an offense to the God who speaks always now, here, and a violation of his own theological principles. For instance, Barth criticized the preaching of his friend Thurneysen because it tended never to change, always hitting the same notes (usually a warning note about finitude and death).

Barth's *Homiletics* is incomprehensible apart from its specific time and place. These lectures were given in the middle of the German church's *Kirchenkamph* that was eventually to force Barth out of Germany. In the summer semester of 1933, Barth was being watched by the Nazis. Barth was appalled that the undistinguished, aging homiletics professor in Bonn had joined with the German Christians. So at the beginning of the semester, Barth announced that he was giving a series of lectures on homiletics. Of course, the homiletics professor was outraged, but Barth forged ahead with a remarkable theological *tour de force*. Difficult times require clear thinking and strong convictions. German preaching had tried to engage its listeners with illustrations from the best of German culture, with high-sounding theological abstractions and assorted delving into the soul of the modern, thinking person. And look what traditional homiletics had produced—the German Christians.

It is clear that Barth felt that German preachers desperately needed some strong, external authorization for their sermons. The preacher must therefore demonstrate that the biblical text for a sermon is laid upon the preacher. The text is an alien word. It therefore must be examined, in the sermon, carefully, line-by-line. In so doing, the preacher stresses the need for complete attention to and obedience to the biblical text without undue elaboration or illustration. So as we read Barth's sweeping denunciations and rather exaggerated assertions, we ought to do so with an image that Barth is talking about preaching in the *Homiletics* with Nazis in the back of the lecture hall.

At the end of the semester, Barth was removed from his teaching post and sent back to Switzerland.

Barth says that the preacher is the witness who has received a gift and merely shares that gift with the congregation:

> The Christian can confront the world only as a witness. His action is wholly dependent on the truth and reality of what he attests. He can only point men to the speaking of Jesus Christ, drawing attention to the fact that He speaks. . . . He cannot . . . come and speak among them as a second Christ, as if Christ spoke through him. He can encounter them only as the friend of the Bridegroom. If Christ speaks through him, giving to his witness the power of His own self-witness, as He can and will, this is not in the Christian's hands and he cannot boast of it to the world. He has no power to baptize with the Holy Ghost, for, even though he may receive and have Him, he does not control Him. Hence it does not stand in his own power to cause the Gospel so to shine that it must enlighten the world, to create and give men the freedom to grasp and appropriate the kingdom of God and therefore their reconciliation, to recognize and confess Jesus Christ as Lord. He cannot convert anyone.[84]

The preacher is unable to convert or to persuade anybody. When preaching "works," when it is true, it is a testimony to the grace of God, an event of divine election, divine vocation, divine justification, and divine sanctification. Barth's stress on preaching as an exercise of justification by faith links him with Reformation thought on preaching. The Reformers were so convinced of the power of the Word to speak for itself that they took a low view of the florid preaching that characterized much of the preaching of the Middle Ages. Though Barth seems not to know the English Puritans and their emphasis upon the "plain style," his *Homiletics* has striking similarities to Puritan anti-rhetorical thought on preaching, though Barth would probably be horrified by this observation.[85]

Barth's belief in the gratuitous, undeserved, yet real gift of revelation leads him into his infamous condemnation of all sermon introductions:

> Basically the sermon should not have an introduction. Only one kind of legitimate introduction is conceivable. When a scripture reading precedes the sermon, a link can be made with this, so that in some sense the sermon proper begins with a pre-sermon consisting of a brief analysis of the lesson that leads up to the real sermon. This is the only possible form of introduction. All others are to be rejected in principle.[86]
>
> The act of proclamation should begin at once. Any additional introduction is a waste of time. Since a sermon cannot go on too long, it is irresponsible. No doubt introductions offer many opportunities for much wit and cleverness, but in any case too much precious time is wasted by intellectual gymnastics of this kind.[87]

> The theological damage of sermon introductions is in any event incredibly extensive, and it is usually an error when preachers use them. For what do they really involve at root? Nothing other than the search for a point of contact, for an analogue in us that can be a point of entry for the Word of God. It is believed that this little door to the inner self must first be found and opened before it is worthwhile to bring the message. No! This is plain heresy. Were we to view the Fall in the framework of Roman Catholic theology, along the lines of prevenient grace or the analogy of being, then an approximation of humanity to God might be possible. But if we understand the Bible after the manner of the Reformers, we know that no such possibility exits. There is only one exception, the contact that is made, of course, by the miracle of God from on high. When the Word has found an entrance into a person, then *God* has worked the miracle, he alone, without any preparation or assistance of ours.[88]

Barth says that when a preacher quotes other people and uses illustrations in a sermon, this only causes listeners' minds to wander.[89] Barth is as opposed to sermon conclusions as to introductions:

> As we reject the special introduction, so there can be no independent conclusion; the sermon has to end with the exposition. If a summary is needed, it is already too late to give it; the mischief has been done. A theoretical sermon cannot be made more practical by a concluding application. Address can never come too soon.[90]

Though Barth does not put the matter this way, I would say that we preachers ought to preach in such a way as to demonstrate the active voice of God. One way to do that is to attempt sermons without introductions or conclusions, leaving the work of making connections and contextualizing the Word in God's hands. We must preach—sans introductions and conclusions—in such a way as to leave room for the grace of God.

We can't preach! When preaching works, it is not because I have had good training in homiletics and have used that training well, but rather as an exemplification of the doctrine of justification of sinners.[91] Christian preaching, as a gift of God's grace, is always in greater danger of failure, always more fragile and defenseless than other forms of public speaking. I say again, Christian preaching is not for the faint of heart.[92]

Nevertheless, we *do* preach and we *do* hear. "In the sphere of reverence before God, there must always be a place for reverence of human grace."[93] While we are revering a Trinitarian God, we must also revere human speech and hearing as gifts of God. Therefore, we are able to speak with great confidence, with an enthusiastic buoyancy that is rooted in the same source as our affirmation of the grace of God. Thus Barth's sermons and thought on homiletics exemplify a robust assurance that we can speak and can hear the Word of God, though not by any rhetorical means.

> To claim that understanding, hearing, and reception by the hearer is up to God and not to us preachers can be a hopeful word for us preachers. Preaching is, thank God, not exclusively in our hands. In my experience, our most conscientious and careful preachers need to hear this word of grace. Our striving ought not to be directed toward concocting the perfect sermon, but rather a striving to keep giving the glory to God in our preaching. The knowledge of God is like manna in the Exodus, says Barth:

>> The knowability of God's Word in faith is not an extraordinary art. Or should one rather say conversely that it is a highly extraordinary art? Its practice does not presuppose any special endowment whether natural or supernatural. The believer is the same ungifted and idle or gifted and busy man he was as an unbeliever and may become again. He believes as the man he is, with the inventory corresponding to his condition . . . It is a possibility given for use, not for putting in an inventory or catalogue, not for storing on ice or placing in a museum.
>> Even in its details the story of the "manna" in Ex. 16 is an illustration of what has to be said about faith in this connexion.
>> The possibility, then, is not one we can exhibit but only one to which we can point, like faith, or the Word of God itself, or the child born of the Virgin Mary in the manger at Bethlehem. The force and seriousness of this pointer must be the force and seriousness of God if we are really to point. Thus the first thing that must be said about the knowability of the Word of God as the possibility given to us in faith is that it arises and consists absolutely in the object of real knowledge.[94]

The Vocation of the Preacher

The Christian life, as depicted by Barth, consists of the willing reception of a divinely bestowed vocation. The significance of the preacher is as someone who has been summoned to be part of a divinely given task. Hunsinger says, "Just as here and now the noetic takes precedence over the experiential aspect of salvation, so also does the reception of the task take precedence over the reception of benefits," making "vocation as the controlling principle of the Christian life. Vocation means that Christians are called primarily to the task of witness."[95] "For this I was born, and for this I came into the world, to testify to the truth" (John 18:37). All human testimony is authentic only to the extent that it remains faithful to the witness of Christ. "You also are to testify because you have been with me from the beginning" (John 15:27). Isaiah says:

Let them bring their witnesses to justify them,
    and let them hear and say, "It is true."
You are my witnesses, says the LORD,
    and my servant whom I have chosen,
so that you may know and believe me
    and understand that I am he. (Isa. 43:9-10)

When God calls people, God tends to call them by their own names and tends to assign them specific tasks. Preaching involves a specific person called to speak to specific people. Thus Paul was called to be a witness to the Gentiles (Acts 9:15). Jeremiah was called to speak to exiles. Mary was called to sing to the rich and the poor. Whereas systematic theologians tend toward systemization, generalization, and abstraction, preachers know that it is the death of preaching to trade in broad generalizations. Barth provides us preachers with theological encouragement to resist all generalized, universalized, generic approaches to the gospel. The gospel, with its identification of Jesus as the specific form of the Word made flesh, necessitates a concrete, specific approach to our preaching:

> After this manner and reality which are spiritual both ontically and noetically, the vocation of man consists decisively in the fact that the living Jesus Christ encounters definite men at definite times in their lives as their Contemporary, makes Himself known to them as the One He is for the world, for all men, and therefore for them too, and addresses and claims them as partners in His covenant and sinners justified and sanctified in Him. He does this in the witness of the prophets and apostles. But in this witness it is He, Jesus Christ, who does it, so that these men may say with the Samaritans: v. 42. The historical process of vocation is thus highly extraordinary and yet also supremely historical event among others, and yet it is distinguished by this manner and content.[96]

Thus we are called to resist, in Hans Frei's term, "mythological readings" of scripture.[97] In mythological reading, the gospel becomes a means of arriving at a deeper understanding of the self, a deeper, broader sense of the sacred. Deeper understanding, enlightenment about the meaning of life, becomes salvation.[98] Frei, following Barth, notes that the gospel does not support such a reading. The unsubstitutable, unique, and decisive identity that is claimed for Jesus is not the stuff of myth. Myth trades in "once upon a time" universals and anywhere and anyplace generalities. Barth stressed, even more than Frei, that it is the peculiar nature of this particular savior, this specific Jew from Nazareth, to save through appointment of others, through calling and commissioning of specific people (the Twelve) who are elected by Jesus to be the specific means of his work in the world. There is, Barth stresses, "the definiteness of the divine decision."[99]

The main work that these apostles are sent to do is to preach the gospel in the world, to announce the kingdom of God and show signs of its enactment and thereby to witness its divine formation.[100] They speak only as those who have heard; they move out only as those who have been called; they represent only as those who have been commissioned. "Their field is the world, and they are only sowers who pass over it. They renounce any self-grounded or self-reposing rightness or importance of their distinctive being and activity. . . . It cannot be otherwise than that . . . in this renunciation they should be a normative pattern to the community gathered by this ministry."[101] Renouncing any self-grounded basis for their words, they also renounce any technique or strategy that presumes to make our words work through our techniques and stratagems. Our vocation, our authorization, and our validation are external to us preachers and our words.

We have noted Barth's lifelong fascination with Grunewald's John the Baptist of the Isenheim Altar. This image embodies Barth's view of preaching. Barth's John the Baptist is the Baptist as rendered in John 1:6-8, in distinction from the Baptist as presented in the synoptic Gospels. John the Baptist in the Fourth Gospel is one who is apostolic, that is, "sent from God" (1:6). His purpose is pure testimony (1:7). Twice it is reiterated that John is not the light but rather a "witness to testify to the light" (1:7-8). When John says that there is one who comes "after [me]," he speaks not chronologically but relationally. Jesus is superior and prior to the witness. John witnesses that no one can know the Father except by the revealing work of the Son (1:18). When John is challenged by the Levites, John calls himself a mere "voice" (1:23). Unlike the synoptics' depictions of the Baptist, we are given none of the moral exhortation of John's preaching, nothing about his appearance or much of the content of his preaching. We are only given John's testimony that, when he saw Jesus, he says that here was the "Lamb of God who takes away the sin of the world" (1:29), and that he saw the Spirit descending upon him like a dove. John's only function, his great purpose and significance, is to be a voice, a transparent witness who simply tells what he has seen (1:34). John's repeated exhortation is simply for people to "Behold the Lamb of God," that is, simply to look and to see what he has seen (1:36 RSV). This "beholding" is enough. At the testimony of John, two disciples "heard him say this, and they followed Jesus" (1:37). This is a good rendition of a Barthian homiletic, the witness who points to the finished, completed work of God in Jesus Christ on the cross.

In fact, the longer Barth preached, the more the theme of faith as the accomplished, finished work of God in our behalf came to the fore. His penchant for preaching a sermon on a single biblical word like "All," or "Nevertheless," which characterizes his last sermons, his complete avoidance of political themes in favor of theological ones, can all be attributed to the way in which God's accomplished reconciliation and redemption (themes in the final volumes of the *Church Dogmatics*) dominates Barth's thought at the end. As Hinrich Stoevesandt says of Barth's last sermons, "The keynote of the later sermons in particular is the faith, promised unconditionally to the listeners, that God's saving work in Christ has been definitively 'accomplished' (John 19:30)."[102]

Just as some have noted that Barth's theology of revelation is related to the Reformation's theology of justification *sola fidei*, so Barth's theology of preaching is based upon a theology of vocation. In the Reformation, vocation is a sort of subspecies of, or another form of, justification *sola fidei*. The preacher is called, commissioned, assigned a word that is never self-derived or self-authenticated by the person of the preacher. The whole church is that gathering that has been called to hear the word and to preach the word. Barth calls the church "apostolic," that is, sent. It is not to seek permanence, stability, some significance of its own, but rather must be content to be apostolic, to serve at the pleasure of the One who calls and commissions. Like the preacher, the church has no continuing, stable, ongoing significance beyond that of being called for a task. The church is pure mission:

> As an apostolic Church the Church can never in any respect be an end in itself, but, following the existence of the apostles, it exists only as it exercises the ministry of a herald. . . . It cannot forget that it cannot do [what it does] for its own sake, but only in the course of its commission—only in an implicit and explicit outward movement to the world. . . . Its mission is not additional to its being. It is, as it is sent and active in its mission. It builds up itself for the sake of its mission and in relation to it.[103]

Proclamation rests upon the Resurrection and Ascension as the decisive acts of divine self-communication. The Resurrection enabled the apostles, who had known Jesus in his "appearance of ignominy and despicability and insignificance,"[104] to know him in his full, true identity. Revelation involves vocation. This knowledge implied a mission that thrust the apostles to communicate him to the world. Each resurrection appearance is not only a validation of faith but also an occasion for vocation, a call to public speaking. The women at the tomb are told not only that "he is risen!" but also to "Go! Tell!"

So Barth says:

> If the [disciples] of the New Testament could think and speak at all of Jesus Christ, if they had any right to do so, it was only as He had given Himself to be known as the One He was in His resurrection and ascension, as [He] was manifested to them in the revealing power of this event. . . . In His resurrection and ascension He gave Himself to be seen and heard and understood by them as the one He was and is.
>
> He became for them not only One who is but One who is also known. And what other ground could they possibly have for thinking and speaking of Him, for going out as His witnesses to Israel and to the Gentiles? As they did it on this ground, they did it as those who were authentically instructed, as those who genuinely knew Him as witnesses of His history and existence whom He had authorized.[105]

Knowledge of God is always in Barth linked to the call of God, communication and disclosure are always linked to commission and call, and revelation divinely given is linked to obedient human response. Our challenge, as preachers, is not to master God's word but rather to develop the skills to listen to God without despising God for speaking to us. The God of the Bible who speaks is the God who commands and one wonders if many of our hermeneutical and homiletical strategies are designed to manage that command. For Barth, every single verse of scripture is a potential act of vocation. The question to be put to any of God's three forms of proclamation is never simply, "Do I understand?" or certainly not, "Do I agree?" but rather, "How am I being called to change and commit through this word?"

God's word is God's act, says Barth, in which God "makes history":

> We are speaking of God's Word. Therefore we have to speak of its power, its might, its effects, the changes it brings about. Because the Word of God makes history, as Word it is also act (Jer. 23:29).
>
> The promise of the Word of God is not as such an empty pledge which always stands, as it were, confronting man. It is the transposing of man into the wholly new state of one who has accepted and appropriated the promise, so that irrespective of his attitude to it he no longer lives without this promise but with it. The claim of the Word of God is not as such a wish or command which remains outside the hearer without impinging on his existence. It is the claiming and commandeering of man. Whatever may be his attitude to God's claim, man as a hearer of His Word now finds himself in the sphere of the divine claim; he is claimed by God.[106]

The Addressed

Aristotle's definition of a human being as "an animal who uses words," underscores that human characteristic that seems most to interest Barth. Christians, as a "people of the book," a "people of the word," resonate with Aristotle's definition of humanity as word-using animal. Is this what being created in "the image of God" means? God, as we first meet God in Genesis 1, is speech, "Let there be light . . ." (Gen. 1:3). This Creator is a great talker who creates through words.

And yet, Barth takes Aristotle's definition a step further. When we first meet humanity, in Genesis 2, it is not human speech that characterizes this peculiar, crowning act of creation, but rather human *hearing*. It is God who addresses humanity, before humanity musters the courage to say anything to God. When the earthling speaks, what is said is not much, a sort of self-congratulatory, sexist jubilation that the woman is "bone of my bones / and flesh of my flesh" (Gen. 2:23). Self-generated human speech is rarely of great consequence.

Thus, in distinction from Aristotle, Barth has us define humanity as *that animal who is addressed*. First God speaks to the "formless void" with "let there be light"; then God addresses the trees, the seas, the dry land. Finally, God turns for conversation to humanity, addressing humanity in a conversation that has not ended, a long dialogue, despite humanity's resources for evasion and penchant for monologue. Humanity is the creature addressed by God, the creature that has been given the gift of the ability to hear the speech of God, and the gift of something to do in God's continuing Creation ("Be fruitful and multiply"). Human speech tends to be responsive. First God speaks, then the human responds, and in responding the human being becomes truly human, that is, the human being that God intends the human to be.

Whereas Aristotle felt that human beings were distinguished by our rational qualities, our *episteme*, Genesis seems to assume that it is our hearing, our responsiveness that is most interesting. After calling all fish and fowl, all animals and creeping things into being, God turns exclusively to humanity for conversation. The animals are addressed in Genesis, given their vocation by God, but only humanity responds, dares to enter into conversation, and grows and develops in the process.[107]

History begins, not with our first actions and decisions, but in our being encountered by God: "The history of a being begins, continues and is completed when something other than itself and transcending its own nature encounters it, approaches it and determines its being in the nature proper to it, so that it is compelled and enabled to transcend itself in response and in relation to this new factor."[108] Our history begins to mean something, begins to move and receive its impetus only when we are freed from being locked up in ourselves, only in address, only in the invitation to be in dialogue. Who is a human being? Someone who is "summoned by this Word."[109] Our great, God-given dignity is that God wants to talk to us. God speaks to us and what God says is, "I will be your God and you will be my people."

CHAPTER SEVEN

HERALDS OF GOD

Barth began his second edition of *Romans* with a commentary on Romans 1:1, "Paul, a servant of Jesus Christ, called to be an apostle." Barth says that Paul "is no 'genius rejoicing in his own creative ability' (Zündel). The man who is now speaking is an emissary, bound to perform his duty; the minister of his King; a servant, not a master. However great and important a man Paul may have been, the essential theme of his mission is not within him but above him—unapproachably distant and unutterably strange. . . . He is—called by God and sent forth."[1] He has no significance of his own other than that he has been sent forth. Here, in Paul, is Barth's image of the preacher—someone who has miraculously been given a word from above.[2]

Preachers are called to be heralds of God, says Barth, witnesses, instruments whereby the divinely initiated conversation continues, the conversation that gives humanity to the earthlings in the first place. Heralds are those "who have something to relate about [God], the freedom of confessors who cannot keep silent but must speak of Him, their freedom to expose themselves to his glory, to commit themselves to His honour with clear and definite words, to be serviceable to Him in and with these words, to be His declared and decided partisans."[3]

The preacher preaches into a kind of human vacuum. The preacher cannot, through rhetorical strategies, prepare the hearers for the Word of God; only God can do that. Fortunately for the herald, God is active. Beyond affirmation of God's speech, the preacher can go no further. There is a border to our theological speculation.[4] The preparation required of the herald is attentiveness, notice, the courage to listen. The German word *Wahrnehmen*—to perceive, to observe, to be attentive—this is the homiletical preparation required of the herald: "Behold!"

Barth got his herald image primarily from Paul. Paul gives us the image of a herald running ahead of the royal entourage to proclaim the king's arrival. *Kerygma* refers both to the act of proclamation (1 Cor. 2:4) and also to the content of what is proclaimed (1 Cor. 15:4). The heralds proclaim only what the king authorizes. The word of the herald is a partisan word in behalf of the king. "So we are ambassadors for Christ, since God is making his appeal through us" (2 Cor. 5:20). Jesus Christ is therefore present in the kerygmatic occasion. He is present not as an empirical object, but as the saving power of the gospel. He is present not simply as the subject who is proclaimed but as the abiding agent of proclamation. "No one has ever seen God. It is God the only Son, who is close to the Father's heart, who has made him known" (John 1:18). Heralds witness to the arrival of Christ; he has sent us on ahead, in advance of his arrival, to "where he was about to go."

Barth says that God speaks through us preachers so that God's people might be in conversation with God:

> Proclamation is human language in and through which God Himself speaks, like a king through the mouth of his herald, which moreover is meant to be heard and apprehended . . . in faith as the divine decision upon life and death, as the divine judgment and the divine acquittal, the eternal law and the eternal gospel both together.[5]

This is indeed an actively theological view of preaching since, through the words of the preacher, God is doing the preaching, "making his appeal through us." In preaching, there is a voice beyond the voice of the preacher, that is, the very voice of God. The herald ought not to embellish or elaborate on the kingly proclamation.[6] The herald ought simply to speak it, to preach what the herald has been told to preach:

> We have simply to assume the attitude of a messenger who has something to say. We have no need to build a slowly ascending ramp, for there is no height that we have to reach. No! Something has to come down from above. And this can happen only when the Bible speaks from the very outset. We have then done what we could.[7]

The herald is not troubled by what the listeners need, or think they need. The listeners have no way of knowing who they are or what they need before they are addressed.[8] The herald need not be concerned with rhetorical stratagems or oratorical niceties (a "slowly ascending ramp"), because the Word of God makes its own way. The herald seeks only to be a faithful vehicle, a servant of the Word.[9] The herald's job is to proclaim the royal proclamation. Courage, rather than art or craft, is the prerequisite for good preaching.

For Barth, preaching is an act of divine self-disclosure, grace, revelation. What makes preaching interesting and important is not what the preacher says but what God says. The message determines the medium and is infinitely more significant than the messenger. The herald must get that divinely given message as clear as possible, then have the courage to stand up and speak it, and then sit down and let God do the work. As Barth says, in the opening pages of his *Homiletics*:

> He himself wills to attest his revelation. He himself—not we—has done this and wills to do it. Preaching, then, takes place in listening to the self-revealing will of God. Preachers are drawn into this event. It is of concern to them. They are called by this event. The event becomes a constituent part of their own existence. Because God has revealed himself and wills to reveal himself, and because preachers are confronted by this event, their preaching—if they are commissioned to preach—is necessarily governed by it in both content and form, in the logical content of what is said and in their relation to the fact that God has revealed himself and will reveal himself. Preaching is not a neutral activity. It is not an action involving two equal partners. It can mean only Lordship on God's side and obedience on ours.[10]

The listening of the herald is thus prior to the herald's speaking. Essential disciplines for the preacher are the disciplines of hearing—prayerful, attentive, focused, obedient, and courageous receptivity—rather than the disciplines of delivery and address.[11]

David Bartlett says that the main continuity throughout the New Testament concerning the gospel is that the gospel "is still always the herald's announcement of God's victory." Bartlett goes on to note that the term "gospel," *euangelion*, which the earliest Christian writers used as a description of the Christian message, may have been a word they borrowed from the surrounding classical culture. "There the term refers to a message delivered by a herald, sometimes the message of a royal birth, sometimes the message of military victory. It was an announcement (an *aggelion*), and it was a good announcement (a *euaggelion*)."[12] Mark says that Jesus began his ministry calling on people to believe "the good announcement." In Galatians 1:11-12, Paul says that he is a herald who brings an announcement, "for I want you to know, brothers and sisters, that the gospel that was proclaimed by me is not of human origin; for I did not receive it from a human source, nor was I taught it, but I received it through a revelation of Jesus Christ." In other words, Paul claims that his gospel is miraculous in origin.

The message of God is more than a set of words spoken over a congregation, something delivered to them; the message is an event, something that happens to them, a lightning bolt of divine disclosure that is beyond the control of the preacher.

Thomas G. Long has developed the preacher-as-witness image in his influential homiletical textbook, *The Witness of Preaching*: "Consider what happens in a court trial. The trial is conducted in a public place because what happens is a public matter. A trial is designed to get at the truth, and the people have a vested interest in the truth. In order to get at the truth, a witness is brought to the stand to testify. Now this witness is in every way one of the people, but he or she is placed on the stand because of two credentials: The witness has seen something, and the witness is willing to tell the truth about it—the whole truth and nothing but the truth. In one sense, the personal characteristics of the witness do not matter. The court is interested in the truth and in justice, not in the witness per se. In another sense, however, the character of the witness is crucial. If the witness lies—bears false witness— the ability of the people to discover the truth will receive a grievous blow. 'False testimony,' writes Ricoeur, 'is a lie in the heart of the witness. This perverse intention is so fatal to the exercise of justice and to the entire order of discourse that all codes of morality place it very high in the scale of vices.'"[13]

Expanding the witness metaphor, Long says that "the court has access to the truth only through the witness. It seeks the truth, but it must look for it in the testimony of the witness. The very life of the witness, then, is bound up into the testimony. The witness cannot claim to be removed, objectively pointing to the evidence. What the witness believes to be true is a part of the evidence, and when the truth told by the witness is despised by the people, the witness may suffer, or even be killed, as a result of the testimony. It is no coincidence that the New Testament word for 'witness' is *martyr*."

The preacher's authority rests upon something that the preacher has seen and heard. The preacher goes to the biblical text, in service to the congregation, hoping there to be encountered by a voice, a living presence. This gives the preacher something to witness. The preacher has been ordained as one who is a reliable, dependable witness. The preacher's training is training in those disciplines necessary to be a witness.

Long stresses that the objective otherness of the preacher's message has rhetorical implications for how the preacher will form the message: "The witness image carries with it guidance about the rhetorical form of preaching. The witness is not called upon to testify in the abstract but to find just those words and patterns that can convey the event the witness has heard and seen. One can even say that the truth to which the witness testifies seeks its own verbal form, and the responsibility of the witness is to allow that form to emerge. Most often the witness is invited to 'tell your story'; thus the prominence given to narrative in the storytelling image is also implied in the image of witness. On other occasions, though, the truth will demand another form. Preaching, in other words, will assume a variety of rhetorical styles, not as ornaments but as governed by the truth to which they correspond. The shape of the witness's sermon should fit the character of the testimony."[14]

The witness image is thus a reminder that we preachers are radically dependent on something other than ourselves in order to have something to say. The witness is always subordinate to that which is witnessed.[15] God is always out ahead of us, enlisting and empowering us to lead in the work of the Word

> by sending [the church] among the peoples as his own people, ordained for its part to confess him before all human beings, to call them to him and thus to make known to the whole world that the covenant between God and man concluded in him is the first and final meaning of its history, and that his future manifestation is already here and now its great, effective, and living hope.[16]

As the Barthian commentator Hinrich Stoevesandt says, "The sermon is never more than a 'hint' (*Hinweis*—that is, a pointing to, a calling to attention) of the presence of God himself."[17] My only quibble with Stoevesandt's definition is in his "never more than." It takes a considerable amount of courage, in a society in which everyone is pointing in a different direction (usually toward themselves), for the herald to point in a distinctly divine direction and say, "Look, here! Here is the Word of God."

The Eventful Vocation

Earlier we noted that Barth teaches that revelation is an "event." Our descriptions of revelation are like attempts to draw a bird in flight or to describe lightning when all we have to go on is what is left after lightning strikes. Barth continuously stresses that revelation is not something that we have or hold, but always something that God gives, fresh, new each day, each moment of revelation.

I remind you that the event of revelation also has a twofold aspect in Barth—divine gift and human response. God graciously makes Godself to be objectively known to us through the three forms of proclamation and also, through the Holy Spirit, enables us to respond in faith to that divine self-manifestation. Again we ought to remind ourselves of what has been said before (Barth never tires of these reminders of what has been said before): "revelation" has both objective and subjective aspects. Revelation is both God's self-manifestation and also the gift of faith through which we receive and obey what we have heard.[18] Revelation is God's speaking and our response, God's command and our obedience.

It is not true that Barth has no interest in the response of our hearers to our preaching:

> The witness of the community must be evangelical address, i.e., address in which men are claimed in advance for what is to be made known to them as the content of the Gospel. This content must form not only the declaration and explanation but the appeal with which the community turns to the world. . . . To address men evangelically is decisively to present to them the great likeness of the declaration and explanation of the Gospel in such a way that they come to see its crucial application to them, that so far as any human word can do so it pricks their heart (v. 37), that it brings them to realize that the reference is to them, or to a supremely general truth which as such demands their personal cognizance and knowledge.[19]

Barth ends one of his prison sermons with this recognition of the possibility, even the necessity of response:

> What shall we do now? Shall we continue in our old ways, in absentmindedness, in disbelief, perhaps in some lofty Christian sentiments? Or shall we awake and rise, set out on our journey and turn about? The angel of the Lord does not compel anybody. Even less can I compel! A forced listening to the Christmas story, a forced participation in the story, is of no avail. We must willingly listen, and willingly participate.[20]

This objective-subjective, gift-response event happens as pure, undeserved act of God, an event by which we find ourselves drawn into the circle of God's knowing, into that constant communication that goes on in the very heart of the Trinity. Knowledge of God, conversation with God, cannot be summoned by human beings, even those who practice noble spiritual disciplines. It cannot be frozen and codified, systematized and examined like a cadaver on a table. It cannot be printed in a sermon to be coolly considered later at one's leisure. We can only live by faith in God's promise that the lightning that has struck in the past will strike again in the future. We are free to cherish and to identify the places where revelation has happened and where we believe it possible for it to happen again. We can only trust that the God who raised Jesus from the dead continues to raise the dead and to make alive. But none of those actions on our part guarantees the event, for revelation is always dynamic and gifted.[21]

Gerhard Sauter, student of Barth, in his *Dogmatics*, displays the most Barthian description of the preaching task that I have found among contemporary theologians:

The inner grounding of proclamation is the prevenient action of God. It is only thanks to this action that the presence of God already embraces all of us: speakers, hearers, the people we speak to, the people we pray for. We dare not make this point except in faith, hope, and love. Yet the expectation it gives us is a most powerful weapon against indoctrination, which is the greatest misunderstanding of proclamation. The community on no account should experience exorcism. It confesses its sins, but this does not allow preachers to root out those who must be excluded on account of their "unbelief," and in the way led to "faith."

The prevenient action of God is the presence of his Spirit. God is present with us before we are aware of it. He acts in relation to us even before we are believers, even before we can speak meaningfully about belief and unbelief, even before we know what these terms signify. He has confronted us for a long time. Were we aware of it? Could we be before his message reaches us? He is at work among us, but are we where he is? His promise leads us beyond ourselves into faith, hope, and love.

The fact that proclamation is grounded in the presence of God's Spirit does not usually form part of the content of proclamation, but is does form its theological premise, which can come to view in its fine structure. Proclamation and dogmatics are thus interlocked. Dogmatics unfolds the theological grounding of proclamation. . . .

Pronouncing the message of God's prevenient grace, proclamation is at its heart *kerygma*. . . . missionary preaching signifying that people of all kinds are called into the Christian fellowship, not born into it. Along with this an outward reason is mentioned that is not restricted to mission, namely, Christian communities have arisen, and still arise, as individuals are called out of their particular circumstances and *into* the history that God has founded with humanity *(ecclesia)*. For the sake of this message, ambassadors are needed who will proclaim the fact that Jesus was sent into the world. Proclamation needs messengers to transmit it, to do so plainly and simply, announcing the unknown proximity of God. They will not impart either doleful messages or songs of victory, but the message that has itself been given, the Word that comes from God and will not return to him empty (Isa. 55:11).

This message is new and strange, and not merely for those who have not yet heard it, that is, on the mission field, but also for all those who hear far too many voices, not least their own. The message tells us who God really is, who we ourselves are in his presence, and what is real. It will surprise us often enough, and at times alienate us, but it will at least cause us to address the question: Who are you? How do you live and how will you die? What have you to do or not do?

The inner grounding of proclamation is the inexhaustible fullness of the presence of God's Spirit. . . .

The inexhaustibility of the presence of the Spirit relates to the fact that the Spirit is linked to the Word and thus to the many ways in which the Bible speaks about God. . . . . As proclamation is dependent on dogmatics (so that we do not lose sight of the infinite range of God's action), it is also dependent on the canon. A multitude of voices are heard in the biblical Word, all in tension, yet all in secret agreement as regards God's action. As we listen to these voices, proclamation will show us how manifold is the work of God. . . .

The inexhaustible presence of the Sprit of God intensifies to proclamation, actually demanding that preaching and pastoral counseling be one-sided in their aim at specificity. This is not just because no one can say everything at once. Proclamation is pointed just because it encourages us to go beyond this point. It leads us into unknown territory that may seem to us to be no-man's land at first glance. But we can take this step, for proclamation does not stand alone. It is accompanied by all the other activities of the church. We may take the step indicated by proclamation because it is supported by lament, petition, and intercession, by praise and thanksgiving.

Why is it never enough to hear only one sermon, no matter how incisive for our lives this might be? Proclamation as kerygma extends to us a message from outside that we cannot grasp, that might easily be buried under other things, so that we have to hear it time and time again in various situations and with many nuances. It will always come to us as something new and different, yet it is always the same, for God himself speaks to us. He speaks to us in unexpected ways, and even though we go to meet him, his Word *strikes* us. He finds us in ways that we do not recognize ourselves, or do not want to, and addresses us in ways that we can never speak about ourselves. . . . God's unknown proximity is not uncovered by stages in proclamation. Fresh hearing, then, is always demanded even though it leads us forward. We will never reach an end, however, for the unknown proximity of God is inexhaustible, because he remains concealed in his revelation but, in his concealment he is near to us.

In proclamation God draws near to us.[22]

We preachers resonate to the notion of the eventful quality of revelation. The longer I preach, the more convinced am I that preaching is the most fragile of artistic media. Our words are spoken, they waft out over the congregation, bounce back and forth off the walls of the church, and are heard no more.[23] A sermon cannot be "redone," duplicated. A sermon can be artificially, electronically recorded, but no one, after having heard that sermon preached "live," would confuse that recording of the sermon with the actual event of the sermon itself, any more than we would confuse a stuffed and mounted eagle with a live one. There is no way to reassemble the congregation, the moment, the visual and auditory expressions of the preacher, the interaction with the hearers, or (Barth would want us to say) the particular event when God spoke in and through the sermon and transformed that sermon into revelation and the preached word became God's word. Two persons listen to the same sermon. One says, "That sermon really spoke to me." The other, listening to the same sermon, says, "I didn't get it." It is a fragile, uncontrollable, unpredictable medium.

Nicholas Wolsterstorff notes Barth's "relentless eventism" as Barth's determination to keep revelation in God's hands rather than ours. Barth is determined to keep revelation miraculous.[24] What Barth says of scripture can be transposed directly to preaching:

Only when and as the Bible grasps at us. . . . If the prophets and apostles tell us what they have to tell us, if their word imposes itself on us . . . all this is God's decision and not ours. . . . The Bible is God's Word to the extent that God causes it to be His Word, to the extent that He speaks through it. . . . The Bible, then, becomes God's Word in this event, and in the statement that the Bible is God's Word the little word "is" refers to its being in this becoming.[25]

Stoevesandt gives what he terms a "Barthian" definition of preaching. Note the Barthian stress on preaching as a divine rather than a human act:

> Preaching is speech of those human beings who are empowered to speak to other human beings who gather in the worship service of the congregation, in the middle of the present world, and are addressed by the triune God as an expression of God's presence, on the basis of scripture, by the Holy Spirit, in the hope of God's own work and correction through the sermon.[26]

Bonhoeffer, by the way, was among those who were critical of the Barthian stress upon revelation as "event." Gary Dorrien notes that, while Bonhoeffer recognized that Barth was attempting to honor Kant's warning that God cannot be "an object of knowledge," a thing to be examined like any other object, and while Bonhoeffer agreed that Barth's radical "actualism" wonderfully stressed the sovereignty of God and the prevenience of grace, Bonhoeffer was concerned that Barth had too heavily stressed God's freedom from human constraints in his doctrine of the event of revelation. Barth made God isolated and episodic in God's relations with the world, charged Bonhoeffer. Our God, said Bonhoeffer, is the God who has, in the Incarnation, freely bound himself to the world. We can therefore intelligently speak about the continuity and reliability of God's revelation, not simply its eventfulness. We can, by God's grace, move beyond paradox and nonobjectivity, momentary encounters and episodes of revelation, to receive the self-giving of God.[27]

Yet Barth's "event" language is in great part his attempt to embody the Lutheran theology of justification by faith in his theology of proclamation. Barth closely follows Luther's understanding of salvation not as a process but as a person, an accomplished fact, something to be gratefully acknowledged and received, a gift. There is no soteriological gradualism in Luther or in Barth, no gradual acquisition of a righteous disposition, certainly no "faith development," or any other gradual, sequential process. Salvation is the finished work that God has done for us. And when we sinners comprehend our salvation, it is an event in which we, in a moment, wake up to the facts of what God has done in Jesus Christ.

Barth's belief that our salvation is finished and accomplished has implications for his homiletics. In the sermon, everything is "downhill":

> The real need is not so much to get to the people as to come from Christ. Then one automatically gets to the people. Nothing should be said on any other level than that of the Word made flesh. No position need be taken vis-à-vis the gospel. The preacher should simply believe the gospel and say all he has to say on the basis of this belief. This means that the thrust of the sermon is always downhill, not uphill to a goal. Everything has already taken place.[28]

The sermon proceeds "downhill," working from the summit of our already accomplished salvation in Christ. The sermon does not intend to move people toward salvation but rather to realize that their salvation is the glorious, finished work of God.

Whenever preaching works, it works in much the same way that salvation works in Barth: "It can only be a matter of the unexpected work of grace."[29] Though Bonhoeffer was right in appreciating the dangers of a misuse of the Doctrine of Justification, Barth joyfully risks these dangers in his determination to keep revelation in God's hands and to keep that revelation dynamic and vital. Even though we can work hard, plan, and provide, "we must not arrogate to ourselves that which can be given and received only as a free gift."[30]

Barth says that preaching can never be justified by us:

Preaching on its own makes no sense at all. The fact that it has meaning does not lie in the preaching itself but in the objective substance . . . revelation, church, commission, and ministry. This means that preachers have to rely on the justification of what they do in Christ, the subject of revelation, the Lord of the church, the source of the command and calling. They are thus referred to the necessity of their faith in justification: a faith which grasps it, which stands in strict relation to the act of the God who justifies that which does not have justification; faith, then, in the sense: "Fear not, only believe." Since, however Christ's justification applies to us in our total existence, it means (in the sense of *existere*) our justification in the situation of our stepping out to act, though not as a transformation, as an endowment, as the infusion of a new nature to enrich us from some higher source. From first to last justification is the light of God's countenance on people who are not transformed, who remain the same as they were before.[31]

Thus preaching is not for the theologically tepid or for the rhetorically weak of heart. Against all instrumental, utilitarian Christianity Barth thunders,

Grace is the majesty, the freedom, the undeservedness, the unexpectedness, the newness, the arbitrariness, in which the relationship to God [i.e., *koinonia*] and therefore the possibility of knowing him has opened up to man by God himself. Grace is really the orientation in which God sets up an order which did not previously exist, to the power and benefit of which man has no claim, which has no competence, even subsequently to justify, which in its singularity . . . he can only recognize and acknowledge and actually set up, as it is powerful and effective as the benefit that comes to him.[32]

"I give thanks to God always for you because of the grace of God that has been given you in Christ Jesus, for in every way you have been enriched in him, in speech and knowledge of every kind—just as the testimony of Christ has been strengthened among you" (1 Cor. 1:4-6).

From my observations of contemporary preaching, neither "conservative" nor "liberal" preachers are immune from the temptation to take the grace of God into our hands and justify our sermons on the basis of our own rhetorical efforts, though we do this in different ways. Too many who fancy themselves as "expository," even "biblical" preachers tend first to reduce the bubbling biblical text to a set of propositions, such as "six biblical principles for success" or "ten steps to a happier family life," and then preach those conceivable steps, using bits of the Bible as a sort of gloss on the principles that they derived from contemporary culture rather than from the scripture. Preachers of a more liberal disposition devise some story, an extended illustration, whereby they hope to evoke—more typically, to induce—some feeling of God's nearness to and affirmation of the listener in the listener. Both methods tend to be evasions of the truth that "the just shall live by faith."

True, our God is graciously, dependably self-revealing, but never in a way that relinquishes God's sovereignty over revelation. Thus in *Romans*, citing Kierkegaard and Luther for theological support, Barth writes:

The Gospel requires—faith. . . . It can therefore be neither directly communicated nor directly apprehended . . . it can appear among us, be received and understood by us, only as contradiction. The Gospel does not expound or recommend itself. It does not negotiate or plead, threaten or make promises. It withdraws itself always when it is not listened to for its own sake. . . . "Indeed only when that which is believed on is hidden, can it provide an opportunity for faith. And moreover, those things are most deeply hidden which most clearly contradict the 'obvious experience of the sense'" (Luther).[33]

Elsewhere Barth says, paradoxically, that revelation is always "hidden," because it is a gift from outside our accustomed conceptual frames of reference.

> To deny the hiddenness of revelation even in Scripture is to deny revelation itself, and with it the Word of God. For God's Word is no longer God's Word when the truth that is new every morning . . . is made into sacred reality, when the miracle of God that is encircled with the possibility of offense is made into a marvel to which one may quietly point.[34]

Even as people looked at Jesus and did not see him as the Word made flesh, so our knowledge of God is both veiled and unveiled, constantly. As we preachers point to the Word, we must do so in a way that allows the Word to be kept as lively and itinerant as the Risen Christ.

> Mark's Gospel vividly portrays the difficulty of communication of the gospel. Yet paradoxically, Mark also portrays the gracious miracle of hearing the gospel. Thus Jesus told a parable in Mark 4:26-29 about the sower who sows and sleeps and rises and goes about daily life. But in the invisible, hidden time, God gives a harvest —"automatically," the Greek says. God takes our poor homiletical efforts and gives them results we could not ourselves give them. In Mark 8:17-21, Jesus marvels at his disciples' inability to understand. By our own devices, we are not capable of interpretation, misinterpretation, or reception of the message. Yet at the end of Mark's Gospel (Mark 15:39), the Roman centurion (!) understood.

> Faithful preaching thus inevitably involves the preacher's resistance against the tendency of the church to want to contain and stabilize God. Church furniture tends to be heavier than it needs to be, large, bolted to the floor. Church buildings tend to be built more substantially than is necessary. Perhaps this comes from the church's inchoate knowledge that it is the nature of this God's word to cause oaks to whirl, to shake the foundations, ripping doors off their hinges (Psalm 29; Acts 2). Therefore, preaching is a perfect medium for the communication of this God because of its fragility, its orality, its lack of stability, and its resistance to duplication and definition.

> If preaching works, it can work only in the way that salvation works in Barth: "It can only be a matter of the unexpected work of grace."[35] Even though we can work hard, plan, and provide, "we must not arrogate to ourselves that which can be given and received only as a free gift."[36] Thus preaching is hard for those who like to be in control.

> However, Barth did say, on a rare occasion, that preachers ought to prepare and work on their sermons. It is not enough simply to say, "Preaching is a miracle," and use this as an excuse for homiletical irresponsibility. Barth says that "vengeance is swift" upon the ill-prepared preacher:

> > I once had two experiences closely related in time. The first was on a Saturday evening when I attended a variety show which was perfect in all its items and therefore, so far as I could see, executed with a real righteousness of works. The second was on the following Sunday morning when I listened to an extremely poor sermon, a real piece of theological bungling. Could I resist the impression that, formally at least, the right thing had been done at the place of very secular amusement and not at the place where the Gospel is preached and worship offered? Vengeance is swift if we think that the service of the Christian community is not also a human activity, that it does not fall under the concept of work and the question of right work, and that theological and

ecclesiastical work does not also possess its own distinctive orientation to an end and the resultant objectivity. Vengeance is swift if in virtue of the Holy Spirit we think that we need not do our best in the same modest but definite sense in which this is almost taken for granted by the children of the world and thus constitutes a promising aspect of so much secular activity.

For Barth, the *scandalon* must be allowed to stand, that scandal of the Word made flesh in a form that we did not apprehend but rather apprehended us. God's Word comes to us in fully human form. Yet precisely because it is God in human form, it is veiled from us and becomes real to us only in the event of revelation. The real presence of the Word in human words cannot be guaranteed, coerced, pinned down, or held. As in the Sacraments, it can only be prayed for and received by faith in, with, and under the creaturely elements.

Preaching for Barth is "human talk about God on the basis of the self-objectification of God which is not just there, which cannot be predicted, which does not fit into any plan, which is really only in the freedom of His grace, and in virtue of which He wills at specific times to be the object of this talk, and is so according to His own good pleasure."[37] Preaching is what we do; proclamation is what God does. Proclamation "must be so solely the truth and miracle of God if his Logos, as he does not regard the lowliness of his handmaiden . . . or view the unclean lips of Isaiah as an obstacle . . . does not think it impossible to pitch his tent in what is at best our poor and insignificant and stammering talk about God."[38]

Barth encourages us, therefore, to think of the task of preaching as a human task, as a response to divine grace. By the grace of God preaching is both an objective and subjective event, as God's initiative and as human response. Jesus Christ is not only the One who is proclaimed but also the gracious Proclaimer.[39]

Eventful theology not only ensures that Barth's theology keeps tied to the self-giving of God that overcomes human incapacity but also ensures that his theology is characterized by movement, energy, and vitality. Deep in the *Church Dogmatics*—whether he is dealing with the church, the inspiration of scripture, faith, knowledge, ethical guidance, or preaching—Barth always understands these phenomena as events. Neither self-initiating nor self-sustaining, ungrounded in any ontological or noetic relationship between Creator and creature, they are always events of gracious intrusion, the dynamic result of God's continuing determination to be our God. The Truth who is Jesus Christ is not a static truth, fixed and stated once and for all.[40] This truth is the predicate of God's own living reality as Jesus the Christ. This truth keeps becoming incarnate, keeps assuming human form, stooping to us that we might receive him in faith. We cannot have this Truth in some abstraction or concept, but only in a living relationship and conversation. This Truth speaks for himself.

Because revelation is a divinely given event, Barth says that the appointed herald need only repeat the biblical words; God grants the hearing. There is thus no invention on the part of the herald, no struggle for an appealing homiletical "point of contact," indeed, Barth rejects the notion of even the possibility of such a point of contact. Barth says:

> I have the impression that my sermons reach and "interest" my audience most when I least rely on anything to "correspond" to the Word of God already "being there," when I least rely on the "possibility" of proclaiming this Word, when I least rely on my ability to "reach" people by my rhetoric, when on the contrary I allow my language to be formed and shaped and adapted as much as possible by what the text seems to be saying.[41]

The most interesting thing that happens in preaching is beyond the preacher's devising, or even beyond the congregation's response. The most interesting thing is that God deems to speak through a lowly human medium like preaching.[42] Thus Barth retains the vigorously theological, gracious, miraculous quality of preaching. He rescues preaching from its tendency to degenerate into merely moralistic, anthropological exercises of advice-giving, scolding, and helpful hints for making it through the week. Barth maintains preaching as a godly event, a gift, something "from above"[43] (John 3).

Unapologetic Preaching

The closed circle of Christian communication, the distinctive linguistic world of the Christian faith, and the miraculous "from above" quality of revelation all account for Barth's great enmity to apologetics.[44] Barth's anti-apologetic stance also puts Barth at odds with a major thrust of today's homileticians. Professor of homiletics Craig Loscalzo says that apologetics is one of the chief roles of today's preacher. "The preacher's ideal role resides in *meaning giving* . . . apologetic preaching offers theological meaning to a culture,"[45] desperately seeking significance, "yet not knowing to what or whom to turn to find it." You can imagine all of the reasons Barth would disagree with Loscalzo's description of apologetic preaching—too vague, too anthropological, too general.

Many recent commentators, while believing that apologetics is an important enterprise for the church, believe that preaching is not the best place for apologetics. The philosopher William P. Alston says that philosophic thinking "rarely, if ever, propels one into a condition of faith." What "propels people to belief"? Alston says that belief arises as "a process of responding to a call, of being drawn into a community, into a way of life."[46] That great communitarian Stanley J. Grenz, in his *A Primer on Postmodernism*, in typical postmodern fashion, discounts the value of preaching and stresses the importance of the social, communal aspects of conversion to the gospel:

> Members of the next generation are often unimpressed by our verbal presentations of the gospel. What they want to see is a people who live out the gospel in wholesome, authentic, and healing relationships. Focusing on the example of Jesus and the apostles, a Christian gospel for the postmodern age will invite others to become participants in the community of those whose highest loyalty is to the God revealed in Christ. . . . We must continue to acknowledge the fundamental importance of rational discourse, but our understanding of the faith must not remain fixated on the propositional approach that views Christian truth as nothing more than correct doctrine or doctrinal truth.[47]

The church itself, in its life together, becomes the new apologetics.

In agreement with Barth, I now believe that the church is not here to speak to the world. We preachers do not have as our task to provide the world with some reason for living or some meaning for its worldliness—we do not believe that the world, on its own, can have a reason or a meaning for its life. The church is about a more imperialistic enterprise than a deferential speaking to the world. We are to let God destroy and create a world through our preaching. That creation of a new world is more than an anthropological matter, more than a cultural-linguistic construction. It is a gift of a world-creating God. This is clear in the church's worship that seeks, through ritual, habit, sign, and symbol, to rearrange the most basic of human activities—eating and drinking, bathing, speaking, walking, listening—under its peculiar experience of the world. Time is retaken, rearranged. It is no small thing that the church considers Maundy Thursday more significant than Mother's Day. The church privileges conversion over apologetic, transformation over conversation.[48]

God is proved only by God's speaking, not through natural theology arguments of God's existence. Since the unbeliever lacks the one requisite for true knowledge, that is, faith, there is no wonder why apologetics, which tries to get around the need for faith, doesn't work. Where God fails to convince the unbeliever, there is little that we can do to convince. Barth's famous rejoinder to Emil Brunner in 1929, *"Nein!"* objected to Brunner's formulation (later refined) that "the mere act of 'bearing witness' remains sterile unless it can be integrated with the truth which the listener already possesses."[49] Barth rejected the possibility of some divine-human connection that is located on the human side of the equation. To assert such a starting point is to dignify unbelief, making it more than it is, and to not give proper weight to the primacy of faith. Believers who reach out, in apologetics, to nonbelievers are in danger of assuming the standpoint, the ground that is occupied by the nonbeliever and thus giving away too much territory before the battle begins.[50] It is no good for the believer to act as though he accepts the nonbeliever's presuppositions. That is a lie. Furthermore, in apologetics, believers are often forced (so they think) to argue that their faith is based on evidence or natural theology when it is, in fact, based upon quite other things (relationship, revelation, a sense of what is true on the basis of what has been given them in faith, etc.). So Barth discounted tolerant dialogue as appropriate for the presentation of the Christian faith, for this truth cannot be considered as relative or nonbinding ideas. The truth that is binding upon the Christian preacher is assumed to be equally binding upon the listener. "It is only where adversaries are opposed with genuine dogmatic intolerance that there is the possibility of genuine and profitable discussion. For it is only there that one . . . has something to say to the other."[51]

In the middle of his largely extemporaneous lectures that became *Dogmatics in Outline*, delivered in the ruins of the University in Bonn from which Barth had been earlier expelled, Barth was asked, "Are you not aware that many are sitting in this class who are not Christians?" Barth says that he laughed and said, "That makes no difference to me."[52]

Whereas this statement is sometimes presented as evidence of Barth's arrogant lack of concern for the non-Christian, it is better interpreted as a theological statement that arises out of Barth's peculiar regard for the non-Christian. With so many forces separating "Christians" from "non-Christians," Barth thought it sad to contribute yet one more separation. His Doctrine of Election, among other things, enabled Barth to look at the non-Christian and not tell much difference between the non-Christian and the Christian. He was determined never to take the nonbeliever's disbelief, or the believer's belief, too seriously.[53]

Barth, in expressing admiration for Herrmann's radical Christology, agrees with him that apologetics is a subordinate and passing activity of the church, destined to vanish because "knowledge of God is expression of religious experience wholly without weapons."[54] The only means we have of making sense of the gospel is Christ. Apologetics tends to speak and reason as if the cross and resurrection of Christ were incidental to comprehension of what we have to say, as if Christian claims can be comprehensible even if one rejects the Christian world. In other words, if we ever devised an effective apologetics that enabled us to present the Christian faith without recourse to a God who speaks for himself, then all we would have done is, through our apologetics, convinced people that there is no God who speaks. To put it in another way, apologetics is a sort of backhanded way of saying that what we believe about God is not really true.[55] We have no weapon to defend Christ; he can only defend himself. We have no "knock down" arguments for Christ; he himself is the only argument.

Barth criticized nineteenth-century liberal theologians who worried too much about the challenges of contemporary thought and as a result "miss a certain carefree and joyful confidence in the self-validation of the basic concerns of theology. . . . It did not enter into their minds that respectable dogmatics could be good apologetics. Man in the 19th century might have taken the theologians more seriously if they themselves had not taken him so seriously."[56]

"Pray," admonished the Bal Shem Tov during one of Poland's pogroms against his fellow Jews, "that we might fall into the hands of God and not into the hands of men." This is a good prayer to be prayed by every preacher at the beginning of every sermon, a prayer for deliverance from the temptation to apologetics, the temptation to play God.

Modern epistemologies made Christian speech unintelligible. Christianity found itself assaulted, in modernity, by ways of thinking and comprehending that claimed to be more universal, more public, less tethered to tradition, so that apologetics seemed to be unavoidable. In apologetics, we took up the weapons of the world—positivism, emotivism, Kant, pop-psychology, existentialism, whatever lay close at hand—and attempted to defeat the world's wisdom with the wisdom of the world rather than the foolishness of the gospel. In other words, apologetics is but one more way that we Christians attempted to make ourselves at home in a world that is not our home.

Samuel Wells notes that, amid the intellectual assaults of modernity and Christianity's dismissal from the table of political debate,

> for those who realized that the church's feast was over, there were two ways of ensuring that Christianity maintained a place at the table. One way was to show that Christian faith was reasonable . . . that the story told in the Bible was plausible and broadly (or wholly) true. Meanwhile there began to be work in a more psychological vein designed to show that religious experience was often genuine, and may well correspond to the philosophical claims of the church. The other way was to demonstrate that Christianity was useful. It became common to show how the historical Jesus embodied and espoused the virtues most highly valued by contemporary society; the church could be seen as a community of ordered love promoting a society of sustainable peace. In short, whether or not Christianity was true, it certainly made people behave better. . . . This argument proved very attractive to many of those in power.[57]

These, according to Wells, were the predominant options for those who attempted to gain a hearing for the Christian faith. I recently thumbed through a collection of "best sermons" for this past year and was surprised that well over half of the sermons fit either or both of Wells's apologetic categories—the faith argued as reasonable or useful. In these sermons the faith is argued, not on the basis that "Jesus Christ is Lord," but rather that the values of the preponderate social order—history, human rationality, social utility—are lord.

Hans Frei must have been the first to note that Barth tends to narrate rather than argue in his theology.[58] Barth reasserts, repeats, redescribes rather than argues or explains. Hauerwas astutely notes that Barth's narrative style is, in itself, an argument: "Barth just cannot provide the kind of 'knock down' argument so many desire; but that he cannot is both theologically and philosophically justified." That is, Barth wants to work in such a way that the three forms of revelation are at work through the Holy Spirit, rather than his logical, well-formed arguments. Barth speaks the way he speaks for theological reasons.

Hauerwas was generous enough to apply a similar insight to my preaching in explaining, "Why Willimon Never Explains."[59] Whereas some (Marva Dawn) have accused my preaching of being unorganized, lacking good transitions and orderly presentation, Hauerwas says that I attempt to leave room for God to work—if there is a living God. I hope that he is right about my preaching. I really do believe that our preaching must not be so polished, so complete, so well reasoned and astutely presented that there is nothing left for God to do to make our preaching "work." I really do believe that if we could come up with an apologetic "knock down" argument for a crucified God, then we would have no need for a crucified God.

All of that said, I am unsure that we must join Barth in so completely rejecting apologetics. With Barth, I disapprove of apologetics, but I still do it on most Sundays. Reasons and defenses of faith can be clarifying, and possibly confirming, *for believers,* though I am uncertain of their value for nonbelievers.[60] In the disruptive aftermath of the exploding bomb and the descent of the dove—that is, *faith*—are believers and their preachers wrong to attempt to articulate and describe that explosion, that descent with whatever metaphorical and analogical resources that we have? Can we not "plunder the Egyptians," using the world's terms to describe something the world does not know?

Even with nonbelievers, perhaps our rationales and justifications for our faith are a sort of testimony, a front door, a modest beginning to more interesting theology. Not taking nonbelievers too seriously surely involves not too dramatically overstating the impossibility of a soft apologetic appeal to them. Cannot God deem to use apologetics as a means of grace, though prevenient, incomplete, but still grace? Can an anti-apologetic stance be, in a sense, an apologetic? In mocking the world, in rebuking the world, have we thereby devised an effective apologetic to the world's cultured despisers? Sometimes the Christian faith attracts those who are giving up on the world by speaking to the world in mocking and sarcastic tones in encouragement of their relinquishment of the world.

I feel fairly confident that Barth would not support me in any attempt to redeem apologetics. Barth believed that the gospel needs from us preachers only restatement, not justification. Hans Frei was among the first to call attention to the Barthian propensity for restatement rather than apologetics. Frei conducted one of the first rhetorical analyses of Barth's theology, saying that Barth "took the classical themes of communal Christian language molded by the Bible, tradition and constant usage in worship, practice, instruction and controversy, and he restated or redescribed them, rather than evolving arguments on their behalf."[61] Frei says that Barth—rather than attempting to build bridges to the discourse of the modern world, or to construct arguments with the modern world on the basis of its reigning ideologies—had to "recreate a universe of discourse."[62] The reader is placed in Barth's "strange new world of the Bible" by showing, not by explaining or arguing. Quite unapologetically, Barth's reader was required by Barth fully to enter a world that had its own linguistic integrity, its own closed circle of meaning, a world that could not be accessed by the use of words from other linguistic worlds. "In much the same way as the now old-fashioned 'newer' literary critics he set forth a textual world which he refused to understand by paraphrase, or by transposition of 'translation' into some other context."[63] Redescription, rather than translation, was Barth's assignment, says Frei, transference of the hearer to the "linguistic world" of the Christian faith. Frei characterized Barth's theology as "Christian self-description" rather than correlation with some allegedly universal "human, cultural quests for ultimate meaning."[64]

Barth noted that his teacher, Anselm, failed to make an argument in the *Proslogion.* Barth says that the key to that classic text is its beautiful opening and closing prayers, not its philosophic arguments. Anselm practiced, in the words of Gary Dorrien, "theology without crutches." Theology arises from prayer, not analysis or argument, as a gift, not as a heroic intellectual construction.[65] Barth is being more than pious here; he is making the intellectual claim that accurate statements about God are possible only because of God's prevenient grace. The ontic precedes the noetic. God's being determines the means of God's knowing; theology must be willing to be mastered by its subject if it is to know anything. Theology is a response to the God who is there; it does not create, it only responds. This is why theology cannot apologetically defend Christian truths in some misguided attempt to convert the nonbeliever. Conversion is exclusively a work of the mysterious movement of God's grace. Since theology speaks only from faith, it cannot speak to non-faith, except indirectly, by properly describing faith.

As Hauerwas says, "Barth was engaged in a massive attempt to overturn the epistemological prejudices of modernity."[66] And he cannot do that without repeating himself, without taking in hand the philosophical weapons whereby modernity had sought to silence Christianity. So Barth announces as early as *Church Dogmatics* II, 1 that he must repeat himself. The truth of God tends to be circular. No synthesis or system must be attempted by us. Preaching begins, not with our questions put to God, but rather in faith that God has spoken and that God's words need to be heard:

> We can only describe Him again and again, and often, and in the last resort infinitely often. If we try to speak conclusively of the limits of our knowledge of God and of the knowledge of God generally, we can come to no conclusion. We can only speak of it again and again in different variations. . . . We have definitely no last word to speak. If we think we have, we have already pronounced our own judgment, because we have denied faith. . . . Jesus Christ is really too good to let Himself be introduced and used as the last word of our self-substantiation.[67]

Because the Word of God originates exclusively with God, preaching must always be, in a certain sense, repetition:

> The problem of the Word (that is, of course, the Word of God) in theology I understand to be the question of whether and how far theology recognizes its obligation of directing Christian preaching to the repetition in human words of what is said to men through God himself about God, in distinction to all which man can say to himself about God.[68]

His great concern that we not be apologists but rather repeaters of the Word arose in part out of Barth's great fear that we preachers would, through our best intentioned rhetorical devices, "domesticate" the wild Word of God. He feared that we would engage in

> the domesticating of revelation . . . the process of making the Gospel respectable. When the Gospel is offered to man, and he stretches out his hand to receive it and takes it into his hand, an acute danger arises which is greater than the danger that he may not understand it and angrily reject it. The danger is that he may accept it and peacefully and at once make himself its lord and possessor, thus rendering it innocuous, making that which chooses him something which he himself has chosen, which therefore comes to stand as such alongside all the other things that he can also choose, and therefore control.[69]

The would-be apologist has no means of making the Christian faith more accessible than it is. Conversion means in part a willingness to enter the new linguistic world that is the Christian faith. All the evangelist can do is redescribe and point to that world, to invite the nonbeliever imaginatively to enter that linguistic universe, but only on the basis of faith itself. Thus Barth fails to make much distinction between "believers" and "nonbelievers," believing that the theological task is the same for both. Theology keeps trying to fear the resourceful, electing, communicating God more than it fears the nonbelieving, rejecting world. Apologetics wrongly takes the alleged unbelief of the unbeliever too seriously.

It is Barth's huge faith in the ultimate triumph of the Word that does not allow him to take unbelief too seriously, or at least to give unbelief any ontological status. Barth taught a revolutionary doctrine of double predestination (but quite unlike that of Luther and Calvin) that helped to blur the distinctions between insiders and outsiders in regard to the Christian faith. The Reformation taught that God elects some for salvation; some for damnation. In volume II, 2 of *Church Dogmatics,* Barth taught that in Jesus Christ, God has, in eternity, elected God's self for rejection, damnation, and death, but sinful humanity for election into salvation, grace, and forgiveness. Jesus Christ is both God's *yes* and God's *no.* God has, in Jesus Christ, chosen rejection for himself but salvation for humanity.

Thus Barth is often charged with *apokatastasis,* universal salvation. He does not directly teach this, but he does believe that the ultimate fate of everyone must remain an open question, that the salvation of all must be our hope, and that this is not an impossible hope considering the triumph of God's grace.[70] The Christian community's responsibility is to testify to God's great *yes* in Jesus Christ. This is our main service to the unbeliever. The main difference between the nonbeliever and the believer is a noetic, not an ontic difference. That is, the Christian knows something, a fact about the world that the non-Christian does not yet know. Believers and unbelievers are bound together both by our solidarity in sin and by our solidarity in grace. Hans Urs von Balthazar said that the central theme of *Church Dogmatics* is "God's eternal Yea and Amen to Himself and His creation." This is how Barth stated our relationship to the unbeliever:

> To the extent that we may be Christians in spite of our non-Christianity, our real distinction from non-Christians will consist in the fact that we know that Jesus Christ himself, and he alone, is our hope as well as theirs, that he died and rose again for those who are wholly or partially non-Christians, that his overruling work precedes and follows all being and occurrence in our sphere, that he alone is the perfect Christian, but that he really is this, and is it in our place.[71]

The nonbeliever "does not yet participate in the knowledge of Jesus Christ and what has taken place in him."[72] For those who do so participate, however, this participation is not just something; it is everything. All have sinned, says Paul, yet, in Jesus Christ, God was reconciling the world to himself. Period. The affirmation that all are enemies of God and that all have been redeemed by the work of God in Christ is the basis for Barth's connection between believers and nonbelievers. Evil, "the Nihil," is thus linked by Barth to stupidity.

Gary Dorrien says that, for Barth, the problem of apologetics was like the problem of candles. We must not attempt to make a ramp up to God through our candles, our organ recitals, or our arguments. With his teacher, Hermann, Barth said that it is a big mistake for Christians to try to convince unbelievers that Christianity is rational, reasonable, or historically credible, because every attempt to defend Christianity inevitably takes its stand at some point outside the Christian faith. The real god of apologetics is the god of reason, or historicity, or some other idol than the living, speaking God of Israel and the church.[73] Faith is a creation of the Word, not of our good arguments. Apologetic appeal to any other basis than the Holy Spirit's gifts is an act of unfaith that produces, not faith, but trust in something other than God to reveal. This applies, I assume, not only to apologetic preaching but also to current apologetic appeals to the Christian community and its sacraments.

In Barth's momentous reply to Emil Brunner, in which Barth famously rejected Brunner's claim of an apologetic "point of contact" that could be useful in homiletical appeals to non-believers, Barth said that his own experience in preaching to "modern youth" taught him that

> in my experience the best way of dealing with "unbelievers" and modern youth is not to try to bring out their "capacity for revelation" but to treat them quietly, simply (remembering that Christ has died and risen also for them), as if their rejection of "Christianity" was not to be taken seriously. It is only then that they can understand you, since they really see you where you maintain that you are standing as an evangelical theologian: on the ground of justification by faith alone.[74]

Stephen Webb says, in quoting this passage, that Barth takes an essentially ironical view of apologetics. If the Christian communicator reaches out to the non-Christian, little of importance will have been exchanged; if the Christian turns away from the world and focuses exclusively on the Word of God, then a real conversation with the unbeliever will have been initiated. As Webb says, Barth may think that by taking this point of view he has thereby avoided the rhetorical problem of tailoring the speech to fit the audience. Barth said that "my sermons reach and 'interest' my audience most . . . when I least rely on my ability to 'reach' people by my rhetoric, when on the contrary I allow my language to be formed and shaped and adapted as much as possible by what the text seems to be saying."[75] As Webb points out, it is curious to see Barth condemning rhetoric in a work like *"No!"* which is so heavily polemical, contentious, and rhetorically charged.

I agree with James F. Kay when he says that Barth attempts to create "a theological rhetoric," rather than to dispose of all rhetoric.[76] This leads Barth to some interesting judgments about homiletics, based on his dogmatics. He notoriously rejects "in principle" sermon introductions. Introductions suggest "a point of contact," some point of entry from human experience into the Word of God. He denounces introductions as "a waste of time," except those introductions that are a brief statement of what the introductory scripture reading is going to be about. Introductions distract listeners and delude listeners into thinking that somehow their experiences, as well as the preacher's acknowledgment of those experiences, are going to be the means by which they will apprehend the Word of God. Use of quotations from various people and illustrations only cause listeners' minds to wander into areas that have no possibility of becoming revelation (Barth, *Homiletics*, pp. 122-23).

However, Barth violates his own principle in many of his sermons, particularly his later prison sermons. Most of the sermons in *Deliverance to the Captives*[77] have extensive and, to my mind, very effective introductions and illustrations. A sermon on the text, "By grace you have been saved!" shows a keen sensitivity to the hearers:

> How strange to have this message addressed to us! Who are we, anyway? Let me tell you quite frankly: We are all together great sinners. Please understand me: I include myself. I stand ready to confess being the greatest sinner among you all; yet you may then not exclude yourself from the group! Sinners are people who in the judgment of God, and perhaps of their own consciences, missed and lost their way, who are not just a little, but totally guilty, hopelessly indebted and lost not only in time, but in eternity. We are such sinners. And we are prisoners. Believe me, there is a captivity much worse than the captivity in this house. There are walls much thicker and doors much heavier than those closed upon you. All of us, the people without and you within, are prisoners of our own obstinacy, of our many greeds, of our various anxieties, of our mistrust and in the last analysis of our unbelief. We are all sufferers. Most of all we suffer from ourselves. We each make life difficult for ourselves and in so doing for our fellowmen. We suffer from life's lack of meaning.

We suffer in the shadow of death and of eternal judgment toward which we are moving. We spend our life in the midst of a whole world of sin and captivity and suffering.

But now listen. Into the depth of our predicament the word is spoken from on high: By grace you have been saved![78]

In the middle of another sermon, Barth notes the assorted comfort that we try to offer ourselves:

Thus all comfort-seeking is overshadowed by the question, "What kind of comfort shall I seek?", or "What is the use of comfort?" I need more than comfort. I need help, I need redemption. But as long as we fail to realize that we may hope in God, we shall go around in circles, constantly trying to seek comfort, constantly discovering that comfort does not help, does not even comfort in the long run! Let me give you a few illustrations.

As you well know, we can comfort ourselves with a cigarette, or with a newspaper, or by turning on the radio, or with a little liquor. Why not? This is called "diversion." There are even nobler diversions like music, work, reading, perhaps reading that involves a great deal of work. Well, diversions are alright, but you know the result. In the end we are back where we were, in our old misery. What comfort shall I seek?

Or we can also seek comfort by comparing ourselves with others. John Doe is no better off than I am, indeed he is no better than myself. Yet ultimately I can only live as I am as an individual, with my heart and my emotions, my suffering and my destiny, and with my conscience. What is the use of comparing? What comfort shall I seek?

We can certainly try to seek comfort in ourselves. All of us do it at times. If all are against me, I will be myself. I will confide in my own strength and be content. Do you know the story of the Negro who had the habit of speaking aloud to himself? When he was asked to explain his odd behavior, he answered, "For one thing, I like to talk to an intelligent person; for another, I like to be addressed by an intelligent one." Or have you heard that other story about the man who believed in the one and only true Church which had but one member for the time being—he himself?[79]

In a sermon on the peace of Christ, Barth recalls the then current armament talks in nearby Geneva:

We might want relentlessly to criticize the four men assembled for a full five weeks at the round table in Geneva. Instead of pronouncing the long expected word of peace and thereby deciding the future of us all they have as yet produced nothing but the same old trite phrases. The same applies, only more so, to their instigators in Moscow, Washington and Bonn, as well as to the newspapers—the Swiss press prominently among them—for agitating the cold war day-in and day-out. Lastly, mankind itself, in the East as in the West, has its share of the blame. Like a herd of sheep it seems to rush toward the precipice, dragging along all and everything. One or the other among you might quite possibly wish to include Christianity in his protest, the Protestant Churches and the Roman Catholic Church along with their spokesmen who so often howled and still howl with the wolves! Again and again they certainly appear as weak as to have better to offer than stone instead of bread.[80]

Once again we see the fallacy of taking Barth's sweeping strictures against introductions and illustrations in *Homiletics* as eternal principles of preaching at all times and places. While he studiously avoids apologetics in his dogmatic theology, Barth seems to know that, when it comes to preaching, some mild form of apologetics is virtually unavoidable.

Dear Church

2 Corinthians 5:1–6:2

Dear Church:
You know me. Church meetings are not my favorite way to spend an evening. Plodding through the business, reading reports to one another. Boredom sets in, I doze, I long to be elsewhere. Lord, deliver me from church meetings.

Except last Wednesday. Now there's a church meeting worth remembering! It's been a long time since the volume got raised that high, along with the temperature. No chairs were thrown, for which I'm grateful. I hope that the argument was productive. It took me until Friday afternoon to cool down and, when asked, "What happened at the Administrative Board meeting on Wednesday?" to answer, "Well, we had ourselves quite a fight—I mean er, productive disagreement."

On my way home after Wednesday's meeting, when I was complaining to the Lord about some of the things some of you said to me, the Lord said, "You're the one who's always complaining about boring church meetings!"

One of your questions stuck in my mind for the rest of the week. I think it encapsulates what was on many of your minds. One of you asked, "Pastor, why are you so vehemently opposed to the war with Iraq?"

I think that was on many of your minds on Wednesday. You wanted me to account for myself—my calling a meeting last Sunday night to discuss our congregation's response to the President's call to arms, and my comments in a couple of sermons this fall.

Church, I know what you're thinking. "He's against the war because he's an incurable sixties radical," or "He's a yellow dog Democrat," or "He's a knee-jerk pacifist who is always against war, and this one too."

Okay. I'll admit all that may have something to do with my repugnance over plans for this war. I didn't vote for George Bush, even though he is my age and a sometime-United Methodist. And my memories of another war in Southeast Asia probably color my thinking.

How well you know me.

"Pastor, why are you so opposed to a war with Iraq?"

It's a question that begs for explanation. I could lay on you my quibbling about U.S. foreign policy in this case—we're being led to war by a President who has never been in war; why Iraq, when a dozen nearby regimes are as corrupt. What on earth do we do once we've won the war—occupy Iraq for the next fifty years? And so forth.

But you would say, "He's no expert of foreign policy. He's nothing but a preacher, and not a great one at that."

And you would be right.

No, I feel the way I do about the proposed war with Iraq, not, I pray, because of something I suspect in George Bush but because of something I know about Jesus. There was a day when I would have thought about these matters from the standpoint of my U.S. citizenship, that is, from an exclusively human point of view. But now I try to think about these matters from the standpoint of my citizenship in a whole New World. From God's point of view.

Let me explain. One day, on a Sunday, or maybe a Wednesday, in my eighteenth year, or maybe my twentieth, I woke up, jumped out of bed, looked out the window and to my surprise I saw a whole new world. I was like Dorothy when, after the tornado, she regains consciousness in Oz and figures out that she is not in Kansas anymore. The world didn't look all green or gold. Just different. No one around me seemed to notice, which at first proved to be disconcerting, as if I had landed on another planet but nobody there knew it was another planet. So I wandered the streets, stumbled along, had to learn to walk, and to count, to talk all over again, like I was born, again.

I had to learn new words, words like reconciliation, atonement, forgiveness, justification. Well-meaning friends told me to "face facts," to "get real." But they were calling to me across a great divide, attempting to lasso me back into the more-confining corral I once called home.

I had moved. It wasn't that I was being unrealistic, it was rather that I had taken up residence in new reality. I still loved "the facts" and thought it important to live in the light of those facts or else appear stupidly out of step.

In short, I had been, was being, am still being, saved. I had been "reconciled to God," as Paul might have put it. At the first, I did not know the words to accurately describe where I was, but that was me, "reconciled to God."

That God, whom I could never reach, had reached to me. That Judge, for whom I could never do enough good deeds, think enough good thoughts, feel enough good feelings, judged me good. The enemy from whom I had fled, raced to me, embraced me, revealed himself as none other than Friend. The Master to whom I owed so much, risked all, bought me in blood.

I won't bore you with the details except to say that, the next day, next year, next decade, I could hardly find my way, so defamiliarized, strange, fresh, and new was the world.

I expect some of you may have had similar born-again, saved, conversion experiences. Even if you have not yet, I bet you will, and whether or not you even experience it, it doesn't change the reality of it. I've been over the mountain. I've seen the other side. It's there for sure. I know folk who've never been to France. Their lack of experience doesn't change the fact of France.

And once you've seen the whole new world, once you know for sure who rules, and who sits on the throne, and where we're all headed, and how the last chapter reads, well, it makes you walk a bit funny.

I don't mean that, as Christians, we are funny. I just mean to say that, as Christians, in the eyes of the world—the old monochrome world of conventionality, governmentally subsidized, officially sanctioned "reality"—we look, well, funny. Odd.

The world still believes that, once you get up that mountain and look over the other side, there's nothing there. So we best take matters in hand and do our best to save ourselves by ourselves. The world thinks the throne is occupied by whomever we elected to sit there and act as if he is in charge. It's up to us to make history come out right, or it won't. Justice is in our hands. (George Bush's first name for his War on Terror was "Operation Infinite Justice.")

That day, that week or whatever when I saw, I moved into a whole New World. When I got reconciled or better, when I woke up to my reconciliation to God, it was like the painted illusory stage backdrop curtain descended and I saw a New World. It had always been there, long before I was given eyes to see it, been there at least since a Friday afternoon, breaking out first at Golgotha, finally broken in to me. But until then, I didn't know.

Because of that first glimpse, I've been reviewing this world ever since, and trying each Sunday, dear church, to get you to do the same. Go ahead and think of Sunday as a weekly attempt to get our vision corrected. Optometrics. We gather in church, not seeking an escape from the "real world" but in order, by the grace of God, to get a gander at reality. Some Sundays, despite my bumbling homiletical efforts, you break free of the confines of convention; you journey to Bethlehem; in you, there is Incarnation; in you, the cross is stamped; and you know that you have been claimed, commandeered for service to a new Kingdom. On other Sundays, our eyes remain shut, no new thing is uttered or heard, and we go back to the same old world from whence we came, bored, but reassured by the routine.

We console ourselves with the slogans of an imperiled empire—can't teach an old dog new tricks, prayer is fine but sometimes you've got to face facts, there is a great struggle between good (us) and evil (them). Roll over and go back to sleep.

Oh, church, forgive me when I overstate the case for a whole new world! Forgive me, in a world at war, for too extravagantly claiming reconciliation. But put my preaching in context. I've tasted new wine that won't fit into old wineskins. I've seen a new world and now refuse to give too much honor to the old one. I've experienced the radical, world-changing power of Christ to get what he wants on the battlefield of my own soul. I'm not going back to business as usual, and I don't want you to either.

And that's my answer to your question. I'm not for the war because I've been introduced to the Prince of Peace. I, who was God's great enemy, have been adopted, embraced, washed, reborn into God's family. I don't worry about who will win this battle or the next one because I already know who has won the war. I'm voting for the Prince.

Paul puts it better than I:

Therefore, knowing the fear of the Lord, we try to persuade others. . . . For the love of Christ urges us on, because we are convinced that one has died for all; therefore all have died. And he died for all, so that those who live might live no longer for themselves, but for him who died and was raised for them.

From now on, therefore, we regard no one from a human point of view; even though we once knew Christ from a human point of view, we know him no longer in that way. So if anyone is in Christ, there is a new creation: everything old has passed away; see, everything has become new! All this is from God, who reconciled us to himself through Christ, and has given us the ministry of reconciliation; that is, in Christ God was reconciling the world to himself, not counting their trespasses against them, and entrusting the message of reconciliation to us. So we are ambassadors for Christ, since God is making his appeal through us; we entreat you on behalf of Christ, be reconciled to God. For our sake he made him to be sin who knew no sin, so that in him we might become the righteousness of God. (2 Cor. 5:11-21)

Presumably, before this war began, the President sent his ambassador to attempt to reason with Saddam. I hope so. When the ambassador is there, it's just like the President himself is there.

Paul says, in Christ, you've had your citizenship in the Old World exchanged for a passport to the new. Not by what you or I did, but by what Christ did, you have been brought close to God. The cross, not the Stars and Bars, gives you your marching orders. The main difference between you and most of the people in Iraq is not that you are a citizen of a righteous, pure, good, and victorious democracy, and they are not. The difference is that you know who sits on the throne, who is in charge, and they don't. Tragically, too many of us act like we're still citizens of the old world. When the U.S. says, "Jump," our only question is, "How high?" That morbid perspective, that "human point of view," is a hard habit to break.

> *Thanks be to God, we're citizens of a new creation. Moreover, we have our marching orders. To us has been entrusted the "ministry of reconciliation." The "message of reconciliation has been entrusted to us." Not just to me, the preacher, but also to you in your new status as "ambassadors for Christ."*
>
> *It's an amazing claim to make for the church. The church is God's embassy, that place from where Christ's ambassadors are sent into the world. My job, as your pastor, is to help you see yourselves as Christ's messengers and to help you get the message.*
>
> *Paul says that in you God is making his appeal. In this letter I'm making my appeal to you. In your peace-making, peace-praying, peace-living, God is appealing to the world. You are God's letter to the world. In you, God is saying, "World, wake up! Open your eyes. This is my world and I'm determined to get back what rightly belongs to me."*
>
> *Though I've not been as good a pastor as you deserved, this has been my vocation while among you, whether I'm in the pulpit, or at a meeting, or beside your beds of pain—to get you to see the world as it is now that Christ has conquered. The way I figure it, if I can just get you to see, you'll figure out what to do. Pray that God will give me what I need to help you claim your ambassadorship.*
>
> *Paul says in his letter what I've been fumbling to say in mine: anyone "in Christ" (that is, us) is a new creation, a minister of reconciliation, a messenger of the good news, an ambassador for Christ, God's letter to the world, the very righteousness of God.*
>
> *So you open your eyes, dare to look at the world as God's, get real, be the righteousness of God!*
>
> *Sincerely,*
>
> *Your Pastor*

More than Heralds

I have found, in my attempts to appropriate Barth's insights for preaching, that there are limits to the Barthian herald image of preaching. When Barth eschews the rhetorical enterprise, he slyly obfuscates the central role that the rhetorical enterprise plays in his own theology. The herald may claim that he is "just preaching," just repeating the words of Scripture, just reiterating what God has already said, but that may mean little more than that the herald either does not know or is unwilling to admit to the herald's own rhetorical goals and strategies.

It is important to acknowledge one's rhetoric because all rhetoric is an exercise of power by the speaker. In any speaking, including preaching, there are decisions to be made all along the way, stratagems, purposes, conscious and unconscious arrangement of material, assumptions about the listeners, things said one way and not another, all of which is the stock and trade of rhetoric. So it is one thing to admit to the peculiarly demanding nature of Christian speech about God, to examine the limits and the sources of such speech, as Barth does so brilliantly. It is another thing to claim that one is merely a neutral, passive vehicle, a mere repeater of words received in speech about God, as Barth does so questionably when he writes about preaching.

Barth so vividly and successfully utilizes rhetorical strategies of irony, narrative, surprise, hyperbole, and many more in his richly metaphorical theological works like *Romans*. And in the *Church Dogmatics* Barth uses a creative, highly complex circular argument. Then he produces sermons that are often so wooden in their presentation. Barth says, of his *Dogmatics*, that he wants to speak to the church. That is a rhetorical strategy of the most basic kind. To speak to the church is to self-consciously speak to a distinctive linguistic community, to work within a peculiar realm of discourse where much of the rhetoric is predetermined but also that forces rhetorical decisions at every turn in the road.

The great test for the validity of Barth's claim that he is willfully disinterested in rhetorical matters, that is, speech from our end of the divine-human conversation, is to ask anyone to pick up a volume of the *Church Dogmatics* and read it. Uninitiated readers, even readers who have been initiated into other attempts at theological discourse, will immediately testify that here they have encountered a queer way of writing. They have not yet been trained in how to read Barth, training that comes from actually reading him and submitting to his vigorous rhetorical demands.

Claims of disinterest in or use of rhetorical strategies by speakers tend to be immoral. That is, the most morally questionable claims are those of the speaker who claims not to have any rhetorical intent—this is, power—in speaking to others. When Aristotle defines rhetoric as speech that persuades, he is noting an inescapable exercise of power in most of our speaking. We all say things to others in the hope of doing things to others in an exercise of power over them.

Perhaps even more damning is my criticism that, in its disdain for rhetorical considerations, Barth's herald image is at odds with a primary form that revelation has been given to us, namely, scripture. As literary criticism of scripture has shown us, scripture employs a rich array of literary forms in order to present the gospel, much richer than one would infer from the sermons of Barth. The Bible was preaching before it was scripture, and its persuasive, proclamatory intentions led biblical writers to reach for a wide range of literary devices to do their proclamation, as Augustine first noted in his *On Christian Teaching*. Scripture's use of these literary devices was not merely to pander to the artistic hungers of the hearers, or an exercise of vanity on the part of the early Christian communicators, but rather art was used to change the hearers, to inculcate the hearers into a complex, linguistically derived world that is called salvation in Jesus Christ. Moreover, there was something about the nature of Jesus Christ that seemed to demand a rich repertoire of linguistic forms in order to do justice to the object of the proclamation.[81]

Each Christmastime, as our congregation gathers to celebrate the Incarnation, I am again impressed by the huge artistic outburst that accompanied the theological claim that "the Word became flesh and dwelt among us." There was something about the Incarnation that demanded a wide array of artistic expression. Preaching participates in that divine enfleshment, delighting in the multiplicity of linguistic forms to which the eternal Logos condescends.[82]

Which is a good place to make the point that Barth is in favor of rhetorical devices and rhetorical activity in sermons, *but only if it is God's activity and device and not that of the preacher*. After eschewing all rhetorical devices by preachers, Barth says, "All these things may well happen in a sermon, of course, but they are acts which God himself wills to perform and which can never, therefore, be a human task." To do so would risk giving the congregation "the impression that the preacher has a corner on Christ and the Spirit. . . . God is not a *Deus otiosus* (inactive God) but an active God," and that fact "imposes upon us a demand for discipline" in our temptation to use rhetorical strategies.[83] Mark's parable of the sower (Mark 4:3-8) is a parable worth remembering at this point. We can read the parable in at least two ways: as a story of the waste of a large amount of seed, or as a story of miraculous growth and harvest. Jesus, when he interprets this parable in Mark's Gospel, has us focus on the latter interpretation. There are many factors arrayed against the hearing and reception of the gospel. And yet it is of the nature of this active, loquacious God to keep sowing, to distribute the Word with reckless abandon. "Other seed fell into good soil and brought forth grain, growing up and increasing and yielding thirty and sixty and a hundredfold" (4:8). The rhetoric of God is miraculously effective.

Despite his love for Mozart, there is in the preaching of Barth a kind of tone-deaf quality in his explication of the biblical text. The style of most of his sermons is direct, upbeat, and declarative. That is often a well-received homiletical style, but it is not the style of the whole of scripture. Barth's sermons assert and announce but they almost never seduce, entice, cajole, and sneak up upon the hearer. The biblical text delights in such allurements.

In an early lecture to preachers Barth said of the gospel:

> This message is as new and foreign and superior to the Church as it is to all the people to whom the Church is supposed to proclaim it. The Church can only deliver it the way a postman delivers his mail; the Church is not asked what it thinks it is thereby starting, or what it makes of the message. The less it makes of it and the less it leaves on it its own fingerprints, the more it simply hands it on as it has received it—and so much the better.[84]

True, the message is "foreign" and "superior" to us preachers, but how might that be known if we do not, perhaps only to some lesser degree, leave our "own fingerprints"? Part of the power of the Gospels themselves is that they are clearly Gospels, self-evidently literary constructions by discernibly different individuals and communities. This mix of voices and variety of perspectives is in itself wonderful testimony to the Trinitarian greatness of their subject—the Word made flesh. Thank goodness the Gospel writers did not attempt to erase their fingerprints or to deny their earthbound reality. They each, like John the Baptist in his full, grizzled humanity, pointed toward the crucified God.[85]

How on earth (that's where preaching occurs, on earth) does Barth think that it is possible to devise a sermon that will be neither picture nor idea but simply a "pointing to Christ himself"?

> We must remember that everything will depend upon the Christians not painting for the non-Christians in word and deed a picture of the Lord or an idea of Christ, but on their succeeding with their human words and ideas in pointing to Christ Himself. For it is not the conception of Him, not the dogma of Christ that is the real Lord, but He who is attested in the word of the Apostles.[86]

While Barth admirably desires that the sermon not be confused with the One toward which the sermon points, and whereas our listeners are promised more than a mere "idea" of Christ or a "picture" of Christ but "Christ Himself," I would argue that if there is one thing more ethically questionable than the sophistic, underhanded use of rhetoric it is the use of rhetoric without acknowledging that one has used a peculiar kind of rhetoric!

Furthermore, as Thomas G. Long notes in his discussion of the homiletics of Barth, "The herald image so stresses that preaching is something which God does, insists so firmly that preaching is divine activity rather than human effort, that the role of the preacher is almost driven from sight."[87]

Even allowing for Barthian hyperbole, Barth's stress upon the Word as independent of, and in no way dependent upon, the gifts or character of the preacher and the listeners seems, in the end, an overstress. The Word is made flesh in Jesus and, in our preaching, the Word is made flesh again, our flesh. Just as there were those who accused Barth of an incipient Nestorianism, in his stress upon the divinity of the Logos (a charge of which Barth acquitted himself by the time he had finished the *Dogmatics*), Barth could also be criticized for a neglect of the human side of preaching, a kind of incipient Docetism. Paul Scott Wilson criticizes Barth's herald image by saying that "it is inaccurate, or at least wishful thinking, to define the preacher's role as nothing more than a mere conduit. . . . We always speak from the limitations of our own time and culture. God's message changes us, and we also change it for those who receive it from us. Mere instrumentality does not exist in preaching."[88] Sermons are as much conversation as proclamation, and no preacher can claim to be always in monologue. Did not Paul boast to his congregation, "I fed you with milk, not solid food, for you were not ready for solid food" (1 Cor. 3:2)?

With all the current worry about the "person of the preacher," one can certainly welcome the Barth's corrective reminder that the messenger's greatest significance is in the speaking of the message. While there is reason for concern about the character, the training, and the competence of the preacher,[89] it is good to be reminded by Barth that nothing commends the messenger to the congregation's attention more than the message.

One does not have to fall back into an Aristotelian stress upon *ethos*, the character of the speaker, to say that Barth has rhetorically overdone his image of the preacher as a mere earthen vessel for the treasure of the gospel. Barthian homiletics requires transparency on the part of the preacher. The congregation must be able directly to see through us to the gospel. But transparency can become just another intolerable burden for the preacher. Now I have to worry, not only that my sermon may be uninteresting, unbiblical, and incomprehensible but also that I may be—through my careful preparation, my astute rhetorical strategies, and my concern over style of delivery—standing in the way of the gospel. The principle of transparency implies that my efforts to be an effective preacher are precisely what hinders me from being a faithful preacher. Even to attempt to be transparent is to not be transparent; transparency can be just another contrivance to speak for God rather than to be transparent to God's speech.

Furthermore, the demand for the preacher to be an unnoticeable vessel—the messenger who is transparent to the message—is not only difficult but also potentially delusional. Beware of the preacher who modestly stands before the congregation and says, "Now I am just giving you the pure Word of God, without any adulteration by my own personality, commitments, limits, or sin." More dangerous than hindering the gospel through the defects in my character is that character defect that deludes me into thinking that I can be a pure vessel for the gospel, that my vocation as a preacher has somehow lifted me out of the mire of sin and self-deceit that infects lesser mortals within the congregation.

Therefore, as a preacher, I ought not to pray to be a pure, untainted vessel, a transparent pane of polished glass (Barth), but rather that God might make me aware of all the ways that I hinder the proclamation of the gospel through my own sin (Luther). Knowing some of the ways that I ought not to be trusted with a biblical text, knowing to some degree the texts that most challenge my own limitations, admitting to some of the ways that I preach myself rather than Christ crucified, can give the preacher a modicum of humility on the way to the pulpit.

As Paul says, in his use of the "earthen vessel" metaphor, "We have this treasure in earthen vessels, *to show that the glory of God belongs to God and not to us*" (2 Cor. 4:7, italics mine). Paul boldly uses himself and his own human corrigibility as a living reminder of the transcendent glory of God. Though he was "the least of the apostles," one "untimely born," as are all of us later-day apostles, Paul saw his humanity as, like the long bony finger of Grünewald's John the Baptist, pointing toward the gracious Christ.

When the all-too-human preacher stands up to preach, in the midst of a congregation who knows the fallibility and finitude of the preacher all too well, the preacher becomes a visible representative of both the reality of the Incarnation and the power of God's redemption in Christ. If God's Word is heard through such a preacher, as it undeniably often is heard, this is glory, and no one knowing the preacher will be deluded into thinking that this glory is somehow derivative of the preacher. That is perhaps a good reason why no one should preach outside of the context of a congregation that is small enough and intimate enough to know— and to be known by—the preacher.[90]

I am certain that Barth would recoil in horror at this suggestion, but I also wonder if his herald image of the preacher, taken to its extreme, might lead to a kind of homiletical irresponsibility in which the preacher forsakes the need for careful, critical work on a sermon because, when it comes down to it, all of the important work on a sermon is either done by God or not. The Barthian sermon comes to us, miraculously, through prayer, as a gift of God, or else it is a vain, impossible human contrivance. The well-known, if perhaps apocryphal, story in which Barth is asked about the meaning of his theology and replies, "Jesus loves me, this I know, for the Bible tells me so," is a silly, and even insidious oversimplification.

The Gospels themselves speak to us in ways that seem to call out for, indeed demand, complex, studied interpretation. When I was once challenged on my interpretation of a Flannery O'Connor short story by a preacher who said that I was "making too much out of a simple little story," I replied that I found O'Connor to be a great writer of parables. O'Connor's stories are written in such a way as to demand interpretation. In her stories, things are not what they seem, and the world is unfamiliar, reality is elusive, and we are thrown into a position where we must ask, "What does this mean?" or else be overwhelmed by a chaos of unknowing. In short, O'Connor writes much like the Gospel of John. One might say that John's Gospel seems so opaque and elusive because of our sin that blinds us to eternal meaning, and that would be one valid response. But we might also say that John's Gospel is opaque because the eternal Logos who is standing before us is so vastly beyond the reach of our experience and conceptual devices, which would also be right. Either way, there is no reading of this text without being called to interpret the text. Too heavily symbolic, overinterpretations are virtually impossible in reading the Fourth Gospel. (And of the writing of books that try to interpret Barth's thought, there shall be no end—the opacity of the thought demands it.)

All of which is to say that preachers are called to the task of faithful listening, of developing those disciplines and skills that are required for listening to this peculiar literature called scripture that is the product of an equally peculiar God named Trinity. There is little that is simple or straightforward about it, as Barth's massive, maddeningly complicated *Dogmatics* shows.

Our preaching is not only our repetition of what we have heard from God, a word delivered by God, through us heralds, pristinely to the congregation; but our preaching is also the result of our pastoral conversation with God. In any conversation there is give and take. True conversation means that each partner in the conversation can be potentially affected by the conversation. One of Barth's distinctive claims is his *patripassianism*, that God feels, hurts, and is changed in God's gracious relationship to us. When Barth speaks of revelation as pure "event," he does not adequately represent the gracious, condescending, conversational quality of revelation as depicted in scripture. The preacher is the one who is called by the church to be in constant, courageous, disciplined conversation with God so that the church might be in conversation with God.

The same is true for preaching. When a preacher speaks, what is spoken is testimony to the sort of conversation and interaction that the preacher has had with the Incarnate Word. Aristotle would call such concerns matters of *ethos*, the character of the speaker. These are not only legitimate rhetorical concerns but also characters deep within the Christian faith (i.e., Moses, Jeremiah, etc.).

One reason there is so little evangelism in today's church, so little heralding of the gospel on the street corners of the world, so little serious engagement in conversation with those of other faiths or those of no faith, is because such cross-cultural conversation can be threatening to the believer. For those of us who, by the sheer grace of God, have heard, our neighbor's frank admission, "I don't hear what you hear," can be perceived as a threat.

Barth speaks of the compulsion that one is under for the sake of the gospel, the compulsion to speak to another, even at the risk of rejection:

> Why I cannot be silent but am required to speak is that I necessarily abandon him and leave him to his own devices if I spare myself what is perhaps the thankless venture, and him the unwelcome penetration of his sphere, and withhold from him that which he definitely ought to know, but cannot know until I tell him. I cannot withhold it, because he encounters me as a man, and I should not take him seriously as a man if I did not seriously try to find the way from me to him.[91]

Noting the role of various Gentiles in the scriptures, Barth says that even the Gentiles can be used for purposes of proclamation:

> We must not overlook the Gentiles also have a place in the redemptive history attested by the Bible. . . . The most remarkable of them—they include Balaam, Rahab, Ruth, Hiram, Cyrus and the Syro-Phoenician woman—is Melchisedek (Genesis 14:18f.; Psalm 110:4), who appears again mysteriously as the representative of an otherwise unmentioned priestly order, by which even the Elect of Yahweh seems to be measured. According to [Hebrews] 5:6, 10; 6:20; 7:1 f., he is the type of Jesus Christ Himself and of His supreme and definitive high priesthood. It is therefore . . . obligatory to regard the figure of Melchisedek as the hermeneutic key to this whole succession. It is not on the basis of a natural knowledge of God and relationship with God that all these strangers play their striking role. What happens is rather that in them Jesus Christ proclaims Himself to be the great Samaritan: as it were, in a second and outer circle of His revelation, which by its very nature can only be hinted at. It must be noted that no independent significance can be ascribed to any of the revelations as we can call them in a wider sense. There is no Melchisedek apart from Abraham, just as there is no Abraham apart from Jesus Christ. They have no Word of God to preach. They are not witnesses of the resurrection. They have no full power to summon to the love of God. In this they differ permanently and fundamentally from the prophets and apostles, as does their function from that of the Church. Their witness is a confirmatory and not a basic witness. . . . If we know the incarnation of the eternal Word and the glorification of humanity in Him, we cannot pass by any man, without being asked whether in his humanity he does not have this mission to us, he does not become to us this compassionate neighbour.[92]

The herald of the gospel may experience rejection, but the herald must be clear that the rejection is not of the herald as a person, as an individual, but rather as a representative of a disputed sovereignty:

> The Christian is not hated as a human individual who is repulsive to the one who hates him on account of his personal being and action. He is hated as the bearer and representative of a specific

claim and cause. . . . It is thus that the disciples are hated by all men and the world. . . . The Christian is accused of *odium humani generis*, and he is also the target of *odium humani generis*. As the witness of Christ he has only good things, indeed, the very best, to say to the world, and he finds himself regarded and treated not only as the bringer of bad news, of that No which is all the world can hear, but also . . . as a malicious disturber of the peace. In attesting Jesus Christ to the world, and therefore its reconciliation with God, he might well think that he is the best and most loyal and useful citizen, but to all his fellow-citizens he is necessarily an odious stranger and fore who is best expelled. He is their friend . . . and yet he must undergo the experience of being treated as their worst enemy. . . . Thus the disciples are regarded and treated as outlaws—not because they are Peter, Paul or John, but because they represent to all men and to the world the alien and intolerable cause of the kingdom, the coup d' etat of God. (IV, 3, pp. 624f.)

In any conversation, even in the conflicted conversation that is preaching, we are forced not only to speak but to listen. Christians believe that our language is provisional, but it is also reliable. It is radically contingent on whether or not there is a God who speaks, but it is also, we have found in our own experience, reliable. At this point, we all become "pragmatists" to a certain degree.

Preachers proclaim the Word to the congregation so that the congregation might respond to the Word, might hear the preacher's words as their divinely given vocation. Note that their vocation, moving from hearing the Word to doing the Word, means that the whole congregation becomes herald:

> The Christian must indicate and attest this word in the act of his whole existence. . . . That he should do this is the concrete goal of his vocation, the *ratio* of his Christian existence. He may be a hearer of the Word to become a doer. But his doing of the Word can consist decisively only in the fact that, commissioned and sent by Christ and himself existing in the world as man, he may turn to the world and other men who have not yet heard this Word, and make known to them what he was enabled to hear.[93]

One way that we "love our neighbor as ourselves" is to talk to the neighbor. We risk misunderstanding and incomprehension in order to make intimate contact with the neighbor. It takes risk to speak across communal boundaries, but it is a risk that the gospel enjoins us to take. God commands us to speak, to testify to what we know. While in conversation with the neighbor, we are forced to consider the possibility of unbelief, the fact that our language may not simply be difficult to understand but may also be unreal. When the neighbor fails to understand our proclamation, it is an opportunity for us to be reminded that much of our neighbor's incomprehension is not due to the neighbor's stupidity but rather to the fact that any hearing and understanding of the gospel, including our hearing and understanding as believers, is a gift of God, not our intellectual achievement.

People listen to us because they are persuaded by our characters, or our competence, or our arguments, or our homiletical arts.[94] Lose says that conversations demand that we speak, and this takes the courage to risk misunderstanding, a willingness to be in monologue, despite our desire for dialogue. The church must cultivate such confidence in our peculiar speech that we are willing to be misunderstood, must cultivate obedience to our vocation as heralds that we fear being unfaithful to our speech more than we fear incomprehension by the world. Matthew 28, the "Great Commission," typifies our bind. We are to "go" into the world with our words, telling the world the story of Christ, but in so doing we are to "make disciples," instructing them, indoctrinating them, forming them, converting them into a new world of discourse by teaching them and by killing them, birthing them, washing and detoxifying them in baptism. The "herald" image is too passive to be adequate to the more aggressive command to "make" disciples.

Conversation demands that we listen. We need critical feedback from our speech in order to speak better. It means allowing the misunderstanding and incomprehension of others to question what we say. Conversation also implies a dynamic process of give-and-take, of growth and understanding, a willingness to risk so that, in speaking, we are also listening and, in listening, we might change.

The danger in the conversation model is that preachers could become confused into thinking that our primary conversation partner is the congregation, our audience. Preaching, and this comes from Barth, must always be conversation *with* God. Preaching, like Barth's theology, is prayer.[95] God initiates this conversation and keeps this particular conversation going. Fortunately God is loquacious. Sometimes we do not hear God's testimony due to our limits, not to God's silence or absence.

One of the maddening, delightful things about conversation with Barth is that as soon as one has found something to criticize in his position, he manages to contradict or to correct that position. Thus, no sooner has he eloquently presented the herald metaphor than he switches to the metaphor of dialogue:

> One should . . . make every effort to ensure that one's sermon is not simply a monologue, magnificent perhaps, not necessarily helpful to the congregation. Those to whom he is going to speak must constantly be present in the mind of the preacher while he is preparing his sermon. What he knows about them will suggest unexpected ideas and associations which will be with him as he studies his text and will provide the element of actuality, the application of his text to the contemporary situation.[96]

Theology must therefore find some means of speaking about the mystery of God while enabling the mystery to remain mystery. "Theology means taking rational trouble over the mystery," he says.[97] We have got to keep ever before us the determination not to deal with thoughts about the divine but rather with God himself.[98] Any talk about God must always take place in the shadow of God's mystery.[99]

Modern homiletics has overly worried about how we can find the words to speak about God. Typically, Barth worries about the wonder of how God found words to speak to us. God has miraculously found just the right words to speak to us so that what ought to be utterly incomprehensible to us—the glory of God—is made available to us. The problem of homiletics is therefore always a problem of our hearing, not our speaking. The homiletical challenge is not preaching. The challenge is distinctively Christian preaching that has its own unique universe of discourse that is determined by its self-revealing subject.

We should therefore pray that it might be said of us, as Martin Buber said of Rabbi Schmelke (d. 1778), "Preaching was his element, because he believed in the transforming reality of the Word." Because he so believed, says Buber, the rabbi "sang new and never before heard melodies . . . awakening many from their snug peace, in order that the congregation might be emboldened."[100] All through the transforming reality of the Word.

CHAPTER EIGHT

TROUBLED PREACHING

"Don't things get dangerous only if and because God is?"
(Barth, in a letter to his brother Peter, 1932)[1]

The Gospels go to rather great lengths to show a world upset by Jesus, even before his resurrection, primarily in Jesus' preaching. His most famous sermon begins with, "Blessed are you poor in spirit." Blessed are you who are deficient in spirit, those of you who are inept in spiritual matters? What's so blessed about that? He might as well have said, "Blessed are you who are poor, hungry, persecuted, unemployed, outcast, and failing"—which is just what he said. Jesus speaks of a world—the kingdom of God—that is so topsy-turvy that any description of that real world is bound to cause conflict with the world we thought we had.

One night, in a student Bible study, we examined Luke 4, Jesus' inaugural sermon at his hometown synagogue. Things go well enough at first, while Isaiah is being read, but then Jesus begins to preach, and all hell breaks loose. Jesus merely repeats to them, in Barthian fashion, stories from scripture, midrash on the prophets, without interpretation and only in description of the peculiar quality of the proclamation of "release to the captives." The sermon ends with the congregation attempting to kill the preacher.

A student hand goes up. "Did you say this was Jesus' first sermon? One might have thought that he would at least have waited until his second or third sermon to say things that so upset the congregation."

So one might have thought, but no—with Jesus, the attack begins in the very first sermon. Jesus, in his preaching, is a troublemaker who brings, not peace, but a sword.

Barth was frequently criticized for his often scornful, severe, harsh criticisms of his critics—and even of some of his friends. Ought not Christian speakers be more charitably disposed to their listeners? Aristotle certainly thought so. In his *Rhetoric* he not only gave directions on how to win the trust and affection of the listeners toward the beginning of a speech, but he also believed that the composition of a speech could go a long way toward lessening the potential dissonance between speaker and hearer. Aristotle believed that through reason we could uncover basic, foundational, uncontested knowledge, at least uncontested among thoughtful, reasonable people. Once the philosopher uncovers these foundations, then most of the speaker's really hard work has been done. One must simply deliver these principles. All rational people will be convinced. If there is dissonance or disagreement with the speech, Aristotle implies, the problem may well be in the faulty reasoning employed by the speaker. The speaker's task is to find the right means of argument whereby the hearers will submit to the claims of the speaker's argument and assent. The purpose of public speaking is to lessen the trouble between the speaker and the hearer.

Barth was so convinced that there is divinely given difficulty between us and God that the Trinity demands such a different and difficult mode of thinking and speaking, that he was suspicious of any rhetorical attempt to assuage that difficulty. The trouble between us and God can be solved only by an act of a forgiving and justifying God. Thus Barth warns against thinking that we can address our sermons to the needs of our people because, outside of the revelation of Christ, we really don't know our people, much less their needs. Barth says,

> The fact that preachers pay attention to the needs, interests, situation, and capacity of the public is no guarantee that they are really addressing man, for in no case, is the man who ought to be addressed and waits to be addressed the public. He is arcane. Secret. Hidden. Sermons which should stir and edify and move him will probably leave this man empty, cold and untouched. By the high-angle fire of the heavy artillery directed above the head of the public, to the more distant entrenched position, this man is perhaps better served in truth than by the all-too jealous pounding of the forward trenches, which he has long since derisively evacuated.[2]

Yet as we noted in the previous chapter, it is not true that, in his sermons, Barth is uninterested in this "arcane" listener. Consider this excerpt from one of his prison sermons, a Christmas sermon. Although this is one of Barth's late sermons, these ruminations typify many of his sermons throughout his life:

> I surely would like to know what went on in your minds when you heard this story! Perhaps two or three among you did not listen very carefully—this happens quite often—and the story passed over their heads like a cloud or a puff of smoke. Should I read the story again for the benefit of these people of wandering thoughts? It is worth repeating twice, even a hundred times! But for today we shall leave it as this.
>
> Or perhaps there are those, men or women, who thought I was telling a nice fairy tale, far removed from the realities of life? Too beautiful to be true? What shall I tell them? Shall I debate with them? I shall gladly do so at any other time. But presently ours is a more important task.
>
> Perhaps also some among you, when they heard the story, were reminded of the days of their youth long since gone-by. They thought of Sunday School where they were told this story for the first time, of the Christmas tree, of the presents and the candies, of how beautiful things were, but are no longer and never will be again. What shall I answer? Shall I put on a serious face and say: Forget about Christmas trees and Christmas sentiments and concentrate on the Christmas story itself? This will not be my reply either.
>
> I only intended to show you, my dear friends, that these are our human reactions to the Christmas story, which truly is the story of us all. It is much more important, more true and more real than all the stories in history books and novels and all the broadcast and printed news put together! A little absentmindedness, a little unbelief and a little Christmas sentiment, these are our reactions, not only yours, but mine as well!
>
> Until the angel of the Lord appears and shakes us up! The angel of the Lord most certainly passed this night through the streets and the homes and the squares of Basel. He was here for those who celebrated Christmas Eve in loneliness and distress, or on the contrary in fun and frivolity. He is here for all those who are still asleep and maybe have something to sleep off. He is passing through the churches of our town this morning. How does he tell the good news to all these people? How do they listen to him or do not listen at all? However, let us not refer to other people, but rather focus on ourselves. The angel of the

> Lord most certainly is here in our midst to speak and to be heard. It only remains for me to make you aware of his presence and attentive to his words, so that together we may listen, and ponder what he has to say.
>
> An angel! That is—a messenger, who has some news for us. You might quite simply think of the mailman bringing you some news. The angel of the Lord is God's messenger carrying the news of the Christmas story. You see, if he announces the news, absentmindedness, unbelief and lofty sentiments are swept away, for the angel of the Lord descends directly from God to us.[3]

Note that, in this sermon, Barth tackles the question "Who defines reality?" Will we have our reality delivered by the evening news or by an angel moving through the city of Basel? Postmodern linguistics has rediscovered the truth that our knowledge is deeply conflicted and that the modern search for secure, nonconflicted, universally acknowledged, consensual definitions of truth and reality are futile. One of the reasons we have rhetoric in the first place is because we have deep disagreements over the question What is real? There are many reasons why people may disagree with our argument—their ignorance is only one of them. We live in differing linguistic worlds, with very different views of reality. Agreement cannot be achieved simply by finding some allegedly universal, all-embracing principles to which all rational people are forced to assent.

Wittgenstein showed us the ways in which we live in linguistic communities, communities that are constructed through various "language games."[4] These language games give a community coherence, a worldview, and an identity. When we speak, we are often speaking across communities, into the different rules of different language games, thus there is much opportunity for dissonance, confusion, and misunderstanding.

In my experience we preachers often work under the misapprehension that we can find a way to proclaim the gospel that lessens interpretive conflict. We like thinking of ourselves as homiletic peacemakers and reconcilers. Yet there are good reasons why a sermon tends to be the provocation of conflict rather than its resolution. For one thing, we speak from one peculiar linguistic community—the church—to many other adversarial interpretive communities—North American democracy, capitalism, the godless academy, and so forth. Conflict is unavoidable.

One might argue that Christian preaching may have more opportunities to be heard in a postmodern world than it had in the modern. The postmodern world exposes *the contingency and caughtness of all language, its political connectedness*. Postmodernism frankly admits to the raggedness of our language, to that which every preacher worth his or her salt knows: *it is hard to be understood, and the possibilities for misunderstanding are limitless*. Postmodernism also points to *the linguistic construction of all reality*. Our speaking and hearing tend to be conflicted because we are always talking across various linguistic communities, and there are deep differences between us. As preachers we have no reason to fear this insight. As Lose says, "Postmodernity renders Christians a tremendous service by clarifying the essential nature of our faith, and realizing the call that Christian claims can rest upon no ultimate foundation, not even that of nonfoundationalism. Rather, Christianity exists solely by confession, the conviction and assertion of revealed truth apart from any appeal to another criterion; we live, that is always by faith alone. . . . The question is ultimately not whether we can speak our faith, but *how*. How, that is, shall we describe the speech that gives voice to faith's deepest convictions? What will be its character?"[5]

Frank acknowledgment of the inherent conflictedness of knowledge can be an important prerequisite for a preacher, particularly a preacher who is afraid of a fight. Christians are commanded by our Lord to forgive our enemies, and preaching is, in part, an exercise in creating enemies who are worth forgiving. Christian preaching is not odd in that it creates dissension and discord; preaching is odd in how it deals with the dissonance. Interpretive peacemaking is God's problem, not ours. Only God can make enemies of the gospel into friends. We are to forgive our enemies, not capitulate or acquiesce to them. Any attempt on our part, as preachers, to render the gospel's enemies into friends will be some coercive, violent rhetorical act. And that is not how the gospel gains its adherents.[6] We work through being clear that our enemies are enemies, thus honoring their enmity. Then, in obedience to Christ, we forgive them as Christ has forgiven us.

William Placher notes how curious it is that we have *four* Gospels. One might have thought that, at some point in the church's life, someone might have said, "It's confusing to have four witnesses to Jesus. Matthew got most of it right, let's go with Matthew and forget Mark, Luke, and John." Someone tried to do that and was promptly condemned as a heretic. No, the church, notes Placher, allowed these four, often conflicted, very different voices to stand. Why? Because, says Placher, the church understood that the way of Christ is a fundamentally nonviolent way and that there was no way to have a unified, coherent, univocal Gospel without doing violence to someone's voice.[7]

Thus, we can see that the Barthian critique of rhetorical strategies can be pushed deeper than even Barth's antipathy toward rhetoric. Any time that we preachers presume to take into our hands "the problem of communication" or "the challenge of preaching," we are circumventing preaching's necessity for miracle. Preaching thus degenerates into a purely human phenomenon and we are forced to seek agreement in the conventional, worldly way—through violence.

In preaching, we always "walk by faith." Christianity is inherently suspicious of all of our claims to knowledge, yet it is convinced and surprised that we do actually know. For Barth, when it comes to revelation from God, our proverbial glass is always more than half full. Every time we rise up and proclaim God's Word, to do so is a kind of witness to the reality of faith. "The possibility of the knowledge of the Word of God relies in the Word of God and nowhere else. . . . This miracle is faith" (*CD*, I, 1, pg. 255). "We declare to you what was from the beginning, what we have heard, what we have seen with our eyes, what we have looked at and touched with our hands, concerning the word of life" (1 John 1:1; see also 2 Cor. 4:13).

In the quite wonderful movie *The Gospel of John*, a three-hour Canadian cinematic exercise in which the movie goes through the entire Gospel of John word-for-word, Jesus is, from the beginning, a serene, enigmatic, but nevertheless mysteriously magnetic figure. People are both drawn to and repulsed by his every move. The moment he sets foot on our landscape (for instance, at the wedding in Cana in John 2) things break out, overflow, and many behold glorious signs and believe in him. He is so effusively, unavoidably theophanous that, by the time the movie gets to the scene with Mary Magdalene at the tomb, the Resurrection appearance, the scene is almost anticlimactic. In most of these religious movies, when things get really spiritual and religious, the camera goes out of focus and everything becomes blurred and bathed in blue light. But in *The Gospel of John*, Mary is stumbling about at the cemetery, sees a man kneeling over by a bush, and, when he speaks to her, calling her name, she realizes that he is none other than the crucified Jesus. In other words, the Resurrection is just another day in our relationship with the Christ. We do not have to wait until the end of the story to receive revelation. From the very first, Jesus is the Lord, the sovereign Proclaimer, the Revealer. To "walk by faith" means in great part to be willing to let our intellectual defenses be broken down, to have our eyes opened, and to have our flat little modern world be continuously flooded by the self-disclosure of God in Christ.

Speaking by faith, without any prior philosophical foundation, we preachers have few interpretive allies in the competing linguistic communities, few means of finding some meta-language whereby we can lessen the necessary conflict between vastly differing ways of construing the world. The nonviolent gospel of Jesus, which has nothing to commend it to the world except a God who works through words, tends to provoke violent reaction against itself, and always has.

Sabbath Unrest[8]

Jeremiah 1:4-10; 1 Corinthians 13:1-13; Luke 4:21-30

The Bible is a very violent book. That's good because we are very violent people. Much of our violence stems from the nature of American democracy. Something about our system of government makes a sizable number of us want, at any given moment, to kill one another. This is the system that we so graciously offer to the people of Iraq. Give the Secretary of Defense an army, and he or she will find somewhere to use it. Give Michael Novak a war, and he'll find Catholic justification for it. Violence is as American as. . . .

But in our Gospel, Luke 4, Jesus' sermon in Nazareth, the case is different. Here, violence is due, not to the aspirations of American democracy or lust for national security, but rather to Jesus. All the Gospels agree—from the first, from the very first, the moment Jesus sets foot in a pulpit—things get nasty.

I've got a friend who is a devotee of His Holiness the Dali Lama. He just returned from an audience with His Holiness in New York.

"When His Holiness speaks, everyone in the room becomes quiet, serene, and peaceful," he claims.

Not so with Jesus. Things were fine at Nazareth, a purpose-driven, seeker-sensitive synagogue, until Jesus opened his mouth and all hell broke loose.

And it was his first sermon! One might have thought that Jesus would have used a more effective rhetorical strategy, that he might have saved his more inflammatory speech until he had taken the time to build trust, to win their affection, that he might have contextualized his message—as we are urged in homiletics classes.

No, first day, first sermon, he hit them right between the eyes with Isaiah, followed by a jab from 1 Kings, right to the jaw, left hook. Beaten, but not bowed, the congregation struggled to its feet, regrouped, and attempted to throw the preacher off a cliff. With that, "Jesus went on his way."

And what a way to go. In just a few weeks, this sermon will end, not at Nazareth but at Golgotha. For now, Jesus has given us the slip. Having preached the sovereign grace of God, grace for a Syrian army officer or a poor pagan woman at Zarephath—you call this "good news"? (Luke 4:18)—Jesus demonstrates that he is free even from the community that professes to be People of the Book. The Book, and its preachers, are the hope of the community of faith, not its pets or possessions. Perhaps the church folk at Capernaum won't put up such a fight (4:31ff.). Jesus moves on, ever-elusive and free.

Those of us who have been professionally trained to make rhetorical peace with the congregation marvel at the freedom of Jesus the Preacher to preach over their heads, to wound in order to heal, to use their own beloved texts against them (surely there were deserving lepers or starving women of our own toward whom God might have been gracious). How sly of the Common Lectionary to pair this linguistic assault by Jesus at Nazareth with Paul's pretty words on love at Corinth (1 Cor. 13). Poor preachers. Sometimes we love our people, in the name of Christ, believing, hoping, enduring just about everything with them (1 Cor. 13:7), and sometimes we love them by throwing the Book at them. No wonder young Jeremiah begged out when God called him to "speak whatever I command you" (Jer. 1:7). Smart boy, young Jeremiah.

Kierkegaard noted that so many great minds of his century had given themselves to making people's lives easier—inventing labor-saving machines and devices—that he would dedicate himself to making people's lives more difficult. He would become a preacher.

Stanley Hauerwas and I were leading a seminar for a group of preachers. I discussed ways to communicate the gospel in sermons; Hauerwas, true to form, discussed ways to make sure that you never communicate the gospel in sermons, at least not to these people.

Toward the end of the seminar, a little pastor said, in plaintive voice, "The bishop sent me to a little town in South Carolina. I preached, one Sunday in Lent, on the challenge of racial justice. In two months, the bishop moved me, so angry were my people. At the next church, I was determined for things to go better. Didn't preach about race. But we had this incident in town. I felt forced to speak." (By this time tears were in his eyes.)

"The Board met that week and voted unanimously for us to be moved. My wife was insulted at the supermarket. My children were beat up on the school ground. It's just so hard."

My pastoral heart went out to this dear, suffering brother.

Hauerwas replied, "And your point is what? We work for the living God, not a false, dead god! Did somebody tell you it would be easy? Next question."

Not one drop of sympathy for this brother, not a bit of collegial concern. Jesus moves right on from Nazareth to Capernaum, another Sabbath, another sermon, where the congregational demons cry out to him, "Let us alone!" (Luke 4:34). But he won't, thank God. He is free to administer his peculiar sort of grace, whether we hear or refuse to hear. This is our good news.

As for us preachers: "See, today I appoint you over nations and over kingdoms, / to pluck up and to pull down, / to destroy and to overthrow" (Jer. 1:10), with no weapon but words.

As Stanley Hauerwas has said, "The church's social task is first of all its willingness to be a community formed by a language that the world does not share. . . . The church's social ethic is not first of all to be found in the statements by which it tries to influence the ethos of those in power, but rather . . . in its ability to sustain a people who are not at home in the liberal presumptions of our civilization and society."[9]

Our speaking must be neither an attempt to lessen all interpretive conflict, nor an attempt to force our principles down every reasonable person's throat, but instead an attempt to reform people into the Christian linguistic community, that community that entails our particular way of talking and construing the world.

We don't have to describe the world through certain allegedly universal categories in order to get people to listen to us. Rather, we speak to a world that is already God's world. That the world does not know that it is God's does not negate the reality that it belongs to God. Therefore we speak into a world that God owns, though the world in its ignorance does not know that, a realm where God is busy getting back what belongs to God, a world always being penetrated by the reach of the Trinity. We speak to others who are outside of our tradition, to those who do not understand our linguistic world, because Christ has commanded us to do so. We speak, not as chaplains of the status quo, but as missionaries in inhospitable territory. It is the content of the Word (Jesus Christ), rather than its form (homiletical diatribe), that causes the trouble. Says Barth:

> The apostle of Jesus Christ not only can but must be a missionary (v. 16). It is not merely the formal necessity of proclaiming the Word of God, nor the humanitarian love which would rather not withhold this Word from others, that forces him to do this. The determining factor is the concrete content of the Word itself. The truth which he knows about Jesus Christ and human life compels him almost as it were automatically to speak wherever it is not yet known. It is like air rushing into a vacuum, or water downhill, or fire to more fuel. Man and his life stand under the sign of God's judgment. This is not just a religious opinion. It is a universal truth. It applies to all of us. It decides concerning every man as such. It leaps all frontiers. It is more urgent and binding than any human insight, however clear and compelling, or any convictions, however enthusiastically embraced. This truth is the driving power behind the Christian mission. Apart from it, there would be no indication where it should be pursued or not pursued. Where it is recognized it bursts all barriers.[10]

Thus, the most engaging aspect of preaching is its peculiar, disruptive content. If we would be interesting and engaging, we must keep close to the substance of Christian preaching (Jesus Christ) and the form and style of Christian preaching (Jesus Christ). Then the gospel will take care of itself.

At the university, a medical ethicist complained to me, "Whenever we get one of you people from the Divinity School over here at the Medical Center for a conversation, I can't tell that you talk any differently from the way we talk. I can't tell the difference between 'Christian' medical ethics and just plain medical ethics. Why bother to be in dialogue with someone who is saying about the same thing that you are saying?" Why indeed? One of the reasons why the world may listen to us is that we are interesting, we are saying something strange that the world cannot hear elsewhere. There are powerful social forces that keep the world safe from the Christian way of construing the world. Furthermore, one of the reasons that we take the trouble to speak to the world, assuming that the world will listen, is because of our conviction that what we say is true, that this is a truthful account of what is really going on in the world, that the world we address is God's.

It is not that Christian speaking is peculiar and limited and other kinds of speaking are universal; it is rather that some peculiar speaking is so socially sanctioned and underwritten by a capitalist economy and a constitutional democracy, that it no longer sounds peculiar. For instance, those who say, quite contrary to claims of the gospel, that "Christianity is only one way of being religious; there are other, equally valid ways," do not say this on their own, as an all-inclusive "fact." In a democratic, capitalist economy, no one is permitted to say anything more interesting about religion than "all religions are just different ways of moving in the same direction." In saying this they are not transcending their linguistic community; they are rather showing their membership in a limited community—the world of secular, democratic, North American capitalism. Everyone stands somewhere when talking. All statements are linked to some specific, socially constrained linguistic community. The question can never be, "Will my statements of truth be limited by some community?" for all of them are. But rather, "Will statements of truth be derived from a truthful community?"

Besides, our story teaches us that we are sinners. We know, or certainly ought to know, some of the myriad of ways that we have perverted God's Word, all the ways that we have evaded and misunderstood, all of the times that we heard but refused to hear. Therefore, we ought to have great sympathy with any resistance to our speaking that we find within the world. We find no resistance to the gospel in the world that we have not met first in our own hearts. The conflict caused by the gospel cuts right through our own souls.

A World Made by the Word

David Ford says that Barth believed that God chooses to bring people to faith through certain stories.[11] Or as Barth says, "When the Bible speaks of Revelation it does so in the form of narrating a story, a series of stories." What makes these biblical stories revelatory for Barth is not their historicity or inerrancy. What makes the stories revelatory is our trust in their subject, a speaking subject who is still alive to confirm them and use them for his purposes.[12]

My teacher of Barth, Robert Clyde Johnson, remembers being in an extended Barth seminar in which there was a heated debate, for well over an hour, among the students, about what Barth was trying to do in his *Church Dogmatics*. Barth smoked his pipe and listened in on the debate. Finally, after a long time he spoke and said, "If I understand what I am trying to do in the *Church Dogmatics*, it is to listen to what Scripture is saying and tell you what I hear." Johnson said that he thought this simplistic statement ought to be taken with utter seriousness by those who wanted to understand Barth.[13]

David Ford demonstrated how Barth can be thought of as a "narrative theologian," not because Barth tells stories in his theology, for he almost never tells stories, but rather because, to enter into conversation with Barth is to be drawn into a particular, peculiar world of discourse, an organized, sustained narrative with beginning and end. Aristotle defined a story as that account of the world which has a beginning, a middle, and an end. A story moves somewhere. A story creates a world. I recall at this point Barth's sermon on the cross of Christ, a cross set between two thieves, interpreting this scene (to the prisoners at Basel) as the precursor of the Christian church:

They Crucified Him with the Criminals, One on Either Side of Him

"They crucified him with the criminals." Which is more amazing, to find Jesus in such bad company, or to find the criminals in such good company? As a matter of fact, both are true! One thing is certain: here they hang all three, Jesus and the criminals, one at the right and one at the left, all three exposed to the same public abuse, to the same interminable pain, to the same slow and irrevocable death throes. Like Jesus, these two criminals had been arrested somewhere, locked up and sentenced by some judge in the course of the previous few days. And now they hang on their crosses with him and find themselves in solidarity and fellowship with him. They are linked in a common bondage never again to be broken, just as the nails that fastened them to the piece of wood would never break. It was

> *as inescapable for them as it was for him. It was a point of no return for them as for him. There remained only the shameful, painstricken present and the future of their approaching death. (Strangely enough, there are many paintings of Jesus' crucifixion where the two criminals are lost to sight. It would perhaps be more appropriate not to represent Jesus' death at all. But if it is done, then the two thieves on the right and on the left must not be left out. In any painting or representation where they are absent, an important, even an essential, element is missing.)*
>
> *They crucified him with the criminals. Do you know what this implies? Don't be too surprised if I tell you that this was the first Christian fellowship, the first certain, indissoluble and indestructible Christian community. Christian community is manifest wherever there is a group of people close to Jesus who are with him in such a way that they are directly and unambiguously affected by his promise and assurance. These may hear that everything he is, he is from them, and every thing he does, he does for them. To live by this promise is to be a Christian community. The two criminals were the first certain Christian community.*[14]

This is church—as much church as it ever gets: Jesus being crucified in the middle of a gathering of criminals.

My world was rearranged in the reading of this sermon. Suddenly I found myself living elsewhere. I not only saw the world differently, but I was in a different world. This is what narrative preaching does when it works—it offers a new world (the kingdom of God) that would be otherwise unavailable to us without the preaching. To be a Christian is to be willing to have your world absorbed by another. Our stories are subsumed into another story named as gospel. And the way we construct worlds, as we see in Genesis 1, is through words. As George Lindbeck puts it, "A scriptural world is . . . able to absorb the universe. It supplies the interpretive framework within which believers seek to live their lives and to understand reality."[15] So we can tell the story, reiterating it, telling it as interestingly and beguilingly as we can, we can testify to the truth as we have witnessed it. However, we do so under the humble and wonder-filled recognition that if people hear, their hearing is a result of God's disclosure and revelation, not ours. Because our hearing is a gift of God, an act of grace, it is miraculous. We cannot specify in advance those who will hear. In fact, every communicative creature knows the surprise of having someone hear when we did not think they would. We also know the disappointment of speaking as correctly and interestingly as we can, and yet there is no hearing. Grace is not grace if it is automatic. Human hearers are sinful. They can't be trusted to know and to receive the gospel on their own.[16] God is known, on occasion, to have "hardened hearts," to have stiffened the resistance of some hearers to the Word of God. We are people who "hearing, refuse to hear." If preaching were a matter of our conscientious rhetorical work, it would be a method. And yet Barth teaches us that preaching is a miracle. This God not only kills but makes alive. Patience is an essential homiletical virtue as we wait upon God to kill and to make alive. Those who wait upon the Lord will mount up with wings like eagles.

As we have noted, Barth does not necessarily teach that the herald is unconcerned about the hearers in the congregation.[17] Rather, the preacher cares about the "real situation" of the congregation in order to subsume the congregation into the biblical story. The congregation's life is to be "taken up in the sermon":

> If preaching is to be congregational, there must also be openness to the real situation of the congregation and reflection upon it so as to be able to take it up into the sermon. Living with their

congregations, preachers live out a history with them, and they are constantly agitated by the question: "How is it with us now?" This does not mean that they are to let themselves be carried along by the stream of life and merely to be the mouthpieces of the congregation. They are not to be popular village sages who know life, who dramatize it, who tell people what is on their hearts. The sermon is not just a transfigured continuation of life, its leading theme. Life must really be taken up into the sermon.[18]

In explaining the massive quantity of Karl Barth's *Church Dogmatics*, Hans Frei noted that Barth was not only just "naturally talkative," but that he was forced to write so much because he attempted to re-create the world. The *Church Dogmatics* is "a universe of discourse, and he had to put the reader in the middle of that world, when instructing him in the use of that language by showing how—extensively, and not only by stating the rules for principles of the discourse."[19] It is the narrative as a whole, its cumulative rhetorical effect, that makes a difference greater than its individual parts.

Barth admitted, when he gave his lectures on preaching, that he believed in linguistic craftsmanship. Because preachers work not only with the Word but also with words, he advises that we are "to nurture speech":

> Let us now focus on the purely linguistic form of the Word that we are to proclaim. We might speak here of the need to nurture speech. Just as cultivation is a needed sphere of life, we can never do enough to cultivate the organ of speech. There is a process of grinding language down which results in our repeating ourselves—using set phrases for certain things. But this leads to people missing what we are saying. An emphatic warning must be given against trying to impress the listener by constant repetition of hackneyed terms. Repetition always robs the content of its force. Shallow reading and newspaper jargon are a danger because they can poison our language from without with their general expressions and modish turns of phrase, which in many cases are totally meaningless. By overhasty and superficial writing we risk ruining the language and letting cliché become a regular disease. The only way to avert this danger is painfully to work on every single word that we ought to use in the sermon. By this work, which cannot be merely a matter of thought, we learn to pay attention to phrases and sentences.[20]

Barth is a narrative theologian in the way he cleverly draws us into the distinctive narrative world of scripture. In so doing, Barth takes our various narratives and renarrates our lives through the talk of a Trinitarian God. Among the devices that he uses in this enterprise are his naive, contemporaneous reading of material that others might read as historical (his switch from the past tense to the present in his discussion of historical material), his constant conversation with the biblical text, always privileging the claims of scripture over contemporary philosophical claims, his use of the biblical text as authority for even his most complicated theological assertions—without seeking authorization from any other philosophical foundation—and his implication that the biblical world is more real than any other world, including our own. Added to this, Barth takes so long to say what he has to say that we find ourselves reading almost nothing but Barth! Faithful preachers are engaged in a complex process of renarration of their congregations' lives in which they find themselves, through God's retelling of their lives, which is scripture, living in a different linguistic world.[21]

As we noted earlier, words make a world. We live in a multiplicity of these linguistic worlds. Preaching is bound to be a conflicted enterprise because preaching is an assault upon the received, socially acceptable, governmentally subsidized worlds by the gospel-induced world. Therefore, conflict comes with the territory, and church can be a conflicted place to be as people are invited to relinquish one world for another. Lindbeck's descriptions of this process as "inclusion" or "absorption" are not violent enough to do justice to this conflicted sort of talk.

In a contemporary university, David Tracy believes that appeals to tradition and authority carry little weight and are quickly dismissed as "obscurantism." In his desperation to be taken seriously by the intellectual community, this means for Tracy that Christian theology must explain and argue in terms that the intellectual community will accept. Beyond the academic community, moreover, there is a pluralistic society debating important moral issues—from feeding the hungry, to abortion, to nuclear disarmament. Tracy wants a "Christian voice" to be heard in those debates, but he thinks that will not happen unless Christians are willing to play by the rules of contemporary society—which means, among other things, not appealing to our own tradition or scripture as if such an appeal settled the issue at hand. Such concern leads Tracy to advocate "public theology."[22]

Tracy sees Barth as the principal representative of what he calls the trajectory of "proclamation," preaching the dual pronouncement of God's judgment and grace, simply stating the argument to the world, rather than attempting to engage the world through speech that is intelligible to the world. This Barthian trajectory of "proclamation" Tracy contrasts with what he calls "manifestation theology," which is more "sacramental" in displaying the means of possible union with humanity through its manifestation of the sacred through earthly means.[23]

Yet Barth, so impressed by the unique, miraculous quality of Christian discourse, would deny manifestation theology's claim for a point of contact with our normal means of making sense of the world. Both the subject matter of Christian proclamation (the Trinity) and the means of proclamation (the Trinity) mean that we cannot find some other, socially accepted means of speaking ("public theology"). This language must be spoken by God or it will not be spoken at all.

I have never liked this talk of "public theology,"[24] finding it naive in its implicit assumption that somehow the "intellectual community" is less closed and peculiar in its linguistic apparatus and more "public" than the church. I find intellectually arrogant the claim that the mode of speaking at the University of Chicago is more "public" than the church's proclamation. In calling what we have to say "proclamation," the church is saying that all of its most important, distinctive speech is "public," never "private" or "parochial." After all, I preach in English and anyone who understands English has, by the grace of God, the possibility of understanding me. Tracy's "public theology" tends to be the speech of those who are limited by the discourse of the University of Chicago. When asked to say something that is relatively public and universal, Christians say "church."

I was surprised when our teacher, James Gustafson, accused Hauerwas and me of "fideism."[25] I suppose that Gustafson believes that the moment we give up trying to justify our beliefs by some philosophical foundation, when we stop attempting to make sense to the world exclusively through the world's means of making sense, we are guilty of being "fideistic" and are sidelined to cultural irrelevancy. Gustafson's critique helped me see how much I agree with Barth that there is an intentional circularity to Christian belief. All our flights of logic in theology finally come back to "the Bible tells us so." But that does not mean to forsake all reason, rather it means to use that reason that is tied (as is all reason) to some particular linguistic community. As David Lose puts this matter of fideism:

> The question . . . is therefore not whether we can escape fideism altogether but whether we stand for a *maximal* or *minimal* fideism. Whereas a minimal—what I will also call a *critical*—fideism places its convictions in the public area for critical scrutiny and evaluation, maximal fideism refuses to enter into a cross-contextual conversation either from disinterest or because it believes such conversation should not take place. (Lose, pg. 39)

I try to practice Lose's minimal fideism because I am willing to explain why I employ a certain viewpoint and play a certain language game, and though these explanations may not be plausible to everyone, they are still public explanations to anyone who is patient and courageous enough to listen to them. All that Christians ought to ask of the world is the patience and the courage to attempt to listen to our public speech and not to rush to judgment on whether what we say is "reasonable" because the world, particularly the North American world, has no means of making that judgment (and we should not attempt to speak as if it has that means of judging).

The postmodernist says that language has no ability to refer beyond itself. Therefore, a kind of critical conversation across the various linguistic worlds is very difficult. The linguistic world created by a language is self-contained, intratextual, and therefore different from another linguistic world. There is a quality of "untranslatability" to our language in which it is difficult for the Christian faith to be translated into more socially acceptable languages like existentialism or feminism (or postmodernism!).

Postmodernism has exposed the way in which our culture privileges some sources of "real" knowledge (like science) and honors some linguistic communities (the university) as being more "public" in their speech than other communities. Christians are notable for being those who are honest about where we privilege the power of language and about which community of language is authoritative for us. That honesty is one of our virtues and one of our contributions to so-called public discourse. One of the exasperating things about many modern linguistic communities (Congress, the university faculty, the evening news, MTV) is their failure to acknowledge the limitations of their own ways of speaking. Some of these communities speak as if they were free, as if they were merely recounting the facts about the world, unconstrained by some linguistic community that has already defined the world before they attempt to describe the facts of the world. Asking our speech to be "public" usually privileges one linguistic world over another, asking Christian speakers to bow to the demands of that other world. Christian speakers are at least honest when we address those who are caught in the linguistic limitations of one world (including the world of academia), when we admit that we would like, by our speaking, to convert them into another linguistic world called the gospel.

I agree with Lose that our language is never utterly, completely distinctive. Lose makes a helpful distinction between our languages being incommensurable and incomparable. Our cultural-linguistic traditions are not as self-contained and complete as we might think. Words and expressions are borrowed, traded, and used. All languages are hybrids. Parasitic. Collage. Whereas language may be a communal construction, our communities are always overlapping. They are not discrete. Therefore, in speaking across communities, we can usually count on the possibility of "relative intelligibility," of being somewhat commensurable.[26] But only somewhat. The moment that a Christian speaker stands up in the context of nearly every other linguistic community and says, "And God said . . . ," we will immediately discover the limits of our ability to make our language commensurable with other differently constituted linguistic communities, though our usage of our distinctive language is in many ways incommensurable.

Preachers know full well the limits of language. Whereas modernists believed that language actually refers to reality with some degree of accuracy, postmodernists believe that language does not refer beyond itself and that reality is a communal, purely symbolic construction. If either of them is absolutely right about language, this spells trouble for the Christian communicator. Postmodernism recognizes the way that language is communally constructed and the way that language constructs the community. This is a primary insight of George Lindbeck and members of the "Yale school" like Hans Frei and Charles Campbell. Lindbeck reminded us that reality is intratextual, self-referential. Language doesn't simply express our thought; language shapes life and thought. Language is a communal phenomenon "that shapes the subjectivities of individuals rather than being primarily the manifestation of those subjectivities."[27]

Yet finally the thing that makes Christian preaching so conflicted is not simply the anthropological observation that proclamation provokes a collision with other linguistic worlds, and that proclamation necessitates inculcation and indoctrination into the peculiar world of the gospel, but rather the more Barthian and therefore more theological observation that preaching deals with a God who is named Trinity.

It is not only that language renders a new world, absorbs us into a new reality, gives us a new grammatical universe, but rather that our reality has been shattered by an external force, the Word of God, that disrupts our linguistically constructed worlds with the Truth, who is Jesus Christ. Our preaching is not only measured by the Lindbeckian standard of how well it inculcates the hearers into a new culture called the church but also how well our speaking conforms to God's speaking that kills and makes alive all cultures, including the one called the church. Preaching has its origin, not in essentially anthropological observations about the way language shapes reality, but rather in the remarkable, "And God said. . . ."[28]

Barth reminds us that Christians are literally conceived of and given birth to by the Word:

> We find all this expressed in the strongest imaginable way in Jas. 1:18, where (cf. also I Pet. 1:23) there is reference to the fact that the Christian is begotten of the word of truth. Then v. 21 goes on logically to speak of an implanted word, i.e., a word which, so to speak, belongs to man himself, without which man, would no longer be himself. And because the word at issue is the Word of God, we must add explicitly that its efficacy, its power to change, is not just relative as in the case of other powers. It is not uncertain. It is not conditioned or restricted by the behaviour of other factors, e.g., man. All this may be true of what it effects in man, of what may be seen of its operation in the life of man. But it is not true of its operation in itself and as such. The power of the Word of God in itself and as such is absolute power.[29]

Christian preaching was both accepted and rejected, not because people were attracted to or repulsed by the strange linguistic world of the early Christian communicators, but rather because of the miraculous work among them of the crucified and Risen Christ. Through him, hearers did not simply find this early preaching helpful but also *truthful*. Christian language not only constituted a new community, but was also constituted by a new agent, a Savior who was counter to all of the world's schemes of salvation. Some of the listeners became convinced that they were being spoken to, not only by the preacher, but by the living God who had, in this speaking, a distinctive identity.

While Lindbeck's observations of the way language has worked in the past are astute, and quite helpful in describing some of the work that we preachers do through our preaching, I doubt that Barth would be content with either Frei's or Lindbeck's accounts. Barth would probably say that Christian language is, in a sense, the end of language as a cultural/linguistic exercise. The thing that interests Barth is not that our language functions in an intratextual way but rather that Christian language is radically extratextual. Christian language does not merely claim to be coherent with the language games and grammatical rules of the Christian faith (Lindbeck) but more importantly claims to be corresponsive to a living reality who makes the language work. Everything is meant to be dependent upon "And God said. . . ."[30]

As the New Testament goes to great pains to demonstrate, the crucified and resurrected Christ is the occasion for severe cognitive dissonance and violent resistance on the part of our hearers. Many of my sermons "fail" neither because of my limitations as a preacher nor the limitations of my congregation, but because of the self-imposed limitations of the God of Israel and the church. It is the nature of this God to be nonviolent, therefore this God will not work with us through any more aggressive means than words. This God has chosen to forgive; therefore, this God will not forsake the very ones who forsake him. This God is intensely loquacious; therefore, this God is always seeking and saving the lost, hoping thereby to initiate a conversation. In other words, this God is troublingly against everything that we are and all that we serve. There is nothing "natural" in the ways of this God, no natural "point of contact" to be made, no way of climbing up to God by the ramp of our innate human interpretive apparatus. Jesus comes to us "without form or comeliness" and stands always before us as the one unknown, the one who—with holes in hands and feet—is an assault on all that we are. He came to us and revealed himself before us, and our collective verdict was and always is, "Crucify him!" We rejected him, not because we did not understand him, but because he understood us all too well. Jesus is the source of preaching's major trouble.

Therefore we preachers must cultivate love for the God who is Trinity more than we love even our congregations. We must nurture a delight in the Trinitarian God, who is so much more interesting than any other subject of speech. There is no way that we can protect our unsuspecting congregations from the ravages of a God who is determined to have them, to use them for his purposes. The courage to preach such conflicted good news comes from the cultivation of love for God, the desire to be a herald for that God, to be an occasion for God's miracle that is Christian preaching. Only this attentive focus, only this passionate love can save us from the fear of failure and rejection that infects most of us preachers. Only such love will enable us to rise above our homiletical success or failure of the moment and to embrace God's words to Jeremiah that, whether they "hear or refuse to hear," at least they will be forced to admit that a real prophet has been among them.

The Virtue of Humility

A few years ago, at a gathering of New Testament scholars who were convened to read and critique the work of my colleague Richard Hays (prior to the publication of Hays's wonderful *New Testament Ethics*), one of the scholars chastised Hays for saying too much, for claiming to know something definitive and certain about the New Testament. The scholar said something to the effect that scholars should be more reticent, more intellectually humble and restrained in their talk about what they know from the Bible and less willing to publish books that imply that they know something that the rest of us don't.

Hays's rejoinder was that this sort of reticence might be fine for biblical scholars, but what about the poor preacher who must stand up, on a regular basis, and actually say something? Preachers don't have the luxury (or is it the temptation?) of being able to infinitely postpone proclamation. At that moment I gave thanks to God that I am called to be a preacher and therefore, despite my reservations and uncertainties, am commanded to sin boldly and on a weekly basis, to stand up and testify, "And God said. . . ."[31]

As we have noted earlier, though Barth speaks of the God who cannot be spoken of, Barth resists apophatic, humble silence before the mystery of the Trinity. God may be an inconceivable mystery, but God is a mystery who has graciously come to us, been born among us, spoken to us, and thus we must speak of this mystery. Respectful silence is not an option.

Barth said that Schleiermacher was "convinced, as few men have been, of the inexpressibility of the divine."[32] And Barth did not mean that as a compliment. The theologian of religious feeling said that he longed for that time when humanity would enjoy such union with the divine that there would be no need for words about God, that faith would be maintained, not by inadequate words, but in that "placid quiet of holy virgins."[33] Schleiermacher said that on Christmas the best Christmas "sermon" would be a flute solo.

Barth was particularly drawn to a Christmas story by Schleiermacher in which one of the characters rejects all "speech-making" about religious matters as "too tedious and cold." Christmas is that which "creates in me a speechless joy, and I cannot but laugh and exult like a child."[34] Of course, with Schleiermacher the problem is thoughts, or too few of them. He cultivated that humble unwillingness to defame God by speaking of God in terms of idea rather than feeling. He describes preaching as a kind of self-expressive poetics, "self-communication" between speaker and hearer. Barth says that "for Schleiermacher proclaiming God means proclaiming one's own piety."[35] This, in Barth's judgment, rendered proclamation into "simply man speaking with himself."[36] Barth believed that Schleiermacher's move left preaching without any norm "from above," making preaching mostly a matter of humble speaking, in that "placid quiet of holy virgins," expressing our innermost spiritual thoughts, rather than bold listening.

Is Barth making too much of God as the God who speaks? There are some who favor a more inarticulate view of God, in fact those who seem to feel that it is of the nature of a true God to be apophatic. But "God" is available to us only in God's self-articulation. A God who does not reveal is not a "god," but only a projection of our selves. If we were listing the attributes of God, which I have no desire to do, surely articulation, that is, self-revelation, would head the list. Just as Aristotle taught that we are not really fully human until we can say what we want and who we are, how could we say that God exists without God's speaking?

And what happens when we have no real notion of God who is external to us? To say that anyone speaks, including to say that God speaks, is to acknowledge a distance, a gap between hearer and speaker. Barth's sense, first articulated in *Romans* but never completely diminished throughout his life, of God's great distance from us, of the infinite qualitative distinction between our ways and God's ways, our speech and God's speech, our lives and God's life, was—in the context of modernity's relentless subjectivity—an act of intellectual courage. That Kantian respect (*Actung*) for the moral law or that Platonic love of the good (*eudaemonia*) both recognize some higher, external judge of all that is human. And this is precisely what is lacking in so much of modern, immanentist thought about God. And, I may say, it is so often lacking in contemporary Christian worship, in my church family at least—that sense of awe, of the grandeur of distance, of the space between here and the throne. It is of the nature of the God who is revealed in scripture to be known as a God who is not known, whose distance and difference are experienced by us precisely in those moments when God speaks.

I am reminded of poor Job who, for so many redundant chapters, pleads with God to speak, only to be devastated by what God says and reveals when God actually speaks. The speaking God, as the living and true God, is a more transcendent, distant God than any silent God.

I agree with those proponents of apophatic, negative theology when they say that attempts to say too much about God, to claim too much knowledge of God, leads to a counterfeit of God.[37] When contemporary Christian preaching takes as its assignment the aggressive overcoming of that distance, when preaching purports to negotiate the space between humanity and the throne of God, we play into the hands of the leveling tendency of the modern.[38] I often hear preachers of a more liberal ilk complain that preachers of a more conservative stripe claim to know too much about God. This is often a fair criticism. But I assume that such criticism also applies to liberal preachers who make facile, sentimental pronouncements that they know that "God is love," or "God cares for us," or "God's love is inclusive," or other saccharine generalities. Generality leads to banality, an attempt to cut God down to our size, whether practiced by those who think of themselves as "progressive" Christians or those who think of themselves as traditionalist Christians. Speech about God should command respect for God, and should empower that respect. The disenchantment of modernity has had devastating consequences for the nobility of preaching.[39]

And yet, we must speak because we have been spoken to, addressed by God. The guard against theological banality and arrogant human attempts to bridge the gap between us and God is attentiveness to the subject and increasingly obedient and faithful descriptions of the subject. The curious sort of inarticulate stammering that characterizes some contemporary preaching presents itself as a kind of respect, a fear of verbal profanation, a sort of humility before the majesty and mystery of God. However, I fear that it is testimony to a kind of modern arrogance that refuses to receive the Word that God has given us, the refusal to take at face value the God who comes to us as a crucified Jew from Nazareth. One does not have to think long to come up with the motivation for such reticence and humility. Better a dumb and apophatic God than one who says to us what the God of Israel and the church is reported to have frequently said. Who wants a God who demands that we take up a cross, and turn the other cheek, and forgive enemies, and trust without reservation?

Without a God who speaks, who says understandable, comprehensible things to us and reveals at least some of God's glory to us, we are left to ourselves, to say that which we damn well please. We are left with that cacophony of voices and images that characterize the confused, but eagerly self-revealing modern self. Any idolatrous people who set up an altar to the "unknown god" (Acts 17:23) is bound to be a people who will worship just about anything if given half a chance to worship something.

Yet if we live in an inarticulate age that is hesitant to assert too much about God, out of false humility about God-talk, then we preachers ought to give God the glory and see this as a fine opportunity to preach. With so many who are so reluctant to say anything declarative about God, the future belongs to those who dare to cause trouble, to speak, who have the guts to declare, "Thus says the Lord. . . ." "And God said. . . ."

Barth thought it highly significant that Schleiermacher put the Doctrine of the Trinity at the very end of his *Dogmatics*. This, said Barth, suggests that Schleiermacher does not believe in any true communication from God—God-talk is what we get after we have first rummaged about within our subjectivity. Barth, of course, puts the Trinity at the beginning of his *Dogmatics* as the very basis for how Christian talk about God can proceed in the first place.[40] It is the relentless self-communication of the Trinity that forms a basis for any hope of communication between God and humanity, that restless divine *perichoresis*. More specifically, it was Barth's stress on pneumatology, the third person of the Trinity, that enabled him to have such confidence in our ability to speak about God because of his confidence in the constant speaking of God.

Barth was accused of arrogance, charged with having a take-it-or-leave-it attitude in regard to revelation, of a tendency to arrogantly say much more about God than ought to be said. John Milbank's statement that "the pathos of modern theology is its false humility"[41] helped me to see that Barth displays the true humility that ought to be expected of a theologian. A truly humble theologian is submissive, not to the limits imposed by modernity, but to the authority of the church's peculiar way of thinking; a falsely humble theologian thinks in a way that will never offend the peace that is enforced by the academic establishment that arrogantly believes that we can come up with something more interesting to say than God. The modern world sought to think without traditional restraints, which, as it turned out, was just another form of enslavement to other sorts of restraints.[42] This is but one of the reasons why it is a good discipline for us preachers to preach using the assigned lessons of the Common Lectionary. We preach, not what the world thinks is a permissible or relevant idea, but rather what we have been told by the church to preach.

Barth believes the toughest task of preaching to be the courage and the discipline to listen. The courage to speak is a gift to those who first summon up the humility to listen.

And God Said . . .

Lindbeck said that most of us, because we live in a society indebted to the thought of philosophical liberalism, mostly listen to ourselves as a source for our "revelation." We have been conditioned by our culture to consider religion as a matter of *"experiential/expressivism."* That is, we think of religion as an institutional means of expressing our personal, inner, innate religious experiences. Religion is merely an expression of a universal human tendency toward the divine. Though there are different religions, these are merely the outward, human-conditioned responses to the inner, innate, universal experience. Preaching in liberalism becomes a means of expressing our inner thoughts about the sacred. Most of the preaching I hear in my own church family, and too much of my own preaching, is essentially in the "experiential/expressivist" mode. We live in a culture, that of liberalism, in which human experience is thought of as the supreme source of most reality, in which religion is seen as a mere accident of birth, a primitive means of expressing a human experience that could be as well-expressed through some other medium. All religions are thus only nominally different, culturally conditioned means of saying the same thing. This is the "well, though you are Muslim and I am Christian, we all believe in God" school of thought. All religions have value mainly as they express various aspects of human experience of the divine. This is contemporary "spirituality" all over.

When religion is viewed in an experiential/expressivist manner, then preaching is mostly a matter of evocation, artistic expression of some sort of subjective sentiment among the listeners. The experiential/expressivist therefore has a theological compulsion to keep all God-talk as vague, inclusive, nonspecific, and general as possible. Lindbeck argued that, though the experiential/expressive manner of construing religion is a popular way of conceiving of religion in our society, it falsifies the way religion actually works among believers. Is it true that religion is merely an expression of an experience that is prior to the religion? Or is it more accurate to say that religion is a way of engendering and forming our experience?

Becoming an adherent to a religion is much like learning to speak a language, says Lindbeck. Thus he proposes what he calls the *"cultural/linguistic"* way of conceiving of religion. To be religious is to be a participant in a culture, a mélange of habits, words, rituals, practices, traditions, and stories that move the participant into a different world than that person would live in without the imposition of the images, vocabulary, practices, and words of a religion. Although liberalism attempted to depict our involvement in religion as something that we choose in order to express our innermost feelings about God, this is not how religion actually works. Although the experiential/expressive mode of conceiving faith depicted us as people who feel certain religious inclinations and then go and shop about for a religion that expresses those inclinations, Lindbeck stressed the cultural/linguistic way that the community of faith forms our inclinations. In this conception of religion, to be converted into a faith is not to discover something within us, but rather to be subsumed into a new culture, to take up a new language that changes what is within us. That the experiential/expressivist thinks that religion is mainly an expression of personal preferences is not an expression of that person's freedom to make judgments about religious people, but rather proof that the experiential/expressivist has been well-inculcated into the limited, though imperialistic, culture of modern Western liberalism.

Lindbeck says religion is more than a projection out of us; it is a cultural imposition that shapes us. Our religion is more than an expression of certain innate inclinations, rather, gradually, over time, religion forms our inclinations. We are enculturated into a system of signs, signals, and symbols, the inculcation of which engenders certain experiences in us, experiences we would never have had without the religion. Becoming a Christian is therefore somewhat analogous to learning French. Just as it is impossible to learn French by reading a French novel in an English translation, so it is also impossible, as Lindbeck notes, truly to learn Christianity by encountering it through the translation of existentialism, or feminism, or the language of self-esteem, American democracy, or whatever. One must learn the vocabulary, must inculcate the moves and gestures of this faith in order to know the faith.[43]

Thus, Lindbeck's categories remind us that *Christianity is a culture.* My penchant for speaking of the church as a "counterculture" does not mean that I believe that the church stands aloof from human culture, pointing a critical finger toward the predominant secular world. Rather, the church itself forms a culture that is counter to the world's ways of doing things. The church does not simply reach out to and speak to the dominant culture; it seeks to disrupt that culture by rescuing some listeners from it, thereby to inculcate those listeners into a new culture called the church.

Building on Lindbeck and Frei, Charles Campbell critiques contemporary homiletics, saying that contemporary homiletics is based upon Enlightenment and Existentialist philosophical presuppositions. The individual self is the criteria for all meaning.[44] Anthropology, rather than theology, becomes the starting point—begin with the alleged limits or potential of the hearers rather than the peculiar claims of the gospel. The primary task of preaching, when anthropological rather than theological criteria set the tone, is to attempt to translate biblical meaning into a contemporary meaning, thereby to enhance "self-understanding."

Jesus Christ becomes a generalized experience of religious feeling, generic "faith," without specific "faith in. . . ."

Barth certainly rejected the notion that faith is something that proceeds from the human self—from our desire for a more meaningful life, or our spiritual yearnings, "faith development." Rather, faith is a gift of God whereby we become miraculously absorbed by the pull of God's yearning for us rather than our yearning for God. Barth says:

The attitude of the men of the Bible and the recipients of revelation . . . is marked by the fact that the strictness with which they are claimed for the things of God is directly paralleled by a particular attraction to the things of God. In the Old Testament prophets and especially in Paul in the New Testament, particularly in the latter case, we do not see anything of the rigidity or Zelotism or anxious zeal, in short, the spiritual cramp which always results when men think and act as if the *causa Dei* were really their own anxiety and concern. They do not really aim to do what God does. They aim only to participate. They do not do the work; they assist. It is in this way that they are the recipients and witnesses of revelation. The commandments which they keep in love to God are God's commandments, and therefore not grievous (v. 3). His yoke is easy and His burden is light (Mt. 11:30). They need not be ashamed of the Gospel, because it does not need their own dynamic. And it does not need it, because it is itself the "power of God," and indeed "to salvation" (Rom. 1:16). (CD, I, 2, pg. 276; see also, IV, 4, pp. 123-27)

So Campbell notes that the average contemporary sermon proposes a human problem, and then sees Jesus, or the general Christian tradition, as a solution to that problem. This makes the sermon more "relevant." Paul Tillich's "Principle of Correlation," becomes the theoretical basis for most sermons. Campbell says, "In the process Christology becomes the function of soteriology, understood as freedom from existential anxiety. A general anthropology sets up the soteriological problem for which Christology becomes the solution. Jesus becomes a good existentialist."[45] Jesus becomes, at best, a representative of some worthy human ideal.

Campbell proposes the work of Frei and Lindbeck as a corrective. He applies an intratextual communal hermeneutic to preaching. Frei praised that premodern reading of scripture that is precritical and "realistic." Precritical reading assumes that the narrative actually describes historical circumstances, that is, scripture is not a purely symbolic exercise. Taken together, the events of the biblical narrative are a single, more or less unified account of what is going on in the world. The world of biblical narratives is, when all is said and done, the one and only real world, and therefore the world that subsumes and consumes the reader's world.[46] Historical criticism is charged by Frei with using the text as a means to reach through it, or behind it, to the "real meaning." But Frei argues that scripture is a "history-like" or "realistic narrative." Scripture is closer to an historical novel, than to some primitive attempt to do modern historiography. Frei asserted that "narrative form and meaning are inseparable, precisely because in both cases meaning is in large part a function of the interaction of character and circumstances."[47]

Frei charges that, because of the "eclipse of biblical narrative"—when that narrative is no longer valued in itself, for what it does to us and for the world it renders—we have similarly devalued Jesus. The text becomes superfluous in its particularities, and so does Jesus. Jesus is valued not so much for who he is but for what he symbolically represents. Frei traces the long and sorry succession of "Christ figures,"[48] in eighteenth- and nineteenth-century biblical interpretation as evidence of this tendency. (Alas, Frei's life was taken from us before he could critique the "Jesus Seminar" and its rehash of this tired theme.)

Frei stresses the formative, transformative intentions of biblical narrative. Biblical reality does not simply want to speak to our present reality, but wants to subsume our reality. The biblical text does not want to make our received reality a bit more bearable, but wants to overcome our reality. Rather than mine biblical texts for certain interesting ideas, we are to fit our lives into its life, to find the structure of our reality rearranged by its structure. This is why Jesus cannot be extricated from the Gospel narratives. He reaches out to us from the narrative as an agent rendered in the Gospel narratives, a subject who speaks for himself. Biblical narrative renders reality; it intends to be self-referential. Rather than deriving its power through correlation with some other reality, biblical reality stands in judgment upon other presumed realities. Barth says, "God must be the subject before he can be the object. . . . We have to be received before we can receive, so that the decisive condition of the existence of Christian preachers is that they must accept the divine address as directed to themselves too."[49]

Frei maintains that of all the events in the Gospels, only the stories of the death and resurrection of Jesus render his full identity. It is this narrative that transcends all other possible analogies within literature and all correlations with our present experience. When all such connections with Jesus to our everyday lives and common sense are transcended and severed, then Jesus is most fully who he is. Frei says, "Jesus' individual identity comes into focus directly in the passion-resurrection narrative rather than in the account of his person and teaching in his earlier ministry. In this final and climatic sequence of the story of Jesus, Jesus is most of all himself, and there—unlike those earlier points at which we can get to his individual identity only ambiguously—we are confronted with him directly as the unsubstitutable individual who is what he does and undergoes and is manifested directly as who he is."[50]

"The primary focus [of the Bible] is not on God's being in itself," claims George Lindbeck, "for that is not what the text is about, but on how life is to be lived and reality construed in the light of God's character as an agent as this is depicted in the stories of Israel and of Jesus."[51]

That is why we must start with the story of the death and resurrection of Jesus, not with alleged universalities of human experience. Jesus must provide the form, and not only the content, of the sermon. Jesus joins the biblical narratives' unique and unsubstitutable identity of the crucified Jesus with the reality of the resurrected Jesus and becomes, in the text, a presence, One who speaks to us.[52] He is thus the form, the content, and the means of our preaching.

Here is a theological empowerment of the Lindbeckian stress on "intratextuality." Our "text" is subsumed into the biblical text, renarrated, rendered into a new reality by the self-revealing work of Christ. As Lose puts it, when we preach, "the biblical reality and our reality are not equal partners engaged in mutual interaction with preaching serving as a thoroughfare between the two, as conceived by contemporary narrative homileticans."[53] Our reality is, through the work of the living Christ, absorbed into, conquered by biblical reality. From the perspective of this cultural-linguistic approach, preaching is training people in the language of faith, narrating their lives in the light of the biblical story, which is more real than any of the stories we can talk about ourselves. Christianity is learning and practicing the language of Christianity. As Lindbeck says, "To become religious . . . is to interiorize a set of skills by practice and training. One learns how to feel, act, and think in conformity with the religious attitude that is, and its intra structure, far richer and more subtle than can be explicitly articulated."[54] Or as Hauerwas told us in his Gifford Lectures, "I believe that

Barth's extraordinary achievement not only helps Christians recover a confidence in Christian speech but also exemplifies how Christian language works. . . . From beginning to end, Barth's theology is designed to make the reader a more adequate knower of God."[55]

Too much of modern preaching focuses upon the individual, whereas Frei and Lindbeck would have us focus upon the community and all the ways in which the practices of the church form us into its peculiar textual world. All "worlds" are textually derived; not just the world of the gospel. But the gospel's textual world is peculiar, as are all textual worlds. Preaching in the community of faith re-creates a universe of discourse and instructs hearers in how to use the language well, that language that asserts that "Jesus Christ is Lord" is a truthful account of reality and other textual accounts, and their various textually rendered lordlets are not.

While Frei, Lindbeck, and Campbell give a helpful, empowering viewpoint to us preachers, ultimately Barth will not allow us to follow them into their intratextual, communally rendered linguistic world. Lose says that, with his stress on communal formation, Campbell is closer to Aristotle than the Bible. Freely using Barth to criticize Campbell, Lose says that Barth reminds us that preaching is never grounded in any anthropological possibility, including the possibility of forming a countercultural Christian community. For preaching to be "theological" means more than that it talks about theology. Preaching is theological when it realizes that it can talk, and it can be heard, only through theological means. When we say that we believe that preaching "works," we do not simply mean that preaching is an effective means of social enculturation, the teaching of a new language and nothing more. It means that Jesus Christ constitutes the only possibility of preaching being heard. Jesus Christ gives the content to the work of the Holy Spirit, the Holy Spirit gives the means of our encounter with the person of Jesus Christ, and that is how we can believe that preaching "works." The major missing element in Lindbeck's analysis is agency.[56] The Holy Spirit is the breath of the Risen Christ:

> The Holy Spirit is simply but most distinctly the renewing power of the breath of His mouth which as such is the breath of the sovereign God and victorious truth. It is the power in which His Word, God's Word, the Word of truth, is not only in Him, but where and when He wills goes out also to us men, not returning to Him empty but with the booty or increase of our faith and knowledge and obedience, and not remaining with Him on its return, but constantly going out again to us to bring back new gain, and thus establishing a communication between Him and us and initiating a history of mutual giving and receiving. (*CD*, IV, 3, pg. 421)

After lamenting the sorry state of Protestant preaching and worship, saying that "there is no lack of good preachers and sermons, but lack of sermons that were meant to be God's Word and are received as such—a lack of (qualified) preaching" (and by "qualified" Barth doesn't mean theologically trained and certified preachers but rather preachers who are qualified by the work of the Trinity in their sermons), Barth says that "Protestants would be better off if we could recover the same attitude toward preaching that Catholics have to the sacrament of Eucharist."[57] In preaching, we experience the real presence of Christ, not a presence to be taken and ingested by us, but rather a presence that reaches out to us. Preaching is the reproduction, the spontaneous adoption of the biblical witness to revelation. Christian preachers are second-rank witnesses. They are neither prophets nor apostles, but witnesses. As witness, preaching relates directly not only to scripture but also to revelation. As scripture is the Word of God in time and history, and as such the presupposition of the church and its preaching, revelation is the eternal Word of God. Both together are the basis of Christian preaching.[58]

Barth uses the man at the pool of Bethesda in John 5 as an analogy for preaching. Without the miraculous intervention of the angel to stir the water, we are merely those fixed and paralyzed lying beside a still, dead pool.[59] Though Frei, Lindbeck, and Campbell may assume this miraculous, divine empowerment of preaching, their observations about preaching, though helpful, are still too anthropological to give the miraculous theological substance that the risk of preaching requires.[60] All our speaking about God rests upon that miraculous event, "And God said. . . ."

Barth Preaches Like Paul

Barth's theological project began as the result of his close reading of Paul, specifically, Paul's very "homiletical" Letter to the Romans. In my own analysis of Barth's sermons, I find more sermons on Pauline texts than on synoptic Gospel texts. I think this propensity for Paul is not only due to Barth's lack of interest in narrative texts of scripture but also due to Barth's theology.[61] Barth, the preacher, encountering Paul, the preacher, is a means of understanding Barth and also a means of underscoring the relevance of Barth's discoveries for today's preacher. The major discovery that Barth made, through his encounter with Paul, was theological and not anthropological. Though it had linguistic implications, its primary energy was theologically derived. Barth met, in Paul, an Agent, the means of Christian preaching.

Earlier we noted Paul's curious lack of interest in the life of our so-called historical Jesus. Paul seems to know nothing and care little about the pre-Resurrection activity of Jesus, other than his crucifixion. We must remind ourselves that Paul's writings are earlier than the Gospels from which some have attempted to mine a "Life of Jesus." On the basis of his proximity to the historical Jesus, one would think that the current Jesus Seminar would have turned to Paul for their attempt to historically reconstruct a "real" Jesus. It turned instead to the less historically interesting synoptic Gospels and, in a rather bizarre move, to the Gospel of Thomas for their reconstructions, thereby showing the limited and prejudiced way with which they have undertaken their reconstruction.

We would do better to turn toward Paul, as he has turned toward us after his encounter with the resurrected Christ. Paul so self-evidently embodies the specter of a man who has been shocked by the Resurrection, his world rocked by an experience of the crucified and Risen Christ. Paul's world believed, with the prophet, "Cursed is everyone who dies upon a tree." Jesus died upon a "tree." He is cursed not only by death but also by an utterly ignoble death.

And yet it was Paul who also, on the Damascus road, was addressed and summoned by the Risen Christ. As many skillful interpreters of Paul have noted, it is not accurate to speak of Paul's "conversion" on the Damascus road, as if Paul moved from one faith to another. It wasn't that Paul stopped being Jewish, for as he said, he was the quintessential Jew among Jews. It was rather that Paul stopped living in the Old World. His eyes were opened, not simply to a new religious insight, but to a whole New World. Paul's later objections to Torah, "the Law" (in Romans and Galatians, etc.), were not so much on the basis of his objections to alleged Jewish "legalism"—that is, an anachronistic interpretation of later readers. Rather, Paul's objections were that the Law was not the Risen Christ. The Law could no longer save one from the grip of an old, false world.

When Acts talks about Paul's encounter on the Damascus road, in Acts 9:22-26, that event is described in interesting, though not hugely significant, differing ways. The differences remind one of the variations in the way that the Gospels narrate the Resurrection. The variations, which have so troubled historical critics of scripture, need not greatly trouble us. In fact, the differences become interesting confirmation of the Resurrection. Be well assured—though those who experience the Risen Christ and his aftermath have difficulty bringing what they have experienced to speech—they have experienced an earthshaking event. If an event can be truly said to be earthshaking, a dismantling and a re-creation, the advent of a whole new world, that event will be by its very nature difficult to describe.

We tend to describe our world on the basis of past experience, speaking about what is on the basis of our experience of certain patterns, repetitions, and conventions that we have experienced in the past. But if the Resurrection is, by its very nature, eschatological, it is the end of "logic," if logic is that which is dependent upon pattern, repetition, and convention. There will, in any faithful description of an earthshaking event, be variation and even logic-bending contradiction. But it is difficult to deny that something has happened. There has been event, an occurrence. It is difficult to speak of the Resurrection as a "historical" occurrence, for we tend to have a limited definition of just what counts as "history." But Paul certainly presents us with a fact, with a kind of irrefutable sense that something has happened, something is there, that has jolted him into residency in a new world.

I am therefore somewhat baffled about why I preach so seldom from the letters of Paul. There is, in my experience, a kind of prejudice, within the liberal, mainline church, against the letters of Paul. I expect that it is a prejudice that is derived from the liberal tendency to avoid theology in favor of anthropology, to reduce the miraculous to the merely moral, mixed with the romantic notion that in the Gospels we have the real usable, retrievable history of the "religion of Jesus." Paul is certainly a challenge to this way of thinking about the matter. Paul seems wonderfully disinterested in the "religion" of Jesus. Those who attempt to write about "Paul's ethics" find it rough going. Paul is like a man who has suffered a head-on collision, like someone who has staggered away from a serious accident on the highway, shaken by an experience of the resurrected Christ. (I am sounding like Barth now.) For Paul, it is too early to speak about ethics, or too late. One gets the impression that, were he allowed another fifty years to write about "the shape of the Christian life" or "practicing the faith," Paul wouldn't do so. When one has suffered a trauma, a deadly blow to the head, when one takes cover in the middle of an earthquake, one does not generally do ethics. (Here, I'm sounding like Flannery O'Connor.) One just tries to hang on, ride it through, and find somewhere to plant one's feet. This is Paul.

Furthermore, we preachers ought to note that all of Paul's "writings" are meant to be heard rather than read. I am sure that his writings were, from the first, used within the assembly of the congregation, read to the congregation as part of its worship. And like all oral communication, his letters have a wonderful spontaneity about them. They are peppered with asides, digressions, unexpected ejaculations ("I entreat Euodice and Synthice to agree in the Lord!" or "You stupid Galatians!"). Paul constantly reaches for metaphors and similes, and uses a wide array of rhetorical devices to move his listeners. Sometimes, as often happens in preaching, Paul becomes entangled in a metaphor. He seems to have a particular penchant for rhetoric derived from the courtroom. He is an attorney arguing his case, "You say, but I submit to you that. . . ."

I have the impression that this oral quality of Paul's writing is more than skillful rhetorical strategy. I believe that Easter makes him do it. Those who have had their world rocked, who genuinely believe that the world as we have attempted to live it is ending and a new one is being born, do not write long books (certainly not books as long as this one!). Thus, there is little of the sage in Paul, none of the measured, reflective, and wise bestowing of wisdom that one finds in biblical books like Proverbs or Ecclesiastes. In Paul things are heated, polemical, sometimes histrionic. It is not so much in Paul that the time is short, as the time is over. Let us be done with vague generalities. There is no more time for the detached, contemplative Greek philosopher, the moderate Aristotelian practitioner of good habits. "You have died! And your life is hidden with Christ in God," says the man who knew not whether to speak of what happened to him on the Damascus road as birth or death. It felt like both at the same time. Paul has staggered away from a bad blow to the head to find himself in an eschatological situation of disorientation, and he talks like it. "Be reconciled!"

Socrates refused to put his philosophy into writing because the written, fixed word promotes false confidence in what is written. The written word, compared with the spoken word, appears to be secure, stable, and eternal. Philosophy feeds on dialectic, conversation, give-and-take, and the dynamic that is inherent in oral interaction. When philosophy lost its Socratic prejudice against the written word, it lost some of its originating dynamic.

Socrates sought not to write philosophy, but to speak it. Thought ought to be alive, always in motion, playful in pursuit of truth, against the fossilized, dead character of written words. Truth is dialogical, dialectical, and interactive. Writing, as soon as it leaves the author's hand, gives the illusion of being eternal. Plato, while he did write, believed that the truths of philosophy are not the words on the written page, but the sparks that the words strike in the soul, the energy that happens between the speaking and the responding. One cannot see a "reader," but a listener is always interacting with the speaker. And, as we have said, the spoken word, by its nature, tends to be more spontaneous, eventful, and actual than the written word. Thus, in a curious way, preaching, the spoken gospel Word is more conducive to the theology of Barth than the written word, academic theology as it is usually practiced.

Martin Luther notes that there is something in the nature of the gospel that tends to be prejudiced toward the oral, noting,

> In the New Testament the sermon should orally and publicly take place with living voice and bring into speech and hearing what was before concealed in the letter and secret visions. . . . Christ himself did not put down his teaching in writing as Moses had done, but he proclaimed it orally and also commanded that it be continued orally, and gave no command that it be written down. The apostles wrote very little. In fact, not all of them wrote . . . and even those who did write did nothing more than direct us into the old scriptures just as the angel directed the shepherds to the manger and the diapers, and the star led those magi to Bethlehem! Therefore, it is not at all according to the New Testament to write books about Christian teaching—but instead of books there should be in all places good, learned, zealous and devout preachers who would draw the living Word out of the old writings and constantly impress it upon the people as did the apostles.[62]

No one writes about preaching better than Luther. A sermon is an event that happens between God, the preacher, and the congregation. It is really not a "sermon" if it is only written. A sermon is not only an auditory but also a visual phenomenon, an event, an encounter with the living Word.

"Last of all, as one untimely born, he appeared to me," says Paul. Paul is a witness to the Resurrection, one who speaks in a voice, shaken but clear, of that which he has seen and heard. Paul was not "converted," as we might say someone was converted from drunkenness to sobriety. If anything, Paul was converted from sobriety to drunkenness. He was called to preach. He had no tortured conscience before this event. He was not "searching for something," other than searching for Christians to persecute. Rather, the Risen Christ was searching for Paul, summoning someone to say a word on his behalf.

It is with some measure of regret that we witness (and we are witnessing the beginning of this movement in the New Testament) the gradual transformation of the Christian experience from being an essentially oral event to a written, literate phenomenon. That Paul speaks mostly in epistolary form helps keep the dialogical, conversational quality of Christian discourse alive, but when those letters become fixed, final canon, there is an almost inevitable process of ossification. The illusory permanence that written language takes enabled written language to give the illusion that there the truth is fixed, there we are dealing with eternal verities; it is there, something to be had, grasped, understood, exposited, held, and practiced. We no longer have to encounter it again, or be encountered by it. We need only to return to the page where it is readily available to our prying eyes anytime we please for analysis and deliberation.

Therefore be thankful that oral communication, like preaching, keeps reminding us that with this faith, after Easter, there is no having, no holding; there is only receiving, encounter, and event. It is with a touch of regret, a sense of loss, that we see the church move, already in Paul, inexorably, quite understandably, from what is said, to what is read. The church, now poring over its written word, excessively arguing about the "correct" interpretation of individual words and phrases, reminds one more of the synagogue, or the mosque, with our scholars poring over a written text, attempting to define or reconstruct rather than being shaken, dislodged, made empty and full by the Resurrection.[63]

How much effort has been expended among scholars in their futile attempts to reconstruct a life of the "historical Paul." That which is interesting about this man is not his precedents, his antecedents, nor his autobiography. The thing that is interesting is that Paul has seen something. He has been encountered, and he has been a witness to the Resurrection.

What can we preachers learn *about* and *from* Paul's letters?

1. They are *occasional*. All of them were occasioned by some dilemma in the church, not meant as abstract, general, timeless truth for all time. As a model for Christian thinking, they suggest to us that the best Christian thinking is not systematic, eternal, large, and universal. The best Christian writing is occasional.

2. They are *communal*. They are addressed to the church; only rarely, in certain brief moments do they become personal or individual. They are official correspondence to a community. They are complex in their composition, dialogical, and conversational, setting up a conversation partner ("you say, but I say . . ."). Romans is a classic diatribe, Paul at his forensic best. Second Corinthians ought to be seen, not as a problematic historical jumble, but as a resourceful mixture of a wide range of rhetorical acts. Paul's letters thus offer a pastoral, dynamic, dialogical view of peculiarly Christian communication. They have tremendous variation. They range in length from Romans to Philemon. They show an extraordinary range of rhetorical resourcefulness, as if that which is being brought to speech demands a huge range of rhetorical devices.

3. Paul's letters *arise out of an experience of the gap, the cognitive dissonance between the congregation's knowledge of and Paul's proclamation of the new age.* Paul is the herald to those who, in their everyday congregational life, are still caught in the old age. If Christ is the redeemer, why don't they look more redeemed? If they are resurrected and living in the new age, why do they still live in the old age? This is the gap, the space where Christian preachers ought to work. On the one hand, we proclaim an accomplished fact, the advent of the new age. On the other hand, we are honest about our continuing, troubling caughtness within the old age.

Paul thus presents us with a marvelous example of the Christian theologian who must "think on his feet." That is a great image of all truly great Christian thinking, improvisation, thinking on our feet, with our mouths open.[64]

The one thing that unites all the witnesses of Jesus is the Resurrection. They may disagree on details about, or even interest in his earthly pre-Resurrection life. They may disagree on the implications of his Resurrection for our lives, current and future. But there is no disagreement among them that they have all experienced the Risen Christ. An event has occurred among them. No witness among them claims that Jesus was a great sage, a moral example, or just a fine spiritual teacher. Why would they universally make such an astounding claim of resurrection if it were not a fact that had occurred to them?

The Acts of the Apostles never mentions that Paul wrote letters! Paul is portrayed as a preacher, a teacher, and an organizer, but never a writer. This is a curious valuation on the part of Acts, possibly an indication of the role that preaching played from the first in the church. Paul wrote letters only because he could not speak to them in person. In this faith, the oral tends to trump the literal.

We have noted that in antiquity one of the most important rhetorical strategies was an argument on the basis of the speaker's character, ethos. Yet New Testament writings are notable for their lack of interest in the character of the speaker. In the Gospels, we are offered little by the evangelists that put forward their credentials to speak to us in this way, other than that God has called them. God has chosen to bring something out of nothing by calling people like them to speak such truth. It is almost as if the evangelists pointedly determined to frustrate any attempts on our part to get behind what they said to the character of those who were doing the evangelical speaking.

True, Paul certainly uses his story as part of his appeal, and his experience of the resurrected Christ as proof of the validity of his argument, even at times urging his hearers to "imitate me." Yet it is a peculiar imitation. As we see in 1 Corinthians, Paul argues that he is not wise, not worthy, and that he is "untimely born." Paul puts forward this negative assessment of his character in order to assert a positive assessment of the transcendent grace of God. Indeed, from Paul we might establish a rule for self-referential remarks in sermons. Only refer to yourself if you are saying something completely deprecating and negative about yourself. This isn't about you. The God of Israel and the church works through weakness, most distinctively, sometimes through limitations of clergy character. Of this, I am a witness.

The Barthian project began with Barth's encounter with Paul and the trouble that occurred in that conversation. The bomb that began the theological revolution was a world-shattering explosion called *Romans*. This is where the trouble started, and it was to Barth's great credit that throughout his life as teacher and preacher he managed to keep close to the trouble. The name of the trouble is Jesus.

CHAPTER NINE

EASTER SPEECH

Ignore the Lord Jesus as long as you can!" advises one of Flannery O'Connor's anti-preachers, "spit out the bread of life!"[1] But we can't. There is something about this forever-reaching God that is determined to draw us into the net. Thus the greatest difficulty in Christian preaching is working with the Risen Christ. It would be one thing to preach about Christ, but "we preach Christ" crucified and resurrected (1 Cor. 1:21-23). We do not preach ideas, precepts, principles, but a person, Jesus Christ.[2] Our challenge is well represented by the movements of Christ in John 20. It is "the first day of the week," that is, the first day of the Jewish workweek, the first day when Israel, including the disciples of Jesus, is attempting to get back to normal after a particularly bloody weekend. This is not to be. Our deadly yearning to get back to business will be disrupted by the Resurrection.

Mary Magdalene comes to the tomb "while it was still dark" (v. 1), that threatening time when Jesus performed some of his most notorious wonders. Mary is literally in the dark. Note that the story begins with a woman, a woman who boldly ventures forth, even in the darkness. Mary Magdalene notices that the stone has been taken from the tomb and apparently assumes that the body has been stolen (v. 2). This will be the first in a long series of misapprehensions and incorrect interpretive conclusions by the disciples after Easter. Whatever has happened here in the darkness will be difficult for them to understand. We, the readers, know what has happened, due to our previous encounters with the text. Our knowledge, and their lack of knowledge, is both a warning and an encouragement to us. It is a warning in that these first witnesses failed to understand, so we also might misunderstand. It is an encouragement in that those who were historically the closest to Jesus did not understand, whereas we who are far removed from these events understand. They did not see, whereas we, hearing their story, see and understand. By the grace of the living God, there is a sense in which we know more about the truth of what's what than even the very first witnesses. Our God is of the living and not the dead. Apparently, history is not our problem with these narratives, so we do well to be suspicious of any who would hand these narratives over to the historians.

Now the men arrive at the tomb after a breathless run. Simon Peter is the first to dare to enter the darkness of the tomb, and there he sees the linen cloths carefully folded and placed by themselves. The careful placement of the cloths is an interesting narrative detail and, especially in John's Gospel but throughout all biblical literature, details are important. Perhaps these carefully folded cloths are proof that the body has not been stolen. Perhaps they are an indication of the careful, deliberate way in which Christ is raised. Who knows? To work with such literature, or to allow such literature to work with us, we must have a high tolerance for ambiguity and a willingness to suspend our desire for sure and immediate comprehension.

When the second disciple follows Peter into the tomb and sees the circumstantial evidence, he also "saw and believed" (v. 8), but what he "believed" is ambiguous for he seems to believe that the body has been stolen because he "did not understand the scripture" (v. 9). Visible evidence in the world is interesting, but not too informative without the gift of revelation.

"Then the disciples returned to their homes" (v. 10). Back to their homes! They "believe" but go back to business as usual, back to the sweet, anesthetizing reassurance of the mundane and the everyday, the predictable and the stable. If there is a resurrection, it is obviously not some projection or wish-fulfillment on the part of the grieving disciples. They are quite content to chalk all of this up to the power of death. The stealing of the body is simply one final indignity worked upon crucified Jesus and his grieving followers.

But Mary stayed, weeping, and stooped to look in the tomb (v. 11). Mary remained, in grief, but still daring to linger, to stoop, and to look. To Mary is given the vision of two angels. The angels have no message for her, only a question about her grief.[3] Unlike some of the other angelic visitations in scripture, these angels are ambiguous messengers who do not directly proclaim resurrection. Mary turns around and sees someone standing there, someone whom she does not know (v. 14). Seeing is not yet believing until the figure speaks to her.[4] Even when the Risen Christ speaks to her, she does not yet know. Revelation, even that which comes through hearing, is hardly ever self-evident, immediate, at least from our point of view. She thinks the speaker is the gardener (v. 15).

Then Jesus calls her by her name, "Mary." That is all he says. He does not tell her about his resurrection, he simply calls her. Yet at that moment of vocation, she hears, she sees, she understands. However, she even yet calls him "Teacher," which may be a term of endearment, and of course Jesus is a teacher, but this may also indicate that Mary is yet on the way to a full recognition of Jesus' identity, moving from teacher to "Lord" (v. 18).

Jesus says, "Do not hold on to me" (v. 17). The Risen Christ is on the move, ascending, restlessly eluding our grasp. He is not to be held, even by those who love him. Perhaps this is a great Johannine-Barthian warning for those of us who are called to talk about the Risen Christ, the great command of the living Lord: "Do not hold me!" We must find a way to talk about Jesus that is faithful to the encounter, that does not attempt to secure, fix, restrain, or limit his movements among us and his movements beyond us.[5]

The Risen Christ is on the move, and now Mary must be on the move. She goes back to the unbelieving, as yet unseeing disciples and preaches to them, "I have seen the Lord." Then "she told them that he had said these things to her" (v. 18). In John's Gospel, this woman is the first evangelist, the first preacher, a striking circumstance in a world where the testimony of women was not even permitted in court.[6] This faith is birthed through the testimony of women, the first who are given the gift of witnessing to the Resurrection. Is not this a summary of all good Christian preaching, the two-point sermon: "I have seen the Lord," and "here is what the Lord has told me to tell you"?

For Mary, seeing is believing, but only when seeing is accompanied by speaking. For Mary, a vision of the Risen Christ is also a commission, a vocation, an assignment from the Risen Christ to go and tell.

Note that Mary must go to the disciples and preach to them what they do not believe. Preaching is always concerned with unbelief, and the first "unbelievers" who need the good news are Jesus' own disciples (the church) who, in their belief, are the first to disbelieve and the most in need of evangelization.

Note also that John does not report the response of the disciples to Mary's "sermon." We are told what Mary, the first "preacher," did and said, but nothing of how the congregation reacted to her words. Presumably their response is not Mary's concern. Presumably their silence is indicative of their disbelief. We learn in the next story, where the Risen Christ must kick through the locked doors of the disciples (church), that they did not believe Mary, for they were cowering behind locked doors "for fear" (20:19-23). So the Risen Christ did for the disciples what Mary alone could not: he came and stood among them and spoke. He breathed upon them (v. 22) and gave them great power. Barth warns that the Risen Christ "passes through closed doors."[7]

Even with the holy breath, even with the commission, even with great power given to them, they did not sally forth as did Mary, who went and told. Perhaps they were even yet afraid, or perhaps now even more afraid than they were earlier. After all, if this is true, if the Risen Christ is determined to have them, if the Risen Christ appears before them in order to speak to them and to give them their marching orders, to send them on a mission that is his mission, well, then they have good reason to fear.

Preaching with Barth

Let us now draw out more implications, both Barthian and biblical, of resurrection for the task of preaching:

To be a preacher is to be accountable to a strange and always challenging story that we name as Easter; it is to be willing to be made strange and unfathomable to the world and sometimes to the church by the substance of that story, to risk frequent misunderstanding and almost weekly incomprehension.

Reading John's Gospel, it is easy to agree with Bultmann that John demonstrates a kind of "realized eschatology." Eternal life is now. The eternal Word is eternal from the very first chapter of John's Gospel, raised and glorified, though his glory is not yet ours to see and to understand. How few people understand Jesus, in John's Gospel or any of the synoptics. And a major source of their misunderstanding is that lack of comprehension that Jesus is not some ideal, some future possibility, but rather is here, now, immediately and concretely demanding. In John 11, Martha seems still to be thinking of "eternal life" as something someday in the future. Jesus corrects her with the astounding pronouncement, "I *am* the resurrection and the life."[8] Preaching is the practice of eternal life now, the eternal becoming eventful in the historical. Note that Jesus speaks in the present tense: "I am the resurrection and the life." Here. Now. Thus Barth's lectures that were printed in 1964 in English, with the title, "God Here and Now." When someone hears and responds to preaching, it is a demonstration of eternal life here and now. In John's Gospel, the *paraclete* can be translated through multiple meanings, but it basically means the Risen Christ *hic et nunc*, here and now. As Barth says, "The statement 'God reveals Himself' must be a statement of utter thankfulness, a statement of pure amazement, in which is repeated the amazement of the disciples in meeting the risen One" (CD, I, 2, pg. 65).

To be a preacher is much more difficult than communicating certain noble ideas and precepts; it is to work with a particularly demanding, moving, immediate, speaking, summoning Presence who refuses to leave us to our own devices.

There are many reasons why our preaching fails, and any preacher knows the frustration of preaching that does not work. Still, "we do see Jesus." The story floods into our time, speaks to us, and that becomes an undeniable datum, an unavoidable claim upon us—a person who speaks, who is present, irrefutably, particularly and personally. Note how curiously we preachers act, how shocked and incredulous we are when our people say, as they say more often than we admit, at the conclusion of one of our sermons, "I have seen the Lord." As we have noted earlier, if there is one thing more frightening to preachers than cruciform homiletical, communicative failure, it is resurrection evangelical success.

Barth said that Christians are those who practice the presence of the living Christ among us. Christ is present:

In practice, at least, it is to be noted that a living Christianity has always in its hymns and prayers, and above all in its administration of baptism and the Lord's Supper, experienced and seen and understood and expounded and proclaimed His presence within it and the world as the presence of the Crucified. Even in the most questionable feature of the Roman Mass, namely, its character as a representation of the sacrifice of Golgotha, we must acknowledge that it does at least make this clear. And Evangelical preaching must never lag behind it in this respect. . . . It is not merely that He was once "touched with the feeling of our infirmities"; He is so still. It is not merely that He was once tempted as we are; He is with us and before us, tempted as we are (v. 15). . . . This is more than recollection, for it speaks of His presence here to-day among us in all our confusion, aberration and abandonment, before all our locked prison doors, at all our sick-beds and gravesides, and, of course, with questioning, warning, restraint and delimitation, in all our genuine or less genuine triumphs. He is still the Friend of publicans and sinners. . . . All this is behind Him, yet it is also continually before Him. It is thus that He is among us and with us: "Slumbering and sleeping, We're safe in His keeping; On our awaking, The glory is breaking, Of His mercy so freely bestowed" (Paul Gerhardt). A man is merciful when he takes to heart the need of another. Jesus Christ has once and for all taken our need to heart. This was His passion. But although He did it once and for all, He did not do it once only. Risen from the dead, He lives and takes it to heart with undiminished severity. This is His passion to-day. (*CD*, IV, 3, pp. 395f.)

Barth made a bold move from his experience of the challenges of preaching to a congregation to the task of teaching and writing theology for the church. Yet he never got far from his homiletical origins. The proclamation of the gospel was the task that consumed the entire *Church Dogmatics*: "The task of dogmatics is an investigation of the church's proclamation with regard to its agreement with the Word of God, with regard to its congruence with that which it wants to proclaim. . . . In dogmatics the church makes itself liable to that which in its proclamation it has undertaken. It puts this undertaking to the test by facing it critically, suspending for a time that claim and expectation insofar as in reflection it separates its proclamation from the Word of God, so that it can measure, not the Word of God by its proclamation, but its proclamation by the Word of God."[9]

And Barth's theology was a sustained critique of preaching's source and goal. In his theology classes in Bonn, Barth insisted that his students begin by reading Feuerbach. It was his way of categorizing and criticizing the project of nineteenth-century theology. Theological reflection, for that project, began with Feuerbach in some aspect of human experience and worked from there to speculate on what could be said about God. Furthermore, the liberals believed that theological talk may be understood exclusively within the terms of that human experience.

Barth's acerbic wit and ironic style were well suited for his assessment of Feuerbach. Of Feuerbach, Barth said,

> He practiced [an] anti-theology. . . . He sought to take Schleiermacher and Hegel seriously, completely seriously, at the point where they concurred in asserting the non-objective quality of God. He wanted, that is, to turn theology . . . completely and finally into anthropology; to turn the lovers of God into lovers of men, the worshippers into workers; . . . he wanted to turn away from heaven towards the earth . . . to transform the theologians into anthropologists—but this time in earnest . . . he is merely affirming God's nature as man's true nature. . . . He affirms, loves and praises man and his will. . . . And it is an open secret that Christianity in its theological form has long since disappeared. . . . [God] is now man's apotheosis.[10]

Barth not only criticized liberals like Feuerbach and Schleiermacher. Under Barth's withering scrutiny, precritical Protestant orthodoxy's claim of having possession of an inerrant biblical text and Roman Catholicism's infallible magisterium were similarly dismissed. These attempts to secure a sure foundation for theology—scriptural orthodoxy, church teaching, human experience—simply validated Feuerbach's charge, according to Barth. With varying degrees of sophistication, both Protestant orthodoxy and the Catholic magisterium were vain efforts to begin talk about God in the sphere of the human, that very sphere that the Resurrected Christ, by definition, transcended. We are forever, quite futilely, like Mary Magdalene attempting to hold Christ, to restrain his movements in a way that is inimical to the energetic, peripatetic Risen Christ.

To be a preacher is to be determined to be a theologian rather than an anthropologist, psychologist, or any other subordinate, humanly derived discipline that is more interested in humanity than in God; it is to discipline ourselves to love God more than our people. The Risen Christ is always a more fit subject for conversation in the church than us. To be a preacher is to relinquish all homiletical assistance other than that given, or not given, by the Holy Spirit.[11]

From the first edition of *Der Romerbrief* (1919), Barth shows a continuing concern both to affirm the reality of revelation and yet to maintain the essential distinction between God and the world. God is distant, far from all of our conceptualization; yet near, Incarnate in the Word. God is known, but only as miracle, as gift of the One who is in heaven to those here on earth.[12] "In Jesus the communication of God begins with a rebuff, with the exposure of a vast chasm, with the clear revelation of a great stumbling block," says Barth.[13] Christ comes to us, but will not be held by us, even by our best theological formulations.

For Barth to say that revelation—God's speaking through our preaching—is a "miracle" enables Barth to claim a great deal for preaching without denying the utter "humanity of its form." Our sinful human limits are not negated by God in speaking; they are miraculously overcome. Barth compares us preachers to the prophets and apostles:

> The prophets and apostles as such, even in their office, even in their function as witnesses, even in the act of writing down their witness, were real, historical men as we are, and therefore sinful in their action, and capable and actually guilty of error in their spoken and written word. If the miracle happened to them that they were called to be witnesses of the resurrection. . . . It was to them it happened, leaving them the full use of their human freedom and not removing the barriers which are therefore posited for them as for all of us. . . . [There is a] truth of the miracle that here fallible men speak the Word of God in fallible human words. (CD, I, 2, pg. 529)

All theological statements have a peculiar logic. They are tied to a specific, peculiar subject of discourse. Theological statements claim to speak about God, not some vaunted area of human life. All our talk about God is therefore responsive rather than initiatory. What we say about God cannot find its source in us or our experience. Faith finds its source in a revealing God, in the self-communication of the Trinity, not in human yearning. All that we know of God comes as gift, as revelation, from above, not from the congregation and not from our subjectivity. God speaks, God is present among us, but the mode of God's presence, the peculiar way that God chooses to be present, is the peculiarity from which theology must move. That peculiar way is through the activity of the Holy Spirit. Barth says, "The Holy Spirit is the authorization to speak about Christ; He is the equipment of the prophet and apostle; He is the summons to the Church to minister the Word. If we ask concerning the mind of the Spirit (Rom. 8:27), we must answer that it consists in the fact that He is the gift of speaking about the 'wonderful works of God.'"[14]

To speak of a "presence" unveiled through the Holy Spirit is also to speak of a transcendence veiled before our prying eyes. God's freedom and sovereignty are such that no part of creation, whether physical or spiritual, can be said to be or to be like God. Against the tendency of nineteenth-century liberalism to degenerate into pantheism (I just heard David Tracy quoted as saying that most contemporary academic theologians are "pan-theists"), Barth pleaded for a more carefully thought-out articulation of God's presence and absence among us, a "radical dedivinization" of the world (*radikale Entgotterung*). Our problem is not atheism, a belief that there is no God to believe in, but rather rampant paganism, a credulous willingness to divinize just about anything and find analogies for God everywhere in the world and in ourselves. If religion is whatever we would sacrifice our daughter for (Luther), then there is much evidence for modernity's religiousness. Barth saw so well that modern humanity is irrepressibly religious. So the one who would proclaim the true and living God must also be one who is willing to be about the business of overturning false gods and mocking their devotees. Jesus driving the money changers from the temple becomes a model for ministry (John 2), because the closer that God comes to us, the more we appreciate the distance between ourselves and God:

> Revelation and it alone really and finally separated God and man by bringing them together. For by bringing them together it informs man about God and about himself. . . . It tells him that this God (no other) is free for this man (no other). . . . The man who listens here, sees himself standing at the boundary where all is at an end. . . . The revelation that crosses this boundary, and the togetherness of God and man which takes place in revelation in spite of this boundary, make the boundary visible to him in an unprecedented way.[15]

Barth gives us preachers a theological means of recovering our nerve. Preaching need not come hat-in-hand before the world, respectfully asking the world what it is able or willing to hear. We do not wait on the world, or the church, to vote on the permissibility of what can be preached. Preaching asserts, assaults, dismantles, remakes the world in its own image. Barth's theology is "homiletical" at its core because Barth believes that the Truth who is Jesus Christ is Truth that can only be proclaimed, not proven, not argued, neither coolly considered nor objectively described. As Bonhoeffer once complained, at times Barth asserts his theology with a "take-it-or-leave-it" attitude. Barth's style was predicated on his theological conviction that the gospel is to be declared, announced, heralded, not argued on the basis of some other authorizing story or some other validating philosophy. Preaching therefore aspires to be an engaging, faithful retelling, a retelling from within the story to those who are being subsumed into the story. Preaching is a declaration from one who is attempting to submit to the story to those who are willing to have their lives renarrated into the story of Jesus and his cross and resurrection. Preaching can never be a detached, cool consideration, certainly not a proof, at least not a proof on the basis of anything outside the story. Therefore preaching need not nervously look for allies in the world outside the gospel story in order to make its point. Making its point is a gift of God, a gift that God gives to those who risk life within this distinctive, interpretive world.[16]

Don't expect help from the historians, be they biblical historians or otherwise. We do not really have a "history" through which we can validate the story. We do not know what our "history" is until his story tells us the truth about our history. As Barth says, "His history is as such our history. It is our true history, more direct and intimate than anything we think we know as our history" (*CD*, IV, 2, pg. 548). His story obliterates what we once thought of as our history, even as it destroys what we once thought of as the facts of life, the status of the world. Preachers therefore cannot move from the world toward the gospel, Jesus' story, using the world's criteria for measurement and truth, but rather we must move the other way around, moving from the gospel toward the world, retelling the world its own true story that the world could not know without our retelling of the gospel.

Again Barth says that it is not our homiletical responsibility to "demythologize" the gospel, reducing its mythological elements to something more palatable to our philosophical perspectives in the way that Bultmann existentialized the gospel or many current preachers politicize or psychologize (in a vain attempt to sanitize) the gospel. True, there is a "demythologizing" that goes on through preaching, but it is not a demythologizing of scripture; it is scripture's demythologizing of us! Through faith our self is "demythologized" (CD, IV, 2 pp. 547, 618).[17] What we thought was our identity—that culturally predominant myth that attempts to tell us who we are—is exchanged for Jesus' revelation of who we are. Through the proclamation of the gospel, we are given our real identity.

To be a preacher is to fail, because success in proclamation is first and last God's self-assumed assignment and not ours. Only God can raise the dead.

Scripture, like John 20 for instance, is a great symphony of comprehension and misunderstanding, of wondrous enlightenment and utter darkness, of shocked recognition and complete bafflement. Barth manages to do justice to the full dialectic of scripture and the Logos as veiled and unveiled revelation. While he asserted the utter distance and unknowability of God, Barth had at the same time a radical sense of God's presence and activity as a "fact" that can be definitively known by humanity.

The peculiar mode of that presence and activity must be subtly explicated by Barth: it is not general but specific, not available always and everywhere but in particular places and at particular times. It is of the nature of a Trinitarian God to elect to be contingent to humanity. It is not a basic condition (*ein Zustand*), not an opening through which any Tom, Dick, or Harry may look into heaven, but a happening (*ein Geschehen*). In the modern world, where we tend to view knowledge mainly as a means of control ("I got it"), it is odd for us to receive knowledge as a gift ("It got me"), as something to be received in humility rather than as a result of our aggressive epistemological methods, as an uncontrollable event rather than as a datum to be uncovered and owned. Knowledge of God tends always to be indirect rather than direct, surprising rather than predictable. Nevertheless God loves us enough to make that knowledge sure and undeniable, for the Trinity is a God who loves to raise the dead in order that the conversation continue.

The self-objectification of God for our sakes is Jesus Christ, the Incarnation. Yet this self-objectification by God requires a fittingly humble reception by humans.[18] That reception is also a gift of God, bestowed by God in the event of revelation. Human receptivity to the Word must be given ever anew; it is not a possession, a state in which humanity comes to reside. In the matter of human knowledge of the divine, all is gift, unexpected, undeserved proclamation by God to us, momentary address, like manna in the wilderness. We preachers can speak only because of the gift of faith that God has spoken; otherwise our speech is silly presumption. Preaching is the result of God having turned to us. "Preaching," said Karl Barth in a seminar held in Bonn in 1932, "cannot try to be a proof of the truth of God. It cannot set out to prove God by an intellectual demonstration, by stating and stressing certain propositions. There can be no other proof of God than that which God himself offers."[19]

When Barth says "revelation," he refers not only to the objective fact of God's self-giving to us but also to God's gracious gift of our reception and obedience in response to God's self-giving. Revelation is not only God's turning to us; it is also our turning to God. Barth constantly unites the subjective-objective aspects of revelation, links the divine subject to the human object, and makes revelation a matter of relationship, an event that is fresh, new each morning. To know this God is to keep acknowledging. We remain, not in knowledge, but in a receptive relationship of acknowledgment. That relationship is based, not upon our desire and yearning, but upon the event of God's active love for us. It cannot be codified any more than it can be grasped through human effort. We can recollect its reception in the past and hope for its gift in the future. We can gratefully name those places and times when it has been offered to us, but we cannot reside in those times and places.

The eventful, sovereign, disruptive quality of this grace is an attack upon much of the current enthusiasm for "spiritual practices."[20] Too often "spiritual disciplines" and "practices" are what we cultivate when we no longer have encounter by the Risen Christ. We can practice a cultivated innocence and openness to this gift, but we cannot develop some series of spiritual disciplines or practices of faith that blunt the disruptive, gifted quality of the revelation. If one can faithfully keep the Sabbath or assiduously pray the rosary, you need not be struck by the Risen Christ, these practices imply.

Contrary to this contemporary stress on spiritual practices, Barth would remind us that the church is created and sustained through proclamation of the Word, not through practices or the formation of allegedly Christian character. The church must rise anew, in each generation, among those who have heard, not simply among those who have been inculcated and indoctrinated. The Word is forever tearing down and rebuilding the church, disrupting, confusing, killing in order to raise us from the dead.

I have even come to believe that much of homiletics' current infatuation with "story" and "narrative," and preaching as "telling the story" may be an attempt to domesticate and tame, to order and to make stable (story defined as that which has a beginning, middle, and end) the Word of God, which is often so exasperatingly disorderly and out of sequence.[21] (Here I have in mind that wonderful ending of Job in which, when God finally speaks to Job, God does so in a way that decisively disrupts the narrative flow—a long series of rather absurd questions with non sequitur answers. Sometimes revelation is the ending of the narrative rather than a result of narrative.) God does not give modern North American people a story just because we are desperate for one.

To use "revelation" to refer to anything other than the dynamic, eventful relationship of divine speaking and human hearing, the giving and receiving, the miracle and wonder, is idolatrously to confuse human substitutes for divine reality. "Jesus Christ is risen," and will not submit to our restraints, even our most loving restraints.

To be a preacher is to risk effective preaching; it is to preach, to witness the reception of the Word, to be scared half out of our wits by the proof that God is alive and determined to have a people, to be delighted that God really means to overturn the present order through ordinary folk like us, and not be completely surprised when preaching actually works. Easter was as great a shock to Jesus' own followers as to anybody else.

There are three forms of proclamation that God uses to be with us and to call us for God's work. Scripture and preaching, humanly considered, are witnesses to God's revelation in Jesus Christ. Jesus Christ *is* and remains God's Word as the incarnation of the Son of God. Scripture and preaching are human realities that, by the grace of God, *become* God's Word as the Incarnate Word enters into them in the event of revelation. Jesus Christ is permanently, indissolubly God; preaching and scripture become manifestations of God as God makes them so. Thus Barth thinks of preaching in terms of John the Baptist pointing away from himself and toward Christ rather than Christ himself preaching. Barth says of Scripture,

"Holy Scripture is God's Word in exactly the same sense in which we have said this of the event of . . . proclamation,"[22] that is, it becomes God's Word through the miracle of God's gracious willingness to make God's own Word known through them. The living Christ is determined to be for us an event, a gift rather than our possession.

Barth's elevation of preaching to equal status and similar function of Scripture is congruent with the Reformed tradition. For while the Reformers with their so-called *sola scriptura* principle elevated the words of biblical writers as the Word of God, Barth claims that they identified the words of preaching in a similar sense. As Bullinger asserts in the Second Helvetic Confession: "The preaching of the word of God *is* the Word of God."

That little word "is," is surely the surprise and the scandal of Barth's view of preaching, the outrageous claim that the words of Christian preachers are identified with God's own Word. The way in which God in Jesus Christ chooses to reveal himself is always a shock and a scandal. In preaching, as in Scripture, fallible human beings speak the Word of God in fallible human words, says Barth, placing the words "fallible" and "God" in closer proximity than we normally like to use them, but no closer than the words "crucifixion" and "God." Preaching is human talk about God, in and through which God speaks about himself,[23] and to which God commits God's self absolutely "in such a way that like the existence of Jesus Christ himself it is God's own proclamation."[24]

We are here again at the Barthian image of veiling and unveiling. God is revealed, but revealed in a way that manages both to hide and to reveal. Thus Barth, citing both Luther and Kierkegaard for support, says in *Romans*:

> The Gospel requires—faith. . . . It can therefore be neither directly communicated nor directly apprehended. . . . It can appear among us, be received and understood by us, only as contradiction. The gospel does not expound or recommend itself. It does not negotiate or plead, threaten or make promises. It withdraws itself always when it is not listened to for its own sake. . . . "Indeed only when that which is believed on is hidden, can it provide an opportunity for faith. And moreover, those things are most deeply hidden which most clearly contradict the obvious experience of the sense" (Luther).[25]

The veil can be lifted only by God. The good news is that God does tear away the veil separating us from the Holy of Holies. As Trevor Hart says, "In the event of revelation God tears the veil away, and makes known the incomprehensible, but as the event is precisely *that*, something which happens and passes and is gone, the veil itself remains formally in place. For those with 'eyes to see' it becomes transparent, but for others it is and remains utterly opaque."[26] For Barth "faith" is something that God does and only secondarily something that occurs in us. Because this Trinitarian God wants to be in existence with us, it is of the nature of this God always to be reaching out, always enabling us to respond, in short, always to be faithful in enabling us to have faith.[27]

To be a preacher is to be willing to be a powerful person; it is to be willing to be a chosen instrument of the God who kills and makes alive, who wounds and heals, who sometimes demands that ordinary folk undertake some terribly dangerous missions—like preaching.

How bold of the Resurrected Christ to demand that the very ones who had so disappointed and betrayed him, in their silence at the cross, be the very ones to proclaim him as resurrected, ruling Lord. This vocation of the powerless to be powerful preachers underscores the miraculous quality of preaching. Preaching as Trinitarian revelation is a miracle, says Barth, a miracle no less than the creation of the world, the virginal conception of Jesus, or the Resurrection. The paradox is the same, the veiling and unveiling as well. That this unveiling happens despite the creatureliness of the form that the Word assumes and (in the instances of scripture and preaching at least) despite its inherent fallibility and sinfulness, is miracle, a miracle of the same sort if not the same magnitude as the Creation *ex nihilo*. The paradox is the same and, even as we preachers are working revelation in our sermons, revelation is working us. We must preach as those who acknowledge that we cannot control that revelation through our preaching. The paradox of revelation must be allowed to stand as paradox.

Without the miracle of revelation ("And God said. . . ."), a Christian conversation with God is in danger of becoming simply conversation with ourselves. Barth was bothered by the way that both pietism and rationalism, both orthodoxy and liberalism were two sides of the same coin—finding revelation elsewhere rather than as a gift of God. Preaching as the Word of God is veiled by its creatureliness and becomes unveiled only in the gracious event of revelation. There is a "real presence of Christ" in preaching, but not as "transubstantiation," *ex opera operato*. We cannot guarantee or coerce preaching as revelation. We can only receive it in faith. What happens in preaching is something theologically akin to what happens in Christ as displayed in Paul's kenosis hymn in Philippians 2:

> Have this mind among yourselves, which is yours in Christ Jesus, who, though he was in the form of God, did not count equality with God a thing to be grasped, but emptied himself, taking the form of a servant, being born in the likeness of men. And being found in human form he humbled himself and become obedient unto death, even death on a cross. Therefore God has highly exalted him and bestowed on him the name which is above every name, that at the name of Jesus every knee should bow, in heaven and on earth and under the earth, and every tongue confess that Jesus Christ is Lord, to the glory of God the Father. (Phil. 2:5-11 RSV)

Trevor Hart comments on the kenotic, Philippians 2 quality of the Barthian concept of revelation in this way:

> Notwithstanding the kenotic aspect of the humanity of the Word, its historically conditioned nature, its contingency, its theological contradictions and limitations, nonetheless, Barth affirms, God's Word is pleased to identify himself with it, to commit himself to it, and, in what can only be described as a miraculous event, to speak through human beings. In this event, wrought by Word and Spirit together, the one as the "objective possibility" of revelation, the other as its "subjective possibility" of revelation, these human words actually *become* the Word of God. God speaks here in such a way that he is heard, as he has spoken here many times before, and promises to do so again and again. As such, both Scripture and preaching may be called Word of God in a straightforward and unqualified manner.
>
> But such a description refers not to an attribute which the words possess in and of themselves, nor even one which they come to possess through grace, but precisely to the event in which they are taken up, assumed, and in which God's Word becomes incarnate once again with revealing and redeeming effect. Thus God is himself the subject of this event as well as the object made known. And as we are drawn into it, actively engaged in knowing, what is in effect taking place is a drawing of us into the very inner heart of God's triune life, into his own self-knowledge, as he posits himself as the Son to be known and loved by the Father in the Holy Spirit. The event of revelation thus has a profoundly Trinitarian structure, although in our case it is a triunity rooted firmly in the historical realm: we are drawn to know God as Father in and through our knowing of and sharing in the life of the human Son, the *Christos*, empowered and sustained by the anointing Spirit. That this miracle should occur, this reconciling and atoning knowing should happen to us or to others is never, of course, within our sphere of influence or responsibility. We

are not called upon to conjure it up genie-like, even from a book rather than a bottle; but simply to point away from ourselves to Christ, to bear witness, to tell the story of redemption. "Only God can talk about God," Barth asserts. "To this extent, in appropriate application of a Christological formulation, we might say of preaching as the Word of God that it is 'conceived by the Holy Ghost.'"[28]

Preachers are called by Christ to be of the same mind as Christ (Phil. 2:5), that is, to be willing to be in self-emptying kenosis with him. We are, as Luther called us, "servants of the Word." We have no real significance, other than that which the Word wants to do through us. The Crucifixion has an epistemological role in refuting all claims to knowledge about God except through the Crucifixion and the Resurrection. In volume IV, section 1 of the *Dogmatics*, "The Obedience of the Son of God" (pp. 224ff.) Barth says that the pattern of the Gospels represents a repetition of the pattern of the Atonement. Only gradually Jesus emerges as superior to his disciples or to those around him. But when we get to the Passion, the roles are reversed. Jesus becomes the servant, the one who is emptied, the one who submits to the acts of the people around him rather than leading them. Instead of judging others, he lets others judge him. He becomes the prodigal son who goes out to the "far country" in order to reach us. The very form that the gospel takes is the pattern through which our recognition comes as God in Christ stoops to us and serves us by making himself available to us. In other words, the shape of the *kenosis* in Philippians 2 is the shape that revelation takes for our sakes. For preachers to preach this kenotic gospel, we must empty ourselves, take the form of a servant, know nothing except what we have been told, and be hesitant to take a stand anywhere other than on that ground that is given us through the Word. And thus we become who we, as heralds, are called to be.

Fortunately, Barth tempers some of his exuberant conviction of preaching as the very Word of God with remarks that seem to draw back a bit from those sweeping claims. He says that "the time of direct, original speech of God Himself in His revelation," was one time, the time of scripture. But the time of the church is another time in which we have not simply a difference in time, but a difference in the "attitude of God to men" (*CD*, I, 1, pg. 145). Today, when we preach, our word is of necessity a derivative word because we are simply repeating the witness of those who lived in a time of more direct address by God. This is all a bit confusing, particularly in the light of all of Barth's Lutheranesque statements about the speaking of God to us, here, now.

Barth is noted for his "Christocentric" theology, and this is true. But in his thought on revelation (and homiletics), Barth is just as interested in the role of the third person of the Trinity in our preaching and hearing. We are not to be overly confident that our words in a sermon are the very words of God. He warned of that "certain assurance of voice, speech and attitude with which, it seems, we think we can work on the new or older field, a certain confidence with which we think we can take those great concepts on our lips and analyze them and interrelate them constructively or in other ways, a certain sprightliness with which we speak about the things denoted by them as those we were speaking about them because we know."[29] The reality of sin, even in its "nothingness"; the eventful quality of revelation; and the high regard for the sovereignty of God are enough to keep Barth or his followers from becoming revelational positivists when it comes to preaching.

Yet what the Word wants to do in us, miracle of miracles, is actually done through us, not every Sunday, but enough to keep us nervous.[30] Every sermon is like a controlled scientific experiment in which we test the proposition that "Christ is risen! He is risen indeed!" We speak, in the sermon, without sufficient rhetorical props, in such a way that there is no way for the sermon to work if Easter is a lie. Thus we participate, almost on a weekly basis, in the dying and rising of Christ, risking the perils of communicative failure, of not being heard, of our sermon meaning nothing to all who pass by; and also risking the perils of homiletical success, of the Word being unleashed among us, and of our sermon prancing out of our hands into God's hands. God tells the prophet that he will "serve as my mouth" (Jer. 15:19). If there is one thing more threatening to a preacher than Good Friday, it is Easter.

Risen Christ, Get Out of Here[31]

1 Corinthians 15:1-11; Luke 5:1-11

Sojourner Jim Wallis, speaking to a pastor's conference, gave a lecture, "The Renewal of the Inner-City Church." Wallis simply stood up and told story upon story of once declining inner-city churches that had, by the grace of God, rediscovered their mission. I was inspired by Wallis's stories of churches that worked. Yet in the conversation afterward, one pastor after another rose to criticize Wallis's speech. They accused him of looking at the church through naive, rose-colored-glasses idealism. One even implied that Wallis lied.

At dinner that evening, I told Wallis that I was appalled by the group's reaction. "I wasn't," he said. "That's the reaction I always get from mainline, liberal pastors. They are amazed when God wins. Just scared to death that Easter just might be, after all, true."

Our gospel is a story of Jesus' homiletical success with a great crowd "pressing in on him to hear the word of God," followed by a frustrating night of fishing failure in which the disciples "caught nothing." Then, just because Jesus speaks, the disciples have astounding, net-bursting success. It's comforting to see Jesus' sermons so well received after that unpleasantness last Sunday at Nazareth (Luke 4:21-30). Next, Jesus is master, not only of the word of God but also of fish. We who so often feel so powerless over the elusiveness of language, the scarcity of natural resources, the horror of world hunger, are thrilled to witness the unveiled, magical power of Jesus.

It's too soon in Luke or the new year for an Easter story. Still, even though it is yet the Season after the Epiphany, any time you are working the night shift with Jesus, be prepared for an outbreak of Easter. We witness what it's like to be astounded by a death-defying Jesus, moved from failure and scarcity to life and triumph. It's wonderful.

Or is it? The reaction of Peter—the premier, though quixotic, disciple, the first of the church—to all this abundance-producing power? "Get out of here; I'm a sinner!" (v. 8). Last Sunday they wanted Jesus out of Nazareth because of his preaching. Now they want Jesus out of Galilee because of his fishing.

Peter moves from the security of fixed, failed reality—"We fished all night and have nothing"—into full, open, new, uncontained reality. But the water is now deep and dark, and the dawn carries with it an odd threat. In a moment Peter senses the gap between his world and the new creation of Jesus. Peter moves from calling Jesus even so exalted a title as "Master" (5:5) to the even more exalted "O Lord!" It's then that things get unmanageable and scary. It's then that Peter comes to see his situation as a lack of faith rather than a lack of fish. It's then that he blurts out, "Get out of here, Jesus," literally in the Greek, "Get out of my neighborhood!"

Time for honesty: I've got a better theology of ministry on Good Friday ("Christ died for our sins in accordance with the scriptures"), with all sorts of sound sociological, psychological reasons for death and defeat, than a pastoral theology robust enough for Easter ("He was raised on the third day in accordance with the scriptures," 1 Cor. 15:3-4). Most of my sermons, even in Epiphany or Easter, work the theme: "Ten reasons why you are not really the Body of Christ even though you thought you were when you came to church this morning." There's a reason why Marcus Borg, in his new book (The Heart of Christianity), labors so to disjoin the "pre-Easter Jesus" from the "post-Easter Jesus." Easier, I think, to be in the boat with Marcus's historical Jesus—wisdom teacher-movement initiator-social prophet—than Jesus the Resurrected Christ who rocks the hell out of my dead and dying world. Though Jesus tells us, "Do not be afraid" (v. 10), when he promises to teach us to fish like him, it's scary. Get out of here, Jesus.

I was not present at the Finance Committee meeting the night they voted on next year's budget. Next morning, got a call from the chair. "Preacher," she said, "great meeting last night. I opened with prayer and it was as if the Holy Spirit just descended on us. With little discussion we unanimously approved next year's budget—a ten percent increase over this year's. It was wonderful! There's a new spirit in this congregation, and we're going to ride with it."

I said, in love, "Let me get this straight. The church that is five percent behind on this year's budget is going to have a ten percent increase next year? That's crazy! I'm the spiritual leader of this congregation. I will tell you when the Holy Spirit gets here. There is no way that you will pledge that budget!"

"Well, you weren't there and we've already voted, so that's that," she replied.

The Sundays that October, in each service, we had a "Stewardship Moment" where the chair reported on the progress, or lack of it, in our pledge campaign. Second Sunday in October she rose at the beginning of the service and said, "I never thought I'd live to see this day in this church. I am pleased to announce that we have pledged next year's budget in full!"

The church erupted in spontaneous applause.

"Which is all the more amazing considering that this is a huge increase over this year's budget." Applause again.

"Now, as I remember, there was somebody who said, 'You will never pledge that budget.' Help me remember. Who said, 'That's crazy, you will never pledge that budget.' Who said that?"

Sometimes I despise the anticlericalism of the laypeople as much as I fear the unwanted intrusions of the Holy Spirit. It isn't easy when you are fishing with Jesus. Get out of here, Jesus.

My friend Hauerwas is fond of saying that this culture is built on one predominant fear—death. He thinks this explains our health care system, our economy, our government, Gold's Gym, and all the rest.

I am now fond of saying that this culture is built on an even greater fear—the threat of being raised from the dead.

Barth says that the church always exists as that event that is a result of God's fresh encounter with humanity:

And so the Church, whose life is sustained by the Gospel story and the apostolic message, can only mediate this beginning, testifying to the individual Christian that this beginning, Jesus Christ, is the beginning of his life too. It has, therefore, nothing else to offer him; nothing of its own, whether old or new. The historical existence of the Church is legitimate only in so far as it refrains from giving specific weight to its own possibilities, developments and achievements, from interesting its members in these things and therefore in itself instead of pointing simply to that beginning in direct and exclusive proclamation of Jesus Christ. The Christian Church exists where it attests to its members and the outside world this beginning and nothing but this beginning. Only as it does this is it the "pillar and ground of the truth" (1 Tim. 3:5). It cannot, therefore, build itself on either its antiquity or its renewals. It cannot consolidate its life around its ministry or dogmas, its cultus or orders. It cannot place its confidence on its ministerial succession or on the religious, intellectual and political lustre of the fathers and saints and doctors and leaders with whom it has been blessed, on the certainty of its doctrinal and constitutional tradition, or on the progressive development of its preaching, institutions or activity. Nor can it insert all these things between that beginning and its contemporary present, between Jesus Christ and the men after His time, as though they had a special and independent value and authority and importance by the side of His. It can understand itself and its history in all its forms only as the context of a service which it has to perform. (*CD*, III, 2, pp. 583f.)

The primary task of the church is to witness to this fresh encounter by praising God through the proclamation of the Word of God, that is, Jesus Christ as God's word to humanity. Church is a choir:

The existence of the community as such and of all Christians has to serve the praise of God. . . . It is not merely insisted that the community should allow the Word of God to dwell in it richly, nor that Christians should sing to God in their hearts, nor that they should do everything in word and deed in His name and therefore with thanksgiving to God the Father but also quite expressly that in wisdom they should teach and admonish one another "in psalms and hymns and spiritual songs." And is it not worth noting that in Mk. 14:26 we are told that the disciples sang a hymn immediately after the last highly significant meal with Jesus and just before the commencement of His passion? The praise of God which constitutes the community and its assemblies seeks bind and commit and therefore to be expressed, to well up and be sung in concert. The Christian community sings. It is not a choral society. Its singing is not a concert. But from inner, material necessity it sings. Singing is the highest form of human expression. It is to such supreme expression that the vox humana is devoted in the ministry of the Christian community. It is for this that it is liberated in this ministry. It is hard to see any compelling reason why it should have to be accompanied in this by an organ or harmonium. It might be argued that in this way the community's praise of God is embedded by anticipation in that of the whole cosmos, to which the cosmos is undoubtedly called and which we shall unquestionably hear in the consummation. The trouble is that in practice instruments seem to be to conceal the feebleness with which the community discharges the ministry of the *vox humana* committed to it. There is also the difficulty that we cannot be sure whether the spirits invoked with the far too familiar sounds of instruments are clean or unclean spirits. In any case, there should be no place for or solos in the Church's liturgy, even in the form of the introductory and closing voluntaries which are so popular. What we can and must say quite confidently is that the community which does not sing is not the community. And where it cannot sing in living speech, or only archaically in repetition of the modes and texts of the past; where it does not really sing but sighs and mumbles spasmodically, shamefacedly and with an ill grace, it can be at best only a troubled community which is not sure of its cause and of whose ministry and witness there can be no great expectation. In these circumstances it has every reason to pray that this gift which is obviously lacking or enjoyed only in sparing measure will be granted afresh and more generously lest all the other members suffer. (*CD*, IV, 3, pp. 865-67)

The theological task of the church is to make sure, as much as is humanly possible, that the word it sings is truly the Word of God, that the praise of the church is orthodox (*orthodoxy* = "right praise"). Theology is the servant of proclamation, the attempt to sing forth a miraculous event. Rarely does theology do justice to the liveliness of God's Word, its miraculous and eventful quality. Invariably, theology sounds more dull and prosaic than the event that it is serving. Still, we preachers must read theology because theology is our necessary critical colleague, as long as theology clearly understands that it is preaching's critical servant and not preaching's master. Theological reflection is that mundane, rather prosaic and at times fastidious and sober reflection that occurs after preaching, rather than a source for preaching.

The free Word of God is the epistemological foundation for the church's theology, its sole source and basis. Any thought about God must be obtained only from God.[32] This occurs through the prophetic office of the Risen Jesus Christ. In the Resurrection, in those fifty days afterward, we see the self-giving of the Risen Christ. The real "Word of God" is Jesus the Christ. Barth says that God may speak "through Russian Communism or a flute concerto, a blossoming shrub or a dead dog,"[33] yet God graciously condescends to speak through Word and Sacrament. Both the Bible and preaching are human activities, but they are human activities in which God has freely, graciously chosen to speak. They are the Word of God where and when God pleases. And, despite our preacherly complaints, it does please God to speak through us more often than our sermons deserve.

CHAPTER TEN

CALLED TO PREACH

The promise of the Word of God is not as such an empty pledge which always stands, as it were, confronting a person. It is the transposing of a person into the wholly new state of one who has accepted and appropriated the promise, so that irrespective of his attitude to it he no longer lives without this promise but with it. The claim of the Word of God is not as such a wish or command which remains outside the hearer without impinging on his existence. It is the claiming and commandeering of the human being. Whatever may be his attitude to God's claim, the person who hears the Word now finds himself in the sphere of the divine claim; he is claimed by God. (CD, I, 2, pg. 152)

Vocation is always linked to proclamation. You can't speak a word so challenging as the gospel without being forced to do it through vocation. You can't pay someone to preach; a person must be called to preach. And proclamation is always linked to vocation. Every word from God is in the vocative. Faith is not only God's gift but also God's assignment. The Word faithfully proclaimed will always be the Word that enables faithful response to the Word. That which keeps Barth's theology tied to our world is vocation, the determined, undeniable, continuing claim of God upon ordinary folk like us. Here, the objective-subjective split is healed. Here, in the event of vocation, any charge that Barth fosters a theology of unreality and detachment is overcome. In vocation, God becomes historical, immanent, and active toward us. In vocation, God keeps creating the world, even as God created the world through vocation ("Let there be. . . .") in Genesis 1. Hear one of the most evocative passages in the *Dogmatics*, written by Barth toward the end of his university career:

> In all the stories of vocation in the Bible, from that of Abraham to that of Paul, while we certainly have to do with works of God or of Jesus Christ towards these men . . . yet because rather than in spite of this we are also dealing in the full sense with the elements in their own individual histories and therefore in the history of the more dear or distant world around them. . . . Upon them, and therefore at once upon the world around them, there came something which had in their lives . . . consequences . . . by which their further course was incisively determined, and in the power of which, wittingly or unwittingly, they exercised an incisive influence on the life of the world around. . . . The call of God makes heroes like Gideon, watchmen like Samuel, kings like David, prophets like Isaiah, Amos, Jeremiah and others, apostles like Paul, seers like John of Patmos—and all with the most far-reaching consequences.
>
> Similarly, for those who came to know and could speak of vocation in the sphere of the Church, it was a work of God which came vertically from above, yet which was also just as real horizontally in their creaturely existence, so that it was an event which determined afresh their own time and that of the surrounding world. Calvin was right when he relentlessly traced back access to Christ to God's eternal election. But for this very reason he took it seriously as his own vocation . . . and gave it prominence in definite acts. . . . Again, John Wesley could give not only the date but the

very hour of his own conversion, yet rightly he understood what happened in terms of the Lutheran doctrine of justification and therefore forensically and in terms of predestination. This did not mean, however, that he was forbidden but rather required to reorientate his life completely . . . and to enter a new way on which he had so revolutionary an external influence that without any exaggeration it has been possible to write a book entitled *England Before and After Wesley*.[1]

The Bible is "God's word" through "the miracle of revelation and of faith when in the proclamation of the church, man's language about God . . . is primarily and decisively God's own language."[2] As we have noted, in Trinitarian fashion, Barth sees God's Word in three forms—the written Word, the proclaimed Word, and the revealed Word. All three forms of revelation are effective but not identical. Jesus Christ is the "objective" aspect of revelation, the Holy Spirit (not our feelings or opinions) is the "subjective" aspect of revelation. Revelation is one of the primary aspects of the relentless self-communicative and self-revealing triune God. Revelation is always "personal," that is, from subject to subject. Faith in a speaking God in Christ entails faith in a hearing, responding person in Christ. The Risen Christ keeps addressing those who thought that, in the cross, God was at last silenced— "Mary," he says, "Go, tell . . ." or, "Peter, feed my lambs"—as address becomes assignment. After 1935, with his expulsion from Germany and return to Switzerland, Barth's thought shows an explicit, disciplined, exuberantly christological nature. Not philosophy, not religion, and not historical method, but rather the crucified and resurrected, speaking Christ becomes the engine that drives Barth's thought. His thought is energized by the living, speaking person of Christ. Barth has been accused of "christomonosm." (He says, "Theology must fundamentally be Christology and only Christology," *CD*, I, 2, pg. 872.) But this is Christology neither as a principle, nor as a system, but as the living person who speaks on the move, Jesus Christ. Preachers are those who, like Mary Magdalene at the tomb, are encountered by the person of Christ and who, in preaching, attempt to be faithful to the summons.

"Not every man can do this [speak the Word of God]. Not every man can speak God's Word. For not every man has heard it,"[3] says Barth. No one speaks anything except what is heard. Everyone who hears can and must speak. Hearing and vocation are inextricably linked. I think it sad that too many contemporary pastors appear to be called only to be pastors—congregational caregivers, managers, organizational leaders—rather than preachers, those who, having heard, have something that they are compelled to say. Much of contemporary homiletics construes preaching as our laborious effort to say something about God. In stressing the divine vocation, Barth's homiletics stresses the miracle of God's drawing near in order to say something to us.

In having heard and being called to speak, the purpose of our preaching is not the conveying of spiritual truth, but an encounter with the One who is the way, the truth, and the life, an encounter that is so real and engaging that the listeners will say "yes." Knowledge leads to acknowledgment. Kant thought that faith and knowledge were opposites. For Barth, faith precedes knowledge, *credere ut intelligere* (Anselm). True knowledge must be unconditionally bound to its object (theology is a "science"). Faith is the human response to the fact, the object of faith *and* our active participation in and acknowledgment of that object. Our acknowledgment is made possible through God's work in us, bringing us to faith. God, not humanity, takes the initiative in any divine-human communication. Communion is the basis for cognition.

Thankfully for us, the Trinity is loquacious. The Risen Christ comes back and speaks, initiates conversation with his disciples. Believing is also a free human act, that is, one which

is not destroyed or disturbed by any magic; but, of course, it is a free act, which as such is conditioned and determined by an encounter, a challenge, an act of lordship that confronts us,
that we cannot bring about ourselves, that exists either as an event or not at all. Therefore
believing is not something arbitrary. It does not control its object. It is a recognizing, knowing, hearing, apperceiving, thinking, speaking, and doing that is overmastered by its object.[4]
Faith, at least that which is Christian, has no development. It is miraculous gift.

As Barth describes faith:

> Faith is not, therefore, a standing, but a being suspended and hanging without ground under our
> feet. Or conversely, in faith we abandon whatever we might otherwise regard as our standing,
> namely, our standing upon ourselves (including all moral and religious, even Christian standing),
> because in faith we see that it is a false and unreal standing, a hanging without support, a waver-
> ing and falling. We abandon it for the real standing in which we no longer stand on ourselves (on
> our moral and religious, or even our Christian state), and in which we obviously do not stand on
> our faith as such but—now at least firmly and securely—on the ground of the truth of God and
> therefore on the ground of the reconciliation which has taken place in Jesus Christ and is con-
> firmed by Him to all eternity. It is a standing which seen from ourselves (but what we see from our-
> selves is a lie) may well appear to be an impossible and intolerable hanging and suspension. We
> will always be afraid of it as we see things from ourselves. We may well try to flee from it as if our
> lives were at stake (as indeed they are, though in the very opposite sense). We shall continually
> surprise ourselves on the flight from faith.[5]

Remembering that Hebrews speaks of faith as "the conviction of things not seen," Barth
interprets "things" to mean those "things whose truth lies in God alone. Hence the believer
who builds her life on such things has God alone and nothing else as his support and basis."[6]

*To be a preacher is to be called to walk by faith; it is to work perilously, without props, without
philosophical justification for our claims, without rhetorical strategies to accomplish our goals, trusting God to speak that which we ourselves cannot speak but must speak.*

Barth tells us poor preachers that we can find continual rejuvenation, confident that
despite our poor preaching and our people's poor listening, the Word of God is forever triumphant:

> [People] with their various (but by nature unanimously hostile) attitudes towards the Word of God
> come and go. Their political and spiritual systems (all of which to some extent have an anti-
> Christian character) stand and fall. The Church itself (in which somewhere the crucifixion of
> Christ is always being repeated) is to-day faithful and to-morrow unfaithful, to-day strong and to-
> morrow weak. But although Scripture may be rejected by its enemies and disowned and betrayed
> by its friends, it does not cease . . . to present the message that God so loved the world that He
> gave his only-begotten Son. If its voice is drowned to-day, it becomes audible again to-morrow. If
> it is misunderstood and distorted here, it again bears witness to its true meaning there. If it seems
> to lose its position, hearers and form in this locality or period, it acquires them afresh elsewhere.
> The promise is true, and it is fulfilled in the existence of the biblical prophets and apostles in virtue
> of what is said to them and what they have to say. The maintaining of the Word of God against
> the attacks to which it is exposed cannot be our concern and therefore we do not need to worry
> about it. Watchmen are appointed and they wait in their office. The maintaining of the Word of
> God takes place as a self-affirmation which we can never do more than acknowledge to our own
> comfort and disquiet. We can be most seriously concerned about Christianity and Christians,
> about the future of the Church and theology, about the establishment in the world of the Christian
> outlook and Christian ethic. But there is nothing about whose solidity we need be less troubled
> than the testimonies of God in Holy Scripture. For a power which can annul these testimonies is
> quite unthinkable.[7]

Under Barth's tutelage, contemporary preaching has the opportunity to recover preaching as an essentially theological endeavor. Preaching is of God. Barth's preacher-as-herald is a high theological view of preaching. Preaching, in Barth's view, is distinctive as a theological activity, not only in substance but also in means. In a day when preaching too often degenerates into moralistic advice, principles for better living, political commentary (whether of the right or of the left), or helpful (but essentially superficial) hints for humanity, Barth recalls us to an idea of preaching as witness to the very voice of God. Preachers, as heralds, "are not to be Luthers, churchmen, prophets, visionaries, or the like. They are simply to be themselves, and to expound the text as such. Preaching is the responsible word of a person of our own time. Having heard myself, I am called upon to pass on what I have heard."[8]

Preaching is more than a rhetorical act, more than what might appear to the outside observer. The "outside observer" is no judge of the value of preaching. The value of preaching, in Barth, is the value that God gives to preaching—God freely using the preacher to speak God's words. Paul marvels at the power of the Word to do that which the Word says: "We also constantly give thanks to God for this, that when you received the word of God that you heard from us, you accepted it not as a human word but as what it really is, God's word, which is also at work in you believers" (1 Thess. 2:13).

Therefore, for preachers who are inspired by Barth, what matters in preaching is the message, the news that makes this news good. The herald's job is to get the story straight, to get the message right. After that, the message creates its own hearers; proclamation makes its own way with the audience. But that message is more than a set of words; it is an event of God's own making, an act of God in and through, beyond and above the words of the preacher. Thus, the preacher has not only a message but also a mandate from God, a command to speak. A principal virtue for the faithful preacher is obedience. Barth speaks about "conformity" as being a demand placed upon both preacher and listener in the sermon process:

> It must be emphasized that the conformity of preaching to ministry cannot be clearly described in psychological terms, whether as regards listener or preacher. Simplicity and relevance may be the marks of this kind of preaching but they do not have to be. Again, the question of success in the sense of a movement and awakening in the congregation cannot be the criterion of true ministry. Right hearing of God's word is the only valid effect of a sermon, but where and when this happens we cannot know, for what we have here is the working of the Word of God that we can only believe.[9]

Faithful preachers are therefore not noted for their creativity; their job is to obediently tell what they have heard, to deliver what they have received, to conform their speaking to the demands of the Word. The rest is God's business. Barthian preachers, it now goes without saying, have a suspicious disposition toward various rhetorical schemes and strategies, so confident are they that God is alive, and that God speaks, and that one of the primary, self-designated means for God's speaking is preaching. Only God can make preaching "true."

Faithful preachers are likewise not always noted for their warm and winning personalities. The message is superior to the messenger. The herald is not called primarily to be somebody but rather to say something. The messenger is a witness to an event, a phenomenon that is more important than the messenger. Not that the messenger is unimportant; matters of the preacher's character are important matters. Yet the moral characteristics required of the messenger are those virtues demanded of a faithful witness—modesty before the facts of the message, transparency, a willingness to be subordinate to the message, a confidence that what we have to say is the most significant thing about who we are, and a greater love for the message than for the congregation. *Ethos* may have been the most important characteristic of Aristotle's rhetor, but the divine Logos is the most important quality in a preacher.

Busch notes that Barth "distinguishes three aspects of human witness to the truth that correspond to the three aspects in which the truth makes itself known to us."[10] First, the work of the witness does not rest upon the affirmation of a general principle or conviction of a simple, straightforward agreement between the witness and that One toward which the witness testifies. *The truth of the witness can never be divorced from the Giver of the truth.*

Second, Barth says that it is typical of a witness to the truth that the testimony of the witness leads the witness to *great distress and discomfort*. Even when the witness does not want to offend, a world that is hostile to the truth may take offense. Barth says that, if a Christian makes a witness, "he cannot avoid disturbing those around, exerting upon them by his witness a pressure to which they can and will react with counterpressure."[11]

Yet, despite the expected affliction, the witness is not too "troubled,"[12] because this affliction is an aspect of ministry.[13] No witness to the truth can ever be "absolutely secured."[14] And confidence of the preacher is confidence in "the Holy Spirit, who will see to it . . . that the truth always remains the truth no matter what people may say against it."[15] Homiletical courage, this implies, rests upon faith in the truthfulness of the testimony, not in any optimism about the world's ability to hear or the witness's ability to speak. In this faith, the witness enjoys "the wonderful possibility, peacefully and joyfully, of having the upper hand over against the totalitarian state and the totalitarian world, not always going around with clenched fists. The church can wait. And it knows that it does not wait in vain. . . . [knowing that] all the totalities of the world and society and the state, which are in truth false gods, are lies. Ultimately one cannot be afraid of lies."[16]

Third, the witness testifies to the validity of the message by showing that she is *completely, single-mindedly claimed by the truth*. By God's grace the witness is delivered "from the ocean of apparently unlimited possibilities" to that truth that is the "only possibility."[17] We are to honor the truth, not the sensibilities of our hearers. This is the great homage we pay to the truth and, in our wholehearted service to the truth, we thereby testify to its veracity. The witness, says Barth, is what causes God Almighty to rejoice. Now that there is Incarnation, "not even the most important or resplendent of things . . . the smallest sigh or laugh of a man is surely more important to Him than the support of the most important institutions, the construction and the working of the most marvelous apparatus, the development of the most lofty or profound ideas."[18] God is staking a great deal in placing such truth upon the lips and in the lives of such witnesses.

Preaching is utterly dependent upon a God who raises the dead and who calls some people to tell about it. If there is no God to make the preacher's sermon "work," then the preacher is the greatest of fools. The messenger is disposable by, dispensable to, and derivative of the message. We have this treasure in earthen vessels. The treasure is more interesting and powerful than the vessel. Today's preachers find themselves in a vulnerable, dangerous situation when a pleasing personality is more important to a congregation than a truthful one, when charm and wit, warmth and "love" become more valued in a preacher than being a person who is willing to stand up and speak the truth as God has given it. The truth that is communicated through personality (Phillips Brooks's definition of preaching) is so much more important than the personality.

In a brief comment on 2 Corinthians 4:7-18, Barth says that all Christians suffer from a confession that is "an impotent stammering":

> It is provided that they always have this treasure in very earthen vessels (v. 7), that their thanks are always very equivocal, that their faith is smaller than a grain of mustard seed, that their knowledge is wrapped in obscurity, that their confession is an impotent stammering. It is provided that their praise of God will always be that "poor praise on earth" in which ultimately they can only pray that it will be received in grace, in the hope that "it will be better in heaven when I am in the choirs of the blessed." There is no perfection in it, only the deep and radical imperfection of the cry, "Abba, Father." Even the voice of this minority is only the voice of the sinful humanity justified only in Jesus Christ, which can only believe in its right as established by Him. It certainly cannot escape a wonderful similarity with its Lord who became a servant. (*CD*, IV, 2, pg. 738f.)

I believe that these theological claims have implications for a sermon design and for the way we say what we say in a sermon. There must be room. I am often accused of not being very well organized in my preaching, not doing a good job on transitions. I am now realizing that I have theological justification for what appears to some as disorder. The three-point sermon, the sermon in which we say all that needs to be said, in which we take some lively, bubbling, and difficult biblical text, and say, "I have three important things to say about this text," or, "We derive five principles from today's scripture," is the sermon which is attempting to fill space that ought to be reserved for the intrusions of the grace of God. As we have noted, we have many ways of evading the grace of God, and one of them is called the careful design and construction of our sermons! Even as Barth was forced to speak and to think dialectically in his early theology in order to keep language fluid and moving, so we preachers are forced to find a way to speak about God that continues to leave room for God to be God.

Indeed, given Barth's stress upon the sermon as a miraculous gift of God, I might have expected Barth to be an advocate and practitioner of extemporaneous preaching. In his limited ecclesiastical setting, Barth probably never experienced a preacher simply standing up and risking the work of the Holy Spirit to give a sermon in that moment. Barth had no experience, so far as I know, with Pentecostal or African-American preaching, which often revels in the exhilarating experience of extemporaneous preaching. Barth's sermons sound like polished, written pieces produced for the eye rather than the ear. And they were. He was noted for being a preacher who plodded through the written text of his sermon, rarely looking up from his manuscript. I have found that Barth's actual sermons are more energetic than the printed texts. Listening to two of Barth's few recorded sermons was helpful. Barth's preaching matched his theology of the eventful, actualistic, dynamic, and miraculous quality of revelation.[19] However, one laments that Barth had limited experience with the richness of the church's homiletical practice. He was Swiss.[20]

To be a preacher is to be called to love God more than our congregations.

Barth underscores the way in which faithful preachers exist in a rather ambiguous, potentially contentious relationship to their congregations. The congregation is the Body of Christ, that gathering whom God has convened to hear the royal proclamation, but the congregation is full of the same incomprehension, cowardice, disbelief, and rebellion that is found in any human gathering when it is assaulted by the Word. We preachers meet no resistance to the Word that was not first encountered in our own hearts. As Barth might put it, the church is just full of "religion" and therefore full of idolatry and credulity, resistance and artful dodging of the Word.[21] Though the church may say that it wants to hear the Word of God—to be addressed by their Lord and Savior—the church lies. Perhaps resistance to the Word is even more pronounced in the church because the church knows firsthand that (1) God's Word is always a summons, an address, a vocation and an obligation,[22] and (2) God has great work in mind for the church, and therefore the church is justified in feeling some fear and consternation in the face of that vocation and therefore is full of resistance to that Word. Church therefore tends to be not only training in discipleship but also in various techniques of avoiding the Word of God.

Although Barth speaks of preaching as an ecclesiastical activity—"Preaching must be done in the sphere of the church, i.e., in concrete connection with the existence and mission of the church"[23]—preaching is prior to and superior even to the church. Preaching is the peculiar speech of the church, but it is not authorized or dependent upon the church and therefore may often be experienced as against the church, in order to be for the church. The words of the sermon are not a congregationally derived Word; that Word comes from God to the church. Preachers must be willing to risk conflict, resistance, and rejection by the church in order to be faithful to the church's peculiar vocation: joyful subservience to the Word. Preachers are to serve the Word, not be acquiescent to the congregation. In a day when pastoral care for and caring about the needs of the congregation has virtually overwhelmed much of Christian ministry, Barth reminds us that the best and most loving service that we clergy can render to our people is utter subservience to the Word.

Guess Where You're Going[24]

Isaiah 6:1-8

> *By the time balloting was completed and the last bishop was elected, it was very late on Friday evening at Jurisdictional Conference, Lake Junaluska. The new bishops were hurriedly assembled behind the stage at the auditorium and the chair of the Episcopacy Committee said, "Give me your cell phone numbers, go home, and try to get some sleep. We will call you sometime before 2 a.m. and tell you where you are being sent."*
>
> *I said, "So when we are bishops and we are appointing pastors we're to say, 'Give me your cell phone number and I'll call you in the middle of the night and tell you where you are being sent?'"*
>
> *He said, "No, don't ever treat your pastors the way we're treating you."*
>
> *Well, we go back to the room. At 3:40 that morning the phone rings. The voice on the other end says, "Good morning, Will. Guess where you're going?"*
>
> *Of course, I don't have a clue.*
>
> *"Birmingham," says the voice.*
>
> *When I sang that beloved new hymn, "Here I am, Lord . . . I have heard you calling in the night . . . ," little did I know it meant 3:40 a.m.!*
>
> *Thus began the journey that brought us here.*
>
> *Now I know that most of you here this afternoon got here differently from the way that we got here, and yet all of us are Christians, disciples of Jesus, so in a sense we all got here the same way.*
>
> *Moses hiding out in Midian (Exod. 3). He killed a man back in Egypt and he's hiding out, working for his father-in-law, a "priest of Midian" who does a little sheep farming on*

the side to augment his ministerial income. Suddenly, a bush bursts into flame. A voice: "I am the LORD your God, the God of Abraham, Isaac, and Jacob. I have heard the cry of my people. I have seen their suffering. I have come down to deliver them. . . . Now guess where you're going?"

Even though Moses had no theological or oratorical gifts or training, even though he was scared to death of the mighty Pharaoh, he went, reluctantly. Who would call a tongue-tied murderer to do a prophet's work?

Little boy Samuel, asleep in the middle of the night (1 Sam. 3). At 3:40 a.m., the child hears his name called—called three times before the child gets the point. Who would call a child to do a grown-up's work? "The house of Eli will be cast down and the voice of God will be spoken to a new generation," says the voice. "Now guess where you're going?"

Young adult Isaiah (Isa. 6). He didn't want to go to church that Sunday, but his mother made him. He didn't get anything out of the sermon, couldn't stand the music. (Bach was not his bag.) Then, without warning, the heavens open, there is a vision, a voice, "Whom shall I send? Who will go for us?"

Young Isaiah says, "Not me! I've got baggage from my freshman year of college. Done things, said things I shouldn't have said."

The voice says, "Perfect. Just the sort of truth-teller my people deserve. Guess where you're going?"

See? Many of you think that you are here because you chose to be here, or your preacher made you feel guilty so you drove over to Birmingham. No. No. You are here because God put you here, in this faith, walking this way, in this ministry. You are here because God said to you, in some way or another, "Guess where you're going?" And you simply said, "Yes."

It is no mere coincidence that all of the Gospels depict Jesus as always on a journey, always on the move. It's rare that Jesus ever sits down and alights somewhere. Get the point?

Jesus walked along a road. Saw some men bending over their nets in the boat. "Follow me!" he called, "Guess where you're going?" And they followed! He took them places they would have never gone by themselves. Know anything about that? I think you do.

Back where I used to work, occasionally some student would wander in and ask me, "How did you get here?" I always found it a threatening question. I wondered if she had been sent to ask that question by the president of the university, "How on earth did you get here?"

I tell them. I was a junior in college, thinking about a lot of things, none of which included the ministry. A friend talked me into going with him to a conference, "Exploring Ministry." I drifted through most of the weekend until late Saturday night: a group of South Carolina pastors sat in a hotel room talking about their lives. These were the days of the Civil Rights Movement. One had been a victim of the Klan—had a cross burned in his yard. Another had a concrete block thrown through the back windshield of his car after a church meeting. The wife and the children of another had been snubbed, persecuted, in a small Southern town.

I, in my low undergraduate imagination, thought, "This sounds great! I didn't know that being a Methodist preacher was this much fun!"

Didn't know it at the time, because I didn't know much about Jesus or the church, but that was my, "Guess where you are going?"

Sometimes, in popular, American, evangelical Christianity, we get this wrong. We say, "Since I took Jesus into my heart . . . ," or "Since I gave my life to Jesus . . . ," or "Since I decided to follow Christ. . . ." That's not the story! The story—Moses, Samuel, Mary, Paul, Peter, you, and me—is that you don't take Jesus anywhere; he takes you places. You can't give your life to Christ. He takes it! It's not all that important that you "decided to follow Christ"; the Bible says that in Jesus Christ, God has decided for you!

Everyone is here because you got put here. For some of you, it was dramatic and life-changing, for others it was a lifetime of quiet leading and coaxing. For every last one of you, God reached in, grabbed you. You got called, summoned.

I got put here as an infant. I can't remember a time when I was not a Methodist Christian. My mother told me I was about three months old when I got baptized. Without my asking, they poured water over my head. I screamed and said, "Boy, I'm glad that's over!"

And in response the church stood and said in unison: "Guess where you're going?"

The last Bush war in Iraq, visiting with a woman, a secretary at the university. She asked me, "Got any yard work that needs to be done? Any chores around the house?" She then told me about how she had befriended an Iraqi student in graduate school at the university. Then the war started and he was cut off, totally without funds. Couldn't go home. Couldn't continue as a student. She and her husband had taken this young man into their home, and she was trying to find him odd jobs so that he could get a little money.

"What does he think about the war?" I asked.

"Oh, he thinks we're terrible and Saddam is just wonderful," she replied.

"Well, I find it interesting that you took this Iraqi into your home, wanted to care for him." With some indignation she replied, "I decided? I wanted?"

"Well, why did you do it?" I asked.

She slammed her fist down on her desk and said, "Because I'm a Christian, darn it! You think it's easy?"

Some of you are here tonight as the ordained. Clergy. But whether you be clergy or lay, we are all here as those under orders. We are here because we've been put here. We are on a mission. The word mission means "to be sent." We are not here because we were searching for deeper meaning in life and stumbled on Jesus. Not here because we did a study of all the world's great religions and decided that Methodism made the most sense. We are here because we got a call and the voice at the other end said, "Guess where you're going?"

Preachers should never talk about their children in a sermon. But, take my daughter. The week after Harriet finished the School of Social Work, she was in a wedding. A Baptist wedding. During the rehearsal party, a fellow bridesmaid said to her, "You're going to be sorry that you wasted all that time and money becoming a social worker. I got my MSW degree. Worst mistake I ever made. Made only twenty-two. I got out and got a good job."

I said, "Harriet, I can't believe she said that to you, and the first week after you had become a social worker. That's terrible!"

Harriet said, "I told her that I would be stupid to go into social work for the money. I'm a social worker because I'm called by God to do this. It's my vocation."

And I said, "The girl has had good preaching!"

Patsy and I are excited about being here and thank the Lord that in the church's wisdom we have been sent to work in a place as good as this with people as good as you. But above

> *all we're excited because we get to work with people who have been called to do good work by a good Lord.*
>
> *It isn't easy work. We are prone sometimes to fail. I'm sure that I won't get everything accomplished that I set out to do with you. You will, before we're done here, see me at my worst, and so will I see you. Thank God we're not called to be successful, or nice, or even friendly. Just faithful. We preachers didn't volunteer to get a raise in salary with each appointment, or to live in a good parsonage; we just pledged to go where we are sent. The good news is that Jesus is going places, and we are the ones who get to go with him.*
>
> *Reporter interviewed me the week after I was elected a bishop. "I've been following your career a long time," she said. "I was a bit surprised by all this."*
>
> *"You and me both," I said.*
>
> *"I never knew that this was part of your plans, that you wanted to be a bishop."*
>
> *And I thought, "You poor, ignorant thing. What I wanted? My plans? That's just not how Methodist preachers think."*
>
> *Jesus is once again on the move. Guess where we're going!*

We do not wait upon the formation of a faithful church in order faithfully to preach. Rather, we preach so that there might be, in each generation, a church. The Reformers were so convinced of the reality of original sin that they did not assume that it was sufficient to be raised in a Christian country. The Word must therefore be preached every Sunday, again and again, repeated afresh in each generation, in order for the Word to be heard and for the grip of sin gradually to be loosed.[25] The church lives and breathes and lives again by preaching, by persuasion, by repetition of the truth, not by sustained tradition or ingrained habits and practices.[26]

In the gathering storm of the mid-1930s, a courageous Brandenburg pastor addressed a meeting of pastors, calling the German Christians "anti-Christs" and Adolf Hitler (calling him by name!) "*the* German anti-Christ." Fourteen days later the pastor was suspended for "medical reasons" and given a three-month absence from his parish. A government official threatened to "take his head off." The embattled pastor wrote to Barth for advice. All this occurred some time after Barth had created a stir in Bonn by criticizing the German Christian movement.

Barth's advice to the embattled pastor is instructive.[27] After a friendly greeting, Barth launches into an attack on the poor man, telling him that he had made "a decisive mistake" in forsaking the purpose of the sermon, namely, to be an exposition of scripture, in order to give a lecture "on your views on Hitler and the German Christians." Thereby he had moved from his vocation to proclaim the gospel to the church to "the region of a subjective systematic theology." Barth ridicules this sort of thing as a "sermon" (in his letter Barth puts the word "sermon" in quotation marks). This sermon is not so much a courageous act, but a yielding to "outside pressure" of the moment. Barth repeatedly says that, while he agrees with the pastor's condemnation of the German Christians, the pastor, in forsaking his obedience to the text of scripture, has acted not too differently from the German Christians he so despises.

While he worries about national socialism "day and night," at the same time Barth chastises the pastor for using the "weapons of Saul" against them, that is, by criticizing them on their own terms—through human teaching rather than through God's Word. He then criticizes the pastor for calling his fellow Christians, even though they be heretical German Christians, "pagans." How does the pastor know this? Did some angel deliver this message to him? They are, like you, baptized. They are, even in error, brothers and sisters in Christ by their baptism. "In calling them 'pagans,' you have negated their baptism in the same way that the German Christians have tried to negate the baptism of some of their fellow Christians." (Here Barth must be thinking of the way that the German Christians argued that Jewish descent negated the baptism of some of their fellow Christians.)

"Your job, when you stand in the pulpit, is to again make well the sick church of Germany. That can be done only by the Word alone. You are to serve that Word and no other. But you can't do that if you sieze upon *Mein Kampf.* . . . Was it not a shame, each minute that you wasted with this book instead of reading the Bible?" Only scripture would give you a word to fight Hitler. Without that Word, I am not a theologian but a dumb dog. Our strongest defense against Hitler and the "pagan" followers of this man is shunning all would-be contemporary prophecies. We speak only from the Word.

"Don't you think that Paul had similar opponents?" Barth asks. "And yet Paul knew only one thing—the cross of Jesus Christ. And that he preached. Perhaps your sermon would have been less angry and more effective if you had let yourself be guided by the Word and not by your own thoughts." The Word can give you a "genuine anger" with or without "growling." I pray, says Barth, that the German church will produce courageous witnesses, but I pray that you will be "a genuine witness."

"See all of this as coming from the heart and with all good wishes from Karl Barth."

This letter represents, as starkly as any document I know, Karl Barth's view of the sovereignty of biblical preaching, particularly as represented in his *Homiletics*, and his faith. Yes, that is *faith* in the power of the Word to subdue all other competing words. I would certainly not have written such an insensitive, seemingly uncompassionate letter to a fellow preacher in such difficulty. But I doubt that my reluctance to speak like Barth is due to my warm pastoral sensitivity. More than likely it is due to my remarkable (in comparison with Barth) lack of faith in the power of the Word and respect for the sovereignty of the preaching office.[28] I do wish that Barth had been more specific that his criticism was not so much that this preacher preached against Hitler, but rather that he preached against Hitler in the wrong way. Barth certainly preached, in word and deed, against Hitler, but he did so in a way that refused to give Hitler the sovereignty that belongs only to God.

What Barth Did Not Know About the Vocation of Preaching

I fear that Barth's emphasis against homiletical rhetoric and style is, in the end, an exaggerated overemphasis. Although Barth objected to organ solos in liturgy and works of art in churches (*CD*, IV, 3, pp. 866f.), his artistic suspicions are curious when one considers Barth's self-consciously "artistic" spiraling arrangement and the vivid style of the *Church Dogmatics*. His sheer verbosity makes him quite an imaginative and even "artistic" theologian. Barth is at his best, stylistically, when using metaphor and story, sometimes excruciatingly turgid when writing in abstract theological concepts. (Blame the stylistic problems on the weighty concepts.) His language is usually vivid, concrete, and often even poetic.[29] The audio recordings of his sermons reveal him to be an energetic, though somewhat unmodulated, reader of sermons. I am sure that Barth would say that his style is demanded by his subject matter, and by the way that the Bible tends to deal with truth, not by any attempt on his part to be artistic or stylistic. Still, I think that Barth's presentation of theology makes all the more odd some of his anti-rhetorical prejudices. It is as if his actual rhetorical practice is better than his anti-rhetorical theory. He evinces a Platonic suspicion that language is a dispensable container for the truth that language means to express rather than an integral part of the truth itself. I believe that the practice of reading and preaching scripture engenders in Christian preachers the conviction that there is something about the God of Abraham, Isaac, Jacob, and Jesus that demands vividness of speech. Barth, at his best, knows this.

For instance, the Trinity, certainly as Barth presents it, is full of energy and movement. Talk about this God, in a sermon, ought also to move. There ought to be some reach from here to there, some sense of descent and ascent. My main criticism of many inexperienced preachers is the lack of movement in their sermons. There is little sense that a sermon is attempting to talk about a living being who is on the move, roaming and free, as we plod from static concept to inert principle. The form of the sermon ought to be tied to the nature of the God to whom we are listening.[30]

My main criticism of Barth's anti-rhetoric is that it is not true to the nature of one of the three forms of revelation. "In many and diverse ways God spoke. . . ." God uses a variety of devices to communicate with us. If we are going to sing the songs of Zion in a strange land, then we must be willing to sing as God has sung to us. Scripture is itself an astute, rhetorically sophisticated product. When Barth says that the Bible is "the form which God Himself in His revelation has assumed in our language, world and humanity" (*CD*, I, 1, pg. 399), this implies that the form of scripture is somehow tied to the form of the Word made flesh and is therefore also indicative of the form of preaching. Besides, it is safe to assume that scripture was preaching before it was scripture, which perhaps accounts for the Bible's creative, resourceful, wide-ranging rhetoric. Word creates world, and scripture apparently wants to create a distinctive linguistic world. In other words, it is impossible to preach biblically and to preach without intentions and effects. Rhetoric is unavoidable in any sort of public speaking, including preaching. Better to be appropriately self-conscious about rhetoric than to deny it. Better to inquire into the character of distinctively Christian rhetoric than to forswear rhetoric. Despite Barth's misgivings about self-conscious style and rhetoric, I think he has much to teach us preachers about rhetoric: Rhetoric is a secondary enterprise to theology (I'm being more Platonic than Aristotelian here). Barth's style suggests to me that the gospel calls for visceral, earthy, real speech devoid of sentimentality and full of energy. Preaching requires repetition. Some things, the really important things, must be reiterated, reworked in an ever-widening circle, restating, expanding, and then stating again.[31] Rather than to act as if we can dispense with rhetorical concerns, we preachers would do well to reflect upon the peculiar sorts of rhetoric that are demanded by the various aspects of the gospel.[32]

Preaching is not only a call to proclamation but also an exercise in the leadership of the formation of a linguistic community.

Perhaps this is the Wesleyan sanctificationist in me, but I believe that preaching is, among other things, about inculcation and indoctrination. Listeners must be trained in the disciplines of hearing the gospel, so strange is the gospel, so against their conventional means of hearing. This implies that the issue for preachers is not, "Should I try to be effective in my preaching?" but rather, "Will the effects of my preaching be responsible to the peculiar truth of Jesus Christ or not?" All sermons are "educational," "formational," for good or ill. Faithful preaching requires some amount of repetitive inculcation of the peculiar speech of the Bible or it is not being true to its intentions. Many of our biblical images and concepts cannot be translated into terms that are readily available in more congenial secular philosophies. Our peculiar speech must therefore be indoctrinated in the lives of our hearers.[33] We preachers must nurture within ourselves and our congregations a love of our peculiar words, a patient willingness not simply to state our Christian convictions but also patiently to unpack them, explain and define them, parse them as best we are able. Barth might remind us that such explanation and definition can be a dangerous business, theologically speaking, for there is always a danger that we will slip into apologetics—confusing our peculiar gospel truth for worldly wisdom, implying to our listeners that they can understand what we are saying without divine help, without conversion, attempting to find support in the world's wisdom—yet we must be teachers while we are being preachers. Barth's theology is rigorous and demanding training in the art of using Christian speech properly, and for Barth to tell us preachers that we ought not to have rhetorical goals and ought not to trouble ourselves over linguistic effects is rather disingenuous of a writer whose writing demands not only that we agree with him but that we be converted into his peculiar way of talking. And Barth's peculiar way of talking is not only due to his attentiveness to the speech of God but also due to his desire to, with his theology, assault the pathologies of twentieth-century German-speaking Christendom.

How well I remember, as a seminarian, hearing a sermon by Ralph Abernathy during the days of the Civil Rights Movement. Abernathy had been asked to speak on a fairly innocuous subject like, "The Next Step in Civil Rights." Instead he came and preached on "Redemption." Abernathy opened up the Civil Rights struggle and redescribed it in theological terms, transforming it from being just another contemporary political struggle into being a spiritual battle, a struggle against the principalities and the powers, an opportunity to experience the lordship of Christ. At one point in the sermon he reflected upon the peculiar Christian word "redemption." Abernathy noted that redemption is a word that Christians stole from the secular world, but that it was made our own, and given utterly unique content, by the sacrifice of Christ on the cross. There, we saw redemption as a gift of God, as a struggle with the principalities and powers that caused the suffering of God. In our redemption on the cross we received a sign that God was not above the fray but in it, with us, for us, on the side of the slaves who long for redemption. Abernathy then repeated the word "redemption" at least twenty times, pronouncing it in different ways, putting the stress first on one syllable then another, his voice growing in volume each time he said it until the sermon ended in a great shout of celebration around the word, "redemption." It was a stunning rhetorical performance, a joyous thanksgiving for, and exercise of, the peculiar speech of Christians, a conversion of an audience that wanted a political speech and got a Christian sermon. Biblical heralds did not only want to say something with their words but also wanted to do something. Whether he openly admits it or not, so does Barth. So do all of us preachers who are worth our salt.

Walter Brueggemann says that preaching involves the nurturance of "alternative modes of speech," and that

> the task and possibility of preaching is to open out the good news of the gospel with alternative modes of speech—speech that is dramatic, artistic, capable of inviting persons to join in another conversation, free of the reason of technique, unencumbered by ontologies that grow abstract, unembarrassed about concreteness. Such speech, when heard in freedom, assaults imagination and pushes out the presumed world in which most of us are trapped. Reduced speech leads to reduced lives. Sunday morning is the practice of a counterlife through counterspeech. The church on Sunday morning, or whenever it engages in its odd speech, may be the last place left in our society for imaginative speech that permits people to enter into new worlds of faith and to participate in joyous obedient life.[34]

Barth's sermons, particularly his later prison sermons, seem to be intent in producing a linguistic community that is careful, understated, deliberative, and graciously upbeat. I find such homiletics appealing, but we ought to note that it is only one type of rhetorical community. Historian Harry Stout has shown how the evangelist George Whitefield, by engaging in open-air preaching, not only developed a new style of preaching that was required for extramural preaching in the open air but also, through such loud, dramatic preaching, formed a new sort of church.[35] Preaching in the open air, says Stout, demanded that Whitefield hold his audiences through entertainment, that he project his voice into as wide a range as possible, that he out-shout competing noise and clamor. It takes physical strength and personal courage to project one's voice into a milling crowd of gaping onlookers. One had to make one's sermon interesting, explosive, and engaging through illustrations and connections. This new kind of preaching produced a new practice of the gospel that Stout says was a strong influence on American evangelicalism to this day.

While it would be wrong to make Whitefield's open-air preaching the norm and standard for all Christian preaching, I wonder if it is also wrong to make the European, Barthian, parochial, in-house preaching (even as he preached in nonparochial settings like the Basel jail) the norm. Barth's *Dogmatics* is always unashamedly *Church* discourse for the sake of the church, but ought preaching be so exclusively parochial? Even in a Sunday congregation, is there not some need for entertainment, illustration, and attempts to retain our hearers? We are commanded by Christ to project our speech beyond the boundaries of the church. The Risen Christ commands that we "go . . . make disciples . . ." (Matt. 28). All Christian preaching is public speech. Do not the evangelical demands of the gospel necessitate a homiletical practice that also thrusts itself into the world with speech that is more assertive and demanding than the image of a herald making an announcement? Timid preaching produces a timid, too deferential and respectful church. Preaching that is comprehended only within the cloistered congregation of the knowledgeable, the well-formed, and the virtuously Christian is bound to be dull.

Thomas G. Long also points out that *the Barthian herald image, in its stress upon preaching as an act of God, an event of God's sole creation rather than ours, ironically "tends to undermine almost all serious thinking about every practical aspect of creating sermons."*[36]

In its stress upon God as the real and only preacher, "the role of the preacher is almost driven from sight." Barth's theological emphasis is, in part, a reaction against the Schleiermachian tendency to tuck homiletics over in the area of "practical theology," that is, second-rate theology, theology for practitioners who could not be bothered by the largely theoretical concerns of dogmatics. Yet in Barth's disdain for practical concerns about sermon construction, delivery, and mechanics, Barth could unintentionally foster the attitude that these practical matters have no theological import.

There is a great difference between saying that the preacher ought not to attempt fully to control and predict the effects of the sermon, ought not to try to be the sole force in the sermon's effectiveness and say that the preacher is not responsible for the sermon. God may be the major actor in a sermon, but the preacher ought not to deny his or her God-given responsibility as well. To be called to be a preacher is to have the vocation not only to guard and protect the beloved words of our faith but also to use those words well for the purposes for which they were intended by God. It is to respect the power that is delivered over to us, to feel a sacred responsibility to the demands of the biblical text, as well as a responsibility to tell the truth within our congregational context.

For instance, Barth states so well that the word "Father," when applied to God, is an analogy that God has applied to us, graciously given us whereby we know God in a way that we could not have known without this gift. We have not, in calling God "Father," taken our human experiences of fatherhood and projected them upon God, rather God has taken up a word that has no theological significance before the Word made Flesh teaches us to address God as "Our Father. . . ." The biblical story of God gives this word meaning that it would not have had without that story. In hearing that story, in using the word "Father" in the context of the gospel, we are being trained to use that word to appropriately describe the nature of the God who has come to us as Father, Son, and Holy Spirit. This word, applied to God, requires not simply that we understand it but rather that we be transformed, converted by using it. This word does not simply speak to my world but significantly enlarges and changes my world. Christian language has a transformative, "political" (that is, Christian speech as an exercise of power) significance that Barth does not adequately note in assigning to that speech the role of heralding and announcing.

Paul calls us "stewards of the mysteries of God." Perhaps *steward*, at this point in our discussion, is a more helpful metaphor than *herald*. These holy mysteries are God's mystery, but God has graciously called us to be stewards of this mystery. A good steward has gratitude for the trust that God has placed in his or her hands. A good steward respects the gift, does not use the powerful gift for personal gain, and does not abuse the trust of the Master. In many of the parables that Jesus told about stewardship, it is clear that the Master holds the stewards accountable for the talents that have been given to the stewards, that the Master means for the stewards to boldly and even rather recklessly invest and use the gifts that have been given in order that God might be glorified.

When we study homiletics, when we carefully craft and prepare our sermons, when we attentively work with the biblical text, attempting to replicate the style and the effects of that text in our sermons, when we thoughtfully and prayerfully consider the possible effects of how we say what we say, we are not necessarily imposing our selfish motives upon the message, nor are we perverting the pure word that we are called to deliver. Rather, the message that has been entrusted to us is of such momentousness that we are required to handle such truth skillfully. The irresponsibility of a sloppily prepared sermon ought not to be blamed upon God. It is part of our vocation carefully to prepare.

It seems ridiculous of me to say this about a complex, dynamic theologian like Barth (and one who wrote so copiously about so much), but his "herald" image, and its implications for preaching, tend to be reductionistic, most "unbarthian" in the single-minded stress upon one biblical metaphor for preaching to the almost total exclusion of others.

Long also wonders whether *Barth's herald image "fails to take adequate account of the context of preaching."*[37] Sometimes a sermon fails to hit a target because it is not aimed, because the preacher has not taken account of the specific cultural and temporal context in which the eternal Word is proclaimed. The congregation shapes the proclamation in subtle but powerful ways, and should. The gospel belongs not just to the preacher but to the whole People of God. We preach on Sunday so that the whole church can preach the rest of the week. Barth tends to speak of "proclamation" in such a way that he seems to imply that this is limited to the sermons of the preacher and not to the witness of the whole church. In our sermons we are "equipping the saints" (Eph. 5–6), so that the specific challenges and needs, the specific location and situation of the saints are appropriate considerations in the construction and delivery of sermons. When Barth preaches dozens of sermons to prisoners in the Basel jail and only rarely refers to the fact that these people are in jail, when Barth says that we must preach, even in the wreckage and misery of World War II "as if nothing happened," then we again are right to wonder whether Barth's purported indifference to the context of preaching is a mistake.

I felt it necessary to begin this study of Barth with a consideration of Barth's biography. What Barth said cannot be adequately understood without knowing something about when Barth said what he said and where he was when he said it. Fair questions about Barth are, Who was his audience? Who were his opponents? Who would have gladly heard Barth, and who would have been offended by him? Who were his antecedents? We are not abusing Barth's thought when we attempt to contextualize him; nor are we abusing a text when we attempt to contextualize it in the congregational context.

When I first read Barth in a college religion class, I was not the least moved by what he had to say. That next summer a pastor in Germany told me of how he, as a young pastor in the 1930s in Westphalia, would excitedly hurry home from the post office, clutching in his eager hands the newest volume of Barth's *Church Dogmatics*, how he would then read all night long until the dawn, too excited and encouraged to stop reading. "Barth gave me the strength to go on when the sky was so dark," he said. I reread Barth with a new ear, having contextualized him.

Barth's ecclesiology may not adequately support the homiletics that Barth demands.

The gathered congregation, the *ecclesia*, is the essential context for preaching. Only within the context of the church do we hear something so strange as the gospel and do we find the resources there for sustained listening to such a strange word. In one of his prison sermons Barth says, "We gathered here this Sunday morning to hear this word: By grace you have been saved! Whatever else we do, praying and singing, is but an answer to this word spoken to us by God himself. The prophets and apostles wrote a strange book, called the Bible, for the very purpose of testifying to this fact before mankind. The Bible alone contains this sentence. We do not read it in Kant or in Schopenhauer, or in any book of natural or secular history, and certainly not in any novel, but in the Bible alone. In order to hear this word we need what is called the Church—the company of Christians, of human beings called and willing to listen together to the Bible and through it to the word of God."[38] The church is that essential place where we are called together to listen.

Barth does not say much more about the church than that the church is a place to listen. In *Resident Aliens*, Hauerwas and I asked why Barth did not have a more sectarian view of the church. His theology suggests a rather radical, sectarian ecclesiology, but Barth never developed that ecclesiology, never seemed too interested in speculating on a different way of being the church than the church as it was presented to him in Germany and Switzerland. In his *Homiletics*, Barth says, "The church is not a tool to uphold the world or to further its progress. It is not an instrument to serve either what is old or what is new. The church and preaching are not ambulances on the battlefield of life." These are wonderfully Barthian statements in their wit and in their high view of preaching. But then he follows that "preaching must not attempt to set up an ideal community, whether of soul or heart or spirit."[39] I wonder if his fear of attempts "to set up an ideal community" led Barth to forsake thinking about the institutional forms of the church. One can be concerned about the church being more faithful in its form and its life together without becoming idolatrous or idealistic in one's thought of the church.

Barth formulates his doctrine of the church during his discussion of the doctrine of election (*CD*, II, 2, par. 34) and the doctrine of reconciliation (*CD*, IV, 1, par. 62; IV, 2, par. 67), thus stressing the church as God's new creation. Yet one of his most interesting sections on the church is in *CD*, I, 2, 215ff. (when Barth is supposed to be talking about the Word of God), also stressing the church as God's creation. Barth says, in *CD*, IV, 1, pg.

644, that thinking about the church is an exposition of the third article of the creed, "I believe in the Holy Spirit," which includes "I believe in the church." The church is the creation of the free working of the Spirit, that is, the Spirit of the actively seeking, lively person of Jesus Christ, who always seeks and saves and thereby calls forth a community (*CD*, IV, 1, pg. 647). The church is never, says Barth, "a human possibility," not the result of human striving, but the result of the free, surprising movement of the Holy Spirit. Thus, our relationship to the church is one of faith. It takes faith to apprehend the church because the church is a theological result of the movement of the Holy Spirit.

And yet (thinking dialectically!), the church also has human form and through the Holy Spirit has become a "phenomenon of world history" (*CD*, IV, 1, pg. 652). Any limp Docetism is thus rejected; we must not attempt at any time to "look penetratingly through this form, as though it was only something transparent and the real Church had to be sought behind it" (*CD*, IV, 1, pp. 653ff.). (Curiously, as we have noted, this is the way we often deal with biblical texts.) Our thought about the church must avoid "refuge from it in a kind of wonderland" (*CD*, IV, 1, pg. 654).

And yet (thinking dialectically) we must not take the Schleiermachian path of reducing the church to some simply historical, psychological or sociological explanation (*CD*, IV, 1, pp. 652, 656). Above all, we must not join with the Roman Catholics in celebrating the visibility of the church, identifying our church as the whole reality of the church (*CD*, IV, 1, pg. 658). When asked, in 1956, about the eternality of the church, Barth replied, "Please not eternally this church, which is so terribly boring to people even on earth."[40]

Barth believes that the church is always threatened by either secularization or sacralization of itself.[41] The only safeguard the church has is constant listening to Jesus Christ. The church is constantly misunderstood by the world, because the world does not understand the One who is head of the church, and the church must take care not to try to lessen the distance between its Lord and the world's lordlets. Only the church's Lord can do that. Yet Barth stresses even more that the church is constantly misunderstood by itself, because the One who is its head is the One who must constantly confront the church. That confrontation cannot be grasped, codified, or systematized because Christ's specific demands vary according to time and place. And yet it can be said that all church thought must be shaped under the church's calling to service, and all church thought is derived from the church's prayer and worship where the living Christ is present. The church's thought is always in motion because the church's Lord is living, vibrant, and moving.[42] In 1946, after confessing his "disgust" at the present church, Barth said that "in the church one is only like a bird in a cage, bumping against the bars time and again. Something greater is at stake than our little bit of preaching, namely the Kingdom of God."[43]

Barth not only spoke of revelation as an "event" but also called the church an "event." The church is not an institution, a form, a continuing community. The church is created afresh in each generation through conversation with the Word:

As the church that is founded on the apostolic word, the church is never a given factor. It has to be repeatedly founded anew by an apostolic word. It can exist only in the event of the speaking and hearing of this apostolic word as God's Word. Thus the church is an institution only as an invitation, as a waiting for the church. In the church we are always on the way to the event of the church. Thus the ministry as the stepping forth of individuals is an act which must repeatedly become a reality by the calling of God. Ordination is a canonical act, but its significance is as a pointer to God's calling to the extent that in ordination the ordained come to hear the Word of God, which, however, they must constantly hear afresh.[44]

While this "event" language is exhilarating, and while we preachers may be pleased (or dismayed) that Barth believes that the church is, in a sense, preached into existence afresh in each generation, I worry that this sort of thinking might lead us to neglect concern with the specific embodiment of the faith that is called the church. At heart the church may indeed be an "event" of faith, but we pastors also know the church as a plodding hippopotamus in the mud (T. S. Eliot) who must not only be preached to but worked with in the mire of life if it is to be faithfully served. We preachers also experience ourselves in the church as birds in a cage, beating our wings against the bars.

He called his *magnum opus Church Dogmatics*, but then presents a rather disembodied theology. The Word of God comes to the church, shatters the church, disturbs the church from without, and in no sense arises from or resides in the church. This Barthian view of the detached Word is different from my own pastoral experience and also differs from the claims of an incarnational faith. We have been given not only a free and eventful Word but also an embodied Word, and we ignore the implications and potential dangers of the form of the Word's embodiment to our peril. Here Barth's disinterest in the history of Jesus seems to have a counterpart in his lack of interest in the institutional, organizational embodied context of the church. Most of us pastors spend our lives not only preaching the sovereign Word but also caring for congregations, which is also an aspect of our preaching. Paul's letters are not only (in fact rather rarely) grand theological exposition but also nitty-gritty pastoral care of specific, forlorn congregations whom Paul unashamedly calls "the Body of Christ." "Now you are the Body of Christ and members of it," Paul says. "Now act more like you are called to be," Paul implies. The church, even in its sorry state and weakness, plays too little role in Barth's homiletic.

Nicholas Healy has a good, critical discussion of Barth's ecclesiology that has homiletical implications.[45] Barth gives us, in Healy's words, three "rules for any ecclesiology." (1) The creedal rule: the church is to be viewed in faith, as a matter of belief (*CD*, IV, 1, pg. 656). (2) The human agency rule: the church is a concrete, visible form of human activity. (3) All thinking about the church is governed by Christology. Just as we can only think about humanity by beginning with Christ, so we can only think about the church by beginning with Christ. We must begin not with a theory of human organization but with the work of the person of Jesus Christ as presented in scripture. He is the center of the circle of theology, as we have noted, and all thought about the church must discipline itself to this center, the Christ, "the source and norm of all truth" (*CD*, II, 2, pg. 4).[46] Any thought about the church that is not christological is not theological and therefore not ecclesiological (*CD*, IV, 1, pg. 666).

In beginning christologically, Barth begins his thought on the church with the eternal election of humanity in Jesus Christ. Before creation there was election, God's determination to be our God. "We can never be too comprehensive as we attempt to understand the election of Jesus as the beginning of all things," says Barth, including the beginning of the church (*CD*, II, 2, pg. 126). That gracious election was done quite independently of anything that we did; certainly it was not based on our response or consent. Our relationship to God, our salvation, is already accomplished as a work of God before creation (see *CD*, IV, 2, pp. 276, 518ff.). If we begin to think about the church sociologically, we are beginning with creation rather than with the prior matter of election, and we will never get from there to here, the church as an aspect of God's eternal election of us in Christ. In the church, and in the doctrine of election, we learn just how radical and far-reaching is the seemingly innocuous statement, "God is love."

Thus quite logically, and quite early in the *Church Dogmatics*, Barth speaks, with Paul (1 Cor. 12:12; Eph. 1:23), of the church as "the Body of Christ" (*CD*, I, 2, pp. 215 ff.). That "body" is not a sociological body but the Body of Christ, that is, a dead, crucified body that is dead without the Holy Spirit. By the Resurrection that Body is made alive through the Holy Spirit (his link of the third article of the creed).

What Barth is avoiding here, says Healy, is some "ecclesial essence" that the church "has," whereby it can be called the Body of Christ. Grace is not ours to own through "apostolic succession," the magisterium, the will of the majority, pure biblical preaching, or any other humanly held possession. The church, humanly viewed, is a place of human sin and little more (*CD*, IV, 3.2, pg. 760). Yet through the event of the Holy Spirit, this sinful gathering really, truly becomes the Body of Christ (*CD*, IV, 1, pg. 650).

The work of the church is "witness," "the sum of what the Christian community has to render."[47] The church, having witnessed God turning to us, in response turns toward the world in speech and action as a witness to the God who is known as God *pro nobis*.[48] The peculiar service of the church is proclamation in the whole life of each of its members.[49] We are to speak the "Yes" that we have witnessed in Jesus Christ. We are, as the church, not the new reality; we are a sign of the new reality. As the church we point to a fact that, though not the kingdom of God as the church, has included the church and made the church, with all its flaws, a likeness of that fact.[50] Yet even though the church is totally dependent upon the Holy Spirit to make it a true "sign," even though the church in no way actively mediates or causes the action or content of the gospel, that to which the sign points, Barth can still say of the church that it is indeed "the earthly-historical existence form of Jesus Christ."[51]

Whereas proclamation is the central role for the church, that is only a human work in response to, and in preparation for the divine work of witness. Whereas, in preaching, there is a limited place for analysis of the sociological condition of those to whom the Word is preached, and a place for some pastoral concern about the health of the institution of the church, none of that is as important as the church as a divine work. We are therefore never to be overly troubled about the success of the church or what form our proclamation should take.[52] Success in the preaching of the church or in the church's life is not our task. Success is a work of the Holy Spirit.

Furthermore, we are constantly to be reminded that Barth's view of the divine address to humanity is universal in scope and not limited to those inside the walls of the church.[53] In fact, being in the walls of the church often means that one has only developed a more complex defense against the Word of God! This means that, no matter how much Barth claims for the necessity of and the ultimate triumph of God in the church, there is always this chastening reminder that God is free, even of the church, that scripture is master of the church, not scripture's servant, that the Magisterium of Rome is no final word.

Hauerwas wonders just how "catholic" Barth's ecclesiology is. I think that Reinhardt Hütter argues well that Barth's ecclesiology is questionable. Barth does not show how the church exists in its embodied, incarnate form.[54] Barth will not let the church be the binding or sole medium where proclamation is done or received. Yet I do think that Barth is a lively corrective to some of the more lapidary ecclesiologies that characterize much of our thinking about the church. Even as preaching is a miracle, an event, a gift, so is the church in Barth. Preaching is prior to, and gives birth to, the church, and preaching is also, in its exclusive attachment to the three forms of proclamation, free of the church and superior to (I suppose Barth would put it this way) the church. As Barth says, "It is the Spirit who upholds the community. . . . But according to the defiant saying in Eph. 6:17, that 'sword of the Spirit' which protects and defends [the community] is the Word of God."[55]

In my present situation as a bishop of the church, I am more convinced than ever that the church is a fallen institution and, if there is a faithful church at any point in our time, then it is a gift, an act of redemption in which God makes our time God's time. Is this sort of Barthian actualism too episodic and eventful? No, because in my present situation as a bishop of the church I see that, by the grace of God, church keeps happening, keeps being offered to us as undeserved, but nevertheless real gift. The "event" language is not used by Barth to stress the discontinuity and the absence of God's presence to the church, but rather to keep stressing that this miraculous presence is never a human possession or achievement. The church's task is not to be established, not to be secure in its life, not even to provide a warm community of disciplined practices for otherwise lonely people. The church is a witness to Jesus Christ. It is the boney finger of John the Baptist that points the world to Christ, so it ought not to be too depressed about its failure to be the very Body of Christ. In the church our greatest prayer ought to be to recognize and acknowledge the church when it happens and to be willing to be subsumed into that church. As Barth wrote in the preface to his very first *Church Dogmatics*, "I believe that to the very day of judgment we shall wait in vain for an Evangelical Church which takes itself seriously unless we are prepared to attempt in all modesty to take the risk of being such a Church in our own situation and to the best of our ability."[56]

Barth, in his introduction to *Romans*, says that the church's proclamation is "no more than a crater formed by the explosion of a shell and seeks to be no more than a void in which the Gospel reveals itself. The people of Christ, His community, know that no sacred word or work or thing exists in its own right: they know only those words and works and things which by their negation are sign-posts to the Holy One."[57] The church "happens" (*geschieht*), it is an "event" (*Ereignis*) as the Holy Spirit draws us into the resurrection.[58] While I am invigorated by this chastened ecclesiology, I do wonder, with Hauerwas, whether "Barth's ecclesiology is sufficient to sustain the witness that he thought was intrinsic to Christianity."[59] It is hard to imagine anyone developing the habits required to theologize with Barth without the church engendering those habits. Say what you will about my church being woefully inept, it at least had the resources to produce Karl Barth and his *Church Dogmatics*, to introduce me to Barth and to enable me to read him with some degree of comprehension. I cannot imagine acquiring the habit of Barth without the church forcing me to do so.

Also, I wonder whether Barth writes within a world that is still so vestigially Constantinian that he did not fully perceive what disestablishment and relinquishment would one day (our day) look like. Just as Barth fought religious subjectivity with his critically realistic theology, I wonder if we might also fight this foe with a renewed emphasis on the church, the Body of Christ, as essential for Christian knowing and living. The post–William James religion-as-subjectivity was the last attempt on the part of many to have a thoroughly disembodied Christ. We therefore may be in a situation in which it is theologically important for us to take seriously that which Barth did not—namely, the form, function, and health of the institutional church. It is difficult to imagine Barth agreeing with me on this, but my only retort would be, "My generation may be among the first in centuries to realize that without the institutional embodiment of the faith there is no imaginable way for the Word to dwell among us richly and for this faith to flourish."

"Christianity in the form we have known it up to now" is ending, wrote Barth as early as 1935.[60] And toward the end of the *Dogmatics,* Barth reiterated, "The Christian West no longer exists."[61] Barth certainly knew that Christendom was gone and that its demise presented a new challenge for Christian proclamation:

> The idea of a Christianity which is automatically given and received with the rest of our inheritance has now become historically impossible, no matter how tenaciously it may linger. . . . The Christian West, i.e., the society in which Christian and non-Christian existence came together, or seemed to do so, no longer exists either in the city or in the peace of the remotest hamlet. . . . A man can no longer be brought up as a member of it. His Christianity can no longer derive from the fact that he is a member of it. Whether he likes it or not, therefore, he is asked to-day whether or not this Christianity of his has some other basis than the scrap of tradition which may still remain as an anachronistic relic. It may thus be argued that to-day even from the historical standpoint there can be no escaping the startling recognition that a man's being as a Christian is either grounded in his vocation or it is simply an illusion which seems beautiful perhaps in the after-glow of a time vanished beyond recall.[62]

Barth goes on, in this same passage, to ridicule those old liberal theologians who continue to try to work within the ruin, attempting to rummage around in the wreckage of Christendom to find a few vestigially Christian principles that might even yet make the faith worth believing without that faith being an act of God.

Until I read this passage I did not know how much Hauerwas and I had been influenced by Barth in our *Resident Aliens.*[63] I would simply add that in my reading of this announcement of the demise of Christendom, there is no grief but rather a joyful sense that Christianity, having lost so many of the intellectual and cultural props that were once provided by an allegedly "Christian culture," is now free to proclaim the gospel utterly dependent upon God for the reception of that gospel, which creates the distinctive culture called "church." Now that Christendom is dead, we no longer have to trouble ourselves over the unbiblical question, "Is there a God?" We can now joyfully witness to the talkative, peculiar living God who is there. We can recover the significance of speaking with a God who is Trinitarian.

I fear that theological conservatives' attempts to restore some of the vestiges of the "Christian culture" only play into the enemy's hands, admitting that we cannot communicate the faith without the cultural, political props to sustain us. Barth surely put this in my head:

> Certainly great membership rolls and good attendances and full churches and halls (and even lecture rooms) are facts which naturally impress us—who can fail to be impressed by them?—but what do they really have to do with the truth? . . . The Scribes and Pharisees were certainly in a majority against Jesus and His disciples, and yet they were wrong. . . . The truth may undoubtedly lie with the minority. . . . It may lie only with the two or three gathered together (Mt. 18:20) in the name of Jesus Christ. That they number several millions is of no avail to those who are not gathered in His name. The whole legitimacy of the Reformation rests upon this possibility. There are some who go further and boldly affirm that the truth will very likely, indeed will fairly (or most) certainly, be found within the minority. An empty church is regarded as a comforting indication

and prejudice in favour of the fact that the pure Gospel is proclaimed in it. . . . In certain circumstances does it not involve a genuine pleasure and exaltation to be in the minority . . . the little flock to which it is the Father's good pleasure to give the kingdom, which is therefore a kind of advance guard of God? In Schiller's words: "What is majority? Majority is folly." Good sense is never found but with the few. But here again we must be careful. There have been minorities whose resistance to the majority has not been legitimate because their cause has had nothing whatever to do with the truth. . . . In the history of the Church . . . there have been far too many little movements of reform instigated by men who appealed readily to the fact that a majority proves nothing, that truth and the good God are more likely to be on the side of the small and even the smallest battalions, and yet in the long run they proved to be no more lasting than a kind of carnival procession. . . . There was something far wrong when the little flock of Lk. 12 became the imperial world-Church Constantine, and many a minority in the Church has lost more than it has gained by becoming a majority, or a big Church instead of small. But it is not fundamentally the case that when the few become many the truth also becomes error. (*CD*, IV, 1, pp. 709f.; cf. also III, 2, pg. 522)

Barth was at least concerned enough with the catholic faithfulness of the church to write the Barmen Declaration in defense of the sanctity and freedom of the church to listen to the Word of God rather than any other words. He also preached that Word no matter what.[64]

And when Barth writes his *Homiletics*, he rejects any positioning, any place to stand except in the church:

The conformity of preaching to revelation cannot be defined in terms of any philosophy and is not a feature that we can confer, we can only consider that what we have here is a specific event that is given to us by grace. Aware of our impotence regarding it, we see that we are directed to a place which we have not first to discover, which we have not to select from any philosophical, political, or aesthetic standpoint, but into which we are simply forced, since it is the only place at which we can stand. This place is the church.[65]

And Barth declares that the church, this "unique place," is the whole point of preaching:

Where the Word of reconciliation creates human hearers for itself, there is the church, the *kyriake ekklesia*, the congregation of those whom the Lord has called. Only in this place where we are set by revelation can there be legitimate preaching, nor will this be on the basis of reflection on humanity, on the situation of the natural and historical cosmos, or the like. Only because the call of revelation goes out and people hear it does the church come into being. In preaching, conformity to the church follows conformity to revelation. Because preaching is done in this unique place to which the Word of the twofold advent comes and in which we are set with no cooperation on our part, preaching conforms to revelation for no reason that we can give.[66]

Yet it is not clear that the church, the actual embodiment of the living Word, plays any material role in Barth's homiletic. His stress on the sovereignty and freedom of the word as well as his attempt to preach "as if nothing happened," without regard to the demands of the listeners, will not let concerns about the shape and the politics of the church, or the interaction between the preacher and the congregation, or the role of the congregation as herald, play a large role in his homiletic.

When I spent a few months preaching at a local prison, I quite naturally thought of Barth and his sermons in *Deliverance to the Captives*, and so I quite naturally turned to those sermons for guidance. And yet I was struck by Barth's studied effort not to mention, in his sermons, that he was preaching to incarcerated men. I felt that there was no way I could preach good news to the captives in my particular jail without acknowledging, at least to myself and perhaps sometimes in my sermons, that they were all men, all young, nearly all African-American, nearly all failures in the educational system that had produced me, nearly all poor, and nearly all bereft of any ecclesial formation. The Word has become flesh, our flesh.

Perhaps Barth's lack of ecclesiological reflection was a limitation of Barth's Swiss background. The only church in which Barth appears to have had any experience was the Swiss Reformed Church, the national church of his native land, along with his adversary, the Roman Catholic Church of Germany. He therefore knew firsthand only a quasi-national church. This national church mentality lives on in contemporary preachers who act as if someone has ordained them to preach in a way that is generally relevant and generally comprehensible in the culture at large. They thus assume that their sermons ought to be for anyone and everyone, rather than that their sermons ought to, in some measure, "equip the saints" (Eph. 6).

In a discussion of Matthew 28:16-20, Barth was severely critical of his national church, the church that is no longer distinctive and different but now merely generalized Christendom for anybody and everybody:

> [The church] constitutes . . . a new people in which the members of all peoples do not merely meet but are united. Gathered to it, men are first members of this new people, i.e., Christians, and only then, without disloyalty to their derivation but above all without compromising their unity, are they members of the different nations. A Church whose members sought to regard and conduct themselves first and decisively as members of their own nation and only then as Christians, i.e., a national Church in the strict and serious sense, would necessarily be a sick Church, since it would resist the witness to the fellowship of all nations, not helping to achieve this but making it if anything more difficult. The community which is true to its witness, while it does not question its particular membership of and responsibility to this or that nation, recognizes the primacy of its own citizenship over all others, and eo ipso is not merely one of the uniting factors in the common life of humanity, but the such factor. (*CD*, IV, 3, pp. 874, 899)

I see a tension here among what Barth knows the church ought to be, the theological demand upon the institution of the church, and his unwillingness to ponder the specific institutional embodiment of his theological claims. What difference would it have made to his *Dogmatics* if Barth had known the African-American church that I knew in the days before the Civil Rights Movement in the South, or the South American Pentecostal churches, or the post-apartheid church in South Africa, or for that matter the currently (in my estimate) demoralized Swiss Reformed Church? Barth should have spent more time in careful, theologically informed, critical analysis of the differing demands of the churches in his day. If he had performed such analysis, perhaps Barth would be more listened to today, perhaps his own Swiss Reformed Church would not be in its considerably diminished state.

Let's face it. All of us preachers are placed, by the act of preaching, in the same Barthian tension between the church as it ought to be and the church as it is. Barth had to keep writing theology, patiently circling each doctrine of the church, then circling around again, rather than waiting for the church to catch up with his thought. Likewise, we cannot be faithful preachers without the gift of patience. True homiletical patience is a gift of faith in a God who says what we ourselves can never say, and creates through the Word that which we will never speak into being. Preaching that demands results, preaching that insists upon confirmation within the congregation, preaching that wants to be effective, or hankers for undeniable institutional embodiment in a faithful church is preaching that denies the absolute sovereignty and divinity of the Eternal Word. Faithful preaching will not allow the church, either in its present form, or in its historical form, to define our preaching today as a failure. We keep preaching, patiently saying what we hear God say, because we must not let our hearers, for any of their occasional virtues, define the significance of our preaching. Only God knows what good our preaching does; only God does what good our preaching does.

We must pray for patience, otherwise we will be tempted to foreshorten the gospel into a set of words that get predictable results. Our preaching can never be something we design and control; it can only be an offering to God, confident that God loves a cheerful giver, that God is able to take our pitiful homiletical gifts and miraculously make them more than we could with our own devices. Our sermons end *(eschatos)*, and have their end *(telos)* only at the very end when Jesus shall have the last word. And he shall reign, despite us.

Yet any misgivings that we have about Barth's ecclesiology should be contextualized by the recognition that the last bombshell that Barth dropped on the theologians' playground was in 1967 when he gave permission to publish CD, IV, 4, shortly before his death. There Barth has a scathing rejection of the practice of infant baptism not only because he considered the practice to be unbiblical but also because it represents a cultural accommodation and compromise for the church he knew we ought to be.

We preachers must contextualize our message, despite Barth's warning against inappropriate concern over the context of our preaching. Preachers are called to deliver a message, lovingly to nurture and greatly to respect the pure gospel message. But the gospel message, being an incarnational event, is never "pure." It is always the enfleshment of the Word here, now, to a specific people in a specific time and place. The Christian faith, unlike, say, Islam, has translated its message into hundreds of languages. The gospel is the same message for all, but it cannot be repeated in exactly the same way to all, or it will be an inaudible message. God's miraculous intervention in preaching need not be reduced to the level of translating Greek to English. The gospel resists being utterly transcendent. God loves us enough to call us by our own names.

The recent preoccupation with "inductive preaching" seems to have subsided. Many of the insights of the inductive movement in homiletics were valid and interesting. Preaching must sometimes be an indirect enterprise, "overheard" (Fred Craddock's phrase), rather than directly undertaken; a matter of the heart, not only of the head; a connection with living human experience rather than a deductive assertion of a set of abstract propositions. Yet inductive preaching, in my experience, seems to be most effective among congregations of a certain age that have heard and reheard the gospel, who know the gospel stories, who have been fully indoctrinated into the Christian faith and now enjoy hearing that faith proclaimed in a way that gives them some unexpected insight, or unaccustomed angle of vision on the well-known faith. In short, inductive preaching seems to work best among older, well-formed-in-the-faith congregations, congregations that few of us preachers preach to today.

The similar infatuation with narrative preaching also seems to be in decline. Attempts to narrate the gospel exclusively as story, to make contact with the listeners' stories, evocatively to make it all narrative, tend not to do justice to the complex substance of the gospel or even the needs of the listeners. We are not only telling them stories, in preaching, but also inculcating them into a counter story to the world's stories, the story that is the gospel of Christ. Today's congregations are more than likely ill-formed in the faith, have not heard the first time, do not know the stories of the faith. They are not in need of inductive awakening but rather theological formation. Inductive preaching, narrative preaching, which is essentially evocative preaching, will be less helpful among new Christians, among young Christians, than formative, unashamedly doctrinal, and transformative preaching. (In my experience, inductive homiletical methods are most enthusiastically embraced among churches that are not evangelizing and therefore who are graying and declining.) Therefore more time will need to be taken reiterating the faith, patiently reasserting the distinctive vocabulary of the gospel, telling the stories that scripture has told us. Barth is the quintessential deductive, creatively expository preacher, and therefore a preacher for the present age, even though he did not intend to be.

In my experience, generational, contextual factors account for the varying length of sermons in different congregations. The older the congregation, the larger percentage of members who are over fifty, the shorter the sermon will be. The younger the congregation, the longer the sermon will be. We have a generation who knows that they do not know, who knows that the gospel is so strange, so against their natural inclination, so countercultural, that they must be willing to listen, to take some time with the gospel, to learn what they do not know. I predict that sermons will become less inductive, less evocative, and more didactic and doctrinal because that is what is needed by many in the present moment.[67]

And if I am right in this prediction, then I also predict that Barth will be wonderfully helpful to us preachers in the present context. Barth is a teacher more than a preacher, a teacher who is noted for his tireless reiterations, restatements, and redescriptions of the faith. He loves to tell and retell the stories of the Bible, to walk through them, to wonder at their meaning, and to enjoy them in their strangeness and particularity. In fact, when one considers the theological need of the present generation of young, North American Christians, one might be tempted to say that Barth's way of doing theology is more relevant now than when he wrote theology. Anyone who is concerned with the present state of the church and who prays for a better, more faithful church, will find empowerment in Barth's belief that faithful preaching constitutes the church, fresh, new, and alive in each generation:

> The point is that the church must be built afresh each time. It must constitute itself. Its members must receive the command and be obedient. "By obedience to obedience" is the goal, and it is also the edifying of the church. In the church the congregation is built up as a fellowship, as a congregation standing under revelation and hear the Word of God.[68]

While we can agree with Barth that the message is definitely more significant than the life of the messenger, need we, like Barth, be so utterly unconcerned with the person of the preacher?

To be sure, we have this grand treasure in utterly earthen vessels. While we need not agree with Aristotle that the *ethos* of the preacher is the most important aspect of a speech, and while a Christian sermon is more substantial than Quintilian's definition of a speech as "a good person speaking well," nothing in an incarnational faith suggests that the person of the preacher is irrelevant to the message. Our God comes to us "in the flesh," in our flesh. It is of the greatness of this God to communicate to us through a person, Jesus, and through fleshly means, scripture. We are stewards not only of the gospel but also of the gifts that God has given us—intelligence, voice, physical appearance, personality—and we have a responsibility not to deny or to neglect those gifts but to develop them, to be aware of our strengths and limitations, and to do all that we do to the glory of God. Some of the disciplines that Barth urges upon us preachers are not only intellectual but also ethical—taking the biblical text more seriously than ourselves, listening to the privileged biblical text before we listen to other texts, letting ourselves be subordinate to the proclamation. Our homiletical vocation demands a certain sort of character formation.

I also think that *Barth may have erred in his stress on the sermon as the chief act of worship.* He wants to be a faithful son of the Protestant Reformation in his liturgical thought and, although he carefully qualifies himself on this point, noting the importance of the sacraments in both Luther's and Calvin's thought on worship, it is clear that for Barth, preaching is primary. Barth approvingly quotes Luther on the primacy of preaching in Christian worship:

> The Christian community should never come together, except there God's very Word be preached and prayer made. . . . Therefore where God's Word is not preached, 'tis better people should neither sing nor read, nor come together. . . . 'Tis better to leave out all, save the Word. And nought is better pursued than the Word. For all Scripture showeth that the same should be in full swing among Christians, and Christ also saith Himself, Lk. 10:42 "One thing is needful." For that Mary should sit at Christ's feet and hear His Word daily is the best part to choose, and is never taken away. It is an eternal saying that all else must pass away, however much there is for Martha to do.[69]

Nevertheless, revelation comes in three forms, according to Barth. Barth not only does not give the sacraments or other acts of worship a place in these three forms of revelation but also Barth does not allow even for other acts of worship to assist in preaching. In fact, in places in his *Dogmatics* Barth seems to regard other worship acts as potential distractions to the primacy of the preached word.

To be sure, Barth says that "there is preaching in the full sense only where it is accompanied and explained by the sacraments. What happens in the sacraments is that with visible signs we are pointed to the event of revelation that underlies and is promised to the church, and this in a way which, unlike that of preaching and all else that the church does, is not just a matter of words but of visible, bodily action."[70]

And again: "Only when there is true worship with both sermon and sacrament can the liturgy be given its rightful place, for only then can it fulfill its purpose, namely, to lead up to the sacrament. In every respect the church is a physical, historical entity, with true and visible corporeality, and yet in every respect it is also wholly invisible as the mysterious body of Christ. Because the church is both at one and the same time, there must never in any circumstances be separation between the administration of the sacraments and the proclamation of the gospel."[71]

These statements are notable for their rarity, and I defy anyone to read Barth on worship—his essentially Zwinglian theology of the Eucharist or his later comments on infant baptism, for instance—and say that Barth does justice to the Reformation theology of Word and Table. Like most of the churches of the Reformation, Barth asserts the linkage of preaching and the sacraments and then is unable to do justice to that linkage in actual church practice. He wonderfully asserts the primacy of the Word but too rarely the possibility of a visible Word.[72]

For a sermon to do justice to the fullness and richness of the gospel, the sermon is appropriately preached in the context of the congregation's worship. As the sermon is the Word proclaimed, our acts of worship are the Word performed, embodied, enacted, and responded to. A sermon, carefully and strictly formed on the basis of the biblical text, may preach a word of pure judgment. This word might be theologically questionable, in the larger context of Christian theology, were it not for the word of grace that is offered in the sacraments. A strictly biblical sermon may be a meditation upon some grand biblical idea. When that sermon is followed by the recitation of the Creed, the vows of baptism, even the standing and singing of a hymn, that preached word has the opportunity to become the Word enacted, embodied and acted upon in the lives of the hearers. We thus become not simply hearers of the Word but doers as well. Barth was so intent on keeping his theological thought lively, energetic, and in constant movement. Yet preaching, at least listening to preaching, is a rather sedentary, passive affair, at least in my church. Preaching in the context of the enacted liturgy enables preaching to be as engaging, lively, and active as the gospel demands.

Barth wonderfully stresses the contemporaneous, active, eventful quality of the Word of God. Here is, by the grace of God, no timeless historical abstraction but an event in our own time and place. Preaching participates in that miracle. Yet I wonder if Barth were subjected to some of the current infatuation for "contemporary worship"—with its upbeat pop tunes and uncritical usage of technology and media, its lack of sacramental action and response, its heavy stress on entertainment, and its ubiquitous reference to the first-person-singular personal pronoun—Barth might say that there is also something to be said for preaching's participation in the great historic legacy of the church. Barth loved that historical legacy and mined it well. He knew the empowerment that comes to the church by being surrounded by "so great a cloud of witnesses." Preaching might not be as eventful, as actualistic, and as momentary as Barth presents it. There is a joy in the church's affirmation of truth that is there for us, held by the church in safekeeping until such time that this truth is needed by the church. Even when some scriptural passage does not move us—evoke, provoke, or dislodge us—nevertheless it can still be God's present truth. Some biblical texts seem to want to shake and convict us, and other texts want to console and reassure us. And all biblical truth is able to rise above the merely contemporary, thank God.

Sometimes the context of worship, with its rituals, its beauty, its timeless affirmation of the eternal truths of the faith, becomes the perfect theological foil for the contemporaneous, lively, specific preached word of the sermon. In the sermon these eternal truths of worship become truth for us, here and now, as Barth might put it. Thus liturgy sometimes raises the questions for which the faithful sermon is the answer. Without the preached word our liturgies might float above this time and place as beautiful, timeless pageants of grace. Yet without the context of liturgical signs and acts, our sermons bear too much theological weight if they try to do justice to the full range of notes within the gospel. Word and Table, word and font belong together.

Before Mary Magdalene discovered the Risen Christ in the garden, at the empty tomb in John 20, Jesus discovered another Mary and her brother in John 11. Lazarus was ill (John 11:1). We who live in a health-infatuated society take notice, for illness has become one of the most interesting and expensive things that can happen to us. Illness, and its care, has become the major act of pastoral care, the whole point of much ministry. Today's pastors tend to spend more time visiting in hospitals than preparing sermons. At any rate, Lazarus's sisters, Mary and Martha, send for Jesus (v. 3), but when Jesus receives their summons, he "stayed two days longer in the place where he was" (v. 6). Jesus will not be jerked around by illness.

Finally, Jesus tells his disciples that he will go to Bethany. Though his disciples protest that such a trip is dangerous (v. 8), they go. By the time they get there, Lazarus is dead and entombed. Jesus is "greatly disturbed" (at the misunderstanding and lack of faith of the two sisters?) (v. 33). Jesus goes to the tomb and with no magical actions, with nothing but "a loud voice" (v. 43), Jesus commands, "Lazarus, come out!" (v. 43). It is an Easter story sometime before Easter. It is a story about the power of Jesus' voice, a perfect prelude to John 20 and the other Mary's encounter with the Risen Christ. At his voice, the dead rise.

And yet it is also a story about death. Immediately after this story, the disciples' fears were realized: the forces of death got organized and, "from that day on they planned to put him to death" (v. 53). From that day on, from this prelude of Easter, from the day when Lazarus was raised by the cemetery preaching of Jesus, they decided that Jesus must die. We cannot have some uncredentialed, uncontained, life-giving force let loose with loud voice among us. We must devise all sorts of perfectly good reasons why the Word ought not be allowed such unmediated access to our hearts and minds.

If you do not know why the dramatic, enlivening raising of Lazarus is connected to the initiation of a plot to kill Jesus and keep him quiet, then you have never preached a resurrection faith among people like us.

And yet, as the first chapter of this Gospel so eloquently states, the light, the life-summoning light, "shines in the darkness, and the darkness did not overcome it" (John 1:5). We do, despite ourselves, see Jesus. Preaching works because the Risen Christ is stronger than the forces of silencing death. He, with a voice loud enough to wake the dead, will not leave us to our silences or to the death-dealing lies of government press releases, of the pompous pronouncements of bishops, or of slick advertising slogans. Therein is our hope. Nothing shall defeat the indomitable Word. In the beginning is the Word, and in the end is the Word, and the Word was God. It is that triumphant Word, rather than the words of us preachers, that keeps the church as the Body of Christ:

> As the true church it would always die and perish if he [Christ] did not speak to it, if it did not hear his voice, summoning it to watch and pray: to watch over its being in all its dimensions, in its preaching and doctrine and theology, but also in its constitution and various ministries....what is the good of all its watching if it does not pray that this may take place, that it may, therefore, be or be again a Christian community?[73]

The church is created, sustained, purified, and made church through a voice, and the good news is that despite the death and the resistance, nothing has been able to silence that triumphant voice. Barth's *Dogmatics* remained unfinished at his death, as he predicted it would be. And, in a sense, all of our words about the Word remain unfinished. We preachers often look tired because we know there is always another sermon to be preached if God gives us until next Sunday. We are never done with our preaching. There is always one more sermon to be preached because, in the Resurrection, God is not finished.[74] Amen.

Thus I end my Barthian homiletic as Barth ended his own ruminations on preaching, with that little word "Amen." "Amen," pronounced at the end of the sermon, not only claims the sermon as an act of prayer but also signifies that the sermon is part of a continuing conversation:

> An important, comforting, and critical little word is the "Amen" with which we confess what we have said before God. "Amen" may be a comfort to us after what has been said in weakness. It also causes us to think of the next sermon and summons us back to work. Every sermon thus closes on both a comforting and an unsettling note. From this little word we might unpack the whole doctrine of preaching.[75]

Barth's whole doctrine of preaching in one word: "Amen." On this comforting and unsettling, prayerful little word, let us end this long conversation and, with the next sermon looming before us, let us once again begin, let us hold out our empty hands, let us test the Easter faith, let us be back to work.

Amen.

NOTES

Introduction

1. Barth had much the same effect upon my thinking as upon Trevor Hart's, who says of his student encounter with Barth's thought, "Here was a Christian theologian who, rather than prioritizing 'relevance' and seeking it through the abandonment or total reconstruction of Christian identity, or making a show of having stepped outside the Christian tradition in order to consider it 'critically', was actually convinced that it was necessary to pursue the critical dialogue and hence to rejuvenate that same tradition unashamedly *from within*, and doing so precisely in order to address the wider intellectual, social, political and ethical concerns and challenges of his day. That was surprising and exciting to me twenty years ago, and it is still so today." Trevor Hart, *Regarding Karl Barth* (Downers Grove, Ill.: InterVarsity Press, 1999), pg. x.

2. In his monumental history of Christian preaching, O. C. Edwards Jr. gives only a couple of pages to Barth, noting that, in the history of homiletics, Barth was "not among the most influential" (*A History of Preaching* [Nashville: Abingdon, 2004], pg. 682).

3. Karl Barth, *Karl Barth's Table Talk*, ed. J. D. Godsey (Edinburgh and London: Oliver and Boyd), pg. 196.

4. One of the few books written in English for preachers on Barth was a curious one by Arnold B. Come, *An Introduction to Barth's Dogmatics for Preachers* (Philadelphia: Westminster Press, 1963). Come gives a standard (for that point in time) interpretation of Barth's theology but has surprisingly little to say about Barth and preaching. One of my great challenges will be to exposit Barth's theology so that I can, along the way, finally talk about Barth and preaching. Recent articles about Barth as preacher are few: Frank D. Rees, "The Need and Promise of Christian Preaching," *Evangelical Quarterly*, 66, April 1994, pp. 107-21; Otto Bächli, "Das Gabet der Gemeinde: Ein Beitrag zur Homiletik von Karl Barth," *Theologische Zeitschrift*, 50, No. 1, 1994, pp. 24-40. Michael Trowitzch, "Karl Barths Predigtverständnis," *Pastoral theologie*, 94 (2005), pp. 296-301. G. D. J. Dingemans," Die kommunikative Kraft der Predigt K. Barths und K. H. Miskottes," *Zeitschrift für dialektische Theologie*, 10 (1994), pp. 49-70. Manfred Josuttis, "Das Wort und die Wörter: zur Kritik am Predigtverständnis Karl Barths," *Freispruch und Freiheit* (Munich: Kaiser Verlag, 1973). See also Hartmut Genest, *Karl Barth und die Predigt Darstellung und Deutung von Predigtwerk und Predigtlehre Karl Barths* (Neukirchen-Vluyn: Neukirchener Verlagshaus, 1995). To my mind, the major attempts to embody a Barthian homiletic, at least to think about preaching from a Barthian perspective (in rather wooden and static ways), are J. J. von Allmen, *Preaching and Congregation* (Richmond: John Knox Press, 1962), and Dietrich Ritschl, A *Theology of Proclamation* (Richmond: John Knox Press, 1962).

5. Karl Barth, *Homiletics*, trans. G. W. Bromiley and Donald E. Daniels (Louisville: Westminster/ John Knox Press, 1991).

6. Just as I was finishing this conversation with Barth on preaching, a wonderful collection of essays on Barth as a conversationalist appeared. See John C. McDowell and Mike Higton, *Conversing with Barth* (Hampshire: Ashgate Publishing, 2004).

7. *CD*, IV, 1, pg. x.

8. *CD*, III, pg. 4. Ludwig Wittgenstein (in Tractatus 6.54) said that anyone who understood all of his elucidations recognized them as "nonsensical." They were meant to be used and then used up, as rungs on a ladder, a ladder that ought to be thrown away right after one has climbed up it. Any generalizations, propositions, and categorizations of Barth's thought ought to function in the same way. That is, after we have characterized Barth, let us be done with our characterizations. After we have made generalizations with him, let us discard the generalizations and allow Barth to work with us, without the steps by which we have climbed up to him.

9. Karl Barth, *Protestant Theology in the Nineteenth Century* (Eerdmans, 2002), pg. 1.

10. Ibid., pg. 2.

11. Karl Barth, *The Word of God and the Word of Man*, trans. Douglas Horton (New York: Harper & Row, 1956).

12. Budapest, Museum of Fine Arts, signed and dated: BRVEGEL, MDLXVI.

13. Barth bases his aversion to pictorial representations of religious subjects upon the first commandment, the first and foremost "axiom for theology." Karl Barth, "Das erste Gebot als theologische Axiom" (1933), in Karl Barth, *Theologische Fragen und Antworten* (Zollikon: Evangelischer Verlag, 1957), pp. 127-42. We must have no "images of God" because Christ is the one and only image we have been given. See the excellent analysis of this speech by S. W. Sykes, "Introduction," pp. 1-24, in H. Martin Rumscheidt, ed., *The Way of Theology in Karl Barth* (Allison Park, Pa.: Pickwick Publications, 1986).

14. The standard work on Barth and the Isenheim Altar is Reiner Marquard, *Karl Barth und der Isenheimer Altar* (Stuttgart: Calwer Verlag, 1995). See Andrée Hayum, *The Isenheim Altarpiece: God's Medicine and the Painter's Vision* (Princeton: Princeton University Press, 1989) for the best treatment of the altar from an art history point of view.

15. Anselm Kiefer, *Book with Wings*, 1992–1994, lead, tin, and steel, Modern Art Museum of Fort Worth, acquired by the Sid W. Richardson Foundation Endowment Fund, 2000.

1. Barth the Preacher

1. Eberhard Busch, *Karl Barths Lebenslauf: nach seinen Briefen und autobiographischen Texten* (München: Kaiser, 1976).

2. John Webster, "Introducing Barth," in John Webster, ed., *The Cambridge Companion to Karl Barth* (Cambridge: Cambridge University Press, 2000), pg. 2.

3. Webster, pg. 3. See also Eberhard Busch, *Karl Barth and the Pietists: The Young Karl Barth's Critique of Pietism and Its Response*, trans. Daniel W. Bloesch (Downers Grove, Ill.: InterVarsity Press, 2004) for a good discussion of Barth's indebtedness to Herrmann.

4. Barth to Helmut Thielicke, 7 November 1967, quoted in Busch, *Karl Barth*, pg. 57.

5. Dorrien, pg. 31. For Barth's earliest sermons, see Karl Barth, *Predigten 1913*, ed. Nelly Barth and Gerhard Sauter (Zurich: TVZ, 1976). For the effect of the outbreak of the war on Barth, see Jochen Fahler, *Der Ausbruch des 1. Weltkrieges in Karl Barths fangliche Predigten, 1913–1915* (Frankfurt: Peter Lang, 1979); Busch, *Karl Barth*, pp. 61-63; Arthur C. Cochrane, "The Sermons of 1913 and 1914," *Karl Barth in Re-View: Posthumous Works Reviewed and Assessed*, ed. H. Martin Rumscheidt (Allison Park, Pa.: Pickwick Press, 1981), pp. 1-5. Despite his commitment to preach beyond mere "relevance," Barth says that he preached so much on the First World War that a woman "came up to me and begged me for once to talk about something else and not constantly about this terrible conflict." *Homiletics* (pg. 118).

6. See Dorrien's discussion of Barth and Blumhardt in Gary Dorrien, *The Barthian Revolt in Modern Theology*, pp. 40-41. See also Eberhard Busch, *Karl Barth and the Pietists*, pp. 31-33.

7. Dorrien, pp. 53-54.

8. Francis Watson in the introduction to Karl Barth, *Epistle to the Philippians* (Louisville: Westminster/John Knox Press, 2002), pg. xxx.

9. I am among those who consider it sad that biblical studies have been given over, for the last century or more, to the historians, or would-be historians. The historical-critical method did yield some insights about scripture that were modestly illuminating, and even Barth tends to use the insights of the decades of German historical criticism of scripture. However, he carefully allocates those insights to a secondary position in his theology, using them mostly as a gloss upon his own exegesis, finding a curiosity here and there in the archaeological spadework of the historical critics but refusing to adhere to their methodology. I consider the errant "Jesus Seminar" to be the last gasp of now discredited nineteenth-century German biblical historical-critical scholarship. Fortunately, theological, confessional interpreters of scripture like Richard Hays, Brevard Childs, Walter Brueggemann, and others are

iving us biblical interpretation that preaches. We preachers have been widely criticized for mostly ignoring the pretentious historical-critical "discoveries" in our preaching. Barth would tell us that we were wise to do so. Sounding a bit like Kierkegaard, Barth says that Jesus manages always to be "the same new thing," to those who first heard him or to those of us in the present age. Our trouble with Jesus is more than the difficulty of history. It is the difficulty of his incomprehensibility.

> Those who heard Jesus, whether they believed or not, were confronted with the same new thing, the same alien will and unknown power, at the heart of man's known and customary possibilities and fulfillments. With the same actuality as those who were eye-witnesses of these particular acts of Jesus they stumbled against the kingdom of God drawn near. The Sermon on the Mount . . . was no less a miraculous Word, the irruption and occurrence of something incomprehensible to man, than the raising of the young man at Nain. (CD, IV, 2, pg. 211)

10. These quotes are from the discussion by Eberhard Busch, *Karl Barth and the Pietists*, pp. 70-77.

11. Eduard Thurneysen wrote a well-received book on Dostoevsky that is still most illuminating, *Dostoevsky* (Richmond: John Knox Press, 1966).

12. For explicit references to Dostoevsky or the Grand Inquisitor in *Romans*, see pp. 67-68, 122, 141, 132, 300, 501-2, 504-5.

13. See Alastair McKinnon, "Barth's Relation to Kierkegaard: Some Further Light," *Canadian Journal of Theology* 13 (1967): pp. 31-41.

14. Stephen Webb, *Refiguring Theology*, pp. 63-66.

15. Busch, pg. 63. For a good analysis of Barth's sermons from this period, see Jochen Fahler, *Der Ausbruch des I. Weltkreiges in Karth Barths Predigten 1913–1915* (Bern, Frankfurt am Main, Las Vegas: Peter Lang, 1979). Barth and Thurneysen published a volume of sermons from these years. See *Come Holy Spirit*, trans. G. W. Richards (New York: Round Table, 1933). Barth's sermons are important for any analysis of his theological thought. In the sermons, for example, it is easy to see Barth's penchant for using cutting and even irritating hyperbole for its shock value. See Barth's very honest, "Der Pfarrer, der es den Leuten recht macht," *Die christliche Welt* 30 (1916): pp. 262-67. Also note that although the "Wholly Other" did not become a slogan until 1919, under the influence of Otto, already in his pre-war sermons he is beginning to use this language; for example, see *Predigten* 1913, ed. G. Sauter and N. Barth (Zurich: TVZ, 1976), pp. 168, 249, 305. In his letters, Barth often credits Thurneysen, not Otto, for making him see the centrality of this phrase. Friedrich Wintzer, *Herausgegeben und eingeführt, Predigt: Texte zum Verständnis und zur Praxis der Predigt in der Neuzeit* (Müchen: Chr. Kaiser Verlag, 1989) is a quite wonderful survey of the most important homiletical writing in Germany that helps to locate Barth in the history of German homiletics. For Barth's politics, see George Hunsinger, ed., *Karl Barth and Radical Politics* (Louisville: Westminster/John Knox Press, 1976).

16. Karl Barth, *A Karl Barth Reader*, ed. Rolf Joachim Erler and Reiner Marquard (Grand Rapids: Eerdmans, 1986), pg. 33.

17. Ibid., pg. 34.

18. Busch, pg. 90.

19. Ibid., pg. 87.

20. Barth's correspondence with Thurneysen is a wonderful resource for reconstructing his early movements. It is also a wonderful example of the power of friendship between two preachers. An English selection is in James Smart, ed., *Revolutionary Theology in the Making: Barth-Thurneysen Correspondence, 1914–1925* (Richmond: John Knox Press, 1964).

21. Karl Barth, *The Word of God and the Word of Man*, trans. Douglas Horton (New York: Harper & Brothers, 1957), pp. 28-50. See Webb's discussion of this sermon in Webb, pp. 57-58.

22. Barth said that, as he worked on *Romans*, "it required only a little imagination for me to hear the sound of the guns booming away in the north." From Karl Barth's preface to the English edition of *The Epistle to the Romans*, trans. Edwyn C. Hoskins (London: Oxford University Press, 1968), pg. v.

23. Quoted by Dorrien, pg. 37. I am indebted to Dorrien, pp. 36-41, for my organization of this material and for these quotes from Barth's early years.

24. Ibid., pg. 3.

25. Quoted in Andreas Pangritz, *Karl Barth in the Theology of Dietrich Bonhoeffer*, trans. Barbara and Martin Rumscheidt (Grand Rapids: Eerdmans, 2000), pg. 36.

26. Eberhard Busch has a particularly illuminating discussion of Barth's move in *Romans*, including particularly surprising evidence of his debt to Pietism for that move in his *Karl Barth and the Pietists*, pp 26-68.

27. *Karl Barth-Eduard Thurneysen: Briefwechsel*, vol. 1, pp. 489-92, quoted by Dorrien, pg. 43.

28. Karl Barth, *The Epistle to the Romans*, trans. of 6th ed., Edwyn C. Hoskyns (London: Oxford University Press, 1933, reprint 1975), pg. 225.

29. Quoted by Dorrien, pg. 49

30. Quoted by Dorrien, pg. 51.

31. Dorrien, pg. 53.

32. Ibid., pp. 54-55. See Richard Ernest Burnett, *Karl Barth's Theological Exegesis: The Hermeneutica Principles of the Römerbrief Prefaces* (Tübingen: Mohr Siebeck, 2001), for a detailed view of the reception of *Romans*, pp. 14-23.

33. Which makes interesting that one of the charges made against Barth and this new "Dialectica Theology" was that it was all invigorating but that it would not preach. One of Barth's professors Hermann Kutter, said that "to actually proclaim God to a society that has fallen away from him is quite another thing than to differentiate a correct concept of God from an incorrect concept of God." Quoted in Bockmuehl, *The Unreal God of Modern Theology: Bultmann, Barth, and the Theology of Atheism, a Call to Recovering the Truth of God's Reality*, trans. Geoffrey W. Bromiley (Colorado Springs Helmers & Howard, 1988), pg. 101. How little Kutter understood that Barth was getting the concepts right only in order to get the proclamation going.

34. Dorrien, pg. 50.

35. Ibid., pg. 67.

36. Ibid., pg. 72.

37. Quoted by Busch, *The Great Passion*, pg. 24.

38. Dorrien, pg. 76.

39. Dorrien, pg. 94.

40. Herrmann's neo-Kantian formulation of the closed circle of divine revelation stuck with Barth throughout his theology. For some critics of Barth, this sealing off of revelation to a special realm of scrutiny led Barth into fideism and gave his theology an air of unreality and detachment. This is the thesis of Klaus Bockmuehl in *The Unreal God*. Bockmuehl says that Barth contributed to the detachment and irrelevancy of modern theology because he was guilty of a "deobjectification of theological statements and a surrender of this worldly reality, transferring the content of biblical statements into the supraterrestrial and suprahistorical world of transcendence. He flies above the radar" (pp. 78-79).

41. Barth in "Concluding Unscientific Postscript on Schleiermacher," *The Theology of Schleiermacher*, trans. Geoffrey Bromiley (Grand Rapids: Eerdmans, 1982), pg. 263.

42. George Hunsinger, *How to Read Karl Barth—The Shape of His Theology* (New York: Oxford University Press, 1991), pg. 59. Hunsinger's is the best English introduction to Barth, along with the English translation of Eberhard Busch's *The Great Passion: An Introduction to Karl Barth's Theology*, trans. Geoffrey W. Bromiley, edited and annotated by Darrell L. Guder and Judith J. Guder (Grand Rapids: Eerdmans, 2004). The best introduction in German is Christofer Frey, *Die Theologie Karl Barths: Eine Einführung* (Frankfurt am Main: Athenäum, 1988).

43. Cf. *CD*, I, 2, pg. 720. See also Geoffrey W. Bromiley, *An Introduction to the Theology of Karl Barth* (Grand Rapids: Eerdmans, 1979) for a good walk through the *Church Dogmatics*.

44. This is the point made so decisively in Barth's early (1933, Bonn) slogan, "Theological existence today!" Barth calls us preachers to practice theological existence, that is, exclusive attachment to the Word of God, clarity about to whom we belong and to whom we must listen. See the wonderfully

Barthian critique of contemporary theology and preaching by Gerhard Sauter, *Eschatological Rationality: Theological Issues in Focus* (Grand Rapids: Baker Books, 1996), ch. 4, "Being Human and Being a Theologian."

45. Rolf Ahlers, *The Barmen Theological Declaration of 1934: The archeology of a confessional text* (Lewiston, N.Y.: Edwin Mellen Press, 1986), pp. 6-10. Also, Karl Barth, *Texte zur Barmer Theologischen Erklärung*, Einleitung von Eberhard Jüngel (Zürich: Theologischer Verlag, 1984), pp. 1-5.

46. Ahlers, *Barmen*, pg. 12.

47. Karl Barth, *Deliverance to the Captives* (New York: Harper & Row, 1961).

2. Preaching the Bible with Barth

1. Barth, *Homiletics*, pg. 80.

2. Barth's editors and translators, G. W. Bromiley and T. F. Torrance, compiled a wonderful resource for preachers, *Church Dogmatics, Karl Barth: Index Volume with Aids for the Preacher* (Edinburgh: T. & T. Clark, 1977), that not only gives us a complete index of scripture and subjects in the *Dogmatics* but also a rich selection of exegetical and expository texts from the *Dogmatics* that are keyed to the assigned scripture texts in the German Lutheran lectionary. This is a necessary volume for any preacher who would preach with Barth. *Church Dogmatics. Karl Barth: Preaching Through the Christian Year*, ed. John McTavish and Harold Wells (Grand Rapids: Eerdmans, 1978) contains a judicious selection of passages from the *Church Dogmatics* that are keyed to the seasons of the liturgical year for use by preachers in the preparation of sermons.

3. Barth, "The Strange New World within the Bible," in *The Word of God and the Word of Man*, trans. Douglas Horton (New York: Harper Torchbooks, 1957), pg. 43. The motivation for Barth's theology is stated clearly by Eduard Thurneysen early in his correspondence with Barth: that the Bible should erupt into the consciousness of the church. Barth and Eduard Thurneysen, *Revolutionary Theology in the Making* (Richmond: John Knox Press, 1964), pg. 20. Shortly before his death, Barth told a group of Christian students from Poland that ten students reading the Bible could do more to bring justice to Poland than hundreds of students marching in the streets. Quoted in Bockmuehl, *The Unreal God*, pg. 177.

4. CD, I, 2, pg. 469.

5. CD, I, 2, pg. 730. American evangelicals have tended to attack Barth's notion that the Bible is not the Word of God but *becomes* the Word of God. Donald Dayton says that these evangelicals show their dependence upon the rather stolid thought of B. B. Warfield, who taught that scripture was inspired, *theopneustos*, "God-breathed," in the past tense. John Wesley and other earlier Pietists tended not to draw such a sharp temporal distinction between scripture that was once and for all time inspired and the illumination of scripture when we read it today. Wesley (in his *Explanatory Notes on the New Testament*) said that biblical inspiration is a continuing activity of the Holy Spirit who is the same yesterday, today, and forever. Barth's thought on scriptural inspiration (in those rare places where he worries about such matters) tends to reveal how American evangelicalism bought into a too-staid doctrine of biblical inspiration. See Donald Dayton's introduction to Eberhard Busch's *Karl Barth and the Pietists*, pg. xii.

6. CD, I, 2, pp. 687, 755, 768.

7. "The Strange New World," pg. 65.

8. Webster, pg. 2.

9. Busch, *The Great Passion*, pg. 6.

10. Barth, *Homiletics*, pg. 49.

11. "The Christian church is the community that expects to hear God speaking through its Scriptures." Elizabeth Achtemeier, "The Canon as the Voice of the Living God," in *Reclaiming the Bible for the Church*, ed. Carl E. Braaten and Robert W. Jenson (Grand Rapids: Eerdmans, 1995), pg. 119.

12. Barth, *Homiletics*, pg. 102.

13. Ibid., pp. 102-6, 113.

14. Ibid., pg. 83.

15. Ibid., pg. 126. Barth often speaks of the "self-exposition of scripture" (Karl Barth, *The Knowledge of God According to the Teaching of the Reformation* [London: Hodder and Stoughton, 1938], pg. 181).

16. Barth, *Homiletics*, pg. 81. This divinely initiated, miraculous quality of scripture led many, from the first, to charge that Barth has thereby removed the Bible from the world. Heinz Zahrnt said that Barth "has shown theology the way to the Bible, but he has not with the same intensity shown the way back from the Bible to life." *The Question of God: Protestant Theology in the 20ᵗʰ Century* (New York: Harcourt, Brace, & World, 1969), pg. 117. Most of these critics, like Zahrnt, fail to acknowledge the Bible's peculiar view of "life."

17. *CD*, I, 2, pg. 495.

18. *Romans*, pg. 12.

19. Barth, *Homiletics*, pg. 77.

20. Barth, *The Word of God and the Word of Man*, pp. 65, 75-76, 84. Barth also says of scripture that "it is this hand which is in evidence in the Bible."

21. Barth, *Homiletics*, pg. 77. Barth indicates that the only way to make us potentially puffed up and pompous preachers modest is through the constant study of the scriptures: "Preachers must not be 'clerics' who, puffed up with the sense of their mission, office, and theology, and perhaps 'full of the Holy Ghost,' attempt to represent the interests of the good Lord to the world. The only healing herb that can meet this vice is that of being biblical, i.e., of engaging in real scriptural exposition." Barth, *Homiletics*, pg. 79.

22. Ibid., pg. 78.

23. Ibid.

24. Ibid., pg. 409, pg. 105.

25. Ibid., pg. 126.

26. Ibid., pg. 94

27. Ibid., pg. 96.

28. Ibid., pp. 118-19.

29. I confess some sympathy with those evangelical critics of Barth who charge that, in his insistence upon the eventful quality of revelation, in his determination to keep God's voice free, even from a necessary connection to scripture, Barth gives us a rather fuzzy doctrine of scriptural inspiration. He dismissed such doctrines as attempting "a freezing, as it were, of the relation between Scripture and revelation" (*CD*, I, 1, pg. 124). In his attempt to keep revelation active and moving, has Barth unintentionally demeaned the authority of scripture as a means of God's speaking? Still, when one hears some evangelical scholars speak of the authority of scripture, one does hear a distinct tendency toward ossification. See Nicholas Wolterstorff, *Divine Discourse: Philosophical Reflections on the Claim That God Speaks* (Cambridge: Cambridge University Press, 1995) for an astute discussion of Barth and the problem of scriptural authority.

30. British biblical scholars of another generation like James Barr, John Hick, and John Barton suggested that we should learn "to see scripture as an indispensable resource rather than as binding authority" for the church. (Quoted in Terence E. Fretheim, *The Bible as Word of God* (Minneapolis, Minn.: Fortress Press, 1998), pg. 12. Obviously, Barth would disagree.

31. Karl Barth, *Against the Stream*, pg. 225.

32. David Ford, *Barth and God's Story: Biblical Narrative in the Theological Method of Karl Barth in The Church Dogmatics* (Frankfurt am Main: Verlag Peter Lang, 1981), pg. 316.

33. See William C. Placher, *The Domestication of Transcendence* (Louisville: Westminster/John Knox Press, 1996), pp. 114-16.

34. Barth, *Homiletics*, pg. 106.

35. See Bultmann, *Kerygma and Mythos*, ed. H. W. Bartsch (Hamburg, 1948), I, pg. 150.

36. *CD*, IV, 3, pg. 170.

37. This fairly well devastates just about everything I learned about the interpretation of scripture from my first college Bible class onward.

38. Barth, *Homiletics*, pg. 85.

39. Hans Frei, *The Eclipse of Biblical Narrative: A Study in Eighteenth and Nineteenth Century Hermeneutics* (New Haven: Yale, 1974).

40. It is curious that, just as the liberal, mainline theological establishment was launching a post-modern critique of historical-criticism, so-called biblical conservatives picked up the historical-critical banner as their last hope for making the Bible into uncontested, unassailable, objective truth. This strategy is a capitulation to the faith of modernity rather than modernity's defeat.

41. Ford, pg. 61. Of the biblical text, Barth says, in a wonderful fugue of knowing, that it reaches out to us: "It reveals and discloses itself. It gives itself to be known. It creates the possibility of a seeing and hearing and understanding of it. Or rather, it creates eyes to see it and ears to hear it and a mind to understand it. In this character it is light, . . . it makes itself a known fact. It opens. . . . It reaches out to a subject. It surrounds and encloses this subject" (*CD*, IV, 2, pg. 122). This statement is, of course, based upon Barth's conviction that "wherever there is Christian gnosis it is His work" (pg. 126).

42. See Bruce McCormack, "The Significance of Karl Barth's Theological Exegesis of Philippians" in *The Epistle to the Philippians*, trans. James W. Leitch (Louisville: Westminster/John Knox Press, 2002), pg. v.

43. Edward Farley, *Practicing Gospel: Unconventional Thoughts on the Church's Ministry* (Louisville: Westminster/John Knox Press, 2003), chs. 6–8.

44. David Kelsey, *The Uses of Scripture in Recent Theology* (Philadelphia: Fortress, 1975), ch. 3, pp. 39 ff.

45. Ford, pg. 58.

46. Noted in Ford, pg. 59.

47. Discussed by Kay, pg. 23, in reference to Barth, *Homiletics*, pp. 49, 102-3. I have recently examined a series of sermons by Rick Warren of Saddleback Church. Warren's preferred biblical hermeneutic is to extract certain purposeful principles from a text and then preach those extracted principles. This gives Warren's hearers the modernist illusion that they can choose what scripture says to them, that they are in control of scripture.

48. For an extended discussion of Barth as exegete and hermenute, see James A. Wharton, "Karl Barth as Exegete and His Influence on Biblical Interpretation," *Union Seminary Quarterly Review* 28 (1972), pp. 5-13.

49. On the intellectual, postliberal sophistication of Barth's biblical interpretation, see Mark I. Wallace, *The Second Naïveté* (Macon, Ga.: Mercer University Press, 1990).

50. Cited in Ford, pg. 91.

51. Barth, *Protestant Thought in the Nineteenth Century* (Grand Rapids: Eerdmans, 2002), ch. 19.

52. Ford, pg. 67.

53. James F. Kay, *Christus Praesens* (Grand Rapids: Eerdmans, 1994).

54. Quoted in Kay, pg. 37.

55. Kay, pg. 77.

56. See "Rudolf Bultmann—An Attempt to Understand Him" in *Kerygma and Myth* (Vol. 2, edited by Hans Werner Bartsch, trans. Reginald H. Fuller [London: SPCK, 1962], pp. 95-97).

57. Quoted by Kay, pg. 81.

58. Ibid.

59. Ibid., pg. 90.

60. Ibid., pg. 118.

61. Kay, pg. 176.

62. This sermon was preached at the wrong time and in the wrong place—at the 2004 Duke Pastor's School and Divinity School Alumni Convocation, at 2:00 in the afternoon, in a campus theater, before the assembled alumni and before a panel of homiletics peers (Fleming Rutledge, Stanley Hauerwas, Marva Dawn, and Peter Gomes). The occasion was the publication of a book on my preaching, edited by William Malambri and Michael Turner, *A Peculiar Prophet: William H. Willimon and the Art of Preaching* (Nashville: Abingdon, 2004).

63. James Barr complained of the "countless pages of wearisome, inept, and futile exegesis" in the *Church Dogmatics*. James Barr, *Biblical faith and natural theology: the Gifford lectures for 1991*, delivered in the University of Edinburgh (Oxford: Clarendon Press, 1993), pg. 203. For his part, Barth says that any church that leaves the task of interpreting the Bible exclusively to scholars is slothful and irresponsible (*CD*, I, 2, pg. 715).

64. Ford, pg. 68.

65. "As regards the handling of Old Testament texts, we maintain that for us the Old Testament is valid only in relation to the New." Barth, *Homiletics*, pg. 80. I would challenge Barth's use of "only."

66. George Hunsinger says that in the *Church Dogmatics* "Jesus Christ is understood as the central content of its witness [the scripture's witness]. . . . The one thing said in the midst of everything, the center which organizes the whole, is 'just this: the name of Jesus Christ.'" *How to Read Karl Barth: The Shape of His Theology* (New York: Oxford University Press, 1991), pg. 59. George Hunsinger has called Barth's use of the circular form "the root metaphor in the *Church Dogmatics*." Christ is always the center and our theological assertions surround this center, move toward the center and out from the center. Hunsinger says, "It is the metaphor of the circle comprising center and periphery—a metaphor which is constantly employed to bring out the centrality of Jesus Christ. The task of theology is to make clear at every point that Christ stands at the center of the gospel: 'to explain the Gospel is to expound, unfold and articulate its content, with no effacement of its unity and simplicity, but rather in enhancement of its unity and simplicity. It is to assert and honor it synoptically in all its richness, displaying the place and manner of each individual part. It is also to make known the periphery in each section as that of the true center, and the center as in every respect that of the distinctive periphery' (*CD*, IV, 3, pg. 850). Jesus Christ is understood as the central content of its witness, for Jesus Christ is the name of the God who deals graciously with sinful humanity. 'To hear this is to hear the Bible—both as a whole and in each one of its separate parts. Not to hear this means *eo ipso* not to hear the Bible, neither as a whole, nor therefore in its parts.' The one thing said in the midst of everything, the center which organizes the whole, is 'just this: the name of Jesus Christ'" (*CD*, I, 2, pg. 720). My teacher Brevard Childs is a contemporary biblical interpreter of note who has used Barth's Christocentric interpretation to good effect. Childs briefly criticizes Barth in his *Old Testament Theology in a Canonical Context* (Philadelphia: Fortress, 1985), pg. 4. In that same volume, Childs says that, for Christians, even the Old Testament, just like the New Testament, "functioned as Christian scripture because it bore witness to Jesus Christ" (pg. 64).

67. Brent A. Strawn, "And These Three Are One: A Trinitarian Critique of Christological Approaches to the Old Testament," *Perspectives in Religious Studies*, unpublished paper, 2004.

68. Wolfhart Pannenberg says that "one of Barth's weaknesses was that he didn't have a real appreciation of Biblical Exegesis, especially critical exegesis. Of course, he used scripture quite a bit. But he had a very personal way of interpreting the Bible. I found by involving myself in historical critical exegesis of biblical writings that this wouldn't do. Theology should be based on the Scriptures, of course, but it should be based upon a reading of the Scriptures through historical interpretation." Pannenberg, "Future Perfect: A Conversation with Wolfhart Pannenberg," Interview by Thomas J. Oord, September/October, 2001, *Books & Culture*, pg. 18.

69. See Ford, ch. 5.

70. Ford, pg. 93.

71. Paul McGlasson, *Jesus and Judas: Biblical Exegesis in Barth* (Atlanta: Scholar's Press, 1991).

72. McGlasson cites *CD*, II, 1, pp. 118 ff. and 363 ff. as examples of this sort of conceptual reading.

73. Nicholas M. Healy, "The Logic of Karl Barth's Ecclesiology," *Modern Theology*, 10:3, July 1994, pg. 258.

74. See the discussion of Barth's imaginative exegesis in Timothy J. Gorringe, *Karl Barth Against Hegemony* (Oxford: Oxford University Press, 1999), pp. 283-85.

75. *CD*, IV, 2, pp. 673ff.

76. Barth, *Homiletics*, pg. 128.

77. Busch, *Life*, pg. 259.

3. I Will Give You Words

1. *CD*, I, 1, pg. 188.

2. Thomas G. Long, "And How Shall They Hear?" in *Listening to the Word*, ed. Gail R. O'Day and Thomas G. Long (Nashville: Abingdon Press, 1993), pp. 170-77.

3. Trevor Hart, "The Word, the Words and the Witness: Proclamation as Divine and Human Reality in the Theology of Karl Barth," *Tyndale Bulletin*, 46.1 (1995): pg. 83.

4. Eugene H. Peterson, *Subversive Spirituality* (Grand Rapids: Eerdmans, 1997), pp. 16-31.

5. *Romans*, pg. 44.

6. Ernstpeter Maurer, *Sprachphilosophische Aspekte in Karl Barths, "Prolegomena zur Kirchlichen Dogmatik"* (Frankfurt am Main, Peter Lang, 1989), correlates Barth's ideas about speech and revelation with current linguistic philosophy, showing some surprising "postmodern" parallels. Still, Maurer notes that Barth has no explicit interest in such linguistic theory, rather, Barth attempts a rigorously biblical view of speech.

7. When, immediately after his Sunday sermon, young Karl hastened to his father's deathbed, the last words that his father spoke to him were: "The main thing is not scholarship, nor learning, nor criticism, but to love the Lord Jesus. We need a living relationship with God, and we must ask the Lord for that." Quoted in Busch, *Karl Barth*, pg. 68.

8. I venture this short survey of over two millenia of philosophy because we preachers, whether we acknowledge it or not, are participants in this history. It is important to acknowledge our debts. Barth noted, as he began his own survey of the recent history of theology, that "history is made up of living men whose work is handed over defenceless to our understanding and appreciation upon their death. Precisely because of this, they have a claim on our courtesy, a claim that their own concerns should be heard and that they should not be used simply as a means to our ends." *Protestant Thought in the Nineteenth Century* (Grand Rapids: Eerdmans, 2003), pg. 8. I am not good enough a philosopher to be that fair to the dead, but at least I hope to show that their thought is still alive among us. John Milbank chastises Barth for not engaging philosophy and therefore allowing philosophy to presume to have an autonomous account of "what is." John Milbank, Catherine Pickstock, and Graham Ward, eds., *Radical Orthodoxy: A New Theology* (London: Routledge, 1999), pp. 22, 32. See Joseph L. Mangina's response to Milbank, "Meditating Theologies: Karl Barth between Radical and Neo-Orthodoxy," *Scottish Journal of Theology* 56 (2003): pp. 227-43.

9. Jeffrey Stout, *The Flight from Authority* (Notre Dame: University of Notre Dame Press, 1981).

10. Debra Dean Murphy, "Worship as Catechesis: Knowledge, Desire, and Christian Formation," *Theology Today*, vol. 58, no. 3 (October 2001): pp. 321-32.

11. Rene Descartes, *Discourse on Method*, as quoted in Murphy, "Worship as Catechesis," pg. 322.

12. Rene Descartes, *Discourse on Method and the Meditations*, trans. F. E. Sutcliffe (Harmondsworth: Penguin Books, 1968), pg. 95.

13. *CD*, III, 1, pp. 359-60.

14. *CD*, II, 1, pg. 411.

15. *CD*, III, 1, pg. 348.

16. *CD*, I, 1, pg. 475.

17. Charles Taylor, *Sources of the Self: The Making of Modern Identity* (Cambridge: Harvard University Press, 1989).

18. Karl Barth, *Protestant Thought: From Rousseau to Ritschl* (New York: Simon & Schuster, 1969), pp. 52-54.

19. Barth refers to this insight of Hume briefly in *CD*, III, 1, pg. 405.

20. John Milbank, *Theology and Social Theory* (Oxford: Basil Blackwell, 1990), pg. 1.

21. Ibid., pg. 109.

22. Here I am helped greatly by Lash, *Easter in Ordinary*, pp. 108-12.

23. Schleiermacher, *On Religion: Speeches to its Cultured Despisers*, trans. John Oman (New York: Harper & Row, 1958), pg. 41.

24. Hegel, pg. 284; Lash, pg. 112.

25. *CD*, II, 1, pg. 339. Edward Farley reworks the Schleiermachian notion that our subjectivity is the point of theology when he defines theology as "a deliberate, focused, and self-conscious thinking that has its origin in faith's need to interpret itself and its situation." In other words, theology is self-conscious talk about ourselves. Edward Farley, *Practicing Gospel: Unconventional Thoughts on the Church's Ministry* (Louisville: Westminster/John Knox Press, 2003), pg. 3. I cannot figure out why Farley calls his own theology "unconventional."

26. Lash, *Easter in Ordinary*, pg. 130. See *CD*, I, 2, pp. 288-91. Flannery O'Connor complained to a friend of those who thought that a doctrine of the church "has to satisfy emotionally to be right." She added, "The truth does not change according to our ability to stomach it emotionally." O'Connor, *Collected Works*, pg. 952.

27. Karl Barth, *The Word of God and the Word of Man*, trans. Douglas Horton (New York: Harper & Row, 1957), pp. 195 ff.

28. See the excellent survey by James E. Davison, "Can God speak a Word to Man: Barth's Critique of Schleiermacher Theology," *The Scottish Journal of Theology*, 37, no. 2 (1984): pp. 189-211. The modern turn that became theology's dead end was made by Langdon Gilkey when he insisted that "questions of the reality of God and the possibility of language about him are still our most pressing theological problems, prior to all other theological issues" (*Naming the Whirlwind* [Indianapolis: Bobbs-Merrill, 1969], pg. 104).

29. Stanley M. Hauerwas demonstrated so well, in his Gifford Lectures, that though he did not intend to be, James, for good or ill, is the true father of modern American theology, most notably the atheology of Reinhold Niebuhr. Stanley M. Hauerwas, *With the Grain of the Universe: The Church's Witness and Natural Theology: Being the Gifford Lectures Delivered at the University of St. Andrews in 2001* (Grand Rapids: Brazos Press, 2001).

30. Nicholas Lash, *Easter in Ordinary*, pg. 90.

31. Lash, *Easter in Ordinary*, pg. 272.

32. Ian Ramsey underscores the peculiar nature of Christian knowing as revelation: "We can develop what seem to us the best stories, but we can never guarantee that for a particular person the light will dawn at a particular point, or for that matter at any point in any particular story. Need this trouble us? Is this not only what has been meant by religious people when they have claimed that the 'initiative' in any 'disclosure' or 'revelation' must come from God?" Ian T. Ramsey, *Religious Language* (London: SCM Press, 1957), pg. 56.

33. *CD*, IV, 3, pp. 512ff.

34. Revelation for Barth, as Christina Baxter puts it, "straddles objectivity and subjectivity, and is never completed or finished, for the relationship between God who is giving Himself to be known, and the 'human subject' who is receiving the capacity to know God is a continuing relationship; it has to be 'new every morning' or it is not knowledge of God at all." Christina Baxter, "The Nature and Place of Scripture in the Church Dogmatics," in John Thompson, ed., *Theology Beyond Christendom* (Allison Park, Pa.: Pickwick Publications, 1986), pg. 35.

35. In a wonderful sermon on John 1:4, "The Life Was the Light of Men," Luther notes that there are three kinds of light: the light of the sun, which shines graciously even on "cows and pigs," but humans alone are "endowed with the glorious light of reason and intellect." Finally there is that greater light, "the Word," by which, "He reveals Himself to His elect through the Holy Spirit and the oral Word." Barth surely would approve of this stress upon the "greater light" as the source for our theology and preaching. The sermon is found in the American edition of *Luther's Works*, vol. 22: 5.

36. Trevor Hart, *Regarding Karl Barth* (Downers Grove, Ill.: InterVarsity Press, 1999), pp. 30-31. In this eventual quality of revelation, Barth was so wonderfully Lutheran. Joseph Mangina quotes Luther: "[The gospel] is not an eternal, lasting, static doctrine, but like a moving shower of rain which strikes what it strikes and misses what it misses. Nor does it return or halt, but is followed by the sunshine and warmth which lick it up." Quoted by Mangina, *Karl Barth*, pg. 33. I believe it was Barth's eventful notion of revelation that led him to say that those who are the recipients of revelation therefore must

"never lose a sense of humour in relation to themselves" (CD, IV, 2, pg. 125). We must do our biblical interpretation with a huge dose of self-deprecating humor.

37. George Hunsinger says that "nothing is more likely to lead the reader of the Church Dogmatics astray than a nondialectical imagination. . . . Unlike theologies which banish mystery to certain inexpressible fringes beyond the reach of human language (as though everything Christian theology needs to say can be said within the conventional bounds of reason), Barth proceeds from the premise that, with the advent of the truth of God, the structure of language has been ruptured at the very core . . . deliberate paradox or conjunction of opposites is the fitting vehicle of expression." George Hunsinger, How to Read Karl Barth: The Shape of His Theology (New York: Oxford University Press, 1991), pg. ix.

38. See Buber, "What Is Man," pg. 148.

39. Reinhold Niebuhr, in his The Nature and Destiny of Man, famously quoted Barth's claim that "the problem is not whether God is a person but whether we are. . . . God is really a person, really a free subject." The debate over the eclipse of the person in modernity was taken up by Hauerwas in With the Grain of the Universe, pg. 5, ch. 6. Barth's quote is found in CD, I, 1, pg. 157 (also pg. 138). See also the discussion in Steven Webb, The Divine Voice, pg. 179. The Dogmatics keeps demonstrating Barth's conviction that theological method follows and does not precede theological content. See his development of his theme in CD, I, 2, pg. 853. Theological method is "the unfolding and presentation of the content of the Word of God."

40. Lash, Easter in Ordinary, pg. 201.

41. Buber, The Eclipse of God, pg. 23.

42. Preached on Easter, 2004.

43. I was helped in this sermon by O. Wesley Allen Jr. in his very helpful book Preaching Resurrection (St. Louis: Chalice Press, 2004), pp. 107-8.

44. Karl Barth, Göttingen Dogmatics, vol. 1 (henceforth GD) (Edinburgh: T. & T. Clark, 1991).

45. GD, pg. 47.

46. Ibid., pg. 48.

47. James H. Cone, Black Theology and Black Power (New York: Orbis, 1969), pg. 120.

48. Easter in Ordinary, pg. 91.

49. Barth, Theological Existence Today (London: Hodder and Stoughton, 1933), pg. 9. For a good critique of "experience" as a basis for preaching, see the critique of feminist experiential theology by Katherine Sonderegger, "Barth and Feminism" in Webster, pp. 215 ff.

50. William H. Willimon, ed., The Sunday after Tuesday: Campus Pulpits Respond to 9/11 (Nashville: Abingdon Press, 2002).

51. George Hunsinger, How to Read Karl Barth: The Shape of His Theology (New York: Oxford University Press, 1991), pg. 121.

52. Hunsinger, pg. 122.

53. Barth is certainly being very Pauline when he insists that our knowledge of God begins with God, with God's knowledge of us rather than our knowledge of God. See Gal. 4:9; 1 Cor. 13:12.

54. The eloquent P. T. Forsyth, a British Congregationalist of another century who shared many affinities with Barth, put God's initiative in this way:

> The Gospel descends on man, it does not rise from him. It is not a projection of his innate spirituality. It is revealed, not discovered, not invented. It is of grace, not works. It is conferred, not attained. It is a gift to our poverty, not a triumph of our resource. It is something which holds us, it is not something that we hold. It is something that saves us, and nothing that we have to save. Its Christ is a Christ sent to us and not developed from us, bestowed on our need and not produced from our strength, and He is given for our sin more than for our weakness. (Peter Taylor Forsyth, "Positive Preaching and the Modern Mind," The Lyman Beecher Lectures on Preaching delivered at Yale University in 1907 [Grand Rapids: Baker, 1980], pg. 212)

For Barth on grace, I find this quote to typify his notion that grace always wounds us from above:

> Reproach is the fate of each servant of the Word. He or she must bear the reproach and resistance of the world, a world that always thinks of another god, and attempts to find that god, who only through grace and only as grace is revealed. But he or she must also suffer the reproach and resistance of the church that always wants grace not to be grace. That God is free, that God wants the world, that god remains free, is what the church doesn't want to hear. But that is just what the preacher must say, who must proclaim the kingdom of Christ. thereby comes the reproach and the resistance. If the preacher has nothing to suffer, then the preacher is not a preacher of grace. The priests who serve idols and the preacher of the law have nothing to suffer. (Barth, *Der Dienst am Wort Gottes Theologische Existenz heute* [Heft 13], Munchen, 1934, pg. 17, my translation)

55. Martin Luther, *Lectures on Galatians* [1535] trans. Jaroslav Pelikan, LW, 26:387.

56. Although I have no interest in defending the term "postliberal," as it has been applied to people like me and Hauerwas, I agree with Sam Wells's definition of the term as essentially a statement about how we think about revelation:

> Postliberalism is primarily a statement about revelation. It is a rejection of the Enlightenment assumption that reality can be discovered empirically, and that the 'world' disclosed in the Bible—revelation—is true only to the extent that it coincides with this given empirical world. Instead, postliberals start theological reflection with God's self-revelation. They adopt no *a priori* philosophical understanding of the nature of existence—no 'foundation.' . . . They see the theologian's task primarily to describe how the faith works. In this they differ from those who seek to explain or to justify the faith. (Sam Wells, *Transforming Fate into Destiny: The Theological Ethics of Stanley Hauerwas* [Eugene, Or.: Cascade Books, 2004], pp. 53-54)

57. It is because of this realistic emphasis that Barth was accused of teaching a "positivism of revelation." Revelation must simply be received and reported as it is given. Dietrich Bonhoeffer, *Letters and Papers from Prison*, ed. Eberhard Bethge (London: SCM Press, 1963), April 30, 1944; June 8, 1944. Whatever Bonhoeffer actually meant by this statement is the subject of much debate. See Andreas Pangritz, *Karl Barth in the Theology of Dietrich Bonhoeffer* (Grand Rapids: Eerdmans, 2000), especially chapter 3.

58. Graham White, "Karl Barth's Theological Realism," pg. 60.

59. In a wonderful examination of the Trinity in American preaching (there isn't much), Marguerite Shuster quotes an unfortunate 1970 sermon from Methodist Harold A. Bosley, in which he says, "I will be interested and informed by the experiences of Paul, Augustine, Luther, and Wesley. But I will never, as long as I try to be a morally responsible person, subordinate my experiences to theirs. . . . I simply cannot turn over to anyone else the responsibility for stating the ultimate theological implications of the experiences I have in my own life." Shuster wonders if Bosley would take such self-assured responsibility for the repairing of his car. I am struck by Bosley's statement that it is "morally responsible" to trust only himself for his revelation. "Preaching the Trinity: A Preliminary Investigation," pp. 354-81 in *The Trinity* (Oxford: Oxford University Press, 1999), pg. 363.

60. CD, 1, 2, pg. 4.

61. Michael Buckley, in his *At the Origins of Modern Atheism* (New Haven: Yale University Press, 1987), showed how the Jesuits virtually invented modern atheism by trying to argue for the existence of a God that, as it turns out, the classical Christian tradition did not believe in anyway.

62. Quoted by Lash, *Easter in Ordinary*, pg. 167.

63. Thomas F. Torrance, *Transformation and Convergence in the Frame of Knowledge* (Grand Rapids: Eerdmans, 1984), pg. 292.

64. *CD*, II, 1, pg. 260, where he has his major inquiry into the knowledge of God.

65. *GD*, pg. 61.

66. This sense of revelation as miracle, as undeserved gift of God, is at the base of everything Barth says about God, and by implication, what he says about preaching. When *Romans* appeared, it was this stress on miracle that Bultmann found to be an intellectual evasion. Bultmann complained that Barth overstated the miraculousness of revelation. "Is the paradox [between faith and reason] overdone?" he asked Barth. He said that by making revelation so miraculous, Barth had removed revelation from any process of human consciousness. Bultmann's reactions to Barth's miraculousness are discussed in Bockmuehl, *The Unreal God*, pp. 80 ff.

67. I like Joseph Mangina's way of putting the miraculous matter of revelation in Barth:

> There is no basis for proclamation other than that provided by the Word of God itself. The quest for the human conditions of talk about God is finally illusory. There are no such conditions. Revelation is possible because it occurs—or more concretely, because God is the Lord. In a sovereign act of mercy, God draws our fallen speech (which in itself can never be *other* than speech about ourselves!) into correspondence with his own self-utterance. Human language bears witness to the divine Word. That it should do so lies entirely in God's hands. Yet miraculously, this does happen. Revelation occurs. God speaks. Even more extraordinary, this speech is heard, as the Spirit awakens human beings to faith and obedience. (Mangina, *Karl Barth*, pg. 31)

68. *GD*, pg. 61.

69. Ibid., pp. 46-47.

70. Ibid., pg. 46.

71. Ibid., pg. 49.

72. As noted in Kierkegaard's *Fear and Trembling* (Princeton: Princeton University Press, 1954), pg. 49

73. *GD*, pg. 51.

74. Ibid., pg. 52.

75. Ibid., pg. 53.

76. K. H. Miskotte speaks of the "jubilation of reason" in Barth's *Dogmatics*. *Über Karl Barths Kirchliche Dogmatik*, pg. 59.

77. Gustaf Wingren, trans. Eric W. Wahlstrom, *Theology in Conflict: Nygren, Barth, Bultmann* (Philadelphia: Muhlenberg Press, 1958), pp. 28-29. See also Wingren, *The Living Word: A Theological Study of Preaching and the Church* (Philadelphia: Muhlenberg Press, 1960), pp. 19, 31-32.

78. Wingren, *Theology in Conflict*, pg. 34.

79. Ibid., pg. 37.

80. Ibid., pg. 108.

81. *CD*, IV, 3, pg. 184.

82. Wingren, *The Living Word*, pp. 205-6.

83. In Barth, "conversion" is a decidedly noetic experience, an acknowledgment of the facts, an admission of the way things are now .that God has invaded the world as the Christ. As George Hunsinger puts it,

> The transition effected by the existential moment of salvation is seen as a transition from the opaque mystery of sin to the luminous mystery of faith. It is therefore a transition from nonacknowledgment (whether in the form of ignorance or indifference or hostility) to acknowledgment, from a mode of participating in salvation which is virtual and unresponsive to a mode which is active and alive. Faith as such does not create or contribute anything new. It consists solely in the existential actualization of a salvation which cannot be conceived except as already objectively actualized. From the point of view of eternity, so to speak, the transition is one in which an already actualized salvation is manifested, attested,

and confirmed. Yet from the point of view of the active historical recipient, the transition is clearly one in which all things have become new. As something real, valid, and complete in itself, the objective moment of salvation is existentially manifested, acknowledged, attested, and received with gratitude and self-surrender. The inner unity of the two moments is so con- ceived that the objective does not occur without this free existential reception and response, nor does the existential occur without this sovereign objective precedence and actualization. (George Hunsinger, *How to Read Karl Barth: The Shape of His Theology* [New York: Oxford University Press, 1991], pg. 113)

4. How to Say What God Says?

1. (New York: Fawcett Crest, 1986), pp. 41-42.

2. Stephen H. Webb, *Re-Figuring Theology—The Rhetoric of Karl Barth* (Albany: State University of New York Press, 1991), pg. viii.

3. Maurice Wiles, *Remaking of Christian Doctrine* (London: SCM Press, 1974), pp. 24-25. Geoffrey W. Bromiley says, at the end of this introduction to the *Church Dogmatics*, "Barth as rhetorician can achieve magnificent flights. . . . Barth has achieved a balance and beauty of arrangement seldom if ever excelled in theological history." *Introduction to the Theology of Karl Barth*, pg. 247.

4. Webb, *Re-Figuring Theology*, pg. viii. Webb's vivid description of Barth's rhetoric reminds me of Cardinal Newman's characterization of the style of scripture: "an unexplored and unsubdued land, with heights and valleys, forests and streams, on the right and left of our path and close about us, full of con- cealed wonders and choice treasures." *An Essay on the Development of Christian Doctrine* (Notre Dame: University of Notre Dame, 1989), pg. 71.

5. One of Barth's students remembered his lectures in this way: "Those who would be listening to Barth for the first time at the beginning of the term would not infrequently panic on hearing his pro- nouncedly Basel-Swiss accent. Especially the many foreigners would at first be close to despair. After fifteen minutes Barth would then interrupt himself, shift his glasses half a stage higher and comfort the new students with the assurance that they would get accustomed to his pronunciation. However, he would not make the slightest effort to express himself in a more generally intelligible way." B. A. Willems, O. P., *Karl Barth: An Ecumenical Approach to His Theology*, trans. M. J. van Velzen (Glen Rock, N.J.: Paulist Press, 1965), pg. 117.

6. Karl Barth, *Homiletics*, trans. Geoffrey W. Bromiley and Donald E. Daniels (Louisville: Westminster/John Knox Press, 1991), pg. 47.

7. Edward Farley is among the many interpreters who have noted that most contemporary homilet- ical theory is about rhetoric rather than theology. Farley, *Practicing Gospel*, pp. 73, 100-101. Yet when Farley critiques homiletics and discusses what homiletics ought to be, his comments seem more rhetor- ical than specifically theological (pp. 77-82). The beginning of the modern turn to rhetoric among German homileticians was led by Gert Otto in Predigt als Rede, *Über die Wechselwirkungen von Homiletik und Rhetorik* (Stuttgart: Urban, 1976).

8. The text that led this turn to the listener was Fred B. Craddock, *As One Without Authority* (Nashville: Abingdon Press, 1983). For a survey of homiletical literature on this "turn to the listener," see Ronald J. Allen, "The Turn to the Listener: A Selective Review of a Recent Trend in Preaching," *Encounter* 64 (2003): pp. 167-96. For an attempt to put the "turn to the listener" into practice in preaching, see Ronald J. Allen, *Hearing the Sermon: Relationship/Content/Feeling* (St. Louis: Chalice Press, 2004). In Germany, an explicit turn from Barth toward the congregation was urged by Hans Werner Dannowski, *Die Kompetenz der Gemeinde*, in Friedrich Wintzer, Predigt, pp. 267-69.

9. CD, IV, 2, pp. 793ff. Kierkegaard complained that Luther had overthrown the Pope only to estab- lish the almighty listener in the place of the Pope. Kierkegaard, *Journals of Kierkegaard*, pg. 169.

10. CD, IV, 3, pg. 933.

11. Saint Augustine, *On Christian Teaching*, trans. R. P. H. Green (Oxford: Oxford University Press, 1997).

12. Ibid., pg. 104.

13. Ibid., pg. 105.

14. Ibid., pg. 119.

15. Augustine, *The First Catechetical Instruction*, Ancient Christian Writers, 2, trans. Joseph P. Christopher (New York: Newman, 1946), pg. 35.

16. Aristotle, *Aristotle on Rhetoric*, trans. George A. Kennedy (New York: Oxford University Press, 1991), pg. 9.

17. "Aristotle, Rhetoric" in *Introduction to Aristotle*, ed. Richard McKeona and trans. W. Rhys Robert (Chicago: University of Chicago Press, 1973), pg. 731 (1355b).

18. David Cunningham, *Faithful Persuasion: In Aid of a Rhetoric of Christian Theology* (Notre Dame: University of Notre Dame Press, 1991), pg. 17. Cunningham's is a wonderful study of the theology of rhetoric and the rhetorical implications of theological assertions. Michael Pasquarello's *Sacred Rhetoric: Preaching as a Theological and Pastoral Practice of the Church* (Grand Rapids: Eerdmans, 2005) is also a wonderful demonstration of a truly theological rhetoric.

19. Augustine, *On Christian Doctrine*, IV, pg. 2.

20. Ludwig Wittgenstein, *Tractatus Logio-Philosophicus*, trans. D. F. Pears and B. F. McGuinness (London: Routledge & Kegan Paul, 1964). First published in German, 1921.

21. Wayne C. Booth, *The Rhetoric of Fiction* (Chicago: University of Chicago Press, 1961), pg. 68.

22. Ibid., pg. 116.

23. Elisabeth Schüssler Fiorenza, *Journal of Biblical Literature* (March 1988): pp. 12-14. In 1973 James Barr, in *The Bible in the Modern World* (London: SCM Press, 1973, pg. 63), asked "whether the time is now coming when a more fully literary study of the Bible will begin to assert itself, a study which will really concern itself with the imagery and structure of the text as it stands, probably ruling out as irrelevant for this purpose the historical and intentional concern which have dominated technical biblical scholarship." That time has come in the great interest in literary criticism of scripture in critics like Kermode, Alter, and others. And rhetorical criticism has been one of the most interesting developments in the area of literary criticism. Birth was given to the field by Amos N. Wilder, *The Language of the Gospel: Early Christian Rhetoric* (New York: Harper & Row, 1964). Robert Funk's *Language, Hermeneutic, and the Word of God: The Problem of Language in the New Testament and Contemporary Theology* (New York: Harper & Row, 1966) was a noteworthy contribution. See also, Stephen Prickett, *Words and the Word, Language, Poetics and Biblical Interpretation* (Cambridge: Cambridge University Press, 1986).

24. Sallie McFague, *Speaking in Parables: A Study in Metaphor and Theology* (Philadelphia: Fortress Press, 1975), pg. 40.

25. Harry Emerson Fosdick, *The Living of These Days: An Autobiography* (New York: Harper, 1956), pg. 99.

26. Friedrich Schleiermacher, *Brief Outline on the Study of Theology*, trans. Terrence N. Tice (Atlanta: John Knox Press, 1966), pp. 98-99. Schleiermacher's influential *Brief Outline on the Study of Theology* treats questions of communication and style only briefly in the discussion of the structure of the church service. For a good discussion of Schleiermacher's attitude toward practical theology, and an example of the increasing importance of practical theology in theological circles today, see John E. Burkhart, "Schleiermacher's Vision for Theology," *Practical Theology*, ed. Don Browning (San Francisco: Harper & Row, 1983). Barth's very rhetorical *Epistle to the Romans* was dismissively accused by Julicher of being "merely practical theology." See also Adolf Julicher, "A Modern Interpretation of Paul," *The Beginnings of Dialectical Theology*, ed. James M. Robinson (Richmond: John Knox Press, 1968), pp. 72-81.

27. Von Balthasar, *The Theology of Karth Barth: Exposition and Interpretation* (San Francisco: Communio Books, Ignatius Press, 1992), pg. 67. Barth complained that Balthasar, "like many Protestants," is "interested in certain philosophical structures of my theology instead of in the theology itself" (pg. 112).

28. Wilhelm Pauck, *Karl Barth: Prophet of a New Christianity?* (New York: Harper, 1931), pg. 19.

29. Von Balthasar, *The Theology of Karl Barth*, pp. 23-24.

30. Webb says that the first person to call Barth an expressionist was Adolf von Harnack, in deriding Barth for his sad lack of modern scientific application to theology. The theologian who most explicitly and extensively reflected upon expressionism's theological implications was Paul Tillich, Barth's nemesis. See John Dillenberger, in the introduction to Paul Tillich, *On Art and Architecture*, ed. Dillenberger and Jane Dillenberger, trans. Robert P. Scharlemann (New York: Crossroad, 1987), pg. xvi. I do not think that Tillich really understood expressionism in art. See William H. Willimon, "Tillich and Art: Pitfalls of a Theological Dialogue with Art," *Religion in Life* (July, 1975), pp. 120-31.

31. Steven Webb called my attention to a wonderful rhetorical study of Pascal by Sara E. Melzer in which she shows how Pascal's figurative language is related to his sense of human sinfulness, sinfulness that creates a gap in our abilities to describe God. See *Discourses of the Fall, A Study of Pascal's Pensees* (Berkeley: University of California Press, 1986). Because our sin wreaks havoc on our epistemological ability to apprehend the truth through language, Pascal believes that we can only apprehend such divine truth by the wager of the heart. Barth would surely not agree to this pietistic solution, but would rather advocate God's gracious gift of metaphor in which God elects to give himself to us through certain divinely appropriated figures of our speech. Webb notes that even postmodernist Derrida says that our deep regret over the split between the signifier and the signified is covertly longing for reunion with God; the sign freed from its real world constraints is a result of the fall. "The sign is always a sign of the Fall. Absence always relates to distancing from God." See: Jacques Derrida, *Of Grammatology*, trans. Gayatri Chakraorty Spivak (Baltimore: Johns Hopkins University Press, 1976), pg. 283. For an attempt to put Derrida and Barth in dialogue, see Graham Ward, *Barth, Derrida and the Language of Theology* (New York: Cambridge University Press, 1995).

32. Friedrich Nietzsche, "On Truth and Lying in an Extra-Moral Sense," in *Friedrich Nietzsche on Rhetoric and Language*, ed. and trans. with an introduction by Sander L. Gilman, Carole Blair, and David J. Parent (New York: Oxford University Press, 1989), pg. 250. These essays show that Nietzsche recovered the sense that philosophy is not an escape from rhetoric but rather a practice of a different sort of rhetoric. Rhetoric is inescapable.

33. Paul de Man, *Allegories of Reading* (New Haven: Yale University Press, 1979), pg. 10.

34. *Romans*, pg. 31. In all, there were six editions of *Der Romerbrief* published between 1919 and 1928. My references are to the English translation of the sixth edition (unrevised from the second edition).

35. *CD*, IV, 3, pg. 322.

36. *Romans*, 1922, pg. 30.

37. Ibid., pg. 29.

38. Webb thoroughly exploits Hans Frei's initial notice of Barth's use of metaphor. Webb quotes Frei: "It [the second edition of *Romans*] is not exactly non-objective [art], but the recurring metaphors certainly aren't mimetic. For the most part they are vaguely mathematical. There are points, tiny, disappearing. There are lines, life and death lines bisecting each other; there is talk about empty space between temporally filled spaces, and so forth and so on." *Karl Barth and the Future of Theology*, ed. David L. Dickerman (New Haven: Yale Divinity School Association, 1969), pg. 5.

39. Webb, pp. 66-70.

40. *Romans*, pg. 225.

41. Ibid., pg. 266.

42. Ibid., pg. 168.

43. Augustine's name appears more in the *Church Dogmatics* than any other patristic thinker (205 times). He cites Aquinas 147 times, Luther 320 times, Calvin 297 times, and Schleiermacher 139 times. Whether Barth is approving or disapproving of these thinkers, I think it significant that Augustine and Luther are mentioned so often.

44. These references to *Confessions* are from the translation by Henry Chadwick, (Oxford: Oxford University Press, 1991). See: Bk. 1.8, pg. 7.

45. Ibid., 1.10, pg. 39.

46. Nicholas Wolsterstorff builds his wonderful philosophical reflections, *Divine Discourse*, around this *"Tolle Lege"* episode from the *Confessions*. Wolsterstorff reminds us that this is one of the most "audacious" claims of Jews, Christians, and Muslims—God speaks. Nicholas Wolsterstorff, *Divine Discourse: Philosophical Reflections on the Claim that God Speaks* (Cambridge: Cambridge University Press, 1995). In these lectures, Wolsterstorff also said, "It was Karl Barth who, of all contemporary theologians, spoke most insistently and persistently, and I might add, provocatively, about God speaking" (pg. 58).

47. Ibid., 1.4, pg. 5.

48. For a comprehensive anthology of this shift from the perspective of "analytical" philosophy, see Richard Rorty, ed., *The Linguistic Turn: Recent Essays in Philosophical Method* (Chicago: University of Chicago Press, 1967).

49. William James, *The Will to Believe and Human Immortality* (New York: Dover, 1956), pg. 9.

50. William James, *A Pluralistic Universe* (Cambridge: Harvard University Press, 1977 [1908]), pg. 148.

51. See Richard Rorty, *Philosophy and the Mirror of Nature* (Princeton: Princeton University Press, 1979), especially pp. 11-12, 371. I am indebted to Stephen Webb for pointing me toward Rorty and Heidegger on language.

52. "Man acts as though he were the shaper and master of language, while in fact language remains the master of man." Martin Heidegger, "Building Dwelling Thinking," *Poetry, Language, Thought*, trans. Albert Hofstadtr (New York: Harper & Row, 1971), pg. 146.

53. Nicholas Lash, *Easter in Ordinary: Reflections on Human Experience and the Knowledge of God* (Notre Dame: University of Notre Dame Press, 1988), pg. 13.

54. David S. Cunningham, *Faithful Persuasion: In Aid of a Rhetoric of Christian Theology* (Notre Dame: University of Notre Dame Press, 1990), pg. 68.

55. Chaim Perelmean and Lucie Olbrechts-Tyteca, *The New Rhetoric: A Treatise on Argumentation*, trans. John Wilkinson and Purcell Weaver (Notre Dame: University of Notre Dame Press, 1969).

56. Gary Wills, *Lincoln at Gettysburg* (New York: Simon & Schuster, 1999).

57. CD, I, 2, pg. 825.

58. Bruce L. McCormack, "Graham Ward's *Barth, Derrida and the Language of Theology*," in *Scottish Journal of Theology*, 49, no. 1 (1996): pp. 97-109.

59. Webb says that the bomb analogy is often made and is originally attributed to Karl Adam. See, for example, T. H. L. Parker, *Karl Barth* (Grand Rapids: Eerdmans, 1970), pg. 56.

60. In an introduction to a collection of letters between him and his good friend Thurneysen, Barth admits that their language during their crisis theology phase "was rich, not to say over rich, in images of all kinds, among which quite noticeable the military and particularly those drawn from the field of artillery played a decisive role. One may shake his head in disapproval, but one can do nothing about it! The first world war was at that time still very much alive in our imaginations, and in fairness also it must be recognized that our decidedly embattled situation during those years drew such forms of expression inevitably from our pens." Karl Barth, *Revolutionary Theology in the Making: Barth-Thurneysen Correspondence, 1914–1925*, trans. James D. Smart (Richmond, Va.: John Knox Press, 1964), pg. 71. On the relationship of Barth and Thurneysen's preaching, see Elmer George Homrighausen, Karl Barth "The Preaching of Karl Barth and Eduard Thurneysen," *Religion in Life*, 3, no. 2 (Spring 1934): pp. 231-44.

61. Karl Barth, "Offenbarung, Kirche, Theologie," *Theological Existence Heute* 9 (1934): p. 16.

62. Langdon Gilkey, "An Appreciation of Karl Barth," *How Karl Barth Changed My Mind*, ed. Donald K. McKim (Grand Rapids: Eerdmans, 1986), pg. 152.

63. CD, I, 1, pg. 239.

64. See John Updike, *Roger's Version* (New York: Knopf, 1996), pg. 42.

65. *The Correspondence of Flannery O'Connor and the Brainerd Cheneys*, ed. C. Ralph Stephens (Jackson: University Press of Mississippi, 1986), pp. 180-81.

66. Karl Barth, *Epistle to the Romans*, trans. Edwyn C. Hoskyns (Oxford: Oxford University Press, 1968), pg. 225.

67. John Bowden, *Karl Barth, Theologian* (London: SCM Press, 1983), pg. 13. Herbert Hartwell also uses a musical analogy (without elaboration) to describe Barth's style, calling *The Epistle to the Romans* "a very hymn in praise of the Goodness of God," *The Theology of Karl Barth: An Introduction* (London: Duckworth, 1964), pg. 9.

68. Ibid., pg. 14.

69. Webb, pp. 6-7.

70. Jeffrey Stout has a good discussion of the Cartesian foundation of modernist thought in *The Flight from Authority, Religion, Morality and the Quest for Autonomy* (Notre Dame: University of Notre Dame Press, 1981), Part 1.

71. Quoted by Webb from John Locke, *Essay Concerning Human Understanding*, vol. 2 (Oxford: Clarendon Press, 1894), pp. 146-47.

72. *Romans*, pg. 224.

73. *Romans*, pg. 6.

74. Karl Barth, *The Word of God and the Word of Man*, trans. Douglas Horton (New York: Harper & Row 1956), pg. 184. Hereafter referred to as *WG*.

75. *WG*, pg. 187.

76. Ibid., pp. 198-99.

77. Ibid., pg. 197.

78. Ibid., pg. 186.

79. Nicholas Wolsterstorff, *Divine Discourse: Philosophical Reflections on the Claim That God Speaks* (Cambridge: Cambridge University Press, 1995), demonstrates that one can make no assault on the modern world that is more devastating than this: "And God said. . . . " The notion that God speaks and that God can be directly heard by human beings is a notion that at least two centuries of philosophy has been assaulting. I think that Wolsterstorff mounts a wonderful defense of the claim that God speaks (using Barth as one of his examples).

80. *WG*, pg. 207. In a letter to his friend Georg Merz, Barth said that he hoped "the proud space of the great Hegel not only to reach but also to overtake" through the use of dialectic which will be the "sword to battle against" contemporary theology. Letter in Karl Barth—Archiv, Basel. June 9, 1933. My translation. See the wonderful analysis of Hegel's influence on Barth, as well as its basis for the current debate between "right wing" Barthians and "left wing" Barthians in Gerhard Sauter, *Eschatological Rationality*, ch. 6, "Shifts in Karl Barth's Thought."

81. *WG*, pp. 133-37.

82. *Romans*, pg. 184.

83. Webb, *Refiguring Theology*, pg. 148. This is the move that was much stressed by von Balthasar, the move from dialectical to analogical thinking from the early to the later Barth. Today, most commentators are agreed that many of Barth's expressionistic, dialectical tendencies that characterize *Romans* continued, though to a lesser degree, throughout Barth's life.

84. Webb, pg. 149.

85. Ibid., pg. 150.

86. Karl Barth, *Die christliche Dogmatik im Entwurf, Erster Band: Die Lehre vom Worte Gottes. Prolegomena zur christlichen Dogmatik* (Munich: Chr. Kaiser Verlag, 1927). This untranslated volume should be distinguished from the later *Dogmatik im Grundriss* (Christian Kaiser Verlag, 1947), English translation by G. T. Thomason, *Dogmatics in Outline* (New York: Harper & Row, 1959).

87. I was impressed, in reading some of Barth's early sermons, how often he railed against subjectivism. In Sermon 53, Nov. 20, 1901, he says, "We must overcome egoism; including pious and intellectual egoism." And in Sermon 134, Sept. 1912, he says, "God be thanked, it doesn't matter if I'm converted. It only matters if Christ is working on me." Handwritten sermons in the Karl Barth archives in Basel.

88. Busch, *Life*, pg. 209.

89. Quoted by Webb, pg. 155.

90. Donald Phillips, *Karl Barth's Philosophy of Communication* (New York: Georg Olms Verlag, 1981), pg. x.

91. See: Torrance, *Karl Barth, An Introduction to His Early Theology, 1910–1931*, especially pp. 151-58. Also see: Graham White, "Karl Barth's Realism," *Neue Zeitschrift fur systematisch theologie und Religionsphilosophie* 26 (1984): pp. 54-70, and George Hunsinger, "Beyond Literalism and Expressionism: Karl Barth's Hermeneutical Realism," *Modern Theology* 3 (1987): pp. 209-23.

92. *CD*, I, 2, pg. 125.

93. Barth, *Dogmatics in Outline*, pg. 9.

94. Barth, *Evangelical Theology*, pg. 3.

95. *CD*, I, 2, pp. 866-67.

96. Ibid., I, 2, pp. 866-67.

97. Ibid., I, 2, pp. 125.

98. Gary Dorrien, *Theology Without Weapons: The Barthian Revolt in Modern Theology* (Louisville: Westminster/John Knox Press, 2000), pg. 3.

99. See: *CD*, II, 1, pg. 210; III, 1, pg. 379; IV, 3, pg. 118.

100. Saint Augustine, *On Christian Teaching*, trans. R. P. H. Green (Oxford: Oxford University Press, 1997), pg. 120.

101. George Hunsinger, *How to Read Karl Barth: The Shape of His Theology* (New York: Oxford University Press, 1991), pp. 44-48.

102. Lections for the eighth Sunday after Pentecost, year C.

103. *CD*, II, 1, pp. 7, 24, 249, 251, 439.

104. In an influential essay on Isaiah 43:8-14, Paul Ricoeur says that there are four characteristics of the witness that distinguish the testimony of a witness:

> The witness is not a volunteer, not just anyone who comes forward to give testimony, but only the one who is sent to testify.
>
> The testimony of the witness is not about the general meaning of human experience but about God's claim upon life. God is the subject of this testimony.
>
> The purpose of the testimony is proclamation to all peoples. It is on behalf of the people, for their belief and understanding that the testimony is made.
>
> The testimony is not merely one of the words but rather demands a total engagement of speech and action. The whole life of the witness is bound up in the testimony. (Paul Ricoeur, "The Hermeneutics of Testimony," *Essays on Biblical Interpretation*, ed. Lewis S. Mudge [Philadelphia: Fortress Press, 1980], pg. 131)

105. Thomas G. Long, *The Witness of Preaching* (Philadelphia: Westminster, 1989), pp. 42-47.

106. David L. Bartlett, *What's Good About This News?* (Louisville: Westminster/John Knox Press, 2003), pg. 87.

107. Long, *The Witness of Preaching*, pg. 44.

108. George Hunsinger, *How to Read Karl Barth*, pg. 48.

109. Steven Webb, in arguing for a Christian privileging of the ear over the eye and the spoken word over the artistic image, links a decline in preaching to theological weakness. "The doctrine of the Trinity is the only intellectual bulwark in the West against the apotheosis of the eye." We worship a God who communicates through Word, says Webb, and the ascendancy of film and image over word is an indication of a limp Trinitarianism. Webb, *The Divine Voice*, pg. 214.

110. George Hunsinger, "How to Read Karl Barth: The Shape of His Theology" (Ph.D. diss., Yale University, 1988). Hunsinger, one of our most able contemporary interpreters of Barth, quite helpfully identifies "Six Motifs in Barth's Theology." Although Barth's theology does not lend itself to simple schematization, and although Barth resisted attempts to schematize and categorize his work, Hunsinger's motifs are a helpful guide to those who try to negotiate the circular, repetitive, complex labyrinth of Barth's thought, particularly in the *Church Dogmatics*:

1. ACTUALISM

A human being exists as a divine act. Revelation is God's continual, every moment condescending to humanity. This event is miraculous, ever new. All knowledge of God is a gift of God. There is no "having" in our relationship with God, only God's continual acts of giving and our constant receiving.

2. PARTICULARISM

Only God can speak of God. And God's particular way of speaking is the event called Jesus Christ. Christian thought and speaking must always discipline itself to stay close to this particular revelation, the Eternal Word, and be suspicious of all abstraction and generalization as potential ways of escaping the particular Word made flesh. Jesus Christ is the unique source for all thinking, and the peculiar test for validity of our God statements.

3. OBJECTIVISM

Revelation and salvation are mediated through ordinary creaturely objects. Divine self-giving, self-enactment is "objective"—real, valid, effective whether acknowledged and received by creature or not. Barth therefore rejects so much of modern theology's subjective, inward experience as an inadequate means of talking about God. The Incarnation is a fact that requires only our acknowledgment. Barth emphasizes that revelation is objective, it has a self-existence and an over-againstness in relationship to us. Thus, God must move toward us, for we have no way of moving toward God.

4. PERSONALISM

God comes to us as a personal address—not in abstract or general concepts. Knowledge of God is fellowship with God. Truth is personal (i.e., Jesus the Christ). Justification / sanctification are aspects of vocation; God's personal address to us. Jesus Christ is the objective fact of revelation; the Holy Spirit works that fact in us as a subjective reality. In Barth "subjective" is always a reference, not to our personal experience but to the work of the Holy Spirit in us, to God's subjectivity offered to us, made an "object" to us so that we might commune with God. Truth is encounter, communion, and salvation is always an address, a vocation.

5. REALISM

Theological language, by the grace of God, miraculously refers to God. By the grace of God, our talk about God is no mere projection of our subjectivities but a realistic dealing with reality. Theological language is analogical and actually refers to reality. Barth can thus speak of theology as a "science" in which theology remains tied to a real object of investigation—the self-revealing God.

6. RATIONALISM

Theological language is rational, cognitive. Controlled by its object (God in Jesus Christ), it is a "science," and it follows rational procedures that are congruent with the object of its investigation. Theology need not retreat into the subjective recesses of human feelings. Theology is rational in that it is guided by certain rules of thought dictated by its subject matter (God in Jesus Christ). Salvation is noetic, a fact that is rationally acknowledged as a true fact.

In fairness to Hunsinger, I should note that he says that these themes are "adjectival in force, not substantive" (pg. 31). They are qualifications of Barth's subject matter, he argues, never the subject matter itself. (This critique of Hunsinger is made by Webb, pg. 7.)

111. Joseph L. Mangina, *Karl Barth: Theologian of Christian Witness* (Louisville: Westminster/John Knox Press, 2004), pg. 20.

112. Kornelis Heiko Miskotte, *Über Karl Barths Kirchliche Dogmatik, Kleine Präludien und Phantasien*, Theologische Existenz heute, n.s., vol. 89 (Munich: Chr. Kaiser Verlag, 1961), pp. 17ff. Miskotte has a wonderful analysis of the "fugue-like repetition" of the *Dogmatics*.

113. Mozart's "Serenade for Winds," no. 10, Bb (K 631), seems to me to be a perfect illustration of this tendency.

114. See Theodore A. Gill, "Barth and Mozart," *Theology Today* 43 (1986): pp. 403-11.

115. David Ford, *Barth and God's Story*, pp. 28-29.

116. *CD*, I, 1, pg. 52. In his fine book, *Early Christian Rhetoric*, Amos N. Wilder says that unlike most forms of classical rhetoric, early Christian communicators engaged in revelation, not persuasion. This seems parallel to Barth's emphasis on the preacher as herald rather than on the classical emphasis on the speaker as persuader.

117. *CD*, I, 1 pg. 72.

118. Ibid., pg. 22.

119. Webb, pg. 161.

120. Douglas John Hall in *Confessing the Faith: Christian Theology in a North American Context* (Minneapolis: Fortress Press, 1996) says that preaching suffers today because of a lack of confidence in its message, therefore it becomes the victim of the entertainment age, in which the audience means everything. Hall says, "The first requirement of the preacher is to interpret the scriptures, and the Main Thrust of the Scriptures, moralism in the history of Christianity not withstanding, is not the laying down of precepts and rules for living but the declaration of God's unmerited grace and love. Edification of the faithful, the building up of the Body of Christ, is certainly part of the intention it was at, as of all other aspects of worship; but is not the primary function. First and foremost, preaching is confession" (pg. 361).

121. *CD*, II, 1, pg. 635.

122. *GD*, pg. 269.

123. Karl Barth, *Evangelical Theology: An Introduction*, trans. Grover Foley (New York: Holt, Rinehart & Winston, 1963), pp. 3, 16.

124. Barbara Brown Taylor notes what most preachers sooner or later experience: "Something happens between the preacher's lips and the congregation's ears that is beyond prediction or explanation. . . . There is more going on here than anyone can say." *The Preaching Life* (Cambridge: Cowley Publications, 1993), pg. 185.

125. This is why it is difficult for one to be a faithful Christian preacher if one has a truly conservative temperament. The gospel is always an assault upon the present order. Barth once quipped that it may be possible for political liberals sometimes to be right; for political conservatives, almost never. I believe that he said this, not as a die-hard socialist, but rather as an experienced preacher.

126. Bowden finds Barth's wit a "mixed blessing. At worst it can be a vicious weapon of destruction, so that one American theologian called him a 'verbal sadist.' Even so, provided that one agrees with Barth, his irony and ridicule to the point of maliciousness can be extraordinarily entertaining" (Bowden, pg. 11). It should be noted that though Barth's wit and irony are biting to the point of being sadistic, that same Barthian wit is frequently turned on himself, sometimes in a more biting way than upon his readers or his opponents.

5. Word Makes World

1. *CD*, I, 2, pp. 803, 813.

2. Barth is convinced of the total, universal, completed work of Christ. Jesus makes our redemption so complete that it puts to death human aspiration to make some contribution to our redemption. "We died: the totality of all sinful men, those living, those long dead, and those still to be born, Christians who necessarily know and claim it, but also Jews and heathen, whether they hear and receive the news

or whether they prod and still try to escape it. His death was the death of all, quite independently of their attitude or response to this event" (CD, IV, 1, pg. 295). This sense of the completion of the redemptive work accounts in great part for Barth's lack of interest in the modern stress on listener "response" and "listener reaction" in preaching.

3. These quotes are helpfully assembled by Hunsinger in his good discussion of Barth's epistemology. George Hunsinger, How to Read Karl Barth—The Shape of His Theology (New York: Oxford Press, 1991), pg. 196. Against any apophatic failure to acknowledge the revelation of divine mystery, Barth keeps stressing the mystery of the Trinity, but does not let human mystification impress him. In the Trinity, God is veiled, but God is also unveiled. Too much talk of "mystery" can be simply a form of human agnosticism. The agnostic begins with the assumption that God is unknowable, and works from a false humility.

"Mystery does not just denote hiddenness of God but His revelation in a hidden, i.e., a non-apparent way which intimates indirectly rather than directly. Mystery is the concealment of God in which He meets us precisely when He unveils Himself to us. . . . Mystery thus denotes a divine givenness of the Word of God which also fixes our own limits in which it distinguishes itself from everything that is given otherwise" (CD, I, 1, pg. 165). There is a difference between the mystery of God's scandalous self-disclosure in the Jew from Nazareth and the projection of human mystification. The Trinity helps protect the Christian faith from becoming "spiritual."

Bultmann hoped to foster appropriate speech about God through his program of "demythologizing." But Barth is so impressed, much more so than Bultmann, with the God who speaks. Both want to avoid the danger of the "objectification" of God—projecting limited, workable human categories upon the divine. But Barth goes at it quite differently. We must be careful not to project our images of God onto God, or our prior conceptions, including the prior conception that God is an utterly unknowable mystery.

4. Hunsinger, pg. 197. See also CD, I, 2, pp. 172-73.

5. Göttingen Dogmatics: Instruction in the Christian Religion, edited by Reiffen, trans. by Bromiley, vol. 1 (Grand Rapids: Eerdmans, 1990), pg. 96.

6. The Christian Century, September 13, 1939, pg. 1097.

7. H. van der Geest, Presence in the Pulpit: The Impact of Personality in Preaching (Atlanta: John Knox Press, 1981).

8. Eberhard Jüngel, trans., John Webster, God's Being Is in Becoming: The Trinitarian Being of God in the Theology of Karl Barth, a Paraphrase (Grand Rapids: Eerdmans, 2001), pg. 9.

9. Göttingen Dogmatics: Instruction in the Christian Religion, edited by Reiffen, trans. by Bromiley, vol. 1 (Grand Rapids: Eerdmans, 1990), pg. 135.

10. "The relation to God on our side must always be a wrestling like Jacob's [Gen. 32:35 ff.] in which constantly is sought only in God and not in us." (GD, pg. 189)

11. CD, IV, 2, pg. 23.

12. In a Christmas sermon, Barth depicts the Incarnation as an intrusion into our world:

> Dear Brothers and Sisters, Jesus came into Galilee. The Galilee into which he came was a region where the Jews, mingling with the Gentiles, had in many ways adjusted to Gentile customs and thereby lost their good name. Into this Galilee, and to these people, Jesus came. It is the very-same region where the Jews who call themselves Israelis today live in bitter strife with their Arab neighbors. Jesus came there almost two thousand years ago and he comes there today. We are now in the present. Jesus comes also to Suez and to Port Said where the old European powers and the awakening people of Africa and Asia clash. He comes into Hungary where a whole nation fights for its freedom, desperately and yet not in despair. He comes also into Warsaw, into Prague, into Moscow, where the unity, firmness and security of a system believed indestructible has begun to crack. Yes, Jesus comes also into Switzerland, into Basel, where so much money has been collected and so much good done for the Hungarians during the past few weeks, but where at the same time people have been remarkably content to hurl abuses at the nasty Communists far away, as if this were of much help to anyone. Even more

important, Jesus comes to us too; he comes into this prison house, he comes to all its inmates, governors and wardens. The he comes to all of us is the event of Christmas. Yes, he comes to all and everyone. If he is not welcome, he is nevertheless present as a silent guest and listener, and as a silent yet impartial judge as well. Above all he is here, as the hidden Saviour of each and every one of us, fulfilling all human need. For he is the Lord to whom all power is given on earth as in heaven. That he comes to us all is the event of Christmas. (Karl Barth, *Deliverance to the Captives* [New York: Harper & Row, 1961], pg. 68)

13. *GD*, pg. 136.

14. The idea that knowledge of the eternal is an "event" is one of Barth's debts to Hegel. Truth is in constant movement. Barth said that Hegel, more than any other thinker, sensed the vitality and aliveness of God. Unfortunately, Hegel saw God alive in humanity, an anthropocentrism that Barth could not abide. See Barth, *Protestant Thought in the Nineteenth Century* (Grand Rapids: Eerdmans, 2002), ch. 10.

15. *GD*, pg. 272.

16. George Hunsinger, ch. 11, "The Mediator of Communion: Karl Barth's doctrine of the Holy Spirit" in Webster, *The Cambridge Companion to Karl Barth*, pg. 179.

17. *GD*, pg. 271. Charles Bartow helpfully notes the implications of the Incarnation for the centrality of preaching. Preaching is quite naturally at the center of an incarnational faith. "The Word of God is not *verbum* but *sermo*, not *ratio* but *oratio*. It is a lively, face to face aural-oral discourse and suasory action. . . It is *action divina*, God's self-performance." *God's Human Speech: A Practical Theology of Proclamation* (Grand Rapids: Eerdmans, 1997), pg. 26.

18. *GD*, pg. 175. The results of privileging written language over spoken language in theology and making theologians writers rather than preachers may have resulted in problems for theology. Theology that is only meant to be read—alone, silently—rather than proclaimed, is theology always in danger of fossilization and silencing the active, resourceful voice of God as the source of theology.

19. *GD*, pg. 154.

20. Lash, *Easter in Ordinary*, pg. 48.

21. Walter Brueggemann finds Barth's metaphor of veiling and unveiling to be a helpful hermeneutical guide: "Barth has made clear that the God of the Bible is 'Wholly Other.' In conventional interpretation, the accent has been on 'wholly,' stressing the contrast and discontinuity. When, however, accent is placed on 'other,' dramatic interpretation can pay attention to the dialectical, dialogical interaction in which each 'other' impinges upon its partner in transformative ways. . . . 'Otherness' need not mean distance and severity, but can mean dialectical, transformative engagement with." *The Bible and the Postmodern Imagination: Texts under Negotiation* (London: SCM Press, 1993), note on pg. 106.

22. O'Connor, *Mystery and Manners*, ed. Sally and Robert Fitzgerald (New York: Farrar, Straus, and Giroux, 1969), pg. 146.

23. For Torrance, all of Barth's other motifs and later developments pale in comparison to the motif of realistic objectivity: "It is all-important to realise that for Barth the Word of God refers to the most completely objective reality there is, for it is the Word of God backed with God's own ultimate Being." For Barth, as for Torrance, the content that God directs to us in his Word is his own Being, "the downright actuality of God, the ultimate objectivity." Though I think that finally Torrance makes more of Barth's realist epistemology than Barth, his work helpfully highlights the importance of Barth's attempt to move theology from the subjective to the objective. See Dorrien's critique of Torrance, including these quotes, in Dorrien, pg. 162.

24. Barth says, "I regard the doctrine of the Trinity as the true center of the concept of revelation." But then he says he can also sympathize with those who prefer "to see the doctrine of Incarnation as the nucleus of all theology" (*Göttingen Dogmatics: Instruction in the Christian Religion* edited by Reiffen, trans. by Bromiley, vol. 1 [Grand Rapids: Eerdmans, 1990], pg. 131). I think it important, when discussing Barth's views on revelation, to discuss Incarnation and Trinity at the same time, or at least place them together in the same chapter!

25. Barth, *Romans* (London: OUP, 1933), pg. 39.

26. *GD*, pg. 59.

27. Trevor Hart, *Regarding Karl Barth* (Downers Grove, Ill.: InterVarsity Press, 1999), pp. 40-41.

28. Hart, pp. 43-44.

29. *CD*, I, 1, pg. 92.

30. *GD*, pg. 271.

31. This is Trevor Hart's way of characterizing Baillie's critique of Barth's Christology. Trevor Hart, *Regarding Karl Barth* (Downers Grove, Ill.: InterVarsity Press, 1999), pp. 1-2.

32. Baillie, *God Was in Christ*, pg. 28.

33. Ibid., pg. 53.

34. *CD*, I, 2, pg. 29.

35. See *GD*, pg. 444. "The proclamation of Jesus Christ and its dreadful limitation are together the history which embraces and comprises, and thus controls and determines, the history of the world and the history of each and every man" (*CD*, IV, 3, pg. 191). The history of the world is the history of preaching!

36. *GD*, pg. 366.

37. *GD*, pg. 151.

38. Gustaf Wingren, trans. Eric W. Wahlstrom, *Theology and Conflict: Nygren, Barth, Bultmann* (Philadelphia: Mulhlenberg Press, 1958), pg. 109. "We know of no gospel, nor any other book in the New Testament, in which the birth occupies such a central place in the redemptive event as it does in Barth's theology" (pg. 112).

39. Wingren, pp. 109-10. Wingren calls this "the fundamental mistake" in Barth (p. 28). Wingren encapsulates Barth's theology in this way, "God has a certain nature. Man has a certain nature. The latter has no knowledge of the former, unless the former reveals himself to the latter. . . . This revelation occurred in Jesus Christ. 'The Word became flesh' (John 1:14)."

40. Wingren, pg. 115.

41. "The first and basic act of theological work is prayer," Karl Barth, *Evangelical Theology: An Introduction* (London, 1963), quoted by Charles M. Cameron, "Karl Barth—The Preacher," *Evangelical Quarterly*, vol. LXVI, no. 2 (April 1994): pp. 99-106. See also *CD*, I, 2, pp. 755, 695, 684, 531.

42. *CD*, II, 1, pg. 182.

43. *CD*, II, 1, pg. 20. Cf. also II, 1, pg. 361; *Evangelical Theology*, pg. 90. Dorothy Soelle says, "I suspect that we Christians today have the duty to criticize the entire concept of obedience . . . simply because we do not know exactly who God is or what God, at any given moment, wills." *Beyond Mere Obedience* (New York, Pilgrim Press, 1982), pg. 9. Soelle bases her call to disobedience on epistemological modesty. But mere disobedience does not defeat the problem that, in a sense, we are all obedient to some master or another. For instance, many in our culture regard themselves as "free" when in reality they are servants of the consumeristic economy. The task is to be obedient to the true God rather than a false god.

44. *GD*, pg. 168; *CD*, I, 2, pg. 204. When Barth discusses the meaning of the word "to preach" κειρυσσειν, he stresses obedience, the need for the messenger "to give the message exactly as commissioned. Beyond that all that was needed was a loud and resonant voice" (*CD*, IV, 2, pg. 201). Barth said elsewhere, "We need today ministers who take their work seriously, . . . who are devout—provided devotion means obedience to the call, 'follow me.'" *Word of God, Word of Man*, trans. Douglas Hourton (New York: Harper Torchbooks, 1957), pp. 130-31. See also Katherine Sonderegger, "Et Resurrexit," in McDowell and Higton, *Conversing with Barth*, pp. 193ff. for a good discussion of obedience in Barth. Sonderegger notes that obedience is a fundamental aspect of all of Barth's theological method.

45. In *GD*, pp. 192-93, Barth says,

Faith and obedience vis-a-vis revelation stand face to face first of all with this historical, self-explicating revelation, or else they do not stand before revelation. It would be a comfortable conjuring away of the offence but no more and no less than the conjuring away of revelation itself, if we were to say that we will cling to God himself but will have nothing whatever to do with all the astonishing things that are linked to our being able to cling to God himself. Faith means not only believing in God but also believing in this and that. To put it with all the offence that it involves, it means believing in the Trinity, or in the NT miracles, or in the virgin birth. And obedience means not only uniting our own wills with God's but, for example, keeping the ten commandments.

46. *GD*, pg. 12.

47. *CD*, I, 1, pg.150, "The Speech of God as the Act of God."

48. *CD*, II, 1, pg. 213.

49. Hart, pg. 89.

50. Hart goes so far as to say that, in this temporary indwelling of the Word with preaching and scripture, Barth implies "more a Nestorian union than a Chalcedonian one" (pg. 89). While Barth certainly wants a high view of the theological significance of preaching and scripture, their significance is given by the graciousness of the Word being so willing to use these two forms for the presence of the Word, with no guarantee that it will always occur.

51. Barth, *CD*, I, 2, pg. 529. "Fallibility and God, we tend to suppose, don't mix—any more than passability and God, ignorance and God, crucifixion and God," says Trevor Hart. Yet in Barth they do, again and again. "Preaching is human talk about God . . . in and through which God speaks about himself." Hart, pg. 92.

52. *CD*, I, 2, pp. 745-46.

53. Barth stresses this tensive, paradoxical quality of revelation throughout his entire discussion of the three forms of revelation in *GD*, I, pg. 271.

54. *Romans*, pg. 120.

55. *CD*, IV, 3, pg. 118.

56. *GD*, pg. 96.

57. Karl Barth, "How My Mind Has Changed in this Decade," *Christian Century*, vol. LVI, no. 38 (1939), pg. 1132. The vague, abstract quality of contemporary theology, its lack of incarnational, Trinitarian concreteness and specificity really bothered Barth: "Modernist Protestantism in its entirety has simply been a regression to pre-Nicene obscurities and ambiguities regarding the Spirit" (*CD*, I, 1, pg. 468). I believe that this would be the same withering criticism that Barth would have for our current infatuation with generic "spirituality" that is devoid of incarnational or Trinitarian content.

58. Robert E. Cushman, "Barth's Attack Upon Cartesianism and the Future of Theology." *Journal of Religion*, vol. XXXVI, no. 4 (1956), pg. 212; and Torrance, *Karl Barth*, pg. 153.

59. *CD*, III, 2, pg. 91; I, 1, pp. 214, 226. See also III, 2, pp. 124-25.

60. *CD*, III, 1, pg. 50. By implication this means that the creature was created by a Trinitarian Creator primarily to listen to preaching!

61. *CD*, III, 1, pg. 182. I find it interesting that, whereas Barth sees this report of divine conversation to a revelation of the very heart of God, Augustine is clearly troubled by this "Let there be light." Speaking, for Augustine, is a carnal, temporal activity. How could God both be a creature bound in time and yet the creator of time? How could the sound of God's voice be generated in a world that is, as yet, devoid of matter? Augustine concludes that this "Let there be light" was not really a literal "voice." See the discussion in Augustine, *The Literal Meaning of Genesis*, vol. 1, trans. John Hammond Taylor (New York: Newman, 1982), pg. 28.

62. *CD*, III, 1, pg. 183.

63. *CD*, I, 1, pg. 354.

64. Barth says that God is three, a unity and Trinity, by using the metaphor of repetition (*wiederholung*). "The name of the Father, Son, and Spirit means that God is the one God in three fold repetition." Trinity means that God is one God "only in this repetition" (*CD*, I, 1, pg. 350). Perhaps this helps to indicate why Barth so often repeats himself in his theology, because he strives to make his theology one of repetition, saying again what God has said of God's self.

65. Preached in Duke University Chapel, May 30, 1999.

66. Luther sure meant it. In one of his sermons on the Gospel of John, Luther says that God "condescends to enter the mouth of every Christian who professes the faith." Preaching must be "believed as though God's own voice were resounding from heaven." Martin Luther, *Luther's Works*, vol. 24, *Sermons on the Gospel of St. John, Chapters 14-16*, ed. Jaroslav Pelikan (St. Louis: Concordia, 1961), pp. 66-67. Barth is so very Lutheran in what he says about preaching and the Word of God.

67. Trevor Hart, "The Word, the Words and the Witness: Proclamation as Divine and Human Reality in the Theology of Karl Barth," *Tyndale Bulletin*, 46.1 (May 1995): pp. 81-102.

68. R. D. Williams, "Barth on the Triune God," in S. W. Sykes, editor, Karl Barth, *Studies of His Theological Method* (Oxford: Clarendon, 1979), pg. 188.

69. See *The Trinity*, Allan Torrence, pp. 72ff.

70. Nicholas Wolsterstorff, *Divine Discourse: Philosophical Reflections on the Claim that God Speaks* (Cambridge: Cambridge University Press, 1995), pg. 70.

71. Torrance, pg. 78 in Webster.

72. Quoted in Dorrien, pg. 133. Thielicke's criticisms have been constantly in my mind as I have reflected on the implications of Barth's thought for homiletical practice. His criticisms seem to me a typically homiletically formed critique of Barth.

73. *CD*, IV, 1, pg. 112.

74. *CD*, I, 1, pg. 157.

75. *CD*, II, 1, pg. 272.

76. *CD*, I, 2, pg. 346.

77. *CD*, II, 1, pg. 313.

78. From the early days, pietists and evangelicals argued with Barth on the place of our decision in our salvation, finding Barth's deprecating comments on our "decisions for Christ" to be an attack upon evangelical theology (at least as it was conceived in North America). Barth's view of response to God's grace was a considerably more nuanced than most of his evangelical critics understood. Barth was more worried about the threat of vaunted human subjectivity than they. See the discussion of this debate in Eberhard Busch, *Karl Barth and the Pietists, the Young Karl Barth's Critique of Pietism and Its Response*, trans. D. W. Bloesch (Downers Grove, Ill.: InterVarsity Press, 2004), pp. 307-9.

79. Dorrien, pg. 142.

80. Oration XL, 412; Migne, PGXXXVI, 417 BC. Cited in V. Lossky, *The Mystical Theology of the Eastern Church* (London: J. Clarke, 1957), pg. 46.

81. See John Macquarrie, *God-Talk* (London: SCM Press, 1967), pp. 41-49. See also Donald Evans, "Barth on Talk about God," *Canadian Journal of Theology* 16, no. 3-4 (1970): pp. 175-92.

82. Torrance, *The Trinity*, pg. 80. Much contemporary Trinitarian thought stresses the relational qualities of the Trinity, as I have done in my discussion above. Yet some of this relational analogy troubles me because (1) we live in a society of loneliness that yearns for relationship and community, and also (2) it is quite difficult for a society like ours that stresses individualism to conceive of any sort of relationship that is not a conglomeration of individuals who, out of their loneliness, chose to be in relationship—thus our conception of "relationship" tends to be inadequate when applied to the Trinity. Barth teaches us to beware of all analogical thinking.

83. *Humanity of God* (Richmond, Va.: John Knox Press, 1963), pp. 51-56.

84. *CD*, I, 2, Section 17.

85. *CD*, II, 1 pg. 224.

86. Ibid., pg. 225. See Jüngel's detailed discussion of the problems with analogies, and Barth's carefully qualified use of analogy, in *God's Being Is in Becoming*, pp. 13-53.

87. "To talk about revelation means strictly and exclusively to talk on the basis of revelation. The ontic and noetic basis is one and the same in this matter." *Göttingen Dogmatics: Instruction in the Christian Religion* edited by Reiffen, trans. by Bromiley, vol. 1 (Grand Rapids: Eerdmans, 1990), pg. 109.

88. On those rare moments when we preachers speak about the Trinity, we tend to do so by stress upon the so-called "economic" aspects of the Trinity—of our experiences of the operations of the

Trinity in our history—rather than through the "immanentist" aspects of the Trinity—the inner being of God. I fear this is testimony to our abiding modernist assumption that only our experiences are true sources of knowledge. But it is of the nature of the Trinity, Barth says, to be beyond human analogy, and it does not come to us through our experience. Thus the Trinity is the ultimate "transcendent" aspect of our faith—we could never have come up with this notion of God on our own. Perhaps that is why Barth begins his discussion of proclamation and revelation with talk of the immanent Trinity, the inner life of God, as a way of asserting, right at the beginning, that we proclaim only what is revealed to us, not what we have discovered out of our experience. Perhaps all of us preachers ought to be forced to preach about the Trinity at least once a year, at least on Trinity Sunday, so that we are forced to demonstrate that we are talking about something that is utterly unavailable to us except for a revealing God.

89. Ibid., pp. 232ff.

90. McCormack says, "I am confident that the greatest contribution of Karl Barth to the development of Church doctrine will be located in his doctrine of election." Barth makes election that means of knowing God without human speculation. It removes Incarnation from being a safe historical event, set somewhere in an unreachable past, to being an event that reaches out to us, through election, in the present. Barth replaced Calvin's version of double predestination—some elected to salvation and some to damnation—with universal election to salvation through the Father's election of the Son to crucifixion. Through his surprising reworking of Election, Barth brought about, in the words of McCormack, "a revolution in the doctrine of God." God became both subject and object in election.

91. Ibid., pg. 223.

92. CD, II, 1, pg. 213.

93. Ford, *Barth and God's Story*, pp. 74-75.

94. Evans, "Barth on Talk About God," pg. 190. Some of Evans' objections suggest that Evans has not really understood the nature of divine election. It is quite pointless to ask, "Why does God elect this person and not another?" for the Bible renders a God whose elective choices are inscrutable. It is of the nature of divine election to transcend our judgments about the rationale for divine election.

95. See my citation of the work of Rodney J. Hunter on ministerial resistance to preaching in William H. Willimon, *Worship as Pastoral Care* (Nashville: Abingdon Press, 1979), chap. 4.

96. Karl Barth, *The Christian Life: Church Dogmatics*, IV, 4, Lecture Fragments, trans. Geoffrey W. Bromiley (Grand Rapids: Eerdmans, 1981), pg. 184.

97. *Göttingen Dogmatics: Instruction in the Christian Religion* edited by Reiffen, trans. by Bromiley, vol. 1 (Grand Rapids: Eerdmans, 1990), pg. 83.

98. Barth was often accused of "Christomonism." True, Barth says that "theology must fundamentally be Christology and only Christology" (CD, I, 2, pg. 872). But this is Christology not as a principle, not as a system, but as the person who speaks, Jesus Christ, truth as Trinity.

6. The Talkative God

1. GD, pg. 265.

2. GD, pg. 268.

3. *Letzte Zeugnisse*, Zurich, 1969, pg. 19.

4. T. F. Torrance has argued that the problem of preaching is central to all of Barth's work: "His primary concern then [in Safenwil] as now was the question as to what preaching really is as a task with its own independent right and action." T. F. Torrance, *Karl Barth: An Introduction to His Early Theology, 1910–1931* (London: SCM Press, 1962), pg. 41.

5. CD, III, 2, pg. 260.

6. Ibid.

7. Ibid.

8. "Ist etwa ein einziges meiner Worte das Wort, das ich suche, das ich aus meiner grossen Not und Hoffnung heraus eigentlich sagen mochte? Kann ich denn anders reden als so, das andre wieder

aufheben muss?" Karl Barth, *Der Romerbrief*, 1922 (Zurich: Theologische Verlag, 1940), pg. 243 [my translation].

9. *Göttingen Dogmatics: Instruction in the Christian Religion*, edited by Reiffen, trans. by Bromiley, vol. 1 (Grand Rapids: Eerdmans, 1990), pg. 85. *GD* is so lively, so concerned with the effusive self-revelation of God, that I now say to any preacher who wants an introductory experience of the theology of Barth, "Start with *GD* I." It would take a cold-hearted preacher not to be moved by the theology there, not to find rich resources for preaching therein.

10. Ibid., pg. 3.

11. Ibid., pg. 281.

12. Ibid., pg. 6.

13. Ibid., pg. 201.

14. *The Word of God and the Word of Man* (London: Eerdmans, 1928, 1935), pg. 100.

15. "Introduction" to *Göttingen Dogmatics* by Daniel L. Migliore, pg. xxi.

16. Busch, *Karl Barth*, pg. 147.

17. Letter from Barth to Prof. Norman W. Porteous, October 13, 1931, in Karl Barth—Archive, my translation.

18. *GD*, pg. 385.

19. Ibid., pg. 278.

20. Ibid., pg. 475.

21. Ibid., pg. 320.

22. *CD*, IV, 3, pg. 802.

23. *GD*, pg. 38.

24. Gerhard Sauter, *Gateways to Dogmatics: Reasoning Theologically for the Life of the Church* (Grand Rapids: Eerdmans, 2003), pp. 123-24.

25. *GD*, pg. 88.

26. *CD*, I, 1, pp. 93, 95.

27. "According to the testimony of the New Testament, God does not cease to dwell in the world in definite and distinct ways, i.e., even as omnipresent, and without detriment to His omnipresence" (*CD*, I, 2, pg. 481).

28. *CD*, I, 2, pg. 330.

29. I am indebted to George Hunsinger for pointing out to me how "Lutheran" is Barth's critique of "religion," a form of Luther's stress upon justification by faith. Barth's sustained attack on "religion" as a defense against God echoes Luther's. See George Hunsinger, "Postliberal Theology," pg. 55, in Kevin J. Vanhoozer (ed.), *The Cambridge Companion to Postmodern Theology* (Cambridge: Cambridge University Press, 2003). The Paul-through-Luther character of Barth's theology is amazing, particularly when that theology is applied to homiletics. John Milbank thinks that Barth has used Luther's notions of faith in a way that Luther never intended. See Milbank, *Radical Orthodoxy: A New Theology*, pp. 22-23.

30. See *CD*, I, 2, pg. 302.

31. Ibid., pp. 299-300.

32. Garrett Green, "Challenging the Religious Studies Canon: Karl Barth's Theory of Religion" *Journal of Religion*, 75 (1995): pg. 477.

33. *CD*, IV, 1, pg. 480.

34. Ibid., pp. 485ff.

35. New York: Farrar, Straus, Giroux, 2004.

36. Ibid., pg. 114.

37. Ibid., pg. 153.

38. Recorded casual comments from Eberhard Busch, University of Bonn, sometime in 1991.

39. Reginald Fuller says that preachers "are concerned with two poles—the text and the contemporary situation. It is their task to build a bridge between these poles." *The Use of the Bible in Preaching* (Philadelphia: Fortress Press, 1981), pg. 41. This is the sort of nineteenth-century text-to-sermon move that Barth deplores.

40. Karl Barth, *Witness to the Word: A Commentary on John 1*, trans. Geoffrey W. Bromiley, ed. Walther Fürst (Grand Rapids: Eerdmans, 1986), pg. 66.

41. *Barmen* is a kind of extended exposition of the doctrine of justification and its relevance, not only for preaching but also, by implication, for the relationship of Christian preaching to the state. See Karl Barth, *Community, State, and the Church*, with an introduction by Will Herbert, trans. G. Ronald Howe (Garden City, N.Y.: Anchor, 1960). Gerhard Sauter says that throughout his theology Barth kept close to the doctrine of justification "with iron resolution," drawing out its implications for every aspect of Christian thought. *Eschatological Rationality*, pg. 122. The continuing political relevance of Barmen is demonstrated by Charles Villa-Vicencio, ed., *On Reading Karl Barth in South Africa* (Grand Rapids: Eerdmans, 1988).

42. *CD*, II, 1, pg. 150.

43. See Daniel J. Price, *Karl Barth's Anthropology in Light of Modern Thought* (Grand Rapids: Eerdmans, 2002) for a discussion of Schleiermacher and Barth, pp. 61-84. I also recall that Schleiermacher prepared to preach by meditating for a couple of hours on Saturday morning, then preparing his sermon on the basis of his own meditations on himself. More than once Schleiermacher is reported to have broken down in tears in the middle of his sermons, overcome at the emotional profundity of his own sermon!

44. Daniel J. Price, in his fine work on Barth's anthropology, puts the Barth/Schleiermacher relationship succinctly in terms of either/or: "How then do we explain the origin of religious beliefs? Either we can explain religious beliefs as a projection of human needs for love, or we can explain human love as a reflection of divine love. In Schleiermacher's theology we arrive at God by analyzing religious consciousness. Barth had decided that any attempt to make predications about God based on religious consciousness could only lead theology into a cul-de-sac of subjectivism." *Karl Barth's Anthropology*, pg. 291.

45. *CD*, I, 1, pg. 29.

46. *CD*, III, 2, pg. 134, my paraphrase.

47. Lection for The Baptism of Our Lord, Year C.

48. When William B. McClain defines African-American preaching as "rhetoric, repetition, rhythm, and rest," he is making a rhetorical rather than a theological claim. William B. McClain, *Come Sunday: The Liturgy of Zion* (Nashville: Abingdon Press, 1990), pg. 69. Among the representatives of this rhetorical turn in homiletics are: Richard L. Eslinger, *A New Hearing: Living Options in Homiletic Method* (Nashville: Abingdon Press, 1987); Eugene Lowry, *The Homiletical Plot: The Sermon as Narrative Art Form* (Atlanta: John Knox Press, 1980); and of course the text that helped to initiate this turn to the listener, Fred B. Craddock, *As One Without Authority: Essays in Inductive Preaching* (Enid, Okla.: Phillips University Press, 1974). Also worthy of mention is David Buttrick, *Homiletic: Moves and Structures* (Philadelphia: Fortress Press, 1987), who laid aside his theological commitments and did a lengthy rhetoric of preaching; Christine M. Smith, *Weaving the Sermon: Preaching in a Feminist Perspective* (Louisville: Westminster/John Knox Press, 1989); John S. McClure, *The Roundtable Pulpit: Where Leadership and Preaching Meet* (Nashville: Abingdon Press, 1995); Lenora Tubbs Tisdale, *Preaching As Local Theology and Folk Art* (Minneapolis: Fortress Press, 1997); and Lucy Atkinson Rose, *Sharing the Word: Preaching in the Roundtable Church* (Louisville: Westminster/John Knox Press, 1997). Buttrick asked homiletics "to make up and relate to rhetoric once again" (David Buttrick, *A Captive Voice: The Liberation of Preaching* [Louisville: Westminster/John Knox Press, 1994], pg. 3). James Kay calls this "a re-turn rhetoric" (Kay, "Reorientation," pp. 25-28). Gert Otto led the charge in Germany, which infected American homiletics by stating bluntly, "Preaching is a rhetorical task. Therefore, homiletics is treated in connection with rhetoric. Theological reflection, exegetical or historical or systematic, has its place then without the rhetorical conceptual framework; but theology has neither priority nor superiority. For reflection on formulated homiletical questions, rhetoric is dominant, not theology." (Translated and quoted by Kay, pg. 27 from Otto's book, *Rhetorical Homiletics*, of 1999.) Otto "completely blames Barth for the practical ineffectiveness of modern homiletics" (Kay, pg. 27). Otto says you can describe a sermon any way you want, but a "sermon is a speech." Whether written, or com-

pletely orally delivered, simple honesty necessitates the admission that preaching is a rhetorical act, and participates in the patterns, goals, and concerns of any kind of speech-making. Thus Luther made a rhetorical play on words when he said that the Word ought to be "geschrieen," that is, "shouted," rather than simply "geschrieben," that is, merely written. Noted in Martin E. Marty, *A Cry of Absence: Reflections for the Winter of the Heart* (San Francisco: Harper & Row, 1983), pg. 25.

49. Beverly Zink-Sawyer, "The Word Purely Preached and Heard: The Listeners and the Homiletical Endeavor," *Interpretation*, vol. 51, no. 4 (Oct. 1997): pp. 342-57.

50. John Calvin, *Institutes of the Christian Religion*, vol. 2, ed. John T. McNeill (Philadelphia: Westminster, 1960), pg. 1023.

51. Augustine, *On Christian Doctrine*, trans. D. W. Robertson Jr. (New York: Liberal Arts, 1958), pg. 121.

52. Cited by Zink-Sawyer, "The Word Purely Preached," pg. 34.

53. Cited by Zink-Sawyer from Fosdick's July 1928 essay in *Harper's Magazine*.

54. I really feel that Fosdick is the equivalent, at least in mainline Protestant homiletics, to William James in mainline Protestant theology. It is difficult to overestimate Fosdick's importance for the history of contemporary North American homiletics, at least in mainline protestantism. On the issue of "felt need" among our hearers, Barth might have countered, "Those who speak about God must find a need in people that they do not perceive along with all their other needs. . . . [Preachers] must teach them to ask so that they can give them an answer. They must plunge them into the depths so that they can really lead them to the heights. . . . To speak about God does not fit in with what they are and do even in their best moments" (*GD*, pg. 50).

55. Harry Emerson Fosdick, *The Living of These Days* (New York: Harper & Brothers, 1956), pp. 99-100.

56. In her misreading of Barth's homiletics, Zink-Sawyer appears to be influenced by the interpretation of David G. Buttrick, whom she cites. See Buttrick's *A Captive Voice: The Liberation of Preaching* (Louisville: Westminster/John Knox Press, 1994). Buttrick sees Barth's initiation of the "biblical theology movement" as the curse that has caused the irrelevancy of much of modern preaching. I would not place Barth at the head of any "biblical theology movement," nor would I ascribe to him any affinity whatsoever with Fundamentalism. Ulrich Nembach, *Predigen Heute: Ein Handbook* (Stuttgart: Verlag W. Kohlhammer, 1966), sharply criticizes the inheritance from Karl Barth and Hans Iwand (in Iwand's widely used *Göttingen Preaching Meditations*) for fostering a "debilitating split between the preacher and the hearer."

57. In *Resident Aliens* Hauerwas and I attempt to describe why Barth was so much more innovative and "new" than Tillich or the Niebuhrs. I never thought of Barth as an innovator in homiletics until I read Zink-Sawyer's account in which she demonstrates that homiletics hardly every turned away from concern for the listener except for the rather erratic lurch toward God in the homiletics of Karl Barth!

58. Zink-Sawyer, pg. 352. She cites only Craddock's *As One Without Authority*, which was the only time Craddock ever advocated this "turn to the listener."

59. Ibid., pg. 353. This strikes me not only as a theologically abstract and vague statement but also—considering all this talk about concern over the listener—one that could be construed as an exaggerated view of the role of the preacher. She cites Buttrick, saying that preaching, "can reshape the world in consciousness and transform identity: Preaching can build a faith-world in human consciousness." Sometimes I wish that we preachers, on our own, were that effective. Such clerical wishes, Barth would call sin.

60. Ibid., pg. 355.

61. *Homiletic*, 2001, 24.02, pp. 13-16.

62. Published as James F. Kay, "Reorientation: Homiletics as Theologically Authorized Rhetoric," *Princeton Seminary Bulletin*, vol. XXIV, no. 1, 2003.

63. Lucy Lind Hogan and Robert Reid, *Connecting with the Congregation: Rhetoric and the Art of Preaching* (Nashville: Abingdon Press, 1999).

64. Trans. by Douglas Horton (New York: Harper and Brothers Publishers, 1957).

65. *The Word of God and the Word of Man*, pp. 122-25.

66. Thomas G. Long, "And How Shall They Hear? The listener in contemporary preaching," in Gail R. O'Day and Thomas G. Long, eds., *Listening to the Word, Studies in Honor of Fred B. Craddock* (Nashville: Abingdon Press, 1993), pg. 177.

67. Kay, pg. 22.

68. See Hogan and Reid, pg. 43. See Kay's criticisms of their a-theological rhetoric in Kay, "Reorienting," pp. 27-29.

69. Ibid., pg. 71.

70. Hogan and Reid, pg. 9.

71. Ibid., pp. 55-56.

72. Kay, pg. 29.

73. Ibid.

74. Hogan and Reid, pg. 91.

75. Kay, pg. 31.

76. Ibid.

77. Hogan and Reid, pg. 13.

78. *CD*, I, 2, pg. 294.

79. Hartmut Genest, *Karl Barth und die Predigt: Darstellung und Deutung von Predigtwerk und Predigtlehre Karl Barths* (Berlin: Neukirchener, 1995).

80. Ibid., pg. 92.

81. Ibid., pg. 96.

82. Ibid., pg. 140.

83. A set of four Barth CDs, which include a couple of sermons and a number of radio interviews and a couple of short lectures, are available from Theologischer Verlag Zürich, www.tvz.ref.ch.

84. *CD*, IV, 3, pg. 629.

85. William Perkins, *The Art of Prophesying*, rev. ed. (Edinburgh: Banner of Truth Trust, 1996). Hughes Oliphant Old, *The Reading and Preaching of the Scriptures in the Worship of the Christian Church*, vol. 4, *The Age of the Reformation* (Grand Rapids: Eerdmans, 2002). Barth says, in discussing the truth of Christianity, that we must always assert such truth under the apostolic admission that "when I am weak, then I am strong," and, after a discussion of church history under the rubric of God's saving of sinners, says that "we can speak of the truth of the Christian religion only within the sphere of the iustificatio impii" (*CD*, III, 3, pg. 204).

86. Barth, *Homiletics*, pg. 121.

87. Ibid., pg. 122.

88. Ibid., pg. 124. Ingo Reuter (*Predigt verstenen: Grund lagen einer homiletischen Hermenutik* [Leipzig: Evangelische Verlagan Stalt, 2000]) ascribes to Luther the origins of Barth's notion that the understanding of the hearer is nothing less than pure miracle (pg. 116). Reuter was also among the first to note Barth's "postmodern" relativization of human reason and radical autonomy of God (pp. 127, 129).

89. Barth, *Homiletics*, pp. 122-23.

90. Ibid., pg. 127. By the way, Flannery O'Connor is noted for the lack of satisfying ending of her stories. She ends her stories in such a way as to frustrate any final interpretation of what happens, in a parabolic manner that demands continued interpretation. See Ralph C. Wood, *Contending for the Faith: The Church's Engagement with Culture* (Waco, Texas: Baylor University Press, 2003), pg. 177.

91. When Barth says that the only "justification" for preaching is the same sort of justification by faith that upholds the Christian, he means that preaching works without the world's accustomed justification: "In other words, this means that preaching is exposition of scripture. . . . If it is a fact that the basis and meaning (or justification) of preaching are to be sought in revelation, church, commission, and ministry, then there can be no question at all of preachers' declaiming their own systematic theology or expounding what they think they know about their own lives or human life in general, or society or the state of the world. If they live by justification, by their faith, it is no longer possible for them to offer systematic theology of this kind, or their own knowledge of how things are and how they ought to be, or ideologies by which people think they may live." Barth, *Homiletics*, pg. 75.

92. Barth's hyperbolic statements about preaching have led some, like David Buttrick, to conclude that he destroyed biblical preaching:

Barth in some ways all but destroyed preaching in the name of the Bible. He threw out sermon introductions because they might imply some "point of contact," some natural affinity for the gospel in the human sphere; and he lopped off conclusions because they might express works-righteousness. Above all, he denied social relevance: "The Preacher," he wrote, "must preach the Bible and *nothing* else." As a result, preaching became for Barth the reiteration of a biblical text . . . without much reference to the social world." (David Buttrick, *A Captive Voice: The Liberation of Preaching* [Louisville: Westminster/John Knox Press, 1994], pg. 8)

93. *CD*, I, 2, pg. 301.

94. *CD*, I, 1, pg. 237.

95. George Hunsinger, *How to Read Karl Barth: The Shape of His Theology* (New York: Oxford University Press, 1991), pg. 183. Cf. *CD*, IV/3, pp. 554-614.

96. *CD*, IV, 3, pg. 502; see also IV, 2, pg. 183.

97. Hans W. Frei, *The Identity of Jesus Christ* (Philadelphia: Fortress Press, 1975).

98. For a contemporary rendition of this nineteenth-century project, see Marcus Borg, *The Heart of Christianity* (San Francisco: HarperSanFrancisco, 2003). Borg describes his "emerging paradigm" as understanding that the Bible is "sacred" "*not* because it is a divine product. It is sacred in its *status* and *function*, but *not* in its *origin*. The point is not to believe in the Bible and the Christian tradition, but to live within them as a metaphor and sacrament of the sacred, as a means whereby the Spirit continues to speak to us today" (pg. 15). This is the sort of thing that Frei meant by "mythological reading." Joseph Campbell, father of contemporary mythological spirituality, says, "Read myths. They teach you that you can inward. . . . Myth helps you to put your mind in touch with this experience of being alive." Joseph P. Campbell with Bill Moyers, *The Power of Myth* ed. Betty Sue Flowers (New York: Doubleday, 1988), pg. 5. Note these rather frank admissions that Borg's "sacred" and Campbell's "myth" have no external referent beyond the self.

99. *CD*, II, 2. See David E. Demson, *Hans Frei & Karl Barth, Different Ways of Reading Scripture* (Grand Rapids: Eerdmans, 1997).

100. *CD*, II, 2, pg. 724.

101. Ibid.

102. Hinrich Stoevesandt, "Karl Barth," in William H. Willimon and Richard Lischer, eds., *Concise Encyclopedia of Preaching* (Louisville: Westminster/John Knox Press, 1995), pg. 27.

103. Ibid., pg. 725. B. A. Gerrish, in *Saving and Secular Faith: An Invitation to Systematic Theology* (Minneapolis: Augsburg Press, 1999), pg. 104, says that a major problem with the quest for the "historical Jesus" among the Jesus Seminar crowd is that they "are not mistaken in seeking an historical anchor for faith. The problem is that they look for it in the wrong place and hold faith captive to historical science, as the old doctrine of creation once held a captive to natural science. The historical anchorage is to be found in the life of the church, the confessing community in which the gospel is proclaimed—the body of Christ." Luke Timothy Johnson took much the same line with the "Jesus Seminar" in his *The Real Jesus* (San Francisco: HarperSanFrancisco, 1996). I am sure that Barth would reject Gerrish's attempt to exchange the "anchorage" of historical science for that of the "confessing community." Any attempt to anchor ourselves anywhere other than in the self-proclamation of the living Christ is, for Barth, a form of "religion," that is, idolatry, the attempt to substitute a true, living God for a false, dead god. The just shall live by faith, the faith that is given by Christ, not by their confidence in the church.

104. Ibid., pg. 133.

105. Ibid., pg. 134. We are preachers, says Barth, only in the sense that we are "apostles," those who are sent (*CD*, IV, 2, pg. 207). Barth has a half-dozen pages on preaching right in the middle of his "doctrine of reconciliation." That God speaks and we hear is for Barth a supreme, the supreme instance of revelation as evidence of reconciliation.

106. *CD*, I, 1, pg. 152.

107. Wolfhart Pannenberg, in an interview, stresses the nature of the human being as one who is addressed: "Does 'In the image of God' mean that the thing that makes us human is our conversation

with God? God speaks, more precisely, God calls, we respond, therefore we are. 'I respond, therefore I am' ought to be the Christian response to Descartes. Identical twins who have the same genetic constitution are different, not simply on the basis of different life experiences, but because God calls each of them by name. They are different, because of God's different claim upon them.

"The first reality God addresses is the earth. The earth is called upon to bring forth vegetation. How can an inorganic reality, bring about an organic reality? By the command of God. The second Commandment to the earth is even more bold—to bring forth animals. God at first addresses the earth before humanity! History (biology, cosmology) begins as address. There is no earth before God's address."

("Future Perfect: A Conversation with Wolfhart Pannenberg," interview by Thomas J. Oord, *Books & Culture*, September/October, 2001, pg. 18.)

108. CD, III, 2, pg. 158. James Kay says that Barth preferred the term "announcement" (*Ankündigung*) to "proclamation" (*Verküdigung*) because the former can be understood as some sort of psychological appeal for an existential decision. I'm not sure that Barth really prefers one term to the other, but I do know that he was determined to remove the subjective from center stage of the act of preaching. Kay, "Reorientation: Homiletics as Theologically Authorized," *Princeton Seminary Bulletin*, pp. 16-35.

109. CD, III, 2, pg. 150. Catherine Mowry LaCugna begins her book on the Trinity with, "Theological statements are possible . . . because God has freely revealed and communicatd God's self, God's personal existence, God's infinite mystery" (*God for Us: The Trinity and Christian Life* [San Francisco: Harper SanFrancisco, 1991], pg. 3).

7. Heralds of God

1. *Romans*, pg. 27.

2. "The word of God on the lips of a man is an impossibility; it does not happen. . . . [It is] God's act." Karl Barth, *The Word of God and the Word of Man* (New York: Harper & Brothers, 1957), pp. 124-25.

3. CD, III, 4, pg. 75.

4. The border of theology is a theme that is presented so well by the Barthian theologian Hinrich Stoevesandt, former director of the Karl Barth Archive in Basel. See Hinrich Stoevesandt, *Gottes Freiheit und die Grenze der Theologie* (Zürich: Theologischer Verlag, 1992), pp. 1-23.

5. CD, I, 1, pg. 57.

6. Thus Barth speaks with contempt for those who try to "present the truth of God aesthetically in the form of a picture, an impression, or an aesthetic evocation of Jesus." Barth, *Homiletics*, pg. 48.

7. Ibid., pg. 125.

8. Early in his life, Barth believed that congregations come to church with "a passionate longing to lay hold of *that* which, or rather of *him* who, overcomes the world because he is its Creator and Redeemer. . . . A passionate longing to have the *word* spoken . . . this is which animates church-goers, however lazy, bourgeoise, or commonplace may be the manner in which they express their want in so-called real life." *The Word of God and the Word of Man*, trans. Douglas Horton (New York: Harper & Brothers, 1956), pg. 109. He would later draw back from any positive assessment of the longing of the hearers.

9. Luther's favorite name for preachers was *ministri verbi divini*, "servants of the word." Faith comes as an auditory phenomenon (Luther loved to quote Romans 10:17). Thus Luther calls the church building a *Mundhaus* (mouth-house).

10. Karl Barth, *Homiletics*, trans. Geoffrey W. Bromiley and Donald E. Daniels (Louisville: Westminster/John Knox Press, 1991), pg. 50.

11. Dietrich Bonhoeffer stresses listening as the requisite for preaching: "Christians, especially ministers, so often think they must always contribute something when they are in the company of others, that this is the one service they have to render. They forget that listening can be a greater service than speaking." *Life Together*, trans. J. W. Doberstein (New York: Harper & Row, 1954), pp. 97-99.

12. David L. Bartlett, *What's Good About This News?* (Louisville: Westminster/John Knox Press, 2003), pg. 7.

13. Thomas G. Long, *The Witness of Preaching* (Philadelphia: Westminster, 1989), pp. 128-29. Barth says that the standard of the witness is precisely the attitude "which must be the standard for dogmatics as the model of Church proclamation." The theme of theology as witness is developed by Barth in *CD*, I, 2, pg. 817.

14. Ibid., pp. 42-47.

15. As Reinhard Hütter says, for Barth, "every witness is a limited witness, every witness is an approximation, every witness is just that, a witness." Reinhard Hütter, "Karl Barth's Dialectical Catholicity: *Sic et Non*," *Modern Theology* 16.2 (April 2000): pg. 146.

16. *CD*, IV, 3, pg. 681.

17. "Als rede dieser Art ist die Predigt nie mehr als '*Hinweis*' aug den gegenwärtigen Gott selbst." Hinrich Stoevesandt, *Gottes Freiheit und die Grenze der Theologie*, pg. 57.

18. In a discussion of revelation in scripture in the thought of Barth, Christina Baxter says that Barth's view of revelation, "straddles objectivity and subjectivity, and is never completed or finished, for the relationship between God who is giving Himself to be known, and the 'human subject' who is receiving the capacity to know God is a continuing relationship; it has to be 'new every morning' or it is not knowledge of God at all." "The Nature and Place of Scripture in the *Church Dogmatics*,'" in John Thompson, ed., *Theology Beyond Christendom* (Allison Park, Pa.: Pickwick Publications, 1986), pg. 35.

19. *CD*, IV, 3, pp. 851 and 852f.

20. *Deliverance to the Captives*, pg. 26.

21. David Bartlett says that the first thing that he tells students in his seminary's "Principles and Practices of Preaching" is this: preaching is occasional. "A sermon is not written for all times and for all places, but for this time, this place, this gathered group of people." David L. Bartlett, *What's Good About This News?* (Louisville: Westminster/John Knox Press, 2003), pg. 3. While such a statement might raise questions about just what "principles and practices" are suitable for "occasional" communication like preaching, I agree with Bartlett that it is important for us preachers to recover the sense of the fragile, occasional, eventful, particular, and specific quality of the spoken word in a sermon.

22. Gerhard Sauter, *Gateways to Dogmatics: Reasoning Theologically for the Life of the Church* (Grand Rapids: Eerdmans, 2003), pp. 129-31. The presence of Christ in preaching is a major theme of Bonhoeffer's thought on preaching. Bonhoeffer asserts that the sermon is nothing less than "Christ himself, walking through his congregation as the Word." *Communion of Saints*, trans. R. G. Smith, 1963, pg. 161; and "Christ is . . . present . . . as the Word of the Church, i. e., as the spoken word of preaching" (*Christology*, trans. John Bowden, 1966), pg. 52.

23. Some years ago, when I interviewed dozens of former preachers for a book I was writing on ministerial "burnout," I found that the fragile, unrepeatable quality of preaching was a major reason why many preachers call it quits. It is demanding to give one's life to such a fragile medium, to work on a sermon with no sure guarantee of results, to preach in all sincerity and skill but without any noticeable effects, to have nothing to show for three decades of preaching but a room full of dead words. These preachers seemed to me to have "burned out" because of a lack of faith that their meager words had become the event of God's word, an event without enduring significance. They reminded me of the remarkable degree to which preachers are forced, week-in-week-out, to "walk by faith" or walk not at all. Preaching is one of the most remarkable, public, risky attempts in the church to witness to the truth that the "just shall live by faith."

24. Nicholas Wolsterstorff, *Divine Discourse: Philosophical Reflections on the Claim that God Speaks* (Cambridge: Cambridge University Press, 1995), pp. 71-72.

25. *CD*, I, 1, pp. 109-10.

26. Hinrich Stoevesandt, *Gottes Freiheit und die Grenze der Theologie* (Zürich: Theologischer Verlag, 1992), pg. 49, my translation.

27. Dorrien, pg. 151.

28. Barth, *Homiletics*, pg. 53. As early as a sermon on Sept. 29, 1912, Barth notes, "Paul says, 'You are all children of God' and doesn't say: 'you ought to be, or might be children of God,' and this is true also for all the crowds of sinners, the indifferent and those who deny God." Sermon 134, Barth archive.

29. *CD*, IV, 3, pg. 477.

30. Ibid.

31. Barth, *Homiletics*, pg. 72.

32. *CD*, II, 1, pg. 74.

33. Barth, *Romans* (London: Oxford University Press, 1933), pg. 39.

34. *GD*, pg. 59.

35. *CD*, IV, 3, pg. 477.

36. Ibid.

37. *CD*, I, 1, pg. 92.

38. *GD*, pg. 271.

39. David Bartlett notes that Luke frequently uses the verb "to preach the gospel" (Matthew uses this verb only once, Mark uses the noun eight times but never uses the verb). Whereas in Matthew it is Jesus who first preaches the good news, "in Luke the good news is first preached *about* Jesus" (pg. 78). Rudolf Bultmann has said that development of the Christian tradition took place as "Jesus the proclaimer becomes the proclaimed." With Barth, I want to recover "the proclaimer." I want to recover Jesus as the active agent of the good news. (Rudolf Bultmann, *Theology of the New Testament*, trans. K. Grovel [New York: Scribner's Sons, 1951–55], vol. 1, pg. 33.) David L. Bartlett, *What's Good About This News?* (Louisville: Westminster/John Knox Press, 2003).

40. Because God is a living, actively speaking God, our speaking about God must always be open to adaptation, improvisation, and movement. Thus it is a mistake to regard anything Barth says about preaching as his fixed, final word on the subject. This experimental attitude toward preaching was present with Barth from his first days as a pastor, as early as September 4, 1914, when Barth wrote his lifelong colleague, Swiss pastor Eduard Thurneysen: "Here are two sermons from me. . . . You will look at them not as though they were finished products but only as experiments. We are really all of us experimenting now, each in his own way and every Sunday in a different way, in order to become to some degree masters of the limitless problem." Karl Barth, *The Heidelberg Catechism for Today*, trans. Shirley C. Guthrie, Jr. (Richmond: John Knox Press, 1964), pg. 19.

41. Karl Barth in Emil Brunner and Karl Barth, *Natural Theology*, trans. Peter Fraenkel (London: Centenary Press, 1946), pg. 127.

42. Calvin says that "if God spoke from heaven it would not be suprising if his sacred oracles were to be reverently received without delay by the ears and minds of all. . . . But when a puny man risen from the dust speaks in God's name," then it is real evidence of our piety and of God's grace if "we show ourselves teachable toward his minister, although he excels us at nothing." *Institutes of the Christian Religion*, 2:1054 (4.3.1).

43. When one considers the miraculous nature of preaching, its eventful quality, one can understand how for Bultmann, "the eschatological event" (as Bultmann interpreted Paul and the Gospel of John) was not some "dramatic cosmic catastrophe" but rather "occurring again and again in history, . . . an event repeatedly in preaching and faith. Jesus Christ is the eschatological event not as an established fact of past time but as repeatedly present, as addressing you and me here and now in preaching." (Rudolf Bultmann, *Theology of the New Testament*, trans. K. Grobel [New York: Scribner's Sons, 1951–55], pg. 219.) One can also understand how Marxsen could say that Christ rose in preaching. (Willi Marxsen, *The Resurrection of Jesus of Nazareth*, trans. Margaret Kohl [Philadelphia: Fortress Press, 1970], pg. 128.) Those who accuse Barth of having too little interest in the historicity of the Gospel stories ought to be reminded of the ways in which these scholars completely detach the Resurrection from any historical grounding. Barth believed that revelation was an "event," but not one that had no historical basis. Barth discusses the historicity of the Resurrection (interestingly, as a sort of preface to his ruminations on proclamation) in *CD*, I, 2, pp. 143-53.

44. See *CD*, II, 2, pg. 136. Ronald J. Allen, professor of preaching, says that now more than any moment in church history since the early fourth century, "apologetics has a key place in preaching in postmodern settings. . . . Given the relativism and pluralism of the postmodern world, *why* should persons remain (or become) Christian? Since all perception is interpretation, and since every point of view

can be deconstructed, what makes us think that we can (or should) trust a Christian vision of the world? Apologetic preaching helps strengthen Christian identity. A preacher can help a congregation understand why it makes sense to believe." Ronald J. Allen, "Preaching and Postmodernism" in *Interpretation* (January 2001): pp. 46-47. Italics in original.

45. Craig A. Loscalzo, "Apologizing for God: Apologetic Preaching to a Postmodern World" in *Review and Expositor* (Summer 1996): pg. 416. See Graham Ward, "Barth, Hegel and the Possibility for Christian Apologetics," McDowell and Higton, eds., *Conversing with Barth*, pp. 53-65 for a wonderfully nuanced treatment of Barth and apologetics.

46. William P. Alston, "A Philosopher's Way Back to Faith," pg. 27.

47. Stanley J. Grenz, *A Primer on Postmodernism* (Grand Rapids: Eerdmans, 1996), pp. 169-70.

48. Thus Robert Wilken says, "Today I believe the most significant apologetic task is simply to tell people what we believe and do. We need to familiarize people with the stories of the Bible and to talk about the things that make Christianity distinctive. Many people are simply unaware of the basics of Christianity. They're rejecting something they don't know that much about. . . . We're really leading people to change their love. To love something different. Love is what draws and holds people." Quoted in Ralph C. Wood, *Contending for the Faith: The Church's Engagement with Culture* (Waco, Texas: Baylor University Press, 2003), pg. 106. While I agree with much of this, I do fear that this defense of communitarian apologetics is just another attempt to continue the apologetic task under another guise. We are lonely people who long for "community" more than a community formed in Christ.

49. Cited in Dewey J. Hoitenga, Jr., *Faith and Reason from Plato to Plantinga: An Introduction to Reformed Epistemology* (Albany: State University of New York Press, 1991), pg. 205.

50. *CD*, II, 1, pp. 93-97.

51. *CD*, I, 2, pg. 827.

52. *Dogmatics in Outline*, pp. 93-94.

53. "The young Karl Barth, laboring between his identification with the oppressed workers of his congregation, the spectacle of liberal Europe's self-destruction, and his obligation to preach and preach and keep on preaching, and to do it from the Bible, discovered that the Bible opens into a world of its own and that, however surprising and upsetting the discovery, *that* is the *real* world." Robert W. Jenson, "Scripture's Authority in the Church" in Ellen F. Davis and Richard B. Hays, *The Art of Reading Scripture* (Grand Rapids: Eerdmans, 2003), pg. 37.

54. Quoted by Hauerwas, *With the Grain of the Universe*, chap. 6, pg. 16.

55. "There is no single royal road to Christianity, either as a universal moral principle or in practice. I am convinced that the passionate and systematic preoccupation with the apologetic task of showing how faith is meaningful and/or possible is largely out of place and self-defeating—except as an *ad hoc* and highly various exercise. In this area an ounce of living is usually worth a pound of talk, and especially of writing." Hans W. Frei, *The Identity of Jesus Christ* (Philadelphia: Fortress Press, 1975), pg. xii.

56. Barth, *The Humanity of God*, trans. Thomas Wieser and John Thomas (Richmond: John Knox Press, 1963), pg. 20.

57. Samuel Wells, *Improvisation: The Drama of Christian Ethics* (Grand Rapids: Brazos Press, 2004), pg. 27.

58. See Hauerwas's response in Hauerwas, *With the Grain of the Universe*, chap. 6, pg. 27.

59. In Michael Turner and Will Malambri, eds., *A Peculiar Prophet: William H. Willimon and the Art of Preaching* (Nashville: Abingdon Press, 2004).

60. Many have noted that Barth carries on a lively and multifaceted *ad hoc* apologetics in many of his small print passages.

61. "An Afterword," *Eclipse*, pg. 110.

62. Ibid., pg. 111.

63. Ibid., pg. 115.

64. Hans W. Frei, "Eberhard Busch's Biography of Karl Barth," H. Martin Rumscheidt, ed., *Karl Barth in Re-View* (Allison Park, Pa.: Pickwick Press, 1981), pg. 103.

65. In his introduction to his prison sermons Barth said, "In preparing and conducting the worship services, the prayers I gave were to my mind as essential as the sermons themselves. I hope that this will hold true in turn for those who, through reading this book share in these services" (pg. 11). The prayer that Barth offers before one of his prison sermons is typical of his later sermon prayers: "Continue to have mercy on us and on all men, on our families, on all the suffering and tempted, on the authorities of this town and country, on civil servants, teachers and students, on the judges, the accused and the sentenced, on the pastors and their congregations, on the missionaries and those to whom they are privilege to proclaim thy truth, on the Evangelicals in Spain and in South America and on their misguided oppressors. Where thou dost not build through thy word, Church and world are built in vain. Let thy word run its course and reach many. Let it go to all men with the power to shine, to heal and to which has whenever it is rightly preached and received in the power of thy Holy Spirit. Our father . . .'" (*Deliverance to the Captives*, pg. 50).

I am also reminded of another prayer that Barth prayed at the end of one of his prison sermons: "God, Father, Son and Holy Ghost! Forbid that we depart without thy loving and severe word accompanying us, each one to his place; into his particular experiences, concerns, sorrows and expectation, into this Sunday and into this coming week! Be and remain present and at work in this house, and with all its inmates. Restrain all evil spirits which threaten to overpower us! Keep the light burning which so often is about to go out" (*Deliverance to the Captives*, pg. 92).

66. Hauerwas, *With the Grain of the Universe*, chap. 7, pg. 22.

67. CD, II, 1, pg. 250. Hauerwas's discussion of the theological implications of Barth's repetitiveness is especially evocative. Hauerwas, *With the Grain of the Universe*, chap. 7.

68. Karl Barth, *Theology and Church*, trans. Louise P. Smith (London: SCM Press, 1962), pg. 200.

69. CD, II, 1, pg. 141.

70. To my surprise, I found that Barth did not come late to this belief in the universal triumph of God's grace. A number of sermons as early as 1910 and 1912 display his sort of universalism. In Sermon 58 (Jan. 29, 1911), Barth imagines with scorn an "evangelistic meeting." "On the one side are the faithful, those who are convinced. They try to draw over to their side those who aren't convinced, the so-called unbelievers. Imagine that Jesus would show up at this meeting and would be asked to speak just one word: Blessed are the spiritually poor. On what side does he stand?" Jesus says, in effect, "Blessed are those who know they are not pious." This sounds "like a tune from another world. It startles us greatly because we thought we were already on the 'right side.'" Then Barth says to his little congregation, "You *are* the people of God because you know that you are not."

71. CD, IV, 3, pg. 342.

72. Ibid., pg. 715.

73. While working on this section I came across James M. Gustafson's apologetic, *An Examined Faith: The Grace of Self-Doubt* (Minneapolis: Fortress, 2004). It would be all well and good for Gustafson to doubt himself and his academic community, but he mainly doubts the historic Christian faith while swallowing totally the claims of certain privileged segments of modern science. Would that Gustafson would be as skeptical of science as he is of orthodox Christian theology!

74. *Nein!* pg. 127. Hans Frei notes that Barth believes there is a trustworthy and vibrant "point of contact" between revelation and human thought, "but it takes place in the mystery of God's freedom as He provides His own 'point of contact' and it need not be 'existential' despair over the possibility of achieving genuine responsible human existence, as Brunner had insisted." Frei, "Religion: Natural and Revealed," pg. 317.

75. Quoted by Webb from Barth, *NT*, pg. 127.

76. James Kay, "Reorientation: Homiletics as Theologically Authorized Rhetoric," *Princeton Seminary Bulletin*, vol. XXIV, no. 1, 2003.

77. Karl Barth, *Deliverance to the Captives* (New York: Harper & Row, 1961).

78. Ibid., pg. 37.

79. Ibid., pp. 54-55.

80. Ibid., pp. 154-55.

81. Robert Alter, in *The World of Biblical Literature* (New York: Basic Books, 1992), waxes poetic in his praise for the unique artistic aspects of scripture:

[Scripture is written by] writers who relished the words and the materials of storytelling with which they worked, who delighted, because after all they were writers, in pleasing cadences and surprising deflections of syntax, in complex echoing effects among words, in the kind of speech they could fashion for the characters, and in the way in which the self-same words could be ingeniously transformed as they were passed from narrator to character or from one character to another . . . the lively inventiveness with which they constantly deploy the resources of their narrative medium repeatedly exceeds the needs of the message, though it often also deepens and complicates the message. (pg. 40)

My only challenge to Alter is his statement that biblical narrative "exceeds the needs of the message." I believe that there is something in the quality of the God who speaks that demands such artistic production from those who would listen to and talk about this God.

82. Flannery O'Connor wrote a friend that "one of the awful things about writing when you are a Christian is that for you the ultimate reality is the Incarnation, the present reality is the Incarnation, the whole reality is the Incarnation, and nobody believes in the Incarnation; that is, nobody in your audience. My audience are the people who think God is dead." *Collected Works*, pg. 943.

83. Barth, *Homiletics*, pg. 48.

84. Karl Barth, "The Proclamation of God's Free Grace," *God Here and Now*, pg. 40. Cf. also CD, 1, 2, pg. 862.

85. I find it significant that in Grünewald's painting, there is no place for John the Baptist to stand, no context or background. His significance is exclusively in that to which he points. Again, this is Barth's estimate of the significance of us preachers. We preachers, as heralds, are to be self-consuming artifacts in that, just to the degree that we truly speak of Christ, we remind ourselves and our congregations of our own inadequacy.

86. Barth, *Dogmatics in Outline*, pg. 94. See also CD, I, 1, pg. 210. Barth has the gall to make a statement like this in the middle of one of his most visually appealing, openly homiletical, rhetorically powerful works, volume 1 of the *Church Dogmatics*!

87. Thomas G. Long, *The Witness of Preaching* (Louisville: Westminster/John Knox Press, 1989), pg. 29.

88. Paul Scott Wilson, *The Practice of Preaching* (Nashville: Abingdon Press, 1995), pg. 28.

89. Phillips Brooks, "truth communicated through personality." I have been among those who have expressed concern about pastoral character. William H. Willimon, *Calling and Character* (Nashville: Abingdon Press, 2000).

90. This incarnational, redemptive principle ought to be applied to Karl Barth. I am among those who continue to be deeply troubled by Barth's relationship to, and treatment of, Charlotte von Kirschbaum, and the effect that this relationship had on Nellie Barth. See Renate Köbler, *In the Shadow of Karl Barth: Charlotte von Kirschbaum*, trans. Keith Crim (Louisville: Westminster/John Knox Press, 1989). Barth was wrong in this and there is no way to deny his sin. Only God redeems sin, and I believe God has. I have experienced that redemption of Barth in his theology. In fact, his life, set next to his theology, is for me a powerful validation of Paul's words: we really do, in Barth, have God's matchless treasure demonstrated in a deeply flawed earthen vessel.

91. CD, III, 2, pp. 254-55.

92. CD, I, 2, pp. 425ff.

93. CD, IV, 3, pg. 609. In his first volumes of the *Church Dogmatics*, Barth tends to speak of witnessing as official church proclamation. But here in the fourth volume, he stresses witness as an assignment to all Christians in general. For Barth, the "witness" image catches up not only the necessity of obedient speaking but also the necessity of faithful, heroic listening. Robert Jensen, of all contemporary theologians, develops this theme in a most Barthian way, connecting it masterfully to the Resurrection. Says Jensen, "Theology's question is always: In that we have heard and seen such-and-such discourse as gospel, what shall we now say and do that gospel may again be spoken?" Robert W. Jensen, *Systematic Theology*, vol. 1 (New York: Oxford University Press, 1997), pg. 14.

94. David Lose, *Confessing Jesus Christ: Preaching in a Postmodern World* (Grand Rapids: Eerdmans, 2003), pp. 59-61.

95. "We cannot preach without praying. Since in the last analysis the sermon can have to do with God alone, its words must be spoken in the course of calling upon him, and the congregation, too, must be summoned to pray." Barth, *Homiletics*, pg. 86.

96. Karl Barth, *The Preaching of the Gospel*, trans. B. E. Hooke (Philadelphia: Westminster Press, 1963), pg. 74.

97. *CD*, I, 1, pg. 423.

98. *CD*, II, 1, pp. 44, 326; I, 1, pg. 199.

99. *CD*, IV, 1, pg. 205; II, 1, pp. 310, 348.

100. Martin Buber, *Die Chassidichen Bucher*, Berlin, 1928, pg. 384, cited by Miskotte, *Das Wagnis der Predigt*, edited and trans. by Heinrich Braunachweiger and Hinrich Stoevesandt (Stuttgart: Calwer Verlag, 1998). My translation.

8. Troubled Preaching

1. Busch, *Life*, pg. 91. This title is from Kierkegaard's *Journals*, where he says, "The purely intellectual effort is only concerned with discovering the truth. The 'troubled' truth is certain enough of being the truth but is concerned, or 'troubled,' to communicate it. That is Christianity. . . . " (pg 169).

2. *GD*, pg. 7.

3. *Deliverance to the Captives*, pp. 21-22.

4. Ludwig Wittgenstein, *Philosophical Investigations*, trans. G. E. M. Anscombe (Oxford: Basil Blackwell, 1980), pp. 123, 249, 630.

5. Lose, pg. 62. See also William C. Placher, *Unapologetic Theology: A Christian Voice in a Pluralistic Conversation* (Louisville: Westminster/John Knox Press, 1989), chaps. 1–2.

6. See Stanley M. Hauerwas, "No Enemy, No Christianity: Preaching Between 'Worlds,'" in *Sanctify Them in the Truth* (Nashville: Abingdon Press, 1998), pp. 191-200.

7. Placher, *Unapologetic Theology*, pg. 167. One of the best explications of the inherently conflicted nature of Christian preaching, particularly in postmodernity, is Stanley M. Hauerwas, "No Enemy, No Christianity: Preaching Between 'Worlds,'" in *Sanctify Them in the Truth*, pp. 191-200.

8. Lections for the Third Sunday in Epiphany, Year C.

9. Stanley Hauerwas, *Against the Nations* (Minneapolis: Winston Press, 1985), pp. 11-12.

10. *CD*, III, 2, pg. 607.

11. David Ford, *Barth and God's Story: Biblical Narrative in the Theological Method of Karl Barth in The Church Dogmatics* (Frankfurt am Main: Verlag Peter Lang, 1981), pg. 22.

12. *CD*, I, 1, pg. 362.

13. Recounted in Robert C. Johnson, "The Legacy of Karl Barth," in *Reflection*, vol. 66, no. 4 (May 1969), pg. 4.

14. Karl Barth, *Deliverance to the Captives* (New York: Harper & Row, 1961), pp. 76-77.

15. George A. Lindbeck, *The Nature of Doctrine: Religion and Theology in a Post-Liberal Age* (Philadelphia: Westminster Press, 1984), pg. 117.

16. From his earliest days as a theologian (1916), Barth condemned as a "false prophet," that pitiful pastor who, in his preaching, "sets out to do right by his people." Quoted by Busch, *The Great Passion*, pg. 9.

17. Hans Dieter Bastian accuses Barth of not simply correcting an overemphasis of traditional rhetoric upon the hearers, but totally pushing the hearers out of the homiletical equation (Hans Dieter Bastian, "From the Word to the Words: Karl Barth and the Task of Practical Theology," trans. Richard Ulrich, in *Theology Of the Liberating Word*, ed. Frederick Herzog [Nashville: Abingdon Press, 1971], pg. 48). Bastian is concerned that Barth appears to be oblivious "to the effects or non-effects of the sermon." We now know this to be a misreading of Barth.

18. Barth, *Homiletics*, pp. 84-85.

19. Hans Frei, "Eberhard Busch's Biography, Karl Barth," in Rumscheidt, *Karl Barth in Review*, pg. 111. Barth's theology has been subjected to rhetorical analysis in a way that raises questions about Barth's supposedly anti-rhetorical attitude. Hans Frei began this analysis of Barth's rhetoric in his *The Identity of Jesus Christ: The Hermeneutical Bases of Dogmatic Theology* (Philadelphia: Fortress Press, 1975); also published that same year was David H. Kelsey, *The Uses of Scripture and Recent Theology* (Philadelphia: Fortress Press, 1975), and, as we have noted earlier, Stephen H. Webb, *Re-figuring Theology: The Rhetoric of Karl Barth*. Gret Otto made the most extensive early observations of the way in which Barth's theology is "rhetorically stamped," yet he also says that Barth's use of language "had no consequences for homiletical theory." Quoted in Kay, "Reorientation," pg. 26.

20. Barth, *Homiletics*, pg. 120.

21. In Woody Allen's story, "The Kugelmass Episode," an aging, balding Jewish man named Kugelmass, who longs for a better life, meets a Jewish holy man who has a box. Walk into that box with your favorite book, the holy man tells him, and you will find yourself in the book, a character in the story. Kugelmass walks into the box with Flaubert's *Madam Bovary*. All over America, college students, dutifully studying Flaubert's realist novel, discover a bald, old Jewish man making love to Emma Bovary. Kugelmass loves his newly narrated life, though before the end of Allen's story he finds himself in an elementary Spanish text, lusted after by difficult Spanish verbs. I take this as a parable of the absorptive quality of preaching.

22. See the discussion of Tracy in William Placher, *Unapologetic Theology: A Christian Voice in a Pluralistic Conversation*, pg. 156. For an attempt to embody Tracy's concerns in a homiletic that opposes Barthian (and Reformation) dialectics with Catholic sacramentalism in preaching, see Mary Catherine Hilkert, *Naming Grace: Preaching and the Sacramental Imagination* (New York: Continuum, 1997). Hilkert believes that theologians like Barth have so removed God from our realm of discourse that preaching has been seriously damaged in the process. She commends, as a corrective to Barth, Karl Rahner, Edward Schillebeeckx, and the liberation theologians who are more congenial in their "sacramental imaginations."

23. See David Tracy, *The Analogical Imagination: Christian Theology and the Culture of Pluralism* (New York: Crossroad, 1981), chap. 9.

24. See my arguments against "public theology" in Willimon, *Peculiar Speech: Preaching to the Baptized* (Grand Rapids: Eerdmans, 1992).

25. James M. Gustafson, "The Sectarian Temptation: Reflections on Theology, the Church, and the University," *Proceedings of the Catholic Theological Society* 40 (1985): pp. 93-94. See also the letters in response, "A Challenge to Willimon's Postliberalism," *The Christian Century*, 104 (1987): pp. 306-10.

26. Lose, pg. 51.

27. Lindbeck, *The Nature of Doctrine*, pg. 30.

28. Ronald Thiemann said that in Lindbeck's account there is "the very real danger that in much of Lindbeck's essay talk about text stands in the place of talk about God." "Response to Lindbeck," *Theology Today* 43 (1986): pg. 378. And Sam Wells says that even Stanley Hauerwas, with all of his stress upon the ecclesial and social media of revelation, might be in danger of neglecting "the sovereign power of the Revealer." Sam Wells, *Transforming Fate into Destiny: The Theological Ethics of Stanley Hauerwas*, pg. 80.

29. CD, I, 1, pp. 152ff. "The Speech of God as the Act of God"; cf. also Isa. 55:6-11.

30. I am indebted to Trevor Hart, *Regarding Karl Barth* (Downers Grove, Ill.: InterVarsity Press, 1999), pg. 124, for these particular insights on Lindbeck and Barth. Citing Lindbeck's regard for Reinhold Niebuhr as an "intratextual theologian" (as opposed to Frei's opinion of Niebuhr), Charles Campbell in his *Preaching Jesus* called my attention to a real theological difference and distinction between Frei and Lindbeck and the error in "simplistically lumping Frei and Lindbeck together." Frei has a definite theological referent and agent in mind that is considerably more than intratextuality at work. Campbell, pg. 52.

31. In his introduction to Barth's prison sermons, John Marsh said, "If I were asked to put into one sentence the basic principle that underlies all Barth's theology I think I would say that it is directed,

all the way through, to but one end—*to leave completely undistorted and uncompromised the great, wonderful and mysterious fact that God has spoken to us in his Son, Jesus Christ our Lord. . . .* I think that this is very adequately illustrated in the sermons before us." (Karl Barth, *Deliverance to the Captives* [New York: Harper & Row, 1961], pg. 9.)

32. Karl Barth, *Theology and Church*, trans. Louise P. Smith (London: SCM Press, 1962), pg. 199.

33. Schleiermacher, *On Religion: Speeches to Its Cultured Despisers*, trans. John Oman (New York: Harper & Row, 1958), pg. 8.

34. Quoted by James E. Davison, "Can God Speak a Word to Man: Barth's Critique of Schleiermacher's Theology," *The Scottish Journal of Theology*, 37, no. 2 (1984): pg. 193.

35. Karl Barth, *Protestant Theology in the Ninetieth Century: Its Background and History* (Valley Forge, Pa.: Judson Press, 1973), pg. 454.

36. *CD*, I, 1, pg. 69.

37. See the admirable exercises in apophatic, negative theology in D. Brent Laythan, ed., *God Is Not . . . Religious, Nice, "One of Us," an American, a Capitalist* (Grand Rapids: Brazos Press, 2004). In his essay in this collection, "God Is Not 'A Stranger on a Bus,'" (pp. 23-38), Rodney Clapp uses Barth's critique of "religion" in a way that provides a trenchant critique of popular American religious culture.

38. I have collected some of our favorite axioms, as expressed in books and lectures on preaching, that preaching should: "get down on their level," "make the gospel real and relevant to their needs," "be in straightforward, plain and comprehensible language," "uncover their story as the story of the sacred," etc.

39. Recently I was present in a congregation in which the preacher, a practitioner of "contemporary, biblically based preaching," overused the expression "awesome!" to describe his opinion of a biblical text. This he did, despite the fact that the expression "awesome" was already at least a decade behind us, thus revealing the preacher's age. The irony was that the more he told us how "awesome" was the biblical text, the more apparent his motives to remove any sense of awesomeness from the text.

40. *CD*, I, 1, pp. 348-49.

41. John Milbank, *Theology and Social Theory: Beyond Secular Reason* (Oxford: Basil Blackwell, 1990), pg. 1. Milbank makes this statement at the beginning of his great work. I see it as a thematic sentence that characterizes his whole book. Milbank's work enabled me to see the basic difference between Barth and contemporary theology, as represented by someone like Reinhold Niebuhr, is in the way they think, the source of their words. One is theological; the other is anthropological.

42. A theme of Alasdair MacIntyre's *Three Rival Versions of Moral Enquiry: Encyclopaedia, Genealogy, and Tradition* (Notre Dame: University of Notre Dame Press, 1990), pp. 90-91.

43. Lesslie Newbigin speaks of the necessary "cultural bilinguality" of the Christian life in which we are forced to know one language (the Christian faith) while living with another (secular speech). *The Gospel in a Pluralist Society* (Grand Rapids: Eerdmans, 1989), pp. 55-65.

44. Charles Campbell, *Preaching Jesus: New Directions for Homiletics in Hans Frei's Post-Liberal Theology* (Grand Rapids: Eerdmans, 1997), pp. 122ff.

45. Campbell, pg. 161. Graham Ward wonderfully disposes of correlationist thinking, accusing it of the "diremption" and "liquidation" of theology in its divorce of theology from concrete substance and particular practices. *True Religion*, Blackwell Manifestos (Oxford: Blackwell, 2003), pg. 115.

46. Hans Frei, *The Eclipse of Biblical Narrative: A Study in Eighteenth and Nineteenth Century Hermeneutics* (New Haven: Yale University Press, 1974), pp. 2-3.

47. Ibid., pg. 280.

48. Ibid., pp. 63-73.

49. *CD*, II, 1, pp. 66-67.

50. Frei , *Identity*, pp. 142-43. I have sometimes pondered why Barth, in focusing upon the Isenheim Altar of Grünewald, focuses only upon one part of that altar—John the Baptist pointing to the crucified and dead body of Christ. The altar is more complex, contains so many more images than the crucifixion. For instance, the resurrection of Christ, as Grünewald depicts it there, seems to me quite "Barthian" in its triumphant, radiating vision. I think that Frei's comments on the centrality of the passion as an

explanation for the rest of the story of Jesus helps us see why Barth focused on this part of the altar and not the rest. The cross is the triumph of Christ. In his *Ethics*, Bonhoeffer says that keeping cross and resurrection together is the great challenge of Christian thought and ethics (New York: Macmillan, 1962), pp. 88-89.

51. George A. Lindbeck, *The Nature of Doctrine: Religion and Theology in a Postliberal Age* (Louisville: Westminster/John Knox, 1984), pg. 121.

52. Campbell, *Preaching Jesus*, pg. 193.

53. Lose, pg. 118.

54. Lindbeck, *The Nature of Doctrine: Religion and Theology in a Postliberal* Age (Louisville: Westminster/John Knox Press, 1984), pg. 35. Barth says that, in our preaching, sometimes we are helped by the religious surroundings—the Gothic windows, the robe, and these other accoutrements, but the most effective help for the sermon will be "the crosses in the church yard which quietly look in through the windows to tell you unambiguously what is relevant here and what is not."

55. Hauerwas, *With the Grain of the Universe*, ch. 6, pg. 4. David Buttrick, *A Captive Voice: the Liberation of Preaching*, asks, "How do we rehabilitate the Word of God *extra nous*?" (pg. 53). After criticizing many "conservative" preachers for a too-constricted, unimaginative view of biblical authority, Buttrick extols the creation of Christian identity that results from the gospel being proclaimed in such a way that people come to a new experience of the presence of God. Preaching must be liberated from its "captivity to scripture" with a "hermeneutic of human situations" (pg. 111). Buttrick then contrasts Barth's restricted "biblical preaching" with the "prophetic preaching" of Martin Luther King, in a curious caricature of both the preaching of King and that of Barth. Buttrick says that the "words of God are the words of liberation" (pg. 113).

Buttrick repeats the tendency of many misinterpreters who detach Martin Luther King from the black church that produced him and his preaching as well as to detach him from the biblical formation that King had in that church. Buttrick not only categorizes Barth's homiletic in a way that misrepresents Barth but also categorizes "biblical preaching" in the reductionistic category of "liberation." This seems rather constricted and unimaginative.

56. Joseph Mangina makes a similar critique of the lack of theological basis in Lindbeck's analysis as well as the added insight that Lindbeck tempts us "to substitute talk about the church and about Christian practices for God himself." Mangina, *Karl Barth*, pg. 55.

57. GD, pg. 31.

58. Ibid., pg. 36.

59. Ibid., pg. 272.

60. In an otherwise wonderful theological treatment of scripture, Steven Fowl says that "the authority of scripture is not a property of the biblical texts any more than a meaning or an ideology is a property of those texts." Fowl sees the practices of the church as more theologically significant than the scripture of the church. I fear this stress upon practices that make scripture "work" rather than the divine Agent who makes scripture speak. Fowl, *Engaging Scripture* (Oxford: Blackwell, 1998), pg. 203.

61. See Nancy Lammers Gross, *If You Cannot Preach Like Paul . . .* (Grand Rapids: Eerdmans, 2002) for a good discussion of Barth's use of Paul, pp. 50-51, 64-68.

62. "Church Postill on Matt. 2:1-12," WA 10/1, 625:19–626:18.

63. Barth teaches that the church is the form of the Risen Christ, the church is the embodiment of Easter. See Stoevesandt's "Jesu Christi Irdisch-Geschichtliche Existenzform: Karl Barth's Lehre von der Kirche als Ostertheologie," in *Gottes Freiheit und die Grenze der Theolgie*, pp. 115-42.

64. I am most impressed by Samuel Wells's notion of "improvisation" as a fine characterization of the dynamics of the Christian life and, as he puts it, "the drama of Christian ethics." Christians are given scripture, but we are not given a script. We must improvise as we go, trusting the habits and convictions that have been cultivated in us by the church. It would be interesting to think about homiletics in the same way that Wells thinks about ethics. Wells, *Improvisation*, especially chapters 4, 8, 10.

9. Easter Speech

1. Mason Tarwater to his nephew in *The Violent Bear It Away*.

2. At the beginning of his influential textbook on preaching, H. Grady Davis says that "the truth we preach is not an abstract thing. The truth is a Person." *Design for Preaching* (Philadelphia: Fortress Press, 1958), pg. 19. Other great religious teachers taught a way; only Jesus said, "I am the way."

3. It is not insignificant, at least for us preachers, that Barth has the longest dissertation on angels of any theologian for hundreds of years (*CD*, III, 3). Barth makes the point that angels are real, but angels are completely undeveloped, so far as their individual personalities are concerned. They are completely transparent to the message that they deliver and, having delivered the message, they are heard from no more. Thus Barth's angels, in their subordination of the messenger to the message, could be taken as his ideal preachers.

Barth has similar things to say about Mary and her virginity. Barth explicates Mary's virginity as a demonstrating of the utter incapacity of human beings for God. God always comes to us as a gift, not because of some capacity on our part. Mary, in her incomprehension, incapacity, and virginity is thus for Barth a prime example of undeserved, humble hearing and speaking—again, the ideal preacher (*CD*, I, 2, pg. 188).

4. In even so richly visual and metaphorical a Gospel as that of John, the auditory appears to be priv-ileged over the visual. The visual cannot see what the voice can reveal (see 1:18; 6:63; 8:51). See Werner H. Kelber, "The Authority of the Word in St. John's Gospel: Charismatic Speech, Narrative Text, Logocentric Metaphysics," *Oral Tradition* 2, (January 1987): pp. 108-31. "The one who sent me is true; and I declare to the world what I have heard from him" (John 8:26).

5. I am startled by those who find Barth's theology to be "arrogant." He seems wonderfully humble in his determination to depend on revelation for all that he thinks and says. Richard Hays does a fine job of tying what he calls the "palpable and elusive" Risen Jesus to the peculiar sort of epistemology demanded by the Resurrection. "We are not ourselves in control of the new knowledge we are given. The risen Christ is present where and when he chooses. Paradoxically, our new understanding depends on an event that we cannot possibly understand. Therefore, we are radically dependent on a God who insists on being known on his terms, not ours. . . . A hermeneutic of resurrection, then, will teach us epistemic humility." Richard Hays, "Reading Scripture in the Light of the Resurrection," in Ellen F. Davis and Richard B. Hays, *The Art of Reading Scripture* (Grand Rapids: Eerdmans, 2003), pg. 234. Katherine Sonderegger says that Barth never gets away from the affirmation "that Christ lives," calling it "the governing maxim of the entire *Dogmatics*." See her wonderful treatment of the Resurrection in Barth in "Et Resurrexit Tertia Die: Jenson and Barth on Christ's Resurrection," in John C. McDowell and Mike Higton, *Conversing with Barth*, pp. 191-213.

6. If one is looking for historical validation of the Resurrection (which I have little inclination to do), then it seems to me that one might look for it here. Why would early Christians have based their reports of resurrection on the testimony of women unless that testimony had its basis in historical real-ity? See Marianne Sawicki's exploration of the significance of the women witnesses in *Seeing the Lord: Resurrection and Early Christian Practices* (Minneapolis: Fortress, 1994).

7. Karl Barth, *Dogmatics in Outline* (New York: Harper Torchbooks, 1959), pg. 123.

8. Bultmann, *Theology*, pg. 219.

9. Karl Barth, *Kirchliche Dogmatik*, I, 1, pp. 263-64, my translation.

10. Karl Barth, *Protestant Theology in the Nineteenth Century: Its Background and History* (Grand Rapids: Eerdmans, 2002), trans. Brian Cozens and John Bowden, pp. 520-26.

11. Throughout my conversation with Barth, I have been impressed that, while Barth does not spend any time on a "Doctrine of the Holy Spirit," his assumption throughout is that we know or we speak only through the gifts of the Holy Spirit. I therefore wonder why, in his masterful treatment of the Creed in *Dogmatics in Outline*, Barth did not pause to question the Creed's omission of the Holy Spirit from its narrative of our salvation.

12. See, e.g., "The Preface to the Second Edition," in *The Epistle to the* Romans (Oxford: Oxford University Press, 1933), pp. 10ff.

13. *Romans*, pp. 98-99.

14. *CD*, I, 1, pp. 455ff.

15. *CD*, I, 2, pg. 29.

16. *CD*, I, 1, pg. 158.

17. Barth cites Paul, who says, "One has died for all; therefore all have died" (2 Cor. 5:14), in asserting that in Christ our "self," has died and has been raised to a new selfhood. Now, in Christ, the hidden truth about the human race is made manifest. We are dead people so that we might be raised. This is how Barth can say that our true humanity is to be found, not by rummaging about in ourselves, not in our subjectivity, but objectively in Christ. Barth writes:

> In Christian doctrine . . . we have always to take in blind seriousness the basic Pauline perception of Colossians 3:3 which is that of all Scripture—that our life is hid with Christ in God. With Christ: never at all apart from him, never at all independently of him, never at all in and for itself. We as human beings never at all exist in ourselves. And Christians are the very last to try to cling to existing in themselves. We exist as human beings in Jesus Christ and in him alone; as we also find God in Jesus Christ and in him alone. The being and nature of human beings in and for themselves as independent bearers of an independent predicate, have, by the revelation of Jesus Christ, become an abstraction which can be destined only to disappear. (*CD*, II, 1, pg. 149)

18. *GD*, pg. 168; *CD*, 1, 2, pg. 204.

19. Karl Barth, *Homiletics*, translated by Geoffrey W. Bromiley and Donald E. Daniels (Louisville: Westminster/John Knox Press, 1991), pg. 47.

20. I'm wondering if the thinness of the theology that is found in many of the books on spiritual practices (like Dorothy Bass, *Practicing the Faith: A Way of Life for a Searching People* [San Francisco: Jossey Bass, 1998]) may be inherent in any account of the Christian life that begins with what we ought to do rather than with what God has done and is doing in Christ. Much of the enthusiasm for Christian practices is theoretically based on the work of Alasdair MacIntyre's influential *After Virtue: A Study in Moral Theory* (London: Duckworth, 1984). MacIntyre thinks about the moral life "from below," in Aristotelian fashion. Such accounts tend to be rather pedestrian, lacking little sense of imperative "from above." We must find a way to keep any account of the moral life as miraculous, a work of God rather than our work. Joseph Mangina (*Karl Barth*, pp. 186-88) raises some similar criticisms about the current enthusiasm for "practices" of the church.

21. Stanley Hauerwas stresses the character-producing, good-habit-forming qualities of narrative (see Hauerwas's "Constancy and Forgiveness: The Novel as a School for Virtue" in *Dispatches From the Front: Theological Engagements with the Secular* [Durham, N.C.: Duke University Press, 1994]). His model writer of fiction is Anthony Trollope, great creator of character. Barth has made me pick Flannery O'Connor as my model Christian writer. O'Connor is the great destroyer of character, continuity, and stability.

22. *CD*, I, 1, pg. 109.

23. Ibid., pg. 95.

24. *CD*, I, 2, pp. 745-46.

25. Barth, *Romans* (London: Oxford University Press, 1933), pg. 39.

26. Trevor Hart, *Regarding Karl Barth* (Downers Grove, Ill.: InterVarsity Press, 1999), pp. 40-41.

27. See the astute article by John Webster in "Faith," in *The Blackwell Encyclopedia of Modern Christian Thought*, ed. Alister E. McGrath (Oxford: Blackwell, 1993), pp. 208-10.

28. Trevor Hart, *Regarding Karl Barth*, pp. 44-45.

29. Quoted by Stephen Webb, *The Divine Voice*, pg. 180.

30. "We are now reminded that right throughout the Old Testament, to those to whom He speaks, and by the very fact that He does speak, Yahweh gives a mission and authority, a commission and a

command, that they too should speak. . . . Not every man can do this. Not every man can speak God's Word. For not every man has heard it" (*CD*, I, 2, pp. 490-91). Behind this warning is the affirmation that anyone who actually hears the Word of God can, indeed must, speak the Word of God.

31. Lections for Fifth Sunday after the Epiphany, Year C.

32. Karl Rahner (*Theological Investigations*, 1984, 18:94) said, "God does not offer himself for observation." God is not an object that is easily compared, described, defined, or contrasted with other objects.

33. *CD*, I, 1, pg. 60.

10. Called to Preach

1. *CD*, IV, 2, pp. 498ff. The section on vocation is number 71, "On the Vocation of Man."

2. *CD*, I, 1, pg. 104.

3. *CD*, I, 2, pp. 490-91.

4. Ibid., pg. 506.

5. *CD*, II, 1, pg. 159.

6. *CD*, III, 2, pg. 156.

7. *CD*, I, 2, pp. 680ff.

8. Barth, *Homiletics*, pg. 82.

9. Ibid., pg. 70.

10. Busch, *The Great Passion*, pg. 148-51.

11. *CD*, IV, 3, pg. 636.

12. Ibid., pg. 662.

13. Ibid., pg. 615.

14. Ibid., pg. 645.

15. Quoted by Busch, *The Great Passion*, pg. 149.

16. Ibid., pg. 149.

17. *CD*, IV, 3, pg. 665.

18. Ibid., pg. 666.

19. Barth speaks of preaching as a kind of reading to oneself: "The sermon will be like the involuntary lip movement of one who is reading with great care, attention, and surprise, more following the letters than reading in the usual sense, all eyes, totally claimed, aware that 'I have not written the text.'" While one likes this stress upon strict attentiveness to the text and the objectivity of the text, still this seems a strange depiction of the act of preaching. *Homiletics*, pg. 76.

20. Harry Stout makes much of the theological significance of the rediscovery of extemporaneous preaching among George Whitefield and the Oxford Methodists. John Wesley seems to have accidentally discovered the method in 1735 when, having forgotten his sermon notes, he preached extemporaneously and was stunned by the power of his sermon. Wesley began recommending extemporaneous preaching to all who were courageous enough (and who had a robust enough theology of the Holy Spirit!) to try it. Stout notes how such preaching establishes a unique bond between speaker and hearer. True. But I would also stress that extemporaneous preaching establishes a unique bond with the Holy Spirit. Stout believes that the practice of extemporaneous preaching is one of the unique aspects of American evangelical homiletics. Stout, *Divine Dramatist*, pg. 43.

21. Flannery O'Connor wrote a friend that "the only thing that makes the Church endurable is that it is somehow the body of Christ and that on this we are fed. It seems to be a fact that you have to suffer as much from the Church as for it" (*Collected Works*, pg. 942).

22. See Paul S. Minear, *To Die and to Live: Christ's Resurrection and Christian Vocation*, 1977, pp. 3-35.

23. Barth, *Homiletics*, pg. 56.

24. Preached at the Service of Celebration and Installation for William Willimon as the Bishop of the North Alabama Conference of The United Methodist Church at Canterbury United Methodist Church, Birmingham, Alabama, on November 14, 2004.

25. Steven Webb, *The Divine Voice*, pg. 110.

26. In this assertion I part company with Stanley Hauerwas, who tends to make ecclesial practice the mark and the canon of scripture and preaching rather than scripture and preaching being the mark and the canon of the church. Early in his thought, Hauerwas says that "just as scientific theories are partially judged by the fruitfulness of the activities they generate, so narratives can and should be judged by the richness of moral character and activity they generate." To this assertion of community as a test of scripture, William Placher responds: "We do something because God did something first. Therefore, it cannot be the virtue of our people or the practices of our community that make true the story we tell about what God did." See this discussion in William C. Placher, *Unapologetic Theology* (Louisville: Westminster/John Knox Press, 1989), pp. 164-65. The Bible does not gain its authority from the church, nor does preaching. The truth of what we say in a sermon cannot be made completely dependent upon the performance of the community. The authority of preaching rests solely upon, "And God said. . . ." For a concise description of Hauerwas's views on scripture and the church (with implications for preaching), see his *Unleashing the Scripture: Freeing the Bible from the Captivity to America* (Nashville: Abingdon Press, 1993), pg. 27.

27. Letter in Karl Barth-Archiv, Basel, October 19, 1933, my translation; the letters from the Vikar are from September 29 and October 6, 1933.

28. I find it remarkable that Barth, during the years of 1933–1938, so rarely refers to Hitler, national socialism, or the war in his sermons or even in his letters. Barth really practices what he preaches. In an open letter to his "former students in the German church," of May 10, 1937, Barth mentions, in some detail, his sympathy for their plight in the present regime. Yet he concludes his discussion by saying that they have less to fear from the government than they do from the Word of God. That Word will enable them not only to resist the government but also to instill in them "an even greater love for the people" they serve. The church cannot permit itself "to be driven by politics" but rather the church must always serve in "concrete obedience" to the gospel. Letter in Karl Barth-Archiv. My translation.

29. Demonstrated so well in David Ford, *Barth and God's Story: Biblical Narrative in the Theological Method of Karl Barth in The Church Dogmatics* (Frankfurt am Main: Verlag Peter Lang, 1981).

30. The recovery of the sense of a sermon as an event in time, moving in time, of a sermon as an energetic and dynamic event, is indebted to the work of Eugene L. Lowry in books like *Doing Time in the Pulpit* (Nashville: Abingdon Press, 1985) and *The Sermon: Dancing on the Edge of Mystery* (Nashville: Abingdon Press, 1997).

31. In one of his prison sermons, Barth says that we inculcate biblical truth like "my hope is in the thee," through repetition: "Granted, the people who speak in the Bible, including the man who affirms in the 39th Psalm: 'My hope is in thee!' were rather peculiar people; but peculiar only because God encountered them and dealt with them in his own way. . . . They were peculiarly exposed to the human predicament, much more so than others. . . . You see, it is from this situation—we might also say into this situation—that the people of the Bible affirm: 'My hope is in thee.' They call us to repeat it for ourselves and to repeat it with them: 'My hope is in thee.'" *Deliverance to the Captives*, pp. 54-55.

32. In the name of evangelism and contemporary worship, many churches are uncritically adopting film clips, slideshow presentations, and other forms of electronic media in their Sunday worship. I fear that they are being naive in the rhetorical difficulty involved with the adaptation of these media for Christian worship. The media are controlled by commercial interests. People are conditioned to hear mostly advertising from such media. The medium becomes the message. I wonder if the gospel can be communicated by a medium like television that is so completely dominated by advertising.

33. Sam Wells speaks of the way in which Christians' listening to scripture is a exercise in the formation of distinctive character:

> When Christians listen for God's word in Scripture, they learn to listen for God's word in every conversation. They develop the skill of storytelling, of finding their place and role in the story, . . . of fitting their own small story into the larger story of God. (Sam Wells, *Improvisation*, pg. 82)

34. Walter Brueggemann, *Finally Comes the Poet: Daring Speech for Proclamation* (Philadelphia: Fortress Press, 1989), pg. 3.

35. Harry B. Stout, *The Divine Dramatist: George Whitefield and the Rise of Modern Evangelicalism* (Grand Rapids: Eerdmans, 1991).

36. Thomas G. Long, *The Witness of Preaching*, pg. 29.

37. Ibid. The conventional view of Barth's homiletic is that it cares nothing for the congregational context. David M. Greenhaw's judgment is typical when he says that wherever Barth's view of preaching is appropriated, "it has tended to elevate preaching beyond the reach of the congregation." "Theology of Preaching," in William H. Willimon and Richard Lischer, eds., *Concise Encyclopedia of Preaching* (Louisville: Westminster/John Knox Press, 1995), pg. 480. I think that Stephen Farris does a nuanced treatment of Barth's idea about sermonic context in his book *Preaching That Matters: The Bible and Our Lives* (Louisville: Westminster/John Knox Press, 1998), chap. 2. There never is any "unadulterated proclamation of the Word of God" (*CD*, I, 2, pg. 803). Proclamation always emanates from "the concrete personality of individual preachers and the character of their congregations" (*CD*, I, 2, pg. 802).

38. *Deliverance to the Captives*, pg. 36.

39. Barth, *Homiletics*, pg. 63.

40. Quoted in Busch, from notes by Ch. Von Kirschbaum, on pg. 311 of Eberhard Busch, *Karl Barth and the Pietists*.

41. When asked, in 1961, by an American newspaper, to identify the "false gods" of our age, Barth thought of the church: "The place where the false gods stand and become active, is today as in all times first in the church itself. The churches believe in their own value and power, Tradition, Morals, and Religious Activities. They believe that they are so different from the Indifferent, the Atheists, and the Communists. . . . They are no different from those who worship Money, Sports, Technology, Sexuality or the simple sovereignty of the comfortable existence. The church has to prove that it believes in God himself, which has freed humanity from the worship of all false Gods." (*Karl Barth: Offene Briefe, 1945–1968*, ed. by von D. Koch [Zürich: Gesamtausgabe, Abt. Verlag, 1985], pg. 501. My translation.) Barth really believed that the greatest danger to the church, and by implication the greatest threat to preaching, lay within the church.

42. See *CD*, "Jesus Christ, the Servant as Lord," vol. IV, 2.

43. *Dogmatics in Outline*, pg. 172.

44. Ibid., pg. 173.

45. Nicholas M. Healy, "The Logic of Karl Barth's Ecclesiology: Analysis, Assessment, and Proposed Modifications," *Modern Theology*, 10.3 (July 1994): pp. 253-70.

46. This is the recurring pattern in Barth. We begin with the particularities of Jesus, shunning any attempt to begin in generalities: "It is not the general which comes first, but the particular. The general does not exist without this particular and cannot therefore be prior to the particular. It cannot, then, be recognized and understood as the general prior to it, as if it were itself a particular. Thus we cannot move from the general to the particular, but only in the opposite direction" (*CD*, II, 1, pg. 602).

47. *CD*, IV, 3.2, pg. 843.

48. Ibid., pp. 865 ff.

49. Ibid., pg. 845.

50. Ibid., pg. 844.

51. Ibid., pg. 729.

52. Ibid., pg. 816; *CD*, III, 4, pp. 498ff.

53. Daniel J. Price, *Karl Barth's Anthropology in Light of Modern Thought*, pg. 146.

54. Reinhard Hütter, "Karl Barth's 'Dialectical Catholicism' *Sic et Non*," *Modern Theology* 16, no. 2 (April 2000): pp. 137-58. In 1959 Ernst Käsemann criticized Barth for not being explicit about the way that Christ is tied to the world through his body, the church. "Barth is in danger of speaking of a *regnum Christi* which is abstract from the concrete ministry of believers and the reality of the body of

Christ as the instrument of the *regnum Christi*. This opens the doors to metaphysics and mythology." Quoted in Bockmuehl, *The Unreality of God*, pg. 101.

55. *CD*, IV, 2, pg. 675. This strikes me as a defiantly Lutheran way of putting the matter—the church as subordinate to the Word. When asked, in a letter from Professor Kuwada of Tokyo, to comment on the sources of world peace and the need for nuclear disarmament, Barth says that the source of war is our bad preaching! (*Letters: 1961-1968*, pg. 90.)

56. *CD*, I, 1, pg. xv.

57. Barth, *Romans*, pp. 36-37. Of course it is no more fair to quote the *Romans* Barth as his last word on the church than to quote the *Homiletics* Barth as the last word on preaching. *Romans* was a corrective that stressed the infinite qualitative distance of the wholly other God. When Barth began the *Church Dogmatics*, Barth keeps stressing the real communion that God has with us. By making his theology dynamically Christocentric, a commentary on the constant communication that is implied in the Incarnation and the Trinity, Barth gives us a sure basis from which to enjoy our lives in the church.

58. "The church *is* when it happens to these human beings in common that they may receive the verdict . . . pronounced in the resurrection of Jesus Christ from the dead" (*CD*, IV, 1, pg. 651).

59. Hauerwas, *With the Grain of the Universe*, ch. 1, pg. 44.

60. Quoted by Busch, *The Great Passion*, pg. 242.

61. *CD*, IV, 3, pg. 525.

62. *CD*, IV, 3.2, pp. 524-25.

63. Barth says that we must "accustom ourselves to the idea that it might be better for the cause and ministry of the Church . . . if one day, without being able to rejoice in any acknowledged position . . . it had to exist again in people, society and state as a small . . . group of aliens" (*CD*, IV, 4, pg. 168).

64. Curiously, Jack Forstman judges Barth's determination to listen to the Bible, "with no grounding that could be acknowledged from the outside," as the reason Hitler was not defeated through the *Barmen Declaration*. Outsiders to the Christian faith like Hitler "do not share the premise, they understand themselves to be exempt from the claim of God to whom the Bible witnesses." Poor Barth limited his social activism to the church where he was "limited to one's own enclave." Frostman's is one of the most curious misconstrurals of Barth's intent in *Barmen*. It is also a foundationalist reading that assumes up front that it is always a waste of effort for preachers to speak primarily to the church. I would remind Frostman that it was the German theological liberals, those who expended such effort to speak on the basis of a grounding "that could be acknowledged from the outside" who couldn't tell the difference between the "German Christians" and the Body of Christ. This sort of "false humility" (Milbank), that assumes that the church must first submit its speech to the "outside" is just the sort of thing that made a truly Christian witness to the Nazis (other than in a Bonhoeffer or a Barth) impossible. See Jack Forstman, *Christian Faith in Dark Times: Theological Conflicts in the Shadow of Hitler* (Louisville: Westminster/John Knox Press, 1992), pp. 254-59.

65. Barth, *Homiletics*, pg. 56

66. Ibid., pg. 57. Rowan Williams underscores, in a very Barthian way, the "Reformation principle" that "the Church must be judged by its freedom to witness to the freedom of God" (pg. 69). "The Catholic Church is simply that gathering in which what Christ has promised is spoken and heard" (pg. 67). *Why Study the Past? The Quest for the Historical Church* (Grand Rapids: Eerdmans, 2005).

67. Barth briefly mentions the issue of sermon length. But of course Barth believes that the length of the sermon ought to be determined by nothing but the biblical text. In my comment above, I am not saying that the length of the sermon ought to be determined by the listeners' limits but by the theological substance that is being described in the sermon. "The general maxim that brevity is the soul of wit may be true of any form of speech but is should not be applied to the sermon. The task of the sermon is to create space for the Word of God, which alone can be the criterion for the length of the sermon." Barth, *Homiletics*, pg. 122. Most of Barth's sermons are not what I would regard as overly long, but it is clear that all of these sermons hope to "create space."

68. Barth, *Homiletics*, pg. 65

69. *CD*, I, 1, pg. 70, quoted by Barth from Luther: *Von Ordnung Gottesdienst*, 1523.

70. Barth, *Homiletics*, pg. 58.

71. Ibid., pg. 60. In a letter to Wolf-Dieter Zimmermann (March 28, 1962) Barth says that he insists that his prison sermons be recorded only in the context of a full service of worship, even inviting those who listen to the recordings to join in the singing of the hymns as they listen, in order that the sermon be experienced in its "natural setting." (Karl Barth, *Letters: 1961-1968*, Jürgen Fangmeier and Hinrich Stoevesandt, eds., Geoffrey W. Bromiley, ed. and trans. [Edinburgh: T. & T. Clark, 1981], pp. 37-38.)

72. Mangina makes a similar critique of Barth in *Karl Barth*, pp. 157-58.

73. *CD*, IV, 1, pg. 711.

74. Thus Hauerwas ends his Gifford Lectures with the astounding claim that the trouble with the *Church Dogmatics* is not that it is too long but that it is too short! In Barth's dynamic sense of divine speaking, there is always more to be said in theology because Jesus Christ has been raised from the dead and continues to speak to those who betrayed him.

In Marilynne Robinson's *Gilead* (pg. 173), her old preacher wanders into the deserted sanctuary of his little church and muses, "When this old sanctuary is full of silence and prayer, every book Karl Barth ever will write would not be a feather in the scales against it from the point of view of profundity, and I would not believe in Barth's own authenticity if I did not also believe he would know and recognize the truth of that, and honor it, too."

I believe this to be true. Barth said once that the angels in heaven laughed at old Barth wheeling in yet another volume of theology. Preaching is a most fragile art, standing as it does under the judgments of God. We preachers must never think that we have had the last word, or that our word endures. We have no significance other than what God gives. All of us, including Barth, are no more than John the Baptist's bony finger pointing toward the One who shall have the last, triumphant word.

75. Barth, *Homiletics*, pg. 127. Thus the "Amen" uttered at the end of a sermon is neither a word of completion nor resignation. It is a joyful "Amen!" that is uttered in mid-conversation, and in joy:

> The church must not allow itself to become dull, nor its services dark and gloomy. It must be claimed by, and proclaim, the lordship of God in the kingdom of his dear Son rather than the lordship of the devil or capitalism or communism or human folly and wickedness in general. . . . Who otherwise will believe it when it says that the holy day is made of joy for men and therefore the day of God? (*CD*, III, 4, pg. 69)

Index of Scripture

Genesis

1	101
1:3	144, 165
1:26	144
2:23	165
3:1	147
3:5	118

Exodus

3	245
16	162

Deuteronomy

32:6	139

1 Samuel

3	246
17:23	29

Job

4:12-16,17	78f.

Psalms

14:1	149
29	113, 175
39	312
110:4	193
139:5-6	117

Jeremiah

1:1,4,9	144
1:7	202
15:19	234
23:29	165

Ecclesiastes

3:1,2,11	40

Isaiah

6	245f.

Matthew

2:1-12	308
1:30	215
18:20	259
25	66
28	130, 134, 252, 261

Mark

4:3-8	189
4:26-29	175

Luke

3:21	151
4	197
4:18	201
4:21-30	201, 234
5:1-11	234
10	148
10:42	264
11:1-13	66, 105
12	260
16:8	66
21:13	47
24	145
24:45-49	108

John

1	126, 138
1:6-8	163
1:18	167
1:23	6, 164
1:29	164
2	200
3:30	177

5:2 218
14:16 142
15:27 162
18:37 162
19:30 164
20 223

Acts
2 . . . . .39, 175
9:15 163
9:22-26 219
17 . . . . .41, 212

Romans
1:16 215
1:19-20 50
1:21 150
8:27 227
10:17 299
13:11-12 66

1 Corinthians
1:4-6 174
1:21-23 223
2:4 167
3:2 191
12:12 257
13:7 202
13:12 .67, 277
15:3-4 235
15:4 167

2 Corinthians
4:13 . . . . .47, 200
5:11-6:2 187
5:14 310
5:20 167
11:28 4

Galatians
1:15 84

Ephesians
1:23 257
3:15 200
5-6 . . . . .253, 261
5:14 66
6:17 258

Philippians
2:5-11 232
2:6 120

Colossians
3:3 310

1 Thessalonians
2:13 242
5:5 66
5:24 66

1 Timothy
3:5 236

Hebrews
1:1-2 124
5:6,10 193
6:20 193
7:1 193

James
3:5-10a 83

1 Peter
1:21, 23 209

1 John
1:1 200

Index of Names

Abernathy, Ralph, 243
Achtemeier, Elizabeth, 271
Adam, Karl, 283
Ahlers, Rolf, 271
Alan of Lille, 153
Allen, O. Wesley, 277
Allen, Ronald J., 280, 302
Allen, Woody, 306
Alston, William P., 177, 302
Alter, Robert, 281, 304
Ambrose, 85
Andrews, Jacqueline, 3
Anselm, 19, 180, 240
Aristotle, 40, 48-52, 80, 84, 85, 87, 88, 95, 96, 119, 156, 165, 166, 189, 193, 197, 204, 211, 217, 243, 263
Auden, 64
Augustine, 33, 47, 56, 85, 88, 93, 94, 104, 131-33, 137, 153, 189, 278, 280-82, 285, 291, 296
Aquinas, Thomas, 119, 138, 282

Bach, 101, 246
Baillie, John, 114, 289
Balthasar, H. Urs von, 44, 90, 91, 102, 281, 284
Balzac, 2, 103
Barr, James, 272, 274, 281
Bartlett, David, 108, 168, 285, 299, 300, 301
Bartow, Charles, 289
Bass, Dorothy, 310
Bastian, Hans Dieter, 305
Bauer, 2
Baxter, Christina, 276, 300
Beecher, Henry Ward, 154, 277
Berkeley, George, 54-56
Beuys, Joseph, 115
Blumhardt, J. C., 10-12, 31, 159, 268
Bockmuehl, Klaus, 270, 271, 278

Boethius, 73-74
Bonhoeffer, Dietrich, 14, 95, 173, 174, 228, 270, 278, 299, 300, 308, 314
Booth, Wayne, 89, 281
Borg, Marcus, 235, 298
Bowden, John, 98, 284, 287, 300, 309
Bromiley, Geoffrey, 267, 270, 271, 280, 288, 289, 292, 293, 294, 299, 310, 315
Brooks, Phillips, 244, 304
Bruegel, Pieter, 5-6
Brueggemann, Walter, 251, 268, 289, 313
Brunner, Emil, 17, 136, 159, 178, 183, 301, 303
Buber, Martin, 68, 195, 277, 305
Bullinger, 42, 127, 231
Bultmann, Rudolf, 20, 31, 33, 37-39, 75, 107, 119, 225, 229, 270, 272, 273, 278, 279, 288, 290, 301, 309
Burckhardt, Abel, 24
Burckhardt, Jacob, 24
Burke, Kenneth, 89
Burkhart, John E., 281
Burnett, Ernest, 270
Busch, Eberhard, 268, 269, 270, 271, 274, 275, 284, 292, 294, 302, 305, 306, 311, 313, 314
Bush, George W., 105, 107, 115, 185, 186, 247
Bushnell, Horace, 154
Buttrick, David, 154, 295, 296, 297, 298, 308
Byassee, Jason, 3

Calvin, John, 9, 19, 27, 48, 75, 124, 136, 149, 153, 182, 239, 264, 282, 293, 296, 301
Cameron, Charles M., 290
Campbell, Charles, 209, 214, 215, 217, 218, 306, 307, 308
Campbell, Joseph, 298
Childs, Brevard, 1, 268, 274
Cicero, 33, 87

Come, Arnold B., 267
Clapp, Rodney, 307
Cone, James H., 277
Craddock, Fred B., 154, 262, 280, 295, 296
Crites, Stephen, 34
Cunningham, David, 95, 281, 283
Cushman, Robert E., 291

Dannowski, Hans Werner, 280
Davis, Ellen F., 302, 309
Davis, H. Grady, 309
Davison, James E., 276, 307
Dawn, Marva, 180, 273
Dayton, Donald, 271
Demson, David E., 298
Derrida, Jacques, 95, 282, 283
Descartes, René, 51-53, 56, 64, 68, 71, 88, 98,
    115, 275, 298
Dillenberger, John, 281
Dorrien, Gary, 10, 17, 103, 173, 181, 182, 268,
    269, 270, 285, 289, 292, 300
Dostoevsky, Fyodor, 12, 18, 269

Edwards, Jonathan, 154
Eliot, T. S., 83, 256
Eslinger, Richard L., 295
Evans, Donald, 140, 292, 293

Fahler, Jochen, 268, 269
Farley, Edward, 33-34, 273, 276, 280
Feuerbach, Ludwig, 12, 48, 62, 64, 102, 122, 226,
    227
Finney, Charles G., 154
Fiorenza, Elisabeth S., 89, 281
Flaubert, 306
Ford, David, 37, 41, 44, 64, 110, 134, 204, 216,
    272, 273, 274, 286, 293, 305, 312
Forstman, Jack, 314
Forsyth, P. T., 277
Fosdick, Harry E., 90, 154, 281, 296
Fowl, Stephen, 308
Frei, Hans, 1, 32, 98, 163, 179, 180, 206, 209,
    210, 214-18, 273, 282, 298, 302, 303, 306, 307
Freud, Sigmund, 102
Frey, Christofer, 270
Fuller, Reginald, 273
Funk, Robert, 281

Geest, H. van der, 288
Genest, Hartmut, 267, 297
Gerhardt, Paul, 226

Gerrish, B. A., 298
Gilkey, Langdon, 97, 276, 283
Gill, Theodore A., 286
Gogarten, Friedrich, 17
Gomes, Peter, 273
Gorgias, 50, 86, 87, 146
Gorringe, Timothy J., 274
Green, Garrett, 148, 294
Green, R. P. H., 280, 285
Greenhaw, David, 313
Gregory of Nazianus, 47, 136
Grenz, Stanley J., 177, 302
Gross, Nancy, 308
Grünewald, Matthis, 5, 6, 24, 26, 31, 163, 192,
    304, 307
Gustafson, James M., 207, 303, 306

Hall, Douglas John, 287
Harnack, Adolf von, 10, 146, 158, 281
Hart, Trevor, 48, 67, 119, 121, 122, 124, 126, 134,
    231, 232
Hauerwas, Stanley, 3, 40, 64, 107, 149, 179-81,
    202, 207, 216, 235, 254, 257-59, 273, 276,
    277, 278, 296, 302, 303, 305, 306, 308, 310,
    312, 314, 315
Hayum, Andrée, 268
Hays, Richard B., 210, 211, 268, 302, 309
Healy, Nicholas, 274, 313
Hegel, G. W. F., 61, 62, 140, 226, 276, 284, 289,
    302
Heidegger, Martin, 95, 283
Henry, Pat, 105
Herrmann, Willhelm, 9, 10, 14, 20, 158, 178,
    268, 270
Hick, John, 272
Higton, Mike, 267, 290, 302, 309
Hilkert, Mary C., 306
Hitler, Adolf, 20, 21, 72, 248, 249, 312, 314
Hogan, Lucy, 155-57, 296, 297
Hoitenga, Dewey J., 302
Hollaz, 2
Holmer, 1
Homrighausen, E. G., 283
Hume, David, 52, 56-60, 98, 275
Hunsinger, George, 3, 20, 35, 72, 104, 107, 110,
    117, 119, 126, 162, 269, 270, 274, 276, 277,
    279, 284, 285, 286, 287, 288, 289, 294, 298
Hunter, Rodney J., 293
Hütter, Reinhardt, 257, 300, 313

Isner, Michael, 70

Isocrates, 86-87
Iwand, Hans, 296

James, William, 62-64, 94, 258, 283, 296
Jenson, Robert W., 271, 302, 309
Johnson, L. T., 298
Johnson, R. C., 1, 204, 305
Julicher, Adolf, 17, 281
Jüngel, Eberhard, 118, 288, 292

Kant, Immanuel, 9, 12, 16, 32, 52, 59-61, 64, 68, 88, 94, 119, 138, 173, 179, 211, 240, 254, 270
Käsemann, Ernst, 313
Kay, James F., 37-39, 156-57, 183, 273, 295, 296, 297, 303, 306
Kelber, Werner H., 309
Kelsey, David, 34, 97, 273, 306
Kermode, Frank, 35, 281
Kiefer, Anslem, 7, 268
Kierkegaard, Søren, 13, 18, 77, 79, 100, 119, 121, 174, 202, 231, 268, 269, 280, 305
King, Martin Luther, 155, 308
Kirschbaum, Charlotte, 150, 304, 313
Köbler, Renate, 304
Kutter, Hermann, 270

LaCugna, Catherine Mowry, 299
Lash, Nicholas, 62, 64, 65, 68, 72, 95, 120, 275, 276, 277, 278, 283, 289
Laythan, D. Brent, 307
Leibniz, 54
Lincoln, Abraham, 96
Lindbeck, George, 205-6, 209-10, 213-18, 305, 306, 308
Lischer, Richard, 155, 298, 313
Locke, John, 53-56, 58, 88, 99, 283
Long, Thomas G., 47, 84, 108-9, 156, 169, 190, 252-53, 274, 285, 296, 300, 304, 313
Loscalzo, Craig, 177, 302
Lose, David, 194, 199, 207-8, 216-17, 305, 306, 308
Lossky, V., 292
Lowry, Eugene, 295, 312
Luther, Martin, 4, 18, 21, 48, 76, 81, 82, 119, 121, 131, 136, 157, 173-75, 182, 191, 220, 228, 231, 233, 264, 276, 278, 280, 282, 292, 294, 295, 297, 299, 314

MacIntyre, Alasdair, 307, 310
Macquarrie, John, 292
Mangina, Joseph, 275, 276, 279, 287, 308, 315

Man, Paul de, 282
Manfred, Josuttis, 267
Marquard, Reiner, 268, 269
Marx, Karl, 64
Marxsen, Willi, 301
Maurer, Ernstpeter, 275
McClain, William B., 295
McClure, John S., 295
McCormack, Bruce, 273, 283, 293
McDowell, John C., 267, 290, 302, 309
McFague, Sallie, 90, 281
McGlasson, Paul, 274
Melzer, Sara E., 281
Merz, Georg, 284
Migliore, Daniel, 294
Milbank, John, 60, 213, 275, 294, 307, 314
Minear, Paul S., 311
Miskotte, K. H., 279, 287, 305
Moyers, Bill, 298
Mozart, 5, 39, 110, 190, 286
Murphy, D. D., 275

Nembach, Ulrich, 296
Newbigin, Lesslie, 307
Newton, Isaac, 56, 60
Niebuhr, Reinhold, 64, 276, 277, 296, 306, 307
Nietzsche, Friedrich, 11, 68, 72, 91, 142, 282

O'Connor, Flannery, 97, 120, 192, 219, 223, 283, 289, 297, 304, 310, 311
Olbrechts-Tyteca, L., 283
Otto, Gert, 280
Overbeck, Franz, 11-12, 16

Pangritz, Andreas, 270, 278
Pannenburg, Wolfhart, 274, 298, 299
Parker, T. H. L., 283
Pauch, Willhelm, 91
Perelmean, Chaim, 283
Perkins, William, 297
Peterson, Eugene, 48, 275
Phillips, Donald, 103, 285
Pickstock, Catherine, 275
Placher, William C., 200, 305, 306, 312
Plato, 16, 35, 49-51, 69, 76, 85-88, 110, 124, 211, 220, 250
Porteous, Norman, 294
Price, Daniel J., 295, 313
Prickett, Stephen, 281
Protagoras, 86
Proust, 32

Quintillian, 87, 88, 156, 263

Rabbi Schmelke, 195
Rahner, Karl, 306, 311
Ramsey, Ian, 276
Ramus, Peter, 88
Rather, Dan, 106
Rees, Frank D., 267
Reid, Robert, 156-57, 296, 297
Rhodes, Dan, 3
Ricoeur, Paul, 108, 169, 285
Robinson, James M., 281
Robinson, Marilynne, 149, 315
Rorty, Richard, 94, 282
Rose, L. A., 295
Royce, Josiah, 63
Rutledge, Fleming, 273

Sauter, Gerhard, 147, 171, 268, 269, 270, 284, 294, 300
Sawicki, Marianne, 309
Schleiermacher, F., 2, 10, 14-15, 19, 33, 48, 61-62, 73, 75, 119, 128-29, 136, 150, 158, 211, 213, 226, 255, 270, 275, 276, 281, 282, 295, 307
Schillebeeckx, E., 306
Schopenhauer, 254
Schuster, Marguerite, 278
Smart, James, 269, 283
Smith, Christine M., 295
Socrates, 50-51, 67, 146, 220
Soelle, Dorothy, 290
Sonderegger, K., 290, 309
Stoevesanat, Hinrich, 164, 170, 173, 298, 299, 300, 305, 308, 315
Stout, Harry, 252, 311, 313
Stout, Jeffrey, 51, 275, 283
Strawn, Brent A., 44, 274
Strauss, D. F., 37
Sykes, S. W., 268, 292

Tarwater, Mason, 309
Taylor, Barbara B., 287
Taylor, Charles, 53, 275
Taylor, John Hammond, 291
Teresa, Mother, 106
Thielicke, Helmut, 135, 268, 292
Thiemann, Ronald, 306
Thompson, John, 276, 300

Thurneysen, Eduard, 12, 14-16, 21, 145, 156, 159-60, 269, 270, 271, 283, 301
Tillich, Paul, 34, 48, 83, 97, 104, 107, 215, 281, 296
Tisdale, Lenora Tubbs, 295
Torrance, T. F., 77, 103, 271
Tracy, David, 207, 228, 306
Trollope, Anthony, 310
Trowitzch, Michael, 267

Updike, John, 83, 97, 283

Vermes, Pamela, 120
Villa-Vicencio, 295
Voltaire, 64

Wallis, Jim, 234
Ward, Graham, 275, 282, 283, 302, 307
Warfield, B. B., 271
Warren, Rick, 273
Watson, Francis, 11, 268
Webb, Stephen, 13, 83, 91-92, 97-99, 102, 110, 183, 269, 277, 280, 281-82, 283, 284, 285, 286, 287, 303, 306, 310, 312
Webster, John, 24, 268, 271, 277, 288, 289, 292, 310
Wells, Samuel, 179, 278, 302, 306, 308, 312
Wesley, John, 41, 119, 239-40, 250, 271, 278, 311
Wharton, James A., 273
White, Graham, 43, 76, 278, 284
Whitefield, George, 311, 313
Wilder, Amos N., 281, 286
Wiles, Maurice, 280
Wilken, Robert, 302
Willems, B. A., 280
Williams, R. D., 292
Willimon, William H., 180, 273, 277, 281, 293, 298, 302, 304, 306, 311, 313
Wills, Gary, 283
Wilson, Paul Scott, 304
Wingren, Gustaf, 80-81, 123, 279, 290
Wintzer, Friedrich, 280
Wittgenstein, Ludwig, 76, 89, 199, 267, 281, 305
Wolterstorff, Nicholas, 283, 292, 300
Wood, Ralph C., 297, 302

Zahrnt, Heinz, 271
Zimmerman, W. D., 315
Zink-Sawyer, Beverly, 153-55, 296
Zündel, 167
Zwingli, Ulrich, 19, 264

Index of Subjects

actualism, 19, 28
address, 104f., 165f.
analogy, 137, 142, 136ff.
apologetics, 19, 77, 177-80, 182-84, 301-2
atheism, 61-62, 148ff.

baptism, 151ff.
Barmen Declaration, 150, 260, 314
Black Theology, 71f.

Christian Dogmatics in Outline, 102
Christology, 33, 44, 178, 215, 240, 256, 289, 293, 300
Confessions, The, 93ff.
conflict, 112, 197ff., 201
conversion, 82
correlation, 307
cross, 100

Deism, 141
Dialectical Theology, 15, 101, 158, 270, 281
dogmatics and preaching, 145ff.

ecclesiology, 254ff.
election, 44, 138, 160, 178ff., 239, 293
Enlightenment, 30, 53, 56, 60, 88, 91
epistemology, 49, 56f., 66, 74ff., 98, 119, 127, 129, 136ff.
eschatology, 12, 92
Eucharist, 118, 264
evangelism, 28
event, 27, 38, 65, 145, 170ff., 235f., 256, 258, 285, 287-90, 293, 300, 301, 309, 312
exegesis, 26f., 29, 44, 45
experience, 54ff., 62, 71f., 277
expressionism, 16, 18, 19, 84ff., 99, 104, 109, 281

faith, 59, 120, 124, 164, 174f., 200ff., 241f.
Fideism, 75, 207f.

Göttingen Dogmatics, 2, 90, 128, 145ff., 293f.

grace, 19, 140, 144, 174

herald, 167ff., 188ff.
hermeneutics, 25f.
historical Jesus, 31, 37f., 122
history, 11, 16-17, 30, 36, 166, 228
Holy Spirit, 23f., 28, 36f., 43, 67, 78, 107, 112, 122, 172, 217, 227, 232
humility, 210ff.
hypocrisy, 115f.

idolatry, 118f.
Incarnation, 117ff., 122f., 125ff.
introductions, 161ff., 183
irony, 99f.

Judaism, 120
justification, 80

Kirchenkamph, 160

lectionary, 23, 27, 72
listener, 84ff., 95, 150ff., 168, 197
literalism, 107

Mariology, 118
miracle, 101, 117, 118, 127ff., 140, 151ff., 157, 227, 279
modernity, 31, 32, 49ff., 59, 64, 68, 99, 115ff.
modesty, 40
mystery, 117

naiveté, 24
narrative, 33, 35, 36, 44, 262f.
natural theology, 77, 178
negative theology, 75, 99, 100, 137f., 204ff., 210ff., 306
novel, 12, 33, 35, 103, 310

obedience, 124ff., 263

objectivity, 52ff., 62, 103, 108f., 120, 136, 170f., 229, 289, 300, 311

parable, 28, 192
person of the preacher, 117-18, 127, 191f., 263
persuasion, 87
philosophy, 19, 49ff., 67, 74, 87, 220, 275
politics, 10-1, 13, 112, 312
postliberal, 278
postmodern, 79, 94, 116, 199, 208ff., 275, 297, 301-2
practices, 230f.
prayer, 28, 105ff., 123f.
preaching, 111, 143ff.
preaching, extemporaneous, 245f.
preaching, inductive, 262
preaching, prophetic, 34, 144f.

realism, 32, 76, 102ff., 120, 129, 215, 286
redemption, 116f.
reformation, 260
rejection, 193ff.
religion, 12, 17-18, 64, 148ff.
repetition, 25, 27, 180f.
Resurrection, 32, 38, 39, 68f., 92, 109, 118, 130, 144f., 222, 223ff., 234ff.
revelation, 19f., 23, 29, 53, 57, 62, 75, 76, 77, 78, 79, 80, 96, 116, 120ff., 128, 136ff., 229f., 231f., 240, 249f., 260

rhetoric, 25, 43ff., 83ff., 94f., 99f., 103f., 110, 112f., 150ff., 155ff., 182f., 188ff., 200f., 281, 295
Roman Catholic, 28, 32f., 118
Romans, Epistle to the, 14ff., 92

salvation, 73f., 80, 173
salvation, universal, 182, 303
scripture, 13f., 15, 23ff., 93, 111, 125, 129, 163, 271, 304, 308
sermon, 9, 13
sin, 48, 80f., 118, 204
story (*see* narrative)
subjectivity, 9ff., 33f., 51f., 61ff., 65ff., 102, 258, 276, 292, 295

theology, 11ff., 14, 18
topical preaching, 27f., 36
Trinity, 38, 43f., 67f., 85, 96, 109, 111, 116f., 119f., 121, 128ff., 144ff., 192, 210, 211, 232, 250, 278, 287ff., 291ff., 299
truth, 142

Utilitarian, 179

vocation, 74ff., 138ff., 162ff., 239ff.

witness, 35, 108ff., 162f., 169f., 257f., 285, 300